The Latino/a Condition

The Latino/a Condition

A Critical Reader

Second Edition

EDITED BY

Richard Delgado and Jean Stefancic

New York University Press

NEW YORK AND LONDON

NEW YORK UNIVERSITY PRESS
New York and London
www.nyupress.org

Library of Congress Cataloging-in-Publication Data
The Latino/a condition : critical reader / edited by Richard Delgado and
Jean Stefancic. — 2nd ed.
p.   cm.
Includes bibliographical references and index.
ISBN 978-0-8147-2039-4 (cl : alk. paper) — ISBN 978-0-8147-2040-0 (pb : alk. paper)
1. Hispanic Americans—Social conditions. 2. Hispanic Americans—Politics and
government. 3. Racism—United States. 4. United States—Race relations.
I. Delgado, Richard. II. Stefancic, Jean. III. Title: Latino condition.
IV. Title: Latina condition.
E184.S75L355 2010
305.868—dc22   2010026216

New York University Press books are printed on acid-free paper,
and their binding materials are chosen for strength and durability.
We strive to use environmentally responsible suppliers and materials
to the greatest extent possible in publishing our books.

Manufactured in the United States of America

10 9 8 7 6 5 4 3 2 1

Contents

Acknowledgments

We owe special thanks to Michael Olivas, Gerald López, Kevin Johnson, Juan Perea, Berta Hernández, Frank Valdes, Steve Bender, George Martinez, and Margaret Montoya for support and inspiration. They give new meaning to the term "colleague." Rodolfo Acuña, Derrick Bell, Ronald Takaki, and Ian Haney López, by their example, encouraged us to strive for excellence. Nanette Bradshaw prepared the manuscript with care, precision, and steadfastness. Jonathan LeBlanc pitched in when we needed extra help. Joseph Alvarado, Jennifer Claypool, and Jeanie Lee provided superb research support. Law librarians Tina Ching and Kerry Fitzgerald supplied lightning fast and expert bibliographic services. We thank our four anonymous reviewers for suggestions and critique. We are grateful to the Centrum Institute for the Arts, which provided us with uninterrupted time in a beautiful setting in which to work on the conceptual part of this book, and to Seattle University School of Law for supporting our effort.

As always, we are grateful to our editor, Deborah Gershenowitz, for her support of innovative scholarship, as well as Gabrielle Begue for editorial assistance and Emily Wright and Despina Papazoglou Gimbel for magnificent copyediting and production.

Introduction

Richard Delgado and Jean Stefancic

If you are a Latino, how much do you know about your own group? If you are not a Latino, perhaps a member of the majority race, how much do you know about what is now the largest ethnic group of color in the country? If the answer to either question is, "I would like to know more," this volume is written with you in mind.

With nearly a hundred tightly edited essays, this second edition of a classic collection offers an introduction to the Latino/a condition, including such topics as immigration, popular culture and stereotyping, assimilation, tensions between groups, family life, and the English-only movement. Because many issues vitally affecting Latinos, such as immigration, passports, citizenship, the census, and school, language, and workplace discrimination, end up in the courts, some of the selections are law-themed, although many are not. And with the ones that do address legal issues, we have tried to render them as nontechnically and accessibly as possible. We have placed pieces that address broad, general topics such as identity, immigration, and stereotyping early in the volume, with more specialized areas such as the family, reproduction, religion, and rap music toward the end.

Some of the contents address—or are written by—famous historical figures such as early Communist organizer Emma Tenayuca or poet-visionary-boxer Rodolfo "Corky" Gonzales. Still others are hot-off-the-press pieces addressing contemporary issues such as "sundown towns," media and talk-show racism, and Chicano rap music.

You will learn about the struggles of this growing but multifarious group for recognition, including self-recognition. What, if anything, does this group have in common, including, as it does, Mexican field workers and construction laborers; Puerto Ricans with black features and skin color who speak perfect Spanish and struggle to perfect their English; and light-skinned, well-educated Cubans operating businesses in Miami? How do Latinos see themselves? Are they one group, or many? White? Brown? Black? Or something in between?

You may read about the group's efforts to counter demeaning stereotypes such as the greaser, the bandito, the sleepy Mexican dozing under a cactus, and the romantic Don Juan figure of legend and myth. You will read about interracial marriage and romance, and the struggles of mixed-race children and adults with a foot in two or more cultures.

You will meet activist lawyers, such as the drug-taking, swashbuckling Oscar "Zeta" Acosta, who have struggled to win justice for a group long denied it. You will learn about affirmative action for Latinos, language rights, and workplaces that demand that everyone speak English or be fired.

As we write, black and brown relations are tense, with competition for jobs, slots on city councils and school boards, and admission to top universities. Is the traditional civil rights coalition breaking down, or will old allies join hands once again to combat problems common to both groups? Is civil rights primarily an issue for African Americans, as the reigning black-white binary of race suggests, with Latinos, Asian Americans, and Indians struggling to find a place somewhere in a system designed with blacks in mind? Or will Latinos and, perhaps, other groups demand a new paradigm with roots in immigration, language rights, and respect for cultural difference?

A note about our selection process. Most of the pieces are excerpted from previously published works, although a few are new. We have sharply reduced footnotes, endnotes, references, and similar features contained in the original articles. The reader desiring to find the full pieces need only consult the attribution line, which appears at the bottom of each selection's first page. In general, we included pieces that had something to say and that said it concisely, clearly, and, if possible, entertainingly.

Many fine works could not be included in the volume. Many of these appear in the bibliographies at the end of each part. By the same token, although we aimed at broad coverage, we were unable to address every topic of potential interest to a reader seeking information on Latinos. For example, we include little on voting rights—a highly technical and evolving subject—or cultural studies, other than a few pieces dealing with stereotypes and rap music.

We believe this book will be of interest to readers desiring to become informed about ethnic affairs, demography, political science, and, of course, Latino studies. We hope to induce policy makers and public administrators charged with making decisions about poverty, schools, social services, and immigration to learn more about Latinos. Above all, we hope to reach broad-minded readers seeking to follow developments about race and social justice, and wishing to take part in an ongoing conversation about how to achieve a richer, more inclusive society. It is with all these hopes in mind that we produced this book.

||||||||||||||||||||||||||||||||||||||||||||||||||||||||||||||||||||||||||||||||||||||||

Part I

The Shape of the Latino Group
Who Are We and What Are We Talking about Anyway?

Most readers know that Latinos—persons who trace their ancestry to Latin America or, in some cases, the Caribbean or Spain—are one of the country's fastest-growing minority groups. Constituting about 15 percent of the population (precise numbers are elusive because of the unknown number of undocumented immigrants), Latinos recently surpassed African Americans as the nation's most numerous minority group of color. About two-thirds of U.S. Latinos are Mexican Americans, with Puerto Ricans, Cubans, and Central Americans making up substantial groups as well. Most Mexican Americans reside in the Southwest, California, and the Midwest, most Puerto Ricans in New York and other East Coast cities, and most Cubans in Florida. A relatively young group, Latinos also suffer from poverty and a high rate of school dropout. The chapters in part 1 raise key issues regarding the contours of the Latino group and the way various members of it see and define themselves. Are Latinos a race, an ethnic group, or neither? What are the group's defining characteristics, as seen by itself or by others   the federal government, for example? Are Latinos white? Can one be a Latino or Latina as well as something else—for example, black, or Irish, or gay or lesbian? And if so, what is one, really?

‖‖‖

Chapter 1

Welcome to the Old World

Earl Shorris

We are ordinary people,
we are subject to death and destruction,
we are mortals;
allow us then to die,
let us perish now,
since our gods are already dead.
   —Colloquies of 1524, transcribed by Fray Bernardino de Sahagún

A small group of Dominican artists and intellectuals met in Manhattan in the closing days of 1989 to plan the attack. It seemed less than serious at first, an idea born over drinks and a little smoke in a dark room, whispered, enjoyed, explored over the sound of drums and an old piano. They laughed. Later, the next day and the day after, it became more than an amusement. They hated the imperialists, their whiteness, the soft dough feel of them, their thin hair hanging. And they hated Christopher Columbus most of all.

This was the plan: When the ships arrived to recreate his landing in celebration of the five hundredth anniversary of the discovery of Hispaniola, and all the weaklings, all the ass-lickers, rushed out to greet them, the true Dominicans, hundreds of them in native dress, would rise up out of their hiding places and attack the white invaders. With spears and stones, they would drive the Europeans back to their ships and away from the island of Hispaniola forever.

The Dominicans had overlooked history; they had permitted the symbolism to become confused. No one remembered that by 1570 only the imperialists and their African slaves were left; the genocide of the native population of Hispaniola was virtually complete. It did not occur to the little group of angry romantics in Manhattan that it was themselves they planned to drive away, for the Columbus Day conspirators were the children of conquest, doomed to a life of unendurable irony—Latinos.

Any history of Latinos stumbles at the start, for there is no single line to trace back to its ultimate origin. There are many Edens, a thousand floods, discoveries and conquests in numbers beyond the capability of human memory. Only the smallest fragment of this history survives. We shall never know the Olmecs or read the Mayan books the Spaniards burned; no more is known of the mind of Chief Hatuey of Hispaniola than what a Spanish friar heard; the grandeur of the Yoruba pantheon was not recorded during its reign.

Latino history has become a confused and painful algebra of race, culture, and conquest; it has less to do with evidence than with politics, for whoever owns the beginning has dignity, whoever owns the beginning owns the world. So every version has its adherents, for every human being wishes to be at least equal in his own mind: the African to the Spaniard, the person of mixed blood to the fair-haired descendant of Europeans, the Indian to the person of mixed races, the darker to the lighter, the one with kinky hair to the one with the softly curled hair of Europe to the one with the straight black hair of the Americas.[1]

For some the choice of beginnings is obvious. Imagine a family descended directly from Indians who lived in the Mexican state of Oaxaca: If the family concedes that Columbus "discovered" a New World, they accept the notion that whites (Europeans) come from a superior civilization. On the other hand, if the descendants of Indians say that Latino history began with the Toltecs or the Maya or with the emergence of people from the earth in a place called Aztlán, they raise the value of their own ancestry, making themselves at least equal and possibly superior to the whites.

The choice becomes more difficult for a person of mixed ancestry for whom those small conceits of identity, which are the ordinary rules of chauvinism, do not apply. Should a woman in Chicago who traces her family back to both Chihuahua and Castile identify with Europe or the Americas? According to the rules of conquest, the blood of the conquered dominates, but the rules are not profound; they are written on the skin. If the woman in Chicago appears to be European, she will have to choose where Latino history began, who were the subjects—the ones who acted, the dignified ones—and who were the objects—the people whom the forces of history acted upon.

Her decision will not be frivolous; it will determine her vision of herself, the face she sees in the mirror as well as the one she presents to the world. Her politics, left or right, Democrat or Republican, may depend on what she considers the beginning of history; she may even choose to speak and dress and cook according to how and where she thinks Latino history began. The name by which she identifies herself —Hispanic, Latina, Spanish, chicana, Mexican, Mejicana, Mexican American—will turn on her understanding of the past.

The history of Latinos was not always a difficult one. Until 1920 it was understood that Columbus had discovered the "New World" and begun the process of civilizing its savages and exploiting its natural resources. It was also understood that other savages had been imported from Africa, enslaved, and used to replace the American natives who died in such enormous numbers in the fields and mines of the Caribbean. But the end of the Mexican Revolution of 1910, after almost ten years of war, brought with it the need to integrate the rural Indians into the political economy of the nation. The task was given to one of Mexico's leading intellectuals, José Vasconcelos, who was appointed minister of education. With three words, he proclaimed the integration of the Indian into Mexican society at the most profound level: la raza cosmica.

To explain the notion of this cosmic race to people who could not read, Vasconcelos turned to Mexico's painters. He commissioned Diego Rivera, José Clemente Orozco, and David Alfaro Siqueiros, among others, to paint murals depicting Mexican subjects, and he gave them complete artistic freedom, which they used to attack the government, the colonialists, the capitalists, and the Spanish conquerors. A new version of Mexican history appeared on the walls of public places. For the first time in four hundred years a large number of people began to see the conquest in a different light: Instead of the discovery of a dark, savage continent by intellectually, technologically, morally superior white men, the muralists portrayed the destruction of the glorious civilizations of the Americans by the brutal Spaniards.

After Vasconcelos and his muralists, the victory of the Indianists would seem to have been assured. But there were doubts, even in the mind of the minister of education himself. Vasconcelos wrote that the "blood and soul" of Mexico were Indian, but the language was Spanish. And even more pointedly, the civilization, he said, came from Spain.

NOTES

1. In 1990, Kirkpatrick Sale offered a fascinating revision of the European version of the history of the Americas in *The Conquest of Paradise*. His humanistic, thoughtful work contrasts sharply with a restatement of the old ethnocentric white European view published a year later by Mario Vargas Llosa. As the quincentennial celebration of the Voyage of Columbus drew closer, books, films, television programs and articles appeared in ever-increasing numbers. The Sale and Vargas Llosa books remained at the opposite poles of opinion.

Chapter 2

‖‖

Hispanics? That's What They Call Us

Suzanne Oboler

A person is of Spanish/Hispanic origin if the person's origin (ancestry) is Mexican, Mexican American, Chicano, Puerto Rican, Dominican, Ecuadoran, Guatemalan, Honduran, Nicaraguan, Peruvian, Salvadoran; from other Spanish-speaking countries of the Caribbean or Central or South America; or from Spain.[1]

In the past two decades, the term *Hispanic* has come into general use in the United States to refer to all people in this country whose ancestry is predominantly from one or more Spanish-speaking countries. As a result, millions of people of a variety of national backgrounds are put into a single "ethnic" category, and no allowances are made for their varied racial, class, linguistic, and gender experiences. The term ignores, for example, the distinct and diverse experiences of descendants of U.S. conquest, such as the Chicanos, and those of the Puerto Rican populations, colonized by the United States at the turn of the century. Its users often neglect to contextualize the specific histories and cultures that differentiate these two groups, both from one another and from more recent immigrant arrivals, whether from Mexico, Central or South America, or the Spanish-speaking Caribbean nations. In so doing, they combine longtime native-born U.S. citizens and residents with more recently arrived economic immigrants who may have crossed the U.S. border yesterday.

The term *Hispanic* also lumps together recent political refugees from El Salvador with past political exiles like the first wave of Cubans who arrived in the early 1960s. The latter's upper- and middle-class status and racial composition in turn mask the differences between their entry process and experiences and those of the nonwhite working-class Cuban Marielitos, for example, who arrived in 1980. Moreover, some exiles have today become economic immigrants like the contras and upper- and middle-class Nicaraguans who originally left their country soon after the Sandinista victory of 1979.

While most scholars limit their policy-related research on Latinos to populations with ties to Latin America, the U.S. government census definition that begins this chapter also includes European immigrants from Spain. In addition, the perceptions of the general population compound the sources of definitional confusion about the term *Hispanic*. Unlike government agencies and scholars, many are not aware of the political and cultural implications of the diverse backgrounds of those whom public opinion also unofficially classifies as Hispanics. Among these are the Brazilians who, because of their Portuguese heritage, share neither the language nor the culture of Spanish America, and hence rarely self-identify as "Hispanics."

In addition, the term homogenizes class experiences and neglects many different linguistic, racial, and ethnic groups within the different nationalities themselves: various indigenous populations; the descendants of enslaved Africans; waves of immigrant populations from every country in Europe, Asia, the Middle East. Members of these populations too are increasingly making their way to the United States, ensuring the growing visibility of Latin America's heterogeneity within the Latino populations in this country.[2]

In the current usage by the U.S. census, government agencies, social institutions, social scientists, the media, and the public at large, then, the ethnic label "Hispanic" obscures rather than clarifies the varied social and political experiences in U.S. society of millions of citizens, residents, refugees, and immigrants with ties to Caribbean and Central and South American countries. It reduces their distinct relations among themselves and with U.S. society to an ethnic label that in fact fails to do justice to the variety of backgrounds and conditions of the populations to whom it has been applied. As Martha Giménez put it, the term *Hispanic* "strip[s] people of their historical identity and reduc[es] them to imputed common traits."[3]

Like other ethnic labels currently used to identify minority groups in this country, the term *Hispanic* raises the question of how people are defined and classified in this society and in turn how they define themselves in the United States. It points to the gap between the self-identification of people of Latin American descent and their definition through a label created and used by others.

Given the diversity of the various population groups both in Latin America and in the United States, how *did* the culturally homogeneous representations of people identified as Hispanics become commonplace among scholars, government agencies, the media, and the public at large in this country? Popular reasoning about the origin of the term *Hispanic* usually locates it within the legacy of the Spanish conquest and colonization of the New World. After all, the justification goes, Spanish colonial rule lasted for over three centuries, certainly long enough for the social, ethnic, linguistic, racial, and national experiences of the populations of Latin America and the Caribbean to establish a homogeneous heritage.

But in Latin America itself, the role of the Spanish legacy in shaping a common cultural identity on the continent has been the subject of ongoing debates since that region's independence in the early nineteenth century. Underlying these discussions is the recognition that in spite of the shared Spanish colonial heritage, profound differences mark the various nations' postindependence histories and populations, often overriding cultural or linguistic commonalities they may also share. In many ways, then, the issue of the creation of a unified cultural—and even political and economic —"Hispanic identity" in the United States actually transports to this country a debate that Latin American intellectuals have themselves waged since the nineteenth century in historical essays, social science texts, and their respective national literatures.[4]

NOTES

1. U.S. Bureau of the Census, Population Division, DEVELOPMENT OF THE RACE AND ETHNIC ITEMS FOR THE 1990 CENSUS 51 (New Orleans: Population Association of America, 1988).

2. J. Jorge Klor de Alva, *Telling Hispanics Apart: Latino Sociocultural Diversity*, in THE HISPANIC EXPERIENCE IN THE UNITED STATES: CONTEMPORARY ISSUES AND PERSPECTIVES (Edna Acosta-Belén & Barbara R. Sjostrom, eds.) 107–36 (New York, Praeger, 1988).

3. Martha E. Giménez, *"Latino/Hispanic"—Who Needs a Name? The Case against Standardized Terminology*, INTERNATIONAL JOURNAL OF HEALTH SERVICES 19, no. 3 (1989), p. 41.

4. Simón Bolivar, PARA NOSOTROS LA PATRIA ES AMÉRICA (Caracas: Biblioteca Ayacucho, 1991); José Martí, PÁGINAS ESCOGIDAS (Robert Fernández Retamar, ed.) (Havana, 1985); LA IDENTIDAD CULTURAL DE HISPANOAMERICA: DISCUSIÓN ACTUAL (J. Giordano & D. Torres, eds.) (Santiago de Chile: Monografias del Maitén, 1986); Angel Rama, TRANSCULTURACIÓN NARRATIVA EN AMÉRICA LATINA (Mexico City: Siglo XXI Editores, 1982); Gabriel García Márquez, EL GENERAL EN SU LABERINTO (Madrid, Mondadori, 1989); Julio Cortázar, RAYUELA (Buenos Aires: Ed. Sudamericana, 1967); AMÉRICA LATÍNA EN SUS IDEAS (Leopoldo Zea, ed.) (Mexico City: Siglo XXI Editores/UNESCO, 1987).

Chapter 3

Chance, Context, and Choice in the Social Construction of Race

Ian F. Haney López

The Mean Streets of Social Race

The literature of minority writers provides some of the most telling insights into, and some of the most confused explorations of, race in the United States. Piri Thomas's quest for identity, recorded in *Down These Mean Streets*,[1] fits squarely within this tradition of insight and confusion. Thomas describes his racial transformation, which is both willed and yet not willed, from a Puerto Rican into someone Black. Dissecting his harrowing experiences, piercing perceptions, and profound misapprehensions offers a way to disaggregate the daily technology of race. In the play of race, chance, context, and choice overlap and are inseverable. Nevertheless, I distinguish and explain these terms in order to explore the thesis that a race is best thought of as a group of people loosely bound together by historically contingent, socially significant elements of their morphology and/or ancestry.

Chance

The first terms of importance in the definition of race I advance are "morphology" and "ancestry." These fall within the province of chance, by which I mean coincidence, something not subject to human will or effort, insofar as we have no control over what we look like or to whom we are born. Chance, because of the importance of morphology and ancestry, may seem to occupy almost the entire geography of race. Certainly for those who subscribe to notions of biological race, chance seems to account for almost everything: one is born some race and not another, fated to a particular racial identity, with no human intervention possible. For those who believe in biological race, race is destiny. However, recognizing the social construction of race reduces the province of chance. The role of chance in determining racial identity is significantly smaller than one might initially expect.

From *The Social Construction of Race: Some Observations on Illusion, Fabrication, and Choice*, 29 Harv. C.R.–C.L. Rev. 1 (1994). Originally published in the *Harvard Civil Rights–Civil Liberties Law Review*. Reprinted by permission.

The random accidents of morphology and ancestry set the scene for Piri Thomas's racial odyssey. Seeking better prospects during the depression, Thomas's parents moved from Puerto Rico to Spanish Harlem, where Piri and his three siblings were born. Once in the United States, however, the family faced the peculiar American necessity of defining itself as White or Black. To be White would afford security and a promising future; to be Black would portend exclusion and unemployment. The Thomas family—hailing from Puerto Rico of mixed Indian, African, and European antecedents—considered themselves White and pursued the American dream, eventually moving out to the suburbs in search of higher salaries and better schools for the children. Yet in their bid for Whiteness, the family gambled and lost, because even while the three other children and Piri's mother were fair, Piri and his father were dark skinned. Babylon, Long Island, proved less forgiving of Piri's dark skin than Spanish Harlem did. In the new school, the pale children scoffed at Piri's claim to be Puerto Rican rather than Black, taunting Piri for "passing for Puerto Rican because he can't make it for white,"[2] and proclaiming, "[t]here's no difference . . . [h]e's still black."[3] Piri's morphology shattered not only the family's White dream, but eventually the family itself.

While the family insisted on their own Whiteness as the crucial charm to a fulfilling life in the United States, Thomas, coming of age amid the racial struggles of the 1950s and himself the victim of White violence, fought the moral hypocrisy he saw in their claim to Whiteness. Piri unyieldingly attacked the family's delusion, for example challenging with bitterness and frustration the Whiteness of his younger brother José:

> José's face got whiter and his voice angrier at my attempt to take away his white status. He screamed out strong: "I ain't no nigger! You can be if you want to be. . . . But—I —am—white! And you can go to hell!"

But Piri persisted in attacking the family, one at a time:

> "And James is blanco, too?" I asked quietly.
> "You're damn right."
> "And Poppa?"
> . . . "Poppa's the same as you," he said, avoiding my eyes, "Indian."
> "What kinda Indian," I said bitterly. "Caribe? Or maybe Borinquen? Say, José, didn't you know the Negro made the scene in Puerto Rico way back? And when the Spanish spics ran outta Indian coolies, they brought them big blacks from you know where. Poppa's got *moyeto* [Black] blood. I got it. Sis got it. James got it. And, mah deah brudder, you-all got it. . . . It's a played-out lie about me—us—being white."[4]

The structure of this painful exchange casts a bright light on the power that morphology and ancestry wield in defining races. In the racially charged United States, skin color or parentage often makes one's publicly constructed race inescapable.

Piri's dark features and José's light looks are chance in the sense that neither Piri nor José could choose their faces, or indeed their ancestry. Still, what we look like is not entirely accident; to some extent looks can be altered in racially significant ways. In this respect, consider the unfortunate popularity of hair straightening, blue contact lenses, and skin lighteners. More importantly, however, though morphology and ancestry remain largely matters of chance, those aspects of identity gain their importance on the social, not the physical, plane. Consider, now, the operation of context.

Context

Given Piri's status as a Puerto Rican with ancestral ties to three continents, a certain absurdity inheres in his insistence that he is Black. This absurdity highlights the importance of context to the creation of races. Context is the social setting in which races are recognized, constructed, and contested; it is the "circumstances directly encountered, given and transmitted from the past."[5] At the meta level, context includes both ideological and material components, such as entrenched cultural and customary prejudices, and also maldistributed resources, marketplace inequalities, and skewed social services. These inherited structures are altered and altered again by everything from individual actors and community movements to broad-based changes in the economic, demographic, and political landscape. At the same time, context also refers to highly localized settings. The systems of meaning regarding morphology and ancestry are inconstant and unstable. These systems shift in time and space, and even across class and educational levels, in ways that give to any individual different racial identities depending upon her shifting location. I refer to context in order to explain the phrases "historically contingent" and "socially significant" in the definition of race proffered at the start.

Changes in racial identity produced by the shifting significance of morphology and ancestry are often profoundly disconcerting, as Piri Thomas discovered. In Puerto Rico, prevailing attitudes toward racial identity situated the Thomases, as a family not light enough to be Spanish but not so dark as to be black, comfortably in the mainstream of society. They encountered no social or economic disadvantages as a result of their skin color, and were not subjected to the prejudice that usually accompanies rigid racial constructs. However, the social ideology of race in the United States—more specifically, in New York in the late 1950s—was firmly rooted in the proposition that exactly two biological races existed. Such an ideology forced the Thomas family to define themselves as either White or Black. In the context confronting Piri, "[i]t would seem indeed that . . . white and black represent the two poles of a world, two poles in perpetual conflict: a genuinely Manichean concept of the world."[6] Once in the United States, Thomas came to believe that he and his family were Black as a biological fact, irrespective of their own dreams, desires, or decisions. Yet, Thomas was not Black because of his face or parents, but because of the social systems of meaning surrounding these elements of his identity.

Consider how Thomas came to believe in his own Blackness. In a chapter entitled "How to Be a Negro without Really Trying," Thomas recalls how he and his fair-skinned Puerto Rican friend Louie applied for a sales job. Though the company told Thomas they would call him back, they hired Louie to start Monday morning. Thomas's reflections bear repeating:

> I didn't feel so much angry as I did sick, like throwing-up sick. Later, when I told this story to my buddy, a colored cat, he said, "Hell, Piri . . . a Negro faces that all the time."
>
> "I know that," I said, "but I wasn't a Negro then. I was still only a Puerto Rican."[7]

Episodes of discrimination drove Piri toward a confused belief that he was Black. Aching to end the confusion, Piri traveled to the South, where he hoped to find out for sure whether his hair, his skin, and his face somehow inextricably tied him, a Puerto Rican, to Black America. Working in the merchant marine between Mobile, New Orleans, and Galveston, Piri experienced firsthand the nether world of White supremacy, and the experience confirmed his race: Bullied by his White bosses, insulted by White strangers, confronted at every turn by a White racial etiquette of violence, Thomas accepted his own Blackness. "It was like Brew said," he reflected after his time in the South, "any language you talk, if you're black, you're black."[8] Suffering under the lash of White racism, Thomas decided he was Black. Thomas's Blackness did not flow from his morphology but from traveling the mean streets of racial segregation. His dislocations suggest a spatial component to racial identities, an implication confirmed in Thomas's travel from Spanish Harlem, where he was Puerto Rican, to Long Island, where he was accused of trying to pass, to the South, where he was Black.

Piri and his family were far from the first to face the Manichean choice between White or Black. The Chinese, whose population in the United States rose fifteenfold to 105,465 in the twenty years after 1850, were also initially defined in those stark terms. Thus in Los Angeles circa 1860 the Chinese area downtown was called "Nigger Alley." During their first years in the United States, as Ronald Takaki observes, "[r]acial qualities that had been assigned to blacks became Chinese characteristics."[9] Not only were the supposed degenerate moral traits of Blacks transferred wholesale to the Chinese, but in a fascinating display of racist imagination, Whites also saw a close link between Black and Chinese morphology. Takaki cites a commentator who argued that Chinese physiognomy indicated "but a slight removal from the African race,"[10] and he reprints a startling cartoon contrasting Anglo Uncle Sam with a Chinese vampire replete with slanted eyes, but also with very dark skin, woolly hair, a flat nose, and thick lips.

In California, where the racial imagination included Mexicans and Indians as well as Blacks, Chinese were considered not only in terms of Blackness but also in terms of every non-White race, every rejected and denigrated Other. This point furnishes yet more evidence for the theory that racial identity is defined by its social context. Consider the 1879 play *The Chinese Must Go* by Henry Grimm of San Francisco. Notice the language Grimm ascribes to the Chinese characters, discussing, predictably, their nefarious anti-American plot to destroy White labor through hard work:

Ah Choy: By and by white man catchee no money; Chinaman catchee heap money; Chinaman workee cheap, plenty work; white man workee dear, no work —sabee?

Sam Gin: Me heep sabee.[11]

The Chinese in this Grimm play speak in the language that Whites associated with Indians and Mexicans, making Sam Gin sound remarkably like Tonto playing out the Lone Ranger's racial delusions. Thus, the Chinese were assigned not only their own peculiar stereotypes, like a fiendish desire to work for low wages, but also the degenerate characteristics of all the minorities loathed by Whites. Not coincidentally, three years after Grimm's play, the United States passed its first immigration law: the 1882 Chinese Exclusion Act. In a telling example of law reifying racist hysteria, the Supreme Court upheld the Chinese Exclusion Act in part by citing the threat posed by the Chinese to White labor.[12] The first Chinese, like the Thomas family nearly a century later, entered a society fixated on the idea of race and intent on forcing new immigrants into procrustean racial hierarchies.

The racial fate of Piri and the Chinese turned to a large extent on the social setting into which they immigrated. That setting provides the social meanings attached to our faces and forebears, and for this reason I write that races are groups of people bound together by historically contingent, socially significant elements of their morphology and/or ancestry. A race is not created because people share just any characteristic, such as height or hand size, or just any ancestry, for example Yoruba or Yugoslav. Instead, it is the social significance attached to certain features, like our faces, and to certain forebears, like Africans, which defines races. Context superimposed on chance largely shapes races in the United States.

Choice in Context

Piri's belief that he is Black, and his brother José's belief in his own Whiteness, can in some sense be attributed to the chance of their respective morphology and the context of their upbringing. Yet, to attribute Thomas's racial identity only to chance and context grossly oversimplifies his Blackness. Thomas's father shared not only his social context, but his dark looks as well, making context and chance equal between them. Nevertheless, his father insisted on his Whiteness, and explained this decision to Piri as follows:

I ain't got one colored friend . . . at least one American Negro friend. Only dark ones I got are Puerto Ricans or Cubans. I'm not a stupid man. I saw the look of white people on me when I was a young man, when I walked into a place where a dark skin isn't supposed to be. I noticed how a cold rejection turned into an indifferent acceptance when they heard my exaggerated accent. I can remember the time when I made my accent heavier, to make me more of a Puerto Rican than the most Puerto Rican there ever was. I wanted a value on me, son.[13]

Thomas's father consciously exaggerated his Puerto Rican accent to put distance between himself and Black Americans. Thomas himself also made conscious and purposeful decisions, choices that in the end made him Black. As Henry Louis Gates argues, "one must *learn* to be 'black' in this society, precisely because 'blackness' is a socially produced category."[14]

Choice composes a crucial ingredient in the construction of racial identities and the fabrication of races. Racial choices occur on mundane and epic levels, for example, in terms of what to wear or when to fight; they are made by individuals and groups, such as people deciding to pass or movements deciding to protest; and the effects are often minor though sometimes profound, for instance, slightly altering a person's affiliation or radically remaking a community's identity. Nevertheless, in every circumstance choices are exercised not by free agents or autonomous actors, but by people who are compromised and constrained by the social context. Choice, explains Angela Harris, is not uncoerced choice, "freely given, but a 'contradictory consciousness' mixing approbation and apathy, resistance and resignation."[15] Nevertheless, in racial matters we constantly exercise choice, sometimes in full awareness of our compromised position, though most often not.

Perhaps the most graphic illustration of choice in the construction of racial identities comes in the context of passing. Passing—the ability of individuals to change race—powerfully indicates race's chosen nature. Not infrequently someone Black through the social construction of their ancestry is physically indistinguishable from someone White. Consider Richard Wright's description of his grandmother in *Black Boy*: "My grandmother was as nearly white as a Negro can get without being white, which means that she was white."[16] Given the prevalent presumption of essential, easily recognized phenotypical differences, light-skinned Blacks exist at an ambiguous and often unacknowledged racial border between White and Black. Those in this liminal space often respond along a range from some few who cross the established color line by "passing" to those who identify strongly with their Black status.

For most people, the pervasive social systems of meaning that attach to morphology ensure that passing is not an option. Moreover, for those who do jump races, the psychological dislocations required—suspending some personal dreams, for example childbirth; renouncing most family ties, for instance forgoing weddings and funerals; and severing all relations with the community, for example ending religious and civic affiliations—are brutal and severe. In addition, because of the depth of racial animosity in this society, passing may only succeed in distancing one from her community, not in gaining full acceptance among Whites. In this sense, recall the words of Thomas's father: "I noticed how a cold rejection turned into an indifferent acceptance when they heard my exaggerated accent."[17] Nevertheless, some people do choose to jump races, and their ability to do so dramatically demonstrates the element of choice in the micromechanics of race.

Passing demonstrates not only the power of racial choice, however, but the contingency of the choices people make, thereby reinforcing the point that choices are made in specific contexts. Choices about racial identity do not occur on neutral ground, but instead occur in the violently racist context of American society. Though the decision to pass may be made for many reasons, among these the power of prejudice and self-hate cannot be denied. Thomas's younger brother José reveals the racist hate within him in the same instant that he claims to be White. José shouts at Piri: "I ain't black, damn you! Look at my hair. It's almost blond. My eyes are blue, my nose is straight. My motherfuckin' lips are not like a baboon's ass. My skin is white. White, goddamit! White!"[18]

José's comments are important, if painful to repeat, because they illustrate that a person's choice in the matter of race may be fatally poisoned by ambient racist antipathies. Nevertheless, notice that the context in which passing occurs constantly changes. For example, it may be that today passing as White increasingly does not in fact require that one look White. Recently, many Anglos, committed to the pseudo-integrationist idea that ignoring race equals racial enlightenment, have seemingly adopted the strategy of pretending that the minorities they are friendly with are White. Consider the words of a White Detroit politician: "I seldom think of my girlfriend, Kathy, as black. . . . A lot of times I look at her and it's as if she is white; there's no real difference. But every now and then, it depends on what she is wearing and what we're doing, she looks very ethnic and very Black. It bothers me. I don't like it. I prefer it when she's a regular, normal, everyday kind of person."[19] Even so, passing may be far less common today than it was a hundred years ago. One observer estimates that in the half-century after the Civil War, as many as 25,000 people a year passed out of the Black race. The context in which passing occurs constantly changes, altering in turn the range of decisions individuals face.

Despite the dramatic evidence of choice that passing provides, by far the majority of racial decisions are of a decidedly less epic nature. Because race in our society infuses almost all aspects of life, many daily decisions take on racial meanings. For example, seemingly inconsequential acts like listening to rap and wearing hip hop fashion constitute a means of racial affiliation and identification. Many Whites have taken to listening to, and some to performing, rap and hip hop. Nevertheless, the music of the inner city remains Black music. Rapping, whether as an artist or audience member, is in some sense a racial act. So too are a myriad of other actions taken every day by every person, almost always without conscious regard for the racial significance of their choices. It is here, in deciding what to eat, how to dress, whom to befriend, and where to go, rather than in the dramatic decision to leap races, that most racial choices are rendered. I do not suggest that these common acts are racial choices because they are taken with a conscious awareness of their racial implications, or because they compel complete shifts in racial identity. Rather, these are racial choices in their overtones or subtext, because they resonate in the complex of meanings associated with race. Given the thorough suffusion of race throughout society, in the daily dance of life we cannot avoid making racially meaningful decisions.

NOTES

1. Piri Thomas, Down These Mean Streets (1967).
2. *Id.* at 90.
3. *Id.* at 91.

4. *Id.* at 145.

5. Karl Marx, THE EIGHTEENTH BRUMAIRE OF LOUIS BONAPARTE (1963), quoted in Renato Rosaldo, CULTURE AND TRUTH: THE REMAKING OF SOCIAL ANALYSIS 105 (1989).

6. Frantz Fanon, BLACK SKIN, WHITE MASKS 44–45 (1967).

7. Thomas, at 108.

8. *Id.* at 187–88.

9. Ronald Takaki, IRON CAGES: RACE AND CULTURE IN 19TH-CENTURY AMERICA 217 (1990).

10. *Id.*

11. Quoted in Takaki, at 221.

12. The Chinese Exclusion Case: Chae Chan Ping v. United States, 130 U.S. 581, 595 (1889).

13. Thomas, at 152.

14. Henry Louis Gates, Jr., LOOSE CANONS: NOTES ON THE CULTURE WARS 101 (1992).

15. Angela P. Harris, *Race and Essentialism in Feminist Legal Theory*, 42 STAN. L. REV. 581 (1990) (quoting T. J. Jackson Lears, *The Concept of Cultural Hegemony: Problems and Possibilities*, 90 AM. HIST. REV. 567, 570 [1985]).

16. Richard Wright, BLACK BOY 48 (1966).

17. Thomas, at 152.

18. *Id.* at 144.

19. Kathy Russell, Midge Wilson & Ronald Hall, THE COLOR COMPLEX: THE POLITICS OF SKIN COLOR AMONG AFRICAN AMERICANS 120 (1992).

Chapter 4

||||||||||||||||||||||||||||||||||||||||||||||||||||||||||||||||||||||||||||||||

Latino/a Identity and Multi-Identity
Community and Culture

Leslie G. Espinoza

American society forces individuals to label themselves by race and gender. Not surprisingly, race and gender correlate to power—to the likelihood that one will have educational opportunity, be in a particular income class, be in prison, or be the victim of a violent crime. Race and gender identity are the ways in which we learn to articulate ourselves.

Multi-identity is not an accepted concept in dominant discourse. That discourse is about being "for us or against us," a cowboy or an Indian, an American or an alien, a woman or one of the boys, black or white, Mexican or white, Asian or white, Other or white. The politics of dichotomous categorical identity require individuals to be placed into or to be forced to choose one particular defining identity. Once placed there, the individual is assumed to possess all the characteristics of that category, good and bad. Furthermore, that category is understood by its opposition to another category.

Understanding personal identity, however, often requires the expression of multiple and distinct defining categories and the recognition of a unifying concept—the individual person. Identity may thus seem a paradox. How is group identity possible when each individual is an amalgam of unique characteristics and each community and culture is a mix? The tension between group and individual difference has caused trouble between those with the power to put others into categories such as race, gender, or sexual preference, and those individuals pushed into socially constructed group identities that are both overinclusive and underinclusive. The choice is to assimilate or to be pushed into some distinct category of "other," whether it fits or not. This neat, blanket packaging of people both reflects and perpetuates current power structures. Of course, in reality, most individual outsiders are comfortable with the messy ambiguity of identity—when we are not thinking about it. When we try to counter the socially imposed categories and the oppression they represent, we find that we lack a language to express that which we have learned through experience.

I am a Mexican, Irish, Jewish, Woman, Heterosexual, Aunt, Law Professor, Californian, Bostonian, Tucsonian, middle child, professional; multi-identity is something I

From *Multi-Identity: Community and Culture,* 2 Va. J. Soc. Pol'y & L. 23 (1994). Originally published in the *Virginia Journal of Social Policy and the Law.* Reprinted by permission.

have thought about at length. So much so that often when I try to talk about it, my thoughts seem to all come out in an analytical jumble—a potpourri of personal anecdotes and generalized theory. Yet in all my formulations of self, whether geographical, educational, professional, or familial, the major categories that override all else are race and gender. For me, race and ethnicity should be more complicated; but they are not. The politics of race in America define me as Mexican. It is the identity of social hierarchy. It is the politics of being pushed to the bottom. It is the erasure of the richness of my Mexican/Irish/Jewish mix, and a white-washing of the colorful complexity of meaning in each of my ethnic roots.

Learning Law, Learning Assimilation

I am a teacher, as was my grandmother. Maria Espinoza Cisneros taught in the town of Pitiquito, Sonora, Mexico, at the turn of the century. The oldest of eight children, she fled the Mexican revolution in 1912, settling with her family in Chino, California. My grandmother was the matriarch of her extended family until she died in 1967. After her husband died when he was still young, my grandmother raised her five children through the Great Depression. I never heard my grandmother speak a word of English.

When we were small, she would sit us in her yard and tell us of the Mayan and Aztec kings. She would start sometime around 700 A.D. and recite their names and year of ascension. She would tell us of the Spanish conquest. She would proudly tell us that we were Mexican. The Mayan, Aztec, and Spanish, however, were only part of our heritage. Being Mexican meant to be mixed, to have Indian blood, to be Mestizo. Our Indian ancestors were from three tribes: the Pima, the peaceful poets of the desert; the Tarahumara, the mystics of Northern Mexico; and the Apaches, the warriors of the plains and mountains. Each separate identity combined to create a unique composite. We were a mosaic, each tile separately colored and textured, piecing together a whole identity.

I knew my grandmother, my Nana, in the last years of her life. She was a bent, tiny woman, with well over eighty years behind her. Her hair was like her ideas, always neatly folded in braids and carefully contained in what looked like a frail hairnet. The braids wove a pattern that gave every strand a sense of structure and a knowledge of place and belonging. When she was in the kitchen or crocheting in the living room, it was hard for me to imagine her a "schoolteacher." Yet, she easily assumed her teaching persona when it was time to instruct her grandchildren in their legacy. She had a confidence and assurance that, just as her braids and her ideas fit together with a puzzling strength, her own sense of self would not unravel.

My own hair is short, cropped, and a mess of curls. Like my ideas, it moves every which way. No pattern of braids folds neatly around my head; no organizing net holds everything in place. I find my role transitions equally disarrayed. I am the carefully assimilated, accentless law professor. I move in and out of my other identities, but not smoothly. Like my grandmother, I want to teach my students a legacy. I want to teach them how they can take the pieces of their past and meld them with their developing lawyer persona. This is difficult to do when the discourse of law requires a single hegemonic voice.

We recognize our various identities in our different languages. Language is the vehicle by which others know us and by which we know ourselves. We give labels to our external and internal thoughts and experiences. Through this process of naming, we define our reality. Words are symbols for knowledge. Learning to speak is learning to attach the "right" symbol to the "right" knowing in the "right" context. This is a cultural, political, and personal process.

The problem, however, is that not all of us can learn new languages and keep our fluency in past languages. The story of social hierarchy has been one where the language of social power reinforces that power by muting other languages. Trying to hold on to disempowered identities causes dysfunctionality in the use of the newly learned language of power and assimilation.[1] When race equality means color-blindness that bleaches the concept to mean "the same as white," or when gender equality means "same as men," then socially imposed bias makes those of us with certain identities outsiders. Our consciousness, our way of knowing, through our overlapping identities, cannot coexist with the new language. Our earlier cultural voice is dominated and silenced.

Gender differences provide a concrete example of this type of domination. Women use a special socialized style of speech which Robin Lakoff calls "women's language." This language includes "hedges," "tag questions," and "qualifiers." For example, when asked, "What time is dinner?" women will tend to respond indirectly: "I think that it should be around seven" or "Perhaps seven would be a good time." Alternatively, women will look for affirmation, "Would seven be good?" or "Dinner is at seven, if that's OK?" or "Seven, isn't it?" They might even try to qualify their response: "Assuming you'll be home, seven." Women tend not to respond directly: "Dinner is at seven."

I am intrigued by my grandmother, the teacher. To be a great teacher, she must have had a love for learning. Yet she never learned, or rather admitted to learning, English. She embraced all the different and often warring cultures of her Mexican identity. To the day of her death, she called herself a Mexican—never an American. She seemed to understand the difference of multi-identity in a culture where acceptance means assimilation, and assimilation means the uni-identity, the uni-lingualism of the dominant culture.

Linguistic assimilation has served as a particularly effective instrument in cultural suppression and eventually obliteration. Language domination means that one must learn English in order to participate in the society. More important is the pressure to disuse, and even unlearn, other languages. In 1991, the United States Supreme Court in *Hernandez v. New York*[2] reinforced uni-lingual, cultural domination. The Court held that the prosecutor's use of peremptory challenges during jury selection to exclude all Spanish-speaking, Latino jurors was constitutional—even if the exclusions resulted in all potential Latino jurors being excluded. Of course, all the excluded jurors spoke English. Their infirmity was that they also spoke Spanish. They had taken the first step toward "American identity," but they were not yet trustworthy. The government argued that its challenge to Latino jurors was justified because one of the witnesses at the trial would be testifying in Spanish. The government did not believe that bilingual, Latino jurors would adhere to the official English interpretation.

In *Hernandez*, the jurors were asked if they would abide by the official English translation. They answered that they would. The prosecutor argued, however, that the individual jurors questioned could not be believed. They hesitated and looked away when answering the question. The Supreme Court relied on this notion of individual exclusion to justify its decision. Bilingual Latinos could not be per se excluded. Indeed, bilingual, Latino jurors who promised to rely on the official translation could not be peremptorily challenged—unless they were not believed. As the prosecutor in *Hernandez* testified:

> I believe that in their heart they will try to follow [the official translation], but I felt there was a great deal of uncertainty as to whether they could accept the interpreter as the final arbiter of what was said by each of the witnesses.[3]

In *Hernandez*, the Court tears away the mask of inclusive justice. Ours is not an adjudicatory system where judgment includes the views of peers who speak the same language of multi-identity. Members of the Latino community must not only speak English to be jurors, they must cease to speak Spanish.

The lure to trade our identity for power is strong. We want to be jurors; we want to be lawyers; we want to be law professors. I have this dream. My grandmother and I are speaking Spanish. I wake up but cannot understand what we said. Over the years, I have lost my ability to speak Spanish.

It takes a lot of energy to hide our accents, our idioms, our language. We have to learn to shift between identities, without an overlap. And then comes a time when we feel secure enough in the mastery of the dominant language to experiment with transformative speech—to create a new combination of languages. But can we remember that original language of culture and community? Have we lost all authenticity? I think not. We can try to stay connected to each of our identities. If we become fragmented, if we lose memory, we can endeavor to recapture it. I now understand why my grandmother never spoke English. She wanted to make certain that if we lost our ability to speak in Spanish, we would not lose our ability to dream in Spanish.

NOTES

1. See, e.g., Leslie G. Espinoza, *Masks and Other Disguises: Exposing Legal Academia,* 103 HARV. L. REV. 1878, 1884–86 (1990); Margaret E. Montoya, *Mascaras, Trenzas, y Greñas: Un/Masking the Self While Un/Braiding Latina Stories and Legal Discourse,* 17 HARV. WOMEN'S L.J. 185, 210–15 (1994); Robert A. Williams, Jr., *Taking Rights Aggressively: The Perils and Promise of Critical Legal Theory for Peoples of Color,* 5 LAW & INEQ. J. 103, 106 n.6 (1987).

2. 500 U.S. 352 (1991).

3. *Id.* at 356 (quoting App. 3–4).

Chapter 5

||||||||||||||||||||||||||||||||||||||||||||||||||||||||||||||||||||||||||||||||||||||||||||||||||||

Building Bridges
Latinas and Latinos at the Crossroads

Berta Esperanza Hernández-Truyol

I moved to Albuquerque back in the summer of '82. That is the year when I started teaching at the University of New Mexico. I had been out there to find a place to live in the spring. I fell in love with New Mexico when I first visited the university to interview for the teaching slot. It felt like home, the familiar Spanish influence, the rice and beans, the sunlight and the bright clothing. That summer I arrived the day before my house closing—late, with my dog in tow, and hungry. Starving, really. And when I am hungry I have to eat. But with being in a new place and all, and the excitement of the closing and the furniture arriving, I figured a light meal would do. So I went into the only place I found open and ordered a tortilla, a plain tortilla. There, I was so happy, I could even order food in Spanish. The waitress looked at me kind of funny and asked, simply, "Are you sure all you want is a tortilla?" "Yes," I said. "Plain?" she asked. "Yes," I said, "it's late." So with a shrug of the shoulders she disappeared and promptly returned and put this plate in front of me. Sitting on the plate was this flat thing, white, warm, soft. My turn to ask, "And what is this?" "Your order ma'am." And we stared at each other. I ate this thing, although I did not quite know how I was supposed to do that. I got funny looks when I went at it with fork and knife. I ate, I paid, I left—still hungry and now confused. Clarity arrived several days later when I was formally introduced to the tortilla—that Mexican tortilla anyway, one that I learned to love even plain (well, with some melted butter). But that was not the tortilla I had in mind. That first night I wanted my tortilla, a simple omelette to those of us from the Caribbean.

This is a simple story about complex and diverse peoples. Here we were dealing with the same word: tortilla, and the same language: Spanish. Yet our different cultures give the word different meanings. The existing approach, one that would consider us both the same notwithstanding our common "language" and other cultural similarities, excludes. It denies the different cultural experiences of latinas/os and falsely homogenizes by making us the "same" when we are not. It creates a generic "hispanic" that in reality does not exist. Such a single-trait perspective (and whose

From *Building Bridges—Latinas and Latinos at the Crossroads: Realities, Rhetoric and Replacement*, 25 Colum. Hum. Rts. L. Rev. 369 (1994). Originally published in the *Columbia Human Rights Law Review*. Reprinted by permission.

point-of-view is it anyway?) does everyone a disservice by misinforming. A latina/o can be black, and no less latina/o, just as a woman can be latina/o and no less woman. Prevalent single-trait, uni-perspective methodologies prevent the constructive bridge-building that could occur if the focus were on universality. Yet, our differences need not make us adversaries. A multiple-perspective approach promotes understanding among different peoples by affording them the comfort to talk with each other armed with the knowledge that they will have different perspectives based on their life experiences. A multiple-perspective approach therefore promotes understanding instead of generating conflict.

Typecasting

Stereotyping is one of the greatest problems latinas/os must battle to debunk the myth of a monolithic latina/o. Stereotyping puts people in boxes and creates images that result in false presumptions accepted as incontrovertible truths. To be sure, we have seen how this problem plagues all women and men of color. Latinas/os cannot escape its trap. [See part 4 on media treatment and stereotypes.—Eds.]

The Meat Market

I had an interview I will never forget. It was back in 1981, my first participation in the recruitment conference, back in the days when it was held in Chicago. I had been running around, up and down, a day full of thirty-minute interviews scheduled back to back. My 2:00 P.M. interview was with one of the good, progressive schools. My interviewers were four, what I would then have described as older (but today would describe as middle-aged), white men in lawyer uniform: wing-tips, pin-striped suits, white shirts, red and blue striped ties, dark socks, grey hair parted to the side, and wire-rimmed glasses. I arrived at the door, wearing my costume: a camel hair suit, blouse, pumps, leather briefcase. I knocked. El Jefe (read: dean) answered my knock. A pause ensued as el Jefe and his three colleagues first looked at each other and briefly stared at me, in silence. Then they looked me up and down once, twice, three times. Silence. "Uh," said el Jefe as he proceeded to the door, "you must be at the wrong room. We are scheduled to see a Miss Ber . . . uh Ber . . . uh . . . Ber (mumble, groan) HERnandez." (Unpronounceable name indeed!) My turn. Pause. Extend hand, grip firmly. "I am Berta Esperanza Hernández," I introduced myself and proceeded to enter the interview suite and shake hands with the other three interviewers. Once everyone was seated we engaged in the usual obligatory preliminary chit-chat. We talked law, how exactly would I teach labor law, as I recall. Some ten or fifteen minutes into the interview (which considering its beginnings was proceeding unexpectedly smoothly) el Jefe asked, "Excuse me, do you mind telling us if you are from an academic background?" Young, yes; naive, yes; I still had radar. So I pointed to their hands (each one was holding a copy of my resume), and noted that the resume fully covered my educational experience. "No, no," el Jefe said, speaking for all of them, "we mean are you from an academic (emphasis here with arched eyebrows) background?" I too can play, I thought. "I am afraid I don't understand. I went to law school at . . ." Again the question (with very arched eyebrows). Again my answer, adding, "High School I attended in San Juan, Puerto Rico. St. John's Prep." Until finally el Jefe asked, "Well, er, I, what we mean, is, er, well is your father a professional?" There it was, he said it. "My father is a banker, my mother is a lawyer," I replied. Pause. Long Pause. Very Long Pause. "Um. Er. Well," said el Jefe, "I am afraid that with your background our Chicano students would not be able to relate to you. We are afraid they would consider you elite." Pause, again; long pause again, but this time it was mine. At which point I calmly (I think) stood up and, while shaking their startled hands I said, "Well, I guess we do not have anything else to talk about then."

I can only speculate why the four interviewers concluded that their Chicano students would be unable to relate to me or I to them. However, it is plain that their conclusions, incorrect as they may have been, were driven initially by their pre-conceived image of what a latina law professor should look like and by their presuppositions as to what her family should be like. One thing was clear to me: their view depended upon coded ethnicity-gender and class assumptions. First, their image of latinas was one that did not look like me, and I hate to disappoint any who might infer I look "different"; I am really rather typical looking, if a bit on the tall side: 5'8", dark hair, dark eyes, olive skin. Maybe it was my lawyer uniform that threw them off; although, I must confess, almost everyone who goes to the recruitment conference wears some variant of it. Moreover, latinas/os from educated, professional families did not quite fit their image of who latinas/os are supposed to be. And perhaps because I did not fit their image on either count they decided my "difference" was that I was not Chicana. This is the tragic flaw of homogenizing and stereotyping: somebody else's image of who we are, what our families are like, what we do and what we look like makes us the image. It is this imagery—gender, race, ethnic, color and class stereotyping—that falsely imprisons all of us. And I mean all. Latinas/os too. Read on.

Counting

At a meeting, latina/o colleagues were trying to put together a list of who we were. Because the "final" list was so thin, we started combing available records to see if we had missed someone. I looked at the list carefully and noticed a name missing. The name skipped was someone I knew rather well; we had been in undergraduate school together. In fact our parents had known each other from their university days. So I volunteered, "We failed to include Maria." The chair of that meeting recognized but failed immediately to place the name. So the chair took a moment to ponder and said, "Yes, I know who that is. But she doesn't count, she's Cuban." Not knowing whether to laugh or cry I sat in shocked silence and thought, "And ain't I a Cuban?"

Again, as with the interviewers, a Cuban was deemed not to be one of "us," even among a group of latinas/os. This, of course, is the result of the diversity present even among latinas/os. For example, sometimes the first wave of Cuban refugees, because of their education and professional status, are viewed more like the majority, the privileged.

Thus, one can see that inter-latina/o presumptions about subgroups—subgroups that the majority denies by virtue of the notion of the monolithic latina/o—also hold sway. Such stereotyping, I fear, is the product of this country's divisive race-relations outlook, which, consciously or not, minority groups adopt too often. This model is one that we would be better off changing. Significantly, the majority does not care one bit if you are Cuban, first wave or not, or Mexican or Puerto Rican or anything else. The funny name, the accent, the different culture, and the brown skin are enough —you are an "outsider."

Latinas/os and Language

Language is harmful when it stereotypes in a destructive and isolating way. The poisonous nature of "you do not belong there" is exacerbated because it comes not in terms of a dichotomy of black-white relations but rather in terms that touch deeply on latinas/os' multi-dimensionality. Latinas/os are continually bombarded with the "you are not us" message. The myth tells latinas/os: you are not white, not black, not Asian, not Indian. The reality is that latinas/os can be all of the above.

The result of the complete "otherness" perspective is a silencing of latina/o voices. On the one hand, so-called NLWs [non-Latino whites—Eds.] perceive latinas/os as "minorities"—an "other" who speaks a different language to boot.

On the other hand, non-latina/o blacks see latinas/os as "not black," and perhaps even as white. Professor Derrick Bell, for example, noted that "there is every reason to believe that Spanish-speaking . . . immigrants, like their European predecessors, will move beyond the bottom of the society and leave blacks in the role society has designated for them."[1] Certainly Professor Bell cannot believe that all latinas/os are of European heritage or that they are all white. The history of intermarriages in, for example, the Southwestern states, Puerto Rico, Cuba, and the Republica Dominicana attests otherwise. It is plain that there are many latinas/os of African, Asian, and Indian heritage. Nor can, or should, recent latina/o immigrants be likened to "their European predecessors" even if they are of distant European heritage. Dramatically different issues are at play today than existed in the colonial period or the earlier twentieth-century European immigrations. Nevertheless, the perception exists that because latinas/os are not black, latinas/os and blacks do not share issues and concerns. In reality, this is a great misperception. For example, employment and education are two major concerns shared by the black and the latina/o communities. Nevertheless, the view that these communities do not share issues and concerns strengthens oppositionality.

A June 20, 1993, *New York Times* article entitled "As Hispanic Presence Grows, So Does Black Anger," noted the growing resentment of blacks in Miami against latinas/ os who "take their jobs."[2] The article suggests that the tension increases as the city's latina/o population grows to dominate the economic and political life. As one black woman put it, "They are taking over, and I am a victim of that."[3] This echoes the complaints of her white counterparts about the evils of "affirmative action programs" (code: "minorities," meaning blacks and latinas/os) because they take jobs away from deserving whites.

The tragic flaw of the approach that drives the normative-driven oppositionality is that rather than trying to find a novel solution for a new dilemma—the presence of peoples in this society who do not fit squarely into the dichotomous black-white model's structure—it merely seeks to use the pre-existing model. The black or white model does not fit latinas/os, just as the black or woman model does not fit the black woman. Latinas/os bring different issues into play. Slavery is not the issue; that was theoretically solved by the Thirteenth Amendment. Nor is the problem the consequence of slavery, one that still lacks a solution. Nor is formal equal access to public accommodations, housing, employment, and education the issue. Technically, the 1964 Civil Rights Act crafted the tools to solve that problem, although making these wonderful paper rights a reality is a struggle latinas/os share with the black community. On the other hand, latinas/os need to grapple with the present-day issues of language and immigration. Latinas/os must do battle in order to work—either prove you have a green card when you are a citizen/legal resident or find a way to live without one and still be labeled lazy or a welfare cheat. Additionally, we must face the problems caused by the inhuman conditions in which migrant workers live as well as those that result from the creation of an uninsured underclass of persons who provide domestic help, such as nannies, housekeepers, and gardeners. To be sure, this is not an issue unique to latinas/os, as we may well see analogous problems arise among some of the new groups of immigrants to the United States; so much the more important it becomes that latinas/os who have a long history in this country start working on building bridges.

Latinas/os' racial diversity presents novel issues. Latina/o blacks, for example Afro-Cubans, may identify more with the racially mixed Cuban population than with the racially homogeneous (but culturally diverse) English-speaking black population. Rather than identify solely on the basis of race, Afro-Cubans also identify with their linguistic and cultural heritage. This identification, however, does not, as it cannot, render Afro-Cubans "not black."

Yet another angle to latinas/os as "others" is that some appear "white" in the "Anglo" sense. Of course, this "white look" does not make one bit of difference if the initial interaction is on paper, as are most applications for employment or to institutions of higher education. Given that our society appears to hold a very clear image of what a latina/o looks like, such initial paper contact may well conjure up the stereotypic images of what an applicant should look like. This is very likely the reason a good progressive law school's four interviewers once thought I was not me—not that I look "white" in the NLW sense by any stretch of the imagination; but something about me in my lawyer "costume" must have thrown them off. And then, of course, because my parents are educated professionals—much, I might add, like the parents of most colleagues I have had in my sixteen years in the legal profession—in the eyes of the four interviewers, I somehow did not fit the mold, which I imagine requires having pulled myself out of the working class by being the first in my family to enjoy the privilege of higher education.

These are particularly difficult issues without easy answers. If the law has difficulty understanding the concept of a "blackwoman," what can it do with a "blackCubanwoman" concept? Or a Puertorriquena triguena? By restricting analysis to a single-trait approach, the law isolates and disempowers latinas/os by creating a land-scape where both NLWs and (non-latina/o) blacks see latinas/os as "other." Yet the myth—the sham image—proliferates. Latinas/os are reduced to race-less homogene-ity belonging nowhere. The reality of a culturally and racially diverse people is invis-ible. Rather than have us "torn between two colors," with alienating, isolating con-sequences, the diverse experience of latinas/os can be used to bridge gender, racial, ethnic, cultural, and linguistic differences to translate experiences and expressions. Consider how latinas/os can play a role in enhancing communication and under-standing between and among groups that perceive each as the "other."

Building Bridges

I always have started out as the only latina lawyer or law professor in a workplace. Often, the women emerged as my support group—as if the gender commonality provided the necessary bridge. I remember in one of my myriad careers, I arrived as usual—the only latina. I could sense the otherness with which I was viewed by both black and white. One colleague directly asked once, "You don't really consider yourself hispanic, do you?" This changed when one day I had a close friend come to the workplace to put on a special event. Unbeknownst to all, my friend was African American. Once he arrived it was obvious he was black. After the event, a smashing success, the black colleagues for the first time saw me as me as one of "them"—a person of color.

Here is how latinas/os can help. We can build bridges as we have been doing for years. We are used to being black, white, brown, and every other color and shade. We can help create an understanding within the color spectrum, for we have been doing it among ourselves for years. We speak Spanish, English, Spanglish, regional dialects, and indigenous tongues. We can translate—we have been doing it among ourselves for years. We can promote an understanding of differences by engendering understanding of commonalities—we have been doing it among ourselves for years. The lesson to learn is that people, a composite of their race, gender, ethnicity, class, religion, sexual orientation, ability, and color, are complex. Rarely can we find the best answer (at least for a time) by asking only one obvious question, such as "What is the effect of a practice on an ethnic group?" Rather we will reach the better resolu-tion by asking many questions, including ones that address the conflation of traits. To be sure, undertaking such a course is ambitious, difficult, and likely to be painful as we force ourselves to confront prejudices we would just as soon ignore. Such a multi-layered methodology is certain to result in mistakes. But as long as the mis-takes are honest and made in a quest to learn, they will be forgiven and corrected, and we will all grow. Latinas/os, because of our many components, have experienced multi-dimensionality and thus know the multi-layered approach, although we have not necessarily translated it into actual proposals for change. Let us share it with the rest of society and get on with building bridges to a new place where respect and un-derstanding reign.

NOTES

1. Derrick A. Bell, Jr., *The Permanence of Racism*, 22 Sw. U. L. Rev. 1103 (1993).

2. Larry Rohter, *As Hispanic Presence Grows, So Does Black Anger*, N.Y. Times, June 20, 1993, at A1.

3. *Id.*

Chapter 6

||||||||||||||||||||||||||||||||||||||||||||||||||||||||||||||||||||||||||||||||||||||||||

Life in the Hyphen

Ilan Stavans

What if *yo* were you and *tú fueras* I, Mister?

Born in 1885 in Jalisco, Mexico, the painter Martín Ramírez spent most of his life in a California madhouse, in a pavilion reserved for incurable patients. Since his death in 1960 he has become a symbol in Hispanic immigrant experience and is considered today a leading painter with a permanent place in Chicano visual art. As a young man, Ramírez worked first in the fields and then in a laundry; he later worked as a migrant railroad worker, relocating across the Rio Grande in search of a better life and to escape the dangers of the violent upheaval sweeping his native land. He lost the power to talk around 1915, at the age of thirty, and wandered for many years, until the Los Angeles police picked him up and sent him to Pershing Square, a shelter for the homeless. Diagnosed by doctors as a "deteriorated paranoid schizophrenic" and sent to the Dewitt Hospital, Ramírez never recovered his speech. But in 1945, some fifteen years before his death, he began to draw. Ramírez was fortunate to be discovered by a psychiatrist, Dr. Tarmo Pasto, of the University of California, Sacramento, who, as the legend claims, was visiting the hospital one day with a few pupils when Ramírez approached him, offering a bunch of rolled-up paintings. The doctor was so impressed with Ramírez's work that he made sure the artist had plenty of drawing materials. Soon Pasto began collecting Ramírez's work and showed it to a number of artists, including Jim Nutt, who arranged an exhibit of Ramírez's paintings with an art dealer in Sacramento. Other exhibits soon followed—in New York, Chicago, Sweden, Denmark, and Houston, among other places—and Ramírez, the perfect outsider, was a dazzling revelation at the exposition *Outsiders* in London's Hayward Gallery.

In a controversial text written in June 1986 to commemorate the exhibit *Hispanic Art in the United States: Thirty Contemporary Painters and Sculptors* at the Corcoran Gallery in Washington, D.C., Octavio Paz, the 1990 winner of the Nobel Prize in literature, claimed that Ramírez's pencil-and-crayon drawings are evocations of what Ramírez lived and dreamed during and after the Mexican Revolution. Paz compared the artist to Richard Dadd, a nineteenth-century painter who lost his mind at the end of his life. As Carlos Fuentes, the Mexican novelist and diplomat, claimed in his book *The Buried Mirror*, the mute painter drew his muteness, making it graphic. And Roger Cardinal, the British author of *Figures of Reality*, argued that the artist's

Pp. 7–10, 21–22 from THE HISPANIC CONDITION: REFLECTIONS ON CULTURE AND IDENTITY IN AMERICA by Ilan Stavans. Copyright © 1995 by Ilan Stavans. Reprinted by permission of HarperCollins Publishers.

achievements should not be minimized as psychotic rambling and categorized him as "a *naïf* painter." To make sense of Ramírez's odyssey, Dr. Pasto concluded that Ramírez's psychological disturbances were the result of a difficult process of adaptation to a foreign culture. Ramírez had left Mexico at a turbulent, riotous time and arrived in a place where everything was unfamiliar and strange to him.

Ramírez's plight is representative of the entire Hispanic cultural experience in the United States. Neither a diluted Mexican lost in a no-man's-land nor a fully rounded citizen, Ramírez symbolizes the voyage of millions of silent itinerant *braceros* and legal middle-class immigrants bewildered by their sudden mobility, furiously trying to make sense of an altogether different environment. But Hispanics are now leaving his frustrated silence behind. Society is beginning to embrace Latinos, from rejects to fashion setters, from outcasts to insider traders. New generations of Spanish speakers are feeling at home in Gringolandia. (Etymologically, *gringo*, according to *Webster's Dictionary*, is derived from *griego*, stranger, but it may have been derived from the Spanish pronunciation of a slang word meaning fast-spender, *green-go*). Suddenly the crossroad where white and brown meet, where "yo soy" meets "I am," a life in the Spanglish hyphen, is being transformed. Many of us Latinos already have a Yankee look: We either make a conscious effort to look gringo, or we're simply absorbed by the culture's fashion and manners. And what is more exciting is that Anglos are beginning to look just like us—enamored as they are of our bright colors and tropical rhythms, our suffering Frida Kahlo, our legendary Ernesto "Che" Guevara. Martín Ramírez's silence is giving way to a revaluation of things Hispanic. No more silence, no more isolation. Spanish accents, our *manera peculiar de ser*, have emerged as exotic, fashionable, and even enviable and influential in mainstream American culture.

However, just as Ramírez's art took decades to be understood and appreciated, it will take years to understand the multifaceted and far-reaching implications of this cultural transformation, the move of Hispanics from periphery to center stage. I believe that we are currently witnessing a double-faceted phenomenon: Hispanization of the United States, and Anglocization of Hispanics. Adventurers in Hyphenland, explorers of El Dorado, we Hispanics have deliberately and cautiously infiltrated the enemy, and now go by the rubric of Latinos in the territories north of the Rio Grande. Delaying full adaptation, our objective is to assimilate Anglos slowly to ourselves.

Indeed, a refreshingly modern concept has emerged before American eyes—to live in the hyphen, to inhabit the borderland, to exist inside the Dominican-American expression *entre Lucas y Juan Mejía*—and nowhere is the debate surrounding it more candid, more historically enlightening, than among Hispanics. The American Dream has not yet fully opened its arms to us; the melting pot is still too cold, too uninviting, for a total meltdown. Although the collective character of those immigrating from the Caribbean archipelago and south of the border remains foreign to a large segment of the heterogeneous nation, as "native strangers" within the Anglo-Saxon soil, our impact will prevail sooner, rather than later. Although stereotypes remain commonplace and vices get easily confused with habits, a number of factors, from population growth to a retarded acquisition of a second language and a passionate retentiveness of our original culture, actually suggest that Hispanics in the United States shall not, will not, cannot, and ought not follow paths opened up by previous immigrants.

According to various Chicano legends recounted by the scholar Gutierre Tibón, Aztlan Aztlatlan, the archetypal region where Aztecs, speakers of Nahuatl, originated before their itinerant journey in the fourteenth century in search of a land to settle, was somewhere in the area of New Mexico, California, Nevada, Utah, Arizona, Colorado, Wyoming, Texas, and the Mexican states of Durango and Nayarit, quite far from Tenochtitlán, known today as Mexico City. Once a nomadic tribe, the Aztecs settled and became powerful, subjugating the Haustec to the north and the Mixtec and Zapotec to the south, achieving a composite civilization. Latinos with these mixed ancestries, at least six in every ten in the United States, believe they have an aboriginal claim to the land north of the border. As native Americans, we were in these areas before the Pilgrims of the *Mayflower* and understandably keep a telluric attachment to the land. Our return by sequential waves of immigration as wetbacks and middle-income entrepreneurs to the lost Canaan, the Promised Land of Milk and Honey, ought to be seen as the closing of a historical cycle. Ironically, the revenge of Motecuhzoma II (in modern Spanish: Moctezuma; in its English misspelling: Montezuma) is understood differently in Spanish and English. For Anglos, it refers to the diarrhea a tourist gets after drinking unpurified water or eating chile and arroz con pollo in Latin America and the West Indies; for Hispanics, it describes the unhurried process of the penetration of and exertion of influence on the United States—*la reconquista*, the oppressor's final defeat. Yesterday's victim and tomorrow's conquistadors, we Hispanics, tired of a history full of traumas and undemocratic interruptions, have decided to regain what was taken away from us.

Idiosyncratic differences puzzle me: What distinguishes us from Anglo-Saxons and other European immigrants as well as from other minorities (such as blacks and Asians) in the United States? Is there such a thing as a Latino identity? Ought José Marti and Eugenio María de Hostos be considered the forefathers of Latino politics and culture? Need one return to the Alamo to come to terms with the clash between two essentially different psyches, Anglo-Saxon Protestant and Hispanic Catholic? The voyage to what William H. Gass called "the heart of the heart of the country" needs to begin by addressing a crucial issue: the diversity factor. Latinos, no question, are a most difficult community to describe: Is the Cuban from Holguín similar in attitude and culture to someone from Managua, San Salvador, or Santo Domingo? Is the Spanish we all speak, our *lingua franca*, the only unifying factor? How do the various Hispanic subgroups understand the complexities of what it means to be part of the same minority group? Or do we perceive ourselves as a unified whole?

Culture and identity are a parade of anachronistic symbols, larger-than-life abstractions, less a shared set of beliefs and values than the collective strategies by which we organize and make sense of our experience, a complex yet tightly integrated construction in a state of perpetual flux. To begin, it is utterly impossible to examine Latinos without regard to the geography we come from. We are, we recognize ourselves to be, an extremity of Latin America, a diaspora alive and well north of the Rio Grande. For the Yiddish writer Sholem Aleichem's Tevye the milkman, for instance, America was a synonym of redemption, the end of *pogroms*, the solution to earthly matters. Russia, Poland, and the rest of Eastern Europe were lands of suffering. Immigrating to America, where gold grew on trees and could easily be found on sidewalks, was synonymous with entering Paradise. To leave, never to look back and return, was an imperative. Many miles, almost impossible to breach again, divided the old land from the new. We, on the other hand, are just around the corner: Oaxaca, Mexico; Varadero, Cuba; and Santurce, Puerto Rico, are literally next door. We can spend every other month, even every other week, either north or south. Indeed, some among us swear to return home when military dictatorships are finally deposed and more benign regimes come to life, or simply when enough money is saved in a bank account. Meanwhile, we inhabit a home divided, multiplied, neither in the barrio or the besieged ghetto nor across the river or the Gulf of Mexico, a home either here or within hours' distance. José Antonio Villarreal's 1959 novel *Pocho*, for example, called by some critics "a foundational text" and believed to be the first English-written novel by a Chicano, is precisely about the eternal need to return among Chicanos: a return to source, a return to the self. And Pablo Medina's meticulous Cuban-American autobiography *Exiled Memories*, along the same lines, is about the impossibility of returning to childhood, to the mother's soil, to happiness. But return is indeed possible in most cases. Cheap labor comes and goes back and forth to Puebla and San Juan.

One ought never to forget that Hispanics and their siblings north of the border have an intimate, long-standing, love-hate relationship. Latinos are a major source of income for the families they left behind. In Mexico, for instance, money wired by relatives working as pizza delivery boys, domestic servants, and construction workers amounts to a third of the nation's overall revenues. Is this nothing new, when one ponders previous waves of immigration? Perhaps. Others have dreamed of America as paradise on earth, but our arrival in the Promised Land with strings attached underscores troublesome patterns of assimilation. Whereas Germans, Irish, Chinese, and others may have evidenced a certain ambiguity and lack of commitment during their first stage of assimilation in the United States, the proximity of our original soil, both in the geographic and metaphorical sense, is tempting. This thought brings to mind a claim by the Iberian philosopher José Ortega y Gasset, author of *Rebellion of the Masses*, among many other titles, in a 1939 lecture delivered in Buenos Aires. Ortega y Gasset stated that Spaniards assumed the role of the New Man the moment they settled in the New World. Their attitude was the result not of a centuries-long process, but of an immediate and sudden transformation. To this idea the Colombian writer Antonio Sanín Cano once mistakenly added that Hispanics, vis-à-vis other settlers, have a brilliant capacity to assimilate; unlike the British, for instance, who can live for years in a foreign land and never become part of it, we do. What he forgot to add is that we achieve total adaptation at a huge cost to ourselves and others. We become the New Man and Woman carrying along our former environment. Add the fact that we are often approached as traitors in the place once called home: We left, we betrayed our patriotism, we rejected and were rejected by the milieu, we aborted ourselves and spat on the uterus. Cubans in exile are known as *gusanos*, worms in Havana's eyes. Mainland Puerto Ricans often complain of the lack of support from their original families in the Carribean and find their cultural ties tenuous and thin. Mexicans have mixed feelings toward *Pachucos*, *Pochos*, and other types of Chicanos; when possible, Mexico ignores our politics and cultural manifestations.

Chapter 7

|||||||||||||||||||||||||||||||||||||||||||||||||||||||||||||||||||||||||||||||||||||||

Re-imagining the Latino/a Race

Ángel R. Oquendo

This chapter condemns "racial" subcategories, such as "Black Hispanics" and "White Hispanics," which have been increasingly gaining currency, and ultimately suggests that such categories should be rejected. First, they project onto the Latino/a community a divisive racial dualism that, much as it may pervade U.S. society, is alien to that community. Second, they are falsely premised on the existence of an independent objective concept of race capable of meaningfully classifying individuals as "Black" or "White."

Categorizing on the basis of physical features, of course, is an accepted practice in the United States. In fact, this society has primarily used physiognomy to create the "Hispanic" category. Yet what really unites Latino/as is their unique history of oppression. Unlike other immigrant groups, the largest Latino/a groups—Mexicans and Puerto Ricans—did not come into the United States via Ellis Island; they entered through the brutal process of U.S. imperial expansion. They were militarily attacked, invaded, colonized, and annexed. This common experience has caused them to form a unified community, which now includes other people of Latin American ancestry.

Another factor that bonds the Latino/a community is their common language. Not all Latino/as in the United States speak Spanish, but they all have some connection with it. If they do not speak Spanish themselves, then it is the language of their ancestors. Because they share a language, Latino/as constitute a race in the sense proposed by Spanish philosopher Miguel de Unamuno. In fact, in categorizing Latino/as, the "Anglo" majority has emphasized this common linguistic heritage more than physical appearance. For instance, the derogatory term that cuts across the different Latino/a groups is "spik"—which emphasizes how Latino/as "speak" rather than how they look. More significantly, the anti-Latino/a movement has coalesced politically in reaction to the "English only" movement, which attacks their linguistic identity.

From *Re-Imagining the Latino/a Race,* 12 Harv. Blackletter L.J. 93 (1995). Originally published in the *Harvard Blackletter Law Journal.* Reprinted by permission.

A New Categorization

Soy Mexicana
soy Mexican-American
soy American of Spanish Surname (A.S.S.)
soy Latina
soy Puerto Riquena
soy Cocoanut
soy Chicana[1]

In 1978, during my last high school year in Puerto Rico, I took the SAT. Any test can be intimidating, but one that measures aptitude can make you feel insecure and challenged. These feelings were accentuated in my case because the exam was in English, and more important, was administered by an organization from the United States.

I was nervous, in part, because I was being tested by the people who kept us afloat with their massive economic support, who from afar made important decisions for us, and who generally were successful where we had failed. When they came to our land, they were well-off and they ran many of the large companies. In contrast, when we went to their land, we were poor, did the most menial jobs, and scored the lowest on intelligence tests. Therefore, the test had a greater meaning for me. It symbolized America's continuing dominion and control over Puerto Rico. I was determined to wage a battle that I could ultimately win.

Yet I was caught off guard even before the examination began. While I was filling out the personal information part, I was asked to identify myself racially. This struck me as odd for two reasons. I had never been asked such a question before, and I had never thought of myself in terms of race, even though I was aware of the concept of racial differences. I knew about the history and reality of racism, yet I did not see myself as a member of a particular race.

Fortunately, the SAT authorities were wise or benevolent enough to include "Puerto Rican" among the multiple choices. I had no need to check the color of my skin, feel the texture of my hair, visualize my facial features, or call to mind the physiognomy of my family and relatives. With a sense of relief, I checked "Puerto Rican" and moved on.

At the time, I was only a kid facing an unexpected situation. Today, having lived in the United States for over fifteen years, I have come to regard this kind of questioning as normal. In fact, until recently, I considered myself beyond astonishment with respect to issues of racial categorization. I thought that I would always find a box simply labeled "Puerto Rican," "Hispanic," "Latino," "Spanish Surnamed," or even "Other" with which I could feel comfortable.

However, racial categories have changed in the last few years. I am referring to the relatively recent tendency to subcategorize the category for Hispanics. Ever more often, surveys add to that category the following clarification "(Black and White)"—sometimes "(regardless of race)"—and qualify the White as well as the Black category with the parenthetical "(non-Hispanic)." So the list usually reads as follows: "White (non-Hispanic)," "Black (non-Hispanic)," "Hispanic (Including White and Black Hispanics)," "Asian American," "American Indian," and "Other."

A true bureaucrat's paradise! Granted, the Hispanic category is still being made available to me. But it is more difficult for me to embrace that category with all the added attachments and qualifications. I wonder if I am being told that there is something problematic about my category? Is the message that it, unlike other categories, needs further explanation? Is it implied that after all I do belong objectively to a race but that I am being given a break as a Latino/a for some undisclosed reason? The next step will probably be to create separate classifications for Black Hispanics and White Hispanics and to force Latino/as to choose. The quandary that I narrowly escaped as a child will thus be returning with a vengeance.

The Term "Latino/a"

Some have rejected the term "Hispanic" because of its association with Spanish colonial power. They prefer "Latino" because it lacks any such connotation and is more inclusive and descriptive. "Latino" is short for "latinoamericano." Like its English counterpart, the term refers to the people who come from the territory in the Americas colonized by Latin nations, such as Portugal, Spain, and France, whose languages are derived from Latin. People from Brazil, Mexico, and even Haiti are thus all "latinoamericanos." Individuals who are descendants of the former British or Dutch colonies are excluded.

"Iberoamericanos," in contrast, are individuals who come from American lands once occupied by Portugal and Spain, the two countries on the Iberian peninsula. Brazilians and Mexicans are iberoamericanos, but not Haitians or any of the citizens of countries once claimed by France, Britain, or the Netherlands. Finally, "hispanoamericanos" are persons from the former colonies of Spain in the "New World." The expression "Hispanic" probably derives from "hispanoamericanos."

"Latino" is more inclusive than the term "Hispanic," encompassing as it does those people who are descended from the onetime possessions of not only Spain, but also Portugal and France. However, "Latino" enthusiasts would probably exclude these people from the category because they use it to cover only people from what was once the Spanish empire in America. Therefore, in practical application, the term "Latino" is no more inclusive and descriptive than "Hispanic."

That the term "Latino" should be favored over "Hispanic" because the latter is linked to the brutal Spanish colonization of America is puzzling. "Latino," in the informal sense, is just as bound up with the Spanish colonial enterprise. The formal interpretation of Latino is associated with the similarly objectionable Portuguese and French colonial projects, and both terms slight the rich African and Native American influence on the Latino/a community.

What I do find attractive about the expression "Latino" is, first, that it calls to mind the Latino/a struggle for empowerment in the United States. The leaders of this campaign support "Latino" because it came from the community. The Latino/a people are thus conceived of as not just acquiescing to their christening by the Anglo majority, but rather as giving themselves a name. The adoption of the term "Latino" could be regarded as part of a broader process of self-definition and self-assertion.

Second, "Latino" is a newer term that invites re-thinking and re-defining of what membership in this community is all about. This attitude of re-birth and of facing a new beginning is needed as the Latino/a community in the United States becomes larger and more diverse and strives to find itself. The third reason why "Latino" is a better term is because it is a Spanish word. It accentuates the bond between the Latino/a community and the Spanish language. Furthermore, in insisting upon being called by its Spanish name, the Latino/a community is demanding recognition and respect for its culture.

Racial Dualism

What about racial subcategorization? This trend appears to be an attempt to project U.S. racial dualism onto the Latino/a community as a whole. It is possible to imagine a bureaucrat attempting to defend the move as reasonable on grounds of precision: "The categories are meant to be mutually exclusive. White Hispanics and Black Hispanics, however, are covered by two of the categories. In order to be accurate, they would have to check, in addition to the Hispanic box, either the box labeled 'White' or that labeled 'Black.' We just want to make it clear that for our purposes, they are Hispanic, even if they are additionally White or Black. We want each person to choose only one of the options."

This response is spurious. If the concern were Latino/as who might fall within two categories, it would make sense to stipulate that the rubric "Hispanic" includes people who are "racially" Asian or Indian as well as Black and White. The categories for Asian Americans and Native Americans could be adjusted accordingly to exclude Latino/as explicitly. In this way, Latino/as of Asian extraction as well as those who descend from the indigenous peoples of Latin America would know, without a doubt, which category corresponds to them.

Indeed, I think that it is no coincidence that "Indian" and "Asian" Latino/as have been left out of the picture. The decision to omit these groups reflects "racial dualism." The U.S. racial imagination posits a bifurcated racial universe, in which the Black-White divide overwhelms all other differences. This conception of race is not surprising in light of the prominence in U.S. history of the oppression of people of African ancestry by individuals of European extraction. The institutions of enslavement and discrimination have created and reinforced the perception that the opposition between these two groups is essential and universal. Racial dualism is but the other side of dualist racism.

The subcategorization of Latino/as should be rejected precisely because it projects this foreign racial dualism onto the Latino/a community. Among Mexicans, who constitute by far the majority of all Latino/as, the main physiognomic influences are not even African and European. Mexicans instead tend to descend from the indigenous peoples who populated the southern tip and southwest region of North America and the Spanish who later colonized the territory.

Furthermore, the subcategorization injects a dualism or division of the races that is alien even to those Latino/a groups, e.g., Puerto Ricans, in which the principal ethnic influences are African and European. In the words of Luis Nieves Falcón:

> Because in Puerto Rico prejudices take a subtle and personal form, there is no organized body of customs or practices against Blacks. Because social discrimination seems to operate with equal force against all lower class individuals, regardless of color, there is no sufficient basis for the emergence of racial conflicts along racial lines—though, in any case, racial lines are in fact very fluid. Puerto Ricans—white, brown, or black—have little experience with and a very limited understanding of the racial animosities that divide the North American nation and are, naturally, reluctant to take part in a struggle that is repugnant and meaningless to them.
>
> Interpreting the behavior of Puerto Ricans in the United States with respect to racial matters on the basis of their own particular racial experience, North Americans perceive that behavior as incomprehensible, ridiculous, and cowardly. It seems that they would expect White Puerto Ricans to bond on one side and Blacks on the other. Puerto Ricans are pressured to adopt one or the other racial identity, since North Americans cannot really believe that the integration achieved by Puerto Ricans—imperfect as it may be—is possible.[2]

Puerto Rican society might have been bifurcated along racial lines up to the end of the nineteenth century, when its sense of nationality was still developing. Then, José Luis González insists, the Puerto Rican "nation was so divided racially, socially, economically, and culturally, that we should instead talk of two nations." These two nations—or "ethnic groups that were true castes"—had radically different "cultural traditions" and even "Weltanschauungen."[3]

González himself notes, however, that the U.S. invasion and colonization of Puerto Rico in the twentieth century changed the society's structure in a radical way:

> The progressive dismantling of the Puerto Rican elite's culture under the impact of the transformations that the North American colonial regime brought upon the national society has had as a consequence not the North Americanization of that society but, rather, an internal alteration of the cultural values. The vacuum created by the dismantling of the culture of Puerto Ricans from the top has been filled certainly not by the intrusion of the North American culture but rather by the ever more palpable ascent of the culture of Puerto Ricans from the bottom.[4]

Modern Puerto Rican society, González explains, is dominated by a popular culture in which the African roots are "more important" than the European or Taíno roots and that has "an essentially Afro-Antillean character."[5] González's view was anticipated by the poet Luis Palés Matos in an interview:

> The black essence lives with us physically and spiritually. Its characteristics—which have been filtered into the mulatto essence—influence in an evident way all the manifestations of our popular life. . . . I therefore know no collective feature of our people that

does not show the trace of that delicious mixture from which the Antillean character derives its true tone.[6]

The African heritage is even more pervasive in the Puerto Rican community in the United States. For the Diaspora consists primarily of the impoverished sector of the Puerto Rican society, which includes even more individuals of mostly African extraction than other sectors.

Physiognomically, we find infinite gradations of color, but culturally, a single Afro-Antillean ethos. Thus, if a well-defined Black/White polarity ever existed among Puerto Ricans, none remains today. Even the U.S. Census Bureau realized that the realities and the perceptions of race in Puerto Rico differ from those in the United States. Lawrence Wright reports that "[b]y 1960 the United States census, which counts the population of Puerto Rico, gave up asking the race question on the island because race did not carry the same distinction there that it did on the mainland."[7] More generally, the Latino/a community is not divided along racial lines, in part due to the extent of *mestizaje* or social infusion in Latin America.

This historical background, naturally, had a decisive impact on the racial constitution and attitude of the Latino/a community. Unlike the broader U.S. society, the Latino/a community is not segregated into two "racial" groups, with different cultures, identities, and even dialects. Within this community racial consciousness and even racism endure, but of a different kind. Wright correctly observes that

> [t]he fluid Latin-American concept of race differs from the rigid United States idea of biologically determined and highly distinct human divisions. In most Latin cultures, skin color is an individual variable—not a group marker—so that within the same family one sibling might be considered white and another black.[8]

We thus find no discrete, isolated groups, such as White Latino/as or Black Latino/as, but numerous different and overlapping shades, reflecting the individuals' heritage and to some extent correlating with their socio-economic class.

The subcategorization might, of course, find support among a minuscule minority of "mostly European" individuals, worried that their categorization as Hispanic might be taken to imply a renunciation of their claim to be White. The Latino/a encounter with U.S. racial dualism leads to the development of greater color consciousness. In U.S. society, possessing valid title to Whiteness requires being free from any encumbrances of Blackness. In other words, the most effective way to assert that one is White is by categorically denying any connection or kinship to Blacks: As long as one has "one drop of Black blood," one is taken to be Black. These Latino/as are probably motivated by the desire to distance themselves unequivocally from Black Latino/as. In their zeal to adopt racial dualism they forget about the *mestizaje* that is dominant in their community. They begin to think only in terms of Black or White, neglecting that the majority of Latino/as are Mexicans, whose European blood is strongly diluted not by African but by Aztec blood. Thus, their disassociation has caused them to miscategorize individuals in the tradition of racial dualism.

The Poverty of the Concept of Race

Now, what if the racial dualism bias of the subcategorization were remedied? In other words, what if the re-categorization included specifying that the category Hispanic includes all races and perhaps clarifying that the categories "White," "Black," "Asian American," "Native American," and "Other" do not include "Hispanics"? My bureaucrat could now say: "This is generally a racial classification. For policy reasons Hispanics must be treated separately, even though they do not constitute a distinct race. What we are doing is pulling Hispanics from their corresponding racial categories and artificially creating a separate category for them. The questionnaire simply reflects this reality."

This approach is problematically premised on the existence of an independently meaningful concept of race that applies to all people, including Latino/as. The creation of a separate category for Latino/as is taken to be independent of their status as members of a particular race. They supposedly continue to be Black, White, or another color.

Yet, race is, at best, a highly vague category that generally classifies people in terms of the way they look. Spanish philosopher Miguel de Unamuno reports that the word "race," as used in almost every European language, comes from the Spanish or Castilean word *raza*, which means "ray" or "line." "In Castilla," Unamuno points out, "one speaks of a 'raza' of sun and each thread in a cloth is called a 'raza.'"[9] The modern term "race" apparently came to refer to a mark shared by people who are related by heritage. Not surprisingly, people with resembling physical traits, presumably due to a common genealogy, came to be seen as belonging to the same race.

To the extent that Latino/as physiognomically resemble each other and differ from other groups, they could be taken to constitute a "race." The physiognomic differences among Latino/as are probably not much greater than those among the members of other "racial" groups, such as "Whites" or "African Americans." In light of the inexorable vagueness of the concept of race, the idea of racial cohesion among Latino/as is just as plausible as the notion that Latino/as can be internally segregated by race. The concept of race is incapable of providing a meaningful basis for making significant distinctions between those who fall within and those who fall without a particular race.

The Evils of the Concept of Race

Many have repudiated the concept of race not only because of its inaccuracy but also because of the sinister purposes it has served historically. Unamuno's rejection of "racial materialism" provides a case in point. Racial materialism focuses on material or physical characteristics in defining the concept of race. Unamuno denounces "the materialist cast that is usually given to the anthropological concept of race."[10]

In a 1933 article (published on the Day of the Race, "El dia de la raza"—as Columbus Day is referred to in Spanish-speaking countries) Unamuno asserts that it is the racists who use this material concept of race and adds: "Today I feel an obligation to insist on this point, in light of the . . . barbarity, actually savagery, attained by such racism, especially in Germany."[11] He assails "the barbaric sense" given to the materialist concept of race by "the racists, those supposed Aryans of the gammadion and anti-Christian cross."[12]

If racial categories, in addition to having no intelligible substance, serve mainly as an instrument of oppression, why not just eliminate them altogether? Why not go beyond deleting subcategories, such as "Black Hispanic" and "White Hispanic," and eradicate all the general categories too: e.g., "White," "Black," "Hispanic," etc.? I would argue that these general categories should not be simply quashed, but re-anchored on the cultural or spiritual life of peoples. By reconceptualizing themselves, excluded people will be better able to recapture their identities and to struggle for social justice. Overt or crude racism, which is characterized by openly treating African Americans as inherently inferior, has been termed "old-fashioned" racism. The transition to the more subtle and covert forms of racism that prevail in modern society takes place as old-fashioned racism becomes less acceptable. The injury caused by racism cannot be segregated from the racial classification in place. In fact, racism is unjust because it only allows a person to be identified by empty racial categories. Hence, racism not only deprives people of their income; it robs people of their soul.

NOTES

1. ["I am Mexican/I am Mexican-American/I am American of Spanish Surname (A.S.S.)/I am Latina/I am Puerto Rican/I am Cocoanut/I am Chicana"]. *La Chrisx, La Loca de la Raza Cósmica*, in INFINITE DIVISIONS: AN ANTHOLOGY OF CHICANA LITERATURE 84, 88 (Tey Diana Rebolledo & Eliana S. Rivero eds., 1993).

2. Luis Nieves Falcón, DIAGNÓSTICO DE PUERTO RICO 275 (1972). The translation of this as well as other non-English texts in this chapter are my own.

3. José Luis González, *El país de cuatro pisos*, in EL PAÍS DE CUATRO PISOS Y OTROS ENSAYOS 9, 25–26, 27 (1981).

4. *Id.* at 30; see also *id.* at 34, 36.

5. *Id.* at 19; see also *id.* at 22.

6. Ángela Négron Muñoz, *Hablando con don Luis Palés Matos*, EL MUNDO, Nov. 13, 1932.

7. Lawrence Wright, *One Drop of Blood*, NEW YORKER, July 25, 1994, at 46, 52.

8. *Id.* at 52.

9. Miguel de Unamuno y Jugo, *Hispanidad*, in LA RAZA VASCA Y EL VASCUENCE; EN TORNO A LA LENGUA ESPAÑOLA 264, 266 (1974).

10. Miguel de Unamuno y Jugo, *De nuevo la raza*, in LA RAZA VASCA Y EL VASCUENCE; EN TORNO A LA LENGUA ESPAÑOLA 162, 164 (1974).

11. *Id.* at 162.

12. *Id.* at 163.

Chapter 8

||||||||||||||||||||||||||||||||||||||||||||||||||||||||||||||||||||||||||||||||||||

The Question of Race

Clara E. Rodriguez

According to definitions common in the United States, I am a light-skinned Latina with European features and hair texture. I was born and raised in New York City; my first language was Spanish; and I am today bilingual. I cannot remember when I first realized that the color of one's skin, the texture of one's hair, or the cast of one's features determined how one was treated in both my Spanish-language and English-language worlds. I do know that it was before I understood that accents, surnames, residence, class, and clothing also determined how one was treated.

Looking back on my childhood, I recall many instances when light skin color and European features were the objects of admiration, and terms such as *pelo malo* (bad hair) were commonly used to refer to tightly curled hair. It was much later that I came to see that this Eurocentric bias, which favors European characteristics above all others, was part of our history and culture. In both Americas and the Caribbean, we have inherited and continue to favor this Eurocentrism, which grew out of our history of indigenous conquest and slavery.

I also remember a richer, more complex sense of color than the simple dichotomy of black and white would suggest, a genuine aesthetic appreciation of people with some color and an equally genuine valuation of people as people, regardless of color. Also, people sometimes disagreed about an individual's color and racial classification, especially if the person in question was in the middle range, not just with regard to color, but also with regard to class or political position.

As I grew older, I came to see that many of these clues to status—skin color, physical features, accents, surnames, residence, and other class characteristics—changed according to place or situation. For example, a natural tan in my South Bronx neighborhood was attractive, whereas downtown, in the business area, it was otherizing. I also recall that the same color was perceived differently in different areas. Even in Latino circles, I saw some people as lighter or darker, depending on certain factors such as their clothes, occupation, and families. I suspect that others saw me similarly, so that in some settings, I was very light, in others darker, and in still others about the same as everyone else. Even though my color stayed the same, the perception and sometimes its valuation changed.

I also realize now that some Latinos' experiences were different from mine and that our experiences affect the way we view the world. I know that not all Latinos have multiple or fluctuating identities. For a few, social context is irrelevant. Regardless of the context, they see themselves, and/or are seen, in only one way. They are what the Census Bureau refers to as *consistent*; that is, they consistently answer in the same way when asked about their race. Often, but not always, they are at one or the other end of the color spectrum.

My everyday experiences as a Latina, supplemented by years of scholarly work, have taught me that certain dimensions of race are fundamental to Latino life in the United States and raise questions about the nature of race in this country. This does not mean that all Latinos have the same experiences but that for most, these experiences are not surprising. For example, although some Latinos are consistently seen as having the same color or race, even more are assigned a multiplicity of racial classifications, sometimes in one day! I am reminded of the student who told me after class one day, "When people first meet me, they think I'm Italian, then when they find out my last name is Mendez, they think I'm Spanish, then when I tell them my mother is Puerto Rican, they think I'm nonwhite or black." Although he had not changed his identity, the perception of it changed with each additional bit of information.

Latino students have also told me that non-Latinos sometimes assume they are African American. When they assert they are not black but Latino, they are either reproved for denying their race or told they are out of touch with reality. Other Latinos, who see whites as other-than-me, are told by non-Latinos, "But you're white." Although not all Latinos have such dramatic experiences, almost all know (and are often related to) others who have.

In addition to being reclassified by others (without their consent), some Latinos shift their own self-classification during their lifetime. I have known Latinos who became black, then white, then human beings, and finally again Latino—all in a relatively short time. I have also known Latinos for whom the sequence was quite different and the time period longer. Some Latinos who altered their identities came to be viewed by others as legitimate members of their new identity group. I also saw the simultaneously tricultural, sometimes trilingual, abilities of many Latinos who manifested or projected a different self as they acclimated themselves to a Latino, African American, or white environment.

I have come to understand that this shifting, context-dependent experience lies at the core of many Latinos' life in the United States. Even in the nuclear family, parents, children, and siblings often exhibit a wide range of physical types. For many Latinos, race is primarily cultural; multiple identities are a normal state of affairs; and racial mixture is subject to many different, sometimes fluctuating, definitions.

Some regard *racial mixture* as an unfortunate or embarrassing term, but others consider the affirmation of mixture empowering. Maria Lugones subscribes to this latter view and affirms mixture, *mestizaje*, as a way of resisting a world that emphasizes purity and separation: "Mestizaje defies control through simultaneously asserting the impure, curdled multiple state and rejecting fragmentation into pure parts . . . the mestiza . . . has no pure parts to be 'had,' controlled."[1] Also prevalent in the upper classes is the hegemonic view that rejects or denies mixture and claims a pure

European ancestry. This view also is common among middle- and upper-class Latinos, regardless of their skin color or place of origin. In some areas, people rarely claim a European ancestry, such as in indigenous sectors of Latin America, in parts of Brazil, and in the coastal areas of Colombia, Venezuela, Honduras, and Panama. Recently, some Latinos have encouraged another view in which those historical components that were previously denied and denigrated, such as indigenous and African ancestry, were privileged.

Many people, however—mostly non-Latinos—are not acquainted with these basic elements of Latino life. They do not think much about them, and when they do, they tend to see race as a given, an ascribed characteristic that does not change for anyone, at any time. One is either white or not white. They also believe that race is based on genetic inheritance, a perspective that is just another construct of race.

Whereas many Latinos regard their race as primarily cultural, others, when asked about their race, offer standard U.S. race terms, saying that they are white, black, or Indian. Still others see themselves as Latinos, Hispanics, or members of a particular national-origin group *and* as belonging to a particular race group. For example, they may identify themselves as Afro-Latinos or white Hispanics. In some cases, these identities vary according to setting, but in others they do not.

I have therefore come to see that the concept of race can be constructed in several ways and that the Latino experience in the United States provides many illustrations of this. My personal experiences have suggested to me that for many Latinos, racial classification is immediate, provisional, contextually dependent, and sometimes contested. But because these experiences apply to many non-Latinos as well, it is evident to me that the Latino construction of race and the racial reading of Latinos are not isolated phenomena. Rather, the government's recent deliberations on racial and ethnic classification standards reflect the experiences and complexities of many groups and individuals who are similarly engaged in issues pertaining to how they see themselves and one another.

"Other Race" in the 1980 and 1990 Censuses

It was because of my personal experiences that I first began to write about race and was particularly sensitive to Latinos' responses to the censuses' question about it. The U.S. Census Bureau's official position has been that race and ethnicity are two separate concepts. Thus, in 1980 and in 1990, the U.S. census asked people to indicate their race—white, black, Asian or Pacific Islander, American Indian, or other race—and also whether or not they were Hispanic. Latinos responded to the 1990 census's question about race quite differently than did non-Latinos. Whereas less than 1 percent of the non-Hispanic population reported they were "other race," more than 40 percent of Hispanics chose this category. Latinos responded similarly in the previous decennial census. Although the percentages of the different Hispanic groups choosing this category varied, all chose it more often than did non-Hispanics.

In addition, the many Hispanics who chose this category wrote—in the box explicitly asking for race—the name of their home Latino country or group, to explain their race—or otherness. That these Latino referents were usually cultural or national-origin terms, such as Dominican, Honduran, or Boricua (i.e., Puerto Rican) underscores that many Latinos viewed the question of race as one of culture, national origin, and socialization rather than simply biological or genetic ancestry or color. Indeed, recent studies have found that many Latinos understand race to mean national origin, nationality, ethnicity, culture, or a combination of these and skin color. For many Latinos, the term *race* or *raza* is a reflection of these understandings and not of those often associated with race in the United States, for example, defined by hypo-descent.[2] Studies have found that Latinos also tend to see race along a continuum and not as a dichotomous variable in which individuals are either white or black.

This does not mean that there is only one Latino view of race. Rather, one finds different views of race within different countries, classes, and even families. Latinos' views are dependent on a complex array of factors, one of which is the racial formation process in their country of origin. Other variables also influence their views of race, for example, generational differences, phenotype, class, age, and education. But even though there is not just one paradigm of Latin American race, some basic differences mark the way that Latinos view race and the way it is viewed overall in the United States.

In the United States, rules of hypodescent and categories based on presumed genealogical-biological criteria have generally dominated conceptions of race. Racial categories have been few, discrete, and mutually exclusive, with skin color a prominent element. Categories for mixtures—for example, mulatto—have been transitory. In contrast, in Latin America, racial constructions have tended to be more fluid and based on many variables, like social class and phenotype. There also have been many, often overlapping, categories, and mixtures have been consistently acknowledged and have had their own terminology. These general differences are what Latinos bring with them to the United States, where they influence how they view their own and others' identity.

Although Latinos may use or approach race differently, this does not mean that race as understood by Latinos does not have overtones of racism or implications of power and privilege—in either Latin America or the United States. Indeed, the depreciation and denial of African and Amerindian characteristics are widespread.[3] Everywhere in Latin America can be found "a pyramidal class structure, cut variously by ethnic lines, but with a local, regional and nation-state elite characterized as 'white.' And white rules over color within the same class; those who are lighter have differential access to some dimensions of the market."[4]

Even those countries that subscribe to a racial ideology of *mestizaje*[5] often maintain racial and class hierarchies that favor upper-class interests and political agendas, privilege European components, ignore racialisms, and neutralize expressions of pluralism by indigenous or African-descended groups. As one Jamaican student traveling in the Spanish-speaking Caribbean noted, the attitude there toward race is similarly destructive but strikingly different from that in the United States. Unfortunately, time has not altered the way color and its associated connotations continue to convey and determine the treatment that many receive in the Americas and the Caribbean.

When they migrate to the United States, some Latinos become more aware of the racism of their own country of origin, while others begin to question their conceptions of ethnic, racial, and national identities. This ideological contestation came to the fore when Latinos checked the "other race" category and wrote in their national origins, ethnicity, and so forth on the decennial census forms. Thus, most of the 40 percent of Hispanics who marked the "other race category" and wrote in a Latino referent were asserting that they were "none of the above." Others—non-Latinos—might fit them into one or more of the groups listed on the basis of color, phenotype, or biological or ancestral knowledge of race origin, but culturally or politically these Latinos did not see themselves as white, black, or Asian or Pacific Islander—or just one of these. According to their own, more culturally defined perspective of race, the race groups listed on the census were social groups but did not include their own social group. This is why many Latinos still mark "other" on census forms and fill in the space specifying their national origin. Still others disagree with the race structure mirrored in the census's race question and choose the "other race" category because they are *more* than "one of the above" race categories; that is, they are *mestizo*, mulatto, black Latino, or another mixture.

Although the remaining 60 percent of Hispanics chose one of the census's standard race categories, this does not necessarily mean that they all have assimilated or adopted the United States' racial classification system. Rather, some Latinos believe that this is how they are seen and will always be seen in the United States and accept that this is their race here. Still others are aware of the official pressure to mark one of the standard categories.

Other Hispanics choose the standard race categories for the same reasons that members of other groups do. They determine that biologically, or in terms of blood quantum, they fit into a particular category. Finally, some Hispanics do not want to be (or admit to being) "other than white," "other than black," or "other than *indio*" (i.e., a member of an indigenous nation). That is, they identify culturally and/or politically with members of a particular category.

These "other race" responses presented a problem to the Census Bureau because they differed from previous ones and therefore could not be easily fit into the existing race structure. What was to be done with the nearly 10 million Hispanics who answered the race question in this way? In what category did they belong? How were they to be reported or tabulated? In short, how was this group to be understood? When analyzing these results, references to this data-quality problem were couched in terms of responses in "the other race" category. But the overwhelming majority (97.5%) who chose this category were Hispanic, accounting for 40 percent of that group. How, then, was this "other race" group (or Hispanic component) to be understood or accommodated in a country that for most of its history had employed an overarching dual racial structure with four presumed major color groups, that is, white, black, Asian or Pacific Islanders, and Native American Indian?

This group, moreover, represented a growing number of people. In 1990, those who had checked the "other race" category represented the country's second-fastest growing racial category (after Asian and Pacific Islanders). In addition, the population of Latinos was growing seven times faster than that of the nation as a whole.

The search for solutions to this and other problems has contributed to a radical reexamination of the concept of race by the U.S. government. This reexamination included numerous hearings, conferences, and massive studies of hundreds of thousands of households and resulted in the decision to reverse the Census Bureau's two-hundred-year policy. For the first time, in the 2000 census, respondents were allowed to choose more than one racial group when answering the question about race.

NOTES

1. Maria Lugones, *Purity, Impurity, and Separation,* Signs, Winter 1994, at 458, 460.

2. *Hypodescent* is also referred to as the "one-drop rule," in which "one drop" of "nonwhite or black blood" determines a person's "race."

3. The degree to which racism is perceived and experienced in the Latino framework may be related to phenotype. Consequently, those farthest from either the local mean or the ideal European model may be those most subject to, and therefore most aware of, racism and discrimination. In the dominant U.S. framework, those farthest from the stereotyped "Latin look" may be those most acutely aware of, or in the best position to observe, discrimination.

4. Arleen Torres and Norman E. Whitten, Jr., *Introduction*, in Blackness in Latin America and the Caribbean: Social Dynamics and Cultural Transformations, v.2, at 53 (1998).

5. Martinez-Echazábal uses the word "*mestizaje* as a way of avoiding the English term miscegenation because in Anglo-America, miscegenation refers exclusively to the sexual union of two people of different races while in the Ibero-American contexts it signals both biological and cultural interracial mixing." Lourdes Martinez Echazábal, *Mestizaje and the Discourse of National/Cultural Identity in Latin America, 1845–1959,* 25 Latin American Perspectives 21, 38 (1998).

Chapter 9

||||||||||||||||||||||||||||||||||||||||||||||||||||||||||||||||||||||||||||||||||||

Gateway to Whiteness
The Census and Hispanic/Latino Identity

Gustavo Chacon Mendoza

Recent census projections suggest that by 2050 Whites will make up less than 50% of the United States national population. Latinos are one of the fastest growing groups in the nation. From July 1, 2004 to July 1, 2005, the Hispanic community "accounted for . . . 49% . . . of the national population growth of 2.8 million."

The increasing minority population is threatening the traditional White American identity. This threat arises only by virtue of the inclusive and exclusive manner in which race and ethnicity are currently defined. As the American identity evolves, the decreasing White majority must find new ways to preserve the White national identity. The United States has a long history of reclassifying and redefining race, ethnicity and different sub-groups in America in the census and elsewhere. With the increase of the minority population, the redefining of race and ethnicity emerges as the eventual method of preserving the White American identity. The census will be the tool used to narrow the understanding of ethnicity and broaden the definition of Whiteness in efforts to maintain the current American identity.

The Hispanic/Latino/Spanish population and its multiple sub-groups are the most susceptible to being reclassified and defined as White. Latin America has a history of encouraging the whitening of its national populations, which was pressed upon these societies by strong influential European racial theories between the 1880s and 1930s. In the United States, the census has served as a device to include and exclude groups within the national identity. Mexicans and Puerto Ricans are the largest Hispanic sub-groups within the U.S. Sub-groups with smaller populations in the U.S. may lack the political power to avoid being organized under the Black/White binary and excluded from any separate ethnic categories. Forcing Hispanic groups into the Black/White binary will obscure the rapid increase of the minority population and simultaneously increase the White majority numbers.

The Hispanic grouping is most susceptible to being incorporated solely within the Black/White binary. The influence of Latin American ideology pressed upon many Hispanic group members has created a preference for White identification. Moreover,

From *Gateway to Whiteness: Using the Census to Redefine and Reconfigure Hispanic/Latino Identity in Efforts to Preserve a White American National Identity,* 30 U. La Verne L. Rev. 160 (2008). Originally published in the *University of La Verne Law Review.* Reprinted by permission.

the census's ability to include Hispanic sub-groups into the national identity pushes these groupings to prefer a more specific classification of their own identities. Lastly, a large number of Hispanic group members currently classify themselves within the racial categories as White.

Hispanic groups will not benefit, however, from being considered White. The United States has a long history of discriminating against and negatively stereotyping Hispanic group members. Surnames, language, accents or even physical features will continue to distinguish the Hispanic groups from the White community. If categorized as White, discrimination against members of these groups will only be harder to trace and protection will be more difficult to obtain. White privilege will continue, but Hispanics will not benefit from it the same way many poor White groups have done in the past. Since a larger percentage of Hispanics than Whites are poor, the incorporation will create a permanent poor White sub-class by erasing their ethnicity and incorporating them only within the White racial category.

The Statistical Threat: The Increasing Minority Population

Overall, the United States population could increase from 282.1 million in 2000 to 419.9 million by 2050. By that time, Whites will no longer constitute a majority of this nation's population. African-Americans will account for 15% of the population, Asian-Americans for 8% and Latinos for 24%.

Among the Latino population, the 2000 census found that those of Mexican descent were by far the largest sub-group, accounting for 20.9 million, 59% of the total U.S. Latino population. Those of Puerto Rican descent were the second largest group, a dramatically smaller number of 3.4 million. Other Latinos together accounted for 5.5 million. The Commonwealth of Puerto Rico has an additional 3.8 million Hispanics, who are excluded from the U.S. census count. The U.S. census totals include only the 50 U.S. States and exclude the Puerto Rican Commonwealth and the U.S. Island areas. Although Puerto Ricans are eligible to join the U.S. military, they are not counted by the U.S. census.

The Current State of Race and Ethnicity on the Census

The 2000 census includes one question (question 5) regarding ethnicity and a separate question (question 6) regarding race. Between question 4 and question 5, the form instructs the reader to "please answer both Question 5 and 6." Question 5, the "ethnicity" question, asks, "Is this person Spanish/Hispanic/Latino?" The options are (1) "No, Not Spanish/Hispanic/Latino" (2) "Yes, Mexican, Mexican Am., Chicano" (3) "Yes, Puerto Rican" (4) "Yes, Cuban" (5) "Yes, other Spanish/Hispanic/Latino," with boxes under to fill in. Question 6, the "race" question asks, "What is the person's race?" The respondent can choose from "White," "Black (includes African Am[erican], or Negro)," "American Indian or Alaska Native," a list of Asian races such as Chinese, Filipino, Korean, Vietnamese, and "Some Other Race" with a box to fill in.

The Latino/Hispanic classification in the census has evolved over time. In the 1930

U.S. census, "Mexican" was a distinct racial (not ethnic or nationality) category. The 1940 census removed the Mexican race category and created a different identifier, Spanish as the "mother tongue" category. In the 1950 and 1960 censuses, Latinos were identified indirectly, such as by categorizing "persons of Spanish surname." In 1970, the U.S. census for the first time used the term Hispanic, thereby recognizing and identifying a specific group of people and creating the first ethnicity question on the census questionnaire. However, the version of the 1970 questionnaire that included the ethnicity question was distributed to only "a 5[%] sample of households." The census in 1980 and 1990 asked for "'Spanish/Hispanic origin or descent' and if so, to choose Mexican, Puerto Rican, Cuban, or other Spanish/Hispanic." From the 1990 census to the 2000 census not much changed on the ethnicity question, but the term "Latino" was introduced for 2000.

The biggest question is how Hispanics identify themselves on the census regarding race. According to the 2000 U.S. census, 48% of Hispanics identified themselves as "White" alone. Less than 4% of Hispanics identified themselves as Black (includes African American, Negro). Another 42% of Hispanics marked the "Some Other Race" category. The census found that 6% of Hispanics reported two or more races, and of that number, 81% marked as one of their choices, "Some Other Race." In fact, of the 15.8 million people who marked the "Some Other Race" category, 97% of them were Hispanic. Hence, "Some Other Race" is also functioning as a de facto Hispanic category.

The White American National Identity

The census is a tool in constructing "national identity, group identity and individual identity."[1] The use of race in the census gives rise to a "function of official race classifications . . . [creating] a sense of group membership or even community where there had been none before."[2] The census not only acknowledges existing identities, but also takes particular characteristics to solidify an identity, officially recognizing those in power and those in the minority.

"[T]he idea of 'nation' was made possible in the eighteenth century by the demise of religious and dynastic empires and the rise of vernacular languages and print capitalism."[3] With print capitalism, people began to believe that they were connected with others unknown to them. Similarly, the census provides data to the public which emphasize similarities of a collective and political social body, and strengthen the imagination of a connection between people spread over a broad territory. The census is a composite picture of the nation as a whole, giving a visual depiction and portraying its education, production, lifestyle, and economic patterns. Statistics established a new relationship among people, facts and data, and these categorical interpretations push into existence this imagined average community.

The Census as a Catalyst in the Preservation of the White National Identity

Through the accumulation of statistics and the rapid increase of minority groups, the meaning of Whiteness is necessarily changing. Society will have to redefine Whiteness and include Latinos if Whites are to maintain a numerical majority. History has demonstrated that the United States is willing to redefine and reclassify race and ethnicity. By redefining and broadly interpreting the meaning of White, the racial category can become more inclusive and inflate those numbers. Also by narrowly defining ethnicity and restricting its availability as a census answer, the census will force people to identify themselves in groupings that do not match their social perception and standing.

Due to the framing of questions and limited scope of the census, Whites receive an inflated numerical advantage and perception. An example of how the census can increase numbers in the White racial category is through the formation and layout of questions on the questionnaire. From the inception of the Hispanic ethnic question, the "Other Race" category was the fastest growing racial category in both the 1980 and 1990 census. The Census Bureau reasoned that Hispanics did not understand the race question. It can be inferred that in response to such increasing numbers in the "Other Race" category, the Census Bureau relocated the ethnicity question on the questionnaire in the 2000 census. Instead of being Question 7, the ethnicity question became Question 5, directly before the race question. With the relocation of the ethnicity question, the "Other Race" category declined. By manipulating the formation of the census, fewer people will choose the "Other Race" category, and more Hispanics will continue to fall within the Black/White binary classifications.

The numerical inflation of the White category also results from the census's inclusion of groups which are historically not perceived as White; exclusion of non-White populations; and individual reluctance to being considered Hispanic. For example, in the United States those of Middle Eastern and Arab descent are not viewed socially as White, but the census counts them as such, unless they answer the ancestry question differently. As noted above, the 3.8 million Puerto Ricans living on the Island of Puerto Rico are not counted in the U.S. census totals, which only include the fifty U.S. states. A large number of Hispanics do not fill in the ethnicity question or even, surprisingly, identify as "Not-Hispanic." Among foreign-born persons, 17.2% of those born in Spain, 4% of those born in Central and South America, 50.5% of those born in Brazil, and 89.3% of those born in Portugal and the Azores, filled in "Not-Hispanic." By contrast, approximately 90% of foreign-born Puerto Ricans, Cubans, and Mexicans, and 77% of foreign-born Dominicans, selected the Hispanic ethnicity classification. The statistics demonstrate a divide between certain more and less populous Hispanic sub-groups. This division would make the smaller groups more susceptible to being separated from the larger Hispanic grouping and included solely within the Black/White binary.

Along with the present system of inflating the White majority, certain census proposals have considered the removal of the "Other Race" category. One justification is cost savings. If the 2010 census is conducted the same way as the 2000 version, the cost may reach up to $12.6 billion. Trimming down the number of questions might cut costs. But eliminating the "Other Race" category would force Hispanics to choose one of the standard (i.e., Black/White) racial categories. Since 48% of Hispanics in the 2000 census already chose the White racial category, removing the "Other Race" category would presumably inflate those numbers further.

Will History Repeat Itself and Re-define Race and Ethnicity in Efforts to Preserve the White American Identity?

Since race is subject to being defined and re-defined, the census recognizes its fluidity; societal influence has altered and will continue to change racial classifications. Because of the rapid growth of the Latino community, the fastest way to secure a numerical White majority would be through the inclusion of Latino groups.

Will history repeat itself? Yes, it will. The census has been gradually pushing Hispanics into the White racial category. The census recognizes that race is socially constructed, yet Hispanics have no separate racial category. In the 2000 census, 42% of the Hispanic population perceived themselves as a separate race. Hispanics are only recognized through ethnicity—theirs is, in fact, the only ethnicity acknowledged by the census. Recognizing Hispanic identity as "ethnicity" rather than race, and then requiring Hispanics to choose a recognized race, will force Hispanics to fall in line with the traditional Black/White binary. The census refuses to recognize Hispanics as a race and states that Hispanic recognition as a separate race is based upon the respondents' "confusion" or failure to understand the race question. In 1970, respondents who wrote in Hispanic, Mexican, Cuban, or Puerto Rican in the "Other Race" category were reclassified and tabulated as White, literally forcing these individuals into Whiteness. Either through clever manipulation in questioning, order of questions, or even through force, history is slowly repeating itself.

A simple change of classification does not erase a past filled with discrimination, stereotypes, and stigma. In 1848 the United States promised all Mexicans remaining in the U.S. full citizenship rights, but virtually taxed and licensed them out of existence within the political, economic, and social infrastructures. During the Gold Rush an onslaught of lynchings and murders aimed to force Mexican Americans to release any mining claims they may have had. To this day, Latinos are seen as bringing an inferior welfare and crime-prone culture into the United States. The welfare stereotype continues even though Latino men are employed at a higher rate than any other population group. On television, between 2001 and 2002, Latinos represented only 2% of primetime characters, which is far from actual national population percentages.

It is not hard to find a Latino. Having a Spanish surname is one indication. If an individual is born with the last name Mendoza, unless he denies or changes his last name, he will be classified as Latino, whether or not he claims that group identity. Language use is another way in which Hispanics can be identified. Many children born in the United States to predominantly Spanish-speaking parents speak with an accent. A person who can only speak Spanish, or has an accent deriving from a Spanish-speaking country, will be classified as Hispanic. Physical features can also identify one as Hispanic. A person with a darker tone to her skin or exotic facial features may be characterized as non-White, and possibly Hispanic. Simply because a person is classified as White, or has a fair complexion, does not mean that she will be viewed or treated as White within society.

Latinos are still perceived as distinct from the White majority; because of this perceived difference, Latinos will continue to be discriminated against. For example,

Latinos in California are underserved by the legal profession at three times the rate when compared to Whites. Latinos, "despite their longevity in this nation—continue to show the lowest college-going rates and the lowest economic profile." In 1996, a higher percentage of Latinos lived in poverty than either the White or Black United States population. Since many Latinos can be clearly identified through their surnames, physical features, and accents, they can easily be discriminated against.

Redefining Latino groups will also have an effect on the way federal funds are allocated and affect the data on discrimination methods in collection. More than $100 billion dollars are allocated each year based on census data. The data collected by the census on racial enumeration have supplied the foundation for civil rights enforcement.

If Latinos are defined solely as White, they will not benefit from the same privileges poor White communities did in the past. History demonstrates that White communities benefited economically from the subordination of minority groups. With time, the privileges and effects of slavery and segregation are very slowly diminishing. Since Latinos make up some of the poorest communities in the United States, the only effect of transferring their identity will be to turn a poor Latino into a poor White. The difference is that this poor White will be distinguishable by name, accent, and/or physical features, and continue to be discriminated against based on these differences. There will be no equality in the poor White communities when a former Hispanic, now a poor White, is discriminated against because of his or her differences.

NOTES

1. Naomi Mezey, *Erasure and Recognition: The Census, Race and the National Imagination,* 97 Nw. U. L. Rev. 1701, 1702 (2003).

2. Id. at 1747.

3. Id. at 1707 (identifying certain factors that contributed to the rise of nationality, namely decreasing monarchical legitimacy); see Benedict Anderson, IMAGINED COMMUNITIES: REFLECTIONS ON THE ORIGINS AND SPREAD OF NATIONALISM 16–21 (rev. ed. 1991).

From the Editors *Issues and Comments*

Do all Americans who descend from Spanish-speaking countries have something in common? What can possibly unite such a diverse group, including Cubans, Puerto Ricans, New Mexicans whose families have been here for two hundred years, undocumented migrant laborers, and Central American refugees fleeing political repression?

By what label should Americans who descend from Spanish-speaking countries identify themselves? "Latino"? "Hispanic"? Or something else? How many categories should there be, or should we abolish all categories?

Should the Census designate Latinos as a special class? And, if so, how and with what categories?

Will the government one day force Latinos to classify themselves as white?

Are Latinos more like blacks or like whites?

Historically, any American with a trace of recognizable black ancestry was considered black. Why is there no such "one-drop" rule for Latinos?

Is race—including the Latino race—biological, or a social construct? Note that every feature considered a marker for Latinos, such as olive skin and black hair, is also possessed by many individuals who consider themselves white. If race is a social construct, why do we construct it so? Why does society construct the category "Latino" at all? Are the reasons benign?

If you were a very light-skinned Latino who could, by dressing a certain way and concealing your accent, pass for white, would you do so? What would you give up, and what would you gain?

Suppose that the environment changes radically so that all the white people are sickly, have trouble expressing themselves, and die early in life. Latinos and blacks move into leadership positions and take control of industry. Would whites change their names to Rodriguez and Ramirez and try to "pass" for Latino or black?

Do you agree that higher education can lead to alienation within the Latino group? If you are a Latino student, have others in your group accused you of being different? If you are not a Latino, do you believe you will face similar alienation from friends and family once you earn your degree?

Should light-skinned Latinos be entitled to affirmative action benefits?

How has Latinos' use of Spanish subjected them to discrimination? Have you ever felt threatened by another's use of a language you did not understand? Why is it important to Latinos/as to continue to speak their language?

Suggested Readings

Arce, Carlos H., and Aida Hurtado. "Mexicans, Chicanos, Mexican Americans, or Pochos . . . Que Somos? The Impact of Language and Nativity on Ethnic Labeling." 17 *Aztlán: A Journal of Chicano Studies* 103–30 (1987).

Arce, Carlos H., Edward Murguía, and W. Parker Frisbie. "Phenotype and Life Chances among Chicanos." 9 *Hispanic Journal of Behavioral Science* 19 (1987).

Calderón, José. "'Hispanic' and 'Latino': The Viability of Categories for Panethnic Unity." 19 *Latin American Perspectives* 37–44 (Fall 1992).

Cisneros, Sandra. *The House on Mango Street*. Houston: Arte Publico Press, 1984.

"Directive No. 15, Race and Ethnic Standards for Federal Statistics and Administrative Reporting." 43 *Federal Register* 19,260. Washington, D.C.: National Archives and Records Administration, 1978.

Espino, Rodolfo, and Michael M. Frantz. "Latino Phenotypic Discrimination Revisited: The Impact of Skin Color on Occupational Status." 83 *Social Science Quarterly* 612 (2002).

Ethnic Identity: Formation and Transformation among Hispanics and Other Minorities, edited by Martha E. Bernal and George P. Knight. Albany: State University of New York Press, 1993.

Gomez, Laura E. "The Birth of the 'Hispanic' Generation: Attitudes of Mexican-American Political Elites toward the Hispanic Label." 19 *Latin American Perspectives* 45 (Fall 1992).

Gracia, Jorge J. E. *Latinos in America: Philosophy and Social Identity*. Malden, Mass.: Blackwell, 2008.

Haney López, Ian F. "Race on the 2010 Census: Hispanics & the Shrinking White Majority." 134(1) *Daedalus* 42–52 (2005).

Hayes-Bautista, David. "Identifying 'Hispanic' Populations: The Influence of Research Methodology on Public Policy." 70 *American Journal of Public Health* 353 (1980).

Hayes-Bautista, David, and Jorge Chapa. "Latino Terminology: Conceptual Bases for Standardized Terminology." 77 *American Journal of Public Health* 61 (1987).

Hernández, Tanya Kateri. "Multiracial Discourse: Racial Classifications in an Era of Color Blind Jurisprudence." 57 *Md. L. Rev.* 97 (1998).

Hernández-Truyol, Berta Esperanza. "Borders (En)gendered: Normativities, Latinas, and a LatCrit Paradigm. 72 *N.Y.U. L. Rev.* 882 (1997).

Johnson, Kevin R. *How Did You Get to Be Mexican: A White/Brown Man's Search for Identity*. Philadelphia: Temple University Press, 1999.

Keefe, Susan E., and Amado M. Padilla. *Chicano Ethnicity*. Albuquerque: University of New Mexico Press, 1987.

Klor de Alva, J. Jorge. "Telling Hispanics Apart: Latino Sociocultural Diversity." In *The Hispanic Experience in the United States: Contemporary Issues and Perspectives*, edited by Edna Acosta-Belén and Barbara R. Sjostrom, 107. New York: Praeger, 1988.

Lansdale, Nancy S., and R. S. Oropeza. "White, Black or Puerto Rican? Racial Self-Identification among Mainland and Island Puerto Ricans." 81(1) *Social Forces* 231–54 (2002).

Lopez, Felipe H. "The Construction of Mexican Identity." 54 *Rutgers L. Rev.* 989 (2002).

Medina, Pablo. *Exiled Memories: A Cuban Childhood*. Austin: University of Texas Press, 1990.

Mendible, Myra. "Paradise Lost, Paradise Found: Oral Histories and the Formation of Cuban Identities." 55 *Fla. L. Rev.* 269 (2003).

Murguia, Edward. "On Latino/Hispanic Ethnic Identity." 2(3) *Latino Studies Journal* 8–18 (1991).

Murray, Yxta Maya. "The Latino-American Crisis of Citizenship." 31 *U.C. Davis L. Rev.* 503 (1998).

Obejas, Achy. *We Came All the Way from Cuba So You Could Dress Like This?* Pittsburgh: Cleis Press, 1994.

Oboler, Suzanne. *Ethnic Labels, Latino Lives: Identity and the Politics of (Re)presentation in the United States*. Minneapolis: University of Minnesota Press, 1995.

Office of Budget and Management. *Revisions to the Standards for the Classification of Federal Data on Race and Ethnicity.* Nov. 2, 2000. http://www.census.gov/population/www/socdemo/race/Ombdir15.html.

Padilla, Felix M. *Latino Ethnic Consciousness: The Case of Mexican Americans and Puerto Ricans in Chicago.* Notre Dame, Ind.: University of Notre Dame Press, 1985.

Payson, Kenneth R. "Check the Box: Reconsidering Directive No. 15 and the Classification of Mixed-Race People." 84 *Cal. L. Rev.* 1233 (1996).

Perea, Juan F. "Suggested Responses to Frequently Asked Questions about Hispanics, Latinos and Latinas." 9 *Berkeley La Raza L.J.* 39 (1996).

Prewitt, Kenneth. "Racial Classification in America: Where Do We Go from Here?" 134(1) *Daedalus* 5–17 (2005).

Rodriguez, Clara E. *Changing Race: Latinos, the Census, and the History of Ethnicity in the United States.* New York: New York University Press, 2000.

Rodriguez, Clara E., Aida Castro, Oscar Garcia, and Analisa Torres. 1991. "Latino Racial Identity: In the Eye of the Beholder?"2(3) *Latino Studies Journal* 33–48 (1991).

Rodriguez, Richard. *Brown: The Last Discovery of America.* New York: Viking, 2002.

Rumbaut, Rubén G. "Pigments of Our Imagination: On the Racialization and Racial Identities of 'Hispanics' and 'Latinos.'" In *How the United States Racializes Latinos: White Hegemony and Its Consequences*, edited by José A. Cobas, Jorge Duany, and Joe R. Feagin. Boulder, Colo.: Paradigm Publishers, 2009.

Sandrino-Glasser, Gloria. "*Los Confundidos*: De-Conflating Latinos/as' Race and Ethnicity." 19 *Chicano-Latino L. Rev.* 69 (1998).

Santiago, Esmeralda. *When I Was Puerto Rican.* New York: Vintage, 1994.

Shorris, Earl. *Latinos: A Biography of the People.* New York: W. W. Norton, 1992.

Simon, Lisette E. "Hispanics: Not a Cognizable Ethnic Group." 63 *U. Cin. L. Rev.* 497 (1994).

Skerry, Peter. *Mexican Americans: The Ambivalent Minority.* New York: Free Press, 1993.

"Standards for the Classification of Federal Data on Race and Ethnicity: Advance Notice of Proposed Review and Possible Revision of OMB's Statistical Policy Directive No. 15." 59 *Federal Register* 29,831, 29,832. Washington, D.C.: National Archives and Records Administration, 1994.

Stavans, Ilan. *The Hispanic Condition: Reflections on Culture and Identity in America.* New York: HarperCollins, 1995.

Telles, Edward E., and Edward Murguia. "Phenotypic Discrimination and Income Differences among Mexican Americans." 17 *Social Science Quarterly* 682 (1990).

Thomas, Piri. *Down These Mean Streets.* New York: Knopf, 1967.

Toro, Luis Angel. "'A People Distinct from Others': Race and Identity in Federal Indian Law and the Hispanic Classification in OMB Directive No. 15." 26 *Tex. Tech. L. Rev.* 1219 (1995).

U.S. Census Bureau. *The American Community—Hispanics: 2004* (American Community Survey Reports). February 2007.

Valdes, Francisco. "Diaspora and Deadlock, Miami and Havana: Coming to Terms with Dreams and Dogmas." 55 *Fla. L. Rev.* 283 (2003).

Vasconcelos, José. *The Cosmic Race.* Reprint. Baltimore: Johns Hopkins University Press, 1997.

Waters, Mary C. *Ethnic Options: Choosing Identities in America.* Berkeley: University of California Press, 1990.

Wright, Luther, Jr. "Who's Black, Who's White, and Who Cares: Reconceptualizing the United States' Definition of Race and Racial Classifications." 48 *Vand. L. Rev.* 513 (1995).

Yankauer, Alfred. "Hispanic/Latino—What's in a Name?" 77 *American Journal of Public Health* 15 (1987).

Recent General Works on Latinos

Challenging Fronteras: Structuring Latina and Latino Lives in the United States, edited by Mary Romero, Pierette Hondagneu-Sotelo, and Vilma Ortiz. London: Routledge, 1997.

The Chicano Studies Reader: An Anthology of Aztlan, 1970–2000 (Aztlan Anthology Series, Vol. 2), edited by Chon A. Noriega, Eric R. Avila, Karen Mary Davalos, Chela Sandoval, and Rafael Perez-Torres. Los Angeles: UCLA Chicano Studies Research Center Publications, 2001.

The Columbia History of Latinos in the United States since 1960, edited by David G. Gutiérrez. New York: Columbia University Press, 2006.

A Companion to Latina/o Studies, edited by Juan Flores and Renato Rosaldo. Malden, Mass.; Oxford: Blackwell, 2007.

Encyclopedia Latina: History, Culture, and Society in the United States, edited by Ilan Stavans and Harold Augenbraum. New York: Scholastic Library Publishing, 2005.

Hispanics/Latinos in the United States: Ethnicity, Race, and Rights, edited by Jorge J. E. Gracia and Pablo De Greiff. New York: Routledge, 2000.

Inside the Latino/a Experience: A Latino Studies Reader, edited by Norma E. Cantu and Maria E. Franquiz. New York: Palgrave Macmillan, 2010.

Latinas/os in the United States: Changing the Face of América, edited by Hávidan Rodríguez, Rogelio Sáenz, and Cecilia Menjívar. New York: Springer, 2008.

The Latino Studies Reader: Culture, Economy, and Society, edited by Antonia Darder and Rodolfo D. Torres. New York: Wiley-Blackwell, 1998.

Mexicans in California, edited by Ramon A. Gutiérrez and Patricia Zavella. Champaign: University of Illinois Press, 2009.

The Oxford Encyclopedia of Latinos and Latinas in the United States, edited by Suzanne Oboler and Deena J. González. New York: Oxford University Press, 2005.

Voices of a New Chicana/o History, edited by Refugio I. Rochín and Dennis N. Valdés. East Lansing: Michigan State University Press, 2000.

Voices of the U.S. Latino Experience, edited by Rodolfo Acuña and Guadalupe Compean. Westport, Conn.: Greenwood Press, 2008.

Latino Think Tanks in the United States

Centro de Estudios Puertorriqueños
http://www.centropr.org/home.html

Cuban Research Institute
http://lacc.fiu.edu/centers_institutes/?body=centers_cri&rightbody=centers_cri

CUNY Dominican Studies Institute
http://www1.ccny.cuny.edu/ci/dsi/

Inter-University Program for Latino Research
http://www.nd.edu/~iuplr/

Julián Samora Research Institute
http://www.jsri.msu.edu/

Mauricio Gastón Institute for Latino Community Development and Public Policy
http://www.gaston.umb.edu/

National Association of Latino Elected and Appointed Officials
http://www.naleo.org/

National Community for Latino Leadership
http://www.latinoleadership.org/

National Council of La Raza
http://www.nclr.org/

Pew Hispanic Center
http://pewhispanic.org/

Smithsonian Center for Latino Initiatives
http://latino.si.edu/

Southwest Hispanic Research Institute
http://www.unm.edu/~shri/

Tomás Rivera Policy Institute
http://www.trpi.org/

UCLA Chicano Studies Research Center
http://www.chicano.ucla.edu/

William C. Velasquez Institute
http://www.wcvi.org/index.html

||||||||||||||||||||||||||||||||||||||||||||||||||||||||||||||||||||||||||||||||||||||

Part II

Conquest and Immigration
How We Got (Get) Here

How did Latinos get here? The answer may be easy—conquest or immigration—but the actual routes by which the group arrived here have been accompanied by much pain. Conquest left a legacy and a mark of its own, while immigration presents huge challenges, including acquisition of a new language and culture and separation from family and friends. The United States has not always eased the way, either, ignoring treaty provisions and imposing impossibly high burdens on persons wishing to immigrate. The chapters in part 2 explore Latinos' history of conquest and immigration, delving into such questions as the psychological effect of being a conquered people and the justice—or lack of it—in our official immigration policies. Should the United States admit all comers, or impose some limits? And if some restrictions are in order, what about Latin America, where the United States has been meddling, for good or ill, during much of its history? Does that history place a special obligation on this country to admit immigrants more freely than from other regions, say, Scandinavia?

Chapter 10

|||||||||||||||||||||||||||||||||||||||||||||||||||||||||||||||||||||||||||||||

Occupied America

Rodolfo Acuña

Central to the thesis of this monograph is my contention that the conquest of the Southwest created a colonial situation in the traditional sense—with the Mexican land and population being controlled by an imperialistic United States. Further, I contend that this colonization—with variations—is still with us today. Thus, I refer to the colony, initially, in the traditional definition of the term, and later (taking into account the variations) as an internal colony.

From the Chicano perspective, it is obvious that these two types of colonies are a reality. In discussions with non-Chicano friends, however, I have encountered considerable resistance. In fact, even colleagues sympathetic to the Chicano cause vehemently deny that Chicanos are—or have been—colonized. They admit the exploitation and discrimination, but they add that this has been the experience of most "Americans"—especially European and Asian immigrants and Black Americans. While I agree that exploitation and racism have victimized most out-groups in the United States, this does not preclude the reality of the colonial relationship between the Anglo-American privileged and the Chicano.

The parallels between the Chicanos' experience in the United States and that of other Third World peoples are too similar to dismiss. Attendant to the definition of colonization are the following conditions:

1. The land of one people is invaded by people from another country, who later use military force to gain and maintain control.
2. The original inhabitants become subjects of the conquerors involuntarily.
3. The conquered have an alien culture and government imposed upon them.
4. The conquered become the victims of racism and cultural genocide and are relegated to a submerged status.
5. The conquered are rendered politically and economically powerless.
6. The conquerors feel they have a "mission" in occupying the area in question and believe that they have undeniable privileges by virtue of their conquest.

These points also apply to the relationship between Chicanos and Anglos in Mexico's Northwest Territory.

In the traditional historian's viewpoint, however, two differences impede universal acceptance of the reality of Anglo-American colonialism in this area.

1. Geographically the land taken from Mexico bordered the United States rather than being an area distant from the "mother country."

Too many historians have accepted—subconsciously, if not conveniently—the myth that the area was always intended to be an integral part of the United States. Instead of conceptualizing the conquered territory as northern Mexico, they perceive it in terms of the "American" Southwest. Further, the stereotype of the colonialist pictures him wearing Wellington boots and carrying a swagger stick, and that stereotype is usually associated with overseas situations—certainly not in territory contiguous to an "expanding" country.

2. Historians also believe that the Southwest was won in fair and just warfare, as opposed to unjust imperialism.

The rationale has been that the land came to the United States as the result of competition, and in winning the game, the country was generous in paying for its prize. In the case of Texas, they believe Mexico attacked the "freedom-loving" Anglo-Americans. It is difficult for citizens of the United States to accept that their nation has been and is imperialistic. Imperialism, to them, is an affliction of other countries.

While I acknowledge the geographical proximity of the area—and that this is a modification of the strict definition of colonialism—I reject the conclusion that the Texan and Mexican-American wars were just or that Mexico provoked them. Further, I illustrate that the conditions attendant to colonialism, listed above, accompanied the U.S. take-over of the Southwest. For these reasons, I maintain that colonialism in the traditional sense did exist in the Southwest, and that the conquerors dominated and exploited the conquered.

The colonization still exists today, but as I mentioned before, with variations. Anglo-Americans still exploit and manipulate Mexicans and still relegate them to a submerged caste. Mexicans are still denied political and economic determination and are still the victims of racial stereotypes and racial slurs promulgated by those who feel they are superior. Thus, I contend that Mexicans in the United States are still a colonized people, but now the colonization is internal—it is occurring within the country rather than being imposed by an external power. The territories of the Southwest are states within the United States, and theoretically permanent residents of Mexican extraction are U.S. citizens. Yet the rights of citizenship are too often circumvented or denied outright.

In reality, little differentiates the Chicano's status in the traditional colony of the nineteenth century and in the internal colony of the twentieth century. The relationship between Anglos and Chicanos remains the same—that of master-servant. The principal difference is that Mexicans in the traditional colony were indigenous to the conquered land. Now, while some are descendants of Mexicans living in the area before the conquest, large numbers are technically descendants of immigrants. After

1910, in fact, almost one-eighth of Mexico's population migrated to the United States, largely as a result of the push-and-pull of economic necessity. Southwest agribusinessmen "imported" Mexican workers to fill the need for cheap labor, marking the beginning of even greater Anglo manipulation of Mexican settlements or *colonias*.

The original *colonias* expanded in size with the increased immigration, and new settlements sprang up. They became nations within a nation, in effect, for psychologically, socially, and culturally they remained Mexican. But the *colonias* had little or no control over their political, economic, or educational destinies. In almost every case, they remained separate and unequal to Anglo-American communities. The elected representatives within the *colonias* were usually Anglo-Americans or Mexicans under their control, and they established a bureaucracy to control the political life of the Mexican settlements—for the benefit of the Anglo privileged.

Further, Anglos controlled the educational system. They administered the schools, and taught in the classrooms, and designed the curriculum not to meet the needs of Chicano students but to Americanize them. The police patrolling the colonia lived, for the most part, outside the area. Their main purpose was to protect Anglo property. Anglos owned the business and industry in the *colonias*, and capital that could have been used to improve the *colonias* was taken into Anglo-American sectors, in much the same way that capital is drained from underdeveloped countries by foreign economic imperialists. In addition, the *colonias* became employment centers for industrialists, who were assured of a ready supply of cheap labor.

This pattern is one that emerged in most Chicano communities, and one that contradicts the belief in Anglo-American equality. In sum, even though many Chicanos are native-born U.S. citizens, most Anglo-Americans still considered them Mexicans and outsiders.

In discussing the traditional and internal colonization of the Chicano, it is not my intention to rekindle hatreds, nor to condemn all Anglo-Americans collectively for the ignominies that the Mexican in the United States has suffered. Rather, my purpose is to bring about an awareness—among both Anglo-Americans and Chicanos —of the forces that control and manipulate many millions of people in this country and keep them colonized. If Chicanos can become aware of why they are oppressed and how the exploitation is perpetuated, they can work more effectively toward ending their colonization.

I realize that the initial stages of such awareness might result in intolerance among some Chicanos. However, I caution the reader that this work does not create a rationale for brown power just because it condemns the injustices of Anglo power. Extended visits in Mexico have taught me that Chicano power is no better than any other power. Those who seek power are deprived of their humanity to the point that they themselves become the oppressors. Paulo Freire has written:

> The great humanistic and historical task of the oppressed [is]: to liberate themselves and their oppressors as well. The oppressors, who oppress, exploit, and rape by virtue of their power, cannot find in this power the strength to liberate either the oppressed or themselves. Only the power that springs from the weakness of the oppressed will be sufficiently strong to free you.[1]

It is my hope that *Occupied America* can help us perceive the social, political, and economic contradictions of the power that has enabled Anglo-American colonizers to dominate Chicanos—and that has too often made Chicanos accept and, in some instances, support the domination. Awareness will help us take action against the forces that oppress not only Chicanos but the oppressor himself.[2]

NOTES

1. Paulo Freire, *Pedagogy of the Oppressed* (New York: Herder and Herder, 1972), p. 28.
2. [In later editions, the author modifies his colonization thesis, explaining that the upsurge in Chicano activism makes this necessary. We include this selection in the belief that the thesis still retains great explanatory power, and not just historically—Eds.]

Chapter 11

‖‖

The First U.S. Latinos
White Wealth and Mexican Labor

Joe R. Feagin

Dominant whites usually place each new immigrant group somewhere in the white-to-black hierarchy of wealth and power, as well as in the corresponding white-to-black status continuum. As whites have viewed the social world, the racial hierarchy and status continuum run from "highly civilized" whites to "uncivilized" blacks, from high intelligence to low intelligence, from privilege and desirability to lack of privilege and undesirability. Moreover, the character of the racial oppression confronting an entering group varies depending on its timing of entry, its region of entry, its size, economic resources, cultural characteristics, and physical characteristics. Thus, in the case of Latino and Asian immigrants, whites particularly accent their being culturally "alien" and "foreign."

Viewing Americans of color as alien goes back to the white view of early enslaved Africans as uncivilized, strange, and foreign. Groups entering later have also been viewed as uncivilized, foreign, and threatening to the dominant Anglo-American culture. This was true of groups like the Russian Jews who entered as "alien" and "not white" around the turn of the twentieth century, but who later would become accepted as "white." It has been especially true for immigrants from Asia and Latin America. Thus, Latino immigrants and their descendants have usually been positioned somewhere between whites and blacks—with a negative evaluation on both axes of alienated social relations, that of superior/inferior and that of insider/foreigner. The white view of Latinos sometimes stresses their similarity to black Americans in terms of racial status and inferiority, but at other times accents their "alien" and "foreign" character. It is therefore not surprising that Latino immigrants and their descendants, unlike earlier white European immigrants, have not been allowed to assimilate structurally and fully to white society. All entering groups do not share the same fate, but in all cases it is the dominant white group that generally determines the rate and character of the societal incorporation, as well as the prevailing interpretation of that incorporation.

From *White Supremacy and Mexican Americans: Rethinking the "Black-White Paradigm,"* 54 RUTGERS L. REV. 959 (2002). Originally published in the *Rutgers Law Review.* Reprinted by permission.

The Largest Immigrant Group Ever: Mexicans

Today, large numbers of Latinos make their homes in the United States mainly because of United States government intervention and imperialism in places like Mexico, Cuba, Puerto Rico, and Central America. In this way, Latin American and Caribbean immigrants are not similar to European immigrants, such as those large groups that came from southern and eastern Europe in the decades just before and after 1900. These early European immigrants, like other European immigrants today, are not usually linked to the United States by direct United States imperialism in their home countries, as are most Latin American immigrants. Juan Gonzalez calls this Latin American immigration the "Harvest of Empire":

> [T]he Latino migrant flows were directly connected to the growth of a U.S. empire, and they responded closely to that empire's needs, whether it was a political need to stabilize a neighboring country or to accept its refugees as a means of accomplishing a broader foreign policy objective (Cubans, Dominicans, Salvadorans, Nicaraguans), or whether it was an economic need, such as satisfying the labor demands of particular U.S. industries (Mexicans, Puerto Ricans, Panamanians).[1]

Indeed, the central role of United States employers in aggressively recruiting both legal and undocumented Mexican and other Latin American labor is not well known. Such ignorance allows much anti-immigrant stereotyping to take place unchallenged. From the early twentieth century, as David Gutiérrez notes, United States "employers and their allies in government have worked in close partnership to recruit foreign workers and to ensure that the flow of immigrant workers is regulated for the maximum benefit of American businesses and consumers."[2]

The largest group of Latin Americans ever to be drawn directly into wealth creation within the United States consists of Mexicans and Mexican Americans. Indeed, counting both legal and undocumented immigrants, Mexicans constitute the largest group of immigrants ever to come to the United States from any area of the world. Like African Americans before them, millions of Mexican immigrants and their descendants have been central to wealth creation for United States employers and to cheap services for United States consumers. Because Americans of Mexican origin are by far the largest immigrant group ever drawn from the United States empire, I will examine their history and contemporary situation in some detail.

As noted, the first Mexican residents of the United States did not immigrate, but were brought into the new nation by violent conquest during the Texas rebellion and the Mexican-American War of the 1830s and 1840s. With the end of the Mexican-American War came the incorporation of a hundred thousand Mexicans. Mexicans were forcibly absorbed into the expanding United States empire, which now encompassed a large portion of what was northern Mexico. With great aggression, leading white politicians and economic entrepreneurs sought to dominate the entire continent. In this they were highly successful. World history was shaped by their colonial aspirations and imperialistic actions.

A Long History of Intervention:
Latin America and Mexico

For more than a century and a half, United States imperialism has included both direct colonialism, particularly in Puerto Rico, Cuba, and Hawaii, and neo-colonialism (recurring economic or political intervention) to protect United States economic and political interests in many Latin American countries, such as Mexico. To accomplish United States economic and political domination, military forces have intervened directly or covertly dozens of times in Latin American countries. In order to expand or protect United States interests, this intervention has included protecting dictators sympathetic to United States investors using military aid or tactical intervention, as well as putting down local rebellions seeking to overthrow the United States–supported dictatorships. United States intervention has included the creation of a new country, Panama, to facilitate the building of a canal and thus United States commerce across two oceans.

Accompanying the economic, military, and political intervention in Latin America is a periodic multitude of labor recruiters seeking workers for the growing United States economy. Over time, those who immigrated spread the word as well, thereby extending the recruitment along informal family and friendship networks. Since at least the early 1900s, the United States economy has demanded low-wage immigrant workers in such areas as agriculture, food processing and meatpacking, low-wage manufacturing, construction, and food services. Millions of immigrants have come from Mexico and other countries in Latin America to fill these low-wage jobs.

Most Latin American immigrants are pushed to seek these jobs by serious economic and political problems in their home countries, in which the United States is directly implicated. For example, for decades United States corporations investing and operating in Mexico have helped to generate labor out-migration. Large United States agribusiness firms have built major farming operations in Mexico in order to grow food for export, thereby taking over substantial amounts of arable land. The small Mexican farmers have been forced off their land, which they have traditionally farmed to feed their families. This siphoning off of wealth from Mexico into the pockets of United States corporations has forced many Mexicans, particularly those driven off the land, to migrate to large cities in Mexico. There they often have difficulty finding jobs to support families, and like many before them, they end up migrating to the United States for work.

Moreover, over recent decades United States corporations have built thousands of assembly operations (*maquiladoras*) on the Mexican side of the border region to take advantage of low-wage labor and weak environmental laws. Most who migrate to the border area for work soon learn about ways to access the usually higher wages across the border. Significantly, the Mexicans who perform low-wage jobs in the United States not only create wealth and a better standard of living for many United States citizens, especially affluent Americans, but their wages are usually essential to the survival of their families in Mexico. Indeed, up to one third of Mexico's total revenues comes from the money sent home by these immigrant workers.

Super-Exploitation: Mexican Americans and
"Racial Surplus Value"

Both Adam Smith and, later, Karl Marx saw the workers of a nation as the central source of its enduring creation of wealth. Indeed, Marx developed the idea of "surplus value," which can be seen as that amount of the worth of the productive labor of workers that is not returned to them in the form of wages. As a rule, workers get lower wages than they deserve given the value their work has created. Employers are able to perpetuate this inequity because they have the power to hire, fire, and otherwise control workers in a capitalist society. In addition to this exploitation of workers because of their subordinated class position, there is an added degree of exploitation at the hands of white employers who use the labor of workers of color. Because of their subordinated status, workers of color can be super-exploited, and "racial surplus value" can be extracted from them in addition to the surplus value that is typically taken from workers in a capitalist system. That is, they can be paid lower wages than white workers for the same or similar work. Like the enslaved African Americans on southern plantations, most Mexican and Mexican-American workers have been *super-exploited* by white employers. For a century, many have indeed been "wage slaves."

In the United States many Mexican and Mexican-American manufacturing, domestic, and restaurant workers labor long (for example, fourteen-hour) shifts at hourly wages effectively below the legal minimum. A large proportion of United States service work is now done by immigrants. The meatpacking and fast food industries, among others, would collapse without immigrant labor, especially from Latin America. Investigative reporters have found Mexican and Asian immigrants working under conditions, such as imprisonment in a fenced compound, that are reminiscent of old slave plantations. In addition, growing numbers of affluent households employ gardeners and other lawn workers, domestics, and nannies drawn from Mexico and other parts of Latin America or from the Caribbean. Without these low-wage service workers, many two-earner, white-middle-class households could not function as they do.

Indeed, for more than two centuries, the occupation of "maid" or "servant" has often been racialized, with many such workers being drawn from groups categorized as biologically and culturally inferior by white Americans. For centuries this occupational racialization has had a global dimension, for affluent white families use their wealth to purchase services by workers from poor countries who must work long hours for very low wages. In recent decades, many of these workers have been Latina domestic workers. They pay heavily for servicing many white Americans. As one researcher has recently noted, these costs are "the loss of dignity, respect, and self-esteem; the inability to even live with their [own] children; and the daily hardships of raising families on poverty-level wages. . . ."[3]

NOTES

1. Juan Gonzales, HARVEST OF EMPIRE: A HISTORY OF LATINOS IN AMERICA xiv (2000).

2. David G. Gutiérrez, WALLS AND MIRRORS: MEXICAN AMERICANS, MEXICAN IMMI-GRANTS, AND THE POLITICS OF ETHNICITY 211 (1995).

3. See Pierrette Hondagneu-Sotelo, DOMÉSTICA: IMMIGRANT WORKERS CLEANING AND CARING IN THE SHADOWS OF AFFLUENCE 29–60 (2001).

Chapter 12

‖‖‖

Tracing the Trajectories of Conquest

Juan F. Perea

The conquest of Mexico between 1846 and 1848 has largely disappeared from public consciousness as a significant historical event with contemporary consequences. Yet this conquest resulted in the annexation by the United States of approximately one-half of former Mexico, constituting most of the current southwestern United States. I describe the roles that race and racism played in justifying the conquest and explore some of its current consequences.

One of the defining features of any conquest is the subordination of the conquered. The history of the conquered Mexicans of the Southwest demonstrates this purposeful subordination. Through careful redrafting of the Treaty of Guadalupe Hidalgo, the U.S. Congress reserved to itself discretion over when to admit the conquered territories as states. Congress waited until Mexicans were politically disempowered racial minorities within each territory before admitting the conquered territories as states with political representation. This happened earliest in the cases of Texas (annexed in 1845) and California, and latest in New Mexico, which was denied statehood until 1912.

The minimization of the political power of Mexicans emerges, then, as a prominent theme of the conquest. I believe this theme can be generalized to all Latino peoples subject to U.S. conquest and continues today, in at least three areas. First, nearly four million U.S. citizens resident in Puerto Rico live without voting rights or political representation in the federal government, yet are subject to federal law, violating democratic theory. Second, the intentional, long-term exploitation of undocumented Latino immigrant labor maximizes agricultural profits while minimizing the potential political power of the immigrants. Lastly, attempts to curtail the use of Spanish through Official English laws and other restrictions symbolize the subordination of Spanish speakers and result in less access and use of the democratic process.

These are some of the "trajectories of conquest." This history helps explain why Latino political power always seems less significant than population numbers and demographic projections suggest it should be.

*   *   *

From *A Brief History of Race and the U.S.-Mexican Border: Tracing the Trajectories of Conquest,* 51 UCLA L. REV. 283 (2003). Originally published in the *University of California at Los Angeles Law Review.* Reprinted by permission.

According to a Senate Committee report from 1910, the cohesion of Mexican, Spanish-speaking U.S. citizens of the New Mexican territory, and their ability to retain and pass on their Spanish language, must "be broken up."[1] The report states the interesting proposition that the territory's admission to statehood, and consequently its voting representation in Congress, necessarily meant the dissolution of Mexican American identity. Why was the Senate so concerned about the race and language of Mexican Americans? Why did admission to statehood mean breaking Mexican American identity? And what identity would replace it?

Tentative answers to these questions appear from a study of the history of the border. Race shaped the creation of the border with Mexico in highly significant ways. Southern desire for the expansion of slave territory was crucial to the annexation of Texas and the subsequent disposition of the conquered territories. Racism played an important role in purporting to justify the war of conquest against Mexico and in limiting the political power of Mexicans within the United States. White supremacy was a central component of the ideology of Manifest Destiny, which justified the conquest of Mexico as a divine Anglo-Saxon racial right. The mixed races of Mexicans posed an affront to Anglo ideals of racial purity. Some white politicians believed the mixed races of Mexicans posed a grave threat to democracy itself. Ultimately, these racial factors played a decisive role in determining the amount and location of Mexican territory that the United States would keep as the spoils of war.

Consider an action inextricably tied to conquest: the denial of political power to conquered people. It may seem obvious that the denial of political power inheres in conquest. After all, conquered people rarely have a say in matters of their own conquest. It is less obvious how, in a democracy, the denial of political power is reproduced in subsequent generations. Sociologist Robert Blauner described three conditions associated with colonized minorities in the United States.

> The first condition . . . is that of forced entry into the larger society or metropolitan domain. The second is subjection to various forms of unfree labor that greatly restrict the physical and social mobility of the group and its participation in the political arena. The third is a cultural policy of the colonizer that constrains, transforms, or destroys original values, orientations, and ways of life.[2]

While colonization seems closely related to conquest, colonization refers to temporary seizures of land and displacements as well as to permanent seizures. Temporary cooptation of land and culture allows for some (altered) restoration of original norms. On the other hand, the permanent seizure of land requires processes for the transfer of the land to its new owners. If a conquest seeks the permanent displacement of the original culture, then the conquering power must have processes for inhibiting the survival of the original and its transmission to future generations. Conquest, as I use it, refers to the more or less permanent seizure of land and usurpation of culture, as in the U.S. conquests of Indians and Mexico.

Nevertheless, Blauner's three conditions form a useful framework within which to consider the conquest and subsequent subordination of Mexican and Mexican

American people in the United States. Blauner's conditions also help to explain the current legacies of this conquest affecting many Latinos as well as Mexicans.

Some of the current legacies of conquest include, first, the unremedied colonial situation of Puerto Rico, which demonstrates the purposeful denial of meaningful political power to Puerto Ricans by the United States, a situation with direct links to the strategies used before to deny political power to Mexicans. Second, the longstanding and continuing exploitation of undocumented immigrant Mexican and Latino labor perpetuates an impoverished class of laborers who lack political participation and representation. Lastly, societal campaigns for Official English and English-only rules in the workplace seek to undermine the linguistic heritage of Latinos and to limit the economic and political power of Spanish-speaking Latinos.

Expansionist Desire for Mexico

The manifestation of expansionist desires for Mexican lands began early. Acting through important national figures, the United States persistently sought to obtain Mexican territory. In 1767, even prior to U.S. nationhood, Benjamin Franklin apparently expressed desire for Mexican lands. After the Louisiana Purchase, Thomas Jefferson sought, unsuccessfully, to claim the Rio Grande as the southern boundary of Louisiana. Then in 1826, President John Quincy Adams offered $1 million for Texas, then a northern province of Mexico. Mexico rejected the offer. Subsequently, President Andrew Jackson, an early advocate of Texas's annexation, attempted to purchase Texas for as much as $5 million.

When Texas won its independence in 1835, Mexico protested vigorously and repeatedly the United States' ambitions to annex Texas and incorporate it as a state. Also in 1835, President Andrew Jackson offered to buy San Francisco Bay from Mexico. In 1845, President James K. Polk sent an emissary to try to persuade Californians to follow Texas's example and to secede from Mexico. Polk also sent his representative, John Slidell, to Mexico City in an attempt to purchase California and New Mexico for between $15 and $40 million. Mexico refused even to deal with Slidell.

What could not be had by purchase was taken by force. Polk sent a military force into an area understood to be Mexican, the border area between the Nueces and Rio Grande Rivers, in order to provoke hostilities. Shortly thereafter, Polk got what he wanted. American troops were attacked and killed by Mexican soldiers in the border area under Mexican sovereignty. Polk, however, alleged that "Mexico has passed the boundary of the United States, has invaded our territory and shed American blood upon the American soil." Rather than ask for a formal declaration of war, Polk promptly requested from Congress an unusual resolution recognizing that a state of war already existed "by the act of the Republic of Mexico." Debate on this resolution was severely limited, with dissenting voices given little chance to be heard. Ironically, and revealingly, Polk and his cabinet had agreed to ask Congress to declare war against Mexico before news of the bloodshed reached Washington. Most contemporary historians agree that President Polk provoked the United States' war against Mexico as a pretext for accomplishing his expansionist purposes.

Race and the War against Mexico

Slavery and the southern wish for expansion of the number of slave states played a prominent role in the annexation of Texas, the first seizure of Mexican territory by the U.S. government. Anglo-Americans first began arriving in Mexico's northernmost provinces in the early 1820s. They were, perhaps, some of the first illegal aliens. In 1821, prior to Mexican independence, Spanish authorities allowed American Moses Austin to establish a colony within Texas. Austin was later succeeded by his son, Stephen Austin, who along with other early settlers from slave states brought his slaves with him.

Mexico's declaration of independence from Spain in 1821 cast doubt on the future of slavery in Texas. Eventually, because of the sparse population of its northern provinces, the Mexican government passed legislation encouraging and legalizing the migration of white North Americans into Texas. Although Mexican leaders generally disapproved of slavery and sought to limit slave trading in Texas, they never did anything to effectively abolish it. Furthermore, Mexican laws restricting slavery went unenforced, and American slave owners found ways to evade Mexican law. When Mexicans became concerned about the expansionist desires of Americans and their disrespect for Mexican law and traditions, they passed additional legislation seeking to forbid further immigration by Americans. Yet this too proved ineffective because Americans ignored the laws and continued immigrating illegally into Mexico.

Over time, Mexico's prohibition against slavery became a major irritant between the Mexican government and American immigrants. The President of Mexico outlawed slavery by decree on September 15, 1829. However, Mexican officials effectively excepted Texas from the decree, by choosing to promote Texas's settlement and economic development over the decree's enforcement. Many Americans immigrating into Texas were slave-owning southerners whose slave ownership was illegal under Mexican law. Slave owners attempted to circumvent the law by "freeing" their slaves while simultaneously forcing them to become indentured servants for life. Accustomed to U.S. protections for slave ownership, Americans viewed the abolition of slavery as a deprivation of their individual liberties and of their private property. Although at times critical of slavery, Stephen Austin was a forceful advocate of it in Texas, and "more than any other individual, was responsible for gaining the approval of Mexican authorities for introducing [slavery] there."

John Quincy Adams understood the efforts to annex Texas as "designed primarily for the extension of the area of slavery and the magnification of the power of the slaveocracy in the councils of the nation." The antislavery North saw the annexation of Texas as a national disaster. The expansion of slavery had led to the annexation of formerly Mexican territory, and thereby set a precedent that would facilitate the subsequent war of conquest against Mexico.

White Racism against Mexicans as a Rationale for the War of Conquest

The United States sought Mexican lands for a long time. In addition to slavery's role in the United States' desire for Texas, race played a second role in the creation of the border. The racism of white Americans created the rationale to justify the seizure of the lands from allegedly inferior Mexicans. Mexicans struck white Americans as a mixed-race, mongrel people distinctly inferior to the presumed racially pure whites. According to historian David Weber, "American visitors to the Mexican frontier were nearly unanimous in commenting on the dark skin of Mexican mestizos, who, it was generally agreed, had inherited the worst qualities of Spaniards and Indians to produce a 'race' still more despicable than that of either parent." As Rufus Sage, a newspaperman and Rocky Mountain trapper put it:

> There are no people on the continent of America, whether civilized or uncivilized, with one or two exceptions, more miserable in condition or despicable in morals than the mongrel race inhabiting New Mexico. . . . To manage them successfully, they must needs be held in continual restraint, and kept in their place by force, if necessary,—else they will become haughty and insolent. As servants, they are excellent, when properly trained, but are worse than useless if left to themselves.[3]

Perceived as some incomprehensible mixture of Black, Indian, and Spanish races, Mexicans, by their very existence, violated white American taboos against racial mixing. As such, Mexican people fed the ideology of Manifest Destiny, under which it was the destiny of white Anglo-Saxons to occupy the entire continent without regard for the presence of presumed inferior races.

Race and the Drawing of the Border

In addition to shaping the decision to conquer Mexico, race also influenced the amount of formerly Mexican territory that the United States decided to retain. By the end of the war, the United States occupied much of Mexico, both its northern provinces, which had long been sought by American expansionists, and many interior provinces, including Mexico City. Even under military occupation by the United States, Mexico refused to negotiate the cession of its territory. In response, President Polk considered the possibility of conquering and annexing all of Mexico. The move to annex all of Mexico enjoyed popularity in the United States, but also engendered significant resistance. Many politicians and the American public resisted the annexation of the long-sought northern provinces of Mexico, in large part because of race.

The annexation of Mexican land posed a profound problem for white politicians. Adding Mexican lands to the United States meant adding racially undesirable Mexicans to the population. The prospect of bringing mixed-race Mexicans into the Anglo-Saxon republic of the United States ignited fears of the degradation of white supremacy as well as fears concerning the survival of American democracy. Senator John Calhoun, a prominent southern Democrat, opposed annexation because of these racial implications:

> [I]t is without example or precedent, either to hold Mexico as a province, or to incorporate her into our Union. No example of such a line of policy can be found. We have conquered many of the neighboring tribes of Indians, but we have never thought of

holding them in subjection—never of incorporating them into our Union. They have either been left as an independent people amongst us, or been driven into the forests.

I know further, sir, that we have never dreamt of incorporating into our Union any but the Caucasian race—the free white race. To incorporate Mexico, would be the very first instance of the kind of incorporating an Indian race; for more than half the Mexicans are Indians, and the other is composed chiefly of mixed tribes. I protest against such a union as that! Ours, sir, is the Government of a white race. The greatest misfortunes of Spanish America are to be traced to the fatal error of placing these colored races on an equality with the white race. That error destroyed the social arrangement which formed the basis of society. . . . And yet it is professed and talked about to erect these Mexicans into a Territorial Government and place them on an equality with the people of the United States. I protest utterly against such a project.

Are we to associate with ourselves as equal, companions, and fellow citizens, the Indians and mixed race of Mexico? Sir, I should consider such a thing as fatal to our institutions.[4]

Calhoun could countenance retaining only those Mexican lands that contained no Mexicans:

[O]ur army has ever since held all that it is desirable to hold—that portion whose population is sparse, and on that account the more desirable to be held. For I hold it in reference to this war a fundamental principle, that when we receive territorial indemnity, it shall be unoccupied territory.[5]

The final boundary lines approved in the Treaty of Guadalupe Hidalgo required Mexico to cede to the United States only its northernmost, sparsely populated provinces of New Mexico and California. President Polk had desired all of Mexico. Ultimately, however, he went along with the limited territorial annexation. In his diary, Polk expressed concern about taking land populated by many Mexicans: "I expressed a doubt as to the policy or practicability of obtaining a country containing so large a number of the Mexican population." The racial concerns of Senator Calhoun and others were thus assuaged and the press congratulated Polk for acquiring land "encumbered by only 100,000 Mexicans."

Race and Statehood

The important role of race in the exercise of congressional discretion to grant or withhold statehood is apparent in examining Congress's decisions to approve or deny statehood to the territories taken from Mexico. The speedy annexation of Texas in 1845 was allegedly accomplished to protect white settlers from the threat posed by Mexico.

While Texas and California gained statehood promptly because of white political control in each of the states, New Mexico languished for sixty-two years as a federal territory. Among the principal reasons for denying statehood to New Mexico were that racially mixed, dark-skinned Mexicans lived there and that they spoke Spanish. New Mexicans submitted several formal petitions for statehood. In 1850, New Mexicans held a constitutional convention and drafted a constitution with strong antislavery provisions. The 1850 state constitution enjoyed overwhelming popular support, suggesting strong popular desire for statehood. Because the admission of new slave or free states would alter the balance of power in Congress, debates over new states at this time focused on the issue of whether slavery would be permitted in the state or territory. Under the Compromise of 1850, California was admitted as a free state, but New Mexico was recognized only as a federal territory. Its status with respect to slavery was to be decided at a later time.

It appears that New Mexico did not become a state until a bare majority of its population was English-speaking, which apparently first occurred in 1910. Around this time, congressional concerns over the use of Spanish in the territory were expressed in the New Mexico Enabling Act of 1910. This Act required that public education "shall always be conducted in English" and that the "ability to read, write, speak and understand the English language without an interpreter shall be a necessary qualification for all state officers and members of the state legislature."[6]

The Colonial Status of Puerto Rico

The current status of Puerto Rico as an "unincorporated territory" is closely related to the precedent of the racialized allocation of political power reflected in the Treaty of Guadalupe Hidalgo. Article IX of the Treaty was revised to guarantee Congress the discretion to incorporate the conquered Mexican territories at "the proper time." In the 1898 Treaty of Paris, which settled the Spanish-American War and transferred dominion over Puerto Rico to the United States from Spain, Congress followed and extended the precedent set in its Treaty with Mexico. Consequently, Congress reserved for itself complete control over the political and civil rights of Puerto Ricans. According to Article IX of the Treaty of Paris, "The civil rights and political status of the native inhabitants of the territories hereby ceded to the United States shall be determined by the Congress."[7] This was the first time that a territory had been acquired by treaty with neither an implicit nor an explicit promise of admission to statehood.

Subsequently, in the *Insular Cases* and *Balzac v. Porto Rico*, the U.S. Supreme Court relied on the language of the Treaty of Paris to confirm Congress's dominion over Puerto Rico. In these cases, the Court held that, based on Article IX, Puerto Ricans were not entitled to constitutional protection, but only to such rights as Congress chose to grant. In addition, the Court described Puerto Rico's constitutional status as an unincorporated territory. In part, the Court's reasoning was based on concerns about the race and inferior culture of Puerto Ricans.

Such racial concerns were also prominent in subsequent debates over the Jones Act, which granted statutory U.S. citizenship to Puerto Ricans. As in the case of Mexicans, serious objections were raised about the fitness of mixed-race, part African Puerto Ricans for citizenship. In addition, Congressmen were concerned about the capacity for self-governance of people from tropical climates, the assumption being that democracy was only for white people raised in cold, Nordic climes. Indeed, statutory citizenship was created for Puerto Ricans as a way of showing that they were under U.S. control, rather than for purposes of inclusion.

As with the Treaty of Guadalupe Hidalgo, the Treaty of Paris was implemented to minimize the political participation of Puerto Ricans. To this day, Puerto Ricans remain essentially powerless in U.S. politics. Because Puerto Rico is not a state, it has no voting representation in Congress. Approximately 3.8 million U.S. citizens who reside on the island are ineligible to vote for the President and the Vice President of the United States. Yet, despite their lack of representation in the formulation of federal law, they are subject to all the federal executive and legislative power that is not "locally inapplicable."[8] In addition, Congress has plenary power over Puerto Ricans under the Territorial Clause of the Constitution, which is subject only to rational basis review. These conditions violate a fundamental norm of democratic theory: that citizens should have a voice in the enactment of laws binding them. The unjust contemporary condition of Puerto Ricans is closely related to the race-based allocation of political power evident in the Treaty of Guadalupe Hidalgo.

NOTES

1. COMM'N ON TERRITORIES, AN ACT ENABLING THE PEOPLE OF NEW MEXICO AND ARIZONA TO FORM A CONSTITUTION AND STATE GOVERNMENT, etc., S. Rep. No. 61-454, at 26 (2d Sess. 1910).

2. See Robert Blauner, RACIAL OPPRESSION IN AMERICA 53 (1972).

3. 2 *Rufus B. Sage: His Letters and Papers, 1836–1847*, at 82–87 (LeRoy R. Hafen & Ann W. Hafen eds., 1956), reprinted in FOREIGNERS IN THEIR NATIVE LAND (David J. Weber ed., 1973).

4. Cong. Globe, 30th Cong., 1st Sess. 98 (1848).

5. *Id.* at 96.

6. Juan F. Perea, *Demography and Distrust: An Essay on American Languages, Cultural Pluralism, and Official English*, 77 MINN. L. REV. 269, 322 (1992).

7. Treaty of Paris, Dec. 10, 1898, U.S.-Spain, art. IX, reprinted in 11 TREATIES AND OTHER INTERNATIONAL AGREEMENTS OF THE UNITED STATES OF AMERICA 1776–1949, at 615, 619 (Charles I. Bevans ed., 1974).

8. See Jones Act, ch. 145, §§ 9–10, 39 Stat. 951, 954–55 (1917).

Chapter 13

||||||||||||||||||||||||||||||||||||||||||||||||||||||||||||||||||||||||||||||||||||||||

Latinos in the United States
Invitation and Exile

Gilbert Paul Carrasco

Throughout U.S. history periods of labor shortage have alternated with ones of labor surplus. In times of shortage, the United States has enthusiastically welcomed immigrants to fill gaps in the labor pool. More often than not, however, available employment has included harsh working conditions, enormous amounts of physical labor, and low pay. In addition to abject working conditions, immigrants have also faced discrimination and resentment.

During periods of labor surplus or economic stress, immigrants in the United States have been subjected to particular cruelty. Americans, led by various nativist organizations and movements such as the Know-Nothing Party in the 1850s or, more recently, U.S. English or California's "Save Our State" campaign, have blamed immigrants for the country's economic woes. Such xenophobic bigotry has resulted in calls for anti-immigrant legislation (including restrictions on immigration for whichever group was targeted at the time), attempts to deny public services (including elimination of bilingual education for school-aged immigrants and the American citizen children of undocumented immigrants), and, ultimately, deportation.

Mexican immigrants have usually been the subject of these seesaw trends. One reason is that Mexico and the United States share a common border. The border between the two countries stretches for two thousand miles and is marked in some places by a fence, but at most points merely by an imaginary line in the sand or by the Rio Grande River. Easy to traverse, this border facilitates immigration, both legal and illegal, as well as expulsion.

Due to their great distance from the United States, Europeans historically could not make the journey to where their labor was needed (typically the Southwestern United States) before the need was met. The only immigrants left within reach of the American Southwest were Mexicans and Asians. The Chinese and the Japanese have their own regrettable history of discrimination in the United States. The laws and policies that temporarily ended immigration from Japan and China left Mexico as the only source to fill the labor vacuum. Mexican laborers have since become the United

States' disposable labor force, brought in when needed, only to fulfill their use and be unceremoniously discarded, a trend that has been recurring for over 150 years.

From the Gold Rush to World War I

Early migration into the United States was aided by negligible border restrictions and virtually no immigration laws. The first wave of Mexican laborers was drawn to California by the Gold Rush shortly after Mexico ceded California to the United States under the terms of the Treaty of Guadalupe Hidalgo in 1848. The lure of gold drew people from all over the world, triggering rapid population growth. Because most who flocked to California wanted to strike it rich in their own mines, unskilled manual labor was scarce and laborers were needed to work in Anglo-owned mines, railroads, and farms. The work was backbreaking, low-paying, and often dangerous, so it was difficult to find Anglos who would do it.

In addition to fulfilling labor demands, Mexicans brought with them knowledge of mining. Anglos came to California with dreams of striking it rich but had little practical experience or knowledge of how to do it. Anglos, however, soon acquired the knowledge, tools, and techniques of Latino miners.

Unfortunately for Latinos, a need for their labor and knowledge did not translate into good attitudes toward them. Popular accounts of Latinos during that period were influenced by manifest destiny, "scientific" theories of racial miscegenation, and the Mexican War. These accounts provided the Anglo miner with a negative stereotype of the Latino that led to discrimination, threats, violence, and restrictive legislation directed against Mexicans and Mexican Americans. Posters appeared in mining areas threatening violence to any "foreigners" who remained where "they had no right to be"; vigilante groups expelling Latinos from mines claimed that mineral rights and wealth in America were reserved for "Americans"; a Foreign Miners' Tax Law was imposed; and foreigners were assaulted and lynched.[1]

Anti-Latino attitudes were also fueled by greed for the much coveted gold. Latinos who labored in the fields, on the railroads, or in the mines of Anglos were not as persecuted and discriminated against as those who sought their own fortunes in the mines. Nevertheless, although nonminers were not as persecuted as miners, history records whole towns being put to the torch, rioters shooting any Mexican in sight, random murders, and other vigilante actions throughout this period.

Even while Latinos were being persecuted, their labor was needed, especially in jobs that were low-paying and labor-intensive. Such jobs included ranching, agriculture (especially for crops such as cotton and sugar beets), laying the rails that traverse the Southwest (a task made harder because most of the terrain is desert, semidesert, or mountainous), and mining (where, although their knowledge of mining techniques proved invaluable, they received lower wages for the same work their unskilled Anglo counterparts did).

The demand for Mexican labor in some labor-intensive occupations was so great that employers held Mexicans captive. One such industry was the Colorado sugar beet industry. Sugar beets require attention almost year-round and, therefore, need a semipermanent labor force. When farmers could not persuade Mexican laborers to stay year-round to perform the arduous labor, they resorted to coercion. One tactic was to refuse to make final wage payments to employees so that they were unable to leave; thus, laborers had to remain in the area until the following season to collect their pay. Essentially, farmers had a captive work force without rights of citizenship or the ability to leave.

World War I through the Great Depression

Although economic trouble marked the years 1907 and 1921, when immigrants were blamed for many of the problems, Mexican immigrants were generally welcomed into the United States until the 1930s and the Great Depression. Prior to that time, U.S. immigration policies aimed mainly at keeping out Asians and southern and eastern Europeans, while allowing Mexican laborers to immigrate. For example, within a year of the enactment of the most restrictive immigration legislation in U.S. history —the Immigration Act of 1917—the first foreign labor program came into force.

In response to pressure from agricultural employers in the Southwest, Congress included provisions in the law that allowed entry into the United States of "temporary" workers who would otherwise be inadmissible under the Act. This temporary worker—*bracero*—program was enacted for the duration of World War I and was extended until 1922, four years after the war ended. Although this program did not include the Mexican government's proposals to guarantee the contracts of immigrant workers as did later agreements, it was the blueprint upon which later programs were based.

After the Depression began, Latinos found themselves unemployed and unwanted. Jobs that Latinos had been doing for years were no longer available or were performed by Anglos who were forced to resort to that type of labor. Because Latinos were historically ill-paid, many had few or no financial reserves and no choice but to go on welfare or other relief programs. Because of the Depression, Mexican workers and immigrants were no longer welcomed. In fact, they were so unpopular that many were driven from the country. For example, Latinos in Oklahoma were threatened with being burned out of their homes, in Indiana a mob forced railworkers to "give up their jobs," and in Texas signs warned Mexicans to get out of town.[2]

As the Depression lingered and county, state, and federal budgets dwindled, governments sought ways to cut welfare costs. One method used was to deny welfare benefits to Mexican laborers. This action, labeled "fair and humane" by government agents, was a move to reduce the labor surplus and at the same time to reduce welfare rolls.[3] No longer welcome in the United States, and with no way to sustain themselves, many Mexicans began a mass exodus to Mexico.

The Mexican migration was heralded by governments of various jurisdictions. They decided to expedite this process by sending lawful resident Mexican workers back to Mexico rather than carry them on the public welfare rolls; however, this decision was problematic for a variety of reasons. Legally, to expel Mexicans from the United States was as costly as keeping them afloat when their funds were depleted. Consequently, instead of using costly legal maneuvers such as public hearings and formal deportation proceedings, social workers resorted to betraying Mexicans by telling officials that they wanted to return to Mexico. This duplicitous tactic, of course, lowered the cost of expulsion considerably. It also, however, effectively deprived many of due process.

This treachery continued throughout the Depression. Tragically, some, if not most, of the repatriated Latinos were lawful permanent residents who had lived in the United States for decades, establishing homes and roots. Another result of repatriation was that many families were separated. In some instances, either one or both parents was an "alien," but children, having been born and raised in the United States, were American citizens. In some cases, the children were allowed to stay in the United States while their parents were repatriated, but in many other cases such U.S. citizens were themselves repatriated. By the end of the Depression, over 400,000 Latinos—including thousands of American citizens—were repatriated to Mexico without any formal deportation proceedings.

These repatriation programs naturally sparked protest from the Mexican government. In response, the Los Angeles Chamber of Commerce issued a statement assuring Mexican authorities that the city was in no sense unfriendly to Mexican labor. It insisted further that the repatriation policy was designed solely to help the destitute. This was supposedly the case when invalids were removed from County Hospital in Los Angeles and shipped across the border.

World War II and the Bracero Program

When the Great Depression ended at the onset of World War II, so did the labor surplus the Depression had created. Agricultural growers in the Southwest, however, began as early as 1940 to petition agencies of the United States for permission to use foreign labor to fill shortages, a precedent established during World War I. Shortly after Mexico declared war on the Axis powers on June 1, 1942, the U.S. Department of State contacted the Mexican government about the importation of labor. Mexico doubted that the labor shortage really existed and viewed the efforts of the State Department as a way of obtaining cheap labor.

Cognizant of the deportation and repatriation of Latinos during the Great Depression, the Mexican government, to protect its citizens from harsh treatment and discrimination, entered into a formal agreement with the United States. This protection was provided by a government-to-government accord signed on July 23, 1942. The Mexican Labor Program, or the Bracero Program as it is more commonly known, was first implemented on August 4, 1942, and was funded by the U.S. President's emergency fund. The program was renewed on April 26, 1943.

Under the agreement, Mexico would permit its citizens to work in the United States for temporary, renewable periods under agreed-upon conditions. The conditions stipulated methods of recruitment, transportation, standards of health care, wages, housing, food, and the number of hours the braceros were allowed to work. Discrimination was prohibited. A violation of these conditions was supposed to trigger suspension of the program for the violating area. Unfortunately, the terms were, for the most part, ignored by both the growers and the U.S. government; thus, migrant laborers were subjected to most oppressive working environments.

Braceros across the country were compelled to endure poor food, excessive charges for board, substandard housing, discrimination, physical mistreatment, inappropriate deductions from their wages, and exposure to pesticides and other dangerous chemicals. Although Texas was not the only state that violated the conditions of the agreement, discrimination toward braceros there was so bad that Texas lost its privilege to utilize bracero labor until after the war.

The upshot of the Bracero Program was that the U.S. government provided growers with cheap labor. Agricultural growers preferred hiring braceros to American citizens for two reasons. Growers were able to set the wages that would be paid braceros instead of basing their remuneration on the principle of supply and demand or on collective bargaining agreements. Further, braceros tended to be males who traveled alone, while Americans had their families with them, thus making it easier to provide transportation and housing for braceros.

A secondary effect of the Bracero Program was that it provided the United States with soldiers to fight the war. Although braceros were initially brought in to replace Japanese Americans who were sent to internment camps and Americans who went into the armed services or the defense industry, braceros additionally freed up many Mexican Americans for the armed services. Deferments were given to those who held defense industry jobs, few of whom were Mexican American, while workers in the agricultural industry, heavily staffed by Mexican Americans, were eligible for the draft. In short, Mexican Americans in the agricultural industry were sent off to the war while braceros were imported to replace them.

While in the armed forces, Latinos distinguished themselves as fierce and reliable soldiers. Throughout World War II, no Latino soldier was ever charged with desertion, treason, or cowardice. The bravery of Latino troops was recognized in the many medals awarded to Mexican Americans, including the Congressional Medal of Honor (the United States' highest honor), the Silver Star, the Bronze Star, and the Distinguished Service Cross. Seventeen Mexican Americans received the Congressional Medal of Honor for action in World War II and Korea. These seventeen Latino soldiers represent the highest proportion of Medal of Honor winners of any identifiable ethnic group. Because Mexican Americans seem to have gravitated to the most dangerous sections of the armed forces, they were overrepresented on military casualty lists.

Ironically, when the Mexican American soldiers returned home, they were treated no better than they had been before they left. In Texas, a funeral parlor in Three Rivers refused to bury Félix Longoria, an American soldier decorated for heroism, because he was of Mexican descent. This refusal sparked a storm of controversy that ended with the intervention of then Texas Senator Lyndon B. Johnson, who secured burial for Longoria in Arlington National Cemetery. Sergeants José Mendoza López and Macario García, each awarded the Congressional Medal of Honor, were refused service in restaurants and diners because of their Mexican heritage.

Sergeant García, however, decided to challenge such discrimination against Latinos. García, after being told that he would not be served because he was a "Mexie," admonished the proprietor to serve him, declaring, "[If I am] good enough to fight your war for you, I'm good enough for you to serve a cup of coffee to." The merchant refused and went so far as to attempt physically to remove García from the diner. García defended himself. The altercation ended with the arrival of the police, who sent everyone home and ordered the diner closed for the night. Later, after the incident was recounted over the national news, Sergeant García was arrested and charged with aggravated assault in an attempt by the city to save face.[4]

After the war, American soldiers returned to work, ending the labor shortage. Growers in the agricultural industry were, nonetheless, reluctant to give up bracero labor. With the urging of agribusiness, Congress kept the program alive. The pressure they brought to bear was not enough to keep the program going on indefinitely, however, and the Bracero Program came to an end in December of 1947. Nonetheless, the use of Mexican labor did not end. For the next nine months after the end of the Bracero Program, while no agreement existed between the United States and Mexico, the number of undocumented workers in the United States increased dramatically. Both governments became concerned with the increase and pushed for renewed labor negotiations. These, in turn, led to a new bracero agreement in August of 1949. In addition to providing labor to the United States, the new agreement stressed a reduction in the flow of undocumented workers from Mexico and the legalization of undocumented workers already in the United States.

The program resulted in 238,439 undocumented workers being recruited into the work force between 1947 and 1951. Mass legalization ended for two reasons. First, it was ineffective in stemming the tide of undocumented workers coming into the country. Most importantly, the enactment of Public Law 78 on July 12, 1951, in response to the outbreak of the Korean War, created yet another bracero program.

Under the new program, the U.S. Department of Labor essentially became a labor contractor. Public Law 78 conferred on the Secretary of Labor the responsibility for the certification of the need for the braceros; for authorization of their recruitment in Mexico; for transportation of the braceros to the labor camps; for guaranteeing the terms of their labor contracts; and for setting the prevailing wage. The new agreement also rectified some problems of the prior versions. The braceros were to enter contracts for periods ranging from six weeks to six months instead of year-long contracts. The braceros were also guaranteed work for at least 75 percent of the time for which they had contracted, as well as being paid the wages set by the Secretary of Labor.

From the Korean War to "Operation Wetback"

Public Law 78 did not stem the tide of undocumented workers. Indeed, immigration authorities started finding undocumented workers in industrial jobs, causing labor unions to proclaim undocumented traffic as destructive to their welfare. As a result of these complaints, on June 17, 1954, Herbert Brownell, Jr., the U.S. Attorney General, ordered a crackdown on illegal immigration and a massive deportation drive, "Operation Wetback."

This dragnet proceeded under the direction of Commissioner of Immigration Joseph P. Swing, a retired army general and reputed "professional, long-time Mexican hater." "Operation Wetback" was a two-fold plan that coordinated the border patrol to prevent undocumented aliens from getting into the United States while rounding up and deporting those who were already here.

"Operation Wetback" went beyond its scope, however, and Americans of Mexican descent were also deported, stirring up memories of the mass deportations of the 1930s. Many of those deported were denied the opportunity to present evidence that would have prevented their deportation. Between 1954 and 1959, "Operation Wetback" was responsible for over 3.7 million Latinos being deported. Of those, an unknown number were American citizens. In the haste to deport "illegals," only 63,500 persons were removed through formal deportation proceedings. The rest of the deportees left the United States "voluntarily."

In addition to violating the civil liberties of American citizens via questionable expulsions, the operation violated the human rights of the people being deported. Deportations were characterized by disrespect, rudeness, and intimidation. Reports even mentioned immigration officers "collecting fares" from persons being deported.

Ironically, the bracero program was in effect while "Operation Wetback" was being executed. Public Law 78 was extended until it finally was allowed to lapse in December of 1964. Although the bracero program was originally intended to be an emergency remedy for labor shortages during World War II, it survived the war by almost twenty years. Further, more braceros were hired in single years after the war than were hired during all of the war years combined.

Modern Labor Programs

Even after the bracero program ended, importation of Mexican labor continued under the McCarran-Walter Immigration Act of 1952. Under it, immigrants from Mexico were permanently admitted to the United States to ensure there would be enough laborers. To guarantee there would be a sufficient labor force, the Department of Labor lowered the admission standards for Mexican workers just days before the expiration of Public Law 78 and the Bracero Program.

Although many Mexican citizens received visas or "green cards" allowing them to live and work in the United States, most preferred to reside in Mexico. Known as commuters because they traversed the border regularly to get to work, these workers maintained the bracero lifestyle by working in the United States for days, weeks, or even months at a time, only to return to Mexico. As well as emulating bracero work patterns, these migrant workers performed similar jobs to the braceros' (i.e., low-skilled or service oriented). In 1977, approximately 1 million Mexican resident aliens lived in the United States, according to the Immigration and Naturalization Service. The actual number of commuters is unknown due to inaccurate records and varying numbers of commuters from day to day.

The McCarran-Walter Act also established a fallback Bracero Program. The "H-2 program" revived all the worst features of its predecessors. Under it, the U.S. Department of Labor has power to admit foreign labor for temporary jobs if able, willing, and qualified domestic workers cannot be found at the time and place where they are needed.[5] As were workers in the Bracero Program, these migrants are totally dependent on the growers for employment. If the worker proves himself to be hardworking and faithful, he might be asked to return again the following year; if not, he can be deported without an appeal.

In 1986 the United States went through its most recent mass legalization program. The Immigration Reform and Control Act of 1986 (IRCA) gave legal status to undocumented persons who had been in the United States from January 1, 1982, to the time of application (between May 5, 1987, and May 4, 1988). Like the McCarran-Walter Act, the IRCA provided special status to migrant farmworkers. The IRCA offered legal status to special agricultural workers who could prove that they spent at least ninety "man-days" during a qualifying period doing agricultural work on specified crops. The end result of the IRCA was to legalize millions of undocumented workers and fill a labor shortage caused by the most recent immigrant expulsion, "Operation Jobs."

Obtaining Mexican labor has also been accomplished through the exportation of jobs. Euphemistically called the Border Industrialization Program or, as it is more familiarly known, the Maquiladora Program, this program is a system of concessions that allows manufacturing and assembly plants or maquilas to locate in border towns in Northern Mexico. Other concessions granted by Mexico have included exemptions from labor and environmental regulations.

The exemptions do more than help American companies enter Mexico; they help American companies exploit Mexican labor. The *maquilas* have proven to be a financial success, but only at the expense of Mexican laborers suffering under poor working conditions, inadequate wages, deteriorating environmental conditions, and the inability to take any legal actions against their employers.

NOTES

1. Richard H. Peterson, "Anti-Mexican Nativism in California, 1848–1853: A Study of Cultural Conflict," from *Southern California Quarterly* 62 (1980), reprinted in *Historical Themes and Identity: Mestizaje and Labels* (Antoinette Sedillo López ed., Garland Publishing, 1995), at 181–92.

2. Francisco E. Balderrama and Raymond Rodríguez, *Decade of Betrayal: Mexican Repatriation in the 1930s* (University of New Mexico Press, 1995), 99.

3. Matt S. Meier and Feliciano Rivera, *Readings on La Raza: The Twentieth Century* (Matt S. Meier and Feliciano Rivera eds., Hill and Wang, 1974), 79.

4. Harold J. Alford, "War," from *The Proud Peoples: The Heritage and Culture of Spanish-Speaking Peoples in the U.S.,* reprinted in *Readings on La Raza* at 147–49.

5. See U.S.C. § 1101 (a)(15)(H).

Chapter 14

|||||||||||||||||||||||||||||||||||||||||||||||||||||||||||||||||||||||||||||||||||

Greasers Go Home
Mexican Immigration, the 1920s

Rodolfo Acuña

Opposition to Mexican immigration crystallized in the 1920s. Reaction toward Mexicans intensified as their numbers became larger. In Mexico road and rail transportation was no longer disrupted by the intense fighting of the revolution. Moreover, prices in Mexico rose 300 percent faster than wages. They corresponded with a labor shortage in Colorado, Wyoming, Utah, Iowa, and Nebraska in 1920 that resulted in the heavy importation of Mexicans into those states. Industrialists imported Mexicans to work in the mills of Chicago—first as an army of reserve labor and then as strikebreakers. During the 1919–1920 and 1920–1921 seasons the Arizona Growers Association spent $325,000 recruiting and transporting Mexicans to cotton areas.

Suddenly in early 1921 the bottom fell out of the economy and a depression caused heavy unemployment. If in times of prosperity their numbers had generated hostility, in times of crisis Mexicans became the scapegoats for the failure of the U.S. economy. The corporate interests which had recruited Mexicans felt little responsibility to them, and these capitalists left thousands of Mexicans throughout the country stranded and destitute. In Arizona, although transportation fees had been deducted from the pay of Mexican workers, growers did not give them return passage. *El Universal* of Mexico City on March 5, 1921, reported: "When they arrived at Phoenix a party of Mexican workers were taken to Tempe and introduced to a concentration camp that looks like a dung-heap." According to this source the men were chained and put into work parties. The situation repeated itself in Kansas City, Chicago, and Colorado.

In Fort Worth, Texas, 90 percent of 12,000 Mexicans were unemployed; whites threatened to burn out Mexicans and rid the city of "cheap Mexican labor." Truckloads of Mexicans were escorted to Texas chain gangs. In Ranger, Texas, terrorists dragged a hundred Mexican men, women, and children from their tents and makeshift homes, beat them, and ordered them to clear out of town. In Chicago, employment of Mexicans shrank by two-thirds between 1920 and 1921. Police made frequent raids and strictly enforced vagrancy laws. Conditions grew so bad that Mayor William Hall Thompson allocated funds to ship several hundred families back to the border. The *Denver Post* headlined "Denver Safety Is Menaced by 3,500 Starving Mexicans."

Mexican workers from the Denver area were shipped to the border. Although these workers had been recruited to the United States, the U.S. government did little to ameliorate their suffering. The Mexican government, in contrast, spent $2.5 million to aid stranded Mexicans.[1] Many workers would have starved if it had not been for Mexican President Alvaro Obregón.

Nativist efforts to restrict the entry of southern and eastern Europeans bore fruit with the passage of the Immigration Act of 1921. Many wanted to include Mexicans in the provisions of the act, but Congress felt that the opposition of agribusiness to their inclusion might block passage of the bill. The 1921 act was generally considered too lenient. Nativists replaced it three years later with a permanent quota act that excluded most Asians and drastically cut the flow from southern and Eastern Europe, identified as "racially inferior Europe." The act started a battle between the restrictionists, who wanted to keep the country "Anglo-American" and felt too many foreigners would subvert the "American way of life," and the capitalists, who set aside prejudices for low-cost labor, remembering that the 1917 act had hurt them financially. They opposed any restrictions on the free flow of Mexicans to the United States, especially since the supply of European labor was cut.

In 1923, the commissioner of immigration turned his attention more fully to Mexicans: "It is difficult, in fact impossible, to measure the illegal influx of Mexicans crossing the border." By 1923, the economy had sufficiently recovered to entice Mexican workers to the United States in large numbers again.

This "legal" migration accompanied an avalanche of undocumented workers who were encouraged to avoid the head tax as well as visa charges by U.S. employers and government authorities. The new migration differed from that of earlier years, becoming more permanent. Permanency and large numbers of Mexicans alarmed nativists, who deplored the failure of the Johnson bill, which later became the Immigration Act of 1924, to limit Mexicans. Debate over the issue of Mexican immigration was heated in both houses of Congress. The decision to exclude Mexicans from the quota was a matter of political opportunism. Albert Johnson of Washington, chairman of the House Immigration and Naturalization Committee and sponsor of the bill, bluntly stated that the committee did not restrict the Mexicans because it did not want to hinder the passage of the 1924 Immigration Act. Johnson promised that the committee would sponsor another bill to create a border patrol to enforce existing laws and claimed that a quota alone would not be effective. Representative John E. Raker of California seconded Johnson and saw no need for further legislation to restrict Mexicans. Raker felt that enforcement of existing laws would cut their numbers to a thousand annually, by ending the employers' practice of paying the head tax for them and by excluding illiterates (according to Raker, "from 75 to 90 percent of all Mexicans in Mexico are illiterate").

Nativists were not convinced. Secretary of Labor James J. Davis called for a quota for the Western Hemisphere. Alarmed that Mexican labor had infiltrated into U.S. industries such as iron and steel, he arranged meetings with Samuel Gompers to plan a strategy to remove this "menace." Representative Martin Madden of Chicago, chairman of the House Appropriations Committee, stated, "The bill opens the doors for perhaps the worst element that comes into the United States—the Mexican *peon.* . . .

[It] opens the door wide and unrestricted to the most undesirable people who come under the flag."[2] Representative John O. Box of Jacksonville, Texas, a former Cherokee county judge and ordained Methodist minister, seconded Madden and demanded a 2 percent quota for Mexicans based on the 1890 population as well as additional funds for its enforcement. Box supported an amendment to put only Mexico on a quota basis, exempting the rest of the nations in the Western Hemisphere. The Johnson bill, however, passed the House without the proposed amendment.

In the U.S. Senate, Frank B. Willis of Ohio echoed restrictionist sentiment: "Many of [them] . . . now coming in are, unfortunately, practically without education, and largely without experience in self-government, and in most cases not at all qualified for present citizenship or for assimilation into this country."[3] Senator Matthew M. Neeley of West Virginia charged: "On the basis of merit, Mexico is the last country we should grant a special favor or extend a peculiar privilege. . . . [T]he immigrants from many of the countries of Europe have more in common with us than the Mexicanos have."[4]

Antirestrictionists argued that it would be difficult to enforce such a quota, that Mexicans stayed only temporarily anyway, that they did work white men would not, and that an economic burden would result. However, Pan-Americanism proved to be the most effective argument. Many senators supported Pan-Americanism as a vehicle for establishing the political and economic dominance of the United States over Latin America. Senator Holm Bursum of New Mexico stated that he did not favor disrupting Pan-Americanism, that Mexico was sparsely populated anyway, and "so far as absorbing the Mexican population . . . that is the merest rot."[5]

In 1924, hostility to Mexican immigration peaked. Although border officials strictly applied the $8 head tax, plus the $10 visa fee, Mexicans still entered with and without documents. Johnson's committee, true to its promise, began hearings on the Mexican problem. Reports of the commissioner of immigration underscored that *peones* benefited from the reduction of European immigrants. In 1926, the commissioner wrote that 855,898 Mexicans entered with documents and predicted, "It is safe to say that over a million Mexicans are in the United States at the present time [including undocumented immigrants], and under present laws this number may be added to practically without limit."[6]

An open fight broke out in Congress in 1926. Restrictionists introduced two bills. One proposed by John Box simply sought to apply quota provisions to the whole Western Hemisphere; another, sponsored by Robert L. Bacon of New York, sought to apply them only to Mexico. The Box bill emerged as the main one before the House. Western representatives opposed any attempt to restrict Mexicans. S. Parker Frieselle of California stated that he did not want California based upon a Mexican foundation.[7]

Representative John Nance Garner of Texas emphasized that Mexicans returned home after the picking seasons:

All they want is a month's labor in the United States, and that is enough to support them in Mexico for six months. . . . In our country they do not cause any trouble, unless they stay there a long time and become Americanized; but they are a docile people. They can be imposed on; the sheriff can go out and make them do anything.[8]

In the end, both the restrictionists and the antirestrictionists displayed nativist and racist attitudes. The antirestrictionists wanted an open border because they needed Mexican labor. Box candidly accused opponents of his bill of attempting to attract only the "floating Mexican *peons*" for the purpose of exploiting them, charging that "they are to be imported in trainloads and delivered to farmers who have contracted to grow beets for the sugar companies." Box stated, "They are objectionable as citizens and as residents."[9] During committee hearings, Box questioned a farmer as to whether what he really wanted was a subservient class of Mexican workers "who do not want to own land, who can be directed by men in the upper stratum of society." The farmer answered: "I believe that is about it." Box then asked, "Now, do you believe that is good Americanism?" The farmer replied, "I think it is necessary Americanism to preserve Americanism."[10]

In 1928, the commissioner general of immigration recommended "that natives of countries of the Western Hemisphere be brought within the quota provisions of existing law." The commissioner specifically recommended restriction of Mexicans, stating, "The unlimited flow of immigrants from the Western Hemisphere cannot be reconciled with the sharp curtailment of immigration from Europe."[11] A definite split developed between the Department of Labor, which favored putting Mexicans on a quota system, and the Department of State, which opposed it because the State Department knew that such action would seriously weaken its negotiations with Latin America concerning economic trade treaties and privileges for Anglo-American interests. Anglo-American racism was a sensitive area. Placing Mexicans on a quota would be a legal affirmation of discrimination toward all Latin Americans. State Department officials were engaged in sensitive negotiations with Mexican officials, who threatened to expropriate Anglo-American oil. The State Department, representing Anglo-American foreign investors and exporters, joined southwestern industrialists to kill restrictionist measures. They attempted to sidetrack debates, and for a time congressional debate centered around enforcement of existing immigration laws. Many members of Congress were not satisfied and pushed for numerical restrictions. Anglo-American labor supported the restrictionists, and questioned, "Do you want a mongrel population, consisting largely of Mexicans?"[12]

Growers and other industrialists joined forces with the departments of State, Agriculture, and Interior and formed a solid front to overwhelm restrictionists, heading off the passage of a bill placing Mexicans on a quota. By 1929, conditions changed, lessening Mexican migration to the United States.

Between the turn of the century and the Great Depression, approximately one-tenth of Mexico's population shifted "north from Mexico," in one of the largest mass migrations of people in the history of the world. This movement occurred during a period of great economic and social development which saw the industrialization of the Southwest, the demise of the small farmers, a world war, recessions, and depression. Mechanization and urbanization in the Southwest required cheap labor, which became less abundant as nativist sentiment completely shut off the flow of workers from Asia and drastically limited European immigration. The reception Mexicans received was mixed. Lower- and middle-class Anglo-Americans blamed them for the disorganization of society, which was in fact caused by the restructuring of industry; in contrast, industrialists, rural and urban, saw Mexicans as necessary for building the Southwest.

Mexicans were divided into political, economic, and religious refugees. Those who came before the Mexican Revolution were protesting the dictator Porfirio Díaz and his modernization of Mexico at the expense of political liberties. Many of these refugees offered leadership to the masses of Mexicans who began to flood into the United States at the turn of the century in response to economic conditions in the United States. Perceiving the racism and exploitation of these workers, they used their newspapers to document numerous stories of injustice; they became the vanguard of labor militancy. Many refugees coming to the United States after the revolution were from the middle and upper classes. Those arriving in the 1910s were political exiles, while emigrants in the 1920s were religious refugees. Both groups, although concerned about racism, opposed any type of radical solution.

At the turn of the century, Mexicans overwhelmingly worked in rural occupations; by the 1920s, substantial numbers lived in urban centers. During this transition, the Mexicans' responses changed. Those who worked as seasonal migrants found it difficult to organize, since often the workers' community was limited to their immediate families. Uprooted from friends and associates, they were constantly on the move. Once this migration slowed, Mexicans formed temporary associations, usually *mutualistas*, to solve the most pressing problems. Frequently, Mexican merchants and the consul used these mutual aid societies as a natural vehicle for worker organization. Approaches differed according to the economic conditions in each state or region. In Texas, Mexican Americans formed LULAC (League of United Latin American Citizens), a middle-class and professional group committed to Americanization.

On the eve of the Great Depression, the transition from Mexican to Mexican American manifested itself in the changing character of the new organizations. Mexican American *barrios* now had traceable boundaries. Moreover, the shift from temporary one-issue groups to trade unions and middle-class statewide associations was well underway. The depression would have a dramatic impact on the development of Mexican American organizations, as the nation turned away from the gold standard.

NOTES

1. Lawrence Anthony Cardoso, "Mexican Emigration to the United States, 1900–1930: An Analysis of Socio-Economic Causes" (Ph.D. dissertation, University of Connecticut, 1974), p. 97; Mark Reisler, BY THE SWEAT OF THEIR BROW: MEXICAN IMMIGRANT LABOR IN THE UNITED STATES, 1900–1940 (Westport, Conn.: Greenwood Press, 1976), pp. 39, 50–51, 53; Mark Reisler, "Passing through Our Egypt: Mexican Labor in the United States, 1900–1940" (Ph.D. dissertation, Cornell University, 1973), pp. 84–85; Paul Morgan and Vince Mayer, "The Spanish-Speaking Population of Utah: From 1900 to 1935" (Working Papers, *Toward a History of the Spanish-Speaking People of Utah*, AMERICAN WEST CENTER, MEXICAN-AMERICAN

DOCUMENTATION PROJECT, University of Utah, 1973), pp. 8, 39; *El Universal* quoted in Herbert B. Peterson, *Twentieth-Century Search for Cibola's Post–World War I Mexican Labor Exploitation in Arizona*, in Manuel Servin ed., AN AWAKENING MINORITY: THE MEXICAN-AMERICAN, 2nd ed. (Beverly Hills, Calif.: Glencoe Press, 1974), pp. 127–28.

2. U.S. Department of Labor, Annual Report of the Commissioner General of Immigration (Washington, D.C.: Government Printing Office, 1923), p. 16; Reisler, BY THE SWEAT OF THEIR BROW, pp. 55, 66–69; Job West Neal, "The Policy of the United States toward Immigration from Mexico" (Master's thesis, University of Texas at Austin, 1941), pp. 106, 107–8.

3. Quoted in Neal, p. 112.

4. Quoted in Neal, p. 113.

5. Quoted in Neal, p. 117.

6. U.S. Department of Labor, Annual Report of the Commissioner General of Immigration (Washington, D.C.: Government Printing Office, 1926), p. 10.

7. U.S. Congress, House Committee on Immigration and Naturalization, Seasonal Agricultural Laborers from Mexico: Hearing No. 69.1.7 on H.R. 6741, H.R. 7559, H.R. 9036, 69th Cong., 1st sess. (1926), p. 24.

8. U.S. Congress, Seasonal Agricultural Laborers, p. 190.

9. U.S. Congress, Seasonal Agricultural Laborers, p. 325.

10. U.S. Congress, Seasonal Agricultural Laborers, p. 112.

11. U.S. Department of Labor, Annual Report of the Commissioner General of Immigration (Washington, D.C.: Government Printing Office, 1928), p. 29.

12. Quoted in Robert J. Lipshultz, "American Attitudes toward Mexican Immigration, 1924–1952" (Master's thesis, University of Chicago, 1962), p. 61.

Chapter 15

||||||||||||||||||||||||||||||||||||||||||||||||||||||||||||||||||||||||||||||||||

Ambivalent Reception

Wayne A. Cornelius

If most Americans today do not see immigration as a threat to their personal economic interests, why do they oppose raising legal immigration ceilings, and why do large majorities in national opinion surveys favor tightening border enforcement and imposing stiffer penalties on employers who hire undocumented immigrants? Granted, all available U.S. public-opinion data reveal much less tolerance for illegal immigration than for the legal kind. Therefore, evidence that the flow of illegal entrants—especially from Mexico—continues undiminished despite the buildup of border enforcement resources may feed public concern about immigration levels in general. This is precisely why anti-immigration advocacy groups have labored in recent years to draw a sharp distinction between legal and illegal immigration. But many Americans lump legal and illegal immigration together and do not see significantly different consequences flowing from each.

An alternative way of explaining the persistence of anti-immigrant sentiment in the contemporary United States emphasizes the influence of *noneconomic* factors, especially ethnicity, language, and culture. For example, national survey respondents who have a negative perception of Latinos as an *ethnic group*, not just as immigrants, are more likely to prefer a restrictive immigration policy. Similarly, white respondents in a survey of Los Angeles County residents who saw Latinos as "too demanding" in pushing for equal rights or in seeking assistance from government were more likely to have negative feelings about immigration. Whites in this survey had a more positive perception of Asians, believing the impact of Asian immigration to be less deleterious than that of Latino immigration. The researchers conclude that "whites' attitudes toward the impact of immigration in general are more closely aligned with their perceptions of Hispanics [vs. Asians], suggesting that their anti-*immigrant* feeling may be largely anti-*Hispanic* feeling."

Specifically, what is it about Latinos as an ethnic category that may feed anti-immigration sentiment? Culture and language appear to be important irritants. Although a "culture of multiculturalism" has taken root in the United States to a greater extent than in most West European countries today, the celebration of multiculturalism is by no means universal. A statewide survey of Texas college students found that Anglos who oppose multiculturalism in various forms are more likely to have a negative view of immigration. Among the general U.S. population, those who disapprove of bilingual education or bilingual ballots and who view immigrants as making little effort to learn English are among the most likely to view immigration and its consequences negatively. In California, a county-by-county comparison of the vote for Proposition 63—a 1986 state ballot initiative declaring English to be the only language in which the state government can conduct business—and the vote for Proposition 187 revealed a heavy overlap of supporters. When different economic and policy conditions in the counties were controlled for, there was almost a one-to-one correspondence between county support levels for Propositions 63 and 187.

Language is not the only lightning rod. For example, Latino immigrants' tendency to have larger families and to live in multigenerational households, often crowded into small apartments, clashes with Anglo European concepts of family/household organization. Because of the larger number of income earners in each household unit, many more cars and trucks tend to be parked in driveways and along the streets in neighborhoods where Latino immigrants cluster than in predominantly Anglo neighborhoods. That many recent Latino immigrants are "illegals" lends to the expectation that they will commit other types of crimes. Groups of Latino migrant day laborers waiting on street corners or in shopping centers for contractors to pick them up arouse anxiety and irritation. In sum, a fairly wide range of negative cultural stereotypes and misunderstandings contribute to a less than sympathetic welcome for Latino newcomers. The line between anti-immigrant and anti-Latino sentiment is often blurred, but it is clear from the empirical evidence that the latter contributes significantly to the general public's hostility toward immigration.

Multivariate analysis of data from the National Opinion Research Center's General Social Survey shows that the belief that immigration makes it "harder to keep the country united" (a belief that three-quarters of Americans hold) is a highly significant predictor of anti-immigration policy preferences, independent of other attitudes or personal attributes. The perception of immigration as a source of cultural fragmentation is widely distributed among the U.S. public. A national survey conducted by the *Los Angeles Times* found that a plurality of respondents viewed the increased diversity brought about by immigration as a threat to American culture.

Principled fiscal conservatives can see immigrants as contributing to budget deficits and higher taxes. Holding other attitudes and attributes constant reveals that those who think they pay too much in federal taxes are significantly more likely to prefer reduced immigration. But the concern about immigrants' use of costly public services that respondents express in public-opinion surveys may also be a smoke screen, used to rationalize policy preferences that are actually driven by more deeply felt concerns about national identity, language diversity, and the shifting ethnic and racial composition of the population. For example, MacDonald and Cain's analysis of the vote in California for Proposition 187—which is *not* based on opinion survey data—suggests that concerns about the fiscal impact of immigration on state and local government could explain the especially strong "yes" vote in California's small, rural counties, whose public finances were particularly fragile in 1994. But "pragmatic" fiscal concerns can be triggered or amplified by negative stereotypes of particular ethnic groups and nationalities. According to polling data, the U.S. public believes that Mexicans and other Latin American immigrants are much more likely than Asians and other immigrant groups to end up on welfare. Such beliefs are statistically significant predictors of anti-immigration views.

The perception that immigration to the United States has come to be dominated by a single "problem" nationality, the Mexicans, is also widespread. Since 1965, surveys have shown that Latin America—Mexico in particular—ranks near the bottom in terms of public preferences among sources of U.S. immigration. European immigrants are most favored, and Asians are somewhere in the middle. When a national sample of the U.S. public was asked in 1997 whether there was "any *one* nationality group of recent immigrants you think has done the most to create problems for the United States," Mexicans were the most frequently mentioned (20 percent), followed by Cubans (10 percent), whose image has been tarnished by the Mariel boatlift and its aftermath.

For more than 200 years, new waves of immigrants to the United States have been viewed as a source of disunity or cultural fragmentation. It has been assumed that the cultural baggage carried by the most recently arrived immigrants will cause them to resist assimilation or to assimilate incompletely. Today, Mexicans provoke particular concern because their cultural traditions and Spanish language use are constantly being reinforced through continuing, large-scale immigration from Mexico, making them prime candidates for ethnic separatist movements. The specter of a "Chicano Quebec in the Southwest" is raised even by mainstream U.S. historians.

In contrast to the "classic" American nativism of the 1850–1929 period—a witches' brew of simple racism, xenophobia, and religious intolerance—today's anti-immigration rhetoric stressing issues of ethnocultural balance rarely takes an explicitly racial or xenophobic tack (a conspicuous exception is Brimelow 1995).[1] The basic claim is that the United States is experiencing an immigrant integration crisis, because the latest wave of immigrants—especially Mexicans and people from other Spanish-speaking countries—are clinging stubbornly to their home countries' language and culture and are now numerous enough to change or dilute America's "core culture." In 1997, for example, the national media made a great fuss over the revelation that in the preceding year, for the first time, U.S. shoppers bought more salsa than ketchup!

The empirical evidence indicates that most Latino immigrants eventually learn some English, and "virtually all second- and third-generation descendants have good English language skills." Less than half of second-generation (U.S.-born) eighth- and ninth-grade Latino students in the Miami and San Diego areas were found to be fluent bilinguals. Mexicans are more likely than other contemporary immigrant groups to retain some proficiency in the first generation's language into the second and third generations, but U.S. Census Bureau data show that Mexican-origin persons who were born more recently are much more likely to be monolingual English speakers. Nevertheless, the U.S. public tends to focus on the Spanish-dominant first-generation immigrants in their midst and to see linguistic diversity attributable to Latino immigration as a growing threat to cultural cohesion.

This mind-set is considerably more complex than simple racism. Both economic and noneconomic factors are shaping public opinion toward the latest generation of Latino immigrants. We find a fluid mixture of uncertainty about future job and wage prospects (if one is less-skilled) and stereotypical beliefs about the welfare use, cultural assimilability, and propensity to commit crimes of Latino immigrants (especially Mexicans). Most analysts have concluded that determining the relative weight of these economic and noneconomic factors is virtually impossible within the confines of extant data sets. However, it would be naïve to ignore the strength and persistence of the ethnocultural objection to Latino immigration. Indeed, continuing large-scale immigration from Latin America may be nudging the United States toward what some public-opinion analysts have termed a more restrictive or ethnocultural version of American nationality. Moreover, latent, ethnoculturally grounded anti-immigrant sentiment can still be exploited by entrepreneurial politicians, especially if a prolonged recession raises the perceived economic threat posed by immigration.

NOTES

1. See Peter Brimelow, *Alien Nation: Common Sense about America's Immigration Disaster.* New York: Random House, 1995.

Chapter 16

No Poor Need Apply

Kevin R. Johnson

Although Congress eliminated the racial exclusions from the immigration laws, economic litmus tests, arbitrary annual limits on the number of immigrants per country and other provisions of the current U.S. immigration laws that limit entry into the United States all have racially disparate impacts. Everything else being equal, people from the developing world find it much more difficult under the U.S. immigration laws to migrate to this country than similarly situated noncitizens from the developed (and predominantly white) world. Nonetheless, because of the consistently high demand among people in the developing world to migrate to the United States, people of color consistently dominate the stream of immigrants.

Although racial exclusions are something of the past, firm exclusion of the poor remains a fundamental function of the modern U.S. immigration law, the Immigration and Nationality Act of 1952 (INA). In sharp contrast, domestic laws generally cannot—constitutionally at least—discriminate *de jure* against the poor. The express discrimination against poor and working immigrants by U.S. law, as we shall see, has disparate national origin and racial impacts.

In the first century of this nation's existence, a number of states sought to exclude the poor, as well as criminals and other "undesirables," from their territorial jurisdiction. When the federal government began comprehensively regulating immigration to the United States in the late 1800s, U.S. immigration law from its inception sought to exclude the poor from our shores. The United States also has a long history of restricting entry of certain groups of racial minorities into the country. Not coincidentally, the federalization of the U.S. immigration laws culminated with Congress's decision to exclude the poor *and* specifically target Chinese laborers, as well as criminals, prostitutes, and other noncitizens deemed to be unworthy of admission into the national community.

From *The Intersection of Race and Class in U.S. Immigration Law and Enforcement,* 72 Law & Contemp. Probs. 1 (2009). Reprinted by permission of the author. Originally published in *Law and Contemporary Problems.* Reprinted by permission.

The Public Charge Exclusion

For much of its history, the United States, despite the stated ideal that the nation openly embraces the "huddled masses" from the world over, has not been particularly open to poor and working people seeking admission into the country.

Buried in the American psyche is the deep and enduring fear that without strong measures, poor immigrants will come in droves to the United States, flood the poorhouses, and consume scarce public benefits that many believe should be reserved for U.S. citizens. Responding to that fear, the U.S. immigration laws long have provided that aliens "likely at any time to become a public charge" cannot be admitted into the United States. Over time, Congress has significantly tightened the public charge exclusion and, during the last decade, enforced it with great vigor.

Currently, consular officers must consider the following factors in applying the public charge exclusion to noncitizens seeking entry into the United States: the noncitizen's age, health, family status, assets, resources and financial status, and education and skills. Put differently, prospective entrants must establish that they are and will continue to be self-supporting to lawfully migrate to the United States.

By the same token, employment visas under the Immigration & Nationality Act are much more plentiful for skilled workers than for unskilled ones; indeed, few legal avenues enable unskilled workers without relatives in the United States to lawfully immigrate here. Consequently, many low- and moderately-skilled workers cannot lawfully migrate to the United States unless they are eligible for family visas (and then still must overcome the public charge exclusion). As a result, many enter or remain in the country in violation of the U.S. immigration laws.

Even skilled workers often find it difficult to secure visas. The complexities and delays, as well as the potential for abuse, of the process of certification by the U.S. Department of Labor necessary for many employment visas have been the subject of sustained criticism. Microsoft billionaire Bill Gates regularly testifies before Congress about the difficulties employers experience in seeking to bring skilled immigrant workers to the United States.

Case Studies

Consider some very recent examples of the operation of race and class in the U.S. immigration laws and their enforcement.

The Modern "Sundown" Towns: Prince William County, Virginia, and Escondido, California

The conventional wisdom has been that federal power over immigration is exclusive, with little room for state and local regulation. Nonetheless, in the last few years, a number of state and local governments frustrated with the failure of Congress to enact comprehensive immigration reform, and uneasy with the real and imagined changes brought by new immigrants to their communities, have adopted measures that address undocumented immigration and immigrants. Class and race have influenced the passage of these measures.

PRINCE WILLIAM COUNTY, VIRGINIA

In 2007, Prince William County, Virginia, responded to an increase of Latina/os by adopting a measure that, among other things, required police officers to check the immigration status of anyone accused of breaking the law, whether for speeding or shoplifting, if they believe that the person is in the country unlawfully. Affording such broad discretion, with vague standards, to law enforcement creates the serious potential for profiling. Fearful of the impacts of the enforcement of the new law, Latina/o immigrants and citizens reportedly have moved out of Prince William County, to the dismay of some businesses and the approval of some white residents.

Supporters of local measures have argued that they will promote "self-deportation" of undocumented immigrants. However, the Latina/os moving out of Prince William County appear to be moving to neighboring localities and states rather than returning to their native countries.

ESCONDIDO, CALIFORNIA

The city of Escondido, California, with a Spanish name and location not far from the U.S./Mexico border (and in a part of the state that once was part of Mexico), has also sought to discourage Latina/o immigrants from remaining in its jurisdiction. The means include passing an ordinance, which the city later rescinded in the face of a legal challenge, barring landlords from renting to undocumented immigrants, immigration sweeps, and aggressive enforcement of city codes and other policies.

Escondido currently is attacking undocumented immigration indirectly by, among other things, citing residents for code violations such as garage conversions, graffiti, and junk cars. Like other cities, Escondido city officials considered a policy restricting drivers from picking up day laborers. One of the local police department's most controversial moves was to target unlicensed drivers by means of traffic checkpoints aimed at undocumented immigrants who are ineligible in California (and many other states) to obtain driver's licenses.

Like Prince William County's, Escondido's approach has been described as encouraging "attrition: making life as difficult as possible for undocumented immigrants in the hope that they'll self-deport back home." Again, fulfillment of this hope seems unlikely given that residence is possible in other nearby jurisdictions in the United States. A retired sheriff maintained that the city is "looking for a way to reduce the number of brown people" in Escondido.

THE NEW "SUNDOWN TOWNS"

Local immigration measures like those in Prince William County and Escondido may well be modern-day variants of the old "sundown town," communities in the United States that emerged in the North after the Civil War, when many freed slaves migrated from the South, in which African Americans found themselves systematically excluded from town after sunset. Often enforced through law and threats of violence, sundown laws allowed workers of color to provide labor needed in town without the perceived burden on townspeople of having Blacks living among them.

Ordinances that bar landlords from renting to undocumented immigrants, including ones adopted by Hazleton, Pennsylvania, Valley Park, Missouri, and Farmer's Branch, Texas, have been characterized as the new Jim Crow. The enforcement of these ordinances may result in discrimination against national origin minorities, including U.S. citizens and lawful permanent residents as well as undocumented immigrants.

The elimination of day laborer pick up points, for example, would likely drive the employment of these workers further underground but would not likely dramatically affect, much less eliminate, the informal labor market that helps satisfy the economy's demand for inexpensive labor. The new incarnation of the sundown town, it appears, thus will have unskilled Latina/o immigrant workers by day but will be white-dominated at night.

The Immigration Raids: Postville, Iowa, 2008

Immigration raids are not an entirely new immigration enforcement strategy. At various times in U.S. history, the U.S. government has employed raids as an immigration enforcement device. However, in the last few years, the U.S. government has conducted immigration raids in increasing numbers—with greater aggressiveness—at worksites across the United States.

The May, 2008 raid in Postville, Iowa constituted one of the largest on undocumented workers at a single site in U.S. history. In the raid's aftermath, the U.S. government did not simply seek to deport the undocumented but pursued criminal prosecutions of the workers on immigration and related crimes. The new strategy, which devastated a rural community in America's heartland, proved to be most controversial.

With a massive show of force including helicopters, buses, and vans, agents surrounded the Agriprocessors plant, the nation's largest kosher slaughterhouse and meat packing plant. Officers arrested suspected undocumented immigrants and detained them at the National Cattle Congress grounds, a cattle fairground seventy-five miles from Postville.

According to news reports, immigration authorities arrested 290 Guatemalan, 93 Mexican, 4 Ukrainian, and 2 Israeli workers. Shackled and chained, the workers appeared in court and listened to interpreted court appearances through headsets. An observer of the mass legal proceedings commented that those arrested

> appeared to be uniformly no more than 5 ft. tall, mostly illiterate Guatemalan peasants with Mayan last names, some being relatives . . . , some in tears; others with faces of worry, fear, and embarrassment. They all spoke Spanish, a few rather laboriously. [They presumably were native speakers of indigenous languages.] . . . [A]side from their Guatemalan or Mexican nationality . . . they too were Native Americans, in shackles. They stood out in stark racial contrast with the rest of us as they started their slow penguin march across the makeshift court.[1]

The raid and criminal prosecutions, however, did not end the immigration enforcement activities in Postville. A local teacher reported that, the day after the raid, U.S. Immigration & Customs Enforcement officers searched "every home and apartment that ha[d] a Hispanic name attached to it"; immigration authorities had gone to the local schools seeking student and employee files for any person with a "name that sounded Hispanic."

More than three hundred of those arrested in the Postville raid faced criminal charges for identity theft and related crimes. Most of the Guatemalans could not read or write, and most failed to understand that they were charged with *criminal* offenses, which would make it difficult, if not impossible, for them to ever immigrate lawfully to the United States, rather than simply facing deportation. Court-appointed attorneys had little time to meet with their clients. The human damage of the raid on a small rural town was devastating.

*   *   *

The United States is not exceptional in the racial and class impacts of its immigration laws and their enforcement. The nations that comprise the European Union, for example, have experienced similar public reactions to immigrants from North Africa, with the difference of race and class contributing to sporadic nativist backlashes. However, the United States as a nation has always held itself as committed to more laudable immigration ideals and often purports to embrace the "huddled masses" of the world. It is about time that U.S. immigration laws live up to the nation's lofty ideals.

NOTES

1. See Erik Camayd-Freixas, *Interpreting after the Largest ICE Raid in U.S. History: A Personal Account*, N.Y. TIMES, July 14, 2008.

Chapter 17

The Privatization of Immigration Control

Robert Koulish

At about the same time that Iraqi Prime Minister Nouri al-Maliki announced to the world that he would expel Blackwater Inc. from Iraq after the massacre of 17 unarmed Iraqi civilians at a western Baghdad checkpoint, *Salon* Magazine reported that Blackwater was headed for the US-Mexican border in hopes of expanding its base of operations. According to *Salon*:

> Blackwater is planning to build an 824-acre military-style training complex in Potrero, Calif., a rural hamlet 45 miles east of San Diego. The company's proposal . . . will turn a former chicken ranch into "Blackwater West," the company's second largest facility in the country. It will include a multitude of weapons firing ranges, a tactical driving track, a helipad, a 33,000-square-foot urban simulation training area, an armory for storing guns and ammunition, and dorms and classrooms. And it will be located in the heart of one of the most active regions in the United States for illegal border crossings.[1]

Blackwater has been bringing its private "war on terror" home to the U.S., seemingly, hoping to move into the area of immigration control, five years after Paul Wolfowitz first positioned the "home-front" as the first defense against terrorism.

It makes sense that the private war that followed the troops to Iraq would now be establishing a paramilitary infrastructure on domestic turf. A large immigration industrial complex is an offshoot of a post-9/11 neo-liberal regime that is designed to re-territorialize and privatize the war on terror.

The regime originated in 2003 when immigration control shifted from the Department of Justice (DOJ) to the new Department of Homeland Security (DHS). The INS was abolished in March 2003 and its functions transferred into the DHS, in a merger of some 180,000 employees from 22 different agencies. The DHS has a mission to "unite much of the federal government's effort to secure the homeland, with the primary goal being an America that is stronger, safer and more secure." It seeks to "prevent terrorist attacks within the United States, reduce America's vulnerability to terrorism; and minimize the damage and recover from attacks that do occur."[2]

The new Border Patrol mission prioritized efforts to prevent terrorists and terrorist weapons from entering the United States, while also reaffirming the agency's

From *Blackwater and the Privatization of Immigration Control*, 20 St. Thomas L. Rev. 462 (2008). Originally published in the *St. Thomas Law Review*. Reprinted by permission.

traditional mission of preventing the entry of illegal aliens, narcotics, and other contraband.

The decision to include immigration within Homeland Security was no accident. One author suggests that the first major step linking immigration to the war on terror occurred with the creation of DHS, which would include the Border Patrol, port of entry inspectors from Customs, INS, and the Agriculture Department's Animal and Health Inspection Service within the purview of the new Bureau of Customs and Border Patrol (CBP). Also within DHS are Immigration and Customs Enforcement (ICE) and US Citizenship and Immigration Services (USCIS).

Under a 2002 Executive Order a host of sub-governments formed and private actors gained direct access to the immigration control policy process. For example, the Customs and Border Protection's Expedited Removal Program has contracted with KBR [Inc.] to oversee the expansion of the federal government's capacity to detain immigrants. This $385 million contract would set up temporary processing, detention and deportation facilities. Indeed, the KBR deal is part of an extraordinary rush to build new private detention sites. Private prison companies are competing for an immigrant "super jail" facility (2,800 beds) in Laredo, Texas, and in December 2005, Corrections Corporation of America (CCA) announced a contract with ICE to hold up to 600 immigrant detainees in Tyler, Texas.

Privatizing immigrant detention is nothing new. During the early 1980s, the federal government began experimenting with incarcerating people for profit. What is new is the expansiveness of privatization after 9/11 and its use in establishing a social control apparatus ostensibly for non-citizens but applicable to citizens, as well. According to one authority, "In the aftermath of 9/11, the private prison industry has once again experienced a boom as national security has been pressed to sweep up and jail an unprecedented number of immigrants. Immigrants are currently the fastest growing segment of the prison population in the U.S. today."[3]

As an outcome, the private prison industry is increasingly in a position to direct immigration detention policy. Private detention facilities are one-stop shops for immigrant processing. The DHS contracts are to train and supply security guards and screeners and to build, manage and maintain detention facilities. Security guards and screeners make decisions related to political asylum and other forms of relief from deportation, arrest, recommendations on relief from detention, and hold a great deal of everyday power over the conditions of confinement within the detention facility. Guards have control over access to phones, lawyers, visitors, food, restrooms and medical care. Given the logic of private prisons—to keep beds full—privatization threatens the legal integrity of immigrant processing.

Private guards wear badges, uniforms, carry guns and drive cars with sirens; they make arrests and as far as the individual is concerned, represent the coercive force of the state. They wield as much power as any state actor but are not held as accountable to the rule of law. Screeners and guards make decisions with virtually no oversight. Interviews and hearings are closed to the public and family. Non-citizens are secretly shuffled from one detention facility to another around the country, without notice to family or counsel.

Even more troubling are contingency plans that could detain and deport large numbers of immigrants "at the command of the president." The plan contains echoes of Japanese internment camps during WWII, as well as contingency internment plans for middle-eastern non-citizens established during the 1980s. On October 17, 2006, President Bush signed into law the John Warner Defense Authorization Act. It allows the President to declare a "public emergency" and station troops anywhere in America and take control of state-based National Guard units without the consent of the governor or local authorities, in order to "suppress public disorder."

In a manner reminiscent of government raids preceding Japanese internment during WWII and other notorious raids against immigrant communities during times of national insecurity, the Warner Act would facilitate round-ups and detention of protesters, "illegal aliens," "potential terrorists" and other "undesirables" for detention in facilities already contracted for and under construction by Halliburton. In January 2006, the DHS awarded a $385 million contingency contract to KBR to establish temporary Detention and Removal Operation (DRO) facilities. Under the cover of an "immigration emergency" and militarization of the southern border, detention camps are being constructed for anyone who resists the foreign and domestic agenda of the administration.

Current proposals for guest worker programs are also replete with privatization references. Rep. Mike Pence, an Indiana Republican, has proposed deploying private "Ellis Island Centers" in foreign countries for the purpose of recruiting and managing guest workers. Such mechanisms share proprietary interests with some of the Iraq war's more notorious privateers.

After more than a decade of border militarization, the federal government in May 2006 solicited bids from military contractors Boeing, Lockheed Martin, Raytheon, Ericsson and Northrop Grumman, for a multibillion-dollar contract to build a "virtual fence" of unmanned aerial vehicles, ground surveillance satellites, motion-detection video equipment and databases to store information on the identity of millions of non-citizens along the border.

Such militarization is not new. During the 1970s and 80s, the militarization of the border made do with Vietnam-era technology. During the Reagan era, the INS introduced high tech air support, OH-6 spotter-observation helicopters from the US Army, night-vision and infrared scopes, and low light television surveillance systems. Within short order the border patrol introduced SWAT teams, military trained and armed Border Patrol officers who ride in armored personnel carriers, shoot M-16s and keep grenade launchers handy.

Boeing plans to delegate some of its workload and authority to subcontractors including Unisys and a division of L-3 Communications Holdings Inc., Perot Systems, Lucent, and others. According to Unisys Vice President of Homeland Security, Brian Seagrave, Unisys will be in charge of the SBInet systems engineering, infrastructure, and configuring and installing key software, including the "common operating picture," which Seagrave describes as SBInet's brain. Unisys' experience in this field includes police department systems and a range of surveillance and detection contracts.

The virtual fence gets its cachet from its ability to track non-citizens long after they pass through the border. As such, it becomes a metaphor for the entire border industrial complex. According to Washington Technology, "the system will create a virtual border that operates beyond U.S. boundaries to help DHS assess the security risks of all US-bound travelers and try to prevent potential threats from reaching the country's borders."

After the collection process, the data are stored in government sites in agencies throughout the federal, state, and local governments. As of May 2005, about twenty-five million individuals have submitted data, 590 of whom have been denied admission for crimes and immigration violations. According to one authority, "there is no evidence that US-VISIT has caught a wanted terrorist."

The US-VISIT program is also experimenting with Radio Frequency Identification (RFID), minuscule microchips (half the size of a grain of sand). The RFID tag can be read silently and invisibly by radio waves from up to a foot or more away, even through clothing. It can also link to medical records and serve as a payment device when associated with a credit card. RFIDs provide additional capacity for tracking non-citizens already in this country. Embedded in I-94 entry documents, passports and border crossing cards, non-citizens are urged to carry them at all times. The future use of RFIDs as an immigration control mechanism was not lost on former Secretary of Homeland Security Tom Ridge, who became head of Savi Technologies, an RFID design and manufacturing company.

It is important to note that RFIDs and other forms of technology-based monitoring systems are easily transferable from US-VISIT to other immigration programs, for example, proposed guest worker programs. The RFID watchdog group, "Spychips. com," reported May 18, 2006 that the Board Chairman of VeriChip Scott Silverman

> bandied about the idea of chipping foreigners on national television Tuesday, emboldened by the Bush Administration call to know "who is in our country and why they are here." He told Fox & Friends that the VeriChip could be used to register guest workers, verify their identities as they cross the border, and "be used for enforcement purposes at the employer level." He added, "We have talked to many people in Washington about using it. . . ."[4]

With corporations competing to put "feet on the ground" along the border, one foresees a virtual fence that has private contractors, guns for hire, the National Guard and Border Patrol welcoming newcomers at ports of entry. Few are well trained; fewer are accountable to the Constitution, and some are not liable for the misuse of coercive force.

NOTES

1. See Eilene Zimmerman, *Blackwater's Run for the Border*, SALON, Oct. 23, 2007, http://www.salon.com/news/feature/2007/10/23/blackwater_border/print.html.
2. John Parachini & Lynn Davis, HOMELAND SECURITY: A COMPENDIUM OF PUBLIC AND PRIVATE ORGANIZATIONS' POLICY RECOMMENDATIONS 5 (RAND 2003).

3. See Deepa Fernandes, TARGETED: HOMELAND SECURITY AND THE BUSINESS OF IMMI-GRATION 170 (Seven Stories Press 2007).

4. See Press Release, *Verichip Injects Itself into Immigration Debate,* http://www.spychips .com/press-releases/verichip-immigration.html (May 18, 2008) (on file with author).

Chapter 18

|||||||||||||||||||||||||||||||||||||||||||||||||||||||||||||||||||||||||||||||||||||||||||

Puerto Rico and the Federal Government

Roger Daniels

Since the United States annexed Puerto Rico in the aftermath of the Spanish-American War of 1898, Puerto Ricans are not, strictly speaking, immigrants. They were American nationals and, after 1917, American citizens by birth, and their comings and goings were not affected by immigration legislation. Between annexation and the end of World War II, few Puerto Ricans migrated to the United States despite extreme poverty on the island and the absence of legal restraints keeping them out. There were no cheap means of transportation between the territory and the mainland.

In Puerto Rico itself population growth since annexation has been rapid. An 1899 census found nearly a million people on the island, which has 3,435 square miles, a little over one-third the size of Vermont. By 1980, despite massive migration to the mainland, the population had grown to more than three million. Thus, there are over five million Puerto Ricans and, given the continuing migration, there may soon be more persons of Puerto Rican birth on the mainland than in the Caribbean commonwealth. Already more Puerto Ricans make their home in New York City than in San Juan, the island's capital and largest city.

The legal relationship between the United States and Puerto Rico, dictated by the American Congress—in which Puerto Ricans are not represented—has evolved over the years.

For a brief period after the almost bloodless conquest of 1898 a military government ruled the island. In 1900 the Foraker Act gave the island a modicum of local government: Under it Puerto Ricans were nationals, not citizens, like contemporary Filipinos. The Jones Act of 1917 declared all Puerto Ricans citizens unless they formally rejected that status.

In 1950 the Puerto Rican Federal Relations law enabled Puerto Ricans to draft a constitution as they saw fit, except that the options of either independence and statehood could not be exercised. Such a constitution was drawn up, approved by Congress, accepted by Puerto Ricans in a referendum in 1951 and put into effect in 1952. Under its provisions Puerto Rico is an *estado libre asociado*, literally, "associated free state" but translated as commonwealth. Under its provisions Puerto Rico remains a U.S. possession subject to most federal laws, including the draft. Puerto

Ricans may not vote in presidential elections and have no senators or representatives, although they do elect a resident commissioner who sits with Congress but has no vote. Puerto Ricans tax themselves, and they, and business in Puerto Rico, pay no federal income taxes.

The status of Puerto Rico has been discussed by the United Nations more than once and will undoubtedly be discussed again. In 1953 the UN General Assembly refused to categorize the island as "non-self-governing," because of the 1952 constitution. In 1977, without significant effect, all three major Puerto Rican political groups came before the UN Trusteeship Council to protest the island's status. The ruling Popular Democratic Party complained because it did not have statehood; the Popular party, because autonomy had not been extended; and the several parties that supported independence, because that had not been granted. One wing of the relatively small independence movement has resorted to violence, most spectacularly in an attempt to assassinate President Harry S. Truman in 1950.

The most compelling reason why independence does not enjoy majority support is an economic one. Without the infusion of federal dollars, Puerto Rico would be even poorer than it now is. In 1984, for example, the U.S. Treasury recorded transfer payments to individuals and governments in Puerto Rico of $3.4 billion, amounting to almost a quarter of the island's gross domestic product.

All of this raises the question of just how poor Puerto Rico is. On a Latin American/Caribbean scale, not so poor. Puerto Rico has one of the highest, if not the highest, per capita incomes of any place in the region. But by American standards it is quite low, much lower than that in the poorest American state. And it must not be imagined that all the effects of the relations with the United States have been beneficial: Some of Puerto Rico's problems are caused by, not eased by, that relationship. Not surprisingly migration and remigration between the island and the mainland are constant. A segment of that remigration consists of school-age children raised in the United States whose Spanish is so poor that they cannot function effectively in the island's schools and need remedial attention. Many of these children, in fact, cannot perform well in either language.

Puerto Ricans in the United States

Most Puerto Ricans who have come to or been born in the United States face two related problems: poverty and race prejudice. Puerto Ricans are a racially mixed group. The indigenous Amerindian population of the island was largely killed by the Spanish conquerors and the diseases they brought. The Spanish introduced African slavery to Puerto Rico in 1511—it lasted until 1873—and there is a large admixture of white and black ancestry in the island's population. Although Puerto Rico is not without color prejudice, it is less pervasive and total than that existing on the mainland, and for many newcomers the experience of American-style race prejudice in which one is either black or white is a shock and a major social problem. In the view of social theorists, blacks and Puerto Ricans in New York City and elsewhere ought to be political allies but in fact are more often rivals.

They are also rivals in another sense: They "compete" for places at the lower end of the poverty spectrum. This is complicated by the fact that the Census Bureau puts many Puerto Ricans in two categories: black and Puerto Rican. Among Hispanic groups, Puerto Ricans are at the bottom or near the bottom according to most of the criteria by which the disadvantaged are measured.

Many data demonstrate that second- and third-generation Puerto Ricans, like the second and third generations of most immigrant groups, have tended to improve their economic and educational standing and, as was also true for most immigrant groups, that those who moved away from the established center of immigration—for Puerto Ricans, New York City—tended to have higher incomes. This was true of modest-size Puerto Rican communities in San Francisco, Los Angeles, and Lorain, Ohio. The latter community, attracted there by industry, including steel mills and a Ford plant, has shown high social mobility: In the 1970s more than half the families owned their own homes, and women headed only 7 percent of Puerto Rican families there. But it is New York City—and to a lesser degree its environs—which is crucial to the Puerto Rican experience.

Like so many ethnic Catholics who have come to the United States, Puerto Ricans have felt alienated from the American church. Unlike so many other groups, Puerto Ricans do not count significant numbers of priests migrating with them, and even on the island only about one-third of the Catholic clergy are ethnic Puerto Ricans. The American hierarchy has been more than reluctant, in recent decades, to establish ethnic parishes as it once did. The United States Catholic Conference, as well as a number of dioceses in the East and Southwest, has established bureaucratic organizations to try to meet the needs of its Spanish-speaking communicants, but for the Puerto Ricans these have not been particularly effective. Beginning in 1976 there have been national meetings of Spanish-speaking laity, but these, like so many national organizations of the Spanish speaking, have been dominated by Mexican Americans. Of the first six bishops of Hispanic origin, only one was in New York, the center of Puerto Rican population, and he was a native of Spain. And although as many as half of the Catholics in Manhattan and Brooklyn are Spanish speaking—and Puerto Ricans are the largest segment of those—the hierarchy is, from top to bottom, dominated by European ethnics, especially Irish Americans.

As the data for economic status suggest, relatively few Puerto Ricans have thus far enjoyed the upward social mobility that has been the unifying theme of the American immigrant experience. Puerto Ricans who have become prominent on the mainland seem concentrated in two fields, the arts and politics, although for a while the most prominent Puerto Rican on the mainland was baseball superstar Roberto Clemente (1934–73). Those with entrepreneurial skills, training, and capital are more likely to remain in Puerto Rico where there are, of course, upper and middle classes of considerable size. In the arts, artists and would-be artists tend to come to a metropolis such as New York or Los Angeles for training and performance, just as those from a state such as South Carolina would do. Among the performing artists who have been particularly successful are actors Jose Ferrer and Raul Julia and opera singers Martina Arroyo and Justino Diaz. In mainland politics, Puerto Ricans have achieved prominence in a number of state and local positions in and around New York City and in the House of Representatives; none has yet been elected a state governor or a United States senator. [Eds.—Sonia Sotomayor, a Puerto Rican, was, however, recently confirmed to the U.S. Supreme Court.]

This brief account of one of the earliest Spanish-speaking minorities in the United States shows how artificial the census aggregate "Hispanic" is. Many Mexican Americans and Puerto Ricans share, in addition to language, a common religion and a common poverty. But they share little else. They live in different regions, have different traditions, and, in the color-conscious United States, are regarded as being of different races: Most Puerto Ricans are regarded as being black and most Mexican Americans as being white, although each group is more accurately described as being of mixed racial origin.

The regions in which most of them live are vastly different, with different traditions of dealing with minority groups. And these regional traditions as well as their premigratory history help explain some of the differences in their adaptations to life in America. One way of explaining the difference in the school dropout rate, for example, is to note that in Puerto Rico, American-style school systems and attendance patterns have been established for almost a century and that the school system in New York City has long been conditioned to the notion of integrating a kaleidoscopic procession of ethnic groups. The California pattern was, for decades, to segregate or exclude Mexican Americans. The economic differences are at least in part explainable by the fact that most Mexican Americans live in what is now styled the Sun Belt, which has been, in recent years, the most economically dynamic part of the United States. Puerto Ricans, to the contrary, are centered in an area of slower growth with little work for the relatively unskilled. We thus have the anomaly, by American standards, of better-educated Puerto Ricans—one might put that, "less poorly educated" —earning less money than less-well-educated Mexican Americans.

Both groups suffer from a common phenomenon different from that faced by earlier immigrant groups. Most of the latter also arrived relatively poor and uneducated, but they came to an America in which a person—particularly a young adult male —could earn a modest income without markedly improving his skills. In addition, most of his competitors in the labor force were similarly situated, and he could expect more "greenhorns" to come who would be even less acculturated than he. Those conditions no longer apply. Outside of the shrinking and poorly paid agricultural sector such jobs no longer exist. And the second and third generations of Puerto Ricans and Mexican Americans (along with the native black poor) find that most of the growing number of immigrants in post–World War II America arrive with significantly more skills, education, and acculturation to postindustrial capitalism than they themselves possess.

||||||||||||||||||||||||||||||||||||||||||||||||||||||||||||||||||||||||||||||||

Chapter 19

The Cuban American Exile Ideology

Guillermo J. Grenier

During the past decades, Cuban Americans have attracted more than their share of attention from both the press and the scholarly community. Their visibility has exceeded the demographic reality. The slightly more than one million persons of Cuban origin or descent account for approximately 5 percent of the Hispanic-origin population of the United States.

What accounts for the relatively conspicuous presence of Cuban Americans within the U.S. Latino population?

1. Cubans are primarily responsible for the growth and development of the third-largest Latino community—Miami—in the United States. Their concentration in Greater Miami has created a Latino presence that accounts for over half of the total population of a metropolitan area that is frequently regarded as a harbinger of immigrant America in the twenty-first century.
2. The socio-economic selectivity of migration from Cuba during the past forty-plus years has created a community with relatively large numbers of professionals and entrepreneurs. This socioeconomic profile, although at times overstated, has had implications for the participation of Cubans in leadership positions within the national Latino population, especially in such visible sectors as media and government.
3. As a self-defined exile community, Cuban Americans have developed a set of political institutions and political culture that differ sharply from those of other Latino groups. The political behavior of Cuban Americans has garnered considerable attention from the press, while many of the leading political figures and organizations of the Cuban-American community have been prominent at the national level in furthering the exile political agenda.

Waves of Migration

The first wave of Cubans, approximately 250,000, arrived from 1959 to 1964. As with most revolutions, the first to leave Cuba were those in the middle and upper classes.

From *The Creation and Maintenance of the Cuban American "Exile Ideology": Evidence from the FIU Cuba Poll 2004*, 25(2–3) JOURNAL OF AMERICAN ETHNIC HISTORY 209–24 (Winter/Spring 2006). Reprinted excerpts from pp. 209–10, 212–14, 217, 219–23 by permission of the publisher.

The second wave of Cubans, about 300,000, arrived during the "freedom flights" from 1965 to 1973. The first two cohorts laid the foundation for the creation of a viable Cuban economic enclave in South Florida. The economic enclave founded by middle-class Cubans in these two cohorts accommodated all subsequent arrivals from Cuba and served as a magnet for immigrants from all over Latin America.

The third cohort consists of those who came to the United States between 1974 and 1979, when the migration between the United States and Cuba slowed. The third wave is also highly educated and includes more professionals than post-1980 cohorts.

The seven-year period of reduced migration came abruptly to an end during the Mariel Crisis of 1980. After Peru refused to turn over Cubans who, while crashing through the gates of the Peruvian Embassy, had killed a guard, the Cuban government withdrew the remaining guards and thousands of Cubans rushed into the embassy seeking asylum. Subsequently, Cuban officials opened the port of Mariel to allow all Cubans who wanted to leave the island to do so in an orderly fashion. While the exodus proceeded rather chaotically, 124,776 Cubans did leave from the port of Mariel, most of them ultimately settling in South Florida. Unlike the earlier cohorts, these 1980 Cubans lived most of their adult lives in Cuba's new revolutionary society. This has prompted some analysts to conclude that this migration included more individuals "pushed" by economic necessity rather than by political motives. Although felons comprised less than 3 percent of the Mariel Cubans, this cohort received a hostile reception in the United States. Yet, in spite of the odds against them, they demonstrated patterns of adaptation similar to those of the Cubans who had arrived earlier.

After the Mariel Crisis, the migration between the United States and Cuba slowed again from 1981–1989. The few Cuban Americans who came to the United States during this period constitute the fifth wave. The sixth cohort consists of those who came to the United States between 1990 and 1995. After the fall of the Soviet Bloc in 1989, Cuba's importance to U.S. interests shrank. However, in 1994 a large influx of migrants from Cuba facilitated the historic policy change that officially ended the preferential open door for Cuban immigrants and introduced the current "wet-foot/dry-foot" policy (immigrants found at sea are returned to the island, while those who make it to land receive asylum), which characterizes the entry pattern of the seventh cohort, as well as established the minimum number of visas to be granted to Cubans on the island at 20,000. The cohort is different from previous Cuban immigrants in that they left their homeland with tacit approval from the Castro government. Black and mixed race Cubans are more prominent in this cohort as are many who considered themselves revolutionaries for many years until the opportunity to emigrate presented itself. Consequently, the cultural diversity within the Cuban community is now greater than ever.

The Primacy of the Homeland

In exile ideology, the affairs of the homeland represent the community's foremost priority. The public discourse is largely preoccupied with the political status of the homeland. A key element of any exile consciousness is that the members of the community were forced out of their country; emigration was not a choice, as with so many other immigrants, but a survival strategy allowing them to live and fight another day. Seen in this light, emigration is part of an enduring conflict. The importance of Cuba for the Cuban-American community is often ridiculed because, to the general public, Cuba often is seen as an issue far removed from more pressing foreign policy matters.

This obsession with Cuba spills over into the political process. Many Cuban Americans use the Cuba issue as a litmus test for evaluating candidates for local office. "If you want to run for dog catcher," said a Cuban-American patron at a sidewalk coffee stand, "you'd better take a hard-line position towards Cuba or you'll never get elected." While it may not be that extreme, it is true that Miami politics dances to a Cuban beat. A majority of Cuban Americans (54 percent) still considered a candidate's position on Cuba as "very important" when casting their vote. In this respect, the 1965–1973 sample exhibits the highest percentage among the various wave cohorts. The salience of Cuba falls dramatically among second-generation Cuban Americans, only 33 percent of whom consider a candidate's position on Cuban issues as "very important."

Support for the Republican Party

The primacy of the homeland explains the overwhelming preference for the Republican Party, a trait that sets Cubans apart from other Latino groups. Unlike most other Latinos, who have been traditionally Democrats, a majority of Cubans have traditionally voted Republican—due largely to the GOP's opposition to Fidel Castro. Indeed, their initial attraction to the Republican Party has been motivated by their desire to influence policy towards the island, particularly during the presidency of Ronald Reagan. Their high voter registration and voting rates stand as examples of Cuban Americans' unique political culture.

In fact, if Cuban Americans were to view themselves as immigrants in this country, rather than as political exiles, and made judgments about political parties based upon their needs and aspirations as immigrants in the United States, they would be Democrats in overwhelming numbers. This would be true not only because of the general social agenda of the Democrats but also because of the specific experience of Cuban migration. The measures that have greatly facilitated Cuban immigration and the adjustment of Cuban Americans in the United States all have been enacted by Democratic administrations: the Cuban Refugee Emergency Program and its resettlement efforts, the assistance given to the Cuban elderly and the dependent, the establishment of the Airlift or Freedom Flights, and permission for the Mariel boatlift to take place, among others. That Cubans are overwhelmingly Republican is therefore a testimony to the importance of homeland issues and the perception that Republicans are more in tune with the anti-Castro agenda.

Conclusion

Although an exile ideology persists and dominates, not all Cuban Americans share it to the same degree. Departures from the traditional exile ideology began to manifest themselves at the end of the Cold War. With the fall of the Berlin Wall, Cuban exiles who long had struggled to overthrow an entrenched socialist regime now had in Eastern Europe an operational model of how such a change might come about. Rather than an overnight "rupture" scenario traditionally envisioned by the exiles, the new model took the form of an evolution that might be led by elements from within "the system," a process that could be helped by openness rather than hostility and isolation. Consequently, some Cuban Americans, including some traditional hard-liners, began to espouse relaxation of tensions with Havana and engagement with elements within Cuba. The rise of this new orientation led in the 1990s to the establishment of several organizations that, in different ways, conceptualized anti-Castro activism in more moderate terms, emphasizing constructive relations with the Cuban government. These new organizations have been committed to a peaceful transition to democracy that would not be based on confrontation and hostility.

Ultimately, the Cuban-American story in the United States is paradoxical. On the one hand, Cuban Americans are held up as examples of the "immigrant success story." As an immigrant chronicle, the Cuban-American story is one of achievement and victories. It is the story of an immigrant group that has made unprecedented gains in empowering themselves in the new country. The well-documented economic success as well as equally impressive achievements through the ballot box have resulted in the creation of a solid ethnic enclave in a region that is often considered to be the harbinger of the multi-ethnic American future. These achievements have earned praise and respect from others and have created a positive image of Cuban Americans as strong entrepreneurs with extraordinary political influence in South Florida.

However, the Cuban-American identity is not an immigrant one, but one of exiles. As such, Cuban Americans often behave in ways that the rest of the country finds unreasonable and even irrational. The exile story is one of the relentless and enduring pursuit of recovering the homeland by triumphing over the regime, or more accurately, the person, who is responsible for their exile. It is a story of frustration, misunderstandings, and resentment.

If the goal of exiles is to recover the homeland and the job of immigrants is to adjust economically and empower themselves in the new country, then we can reach the conclusion first formulated by our colleague, Max Castro: Cubans in the United States have been a failure at what they say they are, and a success at what they say they are not.

From the Editors *Issues and Comments*

Are Latinos in the United States an internal colony?

Is the United States today, as a number of authors assert, at least in part responsible for the influx of immigrants from Mexico? If so, by virtue of what past actions?

What role did nativism against southern Europeans and Asians play in opening the door to Mexican workers?

Is Mexico's failure to govern itself properly part of the reason for the immigration explosion in the United States?

What is the push-pull theory of immigration?

If Carrasco's numbers are correct, the United States deported almost four million Mexicans in two xenophobic waves coinciding with hard times or antiforeign fervor, all in a twenty-year period. This total rivals in extent, if not in savagery, better-known episodes of ethnic purging such as the Turkish war against the Armenians or the Serbian campaign against Bosnians. The United States has never admitted fault, even though many of those deported were United States citizens in good standing whose sole sin was looking Mexican.

Is the United States experiencing a revival of hostility toward immigrants and, if so, why?

Why would an undocumented immigrant be so highly motivated to come to the United States that he or she runs such a high risk of death or, at least, extreme discomfort, in order to immigrate here?

Are blue-collar immigrants and farm workers an oppressed class, locked in a form of peonage?

Are measures such as Proposition 187, stepped-up border enforcement, and sundown towns racist? Or are they only legitimate measures aimed at getting control over our borders?

If, as most economists believe, immigration, even of the illegal kind, benefits the nation as a whole, what if it ends up costing a particular state or region more than it can afford in the cost of social services?

Peter Brimelow's *Alien Nation* argues that any nation has the right to determine its own ethnic and cultural composition by restricting immigration. Do you agree?

The "plenary power" doctrine allows Congress to pass racist immigration laws, such as the Chinese Exclusion Act or quotas favoring northern Europeans, without the possibility of judicial review. Does immigration law, then, hold a mirror to U.S. racial attitudes, showing how we would treat even domestic minorities if we were not limited by the Thirteenth and Fourteenth Amendments and civil rights legislation?

Do you favor continued neocolonial status for Puerto Rico? Normalization of relations with Castro's Cuba? Why or why not?

Suggested Readings

Acuña, Rodolfo F. *Corridors of Migration: The Odyssey of Mexican Laborers, 1600–1933*. Tucson: University of Arizona Press, 2008.

Barajas, Manuel. *The Xaripu Community across Borders: Labor Migration, Community, and Family*. Notre Dame, Ind.: University of Notre Dame Press, 2009.

Beirich, Heidi. "Immigration: Getting the Facts Straight." *Intelligence Report*, Summer 2007, at 37.

Between Two Worlds: Mexican Immigrants in the United States, edited by David G. Gutiérrez. Wilmington, Del.: Scholarly Resources, 1996.

Borjas, George J. *Heaven's Door: Immigration Policy and the American Economy*. Princeton, N.J.: Princeton University Press, 1999.

Bosniak, Linda S. "Exclusion and Membership: The Dual Identity of the Undocumented Worker under United States Law." 1988 *Wis. L. Rev.* 955.

———. "Opposing Prop. 187: Undocumented Immigrants and the National Imagination." 28 *Conn. L. Rev.* 555 (1996).

Cabranes, José A. *Citizenship and the American Empire*. New Haven, Conn.: Yale University Press, 1979.

Carens, Joseph H. "Aliens and Citizens: The Case for Open Borders." 49 *Review of Politics* 251 (1987).

Castro, Max J. "Making Pan Latino: Latino Pan-Ethnicity and the Controversial Case of the Cubans." 2 *Harv. Latino L. Rev.* 179 (1997).

Chavez, Leo R. "The Power of the Imagined Community: The Settlement of Undocumented Mexicans and Central Americans in the United States." 96 *American Anthropologist* 52 (1994).

———. *Shadowed Lives: Undocumented Immigrants in American Society*. 2d ed. Fort Worth, Tex.: Harcourt Brace, 1998.

Clark, Juan M. *The 1980 Mariel Exodus: An Analysis and Prospect*. Washington, D.C.: Council for Inter-American Security, 1981.

Conover, Ted. *Coyotes: A Journey through the Secret World of America's Illegal Aliens*. New York: Vintage, 1987.

Coutin, Susan Bibler. *Legalizing Moves: Salvadoran Immigrants' Struggle for U.S. Residency*. Ann Arbor: University of Michigan Press, 2000.

———. *Nations of Emigrants: Shifting Boundaries of Citizenship in El Salvador and the United States*. Ithaca, N.Y.: Cornell University Press, 2007.

Crossings: Mexican Immigration in Interdisciplinary Perspective, edited by Marcelo Suárez-Orozco. Cambridge, Mass.: Harvard University Press, 1998.

Cruz, José E. *Identity and Power: Puerto Rican Politics and the Challenge of Ethnicity*. Philadelphia: Temple University Press, 1998.

Daniel, Cletus E. *Bitter Harvest: A History of California Farm Workers, 1870–1941*. Ithaca, N.Y.: Cornell University Press, 1981.

Davis, Marilyn. *Mexican Voices/American Dreams: An Oral History of Mexican Immigration to the United States*. New York: Henry Holt, 1990.

De León, Arnoldo. *The Tejano Community, 1836–1900*. New ed. Dallas: Southern Methodist University Press, 1997.

Eckstein, Susan. *The Immigrant Divide: How Cuban Americans Changed the U.S. and Their Homeland*. New York: Routledge, 2009.

Ellingwood, Ken. *Hard Line: Life and Death on the U.S.-Mexico Border*. New York: Pantheon, 2004.

Fan, Stephen Shie-Wei. "Immigration Law and the Promise of Critical Race Theory: Opening the Academy to the Voices of Aliens and Immigrants." 97 *Colum. L. Rev.* 1202 (1997).

Fix, Michael, and Jeffrey S. Passel. *Immigration and Immigrants: Setting the Record Straight*. New York: Urban Institute, 1994.

Flores, Juan. *Divided Borders: Essays on Puerto Rican Identity*. Houston: Arte Publico Press, 1993.

Galarza, Ernesto. *Farmworkers and Agribusiness in California, 1947–1977*. Notre Dame, Ind.: University of Notre Dame Press, 1977.

———. *Merchants of Labor: The Mexican Bracero Story, an Account of the Managed Migration of Mexican Farm Workers in California, 1942–1960*. Charlotte, N.C.: McNally & Loften, 1964.

Gamio, Manuel. *The Life Story of the Mexican Immigrant: Autobiographical Documents*. Chicago: University of Chicago Press, 1931. Reprint, New York: Dover Publications, 1971.

———. *Mexican Immigration to the United States: A Study of Human Migration and Adjustment*. Chicago: University of Chicago Press, 1930. Reprint, New York: Dover Publications, 1971.

Garcia, Maria Cristina. *Havana USA: Cuban Exiles and Cuban Americans in South Florida, 1959–1994*. Berkeley: University of California Press, 1996.

Garcia, Mario T. *Desert Immigrants: The Mexicans of El Paso, 1880–1920*. New Haven, Conn.: Yale University Press, 1981.

Garcia, Ruben J. "Critical Race Theory and Proposition 187: The Racial Politics of Immigration Law." 17 *Chicano-Latino L. Rev.* 118 (1995).

Golden, Renny, and Michael McConnell. *Sanctuary: The New Underground Railroad*. Maryknoll, N.Y.: Orbis Books, 1986.

Gomez, Laura E. *Manifest Destinies: The Making of the Mexican American Race*. New York: New York University Press, 2007.

Gomez, Luis G. *Crossing the Rio Grande: An Immigrant's Life in the 1880s*. College Station: Texas A&M Press, 2006.

Gonzalez, Gilbert G., and Raul A. Fernandez. *A Century of Chicano History: Empire, Nations, and Migration*. New York: Routledge, 2003.

Gonzalez, Juan. *Harvest of Empire: A History of Latinos in America*. New York: Viking, 2000.

Gonzales, Manuel G. *Mexicanos: A History of Mexicans in the United States*. 2d ed. Bloomington: Indiana University Press, 2009.

Grenier, Guillermo J., and Lisandro Peréz. *The Legacy of Exile: Cubans in the United States*. Boston: Allyn & Bacon, 2003.

Griswold del Castillo, Richard. *The Treaty of Guadalupe Hidalgo: A Legacy of Conflict*. Norman: University of Oklahoma Press, 1990.

Grosfoguel, Ramón. *Colonial Subjects: Puerto Ricans in a Global Perspective*. Berkeley: University of California Press, 2003.

Gutiérrez, Ramon. "Internal Colonialism: An American Theory of Race." 1(2) *Du Bois Review* 281–95 (2005).

Hellman, Judith Adler. *The World of Mexican Migrants: The Rock and the Hard Place*. New York: The New Press, 2009.

Illegal Immigration in America: A Reference Handbook, edited by David W. Haines and Karen E. Rosenblum. Westport, Conn.: Greenwood Press, 1999.

Johnson, Kevin R. "Civil Rights and Immigration: Challenges for the Latino Community in the Twenty-First Century." 8 *La Raza L.J.* 42 (1995).

———. "An Essay on Immigration Politics, Popular Democracy, and California's Proposition 187: The Political Relevance and Legal Irrelevance of Race." 70 *Wash. L. Rev.* 629 (1995).

———. "Fear of an 'Alien Nation': Race, Immigration, and Immigrants." 7 *Stan. L. & Pol'y Rev.* 111 (1996).

———. "Free Trade and Closed Borders: NAFTA and Mexican Immigration to the United States." 27 *U.C. Davis L. Rev.* 937 (1994).

———. *The Huddled Masses Myth: Immigration and Civil Rights*. Philadelphia: Temple University Press, 2003.

———. "Los Olvidados: Images of the Immigrant, Political Power of Noncitizens, and Immigration Law and Enforcement." 1993 *BYU L. Rev.* 1139 (1993).

———. "Open Borders?" 51 *UCLA L. Rev.* 193 (2003).

———. *Opening the Floodgates: Why America Needs to Rethink Its Borders and Immigration Law*. New York: New York University Press, 2007.

———. "Race and the Immigration Laws: The Need for Critical Inquiry." In *Crossroads, Directions, and a New Critical Race Theory* 187, edited by Francisco Valdes, Jerome McCristal Culp, and Angela P. Harris. Philadelphia: Temple University Press, 2002.

———. "Race Matters: Immigration Law and Policy Scholarship, Law in the Ivory Tower, and the Legal Indifference of the Race Critique." 2000 *U. Ill. L. Rev.* 525.

Lazos Vargas, Sylvia R. "History, Legal Scholarship, and LatCrit Theory: The Case of Racial Transformations circa the Spanish American War, 1896–1900." 78 *Denv. U. L. Rev.* 921 (2001).

———. "'Latina/o-ization' of the Midwest: Cambio de Colores (Change of Colors) as Agromaquilas Expand into the Heartland." 13 *Berkeley La Raza L.J.* 343 (2002).

López, Gerald P. "Undocumented Mexican Migration: In Search of a Just Immigration Law and Policy." 28 *UCLA L. Rev.* 615 (1981).

Lowenstein, Roger. "The Immigration Equation." *N.Y. Times Magazine*, July 9, 2006, at 36.

Luna, Guadalupe T. "'Agricultural Underdogs' and International Agreements: The Legal Context of Agricultural Workers within the Rural Economy." 26 *N.M. L. Rev.* 9 (1996).

———. "Chicana/Chicano Land Tenure in the Agrarian Domain: On the Edge of a 'Naked Knife.'" 4 *Mich. J. Race & L.* 39 (1998).

———. "On the Complexities of Race: The Treaty of Guadalupe Hidalgo and Dred Scott v. Sandford." 53 *U. Miami L. Rev.* 691 (1999).

Malavet, Pedro. *America's Colony: The Political and Cultural Conflict between the United States and Puerto Rico*. New York: New York University Press, 2004.

Marcelli, Enrico. *California in Denial: A Political Economy of Unauthorized Mexican Immigration*. Boulder, Colo.: Westview Press, 2002.

Martinez, Ruben. *Crossing Over: A Mexican Family on the Migrant Trail*. New York: Metropolitan, 2001.

Massey, Douglas S. *Beyond Smoke and Mirrors: Mexican Immigration in an Era of Economic Integration*. New York: Russell Sage Foundation, 2003.

McWilliams, Carey. *Factories in the Fields: The Story of Migratory Farm Labor in California*. Boston: Little, Brown, 1939.

———. *Southern California: An Island on the Land*. Santa Barbara, Calif.: Peregrine Smith, 1946.

Meeks, Eric V. *Border Citizens: The Making of Indians, Mexicans, and Anglos in Arizona*. Austin: University of Texas Press, 2007.

Menjívar, Cecilia. *Fragmented Ties: Salvadoran Immigrant Networks in America*. Berkeley: University of California Press, 2000.

Miami Now! Immigration, Ethnicity, and Social Change, edited by S. Guillermo J. Grenier and Alex Stepick III. Gainesville: University Press of Florida, 1992.

Moran Rachel F. "Demography and Distrust: The Latino Challenge to Civil Rights and Immigration Policy in the 1990s and Beyond." 8 *La Raza L.J.* (1995).

Neuman, Gerald L. "Aliens as Outlaws: Government Services, Proposition 187, and the Structure of Equal Protection Doctrine." 42 *UCLA L. Rev.* 1425 (1995).

Olivas, Michael A. "Immigration Related State and Local Ordinances: Preemption, Prejudice, and the Proper Role for Enforcement." *U. Chi. L. Forum* 27 (2007).

———. "Plyler v. Doe: The Education of Undocumented Children and Polity." In *Immigration Stories* 197, edited by David H. Martin and Peter A. Schuck. New York: Foundation Press, 2005.

Pedraza, Silvia. *Political Disaffection in Cuba's Revolution and Exodus.* New York: Cambridge University Press, 2007.

Pitt, Leonard. *The Decline of the Californios: A Social History of the Spanish-Speaking Californians, 1846–1890.* Berkeley: University of California Press, 1966.

Portes, Alejandro, and Robert L. Bach. *Latin Journey: Cuban and Mexican Immigrants in the United States.* Berkeley: University of California Press, 1985.

The Puerto Rican Diaspora: Historical Perspectives, edited by Carmen T. Whalen and Victor V. Hernandez. Philadelphia: Temple University Press, 2005.

Quinones, Sam. *Antonio's Gun and Delfino's Dream: True Tales of Mexican Migration.* Albuquerque: University of New Mexico Press, 2007.

La Raza: Forgotten Americans, edited by Julian Samora. Notre Dame, Ind.: University of Notre Dame Press, 1966.

Reisler, Mark. *By the Sweat of Their Brow: Mexican Immigrant Labor in the United States, 1900–1940.* Westport, Conn.: Greenwood Press, 1976.

Riley, Jason L. *Let Them In: The Case for Open Borders.* New York: Gotham Books, 2008.

Roman, Ediberto. "Empire Forgotten: The United States's Colonization of Puerto Rico." 42 *Vill. L. Rev.* 1119 (1997).

Romantico (film). Kino International, 2004.

Romo, Ricardo. *East Los Angeles: History of a Barrio.* Austin: University of Texas Press, 1983.

———. "Responses to Mexican Immigration. 1910–1930." 6 *Aztlán: International Journal of Chicano Studies Research* 173 (1975).

Sale, Kirkpatrick. *The Conquest of Paradise: Christopher Columbus and the Columbian Legend.* New York: Knopf, 1990.

Samora, Julian, with Jorge A. Bustamente and Gilbert Cardenas. *Los Mojados: The Wetback Story.* Notre Dame, Ind.: University of Notre Dame Press, 1971.

Sartori, Maria E. "The Cuban Migration Dilemma: An Examination of the United States' Policy of Temporary Protection in Offshore Safe Havens." 15 *Geo. Immigr. L.J.* 319 (2001).

Schuck, Peter H., and Rogers M. Smith. *Citizenship without Consent: Illegal Aliens in the American Polity.* New Haven, Conn.: Yale University Press, 1985.

Sealing Our Borders: The Human Toll. Philadelphia: American Friends Service Committee, 1992.

Smith, Robert C. *Mexican New York: Transnational Lives of New Immigrants.* Berkeley: University of California Press, 2005.

Stephen, Lynn. *Transborder Lives: Indigenous Oaxacans in Mexico, California, and Oregon.* Durham, N.C.: Duke University Press, 2007.

Taylor, Paul S. *Mexican Labor in the United States.* 3 vols. Berkeley: University of California Press, 1928–1934.

Torres-Saillant, Silvio, and Ramona Hernandez. *The Dominican Americans*. Westport, Conn.: Greenwood Press, 1998.

Trías Monge, José. *Puerto Rico: The Trials of the Oldest Colony in the World*. New Haven, Conn.: Yale University Press, 1997.

Urrea, Luis Alberto. *The Devil's Highway: A True Story*. Boston: Little, Brown, 2004.

Vélez-Ibáñez, Carlos G. *Border Visions: Mexican Cultures of the Southwest United States*. Tucson: University of Arizona Press, 1996.

Villazor, Rose Cuison. "What Is a Sanctuary?" 61 *S.M.U. L. Rev.* 133 (2008).

Walking the Line (film). Two-Headed Productions, 2005; www.walkingthelinefilm.com.

Weber, David J. *The Mexican Frontier, 1821–1846: The American Southwest under Mexico*. Albuquerque: University of New Mexico Press, 1982.

Wood, Michael. *Conquistadors*. Berkeley: University of California Press, 2002.

Part III

Nativism, Racism, and Our Social Construction as a "Problem" Group

*How Once We Were Here, We Were
Racialized by the Dominant Culture*

Latinos, especially newcomers, have in many periods been demonized and treated in discriminatory fashion, almost as exiles in their own land. How and why has this been so? The chapters in part 3, written by leading social scientists, historians, and lawyers, examine what lies behind the treatment many Latinos have received at the hands of the American government and citizenry. The term "nativism" describes the periodic waves of anti-immigrant sentiment that sweep the nation, making things difficult for groups perceived as foreign. We seem to be in the midst of such a period again today; what does it have in common with earlier ones? Is it more extreme, and, if so, in what respects? The chapters that follow address these questions and explore whether nativism has an economic or racial base, and what Latinos ought to do about it.

Chapter 20

|||||||||||||||||||||||||||||||||||||||||||||||||||||||||||||||||||||||||||||||||||||

A Separate and Inferior Race

José Luis Morín

Knowledge of the history of relations between the United States and Latin America and the Caribbean is indispensable to putting into focus the often forgotten events and circumstances that account for the Latino/a presence here. In many instances, U.S. policies toward Latin America have been directly responsible for the influx of Latinos/as into the United States. But many today misconstrue that presence as solely based on immigration when, in fact, Latinos/as inhabited what now comprises the Southwestern and Western states of the United States—approximately one-third of its continental territory—long before European settlements in North America.

Absent from the collective consciousness of the United States are the wars of territorial conquest that took place in the 1800s. At the end of the U.S.-Mexican War in 1848, Mexicans were absorbed into the United States along with the land that was previously sovereign Mexican territory. Following the war with Spain in 1898, Puerto Ricans became subjects of the United States and their land a possession of that country, even though in 1897 they had already obtained political autonomy from Spain. Similarly, the colonization of Puerto Rico by the United States has played a direct role in causing Puerto Ricans to come the United States, not as "immigrants," but under a second-class form of citizenship. Thus, immigration alone does not account for the number of Latinos/as currently in the United States. In point of fact, recent census data reveal that three in five Latinos/as are U.S. born.

The conspicuous lack of awareness of this history provides fertile ground for prejudice and discrimination that inhibit the realization of full and equal rights and justice for Latinos/as. Close study of that history can better inform our understanding of the present-day condition of Latinos/as in the United States.

U.S. Imperial Designs on Latin America

At the onset, it is necessary to clarify that the United States, notwithstanding its anti-colonial beginnings, occupies a place in history as one of the world's greatest empires. Its ascent to this status was not accidental. By the end of the nineteenth century, the

From Latino/a Rights and Justice in the United States: Perspectives and Approaches, 2d ed., by José Luis Morín, pp. 19–37. Copyright © 2009 by José Luis Morín. Reprinted by permission of Carolina Academic Press.

United States had successfully positioned itself as an imperial power with territorial possessions around the globe. It had also claimed a dominant role over all of the Americas—a role that it maintains to the present. It is well established that U.S. imperialism was not a passive endeavor or accidental, but a concerted effort to expand U.S. territorial reach for new markets and to secure other economic, social, and political gains.

However much it has been couched in benevolent terms or in the name of spreading democracy, acquiring territories through wars of conquest places the United States squarely in the league of other imperial powers in world history that have engaged in the systematic violation of the right of self-determination of peoples. Indeed, as with all such powers, the United States has used war and the threat of it as indispensable instruments for the attainment of hegemony. Stated clearly, it was through military conquests that the United States was able to wrest approximately half of the lands of Mexico and gain control over a series of island nations—including Puerto Rico, Cuba, the Philippines, Guam, and Hawaii—by the end of the 1800s.

The conquests of the 1800s were rooted in the longstanding and deeply held desire of many founders of the United States to construct an empire. As early as 1767, Benjamin Franklin articulated aspirations for the expansion of U.S. territory, including intentions to make Mexico and Cuba part of the United States. Thomas Jefferson contended that the United States "has a hemisphere to itself. It must have a separate system of interest which must not be subordinated to those of Europe." By the 1780s, Jefferson avowed that the U.S. should take over the Spanish empire "peice by peice [sic]." These expansionist designs were not simply a whim of Franklin and Jefferson; they became an integral part of the ambitions of U.S. policymakers who followed. The goal of seizing other lands to advance U.S. global economic and political interests could not be clearer than in 1891 when Secretary of State James Blaine wrote in a letter to President Benjamin Harrison, "I think there are only three places that are of value enough to be taken that are not continental. . . . One is Hawaii and the others are Cuba and Porto Rico."

Racial Justifications for U.S. Imperialism

U.S. domination over Latin American lands and peoples was made palatable to the U.S. public in large measure through the perpetuation of racist ideologies. "Manifest Destiny," a dominant and influential belief system boldly advanced in the 1800s, touted the divine right of Anglo-Saxon U.S. citizens to territorial expansion based on supposed racial and cultural superiority. The influence of the racist assumptions inherent in the notion of the "White Man's Burden," together with "Manifest Destiny," provided the requisite justification for Anglo-American territorial conquests and domination.

Policymakers and the major news media combined to further the idea that the United States was governed by persons of a superior race, religion, and culture distinguishable from all others and that, therefore, the United States was uniquely and rightfully entitled to claim dominance over other lands and peoples. So deeply held were these beliefs that all non–Anglo Saxons, even those from Europe, were considered threats to the nation. By 1751, Benjamin Franklin had already voiced his beliefs about the racial and cultural threat that non–Anglo Americans posed, including German immigrants, who in his words "will shortly be so numerous as to Germanize us instead of our Anglifying them, and will never adopt our Language and Customs, any more than they can acquire our complexion."

Very early in U.S. history, Latin Americans were singled out as racially inferior to Anglo-Saxon Americans. James Buchanan denounced "the imbecile and indolent Mexican race," and in the press, the *New York Evening Post* in the late 1840s categorized Mexicans as "*Indians*—Aboriginal Indians. Such Indians as Cortez conquered three thousand [*sic*] years ago, only rendered a little more mischievous by a bastard civilization. . . . They do not possess the elements of an *independent* national existence . . . and they must share the destiny of their race."

As historian Howard Zinn documents, major U.S. newspapers and political leaders repeatedly championed the idea of Anglo superiority as justification for the conquest of Mexico. In 1847, the *New York Herald* stated unequivocally: "The universal Yankee nation can regenerate and disenthrall the people of Mexico in a few years; and we believe it is part of our destiny to civilize that beautiful country." Invoking God as further justification, Senator H. V. Johnson stated:

> I believe we should be recreant to our noble mission, if we refuse acquiescence in the high purposes of a wise Providence. War has its evils . . . but however inscrutable to us, it has also made, by the All-wise Dispenser of events, the instrumentality of accomplishing the great end of human elevation and happiness. . . . It is in this view, that I subscribe to the doctrine of "manifest destiny."[1]

The notion that racial and cultural deficiencies rendered Latin American peoples unable to govern their own nations effectively laid the foundation for a foreign policy grounded on achieving and maintaining U.S. hegemony over the Americas. The foreign policy initiative that encapsulated the idea of U.S. hegemony over the Western Hemisphere was the Monroe Doctrine of 1823. It is a policy statement that validated the establishment of a U.S. sphere of influence over the region—particularly over Latin America and the Caribbean—and it is a doctrine that many historians agree still remains influential in U.S.–Latin American relations. In the 1800s, it was not only racially negative characterizations of Latin Americans that helped justify the wars of conquest against Mexico and Spain, these were complemented by U.S. government policies, practices, laws, and judicial decisions that relegated other Latin Americans subordinate to Anglo Americans.

The acceptance in the United States that Latin Americans were a separate and inferior "race" made numerous military interventions throughout Latin America uncontroversial. In the case of Cuba, Orville H. Platt, author of the notorious Platt Amendment, vehemently opposed Cuba's incorporation into the United States because "[t]he people of Cuba, by reason of their race and characteristic, cannot be easily assimilated. . . . Their presence in the American union, as a state, would be most disturbing." Since Cubans were unworthy of incorporation into the union, they also could not be trusted with full political independence. As a result, the Platt Amendment of 1904 relegated Cuba to neocolonial status and insured complete U.S. authority to intervene in Cuba's internal affairs, including its economy and politics. While the Platt Amendment was in effect (1904–1932), U.S. military forces invaded and/or occupied Cuba from 1906–1909, in 1912, and from 1917–1922.

Throughout the nineteenth century and into the twentieth century, in Washington and throughout the United States Latin Americans were openly and continually depicted as inferior and racialized "others," who were prone to uncivilized behavior and undeserving of self-government. The U.S. public received a steady diet of news stories and media portrayals that vividly reinforced the idea that in pursuing its colonial agenda the U.S. government was acting benevolently and justifiably.

In the 1800s, political cartoons in leading newspapers around the country were rife with demeaning and racist stereotypes of the peoples of Cuba, Puerto Rico, Hawaii, and the Philippines. Cartoons depict Uncle Sam (the United States) at the head of a classroom scolding Cuba, Puerto Rico, Hawaii, and the Philippines, represented by the dark-skinned, ugly, and unruly children. The caricature of Cuba, Puerto Rico, Hawaii, and the Philippines as revolting and ignorant children is consistent with racist images of African Americans, Native Americans, and Asians that were widespread at the time.

An analysis of political cartoons by Frederic W. Gleach of Cornell University pinpoints the purpose of the degrading images of the conquered peoples of these island nations around the world: "Racialization, infantilization, primitivization, and feminization were all used to construct our newly interior Others as inferior to real Americans. . . . This was not a passing way of viewing them, but a persistent one—and a problematic one, even to the present." By casting Latin Americans as racialized "others," U.S. public opinion was galvanized in support of their government's actions around the globe. These powerful images offered a vision of a government carrying out a benign mission among inherently inept peoples. Thus, U.S. policies were not to be interpreted as those of a colonial power acting in contravention of its own founding democratic principles, but in furtherance of those ideals.

Racism and a racialized vision of the peoples of the developing world also proved useful in the establishment of a framework for the unequal application of the law to Latinos/as in the United States. In the case of Puerto Ricans, U.S. Supreme Court decisions on the rights of Puerto Ricans have been compared to the separate and unequal treatment accorded to African Americans in the United States for more than half a century. Indeed, virtually the same group of Supreme Court justices responsible for *Plessy v. Ferguson*, 163 U.S. 537 (1896)—the case establishing the notorious legal doctrine of "separate but equal"—decided the *Insular Cases*, which continue to delimit the rights of Puerto Ricans. As with the *Plessy* case, the restrictions the *Insular Cases* imposed on the rights of Puerto Ricans were grounded in the racist and racialized perceptions of Puerto Ricans and Latin Americans that prevailed throughout all branches of the U.S. government. Unlike *Plessy*, however, the *Insular Cases* have never been overturned. As a result, the most fundamental rights of the peoples of Puerto Rico are still significantly limited.

During the Congressional debate in 1900 about whether to extend constitutional protections to them, Puerto Ricans were characterized as follows:

> They are of the Latin race, and are of quick and excitable tempers, but they are at the same time patient, docile, frugal, and most of them industrious.

Given such characterizations, it is not surprising that Puerto Ricans did not receive full constitutional rights, and have not to this very day. As persons perceived as collectively comprising a racially inferior group, the conclusion drawn was that Latin Americans present a danger to the dominant, white U.S. population and its institutions. Therefore, to insure Anglo-American power and authority over the status and condition of Latinos/as in the United States it was imperative to restrict their rights through legislation and other legal obstacles.

U.S. Conquests in Mexico and Puerto Rico

At present, the two largest Latino/a populations in the United States, Mexicans and Puerto Ricans, share a history inexorably linked to the U.S. imperial expansion of the 1800s. Familiarity with the historical experiences of these two groups is essential to understanding the treatment of more recent Latin American arrivals to the United States and the contemporary situation of Latinos/as in this country.

Contrary to the depiction of Latinas and Latinos primarily as "illegal immigrants" to the United States, many Mexicans lived on the lands that presently comprise roughly one-third of the continental United States, including the present-day states of California, Texas, New Mexico, Arizona, Nevada, and parts of Colorado, Utah, and Kansas. At the end of the U.S.–Mexican War in 1848, approximately 75,000 Mexicans living on the lands acquired by the United States through war were forced to decide whether to become U.S. citizens.

The conquest of these lands and the people who inhabited them was possible through the efforts of President James K. Polk. By stationing troops at its border, Polk intentionally instigated hostilities with Mexico. In view of the vast territories and resources taken as part of the Treaty of Guadalupe Hidalgo that ended the U.S.–Mexican War, the $15 million payment to Mexico at the conclusion of this war was little more than a crude attempt to legitimize a land grab that violated the sovereignty of another nation.

Drafted by a victorious U.S. government after Mexico's military defeat, the Treaty of Guadalupe Hidalgo of 1848 between the United States and Mexico failed to protect the rights of Mexicans who became U.S. citizens. Mexicans within the territories acquired by the United States were reduced to second-class citizenship, subjected to the loss of their lands in spite of preexisting land grants, and denied the right to vote and political representation.

Originally, consistent with international law, the Treaty of Guadalupe Hidalgo aimed to extend full rights to Mexicans, but its final version was significantly modified.

In order to appease concerns raised in Congress over the racial threat that Mexicans represented to Anglo-American rule, article IX of the treaty was amended to grant Congress final say as to when Mexicans would be able to exercise full rights as U.S. citizens. As expressed in that article of the Treaty of Guadalupe Hidalgo (1848):

> The Mexicans who, in the territories aforesaid, shall not preserve the character of citizens of the Mexican Republic, conformably with what is stipulated in the preceding article, shall be incorporated into the Union of the United States and be admitted, *at the proper time (to be judged of by the Congress of the United States)* to the enjoyment of all the rights of citizens of the United States, according to the principles of the Constitution; and in the mean time, shall be maintained and protected in the free enjoyment of their liberty and property, and secured in the free exercise of their religion without restriction [emphasis added].

Any reference to the protection of the Mexicans' liberty and property in the treaty was disingenuous. Not only were full constitutional rights withheld in the amendment to article IX, article X of the Treaty of Guadalupe Hidalgo—expected to protect "[a]ll grants of land made by the Mexican government or by the competent authorities, in the territories previously appertaining to Mexico"—was completely stricken from the final version of the treaty. This omission virtually guaranteed that Mexicans with valid land grants would eventually lose lands to white settlers who systematically challenged and won title over those lands in court.

In 1898, the U.S. war with Spain—presented to the U.S. public by government officials and the news media as a crusade to end brutal Spanish colonial rule in Cuba—resulted in one colonial power substituting another. As with the Treaty of Guadalupe Hidalgo, the Treaty of Paris of 1898, which ended the war, fell short of granting equal rights to the peoples of the lands transferred to the United States as spoils of war. Article IX of the treaty provides that the U.S. Congress shall determine the "civil rights and political status of the native inhabitants of the territories . . . ceded to the United States." The ceded territories included the Philippines, Guam, and other Pacific islands, as well as Puerto Rico. At the time, fears about incorporating these "alien nations" and "mongrel" races into U.S. society were widespread. Hence, the language inserted in the Treaty of Paris by the U.S. government assured that the inhabitants of these conquered lands could not exercise full citizenship and constitutional rights.

In 1917, Puerto Ricans were made U.S. citizens with the adoption of the Jones Act by the U.S. Congress. Yet U.S. citizenship—imposed without the consent of the Puerto Rican people and in disregard for the unanimous vote of the Puerto Rican legislature to preserve Puerto Rican citizenship—has not guaranteed full and equal protection under the U.S. Constitution for the people of Puerto Rico and those residing there. In *Balzac v. People of Porto Rico,* 258 U.S. 298 (1922), the U.S. Supreme Court held that, unless expressly granted by the U.S. Congress, a jury trial and similar rights under the U.S. Constitution are not applicable to the inhabitants of Puerto Rico. The court's reasoning, still upheld today, is that, even after the enactment of the Jones Act, Puerto Rico remains an unincorporated territory of the United States, and thus the

U.S. Congress retains plenary powers to determine the rights of Puerto Ricans under the Territorial Clause of the U.S. Constitution, article IV, section 3, paragraph 2.

As reflected in the legislative history of the Jones Act, Senator Foraker emphatically made clear that the "granting" of U.S. "citizenship" to Puerto Ricans from its inception was never intended to confer to them full rights as citizens:

> We considered very carefully what status in a political sense we would give to the people of [Puerto Rico], and we reported that provision not thoughtlessly. . . . We concluded . . . that the inhabitants of that island must be either citizens or subjects or aliens. We did not want to treat our own as aliens, and we do not propose to have any subjects. Therefore, we adopted the term "citizens." *In adopting the term "citizen" we did not understand, however, that we were giving to those people any right that the American people do not want them to have.* "Citizens" is a word that indicates, according to Story's work on the Constitution of the United States, allegiance on the one hand and protection on the other [emphasis added].

Just as the U.S. government curtailed citizenship rights of Mexicans in the conquered territories in the post-1848 era and the U.S. Supreme Court blocked African Americans from citizenship rights, the United States has effectively subverted the right of Puerto Ricans to claim equal rights under the U.S. Constitution—a condition that Puerto Ricans living on their own homeland today continue to endure.

A review of its legislative history reveals that renaming Puerto Rico a "commonwealth" in the 1950s was never intended to end the colonial relationship between the United States and Puerto Rico. At the time, the House committee overseeing Puerto Rico acknowledged that

> It is important that the nature and scope of S.3336 [the bill that allowed islanders to write a constitution] *be made absolutely clear.* The bill under consideration would not change Puerto Rico's fundamental political, social and economic relationship to the United States [emphasis added].

Not surprisingly, at present all political parties in Puerto Rico denounce Puerto Rico's ongoing colonial status. They have also taken their dissatisfaction with the continuing U.S. colonial scheme to the United Nations. As a result, since its first substantive resolution on Puerto Rico in 1973, the United Nations Special Decolonization Committee responsible for the implementation of General Assembly Resolution 1514(XV) of 1960—commonly regarded as the decolonization Magna Carta—has repeatedly recognized the inalienable right of Puerto Ricans as "peoples" to the exercise of self-determination under U.N. standards for decolonization, standards that the United States has failed to recognize or meet.

Despite United Nations resolutions, U.S. Congressional authority over the island nation and its peoples continues, as it maintains Puerto Rico as a U.S. colony. The United States has fashioned a legal framework that allows it to claim complete power to unilaterally nullify all or parts of the Puerto Rican Constitution. In fact, the U.S. Congress actually eliminated Article 2, Section 20 on economic and social rights from the 1952 Commonwealth Constitution, thus overriding the work of the Puerto Rican Constitutional Convention. Puerto Ricans do not share equal rights with U.S. citizens in the United States: They serve and die in U.S. wars, but cannot vote for the President who can send them into battle; U.S. laws apply to Puerto Rico without the consent of Puerto Ricans; Puerto Ricans have no say in treaties and foreign affairs that affect them; Puerto Ricans have no voting representation in the U.S. Congress; trade, maritime, immigration, and monetary policies in Puerto Rico are all controlled by the United States; the U.S. Federal Court is present in Puerto Rico and operates in English, rather than in the native language of Puerto Rico; and the "commonwealth" status continues out of compliance with United Nations decolonization requirements. This situation led former Chief Justice of Puerto Rico José Trías Monge to conclude that "[t]here is no known noncolonial relationship in the present world where one people exercises such vast, almost unbounded power over the government of another."

Why the United States maintains colonies in the face of the worldwide repudiation of colonialism in the post–World War II era becomes apparent when one considers the enormous benefits that accrue to the U.S. government and U.S. corporate interests. Net profits from Puerto Rico to U.S. corporations surpass the profits of all other industrial countries, including the United Kingdom, Germany and Japan. Puerto Rico serves as a captive market for U.S. goods; its population is a source of low-wage labor; 14 percent of the land is used for U.S. military bases; and Puerto Ricans can be readily drafted or they volunteer to serve and fight in the U.S. military.

Contrary to popular belief, Puerto Rico is not an example of U.S. magnanimity or a model for Third World development. Puerto Rico is an impoverished nation with 60 percent of its people living below the poverty line.

Consolidating U.S. Hemispheric Hegemony

Beyond its exercise of U.S. power over Mexico and Puerto Rico, the history of U.S. relations with Latin America abounds with examples in which the U.S. government has sought to extend its political, economic, and cultural domination through diverse means.

To advance U.S. interests in the Americas, the 1904 Roosevelt Corollary to the Monroe Doctrine laid out the principles that justified U.S. military interventionism. In the words of Theodore Roosevelt:

> Chronic wrong-doing, or an impotence which results in a general loosening of the ties of civilized society, may in America, as elsewhere, ultimately require intervention by some civilized nation, and in the Western Hemisphere the adherence of the United States to the Monroe Doctrine may force the United States, however reluctantly, in flagrant cases of such wrongdoing or impotence, to the exercise of an international police power.

Of course, the "civilized nation" that was to oversee this extension of the Monroe Doctrine was the United States, and its desire to intervene in Latin America was far from reluctant. Commonly referred to as the "Big Stick" doctrine, the Roosevelt Corollary to the Monroe Doctrine legitimized the use of armed force by the United States. Thus, it did little to "civilize" or democratize the region. Between 1898 and 1934, the United States used its military forces to invade and/or occupy Latin American countries on more than thirty occasions and "despite high-minded rhetoric and ostensible nobility of purpose, not a single U.S. intervention led to installation of democracy."

In the Dominican Republic, U.S. military interventions begun under President Theodore Roosevelt's administration spanned many decades and included the U.S military invasions and occupations of 1903, 1904, 1914, 1916–1924, and 1965. These interventions provided direct control over the economy of the Dominican Republic for the benefit of U.S. banking and commercial interests. This was most clearly evident in U.S. seizure of the customhouses. Instead of spreading democracy, U.S. policies supported brutal dictators, as in the case of the Dominican Republic's Rafael Trujillo, who safeguarded U.S. business interests and profits until the early 1960s. In the latter half of the twentieth century, the 1965 U.S. military occupation of the Dominican Republic guaranteed that the democratically elected government of Juan Bosch would never return, paving the way for Trujillo's right-hand man Joaquín Balaguer.

At best, for the United States, adherence to the norms of international law has been an afterthought. As U.S. power and control over the region grew, justifying violations of international law became increasingly insignificant to U.S. government leaders. In a moment of complete candor in reference to his administration's intervention of Panama, Theodore Roosevelt offered no explanation other than "I took the Isthmus." From as early as the 1850s, the U.S. government preferred to recognize William Walker—a North American "filibuster" who orchestrated an illegal coup to install himself as president, declare English the official language, and legalize slavery—as the legitimate president of Nicaragua rather than to respect the rights of Nicaraguans to self-determination. Well into the twentieth century, the United States abused its self-ordained "police power" to impose a brutally racist and autocratic U.S. military regime upon the people of Haiti during its occupation of the country from 1915–1934.

In the name of fighting communism and at the expense of human rights in Latin America, U.S. policy took an especially brutal turn. Using methods similar to those for maintaining a neo-colonial relationship with the Dominican Republic, the United States propped up and sustained ruthless dictators and oligarchs throughout Latin America, such as the autocratic and ruthless regime of General Alfredo Stroessner in Paraguay. In Central America, support of the Somoza family dynasty of Nicaragua which "seized most of the wealth, including a land area equal the size of Massachusetts," and of the infamous "Fourteen Families" of El Salvador who still control almost 60 percent of the land, are among the most notorious examples. In Cuba, the United States backed the government of Fulgencio Batista, a dictator who tolerated gross economic disparities, poverty, unemployment, illiteracy, and racial exclusion for the benefit of U.S. business interests. In these and other instances throughout Latin America, local repression became the means by which social unrest in the face of economic injustice was quelled. Latin American armies and police forces trained and financed by the United States became the surrogates for U.S. marines, who in earlier times were readily called upon to intervene.

Behind the Rhetoric of Democracy

It would seem inconceivable that the United States—a country founded after a war against colonialism—would seek to subjugate other peoples or undermine the very principles of democracy it developed and purports to spread. The juxtaposition of its stated principles and its hegemonic ambitions has been and continues to be a fundamental contradiction of U.S. foreign policy. However, a now familiar pattern established itself early on in Latin America: U.S. global economic interests usually supersede even its best intentions. Smedley Darlington Butler, a U.S. marine in the 1930s, memorialized his recollection of decades of U.S. interventionism as follows:

> I spent thirty-three years, most of my time being a high-class muscle man for big business, for Wall Street and the bankers. In short, I was a racketeer for capitalism. . . . I helped make Mexico, especially Tampico, safe for American oil interests in 1916. I helped make Haiti and Cuba a decent place for the National City Bank boys to collect revenue in. I helped in the raping of half a dozen Central American republics for the benefits of Wall Street. The record of racketeering is long. I helped purify Nicaragua for the international banking house of Brown Brothers in 1909–1912. I brought light to the Dominican Republic for American sugar interests in 1916.[2]

NOTES

1. Howard Zinn, PEOPLE'S HISTORY OF THE UNITED STATES: 1492–PRESENT 155 (2003).
2. Smedley D. Butler, WAR IS A RAQUET 10 (2003 c1935).

Chapter 21

||||||||||||||||||||||||||||||||||||||||||||||||||||||||||||||||||||||||||||||

Anglo-Saxons and Mexicans

Reginald Horsman

The Anglo-Saxon blood could never be subdued by anything that claimed Mexican origin.

—James Buchanan, February 14, 1845

The decisive years in the creation of a new Anglo-Saxon political ideology were from the mid-1830s to the mid-1840s. In these years American politicians and the American population were overwhelmed by a variety of influences, both practical and theoretical, which inspired a belief that the American Anglo-Saxons were destined to dominate or penetrate the American continents and large areas of the world. Americans had faith that they would increase in such numbers that they would personally shape the destiny of other areas.

The catalyst in the overt adoption of a racial Anglo-Saxonism was the meeting of Americans and Mexicans in the Southwest, the Texas Revolution, and the war with Mexico. In confronting the Mexicans the Americans clearly formulated the idea of themselves as an Anglo-Saxon race. The use of *Anglo-Saxon* in a racial sense, somewhat rare in the political arguments of the early 1830s, increased rapidly later in the decade and became commonplace by the mid-1840s. The manner in which the Anglo-Saxon race was being isolated from other peoples was stated with clarity by Senator Benjamin Leigh of Virginia in January 1836 when opposing the abolitionist petitions. After pointing out that his fellow Congressmen had only to remember how the mobs of Cincinnati, Philadelphia, and New York had dealt with the few free Negroes in their midst to appreciate what would follow general emancipation, he candidly sketched the problem: "It is peculiar to the character of this Anglo-Saxon race of men to which we belong, that it has never been contented to live in the same country with any other distinct race, upon terms of equality; it has, invariably, when placed in that situation, proceeded to exterminate or enslave the other race in some form or other, or, failing in that, to abandon the country."[1]

Reprinted by permission of the publisher from RACE AND MANIFEST DESTINY: THE ORIGINS OF AMERICAN RACIAL ANGLO-SAXONISM by Reginald Horsman, pp. 208–10. Cambridge, Mass.: Harvard University Press. Copyright © 1981 by the President and Fellows of Harvard College.

The idea of the Anglo-Saxon race as a distinct, all-encompassing force was expressed with increasing frequency in the late 1830s. In February 1837 William Gilpin wrote to his father from New Orleans that while the town was still Gallic in character the "Anglo-Saxon is pushing aside the Frenchman and eating him up. The big steamers . . . are Anglo-Saxon, the huge stores and warehouses into which [goods] are piled have an Anglo-Saxon look and an Anglo-Saxon ship bears them hence. [Of] all the new part of the city, the only decent part is English."[2] When Horace Bushnell, in August 1837, delivered an oration on the principles of national greatness, he used old and familiar arguments concerning America as a land saved for events of world significance; however, he used a new precision in writing of the origin of the people for whom the New World had been preserved. "Out of all the inhabitants of the world," he said, ". . . a select stock, the Saxon, and out of this the British family, the noblest of the stock, was chosen to people our country." In contrast, the Mexican state, he said, had started with fundamental disadvantages in the character of its immigrants. If the quality of the British people was changed into that of the Mexican, "five years would make their noble island a seat of poverty and desolation." For Bushnell, God had reserved America for a special people of Saxon blood.[3]

By the 1830s the Americans were eagerly grasping at reasons for their own success and for the failure of others. Although the white Americans of Jacksonian America wanted personal success and wealth, they also wanted a clear conscience. If the United States was to remain in the minds of its people a nation divinely ordained for great deeds, then the fault for the suffering inflicted in the rise to power and prosperity had to lie elsewhere. White Americans could rest easier if the sufferings of other races could be blamed on racial weakness rather than on the whites' relentless search for wealth and power. In the 1830s and 1840s, when it became obvious that American and Mexican interests were incompatible and that the Mexicans would suffer, innate weaknesses were found in the Mexicans. Americans, it was argued, were not to be blamed for forcibly taking the northern provinces of Mexico, for Mexicans, like Indians, were unable to make proper use of the land. The Mexicans had failed because they were a mixed, inferior race with considerable Indian and some black blood. The world would benefit if a superior race shaped the future of the Southwest.

By the time of the Mexican War, America had placed the Mexicans firmly within the rapidly emerging hierarchy of superior and inferior races. While the Anglo-Saxons were depicted as the purest of the pure—the finest Caucasians—the Mexicans who stood in the way of southwestern expansion were depicted as a mongrel race, adulterated by extensive intermarriage with an inferior Indian race. Travelers delighted in depicting the Mexicans as an unimprovable breed and were particularly scathing about the inhabitants of Mexico's northern provinces. T. J. Farnham in 1840 wrote of the Californians as "an imbecile, pusillanimous, race of men, and unfit to control the destinies of that beautiful country." No one who knew "the indolent, mixed race of California," he argued, could believe they would long populate, much less govern, the region. The mixed white and Indian races of California and Mexico "must fade away; while the mingling of different branches of the Caucasian family in the States" would produce a race which would expand to cover all the northern provinces of Mexico.[4]

NOTES

1. *Register of Debates*, 24th Cong., 1st sess., p. 201, Jan. 19, 1836.

2. Quoted in Thomas L. Karnes, *William Gilpin: Western Nationalist* (Austin: University of Texas Press, 1970), p. 39.

3. Horace Bushnell, "An Oration, Pronounced before the Society of Phi Beta Kappa, at New Haven, on the Principles of National Greatness" (August 15, 1837), pp. 5, 9, 11, 16.

4. Quoted in Robert F. Heizer and Alan M. Almquist, *The Other Californians: Prejudice and Discrimination under Spain, Mexico, and the United States to 1920* (Berkeley: University of California Press, 1971), p. 140.

||||||||||||||||||||||||||||||||||||||||||||||||||||||||||||||||||||||||||||||||||||||||||||||

Chapter 22

"Occupied" Mexico

Ronald Takaki

Mexicans viewed the conquest of their land very differently. Suddenly, they were "thrown among those who were strangers to their language, customs, laws, and habits." The border had been moved, and now thousands of Mexicans found themselves inside the United States. The treaty permitted them to remain in the United States or to move across the new southern border. If they stayed, they would be guaranteed "the enjoyment of all the rights of citizens of the United States according to the principles of the Constitution."[1]

Most remained, but they felt a peculiar alienation. "Our race, our unfortunate people will have to wander in search of hospitality in a strange land, only to be ejected later," Mexican diplomat Manuel Crescion Rejón predicted. "Descendents of the Indians that we are, the North Americans hate us, their spokesmen depreciate us, even if they recognize the justice of our cause, and they consider us unworthy to form with them one nation and one society, they clearly manifest that their future expansion begins with the territory that they take from us and pushing aside our citizens who inhabit the land." A few years later, Pablo de la Guerra vented his frustrations before the California Senate. The "conquered" Mexicans, he complained, did not understand the new language, English, which was now "prevalent" on "their native soil." They had become *"foreigners in their own land."*[2]

What this meant for many Mexicans was political vulnerability and powerlessness. In California, for example, while Mexicans were granted suffrage, they found that democracy was essentially for Anglos only. At first, they greatly outnumbered Anglos, by about ten to one. But the discovery of gold near John Sutter's mill led to a massive migration into California; by 1849, the Anglo population had reached 100,000, compared to only 13,000 Mexicans.

Dominant in the state legislature, Anglos enacted laws aimed at Mexicans. An antivagrancy act, described as the "Greaser Act," defined vagrants as "all persons who [were] commonly known as 'Greasers' or the issue of Spanish or Indian blood . . . and who [went] armed and [were] not peaceable and quiet persons." A foreign miners' tax of $20 monthly was in practice a "Mexican Miners' Tax." The tax collectors took fees mainly from Spanish-speaking miners, including American citizens of Mexican ancestry.

Many of the miners had come from Mexico, where techniques for extracting gold had been developed. In California, they shared this knowledge with Anglo miners, introducing Spanish mining terms such as *bonanza* (rich ore) and *placer* (deposits containing gold particles). But Anglos resented the Mexicans as competitors, making no distinction between Mexicans and Mexican Americans. "The Yankee regarded every man but a native American as an interloper," observed a contemporary, "who had no right to come to California and pick up the gold of 'free and enlightened citizens.'" Anglo miners sometimes violently defended what they regarded as their "right" to the gold. In his memoir, Antonio Franco Coronel described one frightening experience: "I arrived at the Placer Seco [about March 1849] and began to work at a regular digging. . . . Presently news was circulated that it had been resolved to evict all those who were not American citizens from the placers because it was believed that the foreigners did not have the right to exploit the placers." Shortly afterward, a hundred Anglos invaded the diggings of Coronel and some other Mexicans, forcing them to flee for their lives. "All of these men raised their pistols, their Bowie knives; some had rifles, others pickaxes and shovels."[3]

Though Mexicans were a minority of the state population, they continued to constitute a sizable presence in Southern California. In Santa Barbara, for example, Mexicans represented a majority of the voters and dominated local elections. "The Americans have very little influence in the elections," complained Charles Huse in the 1850s. The Mexicans possessed a majority of the votes. When they were united, they were able to elect whomever they wished. However, Huse predicted that Anglos would have "all the power" in a few years and would not consult the Mexicans about anything. Indeed, Mexicans soon became a minority as Anglos flocked to Santa Barbara. In 1873, Mexican voters were overwhelmed at the polls. Though they elected Nicolas Covarrubias as county sheriff, they lost the positions of county assessor, clerk, treasurer, and district attorney. Politically, the Anglos were now in command. "The native population wear a wondering, bewildered look at the sudden change of affairs," a visitor noted, "yet seem resigned to their unexpected situation, while the conquerors are proud and elated with their conquest." Mexican political participation declined precipitously in Santa Barbara—to only 15 percent of registered voters in 1904 and only 3 percent in 1920.[4]

Compared to California, the political proscription of Mexicans in Texas was more direct. There, Mexicans were granted suffrage, but only in principle. A merchant in Corpus Christi reported that the practice in several counties was to withhold the franchise from Mexicans. A traveler observed that the Mexicans in San Antonio could elect a government of their own if they voted but added: "Such a step would be followed, however, by a summary revolution." In 1863, after a closely contested election, the *Fort Brown Flag* editorialized: "We are opposed to allowing an ignorant crowd of Mexicans to determine the political questions in this country, where a man is supposed to vote knowingly and thoughtfully." During the 1890s, many counties established "white primaries" to disfranchise Mexicans as well as blacks, and the legislature instituted additional measures like the poll tax to reduce Mexican political participation.

Political restrictions lessened the ability of Mexicans not only to claim their rights as citizens, but also to protect their rights as landowners. The original version of the Treaty of Guadalupe Hidalgo had contained a provision, Article X, which guaranteed protection of "all prior and pending titles to property of every description." In ratifying the treaty, however, the U.S. Senate omitted this article. Instead, American emissaries offered the Mexican government a "Statement of Protocol" to reassure Mexicans that "the American government by suppressing the Xth article . . . did not in any way intend to annul the grants of lands made by Mexico in the ceded territories." Grantees would be allowed to have their legitimate titles acknowledged in American courts.

But whether the courts would in fact confirm their land titles was another matter. In New Mexico, the state surveyor general handled conflicts over land claims until 1891, when a Court of Private Land Claims was established. Dominated by Anglo legal officials, the court confirmed the grants of only 2,051,526 acres, turning down claims for 33,439,493 acres. The court's actions led to Anglo ownership of four-fifths of the Mexican land grants.[5]

Similarly, in California, Mexican land titles were contested. Three years after the Treaty of Guadalupe Hidalgo, Congress passed a land law establishing a commission to review the validity of some twenty land grants made under Spanish rule and another five hundred by the Mexican government. The boundaries for these land grants had been drawn without surveying instruments and were loosely marked on maps indicating a notched tree, a spot "between the hills at the head of a running water," a pile of stones, and the like. Frequently, land was measured with the expression *poco más o menos*, "a little more or less." The entire Pomona Valley, for example, was described as "the place being vacant which is known by the name of [Rancho] San Jose, distant some six leagues, more or less, from the Ex-Mission of San Gabriel." U.S. land law, however, required accurate boundaries and proof of legitimate titles.

Such evidence, Mexican landholders discovered, was very difficult to provide. Unfamiliar with American law and lacking English language skills, they became prey to Anglo lawyers. If they were successfully able to prove their claim, they would often be required to pay their lawyers one-quarter of their land. Others borrowed money at high interest rates in order to pay legal fees; after they won their cases, many rancheros were forced to sell their land to pay off their debts. "The *average* length of time required to secure evidence of ownership," historian Walton Bean calculated, "was 17 *years* from the time of submitting a claim to the board." Furthermore, during this time, squatters often occupied the lands, and when the rancheros finally proved their ownership, they found it difficult and sometimes impossible to remove them. In the end, whether or not they won their claims, most of the great Mexican rancheros in northern California lost their lands.

The Internal Borders of Exclusion

Included as laborers, Mexicans found themselves excluded socially, kept at a distance from Anglo society. Like Caliban, they were isolated by the borders of racial segregation. Their world was one of Anglo over Mexican. Even on the large cattle ranches of Texas where Mexicans and Anglos lived together and formed loyalties and sometimes even friendships, integration did not mean equality. J. Frank Dobie, for example, described one of the workers on his family's ranch. This "old, faithful Mexican" had been employed on the ranch for over twenty years and he was "almost the best friend" Dobie had. "Many a time 'out in the pasture' I have put my lips to the same water jug that he had drunk from," he remembered fondly. But Dobie added: "At the same time neither he nor I would think of his eating at the dining table with me."[6]

Racial etiquette defined proper demeanor and behavior for Mexicans. In the presence of Anglos, they were expected to assume "a deferential body posture and respectful voice tone." They knew that public buildings were considered "Anglo territory," and that they were permitted to shop in the Anglo business section of town only on Saturdays. They could patronize Anglo cafes, but only the counter and carry-out service. "A group of us Mexicans who were well dressed once went to a restaurant in Amarillo," complained Wenceslao Iglesias in the 1920s, "and they told us that if we wanted to eat we should go to the special department where it said 'For Colored People.' I told my friend that I would rather die from starvation than to humiliate myself before the Americans by eating with the Negroes." At sunset, Mexicans had to retreat to their barrios.[7]

In the morning, Mexican parents sent their children to segregated schools. "There would be a revolution in the community if the Mexicans wanted to come to the white schools," an educator said. "Sentiment is bitterly against it. It is based on racial inferiority." The wife of an Anglo ranch manager in Texas put it this way: "Let him [the Mexican] have as good an education but still let him know he is not as good as a white man. God did not intend him to be; He would have made them white if He had." For many Anglos, Mexicans also represented a threat to their daughters. "Why don't we let the Mexicans come to the white school?" an Anglo sharecropper angrily declared. "Because a damned greaser is not fit to sit side of a white girl."[8]

In the segregated schools, Mexican children were trained to become obedient workers. Like the sugar planters in Hawaii who wanted to keep the American-born generation of Japanese on the plantations, Anglo farmers in Texas wanted the schools to help reproduce the labor force. "If every [Mexican] child has a high school education," sugar beet growers asked, "who will labor?" A farmer in Texas explained: "If I wanted a man I would want one of the more ignorant ones. . . . Educated Mexicans are the hardest to handle. . . . It is all right to educate them no higher than we educate them here in these little towns. I will be frank. They would make more desirable citizens if they would stop about the seventh grade."[9]

Serving the interests of the growers, Anglo educators prepared Mexican children to take the place of their parents. "It isn't a matter of what is the best way to handle the education here to make citizens of them," a school trustee in Texas stated frankly. "It is politics." School policy answered to the needs of the local growers, he elaborated. "We don't need skilled or white-collared Mexicans. . . . The farmers are not interested in educating Mexicans. They know that then they can get better wages and conditions." A Texas school superintendent explained that not all school boards wanted him to enforce compulsory attendance: "When I come to a new school I always ask the board if they want the Mexicans in school. Here they told me to leave them alone. If I tried to enforce the compulsory attendance law here the board would get sore at me and maybe cause us to lose our places, so I don't say anything. If I got 150 Mexicans ready for school I would be out of a job." Another Texas superintendent explained why schools should not educate Mexican children: "You have doubtless heard that ignorance is bliss; it seems that it is so when one has to transplant onions. . . . If a man has very much sense or education either, he is not going to stick to this kind of work. So you see it is up to the white population to keep the Mexican on his knees in an onion patch."[10]

Consequently, the curriculum for Mexican students emphasized domestic science and manual training. In Los Angeles, they were taught not only manual-labor skills, but also the appropriate attitudes of hard work and disciplined behavior. "Before sending [Mexican] boys and girls out to accept positions," a Los Angeles teacher explained, "they must be taught that, technically expert though they may be, they must keep in mind that their employers carry the responsibility of the business and outline the work, and that the employees must be pliant, obedient, courteous, and willing to help the enterprise."[11]

There were educators who saw that Mexican children were capable of learning. "The Mexicans have good minds and are earnest students," a teacher stated. "The Mexican children generally are as capable intellectually as the Americans, but the Mexicans are poorer than the whites, so the comparison of their present progress in school isn't fair." Some teachers tried to give Mexican children a sense of dignity and self-respect. Ernesto Galarza recalled how his school principal "Miss Hopley and her teachers never let us forget why we were at Lincoln; for those who were alien, to become good Americans; for those who were so born, to accept the rest of us." Galarza and his fellow students discovered "the secrets of the English language" and grieved over the "tragedies of Bo-Peep." Every morning, the students stood and recited the pledge of allegiance to the flag of the United States. In his school, Americanization did not mean "scrubbing away" what made them Mexican. "No one was ever scolded or punished for speaking in his native tongue on the playground." The teachers tried to pronounce their Spanish names. "Becoming a proud American," Galarza said, "did not mean feeling ashamed of being a Mexican."[12]

Galarza's experience in school was exceptional, for Mexican children were not usually encouraged to develop self-esteem. "The Mexican children almost don't receive any education," Alonso Galvan complained to an interviewer in the 1920s. "They are taught hardly anything."[13]

NOTES

1. Rodolfo Acuña, OCCUPIED AMERICA: A HISTORY OF CHICANOS (New York, 1981), p. 199; David J. Weber (ed.), FOREIGNERS IN THEIR NATIVE LAND: HISTORICAL ROOTS OF THE MEXICAN AMERICANS (Albuquerque, N.M., 1973), p. 19. The Treaty of Guadalupe Hidalgo described the newly acquired territory as places "occupied" by U.S. forces. See the terms of the treaty in Wayne Moquin (ed.), A DOCUMENTARY HISTORY OF THE MEXICAN AMERICANS (New York, 1972), pp. 182–87.

2. Acuña, Occupied America, p. 20; Weber (ed.), Foreigners in Their Native Land, p. 176.

3. Robert F. Heizer and Alan F. Almquist, The Other Californians: Prejudice and Discrimination under Spain, Mexico, and the United States to 1920 (Berkeley, Calif., 1971), p. 143; Weber (ed.), Foreigners in Their Native Land, pp. 171–73.

4. Albert Camarillo, Chicanos in a Changing Society: From Mexican Pueblos to American Barrios in Santa Barbara and Southern California, 1848–1930 (Cambridge, Mass., 1979), pp. 23, 46, 41, 187. This is an important community study that provides insights into larger patterns of Chicano experiences.

5. Mario Barrera, Race and Class in the Southwest: A Theory of Racial Inequality (Notre Dame, Ind., 1979), pp. 26–27. This is a very useful integration of theories of race and class and the history of Chicanos.

6. David Montejano, Anglos and Mexicans in the Making of Texas, 1836–1986 (Austin, Tex., 1987), p. 250.

7. Manuel Gamio, Mexican Immigration to the United States (Chicago, 1930), p. 177.

8. Montejano, Anglos and Mexicans, pp. 226–27, 221, 194.

9. Sarah Deutsch, No Separate Refuge: Culture, Class, and Gender on an Anglo-Hispanic Frontier in the American Southwest, 1880–1940 (New York, 1987), p. 141; Rosalinda M. Gonzalez, *Chicanas and Mexican Immigrant Families, 1920–1940: Women's Subordination and Family Exploitation*, in Lois Scharf and Joan M. Jensen (eds.), Decades of Discontent: The Women's Movement, 1920–1940 (Westport, Conn., 1983), p. 66.

10. Montejano, Anglos and Mexicans, pp. 192–93; Paul S. Taylor, An American-Mexican Frontier (Chapel Hill, N.C., 1934), p. 194.

11. Montejano, Anglos and Mexicans, p. 160; Mario T. García, Desert Immigrants: The Mexicans of El Paso, 1880–1920 (New Haven, Conn., 1981), p. 117.

12. Taylor, American-Mexican Frontier, p. 204; Ernesto Galarza, Barrio Boy: The Story of a Boy's Acculturation (Notre Dame, Ind., 1971), p. 211.

13. Gamio, Mexican Immigrant, pp. 222–23; García, Desert Immigrants, p. 125.

Chapter 23

||||||||||||||||||||||||||||||||||||||||||||||||||||||||||||||||||||||||||||||||

Initial Contacts
Niggers, Redskins, and Greasers

Arnoldo De León

The English saw the Spanish as an embodiment of racial impurity. For hundreds of years, racial mixing or *mestizaje* had occurred in the Iberian Peninsula between Spaniards and Moors. At a time when Elizabethans were becoming more and more sensitive to the significance of color—equating whiteness with purity and Christianity, and blackness with baseness and the devil—Spaniards came to be thought of as not much better than light-skinned Moors and Africans.

English immigrants to the North American colonies probably brought those ideas with them and were certainly exposed to them through anti-Catholic and anti-Spanish literature constantly arriving in the new society. Men of letters, ministers, and propagandists helped in disseminating such notions. Military clashes along the Georgia-Florida border in the eighteenth century only intensified the hatred.

As for the Mexican aborigines, the English conceived of them as degenerate creatures—un-Christian, uncivilized, and racially impure. From letters, histories, and travel narratives, English writers put together a portrait that turned the people of Mexico into a degraded humanity. The natives subscribed to heathenism, and witches and other devilish agents permeated their culture. They partook of unholy things like polygamy, sodomy, and incest and rejected Christianity outright. Furthermore, they practiced savage rituals like human sacrifice and cannibalism. Of all the Latin American inhabitants, the Mexican Indians seemed the most beastly, for though they were in many ways the most advanced of all the New World peoples, they exercised the grossest violation of civility by these practices. Stories of Aztec gods like Quetzalcoatl who were half man and half beast and accounts of exotic Aztec rites only convinced the English of the Indians' place on the fringes of humankind, with dubious claims to existence, civilization, and Christian salvation.

While such images of the Mexican natives may not have been as widespread as those held of Spaniards, they were nonetheless familiar to many colonists. In newspapers, recent histories, and re-editions of old propaganda materials, furthermore, colonists were able to read things about the origins of the Mexicans which perpetuated enriched images acquired from the mother country.

From THEY CALLED THEM GREASERS: ANGLO ATTITUDES TOWARD MEXICANS IN TEXAS, 1821–1900 by Arnoldo De León, pp. 5–8, 16–18. Copyright © 1983. Reprinted by permission of the University of Texas Press.

In addition to ideas that had been fashioned vicariously, there were those that arose from intimate contact with other peoples whom whites esteemed no more than the Mexican aborigines or the Spaniards. The long history of hostilities against North American Indians on the frontier and the institution of Afro-American slavery molded negative attitudes toward dark skin, "savagery," "vice," and interracial sex. The majority of those who responded to empresario calls most assuredly thought along those lines, for they came from the states west of the Appalachians and south of the Ohio River—Louisiana, Alabama, Arkansas, Tennessee, Missouri, Mississippi, Georgia, and Kentucky. A significant number were Eastern born, but had been part of the frontier movement before their transplantation into Texas. From the Southern and frontier-oriented culture they had acquired a certain repulsion for dark-skinned people and a distaste for miscegenation. Believing that the mores of their own provincial institutions should apply in the new frontier, they assumed a posture of superiority and condescension toward the natives. By conditioning, they were predisposed to react intolerantly to people they found different from themselves but similar to those they considered as enemies and as inferiors. Along with dislike for Spaniards and the Indians of Latin America, these perceptions produced a mode of thinking that set the contours of the primordial response.

And what particularly provoked this reaction? Most Tejanos were descendants of Tlascalan Indians and *mestizo* soldiers from Coahuila. Additionally, a few in Nacogdoches were the offspring of people from Louisiana and reflected that area's racial amalgam, including Indians and blacks. Throughout the province, Tejanos had intermarried among themselves and with Christianized Indian women from local missions so that the colonists continued as a mixed-blood population. Their contrast to "white" and salient kindred to "black" and "red" made Mexicans subject to treatment commensurate with the odious connotations whites attached to colors, races, and cultures dissimilar to their own.

Manifestly, Americans who immigrated to Texas confronted the native Mexicans with certain preconceptions about their character. Whites believed that the inhabitants of the province had descended from a tradition of paganism, depravity, and primitivism. Mexicans were a type of folk that Americans should avoid becoming.

In reality, whites had little contact with Tejanos up to 1836, for most of the Mexican population was concentrated in the San Antonio and La Bahía areas, quite a distance from the Anglo colonies. But whites knew what they would find in Texas before contact confirmed their convictions. They encountered biologically decadent and inferior people because their thoughts had been shaped by the aforementioned influences. Thus, Mexicans lived in ways that Anglos equated with an opprobrious condition. They inhabited primitive shelters. William F. Gray, a land agent from Virginia, comparing Mexicans with the black American culture he knew, pronounced some of the Mexican homes "miserable shabby *jacales*" scarcely equal in appearance to the Afro-American houses in the suburbs of his state. Mexicans adhered to a different religion: they were completely the "slaves of Popish superstitions and despotism" and religion was understood not as an affection of the heart and soul but as one requiring personal mortification in such superficialities as penances and other rituals. If Anglos and Mexicans were not inherently different peoples, editorialized the

Texian and Emigrant's Guide in 1835, habit, education, and religion had made them essentially so.[1]

Additionally, Texians thought that Mexicans' cultural habits clashed with American values, such as the work ethic. Mexicanos appeared a traditional, backward aggregate, an irresponsibly passive people dedicated to the present and resigned not to probe the universe about them. An American arriving in Nacogdoches in 1833 found the citizens there the most "lazy indolent poor Starved set of people as ever the Sun Shined upon." He could not comprehend their lethargy by day, nor their inclination to play the violin and dance the entire night.[2] J. C. Clopper of Ohio reasoned in 1828 that Mexicanos were "too ignorant and indolent for enterprises and too poor and *dependent* were they otherwise capacitated."[3] Mexicanos habitually succumbed to indolence and ease and indulged themselves in smoking, music, dancing, horse-racing, and other sports, noted David Woodman, a promoter for a New York and Boston land company, while activity, industry, and frugality marched on in the new American settlements.[4] "The vigor of the descendants of the sturdy north will never mix with the phlegm of the indolent Mexicans," Sam Houston (the future hero of the war for independence) argued in January 1835 in an address to the citizens of Texas, "no matter how long we may live among them."[5] In contrast to the newcomers, Tejanos were chained by custom to complacency, and instead of committing themselves to progress, they preferred fun and frolic. Some three years after Mexico opened Texas to Anglo-American settlement, Anthony R. Clark complained that Spaniards in the District of Nacogdoches, "generally of the lower sort and illitterate [*sic*]," would rather "spend days in gambling to gain a few bits than to make a living by honest industry."[6] William B. Dewees, who lived in San Antonio in the late 1820s, found Bexareños totally hedonistic. "Their whole study seems to be for enjoyment. Mirth and amusement occupy their whole time. If one is fond of balls and theatres, he can here have an opportunity of attending one every evening. Almost every species of dissipation is indulged in, except drinking."[7] In Goliad, the Mexicans had such a strong predisposition for gaming that almost all the inhabitants in 1833 were gamblers and smugglers, said empresario Dr. John Charles Beales. And Alexander McCrae, touring Texas in 1835 under the auspices of the Wilmington Emigrating Society, remarked in astonishment: "I for the first time saw females betting at a public gambling table; I do not suppose they were of respectable standing in society, from the company they kept; but I am told that it is not all uncommon for Mexican *ladies* to be seen gambling in public."[8]

Acting further to stimulate negative attitudes was the racial composition of Tejanos, who, in the white mind, were closely identified with other colored peoples. For two hundred years, ideas that black men lusted for white women and notions that slaves were of a heathen or "savage" condition had played upon Americans' fantasies; the result had been the institutional debasement of blacks because of their race. Images of the Indian as fierce, hostile, and barbaric similarly affixed themselves in the thoughts of white settlers, and the constant confrontation over land reinforced these images. Consequently, when whites arrived in Texas, they unconsciously transferred onto the new "colored" folk they encountered a pseudo-scientific lore acquired from generations of interaction with blacks and Indians.

Travelers, who frequently came in contact with Tejanos, plainly discerned the Mexicans' relation to the black and red peoples. At no time did Americans hold up Frenchmen, or Germans, or themselves for that matter, as a people who physically resembled Mexicans—comparison invariably was with Indians and blacks. Several factors steered discussion in that direction: Anglos were not about to elevate Mexicans to the level of European whiteness; their own sense of superiority turned Tejanos into a people lesser than themselves; and obviously, in any comparison, Mexicans were going to resemble their progenitors. Thus, whites often likened Mexicans to Africans and Native Americans. When Clopper mentioned the complexion of the Tejanos, he thought it "a shade brighter than that of the aborigines of the country."[9] On the other hand, the land agent Gray stamped Tejanos as a "swarthy looking people much resembling our mulattos, some of them nearly black." Sam Houston asked his compatriots (in the aforementioned address) if they "would bow under the yoke of these half-Indians,"[10] while abolitionist Benjamin Lundy, in Laredo in 1834, remarked that the Mexicans in the town looked like mulattoes.

What whites were especially sensitive to in connection with interracial sex was that the offspring were not whites but colored people. Certainly, Tejanos did not look like Anglos, and the physical connection to Indian and black left no doubt as to whom Mexicans more closely resembled. Most observers, whether travelers or natives, noted the obvious, considering Tejanos as having bronze complexions, as being of a copper color, of being of tawny hue, or simply as having the color of Native Americans. The more opinionated among them described Tejanos as being "fully as dark as Indians."

Beyond this, fixed perceptions about Indians were transposed and cross-culturally referred. The same "olive" color whites observed in the Indians of the seaboard states, for example, they attributed to the Mexicans of Texas. Frederick Law Olmsted, reporting meticulously on the Mexicans of Central Texas during his trip to the state in the mid-fifties, met an elderly Mexican woman "strikingly Indian in feature, her hair, snow white, flowing thick over the shoulders, contrasting strongly with the olive skin." The complexion of the young *señoritas* he likewise thought "clear, and sometimes fair, usually a blushing olive."[11]

The contemptuous word *greaser* which whites used to identify Mexicans may well have applied to Indians as well, since the Indians' olive color was thought to be a result of their practice of anointing their skins with oils and greases. John C. Reid, passing through Texas as a prospective settler in the 1850s, sought to ascertain the origin of the application of the word upon finding that male Mexicans from Texas to the Pacific coast were called "greasers" and the females "greaser women." He failed to find a satisfactory explanation, learning only that it had something to do with the similarity between the Mexicans' color and that of grease. Another transient, commenting upon the vocabulary used in the El Paso region, supported this explanation: "A 'greaser' was a Mexican—originating in the filthy, greasy appearance of the natives."[12]

Then, there were those others who perceived a vestige of the Africans' coloring in Mexican *castas* as well. One traveler noted, for example, that the range of Mexicans' hues extended to African jet. Justice of the Peace Adolphus Sterne, celebrating in 1842 the rites of matrimony between a Tejano, apparently a *criollo* of the upper class, and a white woman, noticed others of the groom's compatriots in the assemblage who were apparently *mestizos*. "If their hair would be a little curly," he remarked, "they would be taken anywhere for Negroes."[13] Similarly, Benjamin F. McIntyre, a Union officer in Civil War Brownsville, conjectured that "Africa might lay some little claim" to the Mexicans' color. Actually, not too many others made such an association, at least not so explicitly. In the last analysis, however, the Tejanos' pigmentation served to stimulate similar attitudes, even if a physical resemblance between Tejano and Negro was remote. As Oscar M. Addison put it in a letter to his brother, the Brownsville Mexicans in the 1850s were of "a class inferior to common nigers [*sic*]."[14]

Then again, the unhygienic nature that white consciousness associated with the skin color of blacks very naturally extended to Mexicanos. To whites, dark colors connoted filth and therefore Mexicans were a dirty, putrid people, existing in squalor. Thus observers made statements about Mexicans having habits "as filthy as their persons" or living in the "most shocking state of filth."[15] When a cholera epidemic plagued San Antonio in 1849, it hit the Mexican population especially hard. "If you could see the manner in which they live," one visitor commented, "you wouldn't for a moment wonder at their having the colera."

Manifestly, spin-offs from racial attitudes developed and cultivated through repeated interaction with colored peoples on the western frontier were being bestowed upon another caste in a different setting. As Olmsted reported in his notes on Texas society of the 1850s, Mexicans were regarded as "degenerate and degraded Spaniards" or, perhaps, "improved and Christianized Indians." Generally, their tastes and social instincts were like those of Africans. "There are thousands in respectable social positions [in Mexico] whose color and physiognomy would subject them, in Texas, to be sold by the sheriff as negro-estrays who cannot be allowed at large without detriment to the commonwealth," he concluded.[16]

In view of the Southern presumption that individuals with any noticeable trace of African blood were blacks and given the contempt whites had for Indian "half-breeds," it is not surprising that "niggers," "redskins," and "greasers" intimately intermingled in the Anglo-Texan mind. Moreover, whites considered racial mixing a violation of austere moralistic codes. According to Joseph Eve, U.S. chargé d'affaires to the Republic, the Texans regarded Mexicans as a race of "mongrels" composed of Spanish, Indian, and African blood. To Francis S. Latham, traveling in Texas in 1842, Mexicanos were nothing else than "the mongrel and illicit descendants of an Indian, Mexican and Spanish, pencilled with a growing feintline of the Anglo Saxon ancestry."[17] Such feelings about "mongrels" stemmed from the extensive lore American culture had developed concerning the undesirability and supposed peril of miscegenation, especially between whites and blacks. Certainly, the mixed-blood nature of Tejanos concerned Anglo Americans because of their cultural aversion to interracial passion, a subject upon which whites expressed themselves adeptly, albeit with no scientific basis. According to white beliefs, Mexicans resembled the degenerates from whom they descended. Although they inherited both the faults and the good qualities of their ancestors, unfortunately, the darker traits predominated, so that Mexicans by nature were superstitious, cowardly, treacherous, idle, avaricious, and inveterate gamblers. Miscegenation was a very serious matter which held great implications for civilization. William H. Emory, surveying the boundary between the United States and Mexico, related this idea in an incidental remark included as part of his report, finished during the Franklin Pierce administration. Attributing the decline and fall of Spanish domination in Texas and the borderlands to a "baneful" cohabitation between whites and Indians, he continued:

> Where practical amalgamation of races of different color is carried [out] to any extent, it is from the absence of the women of the cleaner race. The white makes his alliance with his darker partner for no other purpose than to satisfy a law of nature, or to acquire property, and when that is accomplished all affection ceases. Faithless to his vows, he passes from object to object with no other impulse than the gratification arising from novelty, ending at last in emasculation and disease, leaving no progeny at all; or if any, a very inferior and syphilitic race. Such are the favors extended to the white man by the lower and darker colored races that this must always be the course of events, and the process of absorption can never work any beneficial change. One of the inevitable results of intermarriage between races of different color is infidelity. The offspring have a constant tendency to go back to one or the other of the original stock; that in a large family of children, where the parents are of a mixed race but yet of the same color, the children will be of every color, from dusky cinnamon to chalky white. This phenomenon, so easily explained without involving the fidelity of either party, nevertheless produces suspicion followed by unhappiness, and ending in open adultery.[18]

This sort of pseudoscience dictated the status of mixed-blood Tejanos in a white state.

NOTES

1. *Texian and Emigrant's Guide* (Nacogdoches), December 26, 1835, p. 4.
2. James Ernest Crisp, "Anglo-Texan Attitudes toward the Mexican, 1821–1845," Ph.D. dissertation, Yale University, 1976, p. 22.
3. J. C. Clopper, *Journal of J. C. Clopper*, 1828, SOUTHWESTERN HISTORICAL QUARTERLY 13 (July 1909): 44–80, p. 76.
4. David Woodman, GUIDE TO TEXAS EMIGRANTS, Boston: M. Hawes, 1835, p. 35.
5. Houston to Soldiers, January 15, 1836, in THE PAPERS OF THE TEXAS REVOLUTION, 1835–1836, gen. ed. John H. Jenkins, 4:30.
6. Ernest W. Winkler, ed., MANUSCRIPT LETTERS AND DOCUMENTS OF EARLY TEXIANS, 1821–1845, Austin: Steck Co., 1937, p. 32.
7. William B. Dewees, LETTERS FROM AN EARLY SETTLER OF TEXAS, Waco: Texian Press, 1968, p. 56.
8. Joshua James and Alexander McCrae, A JOURNAL OF A TOUR IN TEXAS: WITH OBSERVATIONS, ETC., BY THE AGENTS OF THE WILMINGTON EMIGRATING SOCIETY, Wilmington, N.C.: Printed by T. Loring, 1835, p. 15. See also Dewees, LETTERS FROM AN EARLY SETTLER, p. 57, for remarks on the Mexican passion for gambling.
9. Clopper, *Journal*, pp. 71–72.
10. Houston to Soldiers, January 15, 1836, in PAPERS OF THE TEXAS REVOLUTION 4:30.
11. Frederick Law Olmsted, A JOURNEY THROUGH TEXAS: OR, A SADDLE-TRIP ON THE

SOUTHWESTERN FRONTIER, WITH A STATISTICAL APPENDIX, New York: Dix, Edwards & Co., 1857; reprint, Austin: University of Texas Press, 1978, p. 161.

12. John C. Reid, REID'S TRAMP: OR, A JOURNAL OF THE INCIDENTS OF TEN MONTHS' TRAVEL . . . , Selma, Ala.: J. Hardy Co., 1858; reprint, Austin: Steck Co., 1935, p. 38; Albert D. Richardson, BEYOND THE MISSISSIPPI: FROM THE GREAT RIVER TO THE GREAT OCEAN . . . 1857–1867, Hartford: American Publishing Co., 1867, p. 239; Lloyd Lewis, CAPTAIN SAM GRANT, Boston: Little, Brown and Co., 1950, p. 142; Cecil Robinson, MEXICO AND THE HISPANIC SOUTHWEST IN AMERICAN LITERATURE (revised from WITH THE EARS OF STRANGERS: THE MEXICAN IN AMERICAN LITERATURE), Tucson: University of Arizona Press, 1977, pp. 38–39; Américo Paredes, On "Gringo," "Greaser," and Other Neighborly Names, in SINGERS AND STORYTELLERS, edited by Mody C. Boatright et al., Dallas: Southern Methodist University Press, 1961, pp. 285–90. Whatever the origins, the word was used commonly in reference to Mexicans.

13. Adolphus Sterne, HURRAH FOR TEXAS! THE DIARY OF ADOLPHUS STERNE, edited by Archie P. McDonald, Waco: Texian Press, 1969, p. 94.

14. Oscar M. Addison to His Brother, February 14, 1854, Brownsville, Texas, Addison Papers, Barker Texas History Center, University of Texas Archives, Austin.

15. John James Audubon, THE LIFE OF JOHN JAMES AUDUBON, THE NATURALIST, edited by Lucy Audubon, New York: G. P. Putnam's Sons, 1902, p. 410; Emanuel H. D. Domenech, MISSIONARY ADVENTURES IN TEXAS AND MEXICO: A PERSONAL NARRATIVE OF SIX YEARS' SOJOURN IN THOSE REGIONS, London: Longman, Brown, Green, Longmans, and Roberts, 1858, p. 83. For a discussion of the psychological connection between color and dirt, see Joel Kovel, WHITE RACISM: A PSYCHOHISTORY, New York: Vintage Books, 1970, pp. 81–92.

16. Olmsted, JOURNEY THROUGH TEXAS, p. 454.

17. Francis S. Latham, TRAVELS IN TEXAS, 1842, edited by Gerald S. Pierce, Austin: Encino Press, 1971, p. 37.

18. House Exec. Doc. No. 135, 34th Cong., 1st Sess. (Ser. 861), 1:68–70.

Chapter 24

‖‖

"The Mexican Problem"

Carey McWilliams

In the vast library of books and documents about ethnic and minority problems in the United States, one of the largest sections is devoted to "the Mexican Problem." There is a curious consistency about the documents in this section. For one thing, the singular is always used. Presumably, also, no problem existed, singular or plural, prior to 1920. *Readers' Guide* lists fifty-one articles on "the Mexican Problem" from 1920 to 1930 by comparison with nineteen articles on the same subject for the previous decade. When these articles are examined, it will be found that "the problem" apparently consists in the sum total of the voluminous statistics on Mexican delinquency, poor housing, low wages, illiteracy, and rates of disease. In other words, "the Mexican Problem" has been defined in terms of the social consequences of Mexican immigration.

It will also be found that the documents devoted to the problem have been deeply colored by the "social work" approach. With the passage of the 1924 Immigration Act, the immigrant social agencies and Americanization institutes simply had to discover a new "problem" and it was the Mexican's misfortune to appear on the scene, sombrero and all, concurrently with the impending liquidation of these agencies. As a consequence, he was promptly adopted as America's No. 1 immigrant problem. The whole apparatus of immigrant-aid social work, with its morose preoccupation with consequences rather than causes, was thereupon transferred to Mexican immigration with little realization that this immigration might not be, in all respects, identical with European immigration.

Once assembled and classified, this depressing mass of social data was consistently interpreted in terms of what it revealed about the inadequacies and the weaknesses of the Mexican character. The data "proved" that Mexicans lacked leadership, discipline, and organization; that they segregated themselves; that they were lacking in thrift and enterprise, and so forth. A mountainous collection of masters' theses "proved" conclusively that Spanish-speaking children were "retarded" because, on the basis of various so-called intelligence tests, they did not measure up to the intellectual calibre of Anglo-American students. Most of this theorizing was heavily weighted with gratuitous assumptions about Mexicans and Indians. Paradoxically, the more sympathetic the writer, the greater seems to have been the implied condescension. All in all, the conclusion is unavoidable that Mexicans have been regarded as the essence of "the Mexican Problem."

The use of this deceptive, catchall phrase has consistently beclouded the real issues by focusing attention on consequences rather than on causes. Actually the basic issues have always had to do with Anglo-Hispano relations in a particular historical setting as influenced by a specific set of cultural, economic, geographical, and social forces. Once these factors are seen in proper perspective, if only in outline form, the elusive character of "the Mexican Problem" vanishes into thin air.

|||||||||||||||||||||||||||||||||||||||||||||||||||||||||||||||||||||||||||||||||||

Chapter 25

The Mexican Question in the Southwest

Emma Tenayuca and Homer Brooks

A native of San Antonio, Texas, Emma Tenayuca is best known as a political activist who led the 1938 pecan shellers strike. This essay makes explicit the beliefs that under-lined many of her political practices. "The Mexican Question in the Southwest," which she coauthored with her husband Homer Brooks, was originally published in The Com-munist *in 1939. Tenayuca's essay marks one of the first political treatises written by a Mexican American in English to argue for the rights and status of Mexicans in the United States. Writing at the height of the pecan strike, Tenayuca expands upon Marx-ist theories of nationalism, emancipation, and citizenship. It is important to remember that the "Mexican Question" was originally a national "Anglo" inquiry into the rights, lands, and status of Mexicans that became critical with the signing of the Treaty of Guadalupe Hidalgo in 1848, the point from which Tenayuca begins her essay. Tenayuca argues that the Mexicans of the Southwest do not constitute a separate nation; they are inextricably connected not only to each other by race and land, but also to Anglo-Americans and U.S. institutions.*

The war with Mexico, in 1846, following the annexation of Texas, resulted in the conquest of the territory which now makes up the states of California, New Mexico, Arizona, Colorado and part of Utah and Nevada. The forcible incorporation of these areas into the United States was progressive, in that it opened up for development territories which until then had stagnated under the inefficient, tyrannical, and semi-feudal control of Mexico. The predominant influence of the Spanish in the Southwest, particularly in California, New Mexico, Arizona, Colorado and Texas, can be seen in the names of such cities as Los Angeles, Santa Fe, San Antonio, San Diego and San Francisco.

The acquisition of these lands brought into the Union a population originally Spanish and later Mexican, whose customs, language, traditions and culture were es-sentially different from those of the rest of the country. In the border area of the Southwest the Mexicans have always constituted a majority, both before and after the war with Mexico.

The expansion and industrialization that followed the Civil War, lasting until a relatively late period in the Southwest, saw the importation of thousands of Mexican workers into Texas, California, Colorado and Arizona. (To a lesser degree this was true of New Mexico, for geographical reasons. Deserts and mountains bordering Mexico prevented free interrelation with old Mexico; at the same time this border region has not made for the development of large-scale capitalist farming.) Railroad companies alone were responsible for a great number of those imported. Most of the railroads of these five states were built by Mexican labor.

With the development of capitalist farming, particularly in California and Texas, Mexico was again a source of cheap labor. Between 1925 and 1929 the heaviest immigration from Mexico took place. The 1930 census showed 1,500,000 Mexicans residing in the United States. Of these, all but 150,000 were found to be living in the states of California, Texas, New Mexico, Colorado and Arizona. However, these figures include only the foreign-born and first-generation Mexicans. They exclude the large Spanish-speaking population of New Mexico. These figures also exclude Mexicans of the third, fourth, and fifth generations and those descendants of the early Spanish colonists of any of the other four states. Therefore, we can readily state that the Mexican population of the Southwest numbers approximately 2,000,000.

Thus, we can see that the present Mexican population in the Southwest is made up of two groups: descendants of those living in the territory at the time of annexation, and immigrant Mexicans and first- or second-generation native-born drawn from the impoverished peasantry of Northern Mexico to work as super-exploited wage workers in railroad and building construction and in highly developed (capitalist) agriculture in the border area.

However, no sharp distinction marks these two groups, either in their social conditions or in their treatment at the hands of the Anglo-American bourgeoisie. Assimilation among those groups which were here before the conquest of these territories by the United States has been slow, and the Spanish language remains today that of both groups.

The treatment meted out to the Mexicans as a whole has from the earliest days of the sovereignty of the United States been that of a conquered people. From the very beginning they were robbed of their land, a process that has continued even up to the present time. In 1916, immediately following the abortive De la Rosa movement in the Texas lower Rio Grande Valley for an autonomous Mexican regime, Texas Rangers, in cooperation with land speculators, came into small Mexican villages in the border country, massacred hundreds of unarmed, peaceful Mexican villagers and seized their lands. Sometimes the seizures were accompanied by the formality of signing bills of sale—at the point of a gun. So that, where, until 1916, virtually all of the land was the property of Mexicans, today almost none of it is. Many farmers who were well-to-do landowners today barely eke out a living employed as irregular wage workers at 60¢ to 75¢ a day on the very lands they once owned. This land-grabbing has continued under one guise or another throughout the Southwest. In New Mexico fewer than one half of the Mexican or Spanish-American farmers retain any of their ancestral lands.

The Present Social Status of the Mexican People

With the penetration of Anglo-Americans into these states, the Mexicans have been practically segregated into colonies. This is particularly true of Colorado. Disease, low wages, discrimination and lack of educational facilities are typical of these communities.

Mexican labor imported into the United States has uniformly received lower wages than those paid Anglo-American workers. The vast majority of the former are today found doing only the most menial work, the bulk of them having been excluded from skilled crafts. In the cities, although Mexicans are found in the garment industry and laundries and as laborers in building construction, the overwhelming majority are seasonal agricultural workers. This is true of the Mexicans in all states except the Spanish-Americans of New Mexico, where instead of being agricultural workers, the majority are small farmers, tenants or sharecroppers.

In Texas, in the area of Corpus Christi, few if any Mexicans are found working in the extensive oil field discovered there several years ago. Corpus Christi, we may add, is one of the cities that lies within the belt where the Mexicans form the majority of the population. An example of the kind of industry that Mexicans are not excluded from is the pecan industry in San Antonio, which until recently employed 12,000 Mexican workers, with wages averaging two to three dollars a week.

Near-starvation faces thousands of Mexican agricultural workers who must live part of the year in the cities and try to get work on W.P.A. A special clause in the relief appropriation act of 1937, which excludes foreign-born workers who have not taken out citizenship papers, resulted in dismissals of thousands from W.P.A. In El Paso, for example, 600 out of 1800 on W.P.A. were so dismissed.

The reaction of most of the Mexican W.P.A. workers to these dismissals could not lead to acquiring citizenship papers due to language, cost, and other burdensome obstacles. Their resentment was expressed by demanding the opportunity to work on all jobs, regardless of citizenship, a demand which by virtue of their historical rights in this territory is unchallengeable.

Discrimination against the Mexican people also haunts relief appropriations. The Relief Commission of Los Angeles presents a special budget for Mexicans, claiming that diet and living expenses are lower among the Mexicans than among other sections of the population. Since the Mexicans live in houses without electricity or natural gas, they are subject to smaller relief portions in every state in the Southwest.

The conditions of the Mexican agricultural workers can be compared only to those of the Negro sharecroppers in the South. According to the United Cannery, Agricultural, Packing and Allied Workers of America, the average wage of the Mexican beet worker in Colorado is from $100 to $200 per year. The average wage of the Texas cotton picker is considerably less; in 1938 it ranged from 35¢ to 75¢ per 100 lbs. In those places where the U.C.A.P.A.W.A. carried on struggles, the prices were raised.

In New Mexico, where the Mexicans or Spanish-Americans have been engaged in small farming, fully one half of the farmers have lost their land. Another factor which threatens the existence of the farmers of New Mexico and the agricultural workers of the Southwest has been the large migration of Anglo-American farmers from the dust bowl.

The crisis has intensified the competition for jobs; a fact that is resulting more and more in displacing Mexican workers in the cities. For example, the Sun-Tex canneries in Texas, located in a city with an overwhelming majority of Mexicans, hires only Anglo-American workers.

The Mexicans are not only subject to wage differentials and discrimination, but a view of their political status in the five states referred to reveals conditions in many ways comparable to the political status of the Negro people in the South. Denial of voting rights to the foreign born means disfranchisement of nearly half the adult Mexican population. Secondly, the semi-migratory character of the work of most of the Mexican workers disfranchises in addition many of those who are citizens. Finally, in Texas the poll tax disfranchises many of those who would otherwise be able to vote. Thus, due to one or another of the three causes, in San Antonio, a city of 250,000, nearly half of whom are Mexicans, only 8,000 Mexicans were eligible to vote in 1938.

This disfranchisement has resulted in nearly complete Anglo-American domination politically in most of the communities where the Mexican people are a majority. Lack of representation in local or state politics and low economic standards have resulted in poor health conditions and lack of educational facilities. An example of this is Texas, where the death rate among Mexicans is decidedly higher than among Anglo-Americans, and even higher than that of Negroes.

San Antonio has the highest infant mortality rate of any large city in the United States. It likewise has a higher rate of deaths from tuberculosis than any other city in the country.

The unequal treatment that the Mexican people suffer is manifested in all phases of life. The practice of excluding Mexicans from hotels and restaurants is prevalent in all these five states. A few years ago an international incident took place in Victoria, Texas, when an official delegation of students from Mexico was excluded from a restaurant. Signs bar Mexicans from dance halls in Los Angeles. In Colorado small town restaurants display signs: "White Trade Only."

Segregation of Mexican children in small town public schools in Texas is a common practice. Several years ago a group of Mexican taxpayers in San Antonio, by threatening to withhold the payment of school taxes, successfully fought this issue. A few months ago Dr. Juan Del Rio, a resident of San Marcos, had to bring suit against the school board of that city to win the right of his children to attend the school established for Anglo-American children.

The suppression of the Spanish language, of the native culture of the Mexicans, is one of the reasons for the high rate of illiteracy. The most important reason is, of course, the semi-migratory life of the agricultural worker, which forces the children out of school at an early age, and makes school attendance irregular for many.

To summarize, the Mexican people of the Southwest have a common historical background and are bound by a common culture, language and communal life. It should be noted, however, that the Mexican communities exist side by side with

Anglo-American communities within a territory where the populated districts are separated by large but thinly populated mountainous and arid regions.

Should the conclusion, therefore, be drawn that the Mexican people in the Southwest constitute a nation—or that they form a segment of the Mexican nation (South of the Rio Grande)? Our view is no. Historically the Mexican people in the Southwest have evolved in a series of bordering, though separated, communities, their economic life inextricably connecting them, not only with one another, but with the Anglo-American population in each of these separated Mexican communities. Therefore, their economic (and hence, their political) interests are welded to those of the Anglo-American people of the Southwest.

We must accordingly regard the Mexican people in the Southwest as part of the American nation, who, however, have not been so accepted heretofore by the American bourgeoisie; the latter has continued to hinder the process of national unification of the American people by treating the Mexican and Spanish-Americans as a conquered people.

Comrade Stalin's classic definition of a nation states: *A nation is a historically evolved, stable community of language, territory, economic life and psychological make-up manifested in a community of culture* [*Marxism and the National and Colonial Question*]. We see, therefore, that the Mexicans in the United States lack two of the important characteristics of a nation, namely, territorial and economic continuity.

||||||||||||||||||||||||||||||||||||||||||||||||||||||||||||||||||||||||||||||||||||||

Chapter 26

The Master Narrative of
White Supremacy in California

Tomás Almaguer

What were the specific symbolic and material factors that contributed to the economic mobility of certain groups and the disadvantaged status of others? What were the gendered dimensions of these class-specific, racialized histories? How, for instance, were relations between men and women of different cultural groups structurally mediated by the racialization process and the imposition of a new class system? What specific role did sexuality play in the structuring and imposition of racialized class relations among Californians during this period?

The answer to these questions can be found in the way that race and the racialization process in California became the central organizing principle of group life during the state's formative period of development. Although California's ethnic populations were racialized in different ways, and the specific manifestations of racial and ethnic conflict were unique to California, at its most basic level it represented the extension of "white supremacy" into the new American Southwest. Historian George Fredrickson defines white supremacy as "the attitudes, ideologies, and politics associated with blatant forms of white or European dominance over 'nonwhite' populations."[1] The attempt to make race or color a basis for group position within the United States was defined initially during the colonial period when notions of "civility" and "savagery," as well as clear distinctions between "Christians" and "heathens," were used to inscribe racial difference and divide humankind into distinct categories of people. These notions provided the basis upon which European immigrants differentiated themselves from the diverse populations they encountered during their expansion into the Far West.

The cultural division of the world into different categories of humanity led white European Americans in California to arrogantly privilege themselves as superior to non-European people of color. Although European Americans were situated unambiguously at the top of this social hierarchy, the racialized populations did not share a common structural position. Racialized relations in the state reverberated along a number of racial fault lines; they did not assume a simple binary form or erupt along one principal fault. The allocation of "group position" along these social strata was the outcome of both cultural and material considerations.

California Indians, for example, were singled out as the complete antithesis of white Californians and were summarily relegated to the very bottom of the racial hierarchy. White immigrants believed that the indigenous population was the lowest level of humankind imaginable. The California Indians wore little clothing, were perceived as horrendously ugly and dirty, ate foods "Americans" deemed unpalatable, and practiced tribal rituals and ceremonies that were anathema to European Christian practices. In short, they were cast as the extreme incarnation of all that was both uncivilized and heathen.

Other cultural groups were judged less harshly and placed between the extreme ends of the racial hierarchy. Mexicans, for instance, were perceived as much closer culturally to European-American immigrants than to their Indian counterparts. The Mexicans' mixed European ancestry, romance language, Catholic religious practices, and familiar political-economic institutions elevated them above all other cultural groups in the white man's eyes. Moreover, the continued political influence of the powerful *Californio* elite during the latter nineteenth century further attenuated more virulent expressions of anti-Mexican sentiment and allowed Mexicans to challenge Anglo-domination for a time.

Black and Asian immigrants, finally, were culturally deemed to be somewhere between the "half civilized" Mexican and "uncivilized" Indian populations. Although antiblack animosity was widespread, blacks who settled in California were at least Christian, spoke English, and had—after years of enslavement—assimilated important European cultural patterns. Most white immigrants grudgingly acknowledged this, a fact that contributed directly to blacks not becoming the major target of racist initiatives in California that they were elsewhere in the country.

Americans perceived Asian immigrants, on the other hand, to have fewer redeeming qualities and group attributes. While they too were unambiguously deemed nonwhite, these immigrants carried the extra burden of being a "peculiar" people who spoke a completely unintelligible Eastern language, had "abhorrent" culinary tastes, dressed "strangely," and practiced a form of "pagan idolatry" clearly at odds with Judeo-Christian religious traditions. In cultural terms, Chinese and Japanese immigrants, therefore, were perceived initially as more like the uncivilized and heathen Indian population than any of the other cultural minorities in the state.

In sum, European-American immigrants in nineteenth-century California inherited and routinely relied on eurocentric cultural criteria to hierarchically evaluate and racialize the various cultural groups they contended with in California. This process clearly privileged and elevated the status of white immigrants in the social structure and placed below them, in descending order, the Mexican, black, Asian, and Indian populations.

The tremendous immigration of European and non-European immigrants into the state after annexation resulted in a hierarchy of group inequality in which race, not class, became the central stratifying variable. The primary racial division of Californians into white and nonwhite categories cut at right angles across the newly emergent class lines that divided capitalists, petit bourgeois commodity producers, and an increasingly segmented working class composed of free wage laborers and individuals held in precapitalist relations of production.

The imposition of a new racial order and attendant class structure in nineteenth-century California gained impetus from popular ideologies that gave voice to the superordinate political and economic position of European Americans in the state. Two powerful ideas reflecting this white supremacist sentiment were fervently embraced by European-American men during the United States' westward expansion: "Manifest Destiny" and the "free labor ideology."

The United States' usurpation of Mexican territory laid the basis for rapidly transforming what would become the American Southwest along new sociocultural, political, and economic lines. This mission became the "white man's burden"—to extend their dominion over all obstacles placed in their path and to bring civilization and Christianity to the uncivilized heathens they encountered. During this period white Americans widely accepted the idea of populating all of the North American continent with a homogeneous white population. They believed it was their providential destiny to expand to the Pacific coast, bringing with them their superior political institutions, notions of progress and democracy, and their own economic system of production. Public support for extending national boundaries found fertile ground in this tumultuous period of expansion and reached its most explicit political expression in the notion of Manifest Destiny.

During the mid-nineteenth century, white supremacist practices also became intertwined inextricably with economic doctrines concerning the role of "free labor." As historian Eric Foner has shown, a free-labor ideology was widely embraced by European Americans at all class levels. White men in particular enthusiastically supported the vision of the social world this ideology promoted: an expanding capitalist society based on free wage labor. Those fervently advocating free-labor doctrines accepted the right to private property and economic individualism and fervently believed that free labor created all value. Moreover, they maintained that everyone could aspire to and achieve economic independence in a free society and that "today's laborer would be tomorrow's capitalist."[2]

The free-labor ideology associated with the Republican Party during the mid-nineteenth century helped crystallize the beliefs of European-American men about their entitlement to privileged economic mobility in the new territories. It also specifically colored the way Anglo Californians initially assessed the various minority groups they competed with for position in the state's new class structure. Free-labor adherents believed that social mobility and economic independence were only achievable in a capitalist society unthreatened by nonwhite populations and the degrading labor systems associated with them. European Americans repeatedly associated nonwhite people with various unfree labor systems that ostensibly threatened their superordinate social standing and class prerogatives in California.

Like Manifest Destiny, the underlying tenets of the free-labor ideology squarely affirmed the superior position of European-American men and helped delineate the subordinate status that people of color would occupy in the Far West.[3] As a consequence, racial lines in California quickly became linked with class divisions in unexpected and complicated ways. Outward struggles over access and group position within the class system were given concrete form and substance by the underlying racialized struggle among its chief protagonists.

The powerful impact of white supremacist notions like Manifest Destiny and the free-labor ideology had important material consequences for these contesting groups. The competition for access to valued social resources did not result, however, in purely symmetrical hierarchies based on class and race. Far from simply paralleling each other, California's new class hierarchy and racial order were mutually constitutive and intersected in complex and shifting ways that were historically contingent.

How groups were accorded access to the ownership of productive property and proletarianized within the working class was not a random selection process impervious to popular perceptions of racial differences. Who gained access to land, owned businesses, became skilled workers, and, more generally, was subjectively placed in either a "free" wage-labor market or an "unfree" labor system was fundamentally determined on the basis of race. Access to every level of the capitalist system of production introduced in nineteenth-century California was largely determined by this status. Although this capitalist economy became a highly competitive system by the late nineteenth century, it remained an institution that limited social mobility to white, European-American men.

White Californians repeatedly claimed primary access to privileged positions within the system of production and effectively thwarted attempts by the nonwhite population to compete with them on an equal footing. Nineteenth-century legislation enacted in the interest and at the behest of European Americans cemented the placement of California's nonwhite minorities in various unfree labor situations (such as slavery, indentured servitude, contracted labor, etc.) or guaranteed their exclusion altogether from certain skilled occupations and self-employment opportunities. European Americans jealously sought to protect their privileged group position in California through the use of discriminatory social closures that impeded equal access to social mobility. Racial status clearly shaped each group's life chances and served as the primary basis for determining whether one was granted access to different strata within the new class structure.

The judicial decisions that formally conferred racial status in nineteenth-century California, therefore, had important consequences for the historical trajectories of each of these groups in California. As each of these "nonwhite" groups entered into competition with European Americans at different class levels after 1850, a series of protracted conflicts erupted along a number of racial fault lines. This took the form of white opposition to black, Chinese, and Sonoran miners in the 1850s; to Chinese workers in urban industries in the 1870s and 1880s; and to Japanese small farmers at the turn of the century. Racial enmity and bitter economic struggle with white competitors punctuated minority history in California during the nineteenth century. White antipathy crystallized most intensely in the case of Native Americans, Mexicans, Chinese, and, to a lesser extent, African-American and Japanese immigrants.

There emerged during this period a strong symbolic association between different minority groups, on the one hand, and various precapitalist economic formations on the other. White antipathy toward Mexicans, Native Americans, and Chinese and Japanese immigrants was typically couched within the rubric of this "free white labor"/"unfree nonwhite labor" dichotomy: Mexicans became inimically associated with the "unproductive," semi-feudal rancho economy that European Americans rapidly undermined after statehood; Indians with a "primitive" communal mode of existence that white settlers ruthlessly eradicated through violence and forced segregation; and Asian immigrants with a "degraded" unfree labor system unfairly competing with and fettering white labor. The class-specific nature of contention between these racialized groups and the European-American populations were all cast in terms of these symbolic associations.

White economic mobility and dominance in California required both the subordination of minority populations and the eradication of the precapitalist systems of production associated with them. Anglo entitlement to California's bounty could only be actualized when the symbolic and material threat these minority populations posed was effectively neutralized or overcome.

NOTES

1. George M. Fredrickson, WHITE SUPREMACY: A COMPARATIVE STUDY IN AMERICAN AND SOUTH AFRICAN HISTORY (New York: Oxford University Press, 1981), p. xi.

2. Eric Foner, FREE SOIL, FREE LABOR, FREE MEN: THE IDEOLOGY OF THE REPUBLICAN PARTY BEFORE THE CIVIL WAR (New York: Oxford University Press, 1970), p. 20.

3. This summary discussion of the "free-labor ideology" is primarily drawn from Foner's FREE SOIL, FREE LABOR, FREE MEN.

Chapter 27

‖‖

Are Anti-immigrant Statements Racist or Nativist? What Difference Does It Make?

René Galindo and Jami Vigil

The topic of immigration continues to receive considerable attention as the press reports on demographic shifts, proposed immigration laws and policies, and accounts of popular reaction to immigrants including anti-immigrant statements. A key question has been whether or not the statements were racist. However, these media accounts have generally side-stepped the question of whether or not the statements were nativist. Given that immigrants are the targets of anti-immigrant statements, failure to mention nativism is notable. The focus on racism and the absence of nativism in press media accounts reflects a historical amnesia of the recurring patterns of nativism across previous eras of anti-immigrant sentiment in the history of the U.S.

Racism and nativism, although always a part of the American social and political landscape, were each especially prevalent in the public discourse during two distinct and separate historical periods. Racism in the current era was made a pressing issue in racial/ethnic societal relations by the Civil Rights Movement of the 1960s. Nativism, like racism, also has a long-standing history in America, being the prominent societal response to mass immigration during periods such as the Americanization era of the first two decades of the 20th century. The dramatic immigration growth of the last two decades of the 20th century and accompanying anti-immigrant sentiment have provided an occasion for the reemergence of nativism as a major force.

Anti-immigrant statements during a period of renewed nativism provide an opportunity to examine the dynamics of nativism directed against Latinos. Unlike the European immigrants who were the targets of nativism at the turn of the twentieth century, the nativism of the current era targets a group of immigrants who are predominantly people of color from Latin America and other non-European countries. The ethnic/racial backgrounds of these immigrants, which differ from those of the European immigrants, highlight the complexity of the nativism directed against them, which includes elements of both racism and defensive nationalism. In spite of the different histories of Latino immigrants and African Americans, the media view anti-immigrant statements and other forms of nativism directed at Latinos through the black and white dichotomy developed from the African-American historical experience. Such a view ignores the history of discrimination that is unique to Latinos. For example, Mexican-origin Latinos in the Southwest exhibit a unique history of the intersection of racism and nativism due to both their historic presence in the U.S. and their recent immigration. As long-term residents, they have faced discriminatory policies such as segregation, and as recent immigrants they have been targeted by restrictionistic policies such as Arizona's Proposition 200. This history calls for a different lens than the one offered by the black and white dichotomy.

At a minimum, three important reasons urge drawing distinctions between racism and nativism. First, discrimination that is based on nativism often does not appear as such when only viewed through the lens of black and white racism. The non-recognition of discrimination based on nativism obscures current and historical patterns of discrimination directed against Latinos. Secondly, discriminatory practices, such as restrictionistic policies, will continue as long as the defensive nationalism that drives nativism remains unexamined. Finally, the exclusionary definition of national identity defended by nativism will continue to define cultural and linguistic diversity as alien to the nation. Drawing attention to nativism as a term, ideology, and political practice will make visible previous and current patterns of prejudice and discrimination directed against immigrants that proceeded under the cover of defensive nationalism.

Racism and nativism overlap and interact in complex ways which can be understood only by analyzing specific cases. Consider press media coverage of an anti-immigrant incident, with a special focus on editorials—the unsigned opinion pieces that represent a newspaper's official position. Editorials are particularly telling in that they express the analysis, interpretations, opinions, and recommendations of a newspaper's editorial board. As such, editorials are authoritative expressions of how given events should be understood and reacted to.

Nativism

Nativism is generally defined as the favoring of native-born citizens over immigrants with modern nationalism serving as the energizing force. According to John Higham, nationalism, expressed in the continual process of nation-building, which marks distinctions between those who are inside from those who are outside of the nation, is the driving force behind nativism.

Nativism consists of more than personal grudges or individual anxieties. It is a body of interconnected ideas about American government and society, about the past and future of the U.S., and about who counts as an American. More than just xenophobic attitudes of a few isolated individuals, nativism has been one of the most sustained social movements in the U.S., spanning over the last 150 years. Increased nativism was particularly evident following the national tragedy of 9/11. Among the numerous consequences of 9/11, and the following "war on terror," was the view of immigrants as threats to national security.

Immigration policy is viewed primarily as a means for fighting terrorism since 9/11, and immigration policy has lost its own independent policy agenda apart from anti-terrorist measures. The national view of immigrants as threats to national security, and the accompanying policy shift from immigration to terrorism, has strengthened the stance of anti-immigrant border vigilantes who can now mask their nativism with patriotism by claiming the more acceptable concern over national security and border enforcement.

Nativism and Latinos

Nativism directed against Latinos continues to reproduce their social positions as "foreigners" who do not belong to the nation. Even elite Latinos, such as Congressman Luis Gutierrez, are not immune from the nativist refrain, "go back where you came from." In addition to expressions of individual nativist sentiment, federal policy resulted from nativist attitudes during the repatriations of the Great Depression and during "Operation Wetback" of the 1950s when thousands of Mexicans, including some who were citizens, were sent back to Mexico. In addition to anti-immigrant initiatives, a primary expression of nativism directed against Latinos is language discrimination. Examples of language discrimination include work-place restrictions against the use of other languages; anti-bilingual education initiatives passed in California, Arizona, and Massachusetts; and Official English initiatives, such that government agencies cannot provide language assistance to non-English speakers, for instance during driver's license examinations.

The Brock Incident

Chad Brock, a country western singer and former professional wrestler, drew media attention and the ire of the Latino community over comments he made during his concert at the Colorado Independence Stampede, in Greeley, Colorado (about 60 miles north of Denver with 77,000 residents), on July 4, 2002. Brock complained to the crowd of about 7,000 during a break between songs, "Why should we adapt? You are coming over to our country. We don't speak Russian. We don't speak Spanish. We speak English here." The *Greeley Tribune* noted that Brock said, "get the hell out" (*Greeley Tribune*, July 10, 2002). Many Latinos walked out of the concert while other members of the audience cheered Brock's comments. For Latinos in Greeley, his statement reopened old wounds of Mexican segregation and Ku Klux Klan activity in Greeley.

THE CALL FOR AN APOLOGY

Latino activists denounced Brock's comments and were upset that Greeley officials had not condemned his statements. The Independence Stampede rodeo had already gained ill-will with the Latino community due to its decision of a few years to cancel "Fiesta Latina," a portion of the rodeo dedicated to Mexican music and performances.

Latino activists met with representatives from Greeley's Human Relations Commission to air their complaints against Brock. They also held a news conference at which Latino leaders demanded an apology from city officials, the event sponsors, and the Stampede organizers. Jorge Amaya, director of the Northern Colorado Latino Chamber of Commerce, stated, "For some reason the Stampede seems to bring out the worst in the community. It seems like this is the time of year when the closet racists come out" (News Staff, July 9, 2002). He also said that the real problem was a lack of willingness on the part of community leaders to condemn Brock's statement.

Another Latino, a local college professor, said that Brock's comments were "bigoted, inflammatory, and hateful" (*Denver Post*, July 9, 2002). The Mayor of Greeley, Jerry Wones, declined to condemn Brock's comments, stating that although they were ill-advised, Brock had the right to make them.

THE CLARIFICATION

Shortly after the incident, Brock stated that his comments were meant to express his pride in being American and were spurred by a recent court decision regarding the phrase "under God" found in the Pledge of Allegiance. Brock directly addressed the charge of racism, stating, "I am not a racist. I wasn't directing the comments toward any particular group. I was speaking my mind as an American during the 4th of July holiday. But I had no idea that there were so many Hispanics in Greeley. I didn't mean to offend anybody" (*Denver Post*, July 9, 2002). He also added, "I had the guts to speak out, but I think a lot of people feel the same way."

SUPPORT FOR THE STATEMENT

Support for Brock's comments mushroomed on The *Greeley Tribune* website, which received more than 1,622 replies in response to the question, "Do you think that Chad Brock's comments about immigrants were appropriate during Friday night's concert at the Greeley Independence Stampede?" Approximately 75% of the votes supported his comments.

EDITORIALS

Editorials typically address policy-relevant issues and make policy recommendations based on their analysis. On occasion they comment on specific incidents as in the case of the Brock statement. The editorials presented their interpretation of the controversial statements, including whether they consider the statements to be racist, and made recommendations on how to respond to such statements.

BROCK EDITORIALS

The *Greeley Tribune*'s (*GT*) editorial, "Singer's Words Reveal Discord" (July 10, 2002), defined the situation as a controversy that resulted from immigrant-bashing. The *Denver Post*'s (*DP*) editorial, "Y'all Don't Come Back" (July 10, 2002), defined the situation as one in which an offense had been committed and to which Latino activists requested an apology, while The *Rocky Mountain News* (*RMN*) editorial (July 16, 2002), "Is Speaking English a Sign of Patriotism," called it a case of a confused connection between speaking the English language and patriotism.

The *GT* editorial in its opening paragraph wrote that there must be a good country western song amid the controversy—called "brouhaha" by the *GT*—that was sparked by "Brock's tirade." The *GT* editorial lamented that a song would be the only good thing so far to come out of the controversy. In calling the discussion a "brouhaha," the *GT* editorial foreshadowed its final recommendation: the need for reasoned discussion on the topic of immigration with more listening and less name calling. The *DP* interpretation was that Brock had given a "boorish performance" that offended Latinos as well as the editorial board. For its part, the *RMN* editorial's interpretation was that Brock delivered a "patriotic homily."

In spite of calls from the Latino community for an apology, the *RMN* and *DP* wrote that they never thought that Brock was a racist. The *DP* quoted directly from Brock's letter to the editor, "I'm not a racist. I was not directing the comments towards any particular group. I was speaking my mind as an American." Brock claimed his American identity in defense of his comments, as if those offended by his comments were not also Americans and part of the nation. Brock's quote in the *DP* editorial was preceded and followed by reference to the Latinos who were offended and to their growth in Greeley where the Latino population doubled during the 1990s, clearly indicating that they were the affected community.

After defining the situation in evaluative terms, the *GT* editorial presented its recommendation that the best response to ignorance was reason. It called on Hispanic activists to help sort out the mess left behind by Brock. However, the *GT* wrote that Latinos' calls for the Stampede organizers to apologize were misguided. The *GT* next offered an explanation for Brock's speech. The editorial noted that entertainers were often outrageous and the *GT* recalled Brock's former occupation as a wrestler. It explained that "bluster" was common in that profession and that other musical entertainers were also outrageous.

The *GT* further developed its explanation by shifting from the topic of entertainment to free speech. It stated that the First Amendment covered the words that people did not want to hear. The editorial returned to its theme of reasoned discussion and wrote that immigration policy was a complex problem that demanded discussion and not finger pointing. In another characterization of Brock's speech, the *GT* wrote that by "blurting out his frustrations," Brock tapped into the concerns and questions of many Americans regarding the recent large wave of immigration, the unclear border policy, and the cost-benefits of immigration. The *GT* wrote that understanding complex immigration issues was not advanced by jingoistic slogans such as "America: Love it or Leave it." Explaining the larger message of the Brock incident, the editorial wrote that the country's strength lies in dissent without fear of jail (for those who make statements) or pressure to leave (for those who disagree with statements).

The *GT* defended its editorial analysis of Brock's "off-the-cuff political position" that could be easily dismissed as inconsequential by noting that intense community reaction warranted the attention. However, not much attention was given in the editorials to the reaction of Latinos. The *GT* editorial next shifted from explaining Brock's speech to challenging his logic by critiquing the fundamental flaw behind Brock's statement. The *GT* wrote that Brock assumed that immigrants did not want to learn English. The editorial replied that they do, but that it took time. While English will always be the language of the country, the *GT* recommended that bilingualism should be encouraged for all. The *RMN* also commented on this topic noting that Brock had implied that immigrants were cultural separatists when in fact they were "following the trail blazed long ago by millions of previous immigrants." The *RMN* also noted that the complete acquisition of English by immigrants takes more than one generation. The *RMN* further explained that the presence of non-English languages in the U.S. was at one of its highest levels.

In contrast to the other two editorials, the *RMN* alone challenged Brock's logic in linking the speaking of English to patriotism. Quoting from Brock's letter, "if Americans and immigrants to this great nation were to embrace being American (in all its aspects) as we did after the September 11 tragedy, the solidarity might better protect us all from the evil deeds of outsiders. What better way to embrace being American than to speak the language of its government, people and mainstream populace?" The retort from the *RMN* was that it could think of better ways, including having people embrace and understand its representative government. The *RMN* message about Brock's message was that it was a false equation between speaking English and American patriotism.

The *RMN* criticized not only Brock's logic but also the indirectness of his message. If Brock thought that the number of immigrants threatens national unity, the *RMN* wrote that he should say so instead of insulting members of his audience. Also, if Brock's point was that a common language fosters social cohesion, the *RMN* agreed and thought that the vast majority of immigrants would also agree. The *RMN* concluded that these false assumptions were the reason some Hispanics took offense at Brock's statements.

In its conclusion, the *GT* editorial assumed the voice of the majority and advocated the middle road, which was shared by "most Americans," in spite of the "shouting from those on the fringes of the political spectrum." In this middle of the road position, Anglos could question immigration policy without being called racists, and Hispanics could speak out against injustice without being told to leave. In response to the "brouhaha" that followed the Brock incident, the *GT* and the *RMN* recommended "a lot less name-calling and a lot more listening." The *DP* recommended that the Stampede "never book him, or the horse he rode in on, again."

Nativism or Racism, Does It Make a Difference?

The discourse concerning anti-immigrant statements in the press media is filtered through the lens of race-based prejudice, but these statements are actually concerned with nativism and nationalism and may be considered acts of banal nationalism. Charges of racism draw attention to acts of discrimination but not to the process of nation-building, forging national unity at the expense of an internal minority. Evidence of this process of forging allegiances for national unity in the Brock case was the 75% approval rating that Brock received on the *Greeley Tribune* website. Another aspect of nation building is the manipulation of symbols to reproduce a narrow definition of national identity. The primary symbol of national identity in the Brock case is the English language. Nation-building also figured prominently in the 4th of July celebration during which his comments were made. Brock defended speaking English while supporting another national symbol, the Pledge of Allegiance. The *Rocky Mountain News* did not accept Brock's argument of patriotism and challenged his nationalist connection between patriotism and speaking English. In nation-building discourse, patriotism is often a cover for nativism. As a Chicano veteran stated in the Brock case, "It bothers me when people use patriotism to mask their racism." Prejudice or bigotry, the term used in the editorials, is camouflaged by nativism through its defense of national symbols such as the English language.

While society frowns on discrimination based on race, discrimination based on nationalism and fueled by nativism is not always recognized as discrimination. The symbolic-indexical function of a language to represent a national or ethnic group is not always recognized and that makes discrimination on linguistic grounds publicly acceptable, whereas discrimination on ethnic or racial grounds would not be. Attitudes towards immigrants and linkages established during the Americanization period, such as the English language as the key symbol of national identity, appear today as having always existed and as self-evident and not as historically based social constructions. The result is that defense of the English language as a national symbol reaffirms definitions of national identity on ethnic rather than civic terms. An important consequence of not understanding nativism is that anti-immigrant statements are not considered to be discriminatory. Calls for apologies by community members went unheeded and the editorial boards saw no need for an apology. Not recognizing prejudice based on nativism makes it difficult to challenge the view that immigrants are an internal threat to the nation; these attitudes in turn contribute to restrictionistic policies directed against immigrants who are blamed for societal ills.

From the Editors   *Issues and Comments*

Do you agree that the treatment of Mexicans and Puerto Ricans by the United States resembles colonialism? If so, does that of other minority groups resemble it, as well?

Are all immigrant groups racialized and constructed as inferior when they first arrive here? Italian, Greek, and Jewish immigrants were regarded as nonwhite for a time, then eventually became part of the white group. Will this also happen to Latinos? To blacks?

Was the intense racialization of Latinos in this country's early years a function of labor needs, the need to justify conquest, or something else? Why were early immigrants from, say, Norway, not treated in similar fashion to that described in some of the selections?

Did social workers in the 1920s construct Latinos as a problem group? Why?

Do K–12 schools today slate minority students for menial jobs, as they did a hundred years ago?

How would you feel if you were deported by mistake, with no chance to explain that you belong here, to a country that your parents or grandparents happened to be from? Imagine that the government decided to return all the Albanian refugees, and your ancestors were from that country. What if you were deported simply because you showed a resemblance, physically and in your family name, to other Albanians? Would you think it was your fault for not having documentation with you? Do you think the American citizens who were deported to Mexico in past indiscriminate roundups felt similarly? Why did international agreements and treaties, such as that of Guadalupe Hildalgo, not stop these abuses?

Do current U.S. policies remind you of Manifest Destiny? The White Man's Burden? The Monroe Doctrine?

What is the difference between nativism and racism? Are both equally harmful? Equally hard to prove? What if the action takes the form of national-origin discrimination, such as slurs and slights directed at people from Spanish-speaking countries?

Why is anti-Latino sentiment increasing in virulence most sharply in California and in regions with new concentrations of immigrants?

If racialization is not a constant but depends on local attitudes, could a Latino live a relatively racism-free life in, say, North Dakota but not in Texas? If so, does he or she cease to be a Latino while living in North Dakota since, in everyday parlance, *Latino* means a person of Latin-American descent who is racialized by the dominant culture?

Suggested Readings

Acuña, Rodolfo F. *Anything but Mexican: Chicanos in Contemporary Los Angeles.* London: Verso, 1996.

———. *A Community under Siege: A Chronicle of Chicanos East of the Los Angeles River, 1945–1975*. Los Angeles: Chicano Studies Research Center, University of California at Los Angeles, 1984.

———. "Crocodile Tears: Lynching of Mexicans." HispanicVista.com, July 20, 2005.

———. *Occupied America: A History of Chicanos*. 6th ed. New York: Pearson Longman, 2006.

Almaguer, Tomás. *Racial Fault Lines: The Origins of White Supremacy in California*. Berkeley: University of California Press, 1994.

American Committee for the Protection of the Foreign Born. *Our Badge of Infamy: A Petition to the United Nations on the Treatment of the Mexican Immigrant*. N.p., 1959. Reprinted in *The Mexican American and the Law*, edited by Carlos Cortes, New York: Arno Press, 1974.

Andreas, Peter. *Border Games: Policing the U.S.-Mexico Divide*. 2d ed. Ithaca, N.Y.: Cornell University Press, 2009.

Balderrama, Francisco E., and Raymond Rodriguez. *Decade of Betrayal: Mexican Repatriation in the 1930s*. Albuquerque: University of New Mexico Press, 1995.

Barrera, Mario. *Race and Class in the Southwest: A Theory of Racial Inequality*. Notre Dame, Ind.: University of Notre Dame Press, 1979.

Barrera, Mario, Carlos Munoz, Jr., and Charles Ornelas. "The Barrio as an Internal Colony." In *People and Politics in Urban Society*, edited by Harlan Hahn, 465–98. Urban Affairs Annual Reviews, no. 6. Beverly Hills, Calif.: Sage Publications, 1972.

Bender, Steven W. "Old Hate in New Bottles: Privatizing, Localizing, and Bundling Anti-Spanish and Anti-Immigrant Sentiment in the 21st Century." 7 *Nev. L.J.* 883 (2007).

Bennett, David H. *The Party of Fear: From Nativist Movements to the New Right in American History*. Chapel Hill: University of North Carolina Press, 1988.

Blauner, Robert. *Racial Oppression in America*. New York: Harper & Row, 1972.

Border Angels. http://www.borderangels.org/mission.html.

Briggs, Laura. *Reproducing Empire: Race, Sex, Science, and U.S. Imperialism in Puerto Rico*. Berkeley: University of California Press, 2002.

Brimelow, Peter. *Alien Nation: Common Sense about America's Immigration Disaster*. New York: Random House, 1995.

Buchanan, Patrick J. *The Death of the West: How Dying Populations and Immigrant Invasions Imperil Our Country and Civilization*. New York: St. Martin's Press, 2002.

Butler, R. E. "Rusty." *On Creating a Hispanic America: A Nation within a Nation?* Washington, D.C.: Council for Inter-American Security, 1985.

Calavita, Kitty. *Inside the State: The Bracero Program, Immigration, and the I.N.S.* New York: Routledge, 1992.

Camarillo, Albert. *Chicanos in a Changing Society: From Mexican Pueblos to American Barrios in Santa Barbara and Southern California, 1848–1930*. Cambridge, Mass.: Harvard University Press, 1996.

Carleton, Don E. *Red Scare! Right Wing Hysteria, Fifties Fanaticism, and Their Legacy in Texas*. Austin: Texas Monthly Press, 1985.

Carrigan, William D., and Clive Webb. "The Lynching of Persons of Mexican Origin or Descent in the United States, 1848 to 1928." 37(2) *Journal of Social History* 411–38 (2003).

Chacón, Justin Akers, and Mike Davis. *No One Is Illegal: Fighting Racism and State Violence on the U.S.-Mexico Border*. Chicago: Haymarket Books, 2006.

Chavez, Leo R. *The Latino Threat: Constructing Immigrants, Citizens, and the Nation*. Palo Alto, Calif.: Stanford University Press, 2008.

Clark, Walter Van Tilburgh. *The Ox-Bow Incident*. Reprint. New York: Modern Library, 2004.

Clopper, J. C. "Journal of J. C. Clopper, 1828." 13 *Southwestern Historical Quarterly* 44–80 (July 1909).

Cockburn, Alexander. "Zyklon B on the U.S. Border." *The Nation*, July 9, 2007, at 9.

Dana, Richard Henry. *Two Years before the Mast*. Boston: Houghton Mifflin, 1911.

De León, Arnoldo. *They Called Them Greasers: Anglo Attitudes toward Mexicans in Texas: 1821–1900*. Austin: University of Texas Press, 1983.

Diaz, David R. "Public Space and Culture: A Critical Response to Conventional and Postmodern Visions of City Life." In *Culture and Difference: Critical Perspectives on the Bicultural Experience in the United States*, edited by Antonia Darder, 123. Westport, Conn.: Greenwood Press, 1995.

Dow, Mark. *American Gulag: Inside U.S. Immigration Prisons*. Berkeley: University of California Press, 2004.

Dunn, Timothy J. *The Militarization of the U.S.–Mexican Border, 1978–1992: Low-Intensity Conflict Doctrine Comes Home*. Austin: CMAS Books, University of Texas, 1996.

Ebright, Malcolm. *Land Grants and Lawsuits in Northern New Mexico*. Albuquerque: University of New Mexico Press, 1994.

Farnham, Thomas Jefferson. *Life, Adventures, and Travel in California*. New York: Nafis & Cornish, 1847.

Foreigners in Their Native Land: Historical Roots of the Mexican Americans, edited by David J. Weber. Albuquerque: University of New Mexico Press, 1973.

Fuentes-Rohwer, Luis. "The Land That Democratic Theory Forgot." 83 *Ind. L.J.* 1525 (2008).

Garcia, Juan Ramon. *Operation Wetback: The Mass Deportation of Mexican Undocumented Workers in 1954*. Westport, Conn.: Greenwood Press, 1980.

Gomez, David F. *Somos Chicanos: Strangers in Our Own Land*. Boston: Beacon Press, 1973.

Gonzalez, Gilbert G. *Culture of Empire: American Writers, Mexico, and Mexican Immigrants, 1880–1930*. Austin: University of Texas Press, 2003.

Grant, Lindsey, and John H. Tanton. *Immigration and the American Conscience*. Washington, D.C.: Environmental Fund, 1982.

Guerin-Gonzales, Camille. *Mexican Workers and the American Dream: Immigration, Repatriation, and California Farm Labor, 1900–1939*. New Brunswick, N.J.: Rutgers University Press, 1994.

Heizer, Robert F., and Alan J. Almquist. *The Other Californians: Prejudice and Discrimination under Spain, Mexico, and the United States to 1920*. Berkeley: University of California Press, 1971.

Hernández-Truyol, Berta Esperanza. "Natives, Newcomers and Nativism: A Human Rights Model for the Twenty-First Century." 23 *Fordham Urb. L.J.* 1075 (1996).

Higham, John. *Strangers in the Land: Patterns of American Nativism, 1860–1925*. 2d ed. New Brunswick, N.J.: Rutgers University Press, 1988.

Hing, Bill Ong. "The Dark Side of Operation Gatekeeper." 7 *U.C. Davis J. Int'l L. & Pol'y* 121 (2001).

———. *Deporting Our Souls: Values, Morality, and Immigration Policy*. New York: Cambridge University Press, 2006.

Hoffman, Abraham. *Unwanted Mexican Americans in the Great Depression: Repatriation Pressures, 1929–1939*. Tucson: University of Arizona Press, 1974.

Horsman, Reginald. *Race and Manifest Destiny: The Origins of American Racial Anglo-Saxonism*. Cambridge, Mass.: Harvard University Press, 1981.

How the United States Racializes Latinos: White Hegemony and Its Consequences, edited by José A. Cobas, Jorge Duany, and Joe R. Feagin. Boulder, Colo.: Paradigm Publishers, 2009.

Huntington, Samuel P. *Who Are We? Challenges to America's Identity*. New York: Simon & Schuster, 2004.

Immigrants Out! The New Nativism and the Anti-Immigrant Impulse in the United States, edited by Juan F. Perea. New York: New York University Press, 1996.

Johnson, Kevin R. "Maria and Joseph Plasencia's Lost Weekend: The Case of *Landon v. Plasencia*." In *Immigration Stories*, edited by David H. Martin and Peter A. Schuck, 221. New York: Foundation Press, 2005.

———. "Race, the Immigration Laws, and Domestic Race Relations: A 'Magic Mirror' into the Heart of Darkness." 73 *Ind. L.J.* 1111 (1998).

———. "September 11 and Mexican Immigrants: Collateral Damage Comes Home." 52 *DePaul L. Rev.* 849 (2003).

Johnson, Kevin R., and Bill Ong Hing. "National Identity in a Multicultural Nation: The Challenge of Immigration Law and Immigrants." 103 *Mich. L. Rev.* 1347 (2005).

Kropp, Phoebe S. *California Vieja: Culture and Memory in a Modern American Place*. Berkeley: University of California Press, 2006.

Lamm, Richard D., and Gary Imhoff. *The Immigration Time Bomb: The Fragmenting of America*. New York: Truman Tallet Books, E. P. Dutton, 1985.

Larson, Jane E. "Free Markets Deep in the Heart of Texas." 84 *Geo. L.J.* 179 (1995).

Latham, Francis S. *Travels in Texas, 1842*, edited by Gerald S. Pierce. Austin, Tex.: Encino Press, 1971.

Laughlin, Harry H. *Conquest by Immigration: A Report of the Special Committee on Immigration and Naturalization*. New York: Chamber of Commerce of the State of New York, 1939.

Lind, Michael. *The Next American Nation: The New Nationalism and the Fourth American Revolution*. New York: Free Press, 1995.

Loewen, James W. *Sundown Towns: A Hidden Dimension of American Racism*. New York: Touchstone Press, 2006.

Martinez, Sara. "Declaring Open Season: The Outbreak of Violence against Undocumented Immigrants by Vigilante Ranchers in South Texas." 7 *Scholar* 95 (2004).

McWilliams, Carey. *North from Mexico*. New ed. Westport, Conn.: Greenwood Press, 1990. Originally published 1948.

Menchaca, Martha. *The Mexican Outsiders: A Community History of Marginalization and Discrimination in California*. Austin: University of Texas Press, 1995.

Merk, Frederick. *Manifest Destiny and Mission in American History: A Reinterpretation*. New ed. Cambridge, Mass.: Harvard University Press, 1995.

Mirande, Alfredo. *Gringo Justice*. Notre Dame, Ind.: University of Notre Dame Press, 1987.

Montejano, David. *Anglos and Mexicans in the Making of Texas, 1836–1986*. Austin: University of Texas Press, 1987.

Morgan, Patricia. *Shame of a Nation: A Documented Story of Police-State Terror against Mexican Americans in the U.S.A.* Los Angeles: Los Angeles Committee for the Protection of the Foreign Born, 1954.

Morín, José Luis. *Latino/a Rights and Justice in the United States*. 2d ed. Durham, N.C.: Carolina Academic Press, 2009.

Navarro, Armando. *The Immigration Crisis: Nativism, Armed Vigilantism, and the Rise of a Countervailing Movement*. Lanham, Md.: AltaMira Press, 2008.

———. *Mexicano Political Experience in Occupied Aztlan: Struggles and Change*. Lanham, Md.: AltaMira Press, 2005.

Nevins, Joseph. *Operation Gatekeeper: The Rise of the "Illegal Alien" and the Remaking of the U.S.–Mexico Boundary*. New York: Routledge, 2001.

Olivas, Michael A. "The 'Trial of the Century' That Never Was: Staff Sgt. Macario Garcia, the Congressional Medal of Honor, and the Oasis Café." 83 *Ind. L.J.* 1391 (2008).

Olmstead, Frederick Law. *A Journey through Texas; or, A Saddle-Trip on the Southwestern Frontier, with a Statistical Abstract.* New York: Dix, Edwards & Co., 1857. Reprint, Austin: University of Texas Press, 1978.

Peterson, Richard H. "Anti-Mexican Nativism in California, 1848–1853: A Study in Cultural Conflict." 62 *Southern California Quarterly* 309–28 (Winter 1980).

Ramos, Efrén Rivera. "The Legal Construction of American Colonialism: The Insular Cases 1901–1922." 65 *Rev. Jur. U.P.R.* 225 (1996).

Reid, John C. *Reid's Tramp; or, A Journal of the Incidents of Ten Months' Travel . . .* Selma, Ala.: J. Hardy Co., 1858. Reprint, Austin, Tex.: Steck Co., 1935.

Rodriguez, Clara E. *Puerto Ricans: Born in the U.S.A.* Boston: Unwin Hyman, 1989.

Rodriguez, Ruben Rosario. *Racism and God Talk: A Latino/a Perspective.* New York: New York University Press, 2008.

Romero, Mary. "'Go After the Women': Mothers against Illegal Aliens' Campaign against Mexican Immigrant Women and Their Children." 83 *Ind. L.J.* 1355 (2008).

Romero, Mary, and Marwah Serag. "Violation of Latino Civil Rights Resulting from INS and Local Police's Use of Race, Culture, and Class Profiling: The Case of the Chandler Roundup in Arizona." 52 *Clev. St. L. Rev.* 75 (2004–2005).

Romero, Tom I., II. "No Brown Towns: Anti-Immigrant Ordinances and Equality of Educational Opportunity for Latina/os." 12 *J. Gender, Race & Just.* 13 (2008).

Rosenbaum, Robert J. *Mexicano Resistance in the Southwest: "The Sacred Right of Self-Preservation."* Austin: University of Texas Press, 1981.

Sage, Rufus B. "Degenerate Inhabitants of New Mexico." In 2 *Rufus B. Sage: His Letters and Papers, 1836–1847,* edited by LeRoy R. Hafen and Ann W. Hafen. Glendale, Calif., A. H. Clark Co., 1956.

Samora, Julian, Joe Bernal, and Albert Pena. *Gunpowder Justice: A Reassessment of the Texas Rangers.* Notre Dame, Ind.: University of Notre Dame, 1979.

Schlesinger, Arthur M., Jr. *The Disuniting of America: Reflections on a Multicultural Society.* Rev. ed. New York: W. W. Norton, 1998.

Schroeder, John H. *Mr. Polk's War: American Opposition and Dissent, 1846–1848.* Madison: University of Wisconsin, Press, 1973.

Schuck, Peter H. "Alien Rumination." 105 *Yale L.J.* 1963 (1996).

Seguin, Juan N. *Personal Memoirs of John N. Seguin: From the Year 1834 to the Retreat of General Woll from the City of San Antonio.* San Antonio, Tex.: Printed at the Ledger Book and Job Office, 1858.

Shirley, Dame. *The Shirley Letters from the California Mines, 1851–1852.* New York: Knopf, 1949.

Southern Poverty Law Center. "Close to Slavery: Guestworker Programs in the United States." Montgomery, Ala.: Southern Poverty Law Center, 2007.

Sterne, Adolphus. *Hurrah for Texas! The Diary of Adolphus Sterne,* edited by Archie P. McDonald. Waco, Tex.: Texian Press, 1969.

Takaki, Ronald. *A Different Mirror: A History of Multicultural America.* Boston: Little, Brown & Co., 1993.

Tanton, John H. *Rethinking Immigration Policy.* Washington, D.C.: Federation for American Immigration Reform, 1979.

U.S. Commission on Civil Rights. *Mexican American Education Study: Ethnic Isolation of Mexican Americans in the Public Schools of the Southwest.* Washington, D.C.: Government Printing Office, 1971.

Webb, Walter Prescott. *The Texas Rangers: A Century of Frontier Defense.* 2d ed. Austin: University of Texas Press, 1965.

Weston, Rubin Francis. *Racism in U.S. Imperialism: The Influence of Racial Assumptions on American Foreign Policy, 1893–1946.* Columbia: University of South Carolina Press, 1972.

‖‖‖

Part IV

Racial Construction and Demonization in Mass Culture
Media Treatment and Stereotypes

If, as most scholars believe, race is a social construct (as opposed to a biological reality), the content of that construct in the case of Latinos is often highly negative, especially in mass culture, where the media depict Latinos as lazy, criminal, dirty, happy-go-lucky, and uninterested in assuming the role of informed citizenship. Many of the images coined in connection with Latinos seem similar in function to the Sambo, mammy, coon, and uncle one sees in black history, but with some notable differences. How do these images form and proliferate? Do they harm—or should one merely laugh them off? And what can one do, within First Amendment limitations, to combat them?

Chapter 28

|||||||||||||||||||||||||||||||||||||||||||||||||||||||||||||||||||||||||||||||||||

Racial Depiction in American Law and Culture

Richard Delgado and Jean Stefancic

Outsider groups argue that free speech law inadequately protects them against certain types of harm. The two of us agree. For us, conventional First Amendment doctrine is most helpful in connection with small, clearly bounded disputes. Free speech and debate can help resolve controversies over whether a school disciplinary or local zoning policy is adequate, over whether a new sales tax is likely to increase or decrease net revenues, whether one candidate for political office is a better choice than another. Speech is less able, however, to deal with systemic social ills, such as racism, that are widespread and deeply woven into the fabric of society. Free speech, in short, is least helpful where we need it most.

Consider racial depiction, for example. Several museums have featured displays of racial memorabilia from the past. One exhibit toured the United States. Filmmaker Marlon Riggs produced an award-winning one-hour documentary, *Ethnic Notions*, with a similar focus. Each of these collections depicts a shocking parade of Sambos, mammies, coons, uncles—bestial or happy-go-lucky, watermelon-eating—African Americans. They show advertising logos and household commodities in the shape of blacks with grotesquely exaggerated facial features. They include minstrel shows and film clips depicting blacks as so incompetent, shuffling, and dim-witted that it is hard to see how they survived to adulthood. Other images depict primitive, terrifying, larger-than-life black men in threatening garb and postures, often with apparent designs on white women.

Seeing these haunting images today, one is tempted to ask: "How could their authors—cartoonists, writers, film-makers, and graphic designers—individuals, certainly of higher than average education, create such appalling images? And why did no one protest?"

Mexican Americans

Images of Mexican Americans fall into three or four well-delineated stereotypes—the greaser; the conniving, treacherous bandido; the happy-go-lucky shiftless lover of song, food, and dance; and the tragic, silent, tall, dark, and handsome "Spanish"

From *Images of the Outsider in American Law and Culture: Can Free Expression Remedy Systemic Social Ills?* 77 CORNELL L. REV. 1258 (1992). Originally published in the *Cornell Law Review*. Reprinted by permission.

type of romantic fiction—which change according to society's needs. As with blacks, Asians, and Indians, most Americans have relatively few interpersonal contacts with Mexican Americans; therefore, these images become the individual's only reality. When such a person meets an actual Mexican American, he or she tends to place the other in one of the ready-made categories. Stereotyping thus denies members of both groups the opportunity to interact with each other on anything like a complex, nuanced human level.

During and just after the conquest, when the U.S. was seizing and then settling large tracts of Mexican territory in the Southwest, "Western" or "conquest" fiction depicted Anglos bravely displacing shifty, brutal, and treacherous Mexicans. After the war ended and control of the Southwest passed to American hands, a subtle shift occurred. Anglos living and settling in the new regions were portrayed as Protestant, independent, thrifty, industrious, mechanically resourceful, and interested in progress; Mexicans, as traditional, sedate, lacking in mechanical resourcefulness and ambition. Writers both on and off the scene created the same images of indolent, pious Mexicans—ignoring the two centuries of enterprising farmers and ranchers who withstood or negotiated with Apaches and Comanches and built a sturdy society with irrigation, land tenure, and mining codes.

In the late conquest period, depiction of this group bifurcated. Majority-race writers created two images of the Mexican: the "good" (loyal) Mexican peon or sidekick, and the "bad" fighter/greaser Mexican who did not know his place. The first was faithful and domestic; the second, treacherous and evil. As with other groups, the second ("bad") image had sexual overtones: the greaser coveted Anglo women and would seduce or rape them if given the opportunity. Children's books of this time, like the best-selling Buffalo Bill series, were full of Mexican stereotypes used to reinforce moral messages to the young: They are like this, we like that.

The first thirty years of the twentieth century saw heavy Mexican immigration of mainly poor workers. The first Bracero programs—official, temporary importation of field hands—appeared. With increasing numbers, white-only signs and segregated housing and schools appeared, aimed now at Mexicans in addition to blacks. With the increased risk of interaction and intermarriage, novels and newspaper writing reinforced the notion of these immigrants' baseness, simplicity, and inability to assimilate.

The movies of this period depicted Latins as buffoons, sluts, or connivers; even some of the titles were disparaging: for example, *The Greaser's Gauntlet*. Films featured brown-skinned desperadoes stealing horses or gold, lusting after pure Anglo women, shooting noble Saxon heroes in the back, or acting the part of hapless buffoons. Animated cartoons and short subjects, still shown on television, featured tequila-drinking Mexicans, bullfighters, Speedy Gonzalez and Slowpoke Rodriguez, and clowns—as well as Castilian caballeras, light-skinned, upper class, wearing elaborate dresses and carrying castanets.

World War II brought the need for factory and agricultural workers and a new flood of immigrants. Images softened to include "normal," or even noble, Mexicans, like the general of Marlon Brando's *Viva Zapata*. Perhaps realizing it had overstepped, America diminished the virulence of its anti-Mexican imagery. Yet the Western genre, with Mexican villains and bandits, continues; and the immigrant speaking gibberish still makes an appearance. Even the most favorable novel and film of the post-war period, *The Milagro Beanfield War*, ends in stereotypes.

A few Anglo writers found their own culture alienating or sick and sought relief in a more serene Southwest culture. As with the Harlem Renaissance, these creative artists tended to be more generous to Mexicans, but nevertheless retained the Anglo hero as the central figure or Samaritan who uplifts the Mexican from his or her traditional ignorance.

How Could They? Lessons from the History of Racial Depiction

As we have seen, the depiction of ethnic groups of color is littered with negative images, although the content of those images changes over time. In some periods, society needed to suppress a group, as with blacks during Reconstruction. Society then coined an image to suit that purpose—that of primitive, powerful, larger-than-life blacks, terrifying and barely under control. At other times, for example during slavery, society needed reassurance that blacks were docile, cheerful, and content with their lot. Images of sullen, rebellious blacks dissatisfied with their condition would have made white society uneasy. Accordingly, images of simple, happy blacks, content to do the master's work, were disseminated.

In every era, ethnic imagery thus comes bearing an enormous amount of social weight. Nevertheless, we sense that we are in control—that things need not be that way. We believe we can use speech, jiujitsu fashion, on behalf of oppressed peoples. We believe that speech can serve as a tool of destabilization. It is virtually a prime tenet of liberal jurisprudence that by talk, dialog, exhortation, and so on, we present each other with passionate, appealing messages that will counter the evil ones of racism and sexism, and thereby advance society to greater levels of fairness and humanity.

Consider, for example, the debate about campus speech codes. In response to a rising tide of racist incidents, many campuses have enacted student conduct codes that forbid certain types of face-to-face insult. These codes invariably draw fire from free-speech absolutists and many campus administrators on the ground that they would interfere with free speech. Campuses, they argue, ought to be "bastions of free speech." Racism and prejudice are matters of "ignorance and fear," for which the appropriate remedy is more speech. Suppression merely drives racism underground, it is said, where it will fester and emerge in even more hateful forms. Speech is the best corrective for error; regulation risks the spectre of censorship and state control. Efforts to regulate pornography, Klan marches, and other types of race-baiting often meet similar responses.

But modernist and postmodern insights about language and the social construction of reality show that reliance on countervailing speech that will, in theory, wrestle with bad or vicious speech is often misplaced. This is so for two interrelated reasons: First, the account rests on simplistic and erroneous notions of narrativity and change, and second, on a misunderstanding of the relation between the subject, or self, and new narratives.

The First Reason—Time Warp: Why We (Can) Only Condemn the Old Narrative

The racism of other times and places does stand out, does strike us as glaringly and appallingly wrong. But this happens only decades or centuries later; we acquiesce in today's version with little realization that it is wrong, that a later generation will ask "How could they?" about us. We only condemn the racism of another place (South Africa) or time. But that of our own place and time strikes us, if at all, as unexceptionable, trivial, or well within literary license. Every form of creative work (we tell ourselves) relies on stock characters. What's so wrong with a novel that employs a black who . . . , or a Mexican who . . . ? Besides, the argument goes, those groups are disproportionately employed as domestics, are responsible for a high proportion of our crime, are they not? And some actually talk this way; why, just last week, I overheard . . .

This time-warp aspect of racism makes speech an ineffective tool to counter it. Racism is woven into the warp and woof of the way we see and organize the world— it is one of the many preconceptions we bring to experience and use to construct and make sense of our social world. Racism forms part of the dominant narrative, the group of received understandings and basic principles that form the baseline from which we reason. How could these be in question? Recent scholarship shows that the dominant narrative changes very slowly and resists alteration. We interpret new stories in light of the old. Ones that deviate too markedly from our pre-existing stock are dismissed as extreme, coercive, political, and wrong. The only stories about race we are prepared to condemn, then, are the old ones giving voice to the racism of an earlier age, ones that society has already begun to reject. We can condemn Justice Brown for writing as he did in *Plessy v. Ferguson*, but not university administrators who refuse remedies for campus racism, failing to notice the remarkable parallels between the two.

The Second Reason: Our Narratives, Our Selves

Racial change is slow, then, because the story of race is part of the dominant narrative we use to interpret experience. The narrative teaches that race matters, that people are different, with the differences lying always in a predictable direction. It holds that certain cultures, unfortunately, have less ambition than others, that the majority group is largely innocent of racial wrongdoing, that the current distribution of comfort and well-being is roughly what merit and fairness dictate. Within that general framework, only certain matters are open for discussion: How different? In what ways? With how many exceptions? And what measures are due to deal with this unfortunate situation and at what cost to whites? This is so because the narrative leaves only certain things intelligible; other arguments and texts would seem bizarre and far-fetched.

A second and related insight from modern scholarship focuses not on the role of narratives in confining change to manageable proportions, but on the relationship between ourselves and those narratives. The reigning First Amendment metaphor—the marketplace of ideas—implies a separation between subjects who do the choosing and the ideas or messages that vie for their attention. Subjects are "in here," the messages "out there." The pre-existing subjects choose the idea that seems most valid and true—somewhat in the manner of a diner deciding what to eat at a buffet.

But scholars are beginning to realize that this mechanistic view of an autonomous subject choosing among separate, external ideas is simplistic. In an important sense, we are our current stock of narratives, and they us. We subscribe to a stock of explanatory scripts, plots, narratives, and understandings that enable us to make sense of—to construct—our social world. Because we live in that world, it begins to shape and determine us, who we are, what we see, how we select, reject, interpret, and order subsequent reality.

These observations imply that our ability to escape the confines of our own preconceptions is quite limited. The contrary belief—that through speech and remonstrance alone we can endlessly reform ourselves and each other—we call the empathic fallacy. It and its companion, the pathetic fallacy, are both based on hubris, the belief that we can be more than we are. The *empathic fallacy* holds that through speech and remonstrance we can surmount our limitations of time, place, and culture, can transcend our own situatedness. But our examination of the cultural record, as well as postmodern understandings of language and personhood, both point to the same conclusion: The notion of ideas competing with each other, with truth and goodness emerging victorious from the competition, has proven seriously deficient when applied to evils, like racism, that are deeply inscribed in the culture. We have constructed the social world so that racism seems normal, part of the status quo, in need of little correction. It is not until much later that what we believed begins to seem incredibly, monstrously wrong. How could we have believed that?

Racism is not a mistake, not a matter of episodic, irrational behavior carried out by vicious-willed individuals, not a throwback to a long-gone era. It is ritual assertion of supremacy, like animals sneering and posturing to maintain their places in the hierarchy of the colony. It is performed largely unconsciously, just as the animals' behavior is. Racism seems right, customary, and inoffensive to those engaged in it, while also bringing them psychic and pecuniary advantages.

What Then, Should Be Done? If Not Speech, What?

So, what can be done? One possibility we must take seriously is that nothing can be done—that race-based subjugation is so deeply embedded in our society, so useful for the powerful, that nothing can dislodge it. However, we offer four suggestions for a program of racial reform. We do this while underscoring the limitations of our own prescriptions, including the near-impossibility of getting a society to take seriously something whose urgency it seems constitutionally unable to appreciate. First, society should act decisively in cases of racism that we do see, treating them as proxies for the ones we know remain unseen. Second, past mistreatment will generally prove a more reliable basis for remedial action (such as affirmative action or reparations) than future- or present-oriented considerations; the racism of the past is the only kind that we recognize and condemn. Third, whenever possible we should employ and empower minority speakers of color and expose ourselves to their messages. Their reality, while not infallible and certainly not the only one, is the one we must heed if we wish to avoid history's judgment. It is likely to be the one society will adopt in thirty years.

Scholars should approach with skepticism the writings of those neoconservatives, including some of color, who make a practice of telling society that racism is ended. Finally, we should deepen suspicion of remedies for deep-seated social evils that rely on speech and exhortation. The First Amendment is an instrument of variable efficacy, more useful in some settings than others. Overextending it provokes the anger of oppressed groups and casts doubt on speech's value in settings where it is, in fact, useful. With deeply inscribed cultural practices that most can neither see as evil nor mobilize to reform, we should forthrightly institute changes in the structure of society that will enable persons of color—particularly the young—to avoid the worst assaults of racism. As with the controversy over campus racism, we should not let a spurious motto that speech be "everywhere free" stand in the way of outlawing speech that is demonstrably harmful, that is compounding the problem.

Because of the way the dominant narrative works, we should prepare for the near-certainty that these suggestions will be criticized as unprincipled, unfair to "innocent whites," wrong. Understanding how the dialectic works and how the scripts and counterscripts work their dismal paralysis may, perhaps, inspire us to continue even though the path is long and the night dark.

Chapter 29

||||||||||||||||||||||||||||||||||||||||||||||||||||||||||||||||||||||||||||||||||

Hispanic Stereotyping

Charles Ramirez Berg

Ideological Perspectives

One way to read a stereotype is as a negative mirror of dominant values. To be sure, the sloppy, greasy appearance of *el bandido* in any number of Hollywood westerns, coupled with his nearly psychotic savagery and immorality, reflects poorly on Mexicans and Mexican Americans. But this stereotype—standing in sharp contrast to the Anglo hero—has another effect: it reinforces the cleanliness, sobriety, sanity, overall decency, and moral rectitude of the WASP in the white hat. By extension, then, stereotypes identify, justify, and support mainstream (Anglo) beliefs.

Stereotyping in films slips effortlessly into the existing hegemony, the subtle, naturalizing way the ruling class maintains its dominance over subordinate groups. Viewed as a tool of the dominant ideology, the creation and perpetuation of stereotypes in the movies and in the media function to maintain the status quo by representing dominant groups as "naturally" empowered and marginal groups as disenfranchised. In the case of Hispanics, their portrayal as bandits and buffoons, whores and exotic clowns, Latin Lovers and Dark Ladies marks them as symbols of ethnic exclusion. As Richard Dyer puts it, through stereotyping, ruling groups attempt "to fashion the whole of society according to their own world-view, value-system, sensibility and ideology." Stereotypes possess two principal features: ethnocentrism, and the belief in inborn and unalterable psychological characteristics. Hegemony, however, is not static, but active and dynamic, "something that must be ceaselessly built and rebuilt in the face of both implicit and explicit challenges to it." The very existence of subordinated subcultures presents such challenges.

Six Hollywood Stereotypes of the Hispanic

Most Hispanic characters in film and television have usually been one or another of the six basic Hispanic stereotypes. Sometimes the stereotypes combine, but the core, defining characteristics remain remarkably consistent.

El Bandido

The Mexican bandit's roots go back to the villains of the silent "greaser" films. Typically, he is treacherous, shifty, and dishonest. His reactions are emotional, irrational, and usually violent; his intelligence is severely limited, resulting in flawed strategies. He is dirty and unkempt—usually displaying an unshaven face; missing teeth; and disheveled, oily hair. A modern incarnation of this type, the Latin American drug runner, shows superficial changes in the stereotype without altering its essence. He is slicker of course, and has traded his black hat for a white suit and his tired horse for a glitzy Porsche, yet he is still driven to satisfy base cravings—for money, power, and sexual pleasure—and routinely employs vicious and illegal means to obtain them. From the halfbreed villain in *Broncho Billy and the Greaser* (1914) to Andy Garcia's sadistic Cuban American gangster in *Eight Million Ways to Die* (1986), the Hispanic bandit is a demented, despicable creature who deserves punishment for his brutal behavior. Other versions of the bandit stereotype include Latin American rebel leaders, corrupt dictators, and inner-city youth gang members.

The Halfbreed Harlot

The corresponding female stereotype is a familiar stock figure in the American cinema, particularly in westerns. Like the bandit, she is a secondary character, and not always a halfbreed. Lusty and hot-tempered, her main function, as Arthur Pettit (1980) wrote in *Images of the Mexican American in Fiction and Film*, is "to provide as much sexual titillation as current censorship standards will permit." Doc Holliday's woman Chihuahua (Linda Darnell), in John Ford's *My Darling Clementine* (1946), is a classic example of this type. Without a man she is a leaf in the wind, so when Doc is out of town and Wyatt Earp (Henry Fonda) doesn't respond to her flirtations, she helps to cheat him during a poker game. The Halfbreed Harlot is a slave to her passions; her character is based on the premise that she is a nymphomaniac. In true stereotypical fashion, motivation for her actions is not given—she is a prostitute because she likes the work, not because social or economic forces have shaped her life.

The Male Buffoon

This is the second-banana comic relief figure: Pancho in "The Cisco Kid"; Sgt. Garcia in Walt Disney's "Zorro"; Ricky Ricardo in "I Love Lucy"; and Leo Carrillo's characters in his many roles in 1930s films. In this case (as with the female counterpart, described next), many of the same stereotypical characteristics that are threatening in the Bandit reappear, but as targets of ridicule. In the case of these stereotypes, comedy is a way of dealing with the Hispanic male's or female's stereotypically accentuated differences, a way of taming their fearful qualities. What is funny about this character is his simple-mindedness (the bumbling antics of Sgt. Garcia), his failure to master standard English ("Let's went, Cisco!"), his childish regression into emotionality (Ricky's explosions into Spanish).

The Female Clown

The Male Buffoon's counterpart, the Female Clown, represents a way of neutralizing the overt sexual threat posed by the Halfbreed Harlot. The strategy is to negate the Latin female's eroticism by making her an object of comic derision. A key example is the film career of the beautiful Mexican actress Lupe Velez, a comic star in Hollywood in the 1930s. Best known for her role as the dizzy "Mexican Spitfire" in a series of eight films, she also starred in a number of other comedies. Velez's Mexican Spitfire was an alluring dingbat, her antics causing baroque plot complications. Velez's other film roles play variations on the Female Clown theme. In *Palooka* (1934), for example, she is a Big City Vamp, a Latin gold digger who lures the rural prize-fighting champ, Joe Palooka (Stu Erwin), into a life of fast-lane dissipation. Once again, her emotionalism and inability to restrain her baser instincts—indeed, she is controlled by them —conform with the common representation of Hollywood's stereotypical Hispanic woman.

Another well-known Female Clown is Carmen Miranda, with her colorful portrayals of Latin American women. What is operative here is exaggeration, another way to elicit derisive laughter and neutralize the feminine Other. Miranda's multicolored costumes and fruit-covered hats, worn in splashy "Latin" musical numbers, were an instant parody of the folkloric costumes (and customs) of Latin America. Miranda's "Lady in the Tutti-Frutti Hat" number from Busby Berkeley's *The Gang's All Here* (1943) is a campy example of the good neighbor policy that was in the United States' and Hollywood's interest to foster during World War II. Furthermore, it was illustrative of the comic exoticism and eroticism attributed to the Hispanic Female Clown.

Psychologically speaking, these four negative stereotypes are projections of the "bad" self. But, as mentioned, some stereotypes are positive. What is important to remember is that although positive stereotypes emphasize traits highly regarded by the in-group, these are still stereotypes—still overgeneralized simplifications that depict the Other as outside the acceptable. From a Lacanian perspective, they represent that moment when the subject perceives a signifier that can provide wholeness. In American movies, these positive Hispanic stereotypes have typically taken two forms: the Latin Lover and the Dark Lady.

The Latin Lover

This stereotype we owe to one star: Rudolph Valentino. An Italian immigrant, in 1921 he had worked his way up from minor movie parts to a starring role as the protagonist in *The Four Horsemen of the Apocalypse*, a story of the effect of World War I on young Argentinean men. In its famous tango scene, Valentino dances seductively with a woman and finishes by flinging her to the ground. With this and other roles as the dashing and magnetic male Other (in *The Sheik* [1921], *Son of the Sheik* [1926], and as the rising bullfighter in *Blood and Sand* [1922]), he began to define a new kind of screen lover and an Other way of making screen love. Since then, the Latin Lover has been a remarkably consistent screen figure, played by a number of Latin actors, from Cesar Romero, Ricardo Montalbán, Gilbert Roland,

and Fernando Lamas to Gabriel Byrne's version in *Siesta* (1987), all maintaining the erotic combination of characteristics instituted by Valentino: suavity and sensuality, tenderness and sexual danger.

The Dark Lady

Mysterious, virginal, inscrutable, aristocratic—and alluring precisely because of these characteristics—cool distance is what makes her so fascinating to Anglo males. She is circumspect and aloof, whereas her Anglo sister is direct and forthright; she is reserved, whereas the Anglo is boisterous; she is opaque, whereas the Anglo woman is transparent. The characters that Mexican actress Dolores Del Rio played in a number of Hollywood films in the 1930s and early 1940s exemplified this stereotype well. In both *Flying Down to Rio* (1933) and *In Caliente* (1935), for example, she played the fascinating Latin woman who aroused the American leading men's amorous appetites the way no Anglo woman could. By making both the Latin Lover and the Dark Lady embodiments of sexual characteristics manifestly lacking in the Anglo, Hollywood stereotyped and marginalized by idealization.

Understanding the Stereotypes

The purpose of reviewing critical stances and outlining these stereotypes is not to reduce their study and understanding to the mere recognition of one or another of the types or their combinations. Rather, it is important to concentrate on Hollywood's pattern of attributing differential traits to a group, in this case Hispanics, and the implications of such attributions.

As Clint Wilson and Felix Gutierrez (1985) have noted, minorities are typically represented as irrational, prone to violence, lacking in intellectual sophistication, oversexed, morally lax, and dirty. Why does stereotyping continue decade after decade, and in what ways are the stereotypes masked? The object of the game is not simply spotting stereotypes, but analyzing the system that endorses them. Once minority representations are seen and understood for what they are, the invisible architecture of the dominant-dominated "arrangement" comes to light, presenting a chance for a structural "rearrangement." The very persistence of such imagery is revelatory of deep-seated problems within the system.

Countering the Stereotypes: A Problematic Stage

The last ten years or so have witnessed a gradual change in the images of Hispanics in U.S. films, stemming both from Hispanic filmmakers working within the industry and from a demonstrable market for films treating Hispanic themes. Hollywood and Chicano film first came together in an uneasy alliance when Universal Studios backed the production of Luis Valdez's successful stage play *Zoot Suit*. The film enjoyed a limited success, but established a Hollywood precedent upon which Valdez and other Hispanic filmmakers would build.

Beyond its merits as a film—which are not inconsiderable—*Zoot Suit* set the stage for a new era in the history of Hispanic images in Hollywood cinema. The explosion of films with Hispanic themes marked an important watershed, because never before had Hollywood seen so many Hispanics in key creative, decision-making positions. With Valdez's *La Bamba* (1987), Cheech Marin's *Born in East L.A.* (1987), Ramon Menendez's *Stand and Deliver* (1988), and Robert Redford and Moctesuma Esparza's *The Milagro Beanfield War* (1988), Hispanics were for the first time having a say in the creation of their images. The next question is a hard one: Do these films manage to break with dominant Hollywood stereotypes of Hispanics or do they perpetuate them?

An inspirational, "go for it" film such as *Stand and Deliver* seems to be a clear-cut case of stereotype breaking and culture affirmation. And, although far from a perfect film, so does *The Milagro Beanfield War*. If nothing else, it deserves praise for giving the Chicano characters self-actualization and a richly varied social-cultural context. As a matter of fact, *Beanfield* ends up stereotyping Anglos through its portrayals of the greedy land developer, his blonde floozy, and the villainous enforcer. Much more troublesome are films such as *Born in East L.A.*, which could easily be perceived as placing the Male Buffoon in the foreground against the backdrop of an insensitively depicted Mexico.

Distorted Images

One of the most disturbing turns Hispanic cinematic imagery has taken is its degeneration into an unrecognizable, nonhuman form. Consider how the "Aliens" in recent science fiction films are a representation of real-life aliens, and the ethnic Other is disguised as an extraterrestrial. The strain felt in American society by the influx of foreign peoples to our shores, and the new immigration law result in the cinematic representation of Aliens in a host of films from *Close Encounters* (1976) and *Aliens* (1986) to *The Terminator* (1984) and many others. If the Aliens stand as representations of actual aliens, then these films are examples of a sort of neonativism at work, because, by and large, the Aliens are either destroyed or sent back where they came. And, because Hispanics make up the majority of all aliens, naturalized and undocumented, by extension, this new screen image is worrisome indeed. The implications of this sort of symbolic distortion are extremely disturbing.

Conclusion: Effects of the Stereotypes

One of the saddest aspects of stereotyping is that out-group members may begin to believe and accept the stereotype. As a stereotype may serve in-group members by reinforcing the belief of their "natural" superiority over the typed out-group, it is thought also to work on out-group members, causing them to view themselves as they are portrayed by the in-group. Imagine what Hispanic viewers—both inside and outside the U.S. (or for that matter people of color elsewhere in the world)—think when they watch *Raiders of the Lost Ark* and see in the film's opening ten minutes the dashing Anglo hero betrayed four different times by Hispanic underlings. Couldn't this be insidious reaffirmation of a true power structure and an existing social order?

Chapter 30

IIIIIIIIIIIIIIIIIIIIIIIIIIIIIIIIIIIIIIIIIIIIIIIIIIIIIIIIIIIIIIIIIIIIIIIIIIIIIIIIIIIIIIII

Imaging Mexican Americans
Rationalizing Oppression

Joe R. Feagin

In the process of super-exploiting workers of color, most employers and their managerial associates have sought to justify this exploitation. Perhaps for religious reasons, it has not been considered adequate just to exploit a group—some reason must be offered. For example, the taking of Mexican lands and, later, the super-exploitation of Mexican-American labor have been rationalized in terms of the pre-existing white-racist ideology. Most whites initially considered Mexicans and Mexican Americans to be much closer to the inferior (black) end of the dominant racial hierarchy than to the white end. Most white colonizers who came into northern Mexico in the early nineteenth century brought the United States system of racist practices and ideas, and applied them to those they encountered in Mexico. The new whites called Mexicans racist epithets and treated them like black Americans or Native Americans. One of the principal leaders of United States immigrants in northern Mexico in this early period, Stephen F. Austin, viewed Mexicans as a "mongrel Spanish-Indian and negro [*sic*] race." Recall too Senator Calhoun's view, articulated in the 1840s, that the United States had never incorporated "any but the Caucasian race" and that there is "no instance whatever of any civilized colored race . . . being found equal to the establishment and maintenance of free government."

Around the turn of the century, especially during the World War I period, employers recruited ever more Mexican workers for U.S. enterprises in agricultural and urban areas. In this period, most whites still viewed Mexican Americans as occupying a social condition and status much inferior to that of native-born whites. For example, in 1897, a U.S. federal judge ruled that a Mexican-American petitioner could become a naturalized citizen, but only because of the treaty agreements made with Mexico. Indeed, the white judge argued, scientifically the Mexican-American petitioner "would probably not be classed as white." The white-racist ideology was clearly central to white thinking about Americans of color, not only African Americans, but also the new Mexican immigrants and their children.

From *White Supremacy and Mexican Americans: Rethinking the "Black-White Paradigm,"* 54 RUTGERS L. REV. 959 (2002). Originally published in the *Rutgers Law Review*. Reprinted by permission.

Recent Rationalizations: The Cases of Powerful and Ordinary Whites

We can now turn to recent decades. As recently as the 1960s, blatantly racist stereotyping of Mexicans and Mexican Americans could be heard in the comments of powerful white Americans. Thus, George Murphy, a former California senator, once asserted that Mexican workers were "ideal for 'stoop' labor—after all, they are built close to the ground."[1] About the same time, in 1965, a leading U.S. historian, Walter Prescott Webb, wrote that "there is a cruel streak in the Mexican nature. . . . [I]t may and doubtless should be attributed partly to the Indian blood."[2] It has only been since the 1960s that most whites, including business and political leaders, have ceased publicly describing Mexicans and Mexican Americans as mixed-race "mongrels" or inferiors with dangerous Indian and African "blood," views still found in white supremacist groups.

Nonetheless, in the last few years, influential whites have still openly asserted other racist views of this group. Thus, at one 1990s community meeting dealing with Mexican immigration, a California state senator spoke against providing the children of undocumented immigrants with public education. As he put it, "It seems rather strange that we go out of our way to take care of the rights of these individuals who are perhaps on the *lower scale of our humanity*. . . ."[3] Also recently, another state legislator in California circulated to fellow legislators a racist poem, which he thought was humorous. This "Ode to the New California" derided Mexican immigrants with mocking lines such as, "I come for visit, get treated regal, So I stay, who care illegal. . . . We think America damn good place, Too damn good for white man's race."[4] Latino legislators took issue with the white legislator's words, but he would offer no apology.

In addition, surveys of white Americans also show much stereotyping. Thus, one recent survey gave white college students a list of three dozen personal and social characteristics. Comparing whites and Hispanics, these students indicated that in their view, Hispanics were more likely than Anglo whites to be violent, dirty, and criminally inclined. Hispanics were also seen as placing less value on education, mature love, and economic prosperity than whites. Old Mexican stereotypes remain very much alive.

Racial Discrimination: The Continuing Oppression

From the end of the Mexican-American war in the 1840s to the present day, Mexican Americans and other Latinos have faced both legal discrimination and the informal *de facto* variety. Until the 1960s, in U.S. towns and cities, especially in the Southwest, Mexican Americans faced blatant or informal discrimination in employment, housing, and schools. The segregation and informal discrimination were often patterned on that developed by whites for black Americans. Moreover, present-day reactions to Mexican immigrants and their descendants are substantially built on this past history of racial oppression.

As we have seen, from the beginning of large-scale immigration in the early twentieth century, white Americans have been divided in their orientations and actions directed at Mexican immigrants. On the one hand, from the early 1900s to the early 2000s, U.S. employers needing low-wage labor have aggressively sought Mexican workers, and have periodically lobbied Congress for special programs to allow in more such workers or to legalize the undocumented workers who are already here. In addition, many middle-class Americans, especially white Americans, have eagerly sought out Mexican and other Latin American workers to do service work in their homes and also to provide them with other low-cost services. Even as they discriminate against these workers (for example, by providing sub-par wages), white employers and many in the middle class will defend this Mexican immigration and its importance to the nation.

Yet, on the other hand, leading white analysts such as Peter Brimelow and Samuel Huntington seek to keep these same workers out of the nation, contending that the "browning of America" will remove or de-center white domination.

The influential Harvard professor Samuel Huntington has argued that, if multiculturalism ever becomes central in the United States, the nation could "join the Soviet Union on the ash heap of history." According to Huntington, in the past, nativist worries about immigrants assimilating were unwarranted. Today, however, the situation is one where some immigrant

> [g]roups feel discriminated against if they are not allowed to remain apart from the mainstream. The ideologies of multiculturalism and diversity reinforce and legitimate these trends. They deny the existence of a common culture in the United States, denounce assimilation, and promote the primacy of racial, ethnic, and other subnational cultural identities and groupings. They also question a central element in the American Creed by substituting for the rights of individuals the rights of groups, defined largely in terms of race, ethnicity, gender, and sexual preference.[5]

Huntington makes clear in his analysis that he is explicitly concerned that today the immigrants come "overwhelmingly from Latin America and Asia." However, he does not deal with the substantial discrimination and segregation that these Latin American and Asian immigrants receive at the hands of white Americans—actions that doubtlessly reduce the possibility of integration and assimilation.

Influential commentators like business magazine editors and leading Ivy League professors play an important role in creating and circulating negative images of recent immigrants. The immigrants of greatest concern are usually those from Latin America. Moreover, conservative members of the nation's elite are not alone in creating images of threatening aliens who cannot, or do not want to, assimilate to the Anglo-Protestant mainstream. Even a liberal academic like the prominent historian Arthur Schlesinger, Jr., has expressed fears that the United States cannot continue to permit substantial immigration if the new immigrants do not fully assimilate to "the language, the institutions, and the political ideals that hold the nation together."[6] He too has in mind non-European immigrants from Latin America and Asia—those he fears are less oriented to Anglo-American ideas and institutions than those from Europe.

Those non-Latinos who edit and report in major newspapers and magazines play a primary role in communicating negative images of immigrants. For example, one recent study examined many articles in a major West Coast newspaper and discovered numerous reports on Latin American immigrants that used racialized language and metaphors. In these articles, reporters often used metaphors portraying Mexican and other Latin American immigrants as animals, invaders, and disreputable persons. The articles describe the need to "ferret out illegal immigrants," of government programs being "a lure to immigrants," of the appetite for "the red meat of deportation," and of government agents catching "a third of their quarry." Other terms and metaphors portrayed these immigrants as a danger, a burden, dirt, disease, invasion, or waves flooding the nation.

Significantly, the media figures who craft such images of an alien people flooding and threatening the nation are not members of the working class. They are for the most part middle- and upper-middle-class white Americans. Working-class and lower-middle-class whites often absorb, or extend, such negative metaphors of the immigrants coming into the country. Thus, on numerous Internet websites, as well as in videos and books, white supremacists describe Mexican and other Latino immigrants as a "cultural cancer" or a "wildfire." They too are sometimes concerned that Mexicans have a plan to reconquer the United States.

The role of middle- and upper middle-class whites in circulating negative images of Mexican immigrants, other Mexican Americans, and other Latinos can be seen in the commonplace mocking of Spanish and Latino cultures. One research study by leading anthropologist Jane Hill examined the common caricaturing and mocking of the Spanish language across the nation—including made-up terms such as "hasta la vista, baby" and "no problemo," and phrases such as "numero uno" and "no way, José." While this mocking may seem innocuous to some white observers, it reveals "a highly negative image of the Spanish language, its speakers, and the culture and institutions associated with them." Complex caricaturing of Spanish and Spanish speakers is commonplace in board rooms, at country-club gatherings, in gift shops, and in the mass media, where once again, the purveyors are typically middle- and upper-class whites. Moreover, advertising signs and cards in gift shops and similar stores sometimes contain jokes about "cucarachas," the Spanish word for cockroaches and an epithet sometimes used by whites to describe Mexicans.

Degrading images are also found in places where they have more subtle effects. For example, in a recent movie, *Men in Black*, a United States government organization is trying to keep "aliens" from going to other planets. In the movie, the most threatening aliens are cockroaches, who are successfully exterminated by the movie's heroes. Since the movie begins with images of Mexican immigrants, this scenario likely reinforces in moviegoers' minds the association of cockroaches with "alien immigrants."

With the large increase in Latin American immigrants and the Latino population in recent decades—an era where blatantly racist comments are considered impolite by most people in public settings—has come a more subtle way of stereotyping and deriding these new Americans. Such linguistic and cultural mocking often generates or perpetuates degrading stereotypes and images of Latinos.

NOTES

1. See Guillermo V. Flores, *Race and Culture in the Internal Colony: Keeping the Chicano in His Place*, in STRUCTURES OF DEPENDENCY 201 (Frank Bonilla and Robert Girling eds., 1973).

2. See George A. Martinez, *Mexican Americans and Whiteness*, in THE LATINO/A CONDITION: A CRITICAL READER 178 (Richard Delgado & Jean Stefancic eds., 1998).

3. Otto Santa Ana, *Like an Animal I Was Treated: Anti-Immigrant Metaphor in U.S. Public Discourse*, 10 DISCOURSE & SOCIETY 191, 220 n.10 (1999) (emphasis added).

4. Donald Macedo, *Foreword* to Enrique T. Trueba, LATINOS UNIDOS: FROM CULTURAL DIVERSITY TO THE POLITICS OF SOLIDARITY, xviii–xix (1999).

5. Samuel P. Huntington, *The Erosion of American National Interests*, FOREIGN AFFAIRS, Sept./Oct. 1997, at 33–34.

6. Arthur Schlesinger, THE DISUNITING OF AMERICA: REFLECTIONS ON A MULTICULTURAL SOCIETY 121 (1991).

|||||||||||||||||||||||||||||||||||||||||||||||||||||||||||||||||||||||||||||||||

Chapter 31

From El Bandido to Gang Member

Mary Romero

Taco Bell's use of "dinky," the heavily accented Chihuahua imitating the popular pose of Che Guevara, is an updated version of the Latino male as a revolutionary bandit. Unlike the Frito Bandido used to advertise Frito corn chips in a former time, corporations no longer construct racist caricatures by dressing the human body of the "other" but rather rely on their audience's understanding the symbols. The power of the Latino and African American criminal narrative is so dominant in American society that it can arrive through images not embodied by Latinos or African Americans. In the same way that we were able to read the racialized text presented in the "California Raisins" commercial, Taco Bell is able to rely upon the Latino criminal trope without using the Latino physical bodily image. The Chihuahua stands in for the Mexican, the beret replaces the sombrero, and the cigar replaces the weapon. The trope works because after decades of presenting specific stereotypes on the silver screen, the popular racist narrative is easily called forth without calling the image a "bandido."

Taco Bell does not have to mention a hot-blooded, violent-tempered, treacherous, knife-wielding gang banger, or drug-selling *vato*. While based on images of the Mexican struggle for social change and equality, the narrative is constructed by reducing history to individual characters that become a generic revolutionary social bandit. American culture has reduced the Mexican-American War and the history of resistance and struggle against dispossession and oppression to the image of a violent, barbarous, and ferocious Latino bandido. Film portrayal of Latino males is rife with images of gangs, prisoners, drug dealers, wife abusers and other violent characters. Even contemporary writers trying to gain from the interest in the Latinization of American culture have exploited the racist bandido icon to sell books.

The lasting image of the bandido strongly points to the success of American popular culture in wiping collective memory of the history of conquest and the extensive use of armed force to subordinate Mexicans and Mexican Americans in the Southwest. Reference to the southwestern U.S. as "Occupied America" captures the essence of the history from which the Latino criminal stereotype originated. Latino entrance into the U.S. legal and judicial system began as conquered subjects of the violent

From *State Violence and the Social and Legal Construction of Latin Criminality: From El Bandido to Gang Member,* 78 Denv. U. L. Rev. 1081 (2001). Originally published in the *Denver University Law Review.* Reprinted by permission.

Mexican-American War. Fueled by the white supremacy ideology of a Manifest Destiny, the U.S. carried out acts that General Winfield Scott characterized as "atrocities to make Heaven weep and every American of Christian morals blush for his country. Murder, robbery and rape of mothers and daughters in the presence of tied-up males of the families have been common all along the Rio Grande." In regions that did not experience a massive demographic change, such as the California Gold Rush, economic circumstances or control through economic and political means, a reign of terror followed the war and the signing of the Treaty of Guadalupe Hidalgo.

As an occupying force, the U.S. government had to be ready for possible uprisings; however, the primary interest of state repression was the dispossession of land and other resources. The history of conquest in the Southwest, and the extensive use of armed forces to subordinate Mexicans and Mexican Americans subliminally grafted the group in the American psyche as "foreign," even though the land had once belonged to Mexico. While economic and political repression were extremely successful in dispossession and subordination of Mexicans living in occupied territory, state sanctioned violence, which in the early 1900s took the form of lynching, has never entirely been replaced. Resistance against the state violence carried out by the police, military, Border Patrol, and the Arizona and Texas Rangers has included insurgent movements, riots, and other forms of armed protest. The armed resistance against the privatization of communal salt beds by Mexicans and Mexican Americans became known as the El Paso Salt War.

In *Las Gorras Blancas*, an insurgent movement against the privatization and fencing of communal lands in New Mexico united poor white farmers and Native Americans against Anglo carpetbaggers and the *Hispano rico*. The list of social rebels that emerged after the Mexican-American War is long and includes Tiburcio Vásquez, Juan Cortina, Joaquín Murietta, Juan Flores, Francisco "Chico" Barela, Juan and Pablo Herrera, and Gregorio Cortez. The Mexican-American War, the Treaty of Guadalupe Hidalgo, Las Gorras Blancas, El Paso Salt War, Zoot Suit Riots, and struggles up to the 1960s high school walkouts all get depoliticized, and the mythology of the Latino banditry masks protests and resistance to social and economic injustices. Che Guevara becomes one more image of "El Bandido." The media, politicians, and law enforcement frequently used aspects of the bandido stereotype to frame demonstrations, protests, and other political activity during the Chicano Movement. Civil rights leaders and labor activists were frequently characterized as criminal and violent, and state violence was sanctioned by the press and local officials. Civil rights activities carried out by Corky Gonzales and the Crusade for Justice, Reies Lopez Tijerina and La Alianza Federal de Mercedes (The Federal Alliance of Land Grants), and the union organizing activities by César Chavez and the United Farm Workers were frequently construed as Mexican and Chicano criminality.

Since WWII, Latino youth have been constructed as inherently criminal. Although most of the time the construction of youth as criminal has fallen under the gang rubric, political activity in the late 60s and 70s was also treated as criminal activity. The specific focus on Mexican and Mexican-American youth as embodying the bandido violent and treacherous character is well documented in the 1943 Zoot-Suit Riots. The demonization of the youth by the press and police in Los Angeles occurred within days of the removal of the last Japanese to internment camps. Mexican crime, Mexican juvenile delinquency, and Mexican gangs became the new scapegoat group. National and international attention on the targeting of Latino youth in Los Angeles occurred during the trial known as the Case of Sleepy Lagoon and from the work of the Sleepy Lagoon Defense Committee who continued two years after the trial to gain the freedom of the youth convicted. Latinos in the U.S. military stationed throughout the world serving their country in the war effort donated money. In response to political pressure, the press replaced the reference to Mexican and replaced it with "Zoot-Suit" and "Pachuco." However, authorities (military and police) continued to treat Mexican youth as inherently criminal. [See chapter 45 for additional treatment of this period.—Eds.]

The most widely distributed representation of Latino youth today is as a gang member. Although the existence of gangs can be traced back to the Middle Ages in Europe and found throughout the world, the War on Gangs launched over the last few decades by U.S. local police departments has targeted Black and Latino youth. While these authorities exhibit little consistency in defining gangs and gang members, the public's acceptance of racialized versions has resulted in an over identification of gangs in low-income communities of color and has rejuvenated the bandido image. The link between immigration, poverty and urban life that social scientists highlight in theorizing about gangs appears in the popular racialized definitions acted upon by the media and public officials. In the case of Latino youth, primary importance is placed on Chicano culture.

Next to the image of gangs, Latino criminality appears in the American psyche as the "illegal alien" and has become analogous to the "immigration problem." Criminalization of Mexican immigrants stigmatizes the Latino community in the U.S. and reinforces the bandito stereotype.

Chapter 32

|||||||||||||||||||||||||||||||||||||||||||||||||||||||||||||||||||||||||||

The Triple Taboo

Richard Delgado

Ramon, Susie, and a Moonlit Night

"And so imagine the scene," Rodrigo began. "As in plantation society, you would have an Anglo family living in the big house. The Mexican crew would work in the fields and spend the nights in temporary shacks somewhere nearby. But these would be free people. Most of them would be male, many of them young. Some would be transient and would move with the crops. Others would settle down in semi-permanent quarters on the farm or a nearby town."

"I think I know what you are going to say. Society needed a taboo to keep everybody apart?"

"It did. Imagine that it's a moonlit night. Susie, the daughter of the farm family, is out for an after-dinner walk in the orchard. She comes across a seventeen-year-old fieldhand named Ramon. Bronzed from the sun and strong from outdoor work, Ramon is also a bright lad. Neither slave nor peon, merely exploited and underpaid, he has dreams and ambitions. He speaks English. He can sing and play the guitar. He knows how to fix things and how to make plants grow."

"And so Susie and he strike up a friendship?"

"Yes. And that's what the mother and father most fear—Susie running away with a Mexican farmhand. They are both good looking and about the same age. They have a lot in common. Both are repressed. Susie hates the farm. Ramon hungers for something better. They form a bond."

"And this is where the taboo comes in?"

"Yes. Multiply that situation by a thousand. You have early Anglos and their families working in close proximity to young, strapping Mexicans. This could easily lead to intimacy of two types: not only the romantic kind between the young daughters of the ruling family and the male farm workers, but also camaraderie between the Anglo supervisors and the Mexican farmhands. They are all about the same age. They have the same objectives—a healthy crop. They both understand and love nature and plants. Yet farm labor requires intense exploitation: Stoop labor. The short hoe. Broiling sun. Long hours. Low pay."

From *Rodrigo's Corrido: Race, Postcolonial Theory, and U.S. Civil Rights,* 60 Vand. L. Rev. 1691 (2007). Originally published in the *Vanderbilt Law Review.* Reprinted by permission.

"And so Anglo society coins a taboo," I said. "I can imagine what's in it. It would have to be pretty disparaging."

"And it is. The taboo, as I mentioned, is triple. Its main components are three—dirt, sexuality, and jabber—attachment to a mysterious and unfathomable language. There are a few other components, but those are the main ones."

"I'd like to hear about all three," I said. "I gather you think they work together?"

How the Taboos Function

"They do. Each of them—filth, hypersexuality, and jabber—separates dominant society from the Latino. And once in place, this separation would happen naturally. An Anglo wouldn't have to think about it every time. And the Anglos could apply the taboo to groups, like Dominicans, that were not from Mexico. They didn't have to differentiate."

"I see what you mean," I said. "An overseer at a farm or ranch ordinarily might position himself about five or ten feet away from a worker. He's safe. Although the worker is potentially filthy, contagion and smell wouldn't travel that far. Still, the overseer wouldn't get any closer—close enough, for example, for the two to shake hands after completing a stage of the work.

"And young Susie," I continued, "who knows in the back of her mind that Ramon is a potential sex maniac, might engage in repressed conversation with him on a moonlit night, but would make sure she has a ready escape route in case he gets too amorous. But what about jabber?"

"Jabber operates at a different level," Rodrigo replied. "Local authorities, including school boards, needed to do something with all those Mexican kids too young to work in the fields. The belief that they are a backward, superstitious people who will hang onto their culture and language justifies treating them that way in a host of settings. In school, for example, California authorities until fairly recently rationalized separate classrooms and schools for little Mexican kids on the ground that they needed special training because of their language deficiencies. And at worksites, it rationalized a kind of language-based hierarchy. Expert Latino fruit pickers, for example, could serve as low-level middlemen and foremen, but never as crew chiefs. They could occupy minor supervisory roles because their knowledge of Spanish enabled them to give orders and discuss problems with the other workers. But their supposed inability to speak English—actually many spoke it quite well—excluded them from consideration as crew chiefs because the chiefs needed, from time to time, to converse with the outside world—with officials such as the county agricultural agent or the clerk at a local fertilizer store."

"It seems to me that it also justifies suspicion," I added. "If a group is constantly jabbering away in a foreign language, it might be planning some form of resistance, maybe a strike for higher wages."

"Right. The planters were already uneasy about the exploitive conditions they imposed on their workers. Just as slaveowners in the South slept uneasily because they feared a slave rebellion, white landowners in the Southwest also feared the Mexican farmhands who might covet something better. Their speaking to each other in a foreign language fed this fear and justified harsh laws excluding farm workers from unionization or coverage for workplace injuries. Later, it justified English-only laws and workplace rules that operated harshly against all Spanish speakers, not just Mexicans or Puerto Ricans."

Rodrigo Shows That the Taboos Persist and Are in Full Force Today

"That all has the ring of truth," I said. "Taboos like the ones you mentioned would enable Anglo overlords to assure that their supervisors, daughters, and friends kept their distance from the fieldhands. They would permit oppressive labor conditions to continue indefinitely. But what evidence do you have that these taboos remain in force today? Maybe those taboos are just historical curiosities."

"I don't think so. I've been gathering mountains of evidence. I've dug up a lot from popular sources—stories, plays, movies, and other narratives circulating in the dominant society. But also from corridos, actos, skits, cantares, laments, and other tales of the Mexican people, which showed their perception of how the Anglos thought of, and acted toward, them."

"A little bit like the slave narratives," I pointed out.

"Precisely. Both bodies of literature, the slave narratives for blacks and the corridos for Latinos, performed much the same function. Each recorded what the colonized people thought of their condition, of their work life, their hopes and dreams, and especially what they thought of their masters and their masters of them. As I mentioned, the Latino taboo consists of filth, hypersexuality, jabber, and a few others. Its purpose is to make sure that Anglos don't get too close. Close enough to supervise and give orders, but not enough to feel real kinship, real camaraderie, as might happen if Anglos and Mexicans worked side by side, at some hard job."

"Or in little Susie's case, close enough that she might feel sexual attraction toward seventeen-year-old Ramon with his deep tan, strong body, and interesting dreams," I added.

"Exactly. And, in the case of jabber, the taboo justifies suspicion and close supervision."

"It occurs to me that your taboo theory taps into a powerful social science insight that I teach every year, namely the social contact hypothesis."

"I teach that, too."

"So we each know that many social scientists hold that the best way to counteract prejudice is to arrange for people of different types and skin colors to work together in pursuit of common goals. Sports or the military are good examples. Or going to grade school with kids of other races."

"Right," Rodrigo said. "The hypothesis, which formed the basis for institutional desegregation beginning in the sixties, holds that racism is a kind of mistake or cognitive error. The racist individual internalizes the notion that persons of a different race, say blacks, are unlike his group, say whites. They are untrustworthy, stupid, sexually lascivious, lazy, and criminal. They want to spend all day listening to loud music and hanging out with their friends on street corners, hassling white passersby, and so on."

"And so, by placing young people of different races together on a sports team or in a third grade classroom, they learn that people of different ethnicities are much like them—some good, some bad. Some like loud music, others hate it."

"And that's how the taboo acquires its diabolical efficacy," I said. "Someone who fears a member of another race or thinks they will smell bad or will want to have sex with you without your consent will not get close enough to have the easygoing conversations that the social contact hypothesis requires. Relationships will remain formal and impersonal. They will enable the pre-existing hierarchy, white over brown, to remain intact forever, with little strain or pressure."

"I have lots of data on the three components, if you are interested."

"I certainly am. Why don't you start?"

Filth

"Have you heard the phrase, 'dirty Mexican'?" Rodrigo began.

I made a face. "Of course. Everyone has. It's the most common, and unfair, of the stereotypes. You hear it everywhere, almost as an epithet."

"It is unfair," Rodrigo said. "But a thousand plots, stories, and cultural references drive it home. It's also untrue. But you see it everywhere. Steven Bender's book says it—and its close relative, the 'greaser'—is one of the most common of the Latino stereotypes. Even relatively modern movies and stories reinforce it. Historians say they find it in practically every era. Mexicans particularly are invested with this awful image, which includes at least the following ingredients: filthy, unshaven, never bathes, lacking in personal hygiene, and likely to give you a communicable disease. A number of legal opinions actually deemed Mexicans a nuisance. They proceeded under that theory, as though the very presence of a handful of brown-faced people was certain to bring noise, disorder, and stench to a neighborhood."

"I read somewhere that early school authorities would separate Latino and Anglo children for this reason," I said. "In addition to rationalizing that separate education would benefit the Latino kids because of their linguistic difficulties, authorities would separate them in school because the Anglo parents would insist on it for hygienic reasons. Parents thought their kids would catch diseases or contract cooties or fleas."

"And of course the Mexican kids would, in fact, come to school in raggedy clothes, because a farm worker's wages would hardly allow the family to shop at Abercrombie and Fitch during a back-to-school sale."

I recalled how Rodrigo had dressed sharply ever since I had known him. It must have galled him to think of generations of promising young Latino children growing up with a double handicap—unable to dress as stylishly as their Anglo counterparts, and, as a result, thought of as culturally or innately inferior, dirty, and prone to wallow in disease and filth.

Rodrigo continued: "A handbook, entitled 'Your Maid from Mexico' provides guidance for wealthy Anglo families wishing to hire a Mexican maid. But it also provides rules for maids. Two-thirds of them have to do with being clean—using a toothbrush and deodorant, for example. And not touching the guests at a dinner party.

"And in today's anti-immigrant climate, you see evidence of the same thing. Immigration opponents cite, without any statistics whatsoever, the drain on emergency rooms, medical clinics, and other resources in regions with high rates of undocumented Latino immigration. This taps into the belief that Latinos are always getting sick and are prone to suffer diseases, accidents, and injuries. In fact, they are easily the country's youngest and healthiest racial groups and visit doctors and emergency wards in lower proportions than anybody else. First we invest them with an unfair stigma, then we use it against them."

"A double bind," I commiserated. "And the heart-wrenching thing about it is that the stereotype comes about, in part, because of unfair and unsanitary living conditions that society imposes on the immigrants. If your migrant labor camp does not have running water or indoor toilets, as many do not, you will relieve yourself in the fields, behind a tree somewhere. If your camp lacks showers or hot water, you will not look, or maybe be, as clean as some Anglo family living in a suburban house with three bathrooms, each with a hot shower. If your mother has to wash your clothes in a river, they may not look as nice as the clothes of a schoolchild whose mother has a washer and dryer right in the kitchen."

"The taboo creates its own conditions of reinforcement, so that in time it comes to seem true, the way things are," Rodrigo concluded. "After a while, you see virtually every nativist writer—Pat Buchanan, Peter Skerry, Victor Davis Hanson, Peter Brimelow, and Samuel Huntington—casually referring to the same things, as though they were well known truths. The environmental justice movement points out that sewage treatment plants and toxic dump sites are disproportionately found in minority neighborhoods—and nobody bats an eye. But are we ready to move on to the next component?"

"I am," I answered. "I gather that it's sexuality."

"It is. It and filth work together. I'm sure, Professor, that you've known white people who are uncomfortable around blacks. They don't like to sit next to them on buses . . ."

"I see this all the time," I said. "You can get on a bus or train. The only vacant seat is next to a well-dressed, middle-aged black commuter. There can even be a few people standing. None of them wants to take that seat."

"I've seen the same thing. One time, I had just got back to the States after all those years in Italy. I was riding a bus around Manhattan and noticed an empty seat. When I pointed it out to an elderly rider, he shook his head and said he was getting off soon. The seat was next to a black executive, I gathered from his well-tailored suit."

"And did the rider get off at the next stop?"

"No. I don't think he got off at all, and I rode the bus for several miles. I ended up taking the seat myself."

Rodrigo continued: "And I'm sure you know a certain type of person, usually from the South, who won't shake the hand of a black person or will do so only reluctantly."

"I have a colleague like that," I said. "He'll take my hand for just a quick, perfunctory squeeze, then pull his own away like a scalded cat. I don't know whether he does this for everybody or just me. I thought maybe he has a germ phobia."

"More likely, it's a man-of-color phobia." Rodrigo grimaced slightly. "Do you know about the writing of Joel Kovel?"

"I do. He's a famous contemporary social scientist who coined a psychodynamic theory of race. It's quite original and not at all flattering, especially to whites. He holds that many white people have embedded, deep in their psyches, devastating associations with blackness and black skin."

"Indeed. It's of course impossible to prove or disprove a psychoanalytically based theory. But Kovel's theory does seem to work, at least on an explanatory level. He says some white folks equate black and brown skin with dirt and feces. They shy away from it, unconsciously, and are never comfortable with one of us. They can't see us as persons, just as symbols of something they have been taught since childhood not to play with. We're taboo. Don't go there."

"And you were saying that a similar dynamic operates in the case of Mexican sexuality?"

Hypersexuality

"Yes," Rodrigo replied. "Bender catalogs this stereotype as well. He finds several versions of it: the sex-maniac Latino male lusting after white women, the ultimate prize; and the softer-edged soulful Latino lover, romantic and ready to break into song and serenade the Anglo princess on his guitar or take her dancing in the moonlight. For their part, Latina women are the lustful objects of Anglo men's desires."

"Neither type is one you would want to take seriously, or take on as a partner in business. You certainly wouldn't want the men romancing your daughter."

"And so, like the dirty stereotype, it operates to put a distance between Anglos and Latinos, particularly Mexican men, such as the ones you would find around a migrant labor camp or community."

"Or find in town on an errand. Or in grade school," I added. "I gather that's your point."

"It is. And a steady stream of movie plots, stories, TV comedies, and other tales build on the hypersexual Latino or Latina. They both prove the existence of the underlying taboo and reinforce it constantly, so that it doesn't weaken over time. And when Anglos have things well in hand, a second image, related to the first, takes its place."

"Which one is that?"

"Oh, it's the hapless, huddled figure who could not possibly be a sexual competitor. John-Michael Rivera writes that Anglos wanted Mexicans deferential, so they discouraged them from looking you in the eye. They taught them to walk in a shuffling gait and to wear loose clothes that allow no sharp definition of the body line. The sombrero, unlike the Texan ten gallon hat, sat low on the head, limiting the user's horizon, particularly his view up."

"Telling." I shook my head. "And these sexual taboos, do you see evidence of them operating today, as you did for filth?"

"Everywhere. Writings by nativist writers such as the ones we mentioned earlier all call attention to the fast-breeding Latino immigrant. They warn of the swamping of superior Anglo genes by those of the swarthy Latinos and blacks."

"Are you ready for your third component?" I asked. "It had to do with language, did it not?"

Jabber

"Yes, it's jabber," Rodrigo replied. "This one holds that the Latinos operate in a different discourse world from ours. Their very language reinforces their exoticism. It sounds funny, with all those trills and rollings of the tongue. Good old-fashioned Americans cannot, of course, speak it, and it's unreasonable to suppose that we should learn it, as opposed to requiring the Mexicans to stop speaking it and use only English. But not only that, their weird language provides a cover for them to make jokes at our expense and leer at our women."

"Although Spanish is a world language with a literature that includes Cervantes, Lope de Vega, and other writers who rival Shakespeare and Byron," I said, "narratives and stereotypes put the Spanish speaker on the same plane as a group of uncivilized cannibals sitting around a boiling pot, discussing how to cook the well-meaning Western missionary. Not only that, they come so attached to their strange language that they are unwilling to learn English. They even expect us to provide ballots in Spanish so that they can vote in our elections without taking the trouble to learn our language and read campaign material written in it. Most unfair of them."

"It's not just an irony," Rodrigo said. "It takes on real historical force. For example, few civil rights scholars know that Latinos were lynched in the Southwest." [See part 11 for further discussion of this chapter in U.S. history.—Eds.]

"And that may be one reason why Anglos, intentionally or not, suppress Spanish speaking among the Latino community and don't want the kids growing up speaking that language," I added. "It makes their own history too available to them and increases the chance that they might revolt against the established order. It makes sense."

"Not just that," Rodrigo said. "Reducing the ability of the second generation of Latino immigrant kids to speak Spanish creates a divide between generations, in which the young cannot communicate with their elders. Many Latino histories, stories, legends, and tales . . ."

"Such as those in the corridos that you mentioned earlier."

"Indeed. Those and others. Many of those tales are oral and have no written record. They are in danger of being lost if generations cannot communicate with each other. This may be one reason that the second generation of Latino kids exhibits such a high dropout rate. They learn English, with the result that the majority culture with its stereotypes, TV plots with Latino villains, and other depictions that teach self-hatred, is wide open to them. A sensitive Latino child who does not speak Spanish has no defense against this vast cultural brainwash. Language represents continuity, struggle, and ultimately, self-preservation."

|||||||||||||||||||||||||||||||||||||||||||||||||||||||||||||||||||||||||||||||||||||||||||

Chapter 33

The War on Terrorism and
Its Consequences for Latinas/os

Steven W. Bender

In the days following the September 11 terrorist attacks, reports emerged of hate crimes, discrimination, and profiling directed at Arab Americans, Arabs, and Muslims in the United States. Yet, Latinas/os are not immune from these negative sentiments. Given their societal construction as violent, foreign, criminal-minded, disloyal, and as overrunning the border, Americans are beginning to similarly construct Latinas/os as a terrorist threat.

Because undocumented immigrants have now emerged as a national security threat—as would-be terrorists—the longstanding association of Latinas/os with "illegal aliens" causes some Americans to view Latinas/os with suspicion. Even if not viewed as terrorists themselves, Latina/o immigrants have been called into question for their supposed willingness to aid terrorists in anti-American plots. Consider the remarks of the head of a Utah anti-undocumented-immigrant group applauding the pre–Winter Olympics sweep of undocumented airport workers in Salt Lake City, most of them Latina/o:

> [T]his may be stereotyping, but, if you go to an illegal Mexican working at the airport, and he has access to airplanes, or he's manning a baggage check or whatever, and an Arab terrorist walks up to him and says, "I'll give you $10,000 if you plant a 9-millimeter on the airplane for me," well, here's an individual who's never stood up, held his hand over his heart and said, "I pledge allegiance to the flag and to the country for which it stands." You think that Mexican is going to head south with the 10 grand? You betcha.[1]

Fueled by television and cinema, the societal association of Latinas/os with drugs is producing a conception of Latinas/os as "narco-terrorists." In February 2002, the Office of National Drug Control Policy announced its initiative to educate Americans on the link between illicit drugs and international terrorism. Pursuant to this campaign, two commercials debuted during the 2002 Super Bowl warning drug users that they were financing terrorists. According to Congressman Mark Souder (R-IL), "Americans who buy and sell illegal narcotics are lending a helping hand to people

From *Sight, Sound, and Stereotype: The War on Terrorism and Its Consequences for Latinas/os,* 81 Or. L. Rev. 1153 (2002). Originally published in the *Oregon Law Review.* Reprinted by permission.

like those who attacked America on September 11."[2] In order to justify military intervention and policing measures in the national and international war on drugs, government officials need only point to the funding of al-Qaeda terrorist campaigns with
proceeds from heroin produced in Afghanistan, a world leader in opium production.

Latinas/os in Texas remember the tragic consequence of militarizing enforcement
against drugs, especially when it includes placing military troops along the U.S.–
Mexico border. In May, 1997, a camouflaged squad of U.S. Marines patrolling near
the Rio Grande on an anti-drug assignment shot and killed teenager Ezequiel Hernandez who was tending goats on horseback as part of a church project. Ezequiel,
who hoped to become a park ranger, carried an old pump-action .22 rifle to fend off
rattlesnakes and predators. Although the Marines claimed that Ezequiel fired at them
and they acted in self-defense, Ezequiel was shot in the side, an angle inconsistent
with this account. More chilling still, while the Marines waited twenty-two minutes
before rendering first aid or calling for emergency help, young Ezequiel bled to death.
As a consequence of the shooting, then Defense Secretary William Cohen ordered
the disarmament of all federal troops engaged in anti-drug missions at the border.
Though it may be forgotten in the haste to fight terrorism, Ezequiel's death provides
evidence of the folly of militarizing the Mexican border.

In addition to their societal association with drug trafficking, Mexican Americans have been linked to terrorism by at least two other avenues—a revisioning of
their longstanding bandido construction, and their supposed affinity with the image
of suicide bombers that has come to define America's view of Palestinians. Within
days after September 11, the media began to suggest the parallels between the hunt
launched in Afghanistan for Osama bin Laden and the major military mission initiated in 1916 to hunt Mexican General Francisco "Pancho" Villa in Northern Mexico.

A former ally of the United States, as was bin Laden, Villa attacked a New Mexico
town in early 1916 killing seventeen Americans while stealing horses and guns. Villa's
motivation for the raid remains unclear. Most suggest that a change in United States
policy which had previously supported Villa's endeavors in Mexico with guns and
arms led him to attack the town that had formerly supplied him with weapons. A few
even suggest that the United States government orchestrated the raid by payment to
Villa hoping to spark military enlistment and patriotism toward American involvement in World War I. Whatever the raid's motivation, President Woodrow Wilson
responded by mobilizing as many as 150,000 troops and sending battalions into
Mexico with horses, tanks, trucks, and open-cockpit planes in a failed effort to find
Villa in the hill country of Chihuahua, Mexico. Post–September 11 comparisons between Villa and bin Laden were drawn not merely for the similarities in an unfruitful
search by the American military, but also for the terrorist identity of both men. For
example, a relative of one of the dead in New Mexico suggested that while Villa was
considered a "bandit" back then, "[b]y today's terms, he was a terrorist." Emerging
from the physical, cultural, political, and economic displacement of Mexicans in the
U.S.–Mexico war and thereafter, the real-life bandidos at the time have now been recast as bin Laden–like terrorists.

In the 1970s, the Brown Berets, a paramilitary group of Chicanas and Chicanos
dressed in army fatigues and brown berets, modeled after the Black Panthers, helped

create a stereotype of Chicanas/os as violent activists. Today, some American vigilantes frustrated with the government's inability to bring bin Laden to justice have resurrected this image of the violent Chicana/o to construct Mexican Americans and other Latinas/os as a more accessible terrorist enemy on American soil. College campus MEChA organizations, comprised mostly of Chicana/o students, but also of other Latinas/os, have been targeted by hate speech that compares their organizations to al-Qaeda. Ostensibly, these vigilantes point to the supposed campaign by MEChA organizations to liberate the Southwest from the United States and return it to Mexico, as reflected in El Plan Espiritual de Aztlán from 1969, an activist Chicana/o manifesto, which provides in part:

> In the spirit of a new people that is conscious not only of the proud historical heritage but also of the brutal "gringo" invasion of our territories, we, the Chicano inhabitants and civilizers of the northern land of Aztlán from whence came our forefathers, reclaiming the land of their birth and consecrating the determination of our people of the sun, declare that the call of our blood is our power, our responsibility, and our inevitable destiny. . . .
>
> Brotherhood unites us, and love for our brothers makes us a people whose time has come and who struggles against the foreigner "gabacho" who exploits our riches and destroys our culture. . . .

A hate email sent to a West Coast campus MEChA organization quoted part of this Plan in contending that MEChA is a "terrorist organization" of "evil terrorists . . . no better than Osama Bin Laden" seeking to "destroy the country." In April 2002, a conservative talk radio show host in Portland, Oregon strove to construct Chicana/o college students as terrorist operatives. He drew a connection between the struggles of Palestinians for land and nationhood in the West Bank and the supposed Chicana/o mission to reclaim Aztlán, enabling him to transfer his characterization of all Palestinians as suicide bombers to Chicanas/os and other Latinas/os by asking the absurd question: "When will the suicide bombings start in Aztlán?"

After September 11, not only Mexican "bandidos" but also urban Latina/o "gangbangers" are being revisioned as terrorists. This threatening image has roots that extend to media and societal conceptions in 1940s Los Angeles of Mexican American youth known as "Pachucos" who were vilified in local newspapers as a foreign threat during World War II, leading to the so-called Zoot Suit Riots in which off-duty Anglo servicemen, and Anglo civilians, stormed barrio neighborhoods. The recent arrest of Puerto Rican Abdullah al Muhajir, formerly Jose Padilla, once a gang member in Chicago, has come to represent the association of Latino gang members with terrorist operatives. Padilla has been held in military prison as an "enemy combatant" while being interrogated for his role in planning a potential "dirty bomb" attack. A former FBI deputy director of counterterrorism made the leaps from Latina/o ethnicity to Latina/o gang membership to terrorism seem like baby steps in contending "[i]f you look at Padilla's background—Puerto Rican, gang member, time in prison, a convert to Islam—what you see is a potential resource for al-Qaeda."

As public sentiment after September 11 builds toward establishing even tougher immigration restrictions at the Canadian and Mexican borders, migrating workers from Mexico and Central America will face a more perilous gauntlet in their efforts to reach jobs in the United States.

NOTES

1. Kim Murphy, *Olympic Hospitality an Irony for Utah Latinos*, L.A. TIMES, Feb. 8, 2002, at A1 (quoting a statement made by Ken Thompson).

2. Press Release, Office of National Drug Control Policy, National Youth Anti-Drug Media Campaign Links Drugs and Terror (Feb. 3, 2002), available at http://www.whitehousedrugpolicy .gov/news/press02/020302.html.

Chapter 34

‖‖

Latinos, Inc.
The Marketing and Making of a People

Arlene Dávila

"Latinos are hot, and we are not the only ones to think so. Everyone wants to jump on the bandwagon, and why not? We have the greatest art, music, and literature. It's time we tell our stories." With these words, actor Antonio Banderas welcomed all to the first advertising "Up-Front" presentation by the Spanish TV network Telemundo. Summoning advertisers to "jump on the bandwagon," he echoed a promise that is repeatedly heard in corporate headquarters and at advertising conventions alike: that Latinos are the hottest new market and that those who target them will not regret it. That Latinos are hot is not at all surprising. It is becoming increasingly common to see aspects of Latino culture popularized in mainstream culture, with salsa outselling ketchup and taking over dance floors, and a growing number of corporate sponsors interested in Latinos as a target market. That a famous Spaniard like Antonio Banderas should become the spokesman of U.S. Latino culture, which is overwhelmingly Mexican, Puerto Rican, Hispanic Caribbean, and Central American, is also not surprising. Although Latino social movements in the 1960s defined themselves against anything Spanish, such distinctions have since been countered by the growing consolidation of a common Latino/Hispanic identity that encompasses anyone from a Spanish/Latin American background in the United States.

Central to this development is Hispanic marketing and advertising. Long before the current popularization of Latin culture, this industry first advanced the idea of a common "Hispanic market" by selling and promoting generalized ideas about "Hispanics" to be readily marketed by corporate America. Thirty years later, the existence and profitability of this culture-specific market feeds one of the fastest growing sectors of the marketing industry in the United States. Over eighty Hispanic advertising agencies and branches of transnational advertising conglomerates spread across cities with sizable Hispanic populations now sell consumer products by shaping and projecting images of and for Latinos.

Hispanic marketing as a self-identified arena, dominated by corporate intellectuals of Latin American background in the United States and directly tied to the structures of the U.S. economy, serves as a fruitful entry point into an analysis of the complex interests at play in the public representation of this emerging identity. The reconstitution of individuals into consumers and populations into markets are central fields of cultural production that reverberate within public understanding of people's place, and hence of their rights and entitlements, in a given society. Looking at Hispanic marketing is therefore particularly revealing of the relationship among culture, corporate sponsorship, and politics, and moreover can illuminate how commercial representations may shape people's cultural identities as well as affect notions of belonging and cultural citizenship. Latinos and other U.S. minorities have historically lacked access to public venues of self-representation; it is in the market and through marketing discourse that they are increasingly debating their social identities and public standing. These issues are consequently reduced and correlated with their "advertising worthiness and marketability," cautioning us against the facile celebration of Latinos' commercial popularity as an infallible sign of their "coming of age" and political standing.

The growth and popularization of a single ethnic category for peoples of Latin American background in the United States are a relatively new development. First generalized by federal agencies in the 1970s, a common identity for the diversity of "Latino" populations has arrived in the form of census categories, state policies, and the media, prompting questions about the political implications of this development and the ways in which people reject or embrace it. One of the most influential forces behind this identity, however, the Hispanic marketing and advertising industry, remains largely unexamined—seldom have studies looked at marketing as constitutive of U.S. Latinidad. Similarly, most studies on Latinos and the media have tended to focus on the mainstream media, such as Hollywood films and network TV, repeatedly reminding us that Latinos/Hispanics are too often excluded, and that when they are portrayed, appear as narrow and simplistic stereotypes. What research has seldom noted is marketing's influence on the public projection of U.S. Latinos and the complex processes and multiple contradictions behind the production of these representations, such as the involvement of "natives"—that is, of "Hispanics"—in their very production.

As part of their struggle for political enfranchisement since the 1960s, Latino populations have become increasingly concerned with their own representation in all types of media. In this context, the development of culturally specific marketing has been generally regarded as a viable means to correct the former stereotypical commercial portrayal of Latinos. We need only to contrast Latinos' earlier commercial representation as thieves, as in Frito Lay's controversial Frito Bandido character, or as stinky bandidos, as in the Arrid deodorant ads in the 1960s and 1970s, with contemporary Hispanic-generated ads to note their pride-worthy images of beautiful, upscale, affluent, and successful Latinos. Hispanic marketers have even gained praise from media scholars for providing corrective and valuable alternatives to Anglo-generated images, and they themselves have adopted this "politically correct" outlook by marketing themselves and their productions as more aware, informed, and sensitive than those generated by their mainstream counterparts.

However, behind such lavish portrayal of Latinos lies a complex industry that stands at the forefront of contemporary Latino cultural politics and that points to the complex dynamics affecting both their public recognition and continued invisibility in U.S. society. I suggest that this industry's political economy, history, and composition are directly implicated in the global processes and transnational bases that sustain commonplace understandings of Latinos as a "people" and a "culture." The production of Latinos as easily digestible and marketable within the larger structures of corporate America is therefore revealing of the global bases of contemporary processes of identity formation and of how notions of place, nation, and race that are at play in the United States and in Latin America come to bear on these representations.

These processes are evidenced in the discourses of authenticity engendered by this industry to defend the existence and profitability of Hispanics as an authentic and thus commercially valuable market. Primary among such discourses is the promotion of Latinos as a "nation within a nation," with a uniquely distinct culture, ethos, and language. Such ideas are fed and maintained by sources as varied as the precepts of contemporary U.S. multiculturalism, nineteenth-century ideas of Latinidad developed by Latin American nationalist ideologies, and Anglo-held beliefs about "Hispanics" evidencing the varied sources that are strategically put into service in the commercial representation of Latinidad as forever needy of culturally specific marketing. In these constructions the Spanish language emerges as the paramount basis of U.S. Latinidad, as is evident in the industry's common designation of "Hispanic marketing" and "Hispanic-driven media." Its premise and rationale for existence are not only that basic differences mark Latinos and other consumers that need to be addressed through culture- and language-specific marketing, but also that a continuous influx of Spanish-speaking populations would lie beyond reach were it not for this type of marketing. Latinos are also repackaged into images that render them pleasing to corporate clients, such as in the garb of the traditional and extremely family-oriented and stubbornly brand-loyal consumer, which I suggest responds more to mainstream society's management of ethnic others than to any intrinsic cultural attribute of the Latino consumer. Through such strategies Latinos are continually recast as authentic and marketable, but ultimately as a foreign rather than intrinsic component of U.S. society, culture, and history, suggesting that the growing visibility of Latino populations parallels an expansion of the technologies that render them exotic and invisible.

Images

> What I eat is not a clear indication of who I am. It is more important where I go than where I come from. The color of my hair says nothing of me as a person. I AM NOT A STEREOTYPE. I love my family. Have values. Like Rhythm. Have faith. But don't categorize me, don't pigeonhole me. Don't judge me for what I eat, what I wear, by my origin. Believe in me . . . and I will trust you.

So reads an ad published in *Hispanic Business*, *Latina*, and *People en Español*, among other Latina/Hispanic magazines, its final note an exhortation to *trust* Ford Motor Company. Juxtaposed with the narrative are photographs, images of woman, an attractive fortyish brunette, dressed in relaxed contemporary clothes, alongside pictures of a pizza, a hamburger, some palm trees, two teenage youths (her children, perhaps?), and three brands of Ford luxury cars, to underscore the seemingly contradictory picture of a contemporary-looking, middle-aged woman who holds dear her traditional values but nonetheless likes hamburgers and can afford a luxury car.

Clearly, stereotypes are a key concern of the Hispanic marketing industry. To sell themselves and their products, those in this industry have not only drawn from existing stereotypes—after all, the above example rests on a Hispanic female type that is traditionally at odds with luxury cars and hamburgers—but have also positioned themselves as the "politically correct" voice with which to challenge stereotypes and educate corporate clients about Hispanic language and culture. These antithetical processes of reinforcing and challenging stereotypes have gone hand in hand in this industry, where advertising staff have long had to confront, reshape, or reformulate all types of Hispanic conventions in order to maintain a legitimate ethnic niche for this market.

As a vast literature has shown, stereotypes are never intrinsically negative or positive, but are always historically created and produced in conversation with social hierarchies of daily life. They work by restricting the range of interpretations and therefore facilitating the evaluations that reproduce and valorize the social distinctions at play in the greater society. Even when individuals may interpret these images and ideas differently or imbue them with idiosyncratic meaning, these renditions are by necessity framed within dominant social conventions.

Chapter 35

||||||||||||||||||||||||||||||||||||||||||||||||||||||||||||||||||||||||||||||||||||

Repercussions of Latinos'
Colonized Mentality

Laura M. Padilla

Internalized oppression and racism are insidious forces that cause marginalized groups to unconsciously turn on themselves. Sadly, "Mexicans themselves internalize the 'Anything But Mexican' mindset. An internalized racism, popularly called a 'colonized mentality' by Chicano movement activists during the 1960s, splinters Latino and even Mexican unity."[1] To the extent that Latinos internalize negative stereotypes, they cause intra-communal harm. For example, a significant number of Latinos voted in favor of California's Proposition 187, which ended many benefits for immigrants, and Proposition 209, which ended affirmative action in government contracting and public colleges and universities, precisely because they accepted negative stereotypes about themselves. That is, they were seduced into believing that Latino immigrants take but do not give, and that they are subhuman, thus undeserving of education and medical attention. Furthermore, they must have been convinced that our society is now color-blind and measures to ameliorate past discrimination are no longer necessary. More recently, a high percentage of Latinos supported Proposition 227, which proposed to end bilingual education in California. Additionally, a mostly Latino school board in New Mexico fired two teachers for teaching Chicano history to a group of predominantly Latino high school students. These examples illustrate the manner in which Latinos' efforts harmed other Latinos, often to the delight of conservatives. This behavior results from a belief in Latino inferiority and Anglo superiority, both manifestations of internalized oppression and racism.

Internalized racism in the Latino community also reveals itself at the individual level. For example, members of my family, as well as their friends, have attempted to one-up each other about how "*guero*" [light skinned—Eds.] their children or grandchildren are. My mother's best friend once bragged about how *guera* her first granddaughter was as she pulled out a photograph of a hirsute, dark baby with thick black hair. Rather than question why her friend felt compelled to assert her granddaughter's "*guera*-ness," my mother and I instead later compared the granddaughter's "*guera*-ness" to the "*guera*/o-ness" of our own family members. We succumbed to the conditioning that white is better. Latinos also use this grading process to rank

From *Social and Legal Repercussions of Latinos' Colonized Mentality,* 53 U. MIAMI L. REV. 769 (1999). Originally published in the *University of Miami Law Review.* Reprinted by permission.

the acceptability of boyfriends, girlfriends, spouses and partners. Lighter is preferred, darker is acceptable so long as that person is Latino. To go any darker may put you at risk of family alienation.

I married a caucasian and in reflecting on why, I realize that the reasons are many, complex, and positive, and that I never consciously chose to not marry a Latino. However, it is not as clear to me whether I subconsciously chose as I did. While I spent much time with my Latino classmates, especially in connection with the Stanford Latino Law Students' Association, I did not date them. One reason, at least in law school, was that there were not many Latinos to choose from and many of them had girlfriends. Another reason was that I saw too many marriages in my family break up because of the man's infidelity. Of course I did not then assume that all Latino males were unfaithful, but it made me nervous. That nervousness increased when I became active with the La Raza Lawyers Association of San Diego. At parties and out-of-town conferences, I noticed that a significant number of men suddenly lost their wedding rings and seemed to spend much time with women who were not their wives. So I remind myself that this behavior is characteristic of many men, not just Latinos. Am I succumbing to internalized racism by believing negative stereotypes about Latino men or am I being practical? That is one of the dangers of internalized oppression; we frequently do not realize when or how we are prejudiced against ourselves.

Many Latinos inwardly, and sometimes outwardly, question the qualifications of other successful Latinos. It is heartening that this is not uniform—several Latinos I know try to provide a mutual support network. For example, we intentionally and systematically refer business to each other. Nonetheless, too often we not only neglect to provide support but actually conspire against each other. Consider a popular Mexican folk story:

> A man stumbles upon a fisherman who is gathering crabs and placing them in a bucket with no lid. When the passerby asks the fisherman whether he is concerned that the crabs might climb out of the bucket and crawl away, the fisherman replies that there is no need to worry. "You see," he says, "these are Mexican crabs. Whenever one of them tries to move up, the others pull him down."

Internalized racism is also at play when Latinos experience self-doubt upon receipt of either admission into a top university or a prestigious job offer. This impostor syndrome haunts many of us—how did I get here? Do I truly belong? The answers, respectively, are through hard work and perhaps some serendipity, and *yes*. But because of internalized racism, we doubt our qualifications and hard-earned credentials, and succumb to the often not very delicate suggestions that we do not belong.

Overcoming Internalized Oppression and Racism

Internalized oppression and racism are deeply rooted in United States history. Preceding the Mexican-American War of 1848, "Anglo-Americans perceived the Mexicans' military weakness and technology to be evidence of the inferiority of the 'half-breeds' and their inability to govern themselves."[2] Thus began the stereotyping of "Mexicans as stupid and inferior hybrids."[3]

With such a prolonged history of Latino oppression in this country, it will take a concerted effort, including group and individual change, to undo the effects and behavior associated with internalized oppression and racism. These types of changes will be extraordinarily difficult, as are changes that must combat the reconstructive paradox. In essence, the reconstructive paradox posits that the most insidious types of social evil tend to be so ingrained in our society that we barely notice them.[4] Accordingly, it takes a herculean effort to overcome the evil. Moreover, because of the scope of the effort, it is bound to be highly visible, generating resistance and ultimately, backlash. That is not to say that the Latino community should not undertake efforts to overcome internalized oppression and racism. Despite the magnitude of the task, we cannot and should not avoid the effort to overcome internalized oppression and racism.

The first and most essential step is consciousness-raising. If we do not recognize internalized oppression and racism, we cannot overcome or undo them. To recognize these destructive forces, Suzanne Lipsky suggests that we ask ourselves questions like the following:

> What has been good about being . . . [Latina/o]? What makes me proud of being . . . [Latina/o]? What has been difficult about being . . . [Latina/o]? What do I want other . . . [Latina/os] to know about me? How specifically have I been hurt by my own people? When do I remember standing up against the mistreatment of one . . . [Latina/o] by another? When do I remember being strongly supported by another . . . [Latina/o]? When do I remember acting on some feeling of internalized oppression or racism? When do I remember resisting and refusing to act on this basis?[5]

In answering these questions, we can resist others' definitions of "Latina/o" and reconstruct our identity in an affirming way. This will enhance how we see ourselves, how we see other Latinos, and how non-Latinos see Latinos.

One Latina described her feelings and those of other Chicanos as follows:

> I have internalized rage and contempt, one part of the self (the accusatory, persecutory, judgmental) using defense strategies against another part of the self (the object of contempt). As a person, I, as a people, we, Chicanos, blame ourselves, hate ourselves, terrorize ourselves. Most of this goes on unconsciously; we only know that we are hurting, we suspect that there is something "wrong" with us, something fundamentally "wrong."[6]

In light of the racist history of our country, it is not surprising that we experience this self-loathing. When Latinos feel self-contempt or contempt for other Latinos, we must stop, name the feelings and their source, and eradicate race-based contempt and self-doubt.

NOTES

1. Rodolfo F. Acuña, ANYTHING BUT MEXICAN: CHICANOS IN CONTEMPORARY LOS ANGELES 8 (1996).

2. Martha Menchaca, *Chicano-Mexican Cultural Assimilation and Anglo-Saxon Cultural Dominance*, 11 HISPANIC J. BEHAV. SCI. 203, 212 (1989).

3. *Id.*

4. See generally Richard Delgado and Jean Stefancic, *The Social Construction of Brown v. Board of Education: Law Reform and the Reconstructive Paradox*, 36 WM. & MARY L. REV. 547, 558–60 (1995).

5. Suzanne Lipsky, INTERNALIZED RACISM 16 (1987).

6. Gloria Anzaldúa, BORDERLANDS/LA FRONTERA: THE NEW MESTIZA 45 (1987).

From the Editors *Issues and Comments*

Have you ever heard someone speak the term "greaser" or "spic," and how did that make you feel? Did you object? Have you ever tried to intercede when someone was expressing racist ideas?

The chapters in part 4 introduce a number of media stereotypes—the carefree lover of song and dance; the bandito; the lazy, shiftless Mexican who loves to take siestas in the shade of a cactus; the tall, dark, handsome type; the suave, diplomatic Latino; the glamorous señorita with castanets; and others. Are these stereotypes:

- 100 percent false, or do they perhaps contain a grain of truth?
- functional, as two of the authors suggest, serving different purposes for mainstream society at different times?
- harmless, perhaps even necessary, when used as literary devices, because every story or novel requires stock characters?

Should Latino (or black) films portray that community warts and all, showing drugs, crime, and gangs, or should they highlight the positive aspects of the community?

Why can't minorities who object to their characterization in the media just "speak back" to these stereotypes, using freedom of expression in their favor?

Is the system of freedom of expression covertly racist if it tolerates demeaning pictures and stereotypes of minority groups, when a successful reply to such images requires a microphone, TV air time, or expensive ads?

Do Latino or black filmmakers stereotype whites?

Suppose you are interviewing for a position with a small company located in an area of the country with a very small minority population. The position requires a considerable amount of technical knowledge. You have a strong Latino/a heritage, but you are light-skinned and often mistaken for Caucasian. While waiting to be interviewed, you strike up a conversation with a fellow applicant who is a Mexican American with a dark complexion. You discover that your fellow applicant holds a degree, with honors, from an acclaimed technical school as well as having several years' experience in the field in which you are applying. During your interview, you discover that you are extremely underqualified for the position, having no technical degree and very little experience. The interviewer is candid with you about the qualifications of your fellow applicant, but expresses ethnic concerns. Not knowing your Latino/a heritage, the interviewer tells you that according to popular perceptions, Latinos/as are shiftless, lazy people and can't or shouldn't be trusted with responsibility. The interviewer, while impressed with the other applicant, fears that the firm's clients won't want to deal with him and that he won't fit in with the other workers. Even though the other applicant is more qualified, you are the only one to receive an offer. Would you accept it?

If a journalist or survey organization issues a "feel good" report on the Latino condition that emphasizes progress and a rosy future, is that damaging? Suppose a company trumpets a favorable, upscale stereotype of a Latino or Latina to sell cigarettes, liquor, or overpriced luxury items to the Latino market?

Can you think of any examples of portrayals of Latinos/as in the media where they are not stereotyped? What would such a non-stereotyped portrayal of Latino culture and people look like?

What could the Latino community do to prevent their stereotyping and to control their images in the media?

If it is true that perceptions of race are limited by our racist society, how can Latinos begin to combat their "colonized mentalities?"

Suggested Readings

Arriola, Elvia R. "LatCrit Theory, International Human Rights, Popular Culture, and the Faces of Despair in INS Raids." 28 *U. Miami Inter-Am. L. Rev.* 245 (1997).

Bender, Steven W. *Greasers and Gringos: Latinos, Law, and the American Imagination.* New York: New York University Press, 2003.

Berg, Charles Ramírez. "Bordertown: The Assimilation Narrative and the Chicano Social Problem Film." In *Chicanos and Film: Essays on Chicano Representation and Resistance*, edited by Chon Noriega. Minneapolis: University of Minnesota Press, 1992.

———. "Images and Counterimages of the Hispanic in Hollywood." 6 *Tonantzin* 12–13 (November 1988).

———. "Immigrants, Aliens, and Extraterrestrials: Science Fiction's Alien 'Other' as (among Other Things) New Hispanic Imagery." 18 *CineAction!* 3–17 (Fall 1989).

———. *Latino Images in Film: Stereotypes, Subversion, and Resistance.* Austin: University of Texas Press, 2002.

Chavez, Leo. *Covering Immigration: Popular Images and the Politics of the Nation.* Berkeley: University of California Press, 2001.

Chicana (W)rites on Word and Film, edited by María Herrera-Sobek and Helena María Viramontes. Berkeley: Third Woman Press, 1995.

Chicano Cinema: Research, Review, and Resources, edited by Gary D. Keller. Binghamton, N.Y.: Bilingual Review/Bilingual Press, 1985.

Chicanos and Film: Representation and Resistance, edited by Chon Noriega. Minneapolis: University of Minnesota Press, 1992.

Dávila, Arlene. *Latino Spin: Image and the Whitewashing of Race.* New York: New York University Press, 2008.

———. *Latinos, Inc.: The Making and Marketing of a People.* Berkeley: University of California Press, 2001.

Delgado, Richard. "Words That Wound: A Tort Action for Racial Insults, Epithets, and Name-Calling." 17 *Harv. C.R.–C.L. L. Rev.* 133 (1982).

Delpar, Helen. "Mexico, the MPPDA, and Derogatory Films, 1922–1926." 12 *Journal of Popular Film and Television* 34–41 (Spring 1984).

Ethnic Eye: Latino Media Arts, edited by Chon Noriega and Ana M. Lopez. Minneapolis: University of Minnesota Press, 1996.

Fregosa, Rosa Linda. "Born in East L.A. and the Politics of Representation." 4 *Cultural Studies* 264–80 (October 1990).

———. *Bronze Screen: Chicana and Chicano Film Culture.* Minneapolis: University of Minnesota Press, 1993.

———. *MeXicana Encounters: The Making of Social Identities on the Borderlands.* Berkeley: University of California Press, 2003.

From Bananas to Buttocks: The Latina Body in Popular Film and Culture, edited by Myra Mendible. Austin: University of Texas Press, 2007.

Fusco, Coco. "The Latino 'Boom' in American Film." 2 *Centro Bulletin* 48 (1990).

Galería de la Raza. *Cactus Hearts/Barbed Wire Dreams: Media, Myths, and Mexicans,* art exhibition curated by Yolanda Lopez, 1988.

Garcia, Juan R. "Hollywood and the West: Mexican Images in American Films." In *Old Southwest/New Southwest: Essays on a Region and Its Literature,* edited by Judy Nolte Lensink, 75. Tucson: Tucson Public Library (distributed by University of Arizona Press), 1987.

Gaspar de Alba, Alicia. "The Alter-Native Grain: Theorizing Chicano/a Popular Culture." In *Culture and Difference: Critical Perspectives on the Bicultural Experience in the United States,* edited by Antonia Darder, 103. Westport, Conn.: Greenwood Press, 1995.

Hart, James D. *American Images of Spanish California.* Berkeley: Friends of the Bancroft Library, University of California, 1960.

Herrera-Sobek, María. *The Bracero Experience: Elitelore versus Folklore.* Los Angeles: UCLA Latin American Center Publications, University of California, 1979.

Images of Mexico in the United States, edited by John H. Coatsworth and Carlos Rico. San Diego: Center for U.S.–Mexican Studies, University of California, San Diego, 1989.

Johannsen, Albert. *The House of Beadle and Adams and Its Dime and Nickel Novels: The Story of a Vanished Literature.* 3 vols. Norman: University of Oklahoma Press, 1950–1962.

Kanellos, Nicolas. *Thirty Million Strong: Reclaiming the Hispanic Image in American Culture.* Golden, Colo.: Fulcrum Publishing, 1998.

Lacy, James M. "New Mexican Women in Early American Writings." 34 *New Mexico History Review* 1 (1959).

Lamb, Blaine P. "The Convenient Villain: The Early Cinema Views the Mexican-American." 14 *Journal of the West* 75 (1975).

Langum, David J. "Californios and the Image of Indolence." 9 *Western Historical Quarterly* 181–96 (April 1978).

Latin Looks: Images of Latinas and Latinos in the U.S. Media, edited by Clara Rodriguez. Boulder, Colo.: Westview Press, 1997.

López, Gerald P. "Big Time Players." *Newsweek,* October 8, 1992.

Maciel, David R. "The Celluloid Frontier: The U.S.–Mexico Border in Contemporary Cinema, 1970–1988." 5 *Renato Rosaldo Lecture Series Monograph* 1–34 (1989).

———. *El Norte: The U.S.–Mexican Border in Contemporary Cinema.* San Diego: Institute for Regional Studies of the Californias, San Diego State University, 1990.

Mayer, Vicki. *Producing Dreams, Consuming Youth: Mexican Americans and Mass Media.* New Brunswick, N.J.: Rutgers University Press, 2003.

Noriega, Chon A. "Citizen Chicano: The Trials and Titillations of Ethnicity in the American Cinema, 1935–1962." 58 *Social Research: An International Quarterly of the Social Sciences* 413–38 (Summer 1991).

———. *Shot in America: Television, the State, and the Rise of Chicano Cinema.* Minneapolis: University of Minnesota Press, 2000.

Paredes, Américo. "On 'Gringo,' 'Greaser,' and Other Neighborly Names." In *Singers and Story-tellers,* edited by Mody C. Boatright et al., 285–90. Dallas: Southern Methodist University Press, 1961.

Paredes, Raymund A. "The Mexican Image in American Travel Literature, 1813–1869." 52 *New Mexico Historical Review* 5–29 (January 1977).

———. "The Origin of Anti-Mexican Sentiment in the United States." 6 *New Scholar* 130–65 (1977).

Perez, Richie. "From Assimilation to Annihilation: Puerto Rican Images in U.S. Films." 2 *Centro Bulletin* 8 (1990).

Pettit, Arthur G. *Images of the Mexican American in Fiction and Film.* College Station: Texas A&M University Press, 1980.

Portales, Marco. *Crowding Out Latinos: Mexican Americans in the Public Consciousness.* Philadelphia: Temple University Press, 2000.

Reyes, Luis, and Peter Rubie. *Hispanics in Hollywood: A Celebration of 100 Years in Film and Television.* Hollywood, Calif.: Lone Eagle, 2000.

Robinson, Cecil. *Mexico and the Hispanic Southwest in American Literature.* Revised from *With the Ears of Strangers: The Mexican in American Literature.* Tucson: University of Arizona Press, 1977.

Rodriguez, Clara. *Heroes, Lovers, and Others: The Story of Latinos in Hollywood.* New York, Oxford University Press, 2008.

Roman, Ediberto. "Who Exactly Is Living La Vida Loca?: The Legal and Political Consequences of Latino-Latina Ethnic and Racial Stereotypes in Film and Other Media." 4 *J. Gender, Race & Just.* 37 (2000).

Saragoza, Alex M. "Mexican Cinema in the United States, 1940–1952." In *History, Culture, and Society: Chicano Studies in the 1980s,* issued by National Association of Chicano Studies. Ypsilanti, Mich.: Bilingual Press/Editorial Bilingue, 1983.

Still Looking for America: Beyond the Latino National Political Survey, by Luis Fraga et al. Palo Alto, Calif.: Stanford Center for Chicano Research, Public Outreach Project, Stanford University, 1993.

Torres, Luis R. "The Chicano Image in Film." 3 *Caminos* 8 (November 1982).

———. "Distortions in Celluloid: Hispanics and Film." 11 *Agenda: A Journal of Hispanic Issues* 37–40 (May–June 1981).

———. "Hollywood and the Homeboys: The Studios Discover Barrio Gangs." 3 *Nuestro* 27–30 (April 1979).

Trevino, Jesus Salvador. "Latino Portrayals in Film and Television." 30 *Jump Cut* 14–16 (March 1985).

———. "Latinos and Public Broadcasting: The 2% Factor." 28 *Jump Cut* 65 (April 1983).

Trulio, Beverly. "Anglo-American Attitudes toward New Mexican Women." 12 *Journal of the West* 229 (1973).

Valle, Victor, and Rodolfo D. Torres. "The Idea of Mestizaje and the 'Race' Problematic: Racialized Media Discourse in a Post-Fordist Landscape." In *Culture and Difference: Critical Perspectives on the Bicultural Experience in the United States,* edited by Antonia Darder, 139–53. New York: Bergin & Garvey, 1995.

Velvet Barrios: Popular Culture and Chicana/o Sexualities, edited by Alicia Gaspar de Alba and Tomas Ybarra-Frausto. New York: Palgrave Macmillan, 2003.

Weber, David J. "Here Rests Juan Espinoza: Toward a Clearer Look at the Image of the 'Indolent' Californios." 1 *Western Historical Quarterly* 61–68 (January 1979).

Weber, David J. "Stereotyping of Mexico's Far Northern Frontier." In *An Awakened Minority: The Mexican American*, 2d ed., edited by Manuel P. Servin, 18–24. Beverly Hills, Calif.: Glencoe Press, 1974.

Williams, Linda. "Type and Stereotype: Chicano Images in Film." 5 *Frontiers* 14–17 (Summer 1980).

Woll, Allen L. "Bandits and Lovers: Hispanic Images in American Film." In *The Kaleidoscopic Lens: How Hollywood Views Ethnic Groups*, edited by Randall M. Miller, 54–71. Englewood Cliffs, N.J.: Jerome S. Ozer, 1980.

———. *The Latin Image in American Film*. Los Angeles: UCLA Latin American Center Publications, [1977] 1980.

Woll, Allen L., and Randall M. Miller. "Hispanic Americans." In *Ethnic and Racial Images in American Film and Television: Historical Essays and Bibliography*, edited by Allen L. Woll and Randall M. Miller. New York: Garland Publishing, 1987.

Part V

||||||||||||||||||||||||||||||||||||||||||||||||||||||||||||||||||||||||||||||

Counterstories
We Begin to Talk Back and "Name Our Own Reality"

The press, cartoonists, speakers, and filmmakers may have drawn derogatory images of Latinos, but Latino writers and artists have not stood still for such treatment. Instead, they have composed counterstories, narratives, *corridos* (ballads), and *cuentos* (stories) of their own to challenge the pernicious images society created for their people. Even lawyers and legal scholars have written such stories, questioning the dominant narrative or understanding on which the law of race rests. Still others have been unearthing little-known chapters in Latino history and suggesting ways to counter negative stereotypes. Part 5 examines how this process has been taking place. Note that some writers question whether the use of narrative deflects attention from the underlying structural causes of racial oppression, and that others question whether storytelling has any place in legal argument at all.

Chapter 36

||||||||||||||||||||||||||||||||||||||||||||||||||||||||||||||||||||||||||||||||||||||

My Grandfather's Stories and Immigration Law

Michael A. Olivas

The funny thing about stories is that everyone has one. My grandfather had them, with plenty to spare. When I was very young, he would regale me with stories, usually about politics, baseball, and honor. These were his themes, the subject matter he carved out for himself and his grandchildren. As the oldest grandson and his first godchild, I held a special place of responsibility and affection. In Mexican families, this patrimony handed to young boys is one remnant of older times that is fading, like the use of Spanish in the home, posadas at Christmas, or the deference accorded all elders.

Sabino Olivas's world featured three verities, ones that he adhered to his entire life: political and personal loyalties are paramount; children should work hard and respect their elders; and people should conduct their lives with honor. Of course, each of these themes had a canon of stories designed, like parables, to illustrate the larger point, and, like the Bible, to be interlocking, cross referenced, and synoptic. That is, they could be embellished in the retelling, but they had to conform to the general themes of loyalty, hard work, and honor.

Several examples will illustrate the structure of my grandfather's world view, and how, for him, everything was connected and profound. Like other folklorists and storytellers, he employed mythic heroes or imbued people he knew with heroic dimensions. This is an important part of capturing the imagination of young children, for the mythopoeic technique exaggerates characteristics and allows listeners to fill in the gaps by actively inviting them to rewrite the story and remember it in their own terms. As a result, as my family grew (I am the oldest of ten), I would hear these taproot stories retold both by my grandfather to the other kids, and by my brothers and sisters to others. The core of the story would be intact, transformed by the teller's accumulated sense of the story line and its application.

One of the earliest stories was about New Mexico's United States Senator Bronson Cutting, and his death in a plane crash after attempting to help Northern New Mexico Hispanics regain land snatched from them by greedy developers. Growing up near Tierra Amarilla, New Mexico, as he did, my grandfather was heir to a long-standing oral tradition of defining one's status by land ownership. To this day, land

From The Chronicles, *My Grandfather's Stories, and Immigration Law: The Slave Traders' Chronicle as Racial History*, 34 St. Louis U. L.J. 425 (1990). Originally published in the *Saint Louis University Law Journal*. Reprinted by permission.

ownership in Northern New Mexico is a tangle of aboriginal Indian rights, Spanish land grants, Anglo and Mexican greed, treaties, and developer domination. Most outsiders (that is, anyone south of Santa Fe) know this issue only by having seen *The Milagro Beanfield War*, the Robert Redford movie based on John Nichols's book. But my grandfather's story was that sinister forces had somehow tampered with Senator Cutting's plane because he was a man of the people, aligned against wealthy interests. Senator Cutting, I was led to believe as I anchored the story with my own points of reference, was more like Jimmy Stewart in *Mr. Smith Goes to Washington* than like the Claude Rains character, who would lie to get his own greedy way.

Of course, as I grew older, I learned that the true story was not exactly as my grandfather had told it. Land ownership in New Mexico is complicated; the Senator had his faults; and my grandfather ran afoul of Cutting's political enemy, Senator Dennis Chavez. But the story still held its sway over me.

His other favorite story, which included a strong admonition to me, was about how he and other Hispanics had been treated in Texas on their way to World War I. A trainload of soldiers from Arizona and northern New Mexico, predominantly of Mexican origin (both New Mexico and Arizona had only recently become states), were going by train to camp in Ft. Hays, Kansas. Their train stopped in a town near Amarillo, Texas, and all the men poured out of the train to eat at a restaurant that catered to travelers. But only to some. A sign prominently greeted them: "No coloreds or Mexicans allowed," and word spread among them that this admissions policy was taken seriously.

My grandfather, who until this time had never been outside the Territory or the State (after 1912) of New Mexico, was not used to this kind of indignity. After all, he was from a state where Hispanics and Indians constituted a majority of the population, especially in the North, and it was his first face-to-face encounter with racism, Texas style. Shamefacedly, the New Mexicans ate the food that Anglo soldiers bought and brought to the train, but he never forgot the humiliation and anger he felt that day. Sixty-five years later, when he told me this story, he remembered clearly how most of the men died in France or elsewhere in Europe, defending a country that never fully respected their rights.

The longer, fuller version, replete with wonderful details of how at training camp they had ridden sawhorses with saddles, always ended with the anthem, "Ten cuidado con los Tejanos, porque son todos desgraciados y no tienen verguenza" (Be careful with Texans because they are all sons-of-bitches and have no shame). To be a *sin verguenza*—shameless, or without honor—was my grandfather's cruelest condemnation, reserved for faithless husbands, reprobates, lying grandchildren, and Anglo Texans.

These stories always had a moral to them, with implications for grandchildren. Thus, I was admonished to vote Democrat (because of FDR and the Catholic JFK), to support the National League (because the Brooklyn Dodgers had first hired Black players and because the relocated Los Angeles Dodgers had a farm team in Albuquerque), and to honor my elders (for example, by using the more formal *usted* instead of the informal *tú*).

All of this is by way of explaining why I am predisposed to tell stories, and accordingly, to listen to them. Not only were stories profoundly important in my own ethnic heritage, but they were nurtured in Catholic schools and in the seminary, where I studied for eight years to become a Catholic priest (I left before ordination). Even in my graduate work in American literature, I wrote my first book on John Updike, one of the premier observers and storytellers of our time. The scene in *The Centaur*, where Updike's father's classroom becomes a braying, bleating, barking menagerie, remains one of my favorites in all of literature.

My objection, if that is the proper word, to Derrick Bell's *Chronicle of the Space Traders* [in which a force of extraterrestrials offers to trade three treasures in return for all American blacks; the United States quickly votes to accept the trade—Eds.] is not that it is too fantastic or unlikely to occur, but rather the opposite: This scenario has occurred, and occurred more than once in our nation's history. Therefore, it is unintentionally ahistorical. Not only have Blacks been enslaved, as the *Chronicle* sorrowfully notes, but other racial groups have been conquered and removed, imported for their labor and not allowed to participate in the society they built, or expelled when their labor was no longer needed.

Consider the immigration history and political economy of three groups whose United States history predates Bell's: Cherokee removal and the Trail of Tears; Chinese laborers and the Chinese Exclusion Laws; and Mexicans in the Bracero Program and Operation Wetback. [The author's treatment of the first two groups is not included— Eds.] These three racial groups share different histories of conquest, exploitation, and legal disadvantage; but even a brief summary of their treatment in United States law shows commonalities of racial animus, legal infirmity, and majority domination of legal institutions guised as "political questions." I could have also chosen the national origins or labor histories of other Indian tribes, the Filipinos, the Native Hawaiians, the Japanese, the Guamese, the Puerto Ricans, or the Vietnamese; in other words, the distinct racial groups whose conquest, colonization, enslavement, or immigration histories mark them as candidates for the Space Traders' evil exchange.

Mexicans, the Bracero Program, and Operation Wetback

Nineteenth-century Mexican and Mexican American labor history in the United States is one of agricultural labor. In the Southwestern and Western United States, Mexicans picked half of the cotton and nearly 75 percent of the fruits and vegetables by the 1920s. By 1930, half of the sugar beet workers were Mexican, and 80 percent of the farmhands in Southern California were so, as well. As fields became increasingly mechanized, it was Anglo workers who rode the machines, consigning Mexicans to stoop-labor and hand cultivation. One observer noted: "The consensus of opinion of ranchers large and small . . . is that only the small minority of Mexicans are fitted for these types of labor [i.e., mechanized agricultural jobs] at the present time."[1]

Most crucial to the agricultural growers was the need for a reserve pool of workers who could be imported for their work, cast aside when not needed, and kept in subordinate status so they could not afford to organize collectively or protest their conditions. Mexicans filled this bill perfectly, especially in the early twentieth-century southwest, where Mexican poverty and the Revolution forced rural Mexicans to come to the United States for work. This migration was facilitated by United States grow-ers' agents, who recruited widely in Mexican villages, by the building of railroads (by Mexicans, not Chinese) from the interior of Mexico to El Paso, and by labor short-ages in the United States during World War I.

Another means of controlling the spigot of Mexican farm workers was the use of immigration laws. Early labor restrictions through federal immigration law (and state law, as in California) had been aimed at Chinese workers. When agricultural interests pressured Congress to allow Mexican temporary workers during 1917–1921, the head tax (then set at $8.00), literacy requirements, public charge provisions, and Alien Contract Labor Law provisions were waived. By 1929, with a surplus of "native" United States workers facing the Depression, the supply of Mexicans was turned off by reimposing the immigration requirements.

While United States nativists were pointing to the evils and inferiority of Southern European immigrants, Mexicans were characterized as a docile, exploitable, deport-able labor force. As one commentator noted:

> Mexican laborers, by accepting these undesirable tasks, enabled [Southwestern] agricul-ture and industry to flourish, thereby creating effective opportunities for [white] Ameri-can workers in the higher job levels. . . . The representatives of [United States] economic interests showed the basic reason for their support of Mexican immigration[;] employ-ers of the Southwest favored unlimited Mexican immigration because it provided them with a source of cheap labor which would be exploited to the fullest possible extent.[2]

To effectuate control over the Southern border, the Border Patrol began operation in 1924, while the Department of Labor and the Immigration Bureau initiated a pro-cedure in 1925 to regulate Mexican immigration by restricting the flow to workers already employed or promised positions.

During the Depression, two means were used to control Mexican workers: mass deportations and repatriations. Los Angeles was targeted for massive deportations for persons with Spanish-sounding names or Mexican features who could not produce formal papers, and over 80,000 Mexicans were deported from 1929 to 1935. Many of these persons had the legal right to be in the country, or had been born citizens but simply could not prove their status; of course, many of these workers had been eagerly sought for perishable crops. In addition, over one-half million Mexicans were also "voluntarily" repatriated, by choosing to go to Mexico rather than remain in the United States, possibly subject to formal deportation.

By 1940, the cycle had turned: labor shortages and World War II had created the need for more agricultural workers, and growers convinced the United States gov-ernment to enter into a large-scale contract-labor program, the Bracero Program. Originally begun in 1942 under an Executive Order, the program brokered laborers under contracts between the United States and Mexico. Between 1942 and 1951, over one-half million "braceros" were hired under the program. Public funds were used to seek and register workers in Mexico who, after their labor had been performed, were returned to Mexico until the crops were ready to be picked again. This program was cynically employed to create a reserve pool of temporary laborers who had few rights and no vesting of equities.

By 1946, the circulation of bracero labor, both in its certification and its deportation mechanism, had become hopelessly confused. It became impossible to separate Mexican Americans from deportable Mexicans. Many United States citizens were mistakenly "repatriated" to Mexico, including men with Mexican features who had never been to Mexico. To correct these errors, a system of "drying out wetbacks" was instituted, what Ernesto Galarza termed a "dehydration" or "desiccation" process.[3] This modest legalization process gave some Mexican braceros an opportunity to regularize their immigration status and remain in the United States while they worked as braceros.

In 1950, under these various mechanisms, 20,000 new braceros were certified, 97,000 agricultural workers were dehydrated, and 480,000 old braceros were deported back to Mexico. In 1954, over one million braceros were deported under the terms of "Operation Wetback," a "Special Mobile Force" of the Border Patrol. The program included massive roundups and deportations, factory and field raids, a relentless media campaign designed to characterize the mop-up operation as a national security necessity, and a tightening up of the border to deter undocumented immigration.

The Bracero Program, dehydration, and Operation Wetback all presaged immigration programs of the 1980s. During this time, the INS began "Operation Jobs," a massive early-1980s workplace-raid program of deportations; a legalization program under the Immigration Reform and Control Act of 1986, an amnesty as a political tradeoff for employer sanctions; and a re-enacted Bracero-style program of H2A-workers, a labor contracting provision of temporary work visas for needed agricultural workers.

In two of his books based on folktales from Tierra Amarilla, New Mexico, the writer Sabine Ulibarri has re-created the Hispano-Indian world of rural, northern New Mexico. In *Cuentos de Tierra Amarilla* (*Tales from Tierra Amarilla*),[4] he collects a variety of wonderful tales, rooted in this isolated town that time has not changed, even today. My grandfather enjoyed this book, which I read to him in his final years. But his favorite (and mine) was Ulibarri's masterwork, *Mi Abuela Fumaba Puros* (*My Grandmother Smoked Puros* [Cigars]),[5] in which an old woman lights cigars in her house to remind her of her dead husband.

My grandfather loved this story, not only because it was by his more famous *tocayo*, but because it was at once outlandish ("mujeres en Nuevo Mexico no fumaban puros," that is, women in New Mexico did not smoke cigars) and yet very real. Smells were very real to him, evocative of earlier events and cuentos, the way that tea and madeleines unlocked Proust's prodigious memory. Biscochitos evoked holidays, and empanadas Christmas. Had he outlived my grandmother, he would have had mementos in the house, perhaps prune pies or apricot jam.

My grandfather's world, with the exception of his World War I sortie in Texas and abroad, was small but not narrow. He lived by a code of behavior, one he passed to his more fortunate children (only one of whom still lives in New Mexico) and grandchildren (most of whom no longer live in New Mexico). But for me, no longer in New Mexico, reading Derrick Bell's *Chronicle* is like talking to my grandfather or reading Sabine Ulibarri; the stories are at once outlandish, yet very real. I also believe, with Richard Delgado, "Stories, parables, chronicles, and narratives are powerful means for destroying mindset—the bundle of presuppositions, received wisdoms, and shared understandings against a background of which legal and political discourse takes place."[6]

Folklore and corridos have always held a powerful place in Mexican society. Fiction has always held a powerful place in the human experience, and the *Chronicles* will inform racial jurisprudence and civil rights scholarship in the United States in ways not yet evident. Critical minority renderings of United States racial history, immigration practices, and labor economy can have equally compelling results, however, recounting what actually happened in all the sordid details. If Derrick Bell's work forces us to engage these unsavory practices, he will have performed great service —he will have caused us to examine our grandfathers' stories and lives. . . .

As a deterrent to Central American refugees and as "bait" to attract their families already in the United States, the INS began in the 1980s to incarcerate undocumented adults and unaccompanied minors in border camps. One, near Brownsville, Texas, was once used as a United States Department of Agriculture pesticide storage facility. The INS has defied court orders to improve conditions in the camps, and by 1990, hundreds of alien children were being held without health, educational, or legal services. Haitian boat persons were being interdicted at sea, given "hearings" on the boats, and repatriated to Haiti; by 1990, only six of 20,000 interdicted Haitians had been granted asylum. The INS had begun a media campaign to justify its extraordinary practices on land and on sea. The cycle of United States immigration history continued, and all was ready for the Space Traders.

NOTES

1. P. Taylor, MEXICAN LABOR IN THE UNITED STATES IMPERIAL VALLEY 42 (1928).

2. Robert A. Divine, AMERICAN IMMIGRATION POLICY, 1924–1952 at 58–59 (1957).

3. Ernesto Galarza, MERCHANTS OF LABOR: THE MEXICAN BRACERO STORY 63–64 (1964).

4. Sabine Ulibarri, CUENTOS DE TIERRA AMARILLA (1971). Sabine Ulibarri, also a native of Tierra Amarilla, told me he had known of my grandfather because the town was small and because their names were so similar. My grandfather, who never met Ulibarri (who was twenty years younger), called him his *tocayo* (namesake).

5. Sabine Ulibarri, MI ABUELA FUMABA PUROS (1977).

6. Richard Delgado, *Storytelling for Oppositionists and Others: A Plea for Narrative*, 87 MICH. L. REV. 2411, 2413 (1989).

Chapter 37

||||||||||||||||||||||||||||||||||||||||||||||||||||||||||||||||||||||||||||||

Storytelling for Oppositionists and Others

Richard Delgado

Everyone has been writing stories these days. And I don't just mean writing about stories or narrative theory, important as those are. I mean actual stories, as in "once-upon-a-time" type stories. Derrick Bell has been writing "Chronicles"; others have been writing dialogues, stories, and metastories. Many others have been daring to become more personal in their writing, to inject narrative, perspective, and feeling —how it was for me—into their otherwise scholarly, footnoted articles and, in the case of the truly brave, into their teaching.

Many, but by no means all, who have been telling legal stories are members of what could be loosely described as outgroups, groups whose marginality defines the boundaries of the mainstream, whose voice and perspective—whose consciousness— has been suppressed, devalued, and abnormalized. The attraction of stories for these groups should come as no surprise. For stories create their own bonds, represent cohesion, shared understanding, and meanings. The cohesiveness that stories bring is part of the strength of the outgroup. An outgroup creates its own stories, which circulate within the group as a kind of counter-reality.

The dominant group creates its own stories, as well. The stories or narratives told by the ingroup remind it of its identity in relation to outgroups, and provide it with a form of shared reality in which its own superior position is seen as natural.

The stories of outgroups aim to subvert that ingroup reality. In civil rights, for example, many in the majority hold that any inequality between whites and nonwhites is due either to cultural lag, or inadequate enforcement of currently existing beneficial laws—both of which are easily correctable. For many minority persons, the principal instrument of their subordination is neither of these. Rather, it is the prevailing mindset by means of which members of the dominant group justify the world as it is, that is, with whites on top and browns and blacks at the bottom.

Stories, parables, chronicles, and narratives are powerful means for destroying mindset—the bundle of presuppositions, received wisdoms, and shared understandings against a background of which legal and political discourse takes place. These matters are rarely focused on. They are like eyeglasses we have worn a long time. They are nearly invisible; we use them to scan and interpret the world and only rarely examine them for themselves. Ideology—the received wisdom—makes current social

From *Storytelling for Oppositionists and Others: A Plea for Narrative*, 87 MICH. L. REV. 2411 (1989). Originally published in the *Michigan Law Review*. Reprinted by permission.

arrangements seem fair and natural. Those in power sleep well at night—their conduct does not seem to them like oppression.

The cure is storytelling (or as I shall sometimes call it, counterstorytelling). As Derrick Bell, Bruno Bettelheim, and others show, stories can shatter complacency and challenge the status quo. Stories told by underdogs are frequently ironic or satiric; a root word for "humor" is *humus*—bringing low, down to earth. Along with the tradition of storytelling in black culture, there flourishes the Spanish tradition of the picaresque novel or story, which tells of humble folk piquing the pompous or powerful and bringing them down to more human levels.

Most who write about storytelling focus on its community-building functions: stories build consensus, a common culture of shared understandings, and deeper, more vital ethics. Counterstories, which challenge the received wisdom, do that as well. They can open new windows into reality, showing us that there are possibilities for life other than the ones we live. They enrich imagination and teach that by combining elements from the story and current reality, we may construct a new world richer than either alone. Counterstories can quicken and engage conscience. Their graphic quality can stir imagination in ways in which more conventional discourse cannot.

But stories and counterstories can serve an equally important destructive function. They can show that what we believe is ridiculous, self-serving, or cruel. They can show us the way out of the trap of unjustified exclusion. They can help us understand when it is time to reallocate power. They are the other half—the destructive half—of the creative dialectic. Stories and counterstories, to be effective, must be or must appear to be noncoercive. They invite the reader to suspend judgment, listen for their point or message, and then decide what measure of truth they contain. They are insinuative, not frontal; they offer a respite from the linear, coercive discourse that characterizes much legal writing.

Storytelling and Counterstorytelling

The same object, as everyone knows, can be described in many ways. A rectangular red object on my living room floor may be a nuisance if I stub my toe on it in the dark, a doorstop if I use it for that purpose, further evidence of my lackadaisical housekeeping to my visiting mother, a toy to my young daughter, or simply a brick left over from my patio restoration project. No single true or all-encompassing description exists. The same holds true of events, especially ones that are racially charged. Often, we will not be able to ascertain the single best description or interpretation of what we have seen. We participate in creating what we see in the very act of describing it.

How can there be such divergent stories? Why do they not combine? Is it simply that members of the dominant group see the same glass as half full, minorities as half empty? I believe more is at work; stories war with each other. They contend for, tug at, our minds. To see how the dialectic of competition and rejection works—to see the reality-creating potential of stories and the normative implications of adopting one story rather than another—consider the following series of accounts, each describing the same event.

A Standard Event and a Stock Story That Explains It

The following series of stories revolves around the same event: A black(or Latino, or Asian, or Indian) lawyer interviews for a teaching position at a major law school (school X) and is rejected. Any other race-tinged event could have served equally well for purposes of illustration. This particular event was chosen because it occurs on familiar ground—many readers of this chapter are past or present members of a university community who have heard about or participated in events like the one described.

The Stock Story

Setting: A professor and student are talking in the professor's office. Both are white. The professor, Blas Vernier, is tenured, in midcareer, and well regarded by his colleagues and students. The student, Judith Rogers, is a member of the student advisory appointments committee.

Rogers: Professor Vernier, what happened with the minority candidate, John Henry? I heard he was voted down at the faculty meeting yesterday. The students on my committee liked him a lot.

Vernier: It was a difficult decision, Judith. We discussed him for over two hours. I can't tell you the final vote, of course, but it wasn't particularly close. Even some of my colleagues who were initially for his appointment voted against him when the full record came out.

Rogers: But we have no minority professors at all, except for Professor Chen, who is untenured, and Professor Tompkins, who teaches Trial Practice on loan from the district attorney's office once a year.

Vernier: Don't forget Mary Foster, the Assistant Dean.

Rogers: But she doesn't teach, just handles admissions and the placement office.

Vernier: And does those things very well. But back to John Henry. I understand your disappointment. Henry was a strong candidate, one of the stronger blacks we've interviewed recently. But ultimately he didn't measure up. We didn't think he wanted to teach for the right reasons. He was vague and diffuse about his research interests. All he could say was that he wanted to write about equality and civil rights, but so far as we could tell, he had nothing new to say about those areas. What's more, we had some problems with his teaching interests. He wanted to teach peripheral courses, in areas where we already have enough people. And we had the sense that he wouldn't be really rigorous in those areas, either.

Rogers: But we need courses in employment discrimination and civil rights. And he's had a long career with the NAACP Legal Defense Fund and really seemed to know his stuff.

Vernier: It's true we could stand to add a course or two of that nature, although as you know our main needs are in Commercial Law and Corporations, and Henry doesn't teach either. But I think our need is not as acute as you say. Many of the topics you're interested in are covered in the second half of the Constitutional Law course taught by Professor White, who has a national reputation for his work in civil liberties and freedom of speech.

Rogers: But Henry could have taught those topics from a black perspective. And he would have been a wonderful role model for our minority students.

Vernier: Those things are true, and we gave them considerable weight. But when it came right down to it, we felt we couldn't take that great a risk. Henry wasn't on the law review at school, as you are, Judith, and has never written a line in a legal journal. Some of us doubted he ever would. And then, what would happen five years from now when he came up for tenure? It wouldn't be fair to place him in an environment like this. He'd just have to pick up his career and start over if he didn't produce.

Rogers: With all due respect, Professor, that's paternalistic. I think Henry should have been given the chance. He might have surprised us.

Vernier: So I thought, too, until I heard my colleagues' discussion, which I'm afraid, given the demands of confidentiality, I can't share with you. Just let me say that we examined his case long and hard and I am convinced, fairly. The decision, while painful, was correct.

Rogers: So another year is going to go by without a minority candidate or professor?

Vernier: These things take time. I was on the appointments committee last year, chaired it in fact. And I can tell you we would love nothing better than to find a qualified minority. Every year, we call the Supreme Court to check on current clerks, telephone our colleagues at other leading law schools, and place ads in black newspapers and journals. But the pool is so small. And the few good ones have many opportunities. We can't pay nearly as much as private practice, you know. [Rogers, who would like to be a legal services attorney, but is attracted to the higher salaries of corporate practice, nods glumly.] It may be that we'll have to wait another few years, until the current crop of black and minority law students graduates and gets some experience. We have some excellent prospects, including some members of your very class. I'm sure you know Patricia Maldonado, who is an articles editor on your own journal.

Rogers: [Thinks: I've heard that one before, but says] Well, thanks, Professor. I know the students will be disappointed. But maybe when the committee considers visiting professors later in the season it will be able to find a professor of color who meets its standards and fits our needs.

Vernier: We'll try our best. Although you should know that some of us believe that merely shuffling the few minorities in teaching from one school to another does nothing to expand the pool. And once they get here, it's hard to say no if they express a desire to stay on.

Rogers: [Thinks: That's a lot like tenure. How ironic; there are certain of your colleagues we would love to get rid of, too. But says] Well, thanks, Professor. I've got to get to class. I still wish the vote had come out otherwise. Our student committee is preparing a list of minority candidates that we would like to see considered. Maybe you'll find one or more of them worthy of teaching here.

Vernier: Judith, believe me, there is nothing that would please me more.

In the above dialogue, Professor Vernier's account represents the stock story—the one the institution collectively forms and tells about itself. This story picks and chooses from among the available facts to present a picture of what happened: an account that justifies the world as it is. It emphasizes the school's benevolent motivation ("look how hard we're trying") and good faith. It stresses stability and the avoidance of risks. It measures the candidate of color through the prism of preexisting, well-agreed-upon criteria of conventional scholarship and teaching. Given those standards, it purports to be scrupulously meritocratic and fair; Henry would have been hired had he measured up. No one raises the possibility that the merit criteria employed in judging Henry are themselves debatable, chosen—not inevitable. No one, least of all Vernier, calls attention to the way in which merit functions to conceal the contingent connection between institutional power and the things rated.

The discussion gives little consideration of the possibility that Henry's presence on the faculty might have altered the institution's character, helped introduce a different prism and different criteria for selecting future candidates. The account is highly procedural—it emphasizes that Henry got a full, careful hearing—rather than substantive: a black was rejected. It emphasizes certain "facts" without examining their truth—namely, that the pool is very small, that good minority candidates have many choices, and that the appropriate view is the long one; haste makes waste.

The dominant fact about this first story, however, is its seeming neutrality. It scrupulously avoids issues of blame or responsibility. Race played no part in the candidate's rejection; indeed the school leaned over backwards to accommodate him. A white candidate with similar credentials would not have made it as far as Henry did. The story comforts and soothes. And Vernier's sincerity makes him an effective apologist for his system.

Vernier's story is also deeply coercive, although the coercion is disguised. Judith was aware of it but chose not to confront it directly; Vernier holds all the cards. He pressures her to go along with the institution's story by threatening her prospects at the same time that he flatters her achievements. A victim herself, she is invited to take on and share the consciousness of her oppressor. She does not accept Vernier's story, but he does slip a few doubts through cracks in her armor. The professor's story shows how forceful and repeated storytelling can perpetuate a particular view of reality. Naturally, the stock story is not the only one that can be told. By emphasizing other events and giving them slightly different interpretations, a quite different picture can be made to emerge.

[Following two other stories—the one told by the disappointed candidate himself, and the one told by the judge in his order dismissing John Henry's legal complaint—the author continues as follows—Eds.]

None of the above stories attempts to unseat the prevailing institutional story. Henry's account comes closest; it highlights different facts and interprets those it does share with the standard account differently. His formal complaint also challenges the school's account, but it must fit itself under existing law, which it failed to do.

Al-Hammar X's Counter Story

A few days after word of Henry's rejection reached the student body, Noel Al-Hammar X, leader of the radical Third World Coalition, delivered a speech at noon on the steps of the law school patio. The audience consisted of most of the black and brown students at the law school, several dozen white students, and a few faculty members. Chen was absent, having a class to prepare for. The Assistant Dean was present, uneasily taking mental notes in case the Dean asked her later on what she heard.

Al-Hammar's speech was scathing, denunciatory, and at times downright rude. He spoke several words that the campus newspaper reporter wondered if his paper would print. He impugned the good faith of the faculty, accused them of institutional if not garden-variety racism, and pointed out in great detail the long history of the faculty as an all-white club. He said that the law school was bent on hiring only white males, "ladies" only if they were well-behaved clones of white males, and would never hire a professor of color unless forced to do so by student pressure or the courts. He exhorted his fellow students not to rest until the law faculty took steps to address its own ethnocentricity and racism. He urged boycotting or disrupting classes, writing letters to the state legislature, withholding alumni contributions, setting up a "shadow" appointments committee, and several other measures that made the Assistant Dean wince.

Al-Hammar's talk received a great deal of attention, particularly from the faculty who were not there to hear it. Several versions of his story circulated among the faculty offices and corridors ("Did you hear what he said?"). Many of the stories-about-the-story were wildly exaggerated. Nevertheless, Al-Hammar's story is an authentic counterstory. It directly challenges—both in its words and tone—the corporate story the law school carefully worked out to explain Henry's non-appointment. It rejects many of the institution's premises, including we-try-so-hard, the-pool-is-so-small, and even mocks the school's meritocratic self-concept. "They say Henry is mediocre, has a pedestrian mind. Well, they ain't sat in none of my classes and listened to themselves. Mediocrity they got. They're experts on mediocrity." Al-Hammar denounced the faculty's excuse making, saying there were dozens of qualified black candidates, if not hundreds. "There isn't that big a pool of Chancellors, or quarterbacks," he said. "But when they need one, they find one, don't they?"

Al-Hammar also deviates stylistically, as a storyteller, from the others, including John Henry. He rebels against the "reasonable discourse" of law. He is angry, and anger is out of bounds in legal discourse, even as a response to discrimination. Judith and John Henry were unsuccessful in getting others to listen. So was Al-Hammar, but for a different reason. His counterstory overwhelmed the audience. More than just a narrative, it was a call to action, a call to join him in destroying the current story. But his audience was not ready to act. Too many of his listeners felt challenged or coerced; their defenses went up. The campus newspaper the next day published a garbled version, saying that he had urged the law faculty to relax its standards in order to provide minority students with role models. This prompted three letters to the editor asking how an unqualified black professor could be a good role model for anyone, black or white.

Moreover, the audience Al-Hammar intended to affect, namely the faculty, was even more unmoved by his counterstory. It attacked them too frontally. They were quick to dismiss him as an extremist, a demagogue, a hothead—someone to be taken seriously only for the damage he might do should he attract a body of followers. Consequently, for the next week the faculty spent much time in one-on-one conversations with "responsible" student leaders, including Judith Rogers.

By the end of the week, a consensus story had formed about Al-Hammar's story. That story-about-a-story held that Al-Hammar had gone too far, that there was more to the situation than Al-Hammar knew or was prepared to admit. Moreover, Al-Hammar was portrayed not as someone who had reached out, in pain, for sympathy and friendship. Rather, he was depicted as a "bad actor," someone with a "chip on his shoulder," someone no responsible member of the law school community should trade stories with. Nonetheless, a few progressive students and faculty members believed Al-Hammar had done the institution a favor by raising the issues and demanding that they be addressed. They were a distinct minority.

The Anonymous Leaflet Counter Story

About a month after Al-Hammar spoke, the law faculty formed a special committee for minority hiring. The committee contained practically every young liberal on the faculty, two of its three female professors, and the Assistant Dean. The Dean announced the committee's formation in a memorandum sent to the law school's ethnic student associations, the student government, and the alumni newsletter, which gave it front-page coverage. It was also posted on bulletin boards around the law school.

The memo spoke about the committee and its mission in serious, measured phrases—"social need," "national search," "renewed effort," "balancing the various considerations," "identifying members of a future pool from which we might draw." Shortly after the memo was distributed, an anonymous four-page leaflet appeared in the student lounge, on the same bulletin boards on which the Dean's memo had been posted, and in various mailboxes of faculty members and law school organizations. Its author, whether student or faculty member, was never identified.

The leaflet was entitled, "Another Committee, Aren't We Wonderful?" It began with a caricature of the Dean's memo, mocking its measured language and high-flown tone. Then, beginning in the middle of the page the memo told, in conversational terms, the following story:

"And so, friends and neighbors [the leaflet continued], how is it that the good law schools go about looking for new faculty members? Here is how it works. The appointments committee starts out the year with a model new faculty member in mind. This mythic creature went to a leading law school, graduated first or second in his or her class, clerked for the Supreme Court, and wrote the leading note in the law review on some topic dealing with the federal courts. This individual is brilliant, personable, humane, and has just the right amount of practice experience with the right firm.

"Schools begin with this paragon in mind and energetically beat the bushes, beginning in September, in search of him or her. At this stage, they believe themselves genuinely and sincerely colorblind. If they find such a mythic figure who is black or Hispanic or gay or lesbian, they will hire this person in a flash. They will of course do the same if the person is white.

"By February, however, the school has not hired many mythic figures. Some that they interviewed turned them down. Now, it's late in the year and they have to get someone to teach Trusts and Estates. Although there are none left on their list who are Supreme Court clerks, etc., they can easily find several who are a notch or two below that—who went to good schools, but not Harvard, or who went to Harvard, yet were not first or second in their classes. Still, they know, with a degree verging on certainty, that this person is smart and can do the job. They know this from personal acquaintance with this individual, or they hear it from someone they know and trust. Joe says Bill is really smart, a good lawyer, and will be terrific in the classroom.

"So they hire this person because, although he or she is not a mythic figure, functionally equivalent guarantees—namely first- or second-hand experience—assure them that this person will be a good teacher and scholar. And so it generally turns out—the new professor does just fine.

"Persons hired in this fashion are almost always white, male, and straight. The reason: We rarely know blacks, Hispanics, women, and gays. Moreover, when we hire the white male, the known but less-than-mythic quantity, late in February, it does not seem to us like we are making an exception. Yet we are. We are employing a form of affirmative action—bending the stated rules so as to hire the person we want.

"The upshot is that whites have two chances of being hired—by meeting the formal criteria we start out with in September—that is, by being mythic figures—and also by meeting the second, informal, modified criteria we apply later to friends and acquaintances when we are in a pinch. Minorities have just one chance of being hired —the first.

"To be sure, once every decade or so a law school, imbued with crusading zeal, will bend the rules and hire a minority with credentials just short of Superman or Superwoman. And, when it does so, *it will feel like an exception*. The school will congratulate itself—it has lifted up one of the downtrodden. And, it will remind the new professor repeatedly how lucky he or she is to be here in this wonderful place. It will also make sure, through subtle or not-so-subtle means, that the students know so, too."

But (the leaflet continued), there is a coda.

"If, later, the minority professor hired this way unexpectedly succeeds, this will produce consternation among his or her colleagues. For, things were not intended to go that way. When he or she came aboard, the minority professor lacked those standard indicia of merit—Supreme Court clerkship, high LSAT score, prep school background—that the majority-race professors had and believe essential to scholarly success.

"Yet the minority professor is succeeding all the same—publishing in good law reviews, receiving invitations to serve on important commissions, winning popularity with students. This is infuriating. Many majority-race professors are persons of relatively slender achievements—you can look up their publishing record any time you have five minutes. Their principal achievements lie in the distant past, when aided by their parents' upper class background, they did well in high school and college, and got the requisite test scores on standardized tests which test exactly the accumulated cultural capital they acquired so easily and naturally at home. Shortly after that, their careers started to stagnate. They publish an article every five years or so, often in a minor law review, after gallingly having it turned down by the very review they served on as editor twenty years ago.

"So, their claim to fame lies in their early exploits, the badges they acquired up to about the age of twenty-five, at which point the edge they acquired from Mummy and Daddy began to lose effect. Now, along comes the hungry minority professor, imbued with a fierce desire to get ahead, a good intellect, and a willingness to work 70 hours a week if necessary to make up for lost time. The minority person lacks the merit badges awarded early in life, the white professor's main source of security. So, the minority's colleagues don't like it and use perfectly predictable ways to transfer the costs of their discomfort to the misbehaving minority.

"So that, my friends, is why minority professors

(i) have a hard time getting hired; and,
(ii) have a hard time if they are hired.

"When you and I are running the world, we won't replicate this unfair system, will we? Of course not—unless, of course, it changes us in the process."

This second counterstory attacks the faculty less frontally in some respects—for example, it does not focus on the fate of any particular minority candidate, such as Henry, but attacks a general mindset. It employs several devices, including narrative and careful observation—the latter to build credibility (the reader says, "That's right"), the former to beguile the reader and get him or her to suspend judgment (everyone loves a story). The last part of the story is painful; it strikes close to home. Yet the way for its acceptance has been paved by the earlier parts, which paint a plausible picture of events, so that the final part demands consideration. It generalizes and exaggerates—many majority-race professors are not persons of slender achievement. But such broad strokes are part of the narrator's art. The realistically drawn first part of the story, despite shading off into caricature at the end, forces readers to focus on the flaws in the good face the dean attempted to put on events. And, despite its somewhat accusatory thrust, the story, as was mentioned, debunks only a mindset, not a person. Unlike Al-Hammar X's story, it does not call the chair of the appointments committee, a much-loved senior professor, a racist. (But did Al-Hammar's story, confrontational as it was, pave the way for the generally positive reception accorded the anonymous account?)

The story invites the reader to alienate herself or himself from the events described, to enter into the mental set of the teller, whose view is different from the reader's own. The oppositional nature of the story, the manner in which it challenges and rebuffs the stock story, thus causes him or her to oscillate between poles. It is insinuative: At times, the reader is seduced by the story and its logical coherence—it is a plausible counter-view of what happened; it has a degree of explanatory power.

Yet the story places the majority-race reader on the defensive. He or she alternately leaves the storyteller's perspective to return to his or her own, saying, "That's outrageous, I'm being accused of . . ." The reader thus moves back and forth between two worlds, the storyteller's, which the reader occupies vicariously to the extent the story is well-told and rings true, and his or her own, which he or she returns to and reevaluates in light of the story's message. Can my world still stand? What parts of it remain valid? What parts of the story seem true? How can I reconcile the two worlds, and will the resulting world be a better one than the one with which I began?

Why Outgroups Should Tell Stories and Why Others Should Listen

Subordinated groups have always told stories. Black slaves told, in song, letters, and verse, about their own pain and oppression. They described the terrible wrongs they had experienced at the hands of whites, and mocked (behind whites' backs) the veneer of gentility whites purchased at the cost of the slaves' suffering. Mexican Americans in the Southwest composed *corridos* (ballads) and stories, passed on from generation to generation, of abuse at the hands of gringo justice, the Texas Rangers, and ruthless lawyers and developers who cheated them out of their lands. Native American literature, both oral and written, deals with all these themes as well. Feminist consciousness-raising consists, in part, of the sharing of stories, of tales from personal experience, on the basis of which the group constructs a shared reality about women's status vis-à-vis men.

This proliferation of counterstories is not an accident or coincidence. Oppressed groups have known instinctively that stories are an essential tool to their own survival and liberation. Members of out-groups can use stories in two basic ways: first, as means of psychic self-preservation; and, second, as means of lessening their own subordination. These two means correspond to the two perspectives from which a story can be viewed—that of the teller, and that of the listener. The storyteller gains psychically, the listener morally and epistemologically.

The member of an outgroup gains, first, psychic self-preservation. A principal cause of the demoralization of marginalized groups is self-condemnation. They internalize the images that society thrusts on them—they believe that their lowly position is their own fault. The therapy is to tell stories. By becoming acquainted with the facts of their own historic oppression—with the violence, murder, deceit, co-optation, and connivance that have caused their desperate estate—members of outgroups gain healing. The story need not lead to a violent act; Frantz Fanon was wrong in writing that it is only through exacting blood from the oppressor that colonized people gain liberation.[1] Rather, the story need only lead to a realization of how one came to be oppressed and subjugated. Then, one can stop perpetrating (mental) violence on oneself.

So, stories—stories about oppression, about victimization, about one's own brutalization—far from deepening the despair of the oppressed, lead to healing, liberation, mental health.[2] They also promote group solidarity. Storytelling emboldens the hearer, who may have had the same thoughts and experiences the storyteller describes, but hesitated to give them voice. Having heard another express them, he or she realizes, I am not alone.

Yet, stories help oppressed groups in a second way—through their effect on the oppressor. Most oppression, as was mentioned earlier, does not seem like oppression to those perpetrating it. It is rationalized, causing few pangs of conscience. The dominant group justifies its privileged position by means of stories, stock explanations that construct reality in ways favorable to it. The stories are drastically at odds with the way most people of color would describe their condition. Artfully designed parables, chronicles, allegories, and pungent tales can jar the comfortable dominant complacency that is the principal anchor dragging down any incentive for reform. They can destroy—but the destruction they produce must be voluntary, a type of willing death. Because this is a white-dominated society in which the majority race controls the reins of power, racial reform must include them. Their complacency—born of comforting stories—is a major stumbling block to racial progress. Counterstories can attack that complacency.

What is more, they can do so in ways that promise at least the possibility of success. Most civil rights strategies confront the obstacle of otherness. The dominant group, noticing that a particular effort is waged on behalf of blacks or Latinos, increases its resistance. Stories at times can overcome that otherness, hold that instinctive resistance in abeyance. Stories are the oldest, most primordial meeting ground in human experience. Their allure will often provide the most effective means of overcoming otherness, of forming a new collectivity based on the shared story.

Members of outgroups should tell stories. Why should members of ingroups listen to them? They should listen to stories, of all sorts, in order to enrich their own reality. Reality is not fixed, not a given. Rather, we construct it through conversations, through our lives together. Racial and class-based isolation prevents the hearing of diverse stories and counterstories. It diminishes the conversation through which we create reality, construct our communal lives. Deliberately exposing oneself to counterstories can avoid that impoverishment, heighten "suspicion," and enable the listener and the teller to build a world richer than either could make alone. On another occasion, the listener will be the teller, sharing a secret, a piece of information, or an angle of vision that will enrich the former teller; and so on dialectically, in a rich tapestry of conversation, of stories. It is through this process that we can overcome ethnocentrism and the unthinking conviction that our way of seeing the world is the only one—that the way things are is inevitable, natural, just, and best—when it is, for some, full of pain, exclusion, and both petty and major tyranny.

Listening to stories makes the adjustment to further stories easier; one acquires the ability to see the world through others' eyes. It can lead the way to new environments. A willing listener is generally "welcomed with open arms." Listening to the stories of outgroups can avoid intellectual apartheid. Shared words can banish sameness, stiffness, and monochromaticity and reduce the felt terror of otherness when hearing new voices for the first time. If we would deepen and humanize ourselves, we must seek out storytellers different from ourselves and afford them the audience they deserve. The benefit will be reciprocal.[3]

NOTES

1. Frantz Fanon, THE WRETCHED OF THE EARTH (1968).

2. See Derrick A. Bell, Jr., AND WE ARE NOT SAVED 215–21 (1987).

3. Al-Hammar X graduated in the top 15 percent of his class, enrolled in a famous LL.M. program, and plans to become a law professor; Judith Rogers continued to be friendly with Professor Vernier, and actually succeeded in making him more receptive to minority candidates; John Henry was hired at Howard, where he had a long and illustrious career; the students at school X formed a committee to press for more minority and women professors. They did all the things Al-Hammar X suggested except disrupt classes. Two years later, the school hired two black women and a Hispanic male, maintaining, however, that this was not the result of student pressure but rather its own long-term recruiting.

‖‖‖

Chapter 38

I Am Joaquín

Rodolfo "Corky" Gonzales and the Retroactive Construction of Chicanismo

George Hartley

Early in 1967 Rodolfo "Corky" Gonzales published his epic poem, *Yo soy Joaquín,* better known as *I Am Joaquín*. By March the poem had already been adapted to film by the traveling activist troupe Teatro Campesino. The poem was mimeographed and widely circulated in order to be read during public demonstrations and organizing campaigns of what would come to be known as *El Movimiento* or the Chicano Movement. Beyond its immediate public activist function, however, *I Am Joaquín* also functioned as an inaugural work of what is now seen as the Chicano Literary Renaissance, lasting from the late '60s to the mid '70s. *I Am Joaquín* provided the groundwork, then, for much Chicano poetry to come. Yet what is perhaps more interesting is its role in serving as a founding literary work for all previous Chicano literature. What I am saying is that before 1967 Chicano literature did not exist, but after 1967 the whole history of Chicano literature from the 1500s to the 1960s suddenly, retroactively, came into being. Moreover, I contend that prior to moments such as 1967 and publications such as *I Am Joaquín*, Chicanos did not exist, and yet after that moment we can see that they had been around for centuries.

I Am Joaquín was able to perform this magic because through this poem the various elements that would make up Chicano identity came together for one of the first times under the name "Chicano." Prior to this, all of the work for justice, civil rights, farm labor laws, and cultural recognition for Mexican Americans had been carried out by Mexican Americans. But it wasn't until *I Am Joaquín*—which embodied all of these elements under the blanket concept of Chicanismo—that these elements could come into concert in the revolutionary subjectivity of the Chicano as the founding gesture of Chicano identity itself. The term "Chicano" as it functions in *I Am Joaquín* brought the Chicano as such into being. This is not to say that the term "Chicano" became an effective label for an already-existing entity; it is to say, rather, that the entity itself only came into being with the use of the word in the particular context marked in large part by this poem.

From *I Am Joaquín: Rodolfo "Corky" Gonzales and the Retroactive Construction of Chicanismo.* Copyright © 2009 by George Hartley. A former version of this essay appears on the Electronic Poetry Center, http://epc.buffalo.edu.

The term "Chicano," which many scholars suggest derives from a shortened version of the Indian pronunciation of "Mexicanos," was initially used as an insult, signifying a person of lower status and culture. This is in fact the way Mexican Americans were viewed by both Americans and Mexicans. Prior to the late 1960s, even within the Mexican-American community the term "Chicano" was reserved for recently arrived immigrants. New arrivals from Mexico—often poor and more visibly "Other" than the more assimilated earlier Mexicans in America—threatened the status of those Mexican Americans who often fought hard to prove their American identity by distancing themselves from their Mexican and Indian roots. Later, however, the term was appropriated by Mexican-American activists during the 1960s in much the same way as the terms "Black" and then later "nigger" were by African Americans, as a way of transforming an insult into a signifier of ethnic strength and pride and as a refusal to assimilate into mainstream White culture. Now "Chicano" came to serve as a badge of militant identity within and against mainstream Anglo-America.

After 1967, then, the term "Chicano" served a consciously ideological function among young radicals as a designator of oppositional identity. The beauty of the poem *I Am Joaquín* lay in the way Gonzales wove together a wide variety of cultural and historical tropes into one emergent identity. Gonzales recounts the roots of Chicano identity in the long history of Mexican miscegenation through Spanish and Indian contact on up through the U.S. occupation and annexation of northern Mexico. The poem also displays the mytho-cultural icons of Chicano identity growing out of pre-Columbian Amerindian cultures. Then the poem surveys the history of Mexican-American oppression and ends by imagining the future liberation of the Chicanos and their homeland. Through moments like this poem, which was staged (and even filmed) as part of the public presentations of the Chicano civil rights movement, Mexican Americans were transformed into Chicanos.

Critic Juan Bruce-Novoa sees the structure of *I Am Joaquín* as a continual dialectical movement from the present to the past and back to a more enriched and complicated present (*Chicano Poetry* 48–68). He divides the poem into three sections, the first being a lament and retreat into the people, la Raza; the second being a dialectical transformation of Mexican Americans through the interplay of past and present; and finally the third being the declaration of a new revolutionary identity—the Chicano—which will transform the future. All of this movement takes place under the name of Joaquín, the Chicano Everyman who functions as the symbolic unity of the people. The I in *I Am Joaquín*, then, is not an individual but a collective I, much like the self of Whitman's *Song of Myself*. While the resulting politics of the poem will be a nascent Chicanismo as a 1960s variant on the Zapatismo of the Mexican Revolution, the poem's transformative collective identification through the interplay of past and present is itself a separate and constitutive politics, which we could refer to as Joaquínismo. Joaquínismo could be seen, then, as a vanishing mediator, as a mediating moment between the indeterminate sense of oppression and injustice of the early 1960s which marks the poem's opening and the identification with the ideological construct of the Chicano which marks the poem's close.

I Am Joaquín opens as follows:

> I am Joaquín,
> lost in a world of confusion,
> caught up in the whirl of a
> gringo society,
> confused by the rules,
> scorned by attitudes,
> suppressed by manipulation,
> and destroyed by modern society. (ll. 1–8)

The burden of the poem lies in its first line, "I am Joaquín": this statement of identity is exactly what the poem itself must accomplish. In this initial line the statement is meaningless, for we know neither the identity of the I nor of the *Joaquín* with whom the I identifies. This declaration, as a speech act, hides the performative function of what appears as a constative utterance. In other words, a proposition posing as a statement of fact, as the simple pointing out of something already existing in the world, in reality brings into being that which it declares. For prior to this utterance there is no such identity between the I and the Joaquín; nor is there any clue as to what the nature of this identification entails.

We do learn in the lines that follow, however, that the initial grounds of this identity are confusion and chaos in an alien world. The speaker is lost, caught up, confused, scorned, and ultimately destroyed by the oppressive and racist structures of modern Anglo America. The speaker goes on to say: "My fathers / have lost the economic battle / and won / the struggle of cultural survival" (ll. 9–12). This (ultimately masculinist) turn to the fathers begins the poem's movement between present and past, the poem's construction of a heritage that will ground the I's identity and, as such, provide refuge from the whirl of living in an Anglo world. The opposition between economic assimilation and cultural struggle forces the Mexican American to make a choice:

> And now!
> I must choose
>
> between
> the paradox of
> victory of the spirit,
> despite physical hunger,
> or
> to exist in the grasp
> of American social neurosis,
> sterilization of the soul
> and a full stomach.

This sense of forced choice itself is key to setting the retroactive construction of the Chicano in motion: the hunger of the body, it turns out, is not as threatening as the sterilization of the soul. This willingness to sacrifice the body in order to regenerate the soul gives this nascent Chicanismo its urgency and strength. It is this choice itself in the midst of confusion that grounds the new subjectivity of the poem. Or, to put this in a different language, following the subjective destitution which the speaker suffers at the opening of the poem, this forced choice functions as a repressed performative (Zizek 99). In Gonzales's poem, as we have seen, the pure performative that must be repressed under the guise of free choice is the founding rather than found nature of the opening statement itself, "I am Joaquín." The speaker has already noted that the economic battle has been lost, so economic assimilation is not really a choice in a society which systematically excludes Mexican Americans from full participation in its economy. That only leaves the option, then, of addressing the sterilization of the soul, which the speaker interprets as a project of cultural historical reconstruction. But it is precisely through this assumption of the mandate to make a choice which is not really a choice, to assume a supposedly pre-existing identity which has not yet come into being, that a new symbolic order can come into being that will make room for the emergent Chicano.

Now that the stage has been set, the speaker is ready to begin. This beginning demands an initial withdrawal from the "nowhere" of this "monstrous, technical, / industrial giant called / Progress / and Anglo success," a withdrawal into the safety of "the / circle of life / MY OWN PEOPLE," La Raza. This retreat begins with a retrospective account of the history of la Raza. Here Gonzales strings together idealized moments of precolumbian and Mexican cultural and political development in a selective chronological succession:

> I am Cuauhtémoc,
> proud and noble,
> leader of men,
> king of an empire
> civilized beyond the dreams
> of the gachupín Cortés,
> who also is the blood,
> the image of myself.
> I am the Maya prince.
> I am Nezahualcóyotl,
> great leader of the Chichimecas.
> I am the sword and flame of Cortés
> the despot
> And
> I am the eagle and serpent of
> the Aztec civilization.

The key element here is the contradictory nature of this identification: Joaquín is both Cuauhtémoc and Cortés, Aztec and Spaniard, conquered and conqueror. Here we see the enactment of a version of what Gloria Anzaldúa refers to as Mestiza consciousness in her *Borderlands/La Frontera*, the construction of a self-identity which performs as the hybrid embodiment of historically opposed forces now joined by blood,

blood both in the sense of lineage and of destruction. The image Anzaldúa uses is that of a large scab, a wound into which both opposing nation-states—Mexico and the U.S.—bleed. This border region now functions as an amorphous and unstable third entity that threatens the neat, defining limit of the concept of the Nation. American identity is here confronted with its dissolution, its miscegenation, its loss of purity. A frightening new Thing threatens the anglo-eurocentric Nation on two counts: this Thing invades the Nation-space at the same time that it joins that space to the foreign space of Mexico. For the mainstream racist imaginary, this third Thing—the Chicano as the embodiment of this blurred space—is ironically the true defining feature of "American" national identity, for this amorphous, oozing mass gives body to the instability of racialized national identity itself. It is this stain marking both the inside and the outside of the raced national body that is the truth of the (Anglo) Nation in its inherent impossibility of achieving fullness and purity. And it is Chicano nationalism, as laid out later in Gonzales's poem, that embodies this defining impossibility as the threat of the internal alien—as we see in today's anti-immigrant hysteria.

This contradictory fusion can be seen in the role of Christianity in Mexican-American culture. While the Church functioned as the spiritual and cultural arm of Spanish imperialism, it nevertheless gave the Mexican people a sense of unity through brotherhood, as embodied in what Joaquín refers to as that "lasting truth that / Spaniard / Indian / Mestizo / were all God's children." Here we have the syncretism crucial to Chicano iconography, whereby the Aztec deities are transformed into, yet continue to co-exist alongside, Catholic saints. The major Aztec female deity, for example, Tonantzín, is converted into the Virgin of Guadalupe, the latter herself functioning in a syncretistic way in that she is the Brown Virgin who appeared to the Indians and spoke in Nahuatl, the Aztec tongue. Joaquín identifies with these female figures as well as the more visible males of Mexican and Mexican-American revolutionary tradition: "I am / The black-shawled / Faithful women / Who die with me / Or live / Depending on the time and place." Yet in this early moment of the construction of Chicanismo, this "female" identification limits the range of manifestations of the "proper" Chicana-Mexican woman by cloaking her in the black shawl of the faithful woman rather than the ammo-belted *guerrilleras* of Revolutionary iconography. (See Emma Pérez on the function of Mexican Revolutionary iconography in the construction of Chicanismo.) Or—to spin this relationship differently—the twin icons of the black-shawled woman and the (here absent) militant *guerrillera* function together to preclude the possibility of a host of other configurations of Mexican womanhood, such as the armed woman in the black shawl whose "faithfulness" and survival are acted out through armed struggle alongside the traditionally male warrior (see Poniatowska). The question of "faithfulness" itself rings perhaps too closely to the unfaithful figure of la Chingada (see Alarcón), the woman who "betrays" masculinist fantasies of love and revolution—fantasies that would soon come under fire by Chicanas at the National Chicano Youth Liberation Conference in 1969 in Denver.

The male line of the revolutionary tradition lives on through Joaquín as he identifies with Hidalgo, Benito Juarez, Pancho Villa, and Emiliano Zapata. And interestingly, true to the dialectical impulse behind the entire poem, Joaquín also identifies with the Mexican dictators Díaz and Huerta. Perhaps more important as an indigenous example, however, is Joaquín Murrieta, the *Californio* who sought revenge against the gold-rush Anglo-American invaders after they raped and murdered his wife. It is this Joaquín, Gonzales told me in conversation in 2004, who gives the poem's speaker his name.

After a review of this foundational historical retrospective, Joaquín returns to the present in a survey of current-day representatives of the oppressor and the oppressed:

> I stand here looking back,
> And now I see
> The present,
> And still
> I am a campesino,
> I am the fat political coyote—
>
> . . . .
> In a country that has wiped out
> All my history,
> Stifled all my pride.

Having constructed the substance of a Chicano identity from the selected moments of the past, Joaquín turns his attention to the future, for that is where the true hope lies for the Chicano now coming into being. This future is embodied by the children of Joaquín, the future generations who must carry out this symbolic mandate if the Chicano is to be fully realized in its being towards the future.

> I am Joaquín.
> I must fight
> and win this struggle
> for my sons, and they
> must know from me
> who I am.

Joaquín is thus a complex and contradictory identity, yet all of these opposing facets nevertheless unite as one against Anglo-American oppression and aggression. The key to survival, the poem ends up declaring, is endurance and revolutionary faith:

> And now the trumpet sounds,
> The music of the people stirs the
> Revolution.
> Like a sleeping giant it slowly
> Rears its head
> To the sound of
> Tramping feet
> Clamoring voices
> Mariachi strains

Fiery tequila explosions
The smell of chile verde and
Soft brown eyes of expectation for a
Better life.

Up to this point in the poem, the term "Chicano" has never been used. It appears inconspicuously in a list of seeming synonyms, all of which, the speaker claims, refer to the same political subject:

La raza!
Méjicano!
Español!
Latino!
Chicano!
Or whatever I call myself,
I look the same
I feel the same
I cry
And
Sing the same.

The final identifying term is "Chicano," and it is this term that gives name to the cultural manifestation that issues forth from the poem. For it is not the case that, whatever he calls himself, Joaquín looks, feels, cries, and sings the same. The name of Chicano is his primal baptism; yet, precisely because of its performative nature, its constitutive function must remain submerged, appearing only as one more presumably pre-existing name for the entity it seems to point to while bringing into being. Gonzales, poet and civil rights leader, can refer to *I Am Joaquín* as "a revelation of myself and of all Chicanos who are Joaquín" (preface to the 1972 photo-illustrated version). Neither he nor anyone else was Joaquín prior to the poem's existence; neither he nor anyone else was a Chicano. Yet after this moment, extending into the past and out towards the future, we can see the Chicano fighting for cultural existence in a hostile and alien land that was once his nation and homeland.

WORKS CITED

Alarcón, Norma. *Traddutora, Traditora: A Paradigmatic Figure of Chicana Feminism.* CULTURAL CRITIQUE 13 (Autumn 1989): 57–87.

Anzaldúa, Gloria. BORDERLANDS/LA FRONTERA: THE NEW MESTIZA. San Francisco: Aunt Lute, 1987.

Bruce-Novoa, Juan. CHICANO POETRY: A RESPONSE TO CHAOS. Austin: U of Texas P, 1982.

Gonzales, Rodolfo "Corky." I AM JOAQUÍN. Denver: Crusade for Justice, 1967. Reprinted in I AM JOAQUIN: YO SOY JOAQUIN; AN EPIC POEM, New York: Bantam, 1972, and in MESSAGE TO AZTLÁN: SELECTED WRITINGS, edited by Antonio Esquibel, pp. 16–29, Houston: Arte Público Press, 2001.

Pérez, Emma. THE DECOLONIAL IMAGINARY: WRITING CHICANAS INTO HISTORY. Blooming-
ton: Indiana UP, 1999.
Poniatowska, Elena. LAS SOLDADERAS: WOMEN OF THE MEXICAN REVOLUTION. El Paso, Tex.:
Cinco Puntos Press, 2006.
Zizek, Slavoj. ENJOY YOUR SYMPTOM: JACQUES LACAN IN HOLLYWOOD AND OUT. New York:
Routledge, 1992.

Chapter 39

||||||||||||||||||||||||||||||||||||||||||||||||||||||||||||||||||||||||

Borderlands

Gloria Anzaldúa

The actual physical borderland that I'm dealing with is the Texas–U.S. Southwest/ Mexican border. The psychological borderlands, the sexual borderlands, and the spiritual borderlands are not particular to the Southwest. In fact, the Borderlands are physically present wherever two or more cultures edge each other, where people of different races occupy the same territory, where under, lower, middle and upper classes touch, where the space between two individuals shrinks with intimacy.

I am a border woman. I grew up between two cultures, the Mexican (with a heavy Indian influence) and the Anglo (as a member of a colonized people in our own territory). I have been straddling that *Tejas*-Mexican border, and others, all my life. It's not a comfortable territory to live in, this place of contradictions. Hatred, anger, and exploitation are the prominent features of this landscape.

However, there have been compensations for this *mestiza*, and certain joys. Living on borders and in margins, keeping intact one's shifting and multiple identity and integrity, is like trying to swim in a new element, an "alien" element. There is an exhilaration in being a participant in the further evolution of humankind, in being "worked" on. I have the sense that certain "faculties"—not just in me but in every border resident, colored or noncolored—and dormant areas of consciousness are being activated, awakened. Strange, huh? And yes, the "alien" element has become familiar—never comfortable, not with society's clamor to uphold the old, to rejoin the flock, to go with the herd. No, not comfortable but home.

This book, then, speaks of my existence. My preoccupations with the inner life of the Self, and with the struggle of that Self amidst adversity and violation; with the confluence of primordial images; with the unique positionings consciousness takes at these confluent streams; and with my almost instinctive urge to communicate, to speak, to write about life on the borders, life in the shadows. . . .

El otro México / The Homeland, Aztlán

This is my home
this thin edge of
barbwire.
But the skin of the earth is seamless.
The sea cannot be fenced,
el mar does not stop at borders.
To show the white man what she thought of his
arrogance,
Yemaya blew that wire fence down.

This land was Mexican once,
was Indian always
and is.
And will be again.

Yo soy un puente tendido
del mundo gabacho al del mojado,
lo pasado me estirá pa' 'trás
y lo presente pa' 'delante.
Que la Virgen de Guadalupe me cuide
Ay ay ay, soy mexicana de este lado.

The U.S.–Mexican border *es una herida abierta* [an open wound—Eds.] where the Third World grates against the first and bleeds. And before a scab forms it hemorrhages again, the lifeblood of two worlds merging to form a third country—a border culture. Borders are set up to define the places that are safe and unsafe, to distinguish *us* from *them*. A border is a dividing line, a narrow strip along a steep edge. A borderland is a vague and undetermined place created by the emotional residue of an unnatural boundary. It is in a constant state of transition. The prohibited and forbidden are its inhabitants. *Los atravesados* live here: the squint-eyed, the perverse, the queer, the troublesome, the mongrel, the mulatto, the half-breed, the half dead; in short, those who cross over, pass over, or go through the confines of the "normal." Gringos in the U.S. Southwest consider the inhabitants of the borderlands transgressors, aliens—whether they possess documents or not, whether they're Chicanos, Indians, or Blacks. Do not enter, trespassers will be raped, maimed, strangled, gassed, shot. The only "legitimate" inhabitants are those in power, the whites and those who align themselves with whites. Tension grips the inhabitants of the borderlands like a virus. Ambivalence and unrest reside there and death is no stranger.

In the fields, la migra. *My aunt saying, "No corran, don't run. They'll think you're* del otro lao." *In the confusion, Pedro ran, terrified of being caught. He couldn't speak English, couldn't tell them he was fifth generation American.* Sin papeles—*he did not carry his birth certificate to work in the fields.* La migra *took him away while we watched.* Se lo llevaron. *He tried to smile when he looked back at us, to raise his fist. But I saw the*

shame pushing his head down, I saw the terrible weight of shame hunch his shoulders.
They deported him to Guadalajara by plane. The furthest he'd ever been to Mexico was
Reynosa, a small border town opposite Hidalgo, Texas, not far from McAllen. Pedro
walked all the way to the Valley. Se lo llevaron sin un centavo al pobre. Se vino an-
dando desde Guadalajara.

During the original peopling of the Americas, the first inhabitants migrated across
the Bering Straits and walked south across the continent. The oldest evidence of humankind in the U.S.—the Chicanos' ancient Indian ancestors—was found in Texas
and has been dated to 35,000 B.C.[1] In the Southwest United States archeologists have
found 20,000-year-old campsites of the Indians who migrated through, or permanently occupied, the Southwest, Aztlán—land of the herons, land of whiteness, the
Edenic place of origin of the Azteca. . . .

La Conciencia de la Mestiza / Towards a New Consciousness

Numerous possibilities leave *la mestiza* floundering in uncharted seas. In perceiving
conflicting information and points of view, she is subjected to a swamping of her
psychological borders. She has discovered that she can't hold concepts or ideas in
rigid boundaries. The borders and walls that are supposed to keep the undesirable
ideas out are entrenched habits and patterns of behavior; these habits and patterns
are the enemy within. Rigidity means death. Only by remaining flexible is she able to
stretch the psyche horizontally and vertically. *La mestiza* constantly has to shift out of
habitual formations; from convergent thinking, analytical reasoning that tends to use
rationality to move toward a single goal (a Western mode), to divergent thinking,[2]
characterized by movement away from set patterns and goals and toward a more
whole perspective, one that includes rather than excludes.

The new *mestiza* copes by developing a tolerance for contradictions, a tolerance
for ambiguity. She learns to be an Indian in Mexican culture, to be Mexican from an
Anglo point of view. She learns to juggle cultures. She has a plural personality, she
operates in a pluralistic mode—nothing is thrust out, the good the bad and the ugly,
nothing rejected, nothing abandoned. Not only does she sustain contradictions, she
turns the ambivalence into something else.

She can be jarred out of ambivalence by an intense, and often painful, emotional
event which inverts or resolves the ambivalence. I'm not sure exactly how. The work
takes place underground—subconsciously. It is work that the soul performs. That fo-
cal point or fulcrum, that juncture where the *mestiza* stands, is where phenomena
tend to collide. It is where the possibility of uniting all that is separate occurs. This
assembly is not one where severed or separated pieces merely come together. Nor is
it a balancing of opposing powers. In attempting to work out a synthesis, the self has
added a third element which is greater than the sum of its severed parts. That third
element is a new consciousness—a *mestiza* consciousness—and though it is a source
of intense pain, its energy comes from continual creative motion that keeps breaking
down the unitary aspect of each new paradigm.

En unas pocas centurias, the future will belong to the *mestiza*. Because the future depends on the breaking down of paradigms, it depends on the straddling of two or more cultures. By creating a new mythos—that is, a change in the way we perceive reality, the way we see ourselves, and the ways we behave—*la mestiza* creates a new consciousness.

The work of *mestiza* consciousness is to break down the subject-object duality that keeps her a prisoner and to show in the flesh and through the images in her work how duality is transcended. The answer to the problem between the white race and the colored, between males and females, lies in healing the split that originates in the very foundation of our lives, our culture, our languages, our thoughts. A massive uprooting of dualistic thinking in the individual and collective consciousness is the beginning of a long struggle, but one that could, in our best hopes, bring us to the end of rape, of violence, of war.

NOTES

1. John R. Chavez, THE LOST LAND: THE CHICANO IMAGE OF THE SOUTHWEST (Albuquerque: University of New Mexico Press, 1984), 9.

2. Robert Plant Armstrong, THE POWERS OF PRESENCE: CONSCIOUSNESS, MYTH, AND AFFECTING PRESENCE (Philadelphia: University of Pennsylvania Press, 1981), 4.

Chapter 40

||||||||||||||||||||||||||||||||||||||||||||||||||||||||||||||||||||||||||||||

Rodrigo's Chronicle

Richard Delgado

"Excuse me, Professor, I'm Rodrigo Crenshaw. I believe we have an appointment."

Startled, I put down the book I was reading and glanced quickly first at my visitor, then at my desk calendar. The tall, rangy man standing in my doorway was of indeterminate age—somewhere between twenty and forty—and, for that matter, ethnicity. His tightly curled hair and olive complexion suggested that he might be African American. But he could also be Latino, perhaps Mexican, Puerto Rican, or any one of the many Central American nationalities that have been applying in larger numbers to my law school in recent years.

"Come in," I said. "I think I remember a message from you, but I seem not to have entered it into my appointment book. Please excuse all this confusion," I added, pointing to the pile of papers and boxes that had littered my office floor since my recent move. I wondered: Was he an undergraduate seeking admission? A faculty candidate of color like the many who seek my advice about entering academia? I searched my memory without success.

"Please sit down," I said. "What can I do for you?"

"I'm Geneva Crenshaw's brother. I want to talk to you about the LSAT, as well as the procedure for obtaining an appointment as a law professor at an American university."

As though sensing my surprise, my visitor explained: "Shortly after Geneva's accident, I moved to Italy with my father, Lorenzo, who was in the Army. After he retired, we remained in Italy, where he worked as a civilian at the same base where he had been serving. I finished high school at the base, then attended an Italian university, earning my law degree last June. I've applied for the LL.M. program at a number of U.S. law schools, including your own. I want to talk to you about the LSAT, which all the schools want me to take, and which, believe it or not, I've never taken. I'd also like to discuss my chances of landing a teaching position after I earn the degree."

I reflected a moment, then said: "Your situation is somewhat unusual. But I'll do my best. I didn't know Geneva had a brother."

"We're only half-siblings," he explained, "and separated by nearly twenty years. But I've kept in touch as best I could, and I'm grateful to you for bringing her message to

From *Rodrigo's Chronicle*, 101 YALE L.J. 1357 (1992). Originally published in the *Yale Law Journal*. Reprinted by permission of the author.

the attention of your friends. She has a rather acerbic manner, as you know. But she respects you and your work enormously."

"Your sister is a remarkable woman," I said. "I have learned at least as much from her as she from me. You said you are going to be taking the LSAT. What are your concerns about that?"

"The usual," he replied, "including that I don't see why I should have to take it at all. I graduated fourth in my class at a law school even older than yours. I should think it would be obvious to anyone that I can read a case or make a legal argument. But I'm more than a little worried about the cultural bias people tell me the test contains. I'm proficient in English, as you can tell. But I've been away from the United States for nearly ten years; I'm afraid some of the questions may assume information I lack simply because I've taken half my schooling outside the culture."

"I've made the same argument myself in the case of minorities in the United States," I said. "But it goes nowhere. They say the test is not biased because it predicts law school grades, which always seemed like a non sequitur to me. I didn't realize that we required the test for foreign law graduates." I paused, then added, "Maybe they think it provides a check against grades, which might vary from one system to another."

"Yet in each system," Rodrigo countered levelly, "those grades reflect, in most cases, broader and more pervasive forms of cultural power, including the backgrounds and advantages of those who earn them. They also correspond to the law firm jobs and prestigious government positions the students will hold after they graduate. Identifying the LSAT as a predictor of grades, or even of later job performance, tells us only that this narrow test will identify people who thrive in particular types of environments—the ones, of course, that rely on the test to do a certain type of screening."

Not bad, I thought—I hoped he would come to my law school. But instead I asked: "So, what are you going to do? If you skip the test, you can kiss your LL.M goodbye."

"I know, I know," he said, "if I have to take the test, I will. I bought one of those practice books. I'm sure I'll do OK—although I can't help thinking the whole thing is a waste of time."

"I agree—on both scores," I added.

[Rodrigo and the Professor discuss the law school hiring market, then continue as follows—Eds.]

"As I mentioned, my program of studies at Bologna centered on the history of Western culture. I'm mainly interested in the rise of Northern European thought and its contribution to our current predicament. During my early work I had hoped to extend my analysis to law and legal scholarship."

"I think I know what you will say about the latter two. Tell me more about the big picture—how you see Northern European thought."

"I've been studying its rise in the late Middle Ages and decline beginning a few decades ago. I'm interested in what causes cultures to evolve, then go into eclipse. American society, even more than its European counterparts, is in the early stages of dissolution and crisis. It's like a wave that is just starting to crest. As you know, waves travel unimpeded across thousands of miles of ocean. When they approach the shore, they rise up for a short time, then crest and lose their energy. Western culture, particularly in this country, is approaching that stage. Which explains, in part, why I am back."

Rodrigo went on: "I'm sure all the things I'm going to say have occurred to you. Northern Europeans have been on top for a relatively short period—a mere wink in the eye of history. And during that time they have accomplished little—except causing a significant number of deaths and the disruption of a number of more peaceful cultures, which they conquered, enslaved, exterminated, or relocated on their way to empire. Their principal advantages were linear thought, which lent itself to the development and production of weapons and other industrial technologies, and a kind of messianic self-image according to which they were justified in dominating other nations and groups. But now, as you can see"—Rodrigo gestured in the direction of the window and the murky air outside—"Anglo-Saxon-Teuton culture has arrived at a terminus, demonstrating its own absurdity."

"I'm not sure I follow you. Linear thought, as you call it, has surely conferred many benefits." (I thought of countless examples. Just that morning I had read about a new medical breakthrough developed at an American research university. Only two weeks ago I had my car rebuilt by a mechanic who [I hope] was well versed in linear thought. The day before I had baked a batch of brownies following a ten-step recipe.) "And is it really on its last legs? Aside from smoggy air, Western culture looks firmly in control to me."

"So does a wave, even when it's cresting—and you know what happens shortly thereafter. Turn on your computer, Professor," Rodrigo said, pointing at my new desktop. "Let me show you a few things."

For the next ten minutes, Rodrigo led me on a tour of articles and books on the West's economic and political condition. His fingers fairly danced over the keys of my computer. Accessing data bases I didn't even know existed, he showed me treatises on the theory of cultural cyclicity; articles and editorials from *The Economist, Corriere della Sera,* the *Wall Street Journal,* and other leading newspapers, all on our declining economic position; material from the *Statistical Abstract* and other sources on our increasing crime rate, rapidly dwindling fossil fuels, loss of markets, and switch from a production- to a service-based economy with high unemployment, an increasingly restless underclass, and increasing rates of drug addition, suicide, and infant mortality. It was a sobering display of technical virtuosity. I had the feeling he had done this before and wondered how he had come by this proficiency while in Italy.

Rodrigo finally turned away from the computer and looked at me inquiringly. "A bibliography alone will not persuade me," I said. "But let's suppose for the sake of argument that you have made a prima facie case, at least with respect to our economic problems and to issues concerning race and the underclass. I suppose you have a theory on how we got into this predicament?"

"I do," Rodrigo said with that combination of brashness and modesty that I find so charming in the young. "As I mentioned a moment ago, it has to do with linear thought—the hallmark of the West. When developed, it conferred a great initial advantage. Because of it, the culture was able to spawn, early on, classical physics, which, with the aid of a few borrowings here and there, like gunpowder from the

Chinese, quickly enabled it to develop impressive armies. And, because it was basically a ruthless, restless culture, it quickly dominated others that lay in its path. It eradicated ones that resisted, enslaved others, and removed the Indians, all in the name of progress. It opened up and mined new territories—here and elsewhere—as soon as they became available and extracted all the available mineral wealth so rapidly that fossil fuels and other mineral goods are now running out, as you and your colleagues have pointed out."

"But you are indicting just one civilization. Haven't all groups acted similarly? Non-linear societies are accomplishing at least as much environmental destruction as Western societies are capable of. And what about Genghis Khan, Columbus, the cruelties of the Chinese dynasties? The Turkish genocide of the Armenians, the war machine that was ancient Rome?"

"True. But at least these other groups limited their own imperial impulses at some point."

"Hah! With a little help from their friends," I retorted.

"Anyway," continued Rodrigo, "these groups produced valuable art, music, or literature along the way. Northern Europeans have produced next to nothing—little sculpture, art, or music worth listening to, and only a modest amount of truly great literature. And the few accomplishments they can cite with pride can be traced to the Egyptians, an African culture."

"Rodrigo, you greatly underestimate the dominant culture. Some of them may be derivative and warlike, as you say. Others are not; they are creative and humane. And even the ones you impeach have a kind of dogged ingenuity for which you do not give them credit. They have the staying and adaptive powers to remain on top. For example, when linear physics reached a dead end, as you pointed out, they developed relativity physics. When formalism expired, at least some of them developed Critical Legal Studies, reaching back and drawing on existing strands of thought such as psychoanalysis, phenomenology, Marxism, and philosophy of science."

"Good point," admitted Rodrigo a little grudgingly, "although I've already pointed out the contributions of Gramsci, a Mediterranean. Fanon and your Critical Race Theory friends are black or brown. And Freud and Einstein are, of course, Jews. Consider, as well, Cervantes, Verdi, Michelangelo, Duke Ellington, the current crop of black writers—non-Saxons all."

"But Northern Europeans, at least in the case of the two Jewish giants," I interrupted.

"True, people move," he countered.

"Don't be flip," I responded. "Since when are the Spanish and Italians exempt from criticism for Western foibles? What about the exploitive capacity of the colonizing conquistadors? Wasn't the rise of commercial city-states in Renaissance Italy a central foundation for subsequent European cultural imperialism? Most ideas of Eurocentric superiority date to the Renaissance and draw on its rationalist, humanist intellectual, and artistic traditions."

"We've had our lapses," Rodrigo conceded. "But theirs are far worse and more systematic." Rodrigo was again eyeing my computer.

Wondering what else he had in mind, I continued: "What about Rembrandt, Mozart, Shakespeare, Milton? And American popular culture—is it not the envy of the rest of the world? What's more, even if some of our Anglo brothers and sisters are doggedly linear, or, as you put it, exploitive of nature and warlike—surely you cannot believe that their behavior is biologically based—that something genetic prevents them from doing anything except invent and manufacture weapons?" Rodrigo's earnest and shrewd retelling of history had intrigued me, although, to be honest, I was alarmed. Was he going too far?

"The Anglos do all that, plus dig up the earth to extract minerals that are sent to factories that darken the skies, until everything runs out and we find ourselves in the situation where we are now." Then, after a pause: "Why do you so strongly resist a biological explanation, Professor? Their own scientists are happy to conjure up and apply them to us. But from one point of view, it is they whose exploits—or rather lack of them—need explaining."

"I'd love to hear your evidence."

"Let me begin this way. Do you remember that famous photo of the finish of the hundred-meter dash at the World Games? It showed six magnificent athletes straining to break the tape. The first two finished under the world record. All were black."

"I do remember."

"Black athletes dominated most of the events, the shorter ones at any rate. People of color are simply faster and quicker than our white brothers and sisters. Even the marathon has come to be dominated by people of color. And, to anticipate your question, yes I do believe the same holds true in the mental realm. In the ghetto they play 'the dozens'—a game that requires throwaway speed. The dominant group has nothing similar. And take your field, law. Saxons developed the hundred-page linear, densely footnoted, impeccably crafted article—saying, in most cases, very little. They also brought us the LSAT, which tests the same boring, linear capacities they developed over time and that now exclude the very voices they need for salvation. Yet you, Matsuda, Lawrence, Torres, Peller, and others toss off articles with ridiculous ease—critical thought comes easy for you, hard for them. I can't, of course, prove your friends are genetically inferior; it may be their mindset or culture. But they act like lemmings. They go on building factories until the natural resources run out, thermonuclear weapons when their absurdity is obvious and everyone knows they cannot be used, hundred-page law review articles that rehash cases when everyone knows that vein of thought has run dry—and they fail even to sense their own danger. You say they are adaptive. I doubt it."

"Rodrigo," I burst in. "You seriously misread the times. Your ideas on cultural superiority and inferiority will obviously generate resistance, as you yourself concede. Wait till you see how they respond to your hundred-yard dash example; you're sure to find yourself labeled as racist. Maybe we both are—half the time I agree with you. But even the other things you say about the West's predicament and its need for an infusion of new thought—things I strongly agree with—will fall on deaf ears. All the movement is the other way. This is a time of retrenchment. The country is listening to the conservatives, not to people like you and me."

"I know," said Rodrigo. "I've been reading about that retrenchment. We do get the *New York Times* in Italy, even if it comes a few days late."

"It strikes me that this way of thinking is an example of what our psychologist friends call 'perseveration,'" I said.

"Exactly. In my studies, I found that most beleaguered people do this, plus search for a scapegoat—a group they can depict as the source of all their troubles."

"An old story," I agreed ruefully. "Some conservatives, for example, place most of the blame for colleges' troubles at the doorstep of those demanding minorities who, along with a few deluded white sympathizers, have been broadening the curriculum, instituting Third World courses, hiring minority professors, and recruiting 'unqualified' students of color—all at the expense of academic rigor and standards. They say the barbarians—meaning us—are running the place and urge university administrators to hold the line against what they see as bullying and a new form of racism."

"Have you ever thought it curious," Rodrigo mused, "how some whites can see themselves as victimized by us—a pristine example of the sort of post-modern move they profess to hate. I suppose if one has been in power a long time, any change seems threatening, offensive, unprincipled, and wrong. But reality eventually intervenes. Western culture's predicament runs very deep—every indicator shows it. And, one sees straws in the wind, harbingers of hopeful change."

"Rodrigo, I'll say this for you—you've proposed a novel approach to affirmative action. Until now, we've struggled with finding a moral basis for sustaining what looked like breaches of the merit principle, like hiring a less qualified over a more qualified person for racial reasons. But you're saying that white people should welcome nonwhites into their fold as rapidly as possible out of simple self-interest—that is, if they want their society to survive. This is something that they are not accustomed to hearing, to put it mildly. Do you have any support for this assertion?"

"Turn on your computer again, Professor. This won't take but a minute."

I obliged him, and was treated to a second lightning display of technological wizardry as Rodrigo showed me books on Asian business organization, Eastern mysticism, Japanese schooling, ancient Egyptian origins of modern astronomy and physics, and even on the debt our Founding Fathers owed the Iroquois for the political ideas that shaped our Constitution. He showed me articles on the Japanese computer and automobile industries, the seemingly more successful approach that African and Latino societies have taken to family organization and the treatment of their own aged and destitute, and even the roots of popular American music in black composers and groups.

"It's only a beginning," Rodrigo said, switching off my computer. "I want to make this my life's work. Do you think anyone will listen to me?"

"It's hard to say. I don't know if the times are right. Most Americans believe that their economic problems are just temporary and that they have the best, fairest political system in the world—conveniently forgetting a chapter or two of their own history. But never mind that. Let me ask you instead a personal question: If things are really as bad as you say, why are you, who have a choice, thinking of returning? Shouldn't you remain safely in Italy while your native culture self-destructs? When a wave crests, then hits the beach, it creates an immediate commotion. There's a lot of foam, a loud noise, a great expenditure of energy, and sometimes an undertow. I should think someone like you would be at some risk here—particularly if you go around speaking as candidly as you have to me today—notwithstanding our much-vaunted system of free expression."

"I'm back for family reasons. Geneva and my other half-brothers and sisters are here. And since my father died, I have no other relatives in Italy. Your decreasing quality of life and high white-collar crime rate gave me pause. And I could be quite comfortable in Italy, now that I've got my military service out of the way. I suppose I thought, as well, that with a little more training I could do something to ease the pain of my native country as it goes through a difficult transition."

"You mean helping America adjust to its new multiracial character, plus its own shrinking share of world markets?" I asked.

"That and more," Rodrigo answered quietly. "The dominant group will need help. All of us will."

"What if they don't see it that way?" I pressed. "Has a dominant group ever given up power gracefully? Has it ever abandoned the modes of thought, military organization, and extractive industries that brought it to power without a struggle? And if so, how are we—I mean those who believe like you—going to conduct such a campaign? I'm afraid they have all the power. You may think truth and history are on your side. But what if they don't go along?"

"They will," Rodrigo replied with conviction, "as soon as they recognize their own dilemma. The early Visigoths destroyed themselves by warring. We can help the current dominant culture avoid a similar fate. We may even have some friends and allies in the majority group—ones who believe as we do. Maybe we can bill our offerings as 'hybrid vigor'—something they already endorse."

"And, once again—what if they refuse? Paradigms change slowly. What if your transformation requires a hundred years?"

"In that case, we could easily see an outbreak of sabotage and what you call terrorism carried out by desperate individuals hoping to speed things up. The more advanced, the more technologically complex a society becomes, the more vulnerable it is to disruption. Imagine what a few strategic and nonviolent taps on telephone switching stations around the country could do—or a few computer viruses, for that matter. Disruption is economically efficient for the subordinated group. In Italy, the government tried for a time to exclude leftist organizations. A few kidnappings and commando raids, and they were ready for serious negotiation. Something like that could happen here—or do you think I'm wrong, Professor?"

"Rodrigo, I have many doubts about all the things you have said—and particularly this one. If you repeat even half of what you have told me today to your colleagues or students, you will find yourself out of academia on your ear—and probably disbarred to boot."

"I had no idea those were the rules of discourse. On the Continent we discuss these things openly—especially since events in Eastern Europe showed that rapid reform is, in fact, possible. Your society certainly perpetrated plenty of terrorism on blacks, Chicanos, and Indians. Nevertheless, if one cannot discuss these things in —how do you put it?—polite company—I'll keep them to myself and for my close friends. I don't want to be seen as having an attitude problem."

Our conversation soon concluded. I had to prepare for a faculty colloquium I was to give at my new school that afternoon, and Rodrigo quickly excused himself, saying he had to get ready for the LSAT—"that dinosaur relic of an outmoded system of thought"—that coming Saturday. But I couldn't shake his image. Here was a man who spoke what he saw. I feared for him.

||||||||||||||||||||||||||||||||||||||||||||||||||||||||||||||||||||||||||||||||||||

Chapter 41

The Significance of Narrative for Outsiders

George A. Martinez

The use of narrative in law raises a number of issues. Narrative has been used primarily by critical theorists, including critical race theorists, Latino legal theorists, Asian-American legal theorists, feminist theorists, and gay/lesbian legal theorists. They offer narrative as a way to introduce a perspective that is absent in mainstream legal discourse.

Drawing on philosophy, I explain the importance of narrative for outsiders and offer responses to some important philosophical or jurisprudential objections to the use of narrative in law. In particular, I respond to the following claims: (1) the use of narrative is an illegitimate externalist approach to law; (2) the use of narrative is misguided because it does not seek to ascertain truth, but instead seeks to change the law; and (3) the use of narrative is hostile to "reason." This philosophical discussion is especially timely and important because although some of the leading critics of narrative have recognized the relevance of philosophy to the debate over the use of narrative in law, they have refused to squarely confront the philosophical issues implicated in the debate.

The philosopher Jean-Francois Lyotard's notion of the "differend" helps show the importance of narrative for outsiders. Without narrative, minorities experience the differend. Lyotard says that the dominant idea of justice can silence subordinate persons. The differend arises when there is a conflict between two conceptions of justice and there is an effort to judge an individual who does not hold the foundational views of the regime that stands in judgment of the individual. In such a situation, the subordinate person lacks "a forum and a language" which would allow them to express how they have been injured. African Americans have experienced this difficulty. For hundreds of years, blacks had no standing to sue for the injuries they sustained at the hands of the white majority. They sustained more than legal injuries. They were harmed because they had "no forum in which they could speak." In such circumstances, the prevailing conception of justice deprives the person of a "voice that can be heard on terms which the system will understand."[1]

When one experiences an injury that cannot be established in a given system of justice, one is victimized and one's claim "constitutes a differend lying outside the system of justice." The differend cannot be acknowledged or comprehended by those

From *Philosophical Considerations and the Use of Narrative in Law,* 30 Rutgers L.J. 683 (1999). Originally published in the *Rutgers Law Journal.* Reprinted by permission.

who brought it into existence. Many minorities experience the differend: their harms sometimes cannot be recognized by the justice system—i.e., the traditional forms of legal argument.

Consider some examples. Mexican Americans have faced the differend. They have sometimes found that our legal system has not recognized their harms. In *Hernandez v. State*, a Mexican-American man had been convicted of murder. He sought to reverse his conviction on the ground that Mexican Americans had been illegally excluded from serving on the jury. He relied on case law holding that it was a violation of the Equal Protection Clause of the Fourteenth Amendment to exclude blacks from serving on juries. The court, however, found that the Fourteenth Amendment protected only two races: blacks and whites. In this regard, the court held that Mexican Americans are "white." Since the juries that indicted and convicted the defendant were composed of white persons—i.e., members of his own race—there was no equal protection violation. In *Hernandez*, Mexican Americans were confronted with the differend. The system did not recognize the harm they suffered from having no Mexican Americans on juries.

Consider another example. In *Mashpee Tribe v. Town of Mashpee*, a Native American community sought to reclaim certain tribal lands. The Mashpee alleged that the lands had been acquired from them in contravention of the Indian Non-Intercourse Act of 1970. That Act bars the sale of Indian land unless the federal government has approved the sale. The Mashpee argued that its land had been sold without the approval of the United States. In response, the defendant Town of Mashpee contended that the Mashpee were not covered by the Act because they were not a tribe.

In order to prevail, the Mashpee had to establish that they were a "tribe" at the time the land was transferred. Relying on earlier case law, the court defined "tribe" as a "body of Indians of the same or similar race, united in a community under one leadership or government, and inhabiting a particular though sometimes ill-defined territory." Applying this definition, the court held that the Mashpee were not a tribe.

The Mashpee disagreed with the court's definition of a "tribe." They argued that their tribal identity could be established through an alternative conception of a tribe —i.e., one based on their long-term relationship with the land and their maintenance of unique cultural practices. That notion of a "tribe," however, did not find support within the legal system. Thus, the system could not recognize their claim. The Mashpee experienced the differend.

Narrative provides a language for minorities to communicate harms. Without narrative, minorities have no voice to explain how they have been harmed. Their claims cannot, at times, be vindicated within the present system. Thus, minorities face the differend, deprived of a language to express claims that are located somewhere outside of the system.

Consider how narrative might have been useful in the *Hernandez* case. If the Mexican-American defendant had been able to use narrative, he could have shown that he was harmed by the absence of Mexican Americans on the jury. Narrative would have shown that he was not protected by having whites on the jury because white Anglos constructed Mexican Americans as non-white. Two examples of the descriptions that Anglos produced regarding Mexican Americans will suffice. The historian David Weber writes:

> Anglo Americans found an additional element to despise in Mexicans: racial mixture. American visitors to the Mexican frontier were nearly unanimous in commenting on the dark skin of Mexican mestizos who, it was generally agreed, had inherited the worst qualities of Spaniards and Indians to produce a "race" still more despicable than that of either parent.[2]

Through narrative, the defendant in *Hernandez* could have explained how he was injured by not having Mexican Americans on the jury. Since the narrative would have established him as non-white, he could have shown that he was not protected by having whites instead of Mexican-Americans on the jury.

Thus, narrative enables outsiders to highlight injuries that they have sustained. For instance, in an effort to rebut those who argue that we should limit the number of Latinos that are allowed to immigrate into the United States on the ground that they refuse to assimilate into the American mainstream, Kevin Johnson has employed narrative to eloquently describe the psychological damage that is suffered by Latinos who attempt to fully assimilate by relinquishing their cultural traditions. Similarly, Richard Delgado and Derrick Bell have used storytelling to show how minorities are injured by racism that affects the hiring process of law school faculties. Likewise, Mari Matsuda has used narrative to show how minorities are harmed by hate speech.

The philosopher Jacques Derrida's notion of justice is also instructive in explaining the importance of narrative as the voice of the outsiders. For Derrida, justice is a "relation or debt from one person to another." Justice is an "incalculable demand to treat the other on the other's terms." Derrida insists that "[t]o address oneself in the language of the other is, it seems, the condition of all possible justice."[3] Because narrative provides minorities with a way to communicate how they have been harmed, narrative is the language of the other. Since justice requires that we treat the other on the other's terms, outsiders should be permitted to use narrative. For Derrida, justice does not permit a dominant group to force its linguistic practices on a minority group. Thus, it is wrong for a majority to impose its legal language, i.e., the traditional forms of legal argument, on outsider groups.

Narratives and conventional modes of legal argument seem to constitute incommensurable languages. There appears to be no reason to believe that narratives are necessarily translatable into traditional modalities of legal argument. Indeed, the manner in which minorities experience the differend demonstrates this point. Lyotard contends that the differend arises precisely from the untranslatability or "the incommensurability of phrases and phrase systems."[4] He asserts: "There are a number of phrase regimens: reasoning, knowing, describing, recounting, questioning, showing, ordering, etc. Phrases from heterogeneous regimens cannot be translated into the other."[5]

This has important implications. First, it supports the idea that minorities have a different conceptual scheme than the dominant group. One philosopher, Donald Davidson, has argued that one conceptual scheme is different from another if it is not translatable. Since outsider narrative is not necessarily translatable into the mainstream forms of legal argument, it represents an alternative conceptual framework. Outsiders, then, operate from a different conceptual scheme. This different conceptual scheme expressed through narratives explains why it is plausible to suppose that there is a distinctive "voice of color."

The differences in conceptual schemes or world views can be clearly seen in the different ways that whites and outsiders view the world. For example, Richard Delgado has described the white majority's view on race in America as follows:

> Early in our history there was slavery, which was a terrible thing. Blacks were brought to this country from Africa in chains and made to work in the fields. Some were viciously mistreated, which was, of course, an unforgivable wrong; others were treated kindly. Slavery ended with the Civil War, although many blacks remained poor, uneducated and outside the cultural mainstream. As the country's racial sensitivity to black's plight increased, the vestiges of slavery were gradually eliminated by federal statutes and case law. Today, blacks have many civil rights and are protected from discrimination in such areas as housing, public education, employment, and voting. The gap between blacks and whites is steadily closing, although it may take some time for it to close completely. . . . Most Americans are fair-minded individuals who harbor little racial prejudice. The few who do can be punished when they act on those beliefs.[6]

Thus, whites see the world as a place where racism has been overcome. In stark contrast to that world view is the outsider perspective. It holds that the history of

> black subordination in America [is] a history "gory, brutal, filled with more murder, mutilation, rape and brutality than most of us can imagine or easily comprehend." This . . . history continues into the present, implicating individuals still alive. It includes infant death rates among blacks nearly double those of whites, unemployment rates among black males nearly triple those of whites, and a gap between the races in income, wealth, and life expectancy that is the same as it was fifteen years ago, if not greater. It includes despair, crime, and drug addiction in black neighborhoods, and college and university enrollment figures for blacks that are dropping for the first time in decades. It dares to call our most prized legal doctrines and protections shams—devices enacted with great fanfare, only to be ignored, obstructed, or cut back as soon as the celebrations die down.[7]

Minorities, then, view the world as still very much infected with racism. For instance, minority scholars describe a world where racial minorities experience numerous "microaggressions." "Microaggressions" are "subtle, stunning, often automatic, and non-verbal exchanges which are 'put downs' [of minorities]."[8] Members of the dominant group, however, view racism as largely a thing of the past. Consistent with a conceptual framework that does not see race as presenting a significant problem, critical scholars have pointed out that whites see themselves as raceless. Thus, whiteness is said to be transparent. "[T]o be white is not to think about it." In my view, outsiders have written a number of narratives, in part, to show the omnipresence of racism. For example, Patricia Williams describes the racism that she experienced during the ordinary act of shopping when a store employee told her that the shop was closed even though it was early afternoon and whites were visibly shopping in the store. Similarly, Charles Lawrence has described how whites have sought to "praise" him by stating "I don't think of you as a Negro." Likewise, Margaret Chon has observed that Asian Americans experience as racist the often received compliment that they "speak such good English."

Minorities have observed that whites tend to criticize outsiders for raising issues of race. This criticism is understandable once one perceives the different conceptual schemes at work. According to the conceptual scheme of the dominant group, racism is no longer a significant problem in America. Given this, it makes sense that whites are troubled by the outsider's insistence that racism continues to be a problem.

Beyond all of this, the use of narrative is philosophically important for outsiders because it provides a way for them to achieve authenticity. John Calmore has observed that minority intellectuals must "battle to avoid being rendered inauthentic by the pressures of adapting to the white world."[9] Martin Heidegger is one of the leading philosophers of this century who has done important work on the notion of authenticity that is not yet well-known in the legal academy. His discussion of inauthentic human beings helps explain the philosophical significance of narrative for outsiders. It provides a way for minorities to escape from standard practices of the mainstream world and thereby become authentic.

In his major philosophical work, Heidegger sought to ascertain "the meaning of being."[10] People can comprehend the notion of being in two distinct ways, "authentically and inauthentically." The authentic route provides us with the most accurate understanding of what it is to be. Heidegger provides an important analysis of inauthentic human beings. In engaging in specific activities and tasks, we express our societal understanding of what it is to be. In Heidegger's view, we generally do so in an inauthentic way. Part and parcel of this societal understanding of what it is to be is an idea of the appropriateness of our goals and tasks and of the ways in which we carry them out. In general, this sense finds expression in social norms of behavior. These norms reveal themselves in such statements as "One just doesn't do that," "One doesn't do that here, in that manner," or "One always . . ." and so on. For Heidegger, these norms are omnipresent as the possible expressions of the societal notion of what it is proper or fitting to do.

According to Heidegger, we are always and everywhere selecting from among the culturally determined alternatives for acting. In so doing, we often choose to do "what one does." "[W]hen we *choose* to interpret our being in the public way—living in the world of the one, . . . doing what one does, we 'fall' into the inauthentic way of being."[11]

When we fall into an inauthentic way of being, we act as one acts. We engage in activities and interpret the world in the manner that is normal in our society. This limits the possibilities for action to what lies within the realm of a standard world —i.e., the typical, the usual or that which is appropriate. The inauthentic person does precisely what anyone would do in that kind of circumstance. Inauthenticity means that we fall into the "anonymity and dispersion of the one."

With Heidegger's analysis in hand, it is possible to see why narrative serves an important role for outsiders. When outsiders produce narrative as scholarship they are not following the traditional norms of scholarship. They are doing something that does not conform to mainstream practices. Thus, narrative provides a way for minorities to be authentic in their intellectual life because it provides a way to move away from standard practices in scholarship. Producing narrative as scholarship provides a way for minorities to become authentic in Heidegger's sense and escape the banality of the one and the "nullity of inauthentic everydayness."

NOTES

1. *See* Douglas E. Litowitz, POSTMODERN PHILOSOPHY & LAW 119, 120 (1997).

2. FOREIGNERS IN THEIR NATIVE LAND: HISTORICAL ROOTS OF THE MEXICAN-AMERICANS 59–60 (David J. Weber ed., 1973).

3. Litowitz, at 92.

4. *Id.* at 119. "When one genre or phrase system is wrapped over another, the incommensurability produces a differend, a remainder, an injustice, or a wrong that cannot be communicated or translated into the universe of the phrase regime or genre which is responsible for causing the differend." *Id.* at 121.

5. *Id.* at 128.

6. *See, e.g.,* Richard Delgado, *Storytelling for Oppositionists and Others: A Plea for Narrative,* 87 MICH. L. REV. 2411, 2417 (1989).

7. *Id.* at 2417–18.

8. *See* Peggy C. Davis, *Law as Microaggression,* 98 YALE L.J. 1559, 1565 (1988).

9. John O. Calmore, *Critical Race Theory, Archie Shepp, and Fire Music: Securing an Authentic Intellectual Life in a Multicultural World,* 65 S. CAL. L. REV. 2129, 2170 (1992).

10. Harrison Hall, *Intentionality and World: Division I of Being and Time, in* THE CAMBRIDGE COMPANION TO HEIDEGGER 135 (Charles Guignon ed., 1993); *see also* Charles Guignon, *Introduction* to THE CAMBRIDGE COMPANION TO HEIDEGGER 2 (Charles Guignon ed., 1993) ("Heidegger's lofty ambition was to rejuvenate philosophy [and at the same time, Western culture] by clearing away the conceptual rubbish that has collected over our history in order to recover a clearer, richer understanding of what things are all about.").

11. *Id.* at 137. Heidegger writes: "The one as that which forms everyday being-with-one-another . . . constitutes what we call *the public* in the strict sense of the word. It implies that the world is already primarily given as the common world." Martin Heidegger, HISTORY OF THE CONCEPT OF TIME: PROLEGOMENA 246 (1985).

Chapter 42

||||||||||||||||||||||||||||||||||||||||||||||||||||||||||||||||||||||||||||||||

Narrative, Storytelling, and the
Mantra of Intersectionality

Antonia Darder and Rodolfo D. Torres

Consider the emphasis that critical race theory places on "experiential knowledge." Robin Barnes notes that "Critical race theorists . . . integrate their experiential knowledge, drawn from a shared history as 'Other' with their ongoing struggles to transform a world deteriorating under the albatross of racial hegemony." In concert with this privileging of experience, critical race theory employs narratives and storytelling as a central method of inquiry to "analyze the myths, presuppositions, and received wisdoms that make up the common culture about race and that invariably render blacks and other minorities one-down." The results of this storytelling method are theorized and then utilized to draw conclusions meant to influence public policy and institutional practices.

This narrative and storytelling method seeks to critique essentialist narratives in law, education, and the social sciences. In place of a systematic analysis of class and capitalist relations, critical race theory constructs "race"-centered responses to Eurocentrism and white privilege. As Delgado Bernal puts it:

> Western modernism is a network or grid of broad assumptions and beliefs that are deeply embedded in the way dominant Western culture constructs the nature of the world and one's experiences in it. In the United States, the center of this grid is a Eurocentric epistemological perspective based on White privilege.[1]

The narrative method "has become especially successful among groups committed to making the voice of the voiceless heard in the public arena."[2] Nevertheless, scholars who embrace the poetics of the narrative approach often "fail to challenge the underlying socioeconomic, political and cultural structures that have excluded these groups to begin with and have sustained the illusion of choice."[3] Thus, the narrative and storytelling approach can render the scholarship antidialectical by creating a false dichotomy between objectivity and subjectivity, "forgetting that one is implied in the other, [while ignoring] a basic dialectical principle: that men and women make history, but not under the conditions of their own choosing."[4]

We agree that "cultural resources and funds of knowledge such as myths, folk tales, *dichos, consejos*, kitchen talk, [and] autobiographical stories"[5] employed by critical race theory can illuminate particular concrete manifestations of racism. However, we contend that they can also prove problematic in positing a broader understanding of the fundamental macrosocial dynamics which shape the conditions that give rise to the "micro-aggressions" of racism in the first place.

Hence, we believe the use of critical race theory in education and the social sciences in general, despite authors' intentions, can unwittingly serve purposes that are fundamentally conservative or mainstream at best. Three additional but related concerns with the storytelling narrative method are also at issue here. One is the tendency to romanticize the experience of marginalized groups, privileging the narratives and discourses of "people of color," solely based on their experience of oppression, as if a people's entire politics can be determined solely by their individual location in history. The second is the tendency to dichotomize and "overhomogenize" both "white" people and "people of color" with respect to questions of voice and political representation. And the third is the inevitable "exaggerations, excesses and ideological trends for which the only possible name is chauvinism."[6] Unfortunately, these tendencies, whether academic or political, can result in unintended essentialism and superficiality in our theorizing of broader social inequalities, as well as the solutions derived from such theories.

It is not surprising that many of the theories, practices, and policies that inform the social science analysis of racialized populations today are overwhelmingly rooted in a politics of identity. Consequently, this approach—steeped in deeply insular perspectives of "race" and representation—has often ignored the imperatives of capitalist accumulation and the presence of class divisions among racialized populations, even though "identity categories and groups are always [racialized] and gendered and inflected by class."[7]

As we have previously stated, much of the literature on critical race theory lacks a substantive analysis of class and a critique of capitalism. And when class issues come in for mention, the emphasis is usually on an undifferentiated plurality that intersects with multiple oppressions. Unfortunately, this "new pluralism" fails to grapple with the relentless totalizing dimension of capitalism and its overwhelming tendency to homogenize rather than to diversify human experience.

This denial of the totalizing force of capitalism does not simply substantiate the existence of plural identities and relations that should be equally privileged and given weight as modes of domination. The logic of this argument fails to recognize that "the class relation that constitutes capitalism is not, after all, just a personal identity, nor even just a principle of 'stratification' or inequality. It is not only a specific system of power relations but also the constitutive relation of a distinctive social process, the dynamic of accumulation and the self-expansion of capital."[8]

Furthermore, such logic ignores that notions of identity result from a process of identification with a particular configuration of historically lived or transferred social arrangements and practices tied to material conditions of actual or imagined survival.

Unquestionably, racism as an ideology is integral to the process of capital accumulation. The failure to confront this dimension in an analysis of contemporary society as a racialized phenomenon or to continue to treat class as merely one of a multiplicity of (equally valid) perspectives, which may or may not "intersect" with the process of racialization, is a serious shortcoming. In addressing this issue, we must recognize that even progressive African American and Latino scholars and activists have often used identity politics, which generally glosses over class differences and/or ignores class contradictions, in an effort to build a political base. Constructions of "race" are objectified and mediated as truth to ignite political support, divorced from the realities of class struggle. By so doing, race-centered scholars have unwittingly perpetuated the vacuous and dangerous notion that politics and economics are two separate spheres of society which function independently—a view that firmly anchors and sustains prevailing class relations of power in society.

NOTES

1. Dolores Delgado Bernal, *Critical Race Theory, Latino Critical Theory, and Critical Race-Gendered Epistemologies: Recognizing Students of Color as Holders and Creators of Knowledge*, 8 QUALITATIVE INQUIRY 105, 111 (2002).

2. Emilia Viotti da Costa, *New Publics, New Politics, New Histories: From Economic Reductionism to Cultural Reductionism—in Search of Dialectics*, in RECLAIMING THE POLITICAL IN LATIN AMERICAN HISTORY: ESSAYS FROM THE NORTH 21 (Gilbert M. Joseph ed., 2001).

3. Steven Watts, *The Idiocy of American Studies: Poststructuralism, Language, and Politics in the Age of Self-Fulfillment*, 43 AMERICAN QUARTERLY 625, 652 (1991).

4. Viotti da Costa, at 20.

5. Delgado Bernal, at 120.

6. Scott McLemee, C. L. R. JAMES ON THE "NEGRO QUESTION" 86 (1996).

7. John Michael, ANXIOUS INTELLECTS 29 (2000).

8. Ellen Wood, DEMOCRACY AGAINST CAPITALISM: RENEWING HISTORICAL MATERIALISM 246 (1995).

Chapter 43

|||||||||||||||||||||||||||||||||||||||||||||||||||||||||||||||||||||||||||

Insurgent Metaphors

Otto Santa Ana

A review of the Latino responses to California's three anti-Latino referenda, Propositions 187, 209, and 227, reveals implicit assent to the worldview promulgated by conservative—at times nativist—political activists. For whenever references to immigrants as commodities, criminals, invaders, or animals are allowed, or whenever claims that affirmative action is the sole cause of U.S. racism are met with silence, or whenever Spanish is allowed to be called a foreign language, then the view of the social world that is antagonistic to Latinos has been tacitly accepted.

Advocates who speak to social issues of Latinos should mind their metaphors. Discourse is always harnessed to pull for a social agenda. Since conventional metaphors construct the status quo, actions to challenge them may bring about a swifter revision of worldview. This section outlines eight steps for the social activist.

One, silence is egregious assent to anti-Latino metaphors. In the course of direct discourse and debate, whether in front of a television audience, in the corridors of power, or on a ten-minute coffee break, the object of counterhegemonic discourse is to open up new cognitive "space," to offer an alternative view of the social world at the level of metaphor.

Two, metaphor should not be brought to the conscious attention of the audience in debate, since the object is to propose a viable alternative vision of the world, not to talk about discourse, which will be seen as quibbling over semantics. Jeffery S. Mio has conducted experiments on listener response to political metaphors and found that all metaphors are not equal. It seems effective metaphors trigger or resonate with the preexisting underlying symbolic representations of the listener, so that "extending" or verifying and affirming the operative scripts of an audience will garner a stronger response. In other words, the effective insubordinate metaphor is the congruent one.

Three, in my judgment, certain reciprocal actions may judiciously contest the conventional metaphoric worldview. Begin by employing a nonmetaphor to point out the failure of the standard vision of society. This will strip the conventional worldview of its presumed self-evident reality by providing a counterexample that forces the taken-for-granted to be questioned. The nonmetaphor can be a statistic, anecdote, or, even better, a face and a story. Then follow with an insurgent metaphor to recast the social world in more just, and more socially encompassing, terms which are demonstrably comprehensible.

Using a new metaphor without exemplification is just pretty words. For example, if bilingual education or bilingualism is characterized as handicap, illustrate the poverty of this view by presenting an adolescent who exhibits superb control of English (as well as excellent Spanish, Cantonese, or Bengali), and who consequently is better equipped to succeed than a similar English-dependent student. Well-spoken speech which retains a nonstandard accent, either due to second-language acquisition or a social dialect also flouts the linguistic hegemony that a speaker must speak with a standard English accent to be considered well educated or eloquent.

To the charge that immigrants are welfare-seeking invaders, call up a statistic and point to the immigrant entrepreneur who has built an economic base comparable to the president of the local Chamber of Commerce. For instance, cite a study of census data which demonstrated that 17 percent of Latino immigrants in Los Angeles County received public assistance in 1990, compared to 42 percent of non-Latino whites, or that six of fifteen top chief executives of Orange County's manufacturing sector are foreign-born bilinguals.

Once the stereotype is confronted on its own terms, then the time is ripe to articulate a new vision. Offer an alternative metaphor that arguably makes better "common sense." This one-two punch may make the complacent nonpartisan voter reconsider the previously unconsidered conventions of the social order. The aim is to create cognitive dissonance regarding the taken-as-given, in order to open up a bit of cognitive space for a more encompassing alternative view of humanity and nation.

Four, in the intermediate term, calls for the dissolution of nation will not be well received. Rather, seek to construct metaphors that can be linked to the conventional constellations of NATION AS BODY and NATION AS HOUSE. Venerable conceptualizations of national security and national unity can be harnessed to a progressive political agenda, much in the same terms that they have been for a neoconservative agenda. As the continuing skirmishes over the Maastrich Treaty negotiations for the European Union have demonstrated, these medieval notions of NATION will remain viable long into the twenty-first century.

For alternative views of nation, the FABRIC metaphor, such as "the intricate weave of American peoples into the national fabric," may be considered. Textile invokes often complex warps and weaves which can be associated with patterns of relations among social groups as well as individuals. Cloth likewise evokes wholeness and inclusivity. Different threads and strands are woven together to create a "whole cloth" which is greater than the sum of its parts. Indeed, the frequent neoconservative complaint against multiculturalism, that it rends the American social fabric, presumes a totality. Because of this ontology, NATION AS FABRIC does not presuppose social exclusion, the insider/outsider entailment, which is the basis for a social covenant that counts some people in and others out.

Five, to create and promulgate effective insurgent metaphors requires recognizing the current prevailing metaphors that give shape to today's worldview. These prevailing views certainly will not match the worldview of minority activists who matured in alienating and subordinating places in society. Careful scrutiny of general public discourse will repay study.

Six, a disturbing tack appeared in the discourse of anti–Proposition 187 partisans, who impugned the ethics of referendum supporters. The *Times* published disparagements, such as this insult directed at the authors of the Proposition 187 referendum ("two mothballed bureaucrats"), and riffs on the pro-187 organization, Save Our State (SOS) ("Snake-Oil Salesmen," "Snoop or Snitch," and "Soldiers of Satan"). Ad hominem attacks are puny attempts to deprecate opponents, and are consonant with the use of metaphor to degrade immigrants as less than human. Such assaults are inadvisable, since they do not offer a more encompassing view of humanity.

Seven, along these lines, the designer of new metaphors does not ever own the copyrights on these tools of insurgency. In the same way the 1960s RACISM AS DISEASE metaphor was subverted in the 1990s, alternative metaphors are subject to usurpation by a rival. The maker of metaphors must explore their connotations and entailments thoroughly to work them into tools that bring into sharp relief the shortcomings of the conventional metaphoric constructs, all the while cognizant that political rivals will seek to exploit the weaknesses of these same alternative metaphors.

Finally, it is a fatal error to become oblivious to the contingency and naturalizing effect of metaphor. All metaphors, because they are merely links between preexisting semantic domains, are only approximations of far more complex realities. Each metaphor emphasizes some elements of the social world at the expense of others. The metaphor maker, or "strong poet," has two tasks. One is to work the insubordinate metaphor so that the public comes around to a new view. The second task is to keep in mind the contingent nature of all metaphors while continuing to seek better ones.

The chief narrative that promotes hegemonic assent among the U.S. public—particularly its racialized and linguistic minorities—is the faith in inevitable social progress. A requirement for social progress, naturally, is social order and placidity among all parties. For the oppressed, this means deference and restraint, and especially endless patience. Nonetheless, crucial American notions such as progress, race, citizen, and nation, as they are currently defined, will not lead inexorably toward greater equality for or inclusion of minorities. Indeed, the conventional use of these terms led to greater domination and less freedom for Latinos to live fully realized lives. Thus, to believe in unfailing social progress is to consent to the public discourse that sustains and legitimizes today's systems of domination and inequity.

Friedrich Nietzsche viewed the downtrodden as chattel and the powerful as the rightful rulers of the weak. He harbored contempt for the masses, whom he considered sheep for the carnivores of the world to feed on. Nevertheless, he recognized that the seat of power is located, not in individuals, but in the discourse that creates the world order:

> What therefore is Truth? A flexible army of metaphors, metonymies, anthropomorphisms; in short, a sum of human relations which have been poetically and rhetorically intensified, transformed, bejeweled, and which after long usage seem to a people to be fixed, canonical, and binding.

For Nietzsche, metaphor was the key to power. For contrary to the tenets of the En-lightenment, he believed that Truth did not exist, except as metaphor-guided discursive practices that compose society. The society accepts its rulers because it accepts the vocabulary the rulers use to define it, that is, it accepts cultural hegemony.

The master of public discourse is the master of metaphors. Consider St. Paul's metaphorical extension of the Greek term *agape*, which transformed the modest notion "charity" into transcendent Christian love, and Sir Isaac Newton's *gravitas*, which meant human psychological "seriousness," but came to refer to a property of attraction of celestial bodies. To this list we can add Frederick Douglass's re-vision of the Jeffersonian axiom "all men are created equal" to include all God's children, together with Martin Luther King Jr.'s eloquent and sustained diagnosis of the nation's racial illness as CANCER. Thus Miguel de Unamuno's laughing rejection of logic should give pause:

> For a single metaphor, I would discard all the syllogisms and their corresponding *there-fores* on which so much scholastic verbiage is hung. One metaphor teaches me more; it reveals more to me. Above all, I am inflamed beneath a metaphor. Imagination only works where there is fire.

Insurgent metaphors are tools to construct stronger vocabularies to speak this new society. To contest the current regime of discourse requires the creation of insubordinate metaphors to produce more inclusive American values, and more just practices for a new society.

From the Editors *Issues and Comments*

What stories do you have to tell? Do you sometimes have trouble getting people to take them seriously?

In what ways do you use stories to persuade? Do you alter the way you tell a story to suit your audience?

If you are a member of an outsider group, such as Mexican American or Puerto Rican, what stories does the group tell about itself that let you know you are a member?

Do you prefer to hear stories that are familiar—that use plots, events, characters, and themes like those you meet every day? Or do you prefer stories that are unfamiliar or unusual?

Do you agree with Derrick Bell's space-traders allegory? Does Michael Olivas show that something similar happened to Latinos at several points in their history?

In what ways do Olivas's and Rodrigo's stories surprise you or cause you to disagree? Which do you identify with and why?

Do counterstories take a long time to register and be accepted? If so, why?

If you are a member of an outsider group, do you think you will reach more people if you tell counterstories of the dominant group—that is, use the forms of storytelling that people are used to hearing?

Have you ever had the impression that members of a different racial group simply could not hear a certain kind of story? If so, which stories and which groups?

Does storytelling, even when poignant or entertaining, deflect attention from the material forces that sustain and reproduce oppression?

Can a powerful poem, such as *I Am Joaquín*, spark a new social movement? Can a new, inspired metaphor change the direction of a conversation?

Suggested Readings

Anzaldua, Gloria. *Borderlands*/La Frontera: *The New* Mestiza. San Francisco: Aunt Lute Books, 1987.

Baron, Jane B. "Resistance to Stories." 67 *S. Cal. L. Rev.* 255 (1994).

Bell, Derrick A. *And We Are Not Saved: The Elusive Quest for Racial Justice.* New York: Basic Books, 1987.

Broyles-González, Yolanda. *El Teatro Campesino: Theater in the Chicano Movement.* Austin: University of Texas Press, 1994.

Bruce-Novoa, Juan. *Retrospace: Collected Essays on Chicano Literature, Theory and History.* Houston: Arte Publico Press, 1990.

Chavez, John R. *The Lost Land: The Chicano Image of the Southwest.* Albuquerque: University of New Mexico Press, 1984.

Colloquium: "LatCrit Theory: Naming and Launching a New Discourse of Critical Legal Scholarship." 2 *Harv. Latino L. Rev.* 1 (1997).

Considering Counter-Narratives: Narrating, Resisting, Making Sense, edited by Michael Bamburg and Molly Andrews. Amsterdam and Philadelphia: John Benjamins, 2004.

Delgado, Richard. "Brewer's Plea: Critical Thoughts on Common Cause." 44 *Vand. L. Rev.* 1 (1991).

———. "The Ethereal Scholar: Does Critical Legal Studies Have What Minorities Want?" 22 *Harv. C.R.–C.L. L. Rev.* 301 (1987).

———. "The Imperial Scholar: Reflections on a Review of Civil Rights Literature." 132 *U. Pa. L. Rev.* 561 (1984).

———. "The Imperial Scholar Revisited: How to Marginalize Outsider Writing, Ten Years Later." 140 *U. Pa. L. Rev.* 1349 (1992).

———. "When a Story Is Just a Story: Does Voice Really Matter?" 76 *Va. L. Rev.* 95 (1990).

Delgado, Richard, and Jean Stefancic. "Norms and Narratives: Can Judges Avoid Serious Moral Error?" 69 *Tex. L. Rev.* 1929 (1991).

Dunbar, Anthony W. "Introducing Critical Race Theory to Archival Discourse: Getting the Conversation Started." 6(1) *Archival Science* 109–29 (2006).

Espinoza, Leslie G. "Masks and Other Disguises: Exposing Legal Academia." 103 *Harv. L. Rev.* 1878 (1990).

Farber, Daniel A., and Suzanna Sherry. "Telling Stories out of School: An Essay on Legal Narratives." 45 *Stan. L. Rev.* 807 (1993).

Garcia, Alyssa. "Counter Stories of Race and Gender: Situating Experiences of Latinas in the Academy." 3 *Latino Studies* 261–73 (2005).

Garcia, David G. "Remembering Chavez Ravine: Culture Clash and Critical Race Theater." 26 *Chicano-Latino L. Rev.* 111 (2006).

Garza, Ana. "The Voice of Color and Its Value in Legal Storytelling." 1 *Hisp. L. J.* 105 (1994).

Gonzales, Rodolfo "Corky." *I Am Joaquin. Yo Soy Joaquin.* Toronto and New York: Bantam Books, 1972.

Gutierrez-Jones, Carl. *Critical Race Narratives: A Study of Race, Rhetoric, and Injury.* New York: New York University Press, 2001.

———. *Rethinking the Borderlands: Between Chicano Culture and Legal Discourse.* Berkeley: University of California Press, 1995.

Harrison, Melissa, and Margaret E. Montoya. Voices/*Voces* in the Borderlands: A Colloquy on Re/constructing Identities in Re/constructed Legal Spaces." 6 *Colum. J. Gender & L.* 387 (1996).

Herencia: The Anthology of Hispanic Literature of the United States, edited by Nicolás Kanellos. New York: Oxford University Press, 2002.

Kennedy, Randall L. "Racial Critiques of Legal Academia." 102 *Harv. L. Rev.* 1745 (1989).

Kingsolver, Ann E. *NAFTA Stories: Fears and Hopes in Mexico and the United States.* Boulder, Colo.: Lynne Rienner, 2001.

Knight, Michelle G., et al. "The Power of Black and Latina/o Counterstories: Urban Families and College-Going Process." 35(1) *Anthropology & Education Quarterly* 99–120 (2004).

Limón, José. *Mexican Ballads, Chicano Poems: History and Influence in Mexican-American Social Poetry.* Berkeley: University of California Press, 1992.

López, Gerald P. "Lay Lawyering." 32 *UCLA L. Rev.* 1 (1984).

López, Gerardo R. "From Sea to Shining Sea: Stories, Counterstories, and the Discourse of Patriotism." 8(2) *Qualitative Inquiry* 196 (2002).

Massaro, Toni M. "Empathy, Legal Storytelling and the Rule of Law: New Words, Old Wounds?" 87 *Mich. L. Rev.* 2099 (1989).

Matsuda, Mari. "Public Response for Racist Speech: Considering the Victim's Story." 87 *Mich. L. Rev.* 2320 (1989).

Montoya, Margaret E. "Border Crossings in an Age of Border Patrols: *Cruzando Fronteras Metaforicas*." 26 *N.M. L. Rev.* 1 (1996).

———. "Law and Languages(s): Image, Integration, and Innovation." 7 *La Raza L.J.* 147 (1994).

———. "*Mascaras, Trenzas, y Greñas*: Un/Masking the Self while Un/Braiding Latina Stories and Legal Discourse." 17 *Harv. Women's L.J.* 185 (1994); 15 *Chicano-Latino L. Rev.* 1 (1994).

Morin, José R. Lopez. *The Legacy of Américo Paredes*. Austin: University of Texas Press, 2006.

Nelson, Hilde Lindemann. *Damaged Identities, Narrative Repair*. Ithaca, N.Y.: Cornell University Press, 2001.

Oquendo, Ángel R. "Straight from the Mouth of the Volcano: The Lowdown on Law, Language, and Latin@s." 83 *Ind. L.J.* 1485 (2008).

Padilla, Genaro M. *My History, Not Yours: The Formation of Mexican American Autobiography*. Madison: University of Wisconsin Press, 1993.

Paredes, Américo. *Folklore and Culture on the Texas-Mexican Border*, 10th ed., edited by Richard Bauman. Austin: University of Texas Press, 1995.

———. *George Washington Gomez*. Houston: Arte Publico Press, 1990.

———. "*With His Pistol in His Hand*": *A Border Ballad and Its Hero*. Austin: University of Texas Press, 1958.

Perez, Emma. *The Decolonial Imaginary: Writing Chicanas into History*. Bloomington: Indiana University Press, 1999.

Recovering the U.S. Hispanic Literary Heritage. Vol. 1–. Houston: Arte Publico Press, 1993–.

Rendon, Armando B. *Chicano Manifesto*. New York: Collier Books, 1972.

Rivera, John-Michael. *The Emergence of Mexican America: Recovering Stories of Mexican Peoplehood in U.S. Culture*. New York: New York University Press, 2006.

Rosaldo, Renato. *Culture & Truth: The Remaking of Social Analysis*. Boston: Beacon Press, 1989.

———. "Surveying Law and Borders." 48 *Stan. L. Rev.* 1037 (1996).

Saldivar, Ramon. *The Borderlands of Culture: Américo Paredes and the Transnational Imaginary*. Durham, N.C.: Duke University Press, 2006.

Santa Ana, Otto. *Brown Tide Rising: Metaphors of Latinos in Contemporary Public Discourse*. Austin: University of Texas Press, 2002.

Solorzano, Daniel G., and Tara J. Yosso. "A Critical Race Counterstory of Race, Racism, and Affirmative Action." 35(2) *Equity & Excellence in Education* 155–68 (2002).

Torres, Gerald. "Translation and Stories." 115 *Harv. L. Rev.* 1362 (2002).

Weinstein, Stephanie, and Arthur Wolfson. "Toward a Due Process of Narrative: Before You Lock My Love Away, Please Let Me Testify." 11 *Roger Williams U. L. Rev.* 511 (2006).

Williams, Patricia J. *The Alchemy of Race and Rights*. Cambridge, Mass.: Harvard University Press, 1992.

Yosso, Tara J. *Critical Race Counterstories along the Chicana/Chicano Educational Pipeline*. New York: Routledge, 2005.

||||||||||||||||||||||||||||||||||||||||||||||||||||||||||||||||||||||||||||||||||||||

Part VI

Rebellious Lawyering and Resistance Strategies
We Fight Back

Latinos have not always passively accepted the ill treatment described in preceding sections of this book. Lawyers, community activists, scholars, and artists have fought back, demanding fair, nonracist treatment at the hands of the authorities and of fellow citizens. The chapters in part 6 describe some of those strategies and the lives of some notable rebels, including lawyers who broke the law "on principle." The writers also cast doubt on the ability of law to redress Latino harms. Several suggest that activism, struggle, and resistance have proven more useful than lawsuits and voting. The selections present a brief overview of the rich history of activism from the World War II era to the Chicano movement of the 1960s. We also see the beginning of the conflict over tactics between older organizations advocating assimilation, such as LULAC, and younger student protest groups. Central to this struggle was the lawyer Oscar Acosta. Inspired by César Chávez and Rodolfo "Corky" Gonzales, Acosta went on to become a pivotal figure in the trial of the LA Thirteen. His reflections on similarities and differences between Mexican Americans and African Americans also foreshadow the deteriorating relations between the two groups that we will revisit in part 9. Much of that conflict turned on the unresolved question of Mexicans' racial identity, whether they were white and able to assimilate, or black, or something in between. Part 7 takes up that question.

||||||||||||||||||||||||||||||||||||||||||||||||||||||||||||||||||||||||||||

Chapter 44

The Idea of a Constitution in the Chicano Tradition

Gerald P. López

I have lived and worked in various cities and on both coasts. But in some ways (and perhaps even against my will) L.A. is still home—the place where I was born and raised, and the place where my mother, sister, brother, and most of my extended family still live. What I now think about the world around me, not surprisingly, first came to life in the Chicano part of this city, East L.A. In my early East L.A. days, religion meant Catholic, fantasy meant cruising in your own car, glamour meant an ethnicized variation on some Hollywood theme, and fish meant Friday. No less important for a sports-crazy boy, baseball meant Koufax, and basketball meant Baylor and West and, yes, wanting desperately to beat the Celtics for the world championship. I've grown some since those days and changed my mind some too about these and other dimensions of life—except of course about the moral importance of beating the Celtics. But for me, as for you, it remains true that we cannot separate who we are from what we try to understand.

Two memories frame what a constitution meant for me in the tradition of East L.A. life. In one, I am four years old and in a car with my father and mother, canvassing the streets of East L.A., posting flyers on telephone poles. The flyers, in Spanish and English, urge everyone to vote for our candidate in an upcoming election. Like most Chicanos then and now, my parents were Democrats; the candidate was a Republican, the only one I was ever to see my family support. Even at four having to tell the world that "our candidate is a Republican" felt oxymoronic. But with his extraordinary directness, my father explained this switch in allegiance: he told me simply that the candidate would fight—fight both for what Chicanos were and for what we wanted.

In the other memory, I am with my family and thousands of other Chicanos in a park in East L.A. Fireworks, music, speeches, *gritos*, costumes, food and drink abound. Somehow these rituals, in all their ornamental and hyperbolic detail, expressed for me even at nine the collective pride I had come to anticipate and to savor on these patriotic occasions. After all, we were celebrating Cinco de Mayo in the park that day, and in remembering Mexico's small military victory over the French at

From *The Idea of a Constitution in the Chicano Tradition*, 37 J. LEGAL EDUC. 162 (1987). Originally published in the *Journal of Legal Education*. Reprinted by permission.

Puebla, we were observing a moment that had come to signify something spiritually constitutive in the history of our people. My mom and dad even took time off from work—the highest tribute.

These memories obliquely yet accurately portray the idea of a constitution, not only in my early East L.A. days but, I think, in the Chicano tradition of living in this country. My father's reason, his *constitutional* reason, for backing a Republican candidate echoed a more general understanding in our community. Constitutions result from fighting. They establish social arrangements that express both in their original detail and in their ongoing adjustments what fighting continues to be about—not just in elections but in day-to-day living.

If ever you doubt this fighting, take a look through my eyes at the wear and tear on people like my relatives and friends here in East L.A., the homely heroes we Chicanos celebrate in our stories, ballads, and murals. Some of these people have been here for generations, anchored in our habits and ideas, learning from and teaching their grandparents and parents, their children and grandchildren what it means to be self-reliant as a people. Others only recently have arrived, undocumented and "unwanted," except of course to bus our tables, stitch together our clothes, harvest our food, clean our bathrooms, and care for our children. Old-timers and newcomers alike survive only to the extent that they quickly learn to temper the daily fighting with considerable self-irony. Laughter helps counter the fury, desperation, and resignation induced by so many events and so many people. As a largely poor and subordinated people, Chicanos have inevitably struggled against the faults and limits of existing arrangements and thinking, faults and limits reluctantly engraved in constitutions. In this important sense, Chicano tradition in this country—our relationship to work, love, laughter, and to other people—necessarily unites self-realization and transformation.

Yet as important as transforming these arrangements was and is in the Chicano tradition, the Constitution itself had no particularly privileged place in our life in East L.A. or, for that matter, in the Chicano tradition generally. We did celebrate the Fourth of July as well as Cinco de Mayo; the celebrations were not in any crude sense rival observances. But the Cinco somehow expressed who we were, whereas the Fourth and its symbolic siblings, the flag and the Constitution, somehow all heralded the tradition of those with whom we regularly fought. Indeed, the language of the Constitution, particularly then and even now, does not readily afford an explanation for what seem to be the daily realities in Chicano life. To that extent our experience and the Constitution daily marginalize one another, sometimes threaten entirely to abandon each other.

In order literally to survive (to live *in* our history and *through* our practices), we Chicanos in East L.A. and elsewhere nurtured a separate tradition, parallel to the "grand tradition" of constitutional life in this country. For years most of us lived this non-converging tradition, as did our ancestors, only vaguely aware of the resistance it offered to what others would have us become. Over the past three decades, however, living this tradition has itself become a deliberate strategy in our efforts to define, *constitutionally*, what one can most importantly do with one's life. We now acutely appreciate that our tradition, like every other, necessarily represents one argument in the national and historical debate about the meaning of "American destiny."

In Chicano tradition the idea of a constitution differs at its roots from what a constitution means to most people, particularly the fortunate. In the grand tradition most believe that through a constitution we can lift our public life above the fallen and compromised realm of factional politics. Like all faiths, this idea of a constitution embraces rival interpretive dogmas. Living within the grand tradition are strict textualists and loose supplementers, proponents and opponents of judicial activism, those who believe in the structural rebellion expressed through this nation's two reconstructions and those who are skeptical of it. But all engaged in this ideological debate remain within the grand tradition insofar as they share the belief that, at our best and as a people, we can, through a constitution, somehow transcend conflict and heal by rising above our nature.

For all that may be honorable in this grand idea of a constitution, it contradicts Chicano experience in this country. Constitutions have been prominent in our life not for their healing but primarily for the injuries they have permitted and inflicted —in the workplace, on the streets, in the home, and in the minds and hearts of many a struggling and bewildered Chicano. And, if anything, factional politics become more prominent when the stakes get higher, as they frequently do whenever a constitution enters any political conversation. In our experience, constitutional interpretations and constitutional decisions reflect the provisional containment of fighting, not its transcendence. As Chicanos see it, through a constitution we in this country publicly announce that "for the moment, there's no battle here," not always confident the words will create, much less reflect, the reality.

Whatever world Madison presupposed in condemning factions as corruptions of a unified, public-spirited citizenry, today's national community aspires to a simple unity by regularly requiring non-converging traditions like our own to betray themselves. Chicanos know well the not-so-subliminal refrain: Vacate your history, your culture, your relationship to work, love, and others, and join with us as one in America's constitutional tradition. We even hear again these days, not always indirectly, that to be fully public-spirited we would have to change the very way we talk. Most Chicanos, after all, express their experience of the constitution in terms other than doctrinal, and often even in terms other than popular newsspeak or civics-babble. In this sense, we participate in the traditional national faith only inarticulately, through accounts that many find uneducated and confused and treat as somehow not quite part of constitutional discourse. In the eyes of the grand tradition, Chicano accounts of constitutional experiences and ideas somehow lack the "larger-than-life" quality, the "more-all-embracing-than-factional" spirit that distinguishes constitutional talk worth having—in scholarly journals, in the Supreme Court, and in New England town meetings.

Yet that very same talk others find constitutionally inarticulate ironically confirms, if only partially, why living in their own non-converging tradition offers Chicanos more than just a comforting familiarity. For those of us in the Chicano tradition, reminding ourselves through our daily language that we are not somehow "larger than life" through a constitution can be emancipating. We fight about a life constitution-ally worth leading, and we know it. We fight with you and among ourselves, in our kitchens and in the fields, and in the formal constitutional battles we are increasingly entering. Chicanos live a dramatic, and often heated, conversation about things that matter, mundane and monumental. Our tradition embodies the continuity of our conflicts, and draws on their wisdom even as we continue to move against things as they are. At our best, we express in our practices an idea of a constitution at once far more aggressively skeptical and far more romantic than the grand tradition accom-modates: we refuse to accept that you need to believe in transcendence or else give up entirely.

Of course, we are not always at our best. We can and have been corrupted both by the desire to make our struggle disappear and by the promise that "Americanizing" ourselves will make us feel more a part of this country. We recognize that both the desire and the promise are retreats: life holds more than leaving behind your poor past, becoming successful "on your own," expressing yourself freely, and secretly yearning for a utopian world, free of conflict and power. Yet recognizing these vener-able retreats does not always mean avoiding them. They live in each of us, as in each of you, offering themselves as "honorable" and "practical" alternatives to a life fully lived in our own tradition. If, as a people, Chicanos manage generally not to acqui-esce in these retreats, that always fragile achievement may express more a response than a choice—a response to our identity that meets an obligation to which our his-tory, our day-to-day lives, and our aspirations call us.

Returning to the streets of this city reminds me that, over the years, Chicanos have made alliances and even some occasional friendships, most notably with people liv-ing in other non-converging traditions—Asians, feminists, Blacks, Native Americans, other Latinos, and certain members of both the intellectual community and the white working class. Still other moments on these very same streets convince me that, in some ways, each of us continues to find the other's nostalgia faintly ridiculous. You think our spiritual attachment to Cinco de Mayo quaint and quixotic; we think your attachment to the idea of a constitution in the grand tradition self-deluding. The truces we live by, in this city and in this country, apparently can't always disguise or alter residual sentiment.

I do not pretend that the idea of a constitution in Chicano tradition is radically discontinuous with all elements of the grand tradition. Our tradition certainly shares with classical republican thought the somewhat blurry image of a self constituted through others and through its relation to work, and of people making a living while simultaneously battling in public life. But unlike the grand tradition, Chicano tradi-tion fights hard not to accept as settled the present arrangement of institutions and ideas. To acquiesce in what people now live and think would be to abandon the very spirit in us that rebels against all that has degraded our ancestors and contempo-raries, and all that works even now, in newly emerging forms, to subordinate our descendants.

We won't celebrate the constitution's bicentennial in the grand tradition, and we'll be better for it.

|||||||||||||||||||||||||||||||||||||||||||||||||||||||||||||||||||||||||||||||||

Chapter 45

Early Chicano Activism
Zoot Suits, Sleepy Lagoon, and the Road to Delano

Rodolfo Acuña

World War II and the Chicano

Raúl Morin, in *Among the Valiant*, has documented the Chicanos' contribution to the war effort. Morin expressed the sense of betrayal that many Chicano soldiers experienced because of the racism at home. Morin wrote that 25 percent of the U.S. military personnel on the infamous Bataan "Death March" were Mexican Americans and that, in World War II, Mexicans earned more medals of honor than any other ethnic or racial group.

When the war began, about 2.69 million Chicanos lived in the United States, approximately one-third of whom were of draft age. According to Dr. Robin R. Scott, between 375,000 and 500,000 Chicanos served in the armed forces. In Los Angeles Mexicans comprised one-tenth of the population and one-fifth of the casualties.[1]

Throughout the war Mexicans were treated as second-class citizens. For example, Sergeant Macario Garcia, from Sugarland, Texas, a recipient of the Congressional Medal of Honor, could not buy a cup of coffee in a restaurant in Richmond, California. "An Anglo-American chased him out with a baseball bat." The Garcia incident was not isolated.

The "Sleepy Lagoon" case (1942) and the zoot-suit riots (1943) insulted Mexicans throughout the United States. The events in Los Angeles generated sympathy and solidarity from as far away as Chicago. Angelenos as well as other North Americans had been conditioned for these events by the mass deportations of the 1930s. The war-like propaganda conducted during the repatriation reinforced in the minds of many Anglos the stereotype that Mexican Americans were aliens. The events of 1942 proved the extent of Anglo racism. Euroamericans herded Japanese Americans into internment camps. When the Japanese left, Mexicans became the most natural scapegoats.

During the war, Los Angeles became a magnet for the rapid migration of all races to the area. The mass influx overtaxed the infrastructure's ability to serve the expanding population. The Mexican *barrios*, already overcrowded, were the most affected, as the city's economic growth drew many Mexicans from other regions. Whites took higher-paying defense jobs, while Mexicans assumed their place in heavy industry.

Mexicans occupied the oldest housing stock; segregation was common; and many recreational facilities excluded Mexican Americans. For instance, they could not use swimming pools in East Los Angeles and in other Southland communities. Often Mexicans and Blacks could only swim on Wednesday—the day the county drained the water. In movie houses in places like San Fernando, Mexicans sat in the balcony.

In this environment, a minority of Chicano youth between the ages of thirteen and seventeen belonged to *barrio* clubs that carried the name of their neighbor-hoods—White Fence, Alpine Street, El Hoyo, Happy Valley. The fad among gang members, or *pachucos* as they were called, was to tattoo the left hand, between the thumb and index finger, with a small cross with three dots or dashes above it. Many pachucos, when they dressed up, wore the so-called zoot suit, popular among low-income youths at that time. Pachucos spoke Spanish, but also used *Chuco* among their companions. Chuco was the *barrio* language, a mixture of Spanish, English, old Spanish, and words adapted by the border Mexicans. Many experts indicate that the language originated around El Paso among Chicanos, who brought it to Los Angeles in the 1930s.

Although similar gangs existed among Anglo youth, Angelenos with little sense of history called gangs a Mexican problem, forgetting that the Euroamerican urban experience caused the gang phenomenon. The *Los Angeles Times*, not known for its analytic content, reinforced this stereotype and influenced the public with stories about "Mexican" hoodlums.

The "Sleepy Lagoon" case was the most notorious example of racism toward Chica-nos in this era. The name came from a popular melody played by band leader Harry James. Unable to go to the public pool, Chicanos romanticized a gravel pit they fre-quently used for recreational purposes. On the evening of August 1, 1942, members of the 38th Street Club were jumped by another gang. When they returned with their home boys, the rival gang was not there. Later they witnessed a party in progress at the Williams Ranch nearby. They crashed the party and a fight followed.

The next morning José Díaz, an invited guest at the party, was found dead on a dirt road near the house. Díaz had no wounds and could have been killed by a hit-and-run driver, but authorities suspected that some members of the 38th Street Club had beaten him, and the police immediately jailed the entire gang. Newspapers sen-sationalized the story. Police flagrantly violated the rights of the accused, and author-ities charged twenty-two of the 38th Street boys with criminal conspiracy. "According to the prosecution, every defendant, even if he had nothing whatsoever to do with the killing of Díaz, was chargeable with the death of Díaz, which according to the prosecution, occurred during the fight at the Williams Ranch."[2]

The press portrayed the Sleepy Lagoon defendants as Mexican hoodlums. A spe-cial committee of the grand jury, shortly after the death of José Díaz, accepted a re-port by Lt. Ed Duran Ayres, head of the Foreign Relations Bureau of the Los Angeles Sheriff's Department, which justified the gross violation of human rights suffered by the defendants. Although the report admitted that discrimination against Chicanos in employment, education, schooling, recreation, and labor unions was common, it concluded that Chicanos were inherently criminal and violent. Ayres stated that Chicanos were Indians, hence Orientals, and as such had an utter disregard for life. The report further alleged that Chicanos were cruel, for they descended from the Aztecs who supposedly sacrificed 30,000 victims a day! Ayres wrote that Indians considered leniency a sign of weakness, pointing to the Mexican government's treatment of the Indians, which he maintained was quick and severe. He urged that all gang members be imprisoned and that all Chicano youths over the age of eighteen be given the option of working or enlisting in the armed forces. Chicanos, according to Ayres, could not change their spots; they had an innate desire to use a knife and let blood, and this inborn cruelty was aggravated by liquor and jealousy. The Ayres report, which represented official law enforcement views, goes a long way in explaining the events around Sleepy Lagoon.

The Honorable Charles W. Fricke permitted numerous irregularities in the courtroom during the trial. The defendants were not allowed to cut their hair or change their clothes for the duration of the proceedings. The prosecution failed to prove that the 38th Street Club was a gang, that any criminal agreement or conspiracy existed, or that the accused had killed Díaz. In fact, witnesses testified that considerable drinking had occurred at the party before the 38th Street people arrived. If the theory of conspiracy to commit a crime had been strictly pressed, logically the defendants would have received equal verdicts. However, on January 12, 1943, the court passed sentences ranging from assault to first-degree murder.

The Sleepy Lagoon Defense Committee had been organized to protect the defendants' rights. It was chaired by Carey McWilliams, a noted journalist and lawyer. McWilliams and other members were harassed and red-baited by the press and by government agencies. The California Committee on Un-American Activities, headed by State Senator Jack Tenney, investigated the committee, charging that it was a Communist-front organization and that Carey McWilliams had "Communist leanings" because he opposed segregation and favored miscegenation. Authorities, including the FBI, conducted heavy surveillance of the committee and support groups such as El Congreso de los Pueblos de Habla Español (the Spanish-Speaking Congress). The FBI viewed it as a Communist front, stating that it "opposed all types of discrimination against Mexicans."[3]

On October 4, 1944, the Second District Court of Appeals reversed the lower court in a unanimous decision stating that Judge Fricke had conducted a biased trial, that he had violated the constitutional rights of the defendants, and that no evidence linked the Chicanos with the death of José Díaz.

After the Sleepy Lagoon arrests, Los Angeles police and the sheriff's departments set up roadblocks and indiscriminately arrested large numbers of Chicanos on countless charges, the most common being suspicion of burglary. These arrests naturally made headlines, inflaming the public to the point that the Office of War Information became concerned over the media's sensationalism as well as its racism.

The tension did not end there. Large numbers of servicemen on furlough or on short-duration passes visited Los Angeles. Numerous training centers were located in the vicinity, and the glitter of Hollywood and its famous canteen attracted hordes of GIs. Sailors on shore leave from ships docked in San Pedro and San Diego went to Los Angeles looking for a good time. Most were young and anxious to prove their manhood. A visible "foe" was the "alien" Chicano, dressed in the outlandish zoot suit that everyone ridiculed. The sailors also looked for Mexican girls to pick up, associating the Chicanas with the prostitutes in Tijuana. The sailors behaved boisterously and rudely to the women in the Mexican community.

In the spring of 1943 several small altercations erupted in Los Angeles. In April marines and sailors in Oakland invaded the Chicano *barrio* and Black ghetto, assaulted the people, and "depantsed" zoot-suiters. On May 8 a fight between sailors and Chicanos, many of whom belonged to the Alpine, broke out at the Aragon Ballroom in Venice, California, when some high school students told the sailors that *pachucos* had stabbed a sailor. Joined by other servicemen, sailors indiscriminately attacked Mexican youths. The battle cry was; "Let's get 'em! Let's get the chili-eating bastards!" Twenty-five hundred spectators watched the assault on innocent Chicano youths; the police did virtually nothing to restrain the servicemen, arresting instead the victims for disturbing the peace. Although Judge Arthur Guerin dismissed the charges for want of sufficient evidence, he warned the youths "that their antics might get them into serious difficulties unless they changed their attitudes." The press continued to sensationalize the theme of "zoot-suit equals hoodlum."[4]

The "sailors riots" began on June 3, 1943. Allegedly, a group of sailors had been attacked by Chicanos when they attempted to pick up some Chicanas. The details are vague; the police supposedly did not attempt to get the Chicano side of the story, but instead took the sailors' report at face value. Fourteen off-duty police officers, led by a detective lieutenant, went looking for the "criminals." They found nothing, but made certain that the press covered the story.

That same night, sailors went on a rampage, breaking into the Carmen Theater, tearing zoot-suits off Chicanos, and beating the youths. Police again arrested the victims. Word spread that *pachucos* were fair game and that they could be attacked without fear of arrest.

Sailors returned the next evening with some two hundred allies. In twenty hired cabs they cruised Whittier Boulevard, in the heart of the East Los Angeles *barrio*, jumping out of the cars to gang up on neighborhood youths. Police and sheriffs maintained that they could not establish contact with the sailors. They finally did arrest nine, but released them immediately without filing charges. The press portrayed the sailors as heroes. Articles and headlines were designed to inflame racial hatred.

Sailors, encouraged by the press and "responsible" elements of Los Angeles, gathered on the night of June 5 and marched four abreast down the streets, warning Chicanos to shed their zoot suits or they would take them off for them. On that night and the next, servicemen broke into bars and other establishments and beat up Chicanos. Police continued to abet the lawlessness, arriving only after damage had been done and the servicemen had left. Even though sailors destroyed private property, law enforcement officials still refused to do their duty. When the Chicano community attempted to defend itself, police arrested them.

Events climaxed on the evening of June 7, when thousands of soldiers, sailors, and civilians surged down Main Street and Broadway in search of *pachucos*. The mob crashed into bars and broke the legs off stools, using them as clubs. The press reported five hundred "zoot suiters" ready for battle. By this time Filipinos and Blacks also became targets. Chicanos had their clothes ripped off, and the youths were left bleeding in the streets. The mob surged into movie theaters, where they turned on the lights, marched down the aisles, and pulled zoot-suit-clad youngsters out of their seats. Seventeen-year-old Enrico Herrera, after he was beaten and arrested, spent three hours at a police station, where he was found by his mother, still naked and bleeding. A twelve-year-old boy's jaw was broken. Police arrested over six hundred Chicano youths without cause and labeled the arrests "preventive" action. Angelenos cheered on the servicemen and their civilian allies.

Panic gripped the Chicano community. At the height of the turmoil servicemen pulled a Black off a streetcar and gouged out his eye with a knife. Military authorities, realizing that the Los Angeles law enforcement agencies would not curtail the brutality, intervened and declared downtown Los Angeles off limits for military personnel. Classified naval documents prove that the navy believed it had a mutiny on its hands. Documents leave no doubt that military shore patrols quelled the riot, accomplishing what the Los Angeles police could or would not do.

For the next few days police ordered mass arrests, even raiding a Catholic welfare center to arrest some of its occupants. The press and city officials provoked the mob. An editorial by Manchester Boddy on June 9 in the *Los Angeles Daily News* (supposedly the city's liberal newspaper) stated:

> The time for temporizing is past. . . . The time has come to serve notice that the City of Los Angeles will no longer be terrorized by a relatively small handful of morons parading as zoot-suit hoodlums. To delay action now means to court disaster later on.[5]

Boddy's statement taken alone would not mean much; it could be considered to be just one man's opinion. But consider that before the naval invasion of East Los Angeles, the following headlines had appeared in the *Times*:

November 2, 1942: "Ten Seized in Drive on Zoot-Suit Gangsters"
February 23, 1943: "One Slain and Another Knifed in 'Zoot' Fracas"
March 7, 1943: "Magistrate 'Unfrocks' Pair of Zoot-Suiters"
May 25, 1943: "Four Zoot-Suit Gangs Beat Up Their Victims"
June 1, 1943: "Attacks by Orange County Zoot-Suiters Injure Five"

During the assault servicemen were encouraged by headlines in the *Los Angeles Daily News*, such as "Zoot Suit Chiefs Girding for War on Navy," and in the *Los Angeles Times*, such as "Zoot Suiters Learn Lesson in Fight with Servicemen." Three other major newspapers ran similar headlines that generated an atmosphere of zoot-suit violence. The radio also contributed to the hysteria.

Rear Admiral D. W. Bagley, commanding officer of the naval district, took the public position that the sailors acted in "self-defense against the rowdy element." Privately Bagley directed his commanders to order their men to stop the raids and then conducted a low-profile cover-up. Sailors were, however, not the only vandals. Army personnel often outnumbered sailors. According to Commander Fogg, on June 8,

1943, hundreds of servicemen were "prowling downtown Los Angeles mostly on foot —disorderly—apparently on the prowl for Mexicans." By June 11, 1943, in a restricted memo, the navy and army recognized that the rioting resulted from "mob action. It is obvious that many soldiers are not aware of the serious nature of riot charges, which could carry the death sentence or a long prison term."

On June 16 the *Los Angeles Times* ran a story from Mexico City, headlined "Mexican Government Expects Damages for Zoot Suit Riot Victims." The article stated that "the Mexican government took a mildly firm stand on the rights of its nationals, emphasizing its conviction that American justice would grant 'innocent victims' their proper retribution." Federal authorities expressed concern, and Mayor Fletcher Bowron assured Washington, D.C., that no racism was present. Soon afterward Bowron told the Los Angeles police to stop using "cream-puff techniques on the Mexican youths." At the same time he ordered the formation of a committee to "study the problem." City officials and the Los Angeles press became exceedingly touchy about charges of racism. When Eleanor Roosevelt commented in her column that the riots had been caused by "longstanding discrimination against the Mexicans in the Southwest," on June 18 the *Los Angeles Times* reacted with the headline "Mrs. Roosevelt Blindly Stirs Race Discord." The article denied that racial discrimination had been a factor in the riots and charged that Mrs. Roosevelt's statement resembled propaganda used by the communists, stating that servicemen had looked for "costumes and not races." The article said that Angelenos were proud of their missions and of Olvera Street, "a bit of old Mexico," and concluded "We like Mexicans and think they like us."

Governor Earl Warren formed a committee to investigate the riots. Participating on the committee were Attorney General Robert W. Kenny; Catholic bishop Joseph T. McGucken, who served as chair; Walter A. Gordon, Berkeley attorney; Leo Carrillo, screen actor; and Karl Holton, director of the California Youth Authority.

The committee's report recommended punishment of all persons responsible for the riots—military and civilian alike. It took a left-handed slap at the press, recommending that newspapers minimize the use of names and photos of juveniles. Moreover, it called for better-educated and trained police officers to work with Spanish-speaking youth.

Little was done to implement the recommendations of the report, and most of the same conditions still exist in Los Angeles city and county. "The kid gloves are off!" approach of Sheriff Eugene Biscailuz has, if anything, hardened since the 1940s.

During World War II, police authorities sought to strengthen social control of the *barrios* and spied extensively on the Mexican community. Little is known about domestic spying at the local or state levels, since these government units are not required to provide copies of their reports to individuals or organizations.

Dr. José Ángel Gutiérrez has done pioneer research in this area. Through the Freedom of Information Act, he received documents proving that the FBI spied even on patriotic groups such as LULAC (League of United Latin American Citizens) and later the G.I. Forum. In 1941, the FBI's Denver Office reported on the LULAC chapter of Antonio, Colorado. Its officers included a county judge and a town marshal. The FBI also investigated respected leaders such as George I. Sanchez and Alonso Perales, reporting that the Mexican community distrusted Sanchez because he had converted to reformed Methodism.

In May 1946, the FBI infiltrated a Los Angeles meeting of LULAC. An informant asserted that participants had a long history of communist activity but made no effort to document the statement. Early in the 1950s, the FBI again investigated LULAC because it demanded racial integration. In Pecos, Texas, the FBI spied on the local LULAC council because a member wanted to be on the Selective Service Board.

The Road to Delano: Creating a Moment

By the mid-1960s, Chicano militancy concerned growers and other employers. The purpose of immigration policy was to control not only Mexicans but Chicanos. After 1965, this policy became more restrictive, designed to regulate both the flow of workers and the wages paid. Essential to this strategy was the criminalization of Mexican labor. Criminalization intensified the division of labor and resulted in Chicanos, to avoid discrimination, pecking down on the undocumented worker; it also justified increased use of police power against all Mexicans, whether documented or undocumented.

The first step in the criminalization process was the passage of restrictive immigration laws. Liberals such as Senator Edward Kennedy sponsored legislation in 1965 designed to correct the past injustice of excluding Asians from legal entry. Nativists took the opportunity to broaden the legislation and, for the first time, placed Latin America and Canada on a quota system. The law specified that 170,000 immigrants annually could enter from the Eastern Hemisphere and 120,000 from the Western. Up to this time Mexico had been the principal source of Latin American immigration; the new law put a cap of 40,000 from any one nation. Unfortunately, few Chicanos or progressive organizations protested the law. And it was not until the 1970s that its full impact was felt; at that time it became a popular cause for progressives.

Many Chicanos have incorrectly labeled the second half of the 1960s as the birth of the Chicano movement. Mexicans in the United States have responded to injustice and oppression since the U.S. wars of aggression that took Texas and the Southwest from Mexico. Middle-class organizations generally spoke for the community, since its members had the education, money, and stability to maintain more or less permanent associations. Established Anglo power brokers also recognized these organizations.

By the mid-1960s, traditional groups such as LULAC and the G.I. Forum, along with recently formed political groups such as Mexican American Political Association (MAPA) and Political Association of Spanish-Speaking Organizations (PASSO), came under challenges. For better or worse, the established Mexican-American associations had served as agents of social control, setting the norm for conduct. The rise of cultural nationalism challenged assimilation as a goal. Sectors of youth, women, and more militant activists were skeptical of traditional methods of struggle and advocated direct action. They also questioned the legitimacy of established leaders.

For the most part, LULAC and Forum leaders at first rejected "street politics"— marches, walkouts, confrontations, civil disobedience, and so on. Over the years their ties with the system tightened. At the same time, the civil rights, antinuclear, and anti–Vietnam War movements, along with community action programs, legitimated an ideology of confrontation, creating a new awareness among Chicanos that resulted in a demand for self-determination by *los de abajo* (the underdogs) and youth. For their part, sectors of the North American left, as well as government agencies, no longer dealt with established groups exclusively but recognized more militant Chicano organizations. This, for a time, broke the monopoly of the Mexican-American middle class. Moreover, rank-and-file members of LULAC and the Forum grew closer to the new Chicano agenda.

César Chávez and the United Farm Workers

César Chávez gave the Chicano movement a national leader. In all probability Chávez was the only Mexican American to be so recognized by the mainstream civil rights and antiwar movements. Chávez and his farm workers also received support from the center Mexican-American organizations along with the left.

On September 8, 1965, the Filipinos in the Agricultural Workers Organizing Committee (AWOC) struck the grape growers of the Delano area in the San Joaquin Valley. Filipino workers had been encouraged by a victory in the spring of 1965 in the Coachella Valley, where the U.S. Labor Department announced that *braceros* would be paid $1.40 an hour. The domestic pickers received 20¢ to 30¢ an hour less. Joined by Mexicans, the Filipinos walked out, and ten days later they received a guarantee of equivalent pay with *braceros*. When the Filipinos requested the same guarantee in the San Joaquin Valley, growers refused, and led by Larry Itlong, they voted to strike. The strike demands were simple: $1.40 an hour or 25¢ a box. The Di Giorgio Corporation became the major target. The rank and file of the National Farm Workers Association (NFWA) voted on September 16 to join the Filipinos.

Chávez emerged as the central figure in the strike. Born in Yuma, Arizona, in 1927, he spent his childhood as a migrant worker. His father had belonged to farm labor unions, and Chávez himself had been a member of the National Farm Labor Union. In the 1940s he moved to San José, California, where he married Helen Favila. In San José Chávez met Father Donald McDonnell, who tutored him in *Rerum Novarum*, Pope Leo XIII's encyclical which supported labor unions and social justice. Through Father McDonnell, Chávez met Fred Ross of the Community Service Organization (CSO). He became an organizer for the CSO and learned grass-roots strategies. Chávez rose to the position of general director of the national CSO, but in 1962 he resigned, moving to Delano, where he began to organize his union. Chávez went door to door visiting farm workers. Delano was chosen because of its substantial all-year farm-worker population; in 1968, 32 percent of the 7,000 harvest workers lived and worked in the Delano area year round.

Chávez concentrated his efforts on the Mexican field hands, for he knew the importance of nationalism in solidifying an organization. He carefully selected a loyal cadre of proven organizers, such as Dolores Huerta and Gil Padilla, whom he had met in the CSO. By the middle of 1964 the NFWA was self-supporting.

A year later the organization had some 1,700 members. Volunteers, fresh from civil rights activities in the South, joined the NFWA at Delano. Protestant groups, inspired by the civil rights movement, championed the cause of the workers. A minority of Catholic priests, influenced by Vatican II, joined Chávez. Anglo-American labor belatedly jumped on the bandwagon. In Chávez's favor was the growing number of Chicano workers living in the United States. Over 80 percent lived in cities, and many belonged to unions. Many, in fact, belonged to big labor such as the United Auto Workers (UAW).

The times allowed Chávez to make his movement a crusade. The stabilization of a large part of the Mexican-American workforce made the forging of an organization possible. And, finally, the end of the *bracero* program took a lethal weapon from the growers.

The most effective strategy was the boycott. Chávez urged supporters not to buy Schenley products or Di Giorgio grapes. The first breakthrough came when the Schenley Corporation signed a contract in 1966. The Teamsters unexpectedly refused to cross picket lines in San Francisco. Rumors of a bartenders' boycott reached seventy-five-year-old Lewis Solon Rosenstiel, Schenley's president, who decided that a settlement was advisable. Soon afterward Gallo, Christian Brothers, Paul Masson, Almaden, Franzia Brothers, and Novitiate signed contracts.

The next opponent was the Di Giorgio Corporation, one of the largest grape growers in the central valley. In April 1966, Robert Di Giorgio unexpectedly announced he would allow his workers at Sierra Vista to vote on whether they wanted a union and who would represent them. Di Giorgio did not act in good faith and his agents set out to intimidate the workers.

With the support of Di Giorgio the Teamsters opposed the farm workers and demanded to represent the workers. Di Giorgio, without consulting the NFWA, set the date for the election. The NFWA urged its followers not to vote, since it did not have time to campaign or to participate in establishing the ground rules. It needed enough time to return eligible voters to the Delano area. Out of 732 eligible voters only 385 voted; 281 voters specified that they wanted the Teamsters as their union agent. The NFWA immediately branded the election as fraudulent and pressured Governor Edmund G. Brown, Sr., a friend of Di Giorgio, to investigate the election. Brown needed the Chicano vote as well as that of the liberals who were committed to the farm workers. The governor's investigator recommended a new election, and the date was set for August 30, 1966.

That summer an intense campaign took place between the Teamsters and the NFWA. A state senate committee investigated charges of communist infiltration of the NFWA but found nothing to substantiate them. As the election neared, Chávez became more somber. He had to keep the eligible voters in Delano, and he had the responsibility of feeding them and their families as well as the army of strikers and volunteers. The Di Giorgio campaign drained the union's financial resources. Some weeks before the strike vote, Chávez reluctantly merged the NFWA and AWOC into the United Farm Workers Organizing Committee (UFWOC).

Teamsters red-baited the UFWOC and circulated free copies of Gary Allen's John Birch Society pamphlet. The UFWOC passed out excerpts from *The Enemy Within*, in which Robert Kennedy indicted James Hoffa and the Teamsters in scathing terms; association with the Kennedy name helped. Finally the vote was taken. The UFWOC won the election, 573 votes to the Teamsters' 425. Field workers voted 530 to 331 in favor of the UFWOC. Soon afterward the Di Giorgio Corporation and the UFWOC signed a contract.

Other growers proved to be more difficult. In 1967 the Giumarra Vineyards Corporation, the largest producer of table grapes in the United States, was targeted. When Giumarra used other companies' labels to circumvent the boycott, in violation of the Food and Drug Administration rules, the union boycotted all California table grapes. Boycott activities spread into Canada and Europe. Grape sales decreased significantly. Some of the slack was taken up by the U.S. Defense Department. In 1966 U.S. troops in Vietnam were shipped 468,000 pounds of grapes; in 1967, 555,000 pounds; in 1968, 2 million pounds; and by 1969, more than 4 million pounds. Later the U.S. Defense Department spent taxpayers' money to buy large quantities of lettuce when the union boycotted this product. In the summer of 1970 the strike approached its fifth year. In June 1970 a group of Coachella Valley growers agreed to sign contracts, as did a majority of growers. Victories in the San Joaquin Valley followed.

The union then turned to the lettuce fields of the Salinas Valley, where growers were among the most powerful in the state. During July 1970 the Growers-Shippers Association and twenty-nine of the largest growers in the valley entered into negotiations with the Teamsters. Agreements signed with the truckers' union in Salinas were worse than sweetheart contracts: they provided no job security, no seniority rights, no hiring hall, and no protection against pesticides.

Many growers, like the Bud Antle Company (a partner of Dow Chemical), had dealt with the Teamsters since the 1950s. In 1961, in return for a $1 million loan, Antle signed a contract with the truckers. By August 1970 many workers refused to abide by the Teamster contracts, and 5,000 walked off the lettuce fields. The growers launched a campaign of violence. Jerry Cohen, a farm-worker lawyer, was beaten unconscious. On December 4, 1970, Judge Gordon Campbell of Monterey County jailed Chávez for refusing to obey an injunction and held him without bail. This action gave the boycott needed publicity. Dignitaries visited Chávez in jail; he was released on Christmas Eve.

By the spring of 1971 Chávez and the Teamsters signed an agreement that gave the UFWOC sole jurisdiction in the lettuce fields and that allowed George Meany, president of the AFL, and Teamsters president Frank Fitzsimmons to arbitrate the situation. Throughout the summer and into the fall, however, growers refused to disqualify Teamster contracts, and gradually the situation became stalemated.

The fight with the Teamsters hurt the UFWOC since it turned its attention from servicing contracts. Chávez refused help from the AFL, believing that farm workers had to learn from their own mistakes. According to *Fresno Bee* reporter Ron Taylor, although Chávez was a patient teacher, he did not delegate authority and involved himself with too much detail. Farm workers had never had the opportunity to govern themselves and Chávez had to build "ranch committees" from the bottom up. This took time, and the corporate ranchers who ran agribusiness had little tolerance for democracy.

NOTES

1. Raúl Morin, AMONG THE VALIANT (Alhambra, Calif.: Border, 1966), p. 16.

2. Ismael Dieppa, *The Zoot-Suit Riots Revisited: The Role of Private Philanthropy in Youth Problems of Mexican-Americans* (DSW dissertation, University of Southern California, 1973), p. 14; see Carey McWilliams Papers at the Special Collections Library at the University of California at Los Angeles.

3. Robin Fitzgerald Scott, *The Mexican-American in the Los Angeles Area, 1920–1950: From Acquiescence to Activity* (Ph.D. dissertation, University of Southern California, 1971), pp. 223, 225.

4. Dieppa, p. 15, emphasizes the sex motive, stating that there were five servicemen to every girl.

5. FBI report, January 14, 1944. *The Eastside Journal*, June 9, 1943, wrote an editorial defending the zoot-suiters; it pointed out that 112 had been hospitalized, 150 hurt, and 12 treated in the hospitals.

III

"Breaking the Law" on Principle

Michael A. Olivas

A recent article by Professor Martha Minow[1] identifies three risks inherent in the lawyer-client relationship when the client breaks the law to pursue social, political, or legal change: a risk of nonrepresentation, where no accomplished lawyer will take the case; a risk of terminated representation, when ethical requirements may jeopardize an unpopular client's defense; and a risk of truncated representation, where the lawyer's choice of tactics may undermine the very premise of the client's grievance.

Consider the first risk. When unpopular clients break the law, they may face a difficult time in securing representation. If the client is wealthy, however, he or she will be able to secure counsel, however reprehensible or unpopular the crime. Minow does not argue the ethical or constitutional reasons for representation of politically motivated offenders; rather her concern is that for the system to work requires saboteurs to challenge legal complacency, which in turn necessitates lawyers willing to commit themselves.

Undoubtedly, this willingness to test the legal barriers is essential to change. Having excellent counsel certainly increases the likelihood of effecting change through litigation, and makes the change more substantial and precedential. Consider the classic example Minow employs, that of Martin Luther King, Jr., held in jail in Birmingham, Alabama. This particular incident is certainly one of the central events in United States civil rights history. Reverend King's incarceration had great moral and symbolic significance for his political agenda of overturning racial apartheid, and played out on national television, demonstrating how unjust public laws were for blacks. This and similar incidents led to a series of changes in civil rights laws.

In the second scenario, principled would-be law-breakers divulge to their attorney that they intend to break a law. Do lawyers have a "Tarasoff" duty to warn (or withdraw)?[2] Minow poses the question in an example she cites, where a client that would import and distribute RU-486, the "abortion pill" available in Europe, could well violate Food and Drug Administration (FDA) regulations and be held in criminal contempt. Her analysis concludes that the Model Code allows the company's attorneys the discretion to serve their client without disclosing the intended lawbreaking. If consulted before the client violates the law, the lawyer may advise the client on

From *"Breaking the Law" on Principle: An Essay on Lawyers' Dilemmas, Unpopular Causes, and Legal Regimes,* 52 U. PITT. L. REV. 815 (1991). Originally published in the *University of Pittsburgh Law Review.* Reprinted by permission.

the likely or probable consequences of their proposed actions. In so doing, however, Minow warns, legal representation itself risks furthering a fraudulent scheme or ongoing crime.

Minow's third risk is a variation of T. S. Eliot's *Murder in the Cathedral*, doing what may be the right thing for the wrong reasons.[3] This is a paradox of compelling stature, where a client's principles may preclude a defense that could minimize the very real personal harm that the client's conviction would cause. Recent rulings by the Fourth Circuit in Rule 11 proceedings pose just such a dilemma for William Kunstler's attorneys.[4] The famous civil rights litigator filed a suit against prosecutors and public officials in North Carolina, alleging harassment of Native Americans during a criminal investigation. He and his co-counsel held a press conference to draw public attention to the alleged harassment. The prosecutors sought sanctions alleging that Kunstler had filed the suit "for publicity, to embarrass state and county officials, to use as leverage in criminal proceedings, to obtain discovery for use in criminal proceedings, and to intimidate those involved in the prosecution of [the Indian activists]."[5] Kunstler vowed, "I'm not going to pay any fine. I'm going to rot in jail if that's what I have to do to dramatize this thing."[6] The same court also recently upheld Rule 11 sanctions against Julius Chambers, Director of the NAACP Legal Defense Fund (LDF), for charges stemming from an employment discrimination case brought by the LDF against the U.S. Army. The court reduced the $85,000 fine but upheld the sanctions, holding that the attorneys had not met their "responsibility to explore the factual bases for the clients' suits . . . instead charging forward with the litigation in disregard of its manifest lack of merit."[7]

At bottom is Minow's contention that each of these three types of dilemma poses "genuine dangers," particularly if our system is not supple enough to consider principled claims or to accommodate pluralistic approaches to the law. She urges an expanded role for "legal process" courses so that students learn "the historic traditions of lawyers defending people who break the law for political reasons."[8] Consider three further examples:

Case 1: The Case of Unaccompanied Refugee Children: Legal Clinics and the Risk of Cooptation

Thousands of unaccompanied children who have felt the violence in their Central American countries are being detained in refugee camps in the United States, most in shameful conditions without access to basic necessities of education, health care, or legal services. Because immigration procedures, including deportation, are considered civil rather than criminal proceedings, little process is due these alien children under the Constitution. Immigration law requires highly technical legal expertise, yet the Immigration and Naturalization Service (INS) has actively discouraged its detained aliens from getting it. Children are particularly vulnerable in the asylum process; nonetheless, at present, no statutory or common law right guarantees appointed counsel or guardians for children trapped in the immigration labyrinth.

In early 1989, to stem the tide of Central American refugees and asylum seekers, the INS decided to detain these aliens in border facilities and tent-shelters. Earlier, many asylum seekers had been processed quickly in mass adjudications, often conceding their deportability and being sent back to their home country. Under this policy, unaccompanied children awaiting a decision were released to family members, church groups, or other community assistance organizations. The children were unaccompanied either because they had fled their country without adults, they were sent ahead by family members who had hoped to shield them from harm, or they had become separated from adults during flight. The INS policy of detaining children and adults has led to an expansion of detention facilities in rural areas. INS figures for a recent year show over 3,600 aliens in Texas detention facilities, and 2,500 alien children in California. Predictably, the facilities are ramshackle: one site in Texas has been sardonically dubbed "El Corralon" (The Corral), while another is a former Department of Agriculture pesticide storage facility. A study of the children in these facilities revealed that virtually all suffered from advanced and untreated cases of post-traumatic shock syndrome. These children have virtually no access to health care or personal counseling, even though many have been severely traumatized by the war in their country, by the arduous and dangerous trip North, and by their incarceration here. The children receive no educational services, even though every child in Texas is required to enroll in school during the school year. Like the adults, the detained alien children have little access to attorneys, telephones, or other legal means to prepare their cases.

Because the INS couches its actions in national defense terms ("securing our borders" and "intercepting drug trafficking"), little community outrage has been heard over these actions. The Red Cross has been coopted into operating one of the facilities, cloaking the center with legitimacy, while community newspapers have been lulled into believing that the policy is humanitarian. Further, INS officials counted on the remoteness of the camps, the economic incentive to the poor communities, and the distance from legal services to keep their practices from undergoing public scrutiny.

The practice of detaining alien minors has advanced two ulterior motives. First, to discourage other refugees from migrating to the United States.[9] Second, authorities hoped to "bait" undocumented families into revealing themselves to authorities. As a result of these practices, family members in the United States, even those with permission to be in the country, have found it intimidating or impossible to locate their children. In *Flores v. Meese*[10] and *Perez-Funez v. INS*,[11] many of these INS practices concerning children came to light. In these cases, the courts found that the INS had acted to deprive unaccompanied alien minors of their rights to full hearings and due process. In another case, the judge found "a persistent pattern and practice of misconduct," use of "intimidation, threats, and misrepresentation," and evidence of "a widespread and pervasive practice akin to a policy" concerning pressure on Salvadorans to concede their rights.[12]

As a result of the remote locations of the facilities, INS policies on transfer, availability of legal resources, and poor response by organized bars, legal assistance to unaccompanied children is virtually non-existent. For example, even though Laredo, Texas, is hundreds of miles away from San Antonio (the tenth largest city in the United States), over 80 percent of the San Antonio region immigration caseload is in Laredo. To make matters worse, no immigration judge lives in or is appointed on a regular basis in Laredo. Therefore, all hearings are consolidated into alternating weeks when a judge does ride the circuit. This irregular schedule precludes attorneys (most of whom live in San Antonio) from arranging their schedules to synchronize with those of the judges. A visiting federal judge found that aliens were not even provided adequate lists of legal services. For example, the list (in English) included names and numbers of lawyers who did not handle immigration cases, and failed to include a free legal assistance program. He characterized this and other practices as "bad faith."[13] An ABA inspection team issued a report noting that legal services to detained aliens were "grossly inadequate."[14] Even when courts find that detained aliens have been deprived of basic legal information on their rights, and have ordered changes, the INS has "not diligently respected [injunctions and temporary restraining orders], nor were agents disciplined for failing to adhere to terms."[15]

Most troubling has been the practice of transferring aliens as a means of depriving them of counsel.[16] Because the policy of establishing rural detention centers virtually assures that the refugees and asylum seekers will not have access to counsel, transfer to one of them is tantamount to a deprivation of counsel. In a troubling decision, a United States district court upheld the practice, noting INS's discretionary authority to make custodial decisions. In several instances, transfers have even been made after counsel was retained or as a blatant attempt to deny counsel. The policies and practices of INS have ensured that legal services for detainees have been minimal or nonexistent.

At my own law school, we pooled our resources and agreed to try to provide clinical legal assistance. We decided to offer a between-semester clinical credit refugee project, with concentrated instruction in Houston, and a supervised field experience. We arranged for seven students to spend sixty hours in a week on a pro bono bar project in the Valley. Another fourteen students worked in Houston, trying to secure bond redetermination hearings and doing country research necessary for ongoing asylum cases. We sponsored conferences and coordinated course coverage so that more students could train as immigration lawyers. Were we successful? It is hard to say. Student enthusiasm ran high, yet at two o'clock in the morning I could not help but wonder if we are simply legitimizing INS in its pernicious practices, and I recall the faces of the children who fled war only to wind up at El Corralon.

Case 2: The Boycott of Israeli Military Courts by Israeli and Palestinian Lawyers

[Deleted—Eds.]

Case 3: Oscar Z. Acosta, Chicano Lawyer

In the early 1970s, two novels appeared that were widely read and admired, *The Autobiography of a Brown Buffalo* and *The Revolt of the Cockroach People* by Oscar Zeta

Acosta, a lawyer in real life. Acosta became a counter-cultural hero, whose character later figured prominently in Hunter S. Thompson's popular "Fear and Loathing" series, where he became the wild Samoan attorney, Dr. Gonzo. Acosta's two novels have been widely studied by literary scholars, particularly emphasizing his search for identity as a Mexican American, and the bawdy, picaresque depiction of his life in the late 1960s, when Chicano political consciousness arrived on the scene.

In *Brown Buffalo*, he flees from his Legal Aid position and drives across the country and Mexico to find himself and discover his role in life. After a harrowing series of drug- and alcohol-related incidents, he returns to California, determined to become "Zeta, the world-famous Chicano lawyer who helped to start the last revolution."[17] In *Revolt*, Acosta blends historical and political events into his narrative, having decided to become someone of importance:

> I will change my name. I will learn Spanish. I will write the greatest books ever written. I will become the best criminal lawyer in the history of the world. I will save the world. I will show the world what is what and who the fuck is who. Me in particular.[18]

He then sets out on a variety of escapades, deftly meeting and incorporating figures from the times. He runs for Los Angeles County Sheriff; he defends Chicanos charged with political crimes; he testifies before the Los Angeles school board after a student walkout; he sues to get at the truth of a murdered reporter. These events and people become transmogrified into Acosta's tales in prose reeking of anger and a sense of the absurd. Acosta takes on a pseudonym, Buffalo Z. Brown, for its Mexican cultural antecedents and for the wistful significance of the American buffalo, doomed to extinction. As one scholar put it:

> The masks and use of fictionalization in ethnic autobiography are important keys to understand the intent and purpose of the autobiographer, for they help him to evaluate not only himself but also his race. In this particular case, *Brown Buffalo* represents the Chicano's confusion at the start of the Chicano Movement, while *Cockroach People* tells us where he is heading as a result of this Movement. The reader travels with Acosta in his search for an identity because he can relate so strongly with the human emotions the narrator experiences, while at the same time he learns and arrives at an understanding of the history and ideology of the Chicano Movement.[19]

Although ostensibly fiction, Acosta's work, in several instances, draws from the author's real-life experience as a lawyer, as in the poignant portrait of the demoralizing work of a poverty lawyer, and in his handling of political cases, woven into *The Revolt of the Cockroach People*. One of these, *Castro v. Superior Court of Los Angeles County*,[20] actually broke new ground and fits Martha Minow's classification of cases that need to be undertaken for their monkey-wrenching value. In his fictional treatment of the case, all hell is breaking out in East Los Angeles, home to a half-million Mexican Americans. This parallels history. On March 3, 1968, many high school students began a series of walkouts, and by the time the strike was over, a week later, the "blowouts" had given many young Chicano students their first taste of politics:

Overnight, student activism reached levels of intensity never before witnessed. A few Mexican American student activists had participated in civil rights marches, anti–Vietnam War protests, and had walked the picket lines for the farmworker movement. But the high school strike of 1968 was the first time students of Mexican descent had marched en masse in their own demonstration against racism and for educational change. It was also the first time that they had played direct leadership roles in organizing a mass protest.[21]

Several leaders of the strike and ten students were indicted by a grand jury in June 1968 and became known locally as the "LA Thirteen." This entire episode is recounted by Acosta in *Revolt*. Acosta and his co-counsel, in real life, attacked the indictments of the "LA Thirteen" on first amendment grounds, charging that the indictments were politically motivated, that the state educational code provisions under which they had been indicted were overbroad, and that both felony and misdemeanor counts should be dropped. The court of appeals agreed on all points, save the last, and preserved the misdemeanor counts. These misdemeanor counts had already been dismissed during collateral charges brought in municipal court, and the appeals court remanded for fact-finding on whether the District Attorney could press for further prosecution on the misdemeanors. When the charges were not refiled, victory for the "LA Thirteen" was complete.

In *Castro*, Acosta had also challenged the racial composition of the grand jury, but with the decision in the writ proceeding, this issue was set aside. In another, similar case, however, Acosta advanced the argument that because it was a politically motivated prosecution, the appeals court should quash the grand jury indictments on the grounds that the juror selection process was racist in its virtual exclusion of Mexican Americans.[22] Acosta's data, for example, showed that in 1968, when 12.4 percent of Los Angeles County was Hispanic, only 3 grand jurors out of 171 serving that year were Hispanic, or 1.8 percent. This ratio of 6.9 available jurors to 1 juror called exceeded southern black grand juror ratios found discriminatory by the United States Supreme Court in earlier cases.

Los Angeles presented an additional feature in seating its grand juries, as each superior court judge was allowed to nominate two jurors. In 1969, 7 Hispanics had been nominated by 5 judges to the 189 positions. From 1959 to 1969, 25 of 1690 (2.8 percent) grand jurors in Los Angeles county courts were Hispanic. Acosta decided to subpoena the judges to find out why they had nominated so few Hispanics to their grand juries.

The trial court ruled against Acosta, finding that ten "Spanish-surnamed" persons had been nominated, of which a majority were Mexican American. "Therefore, it cannot be said that Mexican-Americans or persons with Spanish surnames were excluded from the 1969 grand jury."[23] Acosta, however, wanted to depose the superior court judges, including the then-presiding judge, about their nominations, which, he argued, were too few for the percentage of Latinos in the Los Angeles population at large. Acosta argued that, "as applied to a county containing over one-half million Spanish-surnamed persons, the peoples' 'explanations' of chronic tokenism in grand jury representation are inadequate, if not racist."[24]

The state had asserted that their low level of education explained why so few Latino jurors had been chosen. Acosta offered counter evidence, drawing from United States Census data and other cases that a sixth-grade education was the minimum education necessary to be called for grand jury duty. As the appeals court noted, Acosta intended to show that, with very few exceptions, the judges of the respondent court were by reason of birth, education, residence, wealth, social and professional associations, and similar factors not acquainted with the qualifications of eligible potential grand jurors of petitioners' class and that they did not make an adequate effort to overcome this alleged deficiency.[25] The appeals court, having found for Acosta on this point, granted the writ.

This was Acosta's last major case before he disappeared off the coast of Mexico in May 1974. In December 1986, he was declared legally dead. In 1989, his son arranged to have his two novels reissued, so that a new generation of readers could appreciate Acosta's lawyering skills. Acosta fit neatly within Minow's typology of lawyers who, through their representation of unpopular clients and causes, force the system to confront its political underpinnings. The Chicanos who became Acosta's clients felt that they had pursued peaceful solutions to improve community conditions. When they exercised their first amendment rights, the full force of the Los Angeles police power, including the political aspirant District Attorney, was directed at them. Acosta's defense tactics, challenging the racial composition of the grand jury process and the racial bona fides of the judges in the appointment process, led to acquittals of the defendants in both trials on all the major charges. His combination of astute political instincts and deft lawyering did not compromise his clients' interests, and largely vindicated them.

NOTES

1. Martha Minow, *Breaking the Law: Lawyers and Clients in Struggles for Social Change*, 52 U. PITT. L. REV. 723 (1991).

2. Tarasoff v. Regents of Univ. of Cal., 17 Cal. 3d 425, 131 Cal. Rptr. 14, 551 P.2d 334 (1976) (therapist had duty to warn identifiable potential victim of potential harm threatened by patient).

3. In *Murder in the Cathedral* the Archbishop is killed, but his ostensibly heroic action is undermined by his hubris, as he sought martyrdom.

4. *In re* Kunstler, 914 F.2d 505 (4th Cir. 1990).

5. *Id.* at 520.

6. Don J. DeBenedictis, *Rule 11 Snags Lawyers*, A.B.A. J., January 1991, at 17.

7. Blue v. United States Dep't. of the Army, 914 F.2d 525, 550 (4th Cir. 1990).

8. Minow, at 750.

9. Press release from Department of Justice, February 23, 1989, reprinted in CENTRAL AMERICAN ASYLUM-SEEKERS: HEARING BEFORE SUBCOMMITTEE ON IMMIGRATION, REFUGEES, AND INTERNATIONAL LAW OF THE HOUSE COMMITTEE ON THE JUDICIARY, 101st Cong., 1st Sess. 51 (1990) (Statement of Alan Nelson, Commissioner, INS) (INS enforcement plan "sends the message loud and clear to those thousands motivated only by economic betterment for themselves who use the asylum application to circumvent the process of awaiting for

immigrant status in their home countries"). Economic hardship is not a criterion for refugee or asylum status.

10. Flores v. Meese, 681 F.Supp. 665 (C.D. Cal. 1988) (routine strip searches of detained alien juveniles violated juveniles' fourth amendment rights). This was overturned in 1990, 913 F.2d 1315 (9th Cir. 1990), but because the Ninth Circuit decided to rehear it en banc, the opinion was withdrawn.

11. 619 F.Supp. 656 (C.D. Cal. 1985).

12. Orantes-Hernandez v. Meese, 685 F.Supp. 1488, at 1504, 1505 (C.D. Cal. 1988).

13. *Id.* at 1498.

14. ABA COORDINATING COMMITTEE ON IMMIGRATION LAW, LIVES ON THE LINE: SEEK-ING ASYLUM IN SOUTH TEXAS 19 (1989).

15. Orantes-Hernandez, 685 F.Supp. 1495.

16. *Id.* at 1509.

17. Oscar Acosta, THE AUTOBIOGRAPHY OF A BROWN BUFFALO 199 (1972).

18. Oscar Acosta, THE REVOLT OF THE COCKROACH PEOPLE 31 (1973).

19. Kimberly Kowalczyk, *Oscar Zeta Acosta: The Brown Buffalo and His Search for Identity*, 16 AMERICAS REV. 198, 206 (Fall-Winter 1988).

20. Castro v. Superior Court, 9 Cal. App. 3d 675, 88 Cal. Rptr. 500 (1970).

21. Carlos Muñoz, Jr., YOUTH, IDENTITY, POWER: THE CHICANO MOVEMENT 65 (1989). Carlos Muñoz, Jr., who knew Acosta and appears in REVOLT as one of the East LA Thirteen, is a professor of ethnic studies at the University of California, Berkeley. I am grateful to him for his assistance during discussions in March 1991.

22. Montez v. Superior Court, 10 Cal. App. 3d 343, 88 Cal. Rptr. 736 (1970). Acosta had raised this issue in Castro, but the judges decided the case without reaching the merits of this argument. The record, however, was well developed, and the transcript for this motion to quash in Castro filled more than a thousand pages. Castro v. Superior Court, 9 Cal. App. 3d 675, 680, 88 Cal. Rptr. 500, 504, 6 (1970).

23. *Id.* at 347 n.6, 88 Cal. Rptr. at 738 n.6.

24. Petitioners' Reply Brief at 4, Montez v. Superior Court, 10 Cal. App. 3d 343, 88 Cal. Rptr. 736 (1970) (Civ. No. 36021).

25. Montez, 88 Cal. Rptr. at 740.

Chapter 47

||||||||||||||||||||||||||||||||||||||||||||||||||||||||||||||||||||||||||||||||

Life in the Trenches

Oscar "Zeta" Acosta

. . . That really affected my whole thing with the result that, when I got out of the service, I attempted suicide. Naturally, I chickened out like everybody else, but I ended up in psychiatry. I started school at San Francisco State and started writing. I was majoring in creative writing and mathematics and I dug both of them. I had one more semester to go to get my degree in math but, by that time, I was halfway through a novel, so I dropped out to finish that and then intended to go back. I never did because by that time it was 1960, the Kennedy campaign and I got involved in that. I hadn't had a political thought up until then. I decided I didn't want to be either a mathematician or a professional writer after that involvement, but I did finish the novel and submitted it to three publishers, all of whom almost accepted it. They all said that I was great, earthy, poetic, the most brilliant unpublished writer in the world, but I was writing about Chicanos at that time—it was a Romeo and Juliet story of Okies and Chicanos in the valley—and that subject wasn't acceptable. So I decided I would write because that is what I am, a writer, but that I didn't want to have to write or to be a professional writer.

Since I was interested in politics and Chicanos, I decided to go to law school then work with Chávez and the farmworkers and be a union organizer. So I did it and got involved in the black civil rights movement for the next four years in San Francisco, but it wasn't really me. I told people that it wasn't just black and white, that there were Chicanos, too, and they laughed at me so I told them to go fuck themselves and they split. I graduated from San Francisco Law School, a night law school, in 1965. I was working at the *San Francisco Examiner* all of this time through college and law school as a copy boy, along with all of the political activity. When I got out, I took the bar exam and flunked it. It was the first time I had flunked an exam in my life and it was the third major trauma, so I ended up back with the psychiatrist. I studied for the bar again and passed it a couple of months later.

I became a legal aid lawyer in Oakland in a half-black, half-Chicano section. I hated it with a passion. I'd wake up in the morning and throw up. All we'd do was sit and listen to complaints. There were so many problems, and we didn't do anything. We didn't have a direction, skills or tools.

After a year, I became totally depressed. I couldn't do anything, so I said fuck it to

From *Autobiographical Essay* by Oscar "Zeta" Acosta, in Oscar "Zeta" Acosta: The Uncollected Works, edited by Ilan Stavans, pp. 7–15. Copyright © 1996. Reprinted by permission of Arte Publico Press.

everything and told the psychiatrist to shove it and to stick the pills up his ass. I said I'd been with him on and off for ten years and that I was still as fucked up as when I began, just taking ten times as many pills. I took off and ended up in Aspen.

I met some people who were pretty nice to me, including Hunter S. Thompson, the writer, and I started dropping acid and staying stoned most of the time and doing all kinds of odd jobs—construction work and washing dishes—and, within about three months my head was clear. I felt like I knew who I was, what I was and what I was supposed to do. I stayed there for about six months, and then I was on my way to Guatemala to smuggle guns to the revolutionaries down there and to write about them. I got stopped in Juárez and thrown in jail. When I got out I called my brother who suggested that I go to Los Angeles. Well, I hated it. Being from up north, I was subjected to this old prejudice between Northern and Southern California, which was ridiculous. I asked my brother why I should go there and about a newspaper called *La Raza*. That was in January 1968. I arrived here in LA in February, intending to stay for a few months, write an article about it and then get out.

Then the high school walkouts occurred and I agreed to take a few misdemeanor cases. Two months later, thirteen of the organizers of the walkouts were busted on sixteen counts of conspiracy which could have resulted in forty-five years in prison for each of them. I agreed to take the case. It was my first major case, my first criminal case and here I am three years later. I haven't been able to get away and I don't think I ever will leave. This is it for me because I've gone through intensive changes in myself and my consciousness has developed about Chicanismo, La Raza, revolution and what we're going to do, so it looks like I'm here to stay. It seems to me that at some point in your life you have to make a stand, and I've decided that I might as well be here as anywhere else. This, East Los Angeles, is the capital of Aztlán, because there are more of us here than anywhere else.

To understand where I am you have to understand how the Chicano Movement has developed. In 1967 and 1968 young Chicano students, both in high school and college, began to identify as Mexican Americans. The first issue was what to call themselves. They began to organize coffee-houses and clubs but were mainly interested in the educational system. So, in March 1968, they had massive high school walkouts from four of the Mexican-American high schools in East Los Angeles. The result was numerous busts and that is when I became involved. Those walkouts were the first major activity by Chicanos as Chicanos in the history of this country. There had been labor groups and political-type groups, but there had never been any group organized to organize and politicize the community as Chicanos on broad-based issues. There are two million Chicanos here in Southern California. I think we're the largest ethnic minority in the Southwest—certainly here in Los Angeles we are. Statistically, we're the lowest in education, with an eighth-grade education being the median, and we're the lowest in housing and jobs. We have the problems here in Los Angeles and the Southwest that the blacks have throughout the country.

But the history of the Southwest is totally different from that of the rest of the country, which is something that most people don't understand, and they don't understand that this historical relationship is what causes the attitudes that exist here today. They tend to see us as immigrants, which is absolutely wrong. We were here before the white man got here. The American government took our country away from us in 1848, when the government of Mexico sold us out. They sold not only the land, but they basically sold us as slaves in the sense that our labor and our land was being expropriated. The governments never gave us a choice about whether or not to be American citizens. One night we were Mexican and the next day we were American. This historical relationship is the most important part of the present day relationships, but it's totally ignored or unknown or rejected by the Anglo society.

In 1968, when we started making a movement toward attaining better education and schools, we wanted the literature to reflect our heritage and our culture. We started meeting with school boards and the city council, and we began to know the enemy. At that point I think that most of us believed we could integrate into the society and get a piece of the action, since nobody denied that we had problems. But now, three years later, there have been few changes. Now there are two assemblymen in the California legislature, one Congressman, and one member of the school board who are Chicanos, and that is it for a class that constitutes 13 percent of the population.

In 1968, our first problem was that of identity. As time went on we no longer questioned that. We had chosen a name—Chicano—whether we had Spanish or Indian blood, and we knew that we existed alone. That is, we relate to Mexico, but in a nostalgic way. We know that when the going gets rough, the Mexican government ain't going to do shit for us. And we know that no other aspect of the broad movement is going to do shit for us. They'll pay lip service, they'll condescend to us, but basically they're just as paternalistic to us as the white racist pigs. For example, I've spoken at numerous rallies for the Panthers, for Angela Davis, and every time I get the same bullshit treatment. I'm the last on the program with five minutes to speak and we get no offers of any real unity or working together.

I think that the Black Movement has been co-opted. Three years ago I used to know a lot of heavy blacks. They're just not around anymore. I'm talking about the Black Panthers. They're just rhetoric; they're just sucking in that money. They talk heavy as hell, but when it comes down to what they're fighting for I don't think even they know what they're fighting for because they're integrating into the society that they despise as fast as that society allows them to. I made this decision during Corky's trial.

Corky González is head of the Crusade for Justice, which is based in Denver. He is also a poet, a street-fighter, a theorist and an organizer, and he is recognized by a lot of Chicanos as the boss, the leader. Chávez is like a grandfather to the Movement. We respect him and love him and would help him anytime he asked, but we don't feel that his progress, his ideology, is Chicano enough. César used the white liberal population quite a bit and, more than anything, this offends the average Chicano. It is bad because they take jobs that Chicanos should be taking, and using them is the easy way out. There were probably more competent white militants three years ago than there were available Chicanos, but we feel that he should have trained his own people more as we do now.

Corky was on trial on a weapons charge arising out of the August 29, 1970 police riot here, where three people, including Rubén Salazar, were killed by the police. Corky had been trying to get away from the violence with his two children when the police busted him for a traffic violation, suspicion of robbery, and a concealed weapons charge. He was on a truck with a lot of people and we never denied that somebody on it had a loaded pistol, but it wasn't Corky. He wouldn't dare carry a goddamn gun around with him. He's a leader. He doesn't have to carry a gun for the same goddamn reason that Nixon doesn't have to. But we didn't stress that point at the trial for fear of alarming the jury and perhaps inflaming the press and cops. Why should we give them an excuse to shoot at Corky like they did at Rubén when they thought that he was a leader?

What I did stress in picking the jury was whether they would be prejudiced if Huey Newton testified for Corky. See, Huey had called and said he wanted to talk to me. I asked him if he'd come down and be a character witness for Corky. I thought it would be a great show of unity. Everybody said he would. Then, after I'd announced it all over town and picked a jury by hammering at that question, he wouldn't come or talk to me on the phone, so I have nothing more to do with the Black Movement. I'm talking about the professional revolutionaries, not the people.

I think in the past year or so the Chicano movement has begun to solidify. After the August 29th thing, there was the National Chicano Moratorium "non-violent march for justice" on January 31, 1971. It was against police brutality and repression and was non-violent until the end, when fighting broke out and the cops swarmed out of the police station with everything, including twelve-gauge shotguns firing buckshot balls straight into the crowd. After two hours, one person was dead, thirty seriously injured, and there was about a half-million dollars' worth of damage, including seventy-eight burned police cars.

Things have gotten heavier since then, and Chicano consciousness is spreading. Everybody in "El Barrio" is a Brown Beret. It's a concept, an idea. M.E.CH.A (Movimiento Estudiantil Chicano de Aztlán): the Chicano-student movement is also growing. Aztlán is the land we're sitting on now. The land where my forefathers lived hundreds of years ago before they migrated to the valley of Mexico. The Aztecs referred to the entire Southwest as Aztlán. Now the Chicano movement has no need for anyone else's ideas but our own. We have a way of life that we've learned from childhood. The concept of *la familia*, the respect for elders, is not Sunday-school bullshit with us. It's part of our culture. A Chicano can no more disrespect his mother than he can himself. Which means he can, but at great cost to himself. The concept of community—of La Raza—isn't a political term to us as I feel it is to black and white radicals. The term brother is a social term to us, one we learn before we learn about politics.

We don't kid ourselves anymore. We know we're headed for a head-on collision with the rest of society. We're absolutely convinced of it and we're not being paranoid or nothing. We know that the main thing we want now is not better education or better jobs or better housing, because we know that they are not possible to achieve. It is not possible as the result of the history of human nature and the animal instinct against the races integrating in the liberal sense of the word.

You can't be a class or a nation without land. Without it, it doesn't have any meaning. It's that simple. So we are beginning to see that what we're talking about is getting land and having our own government. Period. It is that clear-cut. As to what land, that is still in the future. We have to develop the consciousness of land as the principal issue, just as three years ago we had to develop the consciousness of identity as the principal issue.

The black man came here as a slave. He is not of this land. He is so removed from his ancestry that he has nothing but the white society to identify with. We have history. We have culture. We had a land. We do feel solidarity with the American Indians because we are Indians. We have a total unification in ideology but no unification organizationally. I look upon them as my blood brothers. It is the Indian aspect of our ancestry that gives meaning to the term "La Raza." We are La Raza. Of course there is Spanish and European blood in us, but we don't always talk about it because it is not something that we are proud of. For me, my native ancestry is crucial. This consciousness is beginning to develop now, symbolized in the word *tierra*. We want our land back and this is what we are going to be fighting for.

I don't think you're going to see too much more of demonstrations against education or things of that sort. I think that has petered itself out. A lot of kids have gotten into OEO projects and school projects as a result of the movement, so they've been in college for a few years now and they are as hip to what's being taught in the colleges as the white radicals have been for some years now. They think it is a waste of time, that it takes away what little you have of your identity.

A perfect example is the National La Raza Law Students Association, here in Los Angeles, which I am pretty much associated with. The very first day they started school here on some OEO project I went in and spoke and told them, "Half of you will never be lawyers. Those of you that do are going to become so only because of your race. You got into these programs because you're Chicano. So you owe something to your Raza. Yet, I predict that in three years I'm going to be fighting 50 percent of you guys. You're going to be my enemies." They laughed. But it is a fact. This past year I've been working on these major cases of importance to Chicanos not only organizationally but legally, and often I've been unable to get the assistance of the Chicano law students. My prophecy to them has come true, except I was wrong in one respect. It is not 50 percent I'm fighting. It is about 75 percent. This is why I'm no longer pushing for more school programs, more handouts, more welfare. I think that will destroy the movement. They are attempting with those to do the same things they did to blacks.

For example, with the law students when I was doing this judges' thing in 1971, they didn't want to be associated with it because they were afraid that it might affect their future, their careers. That judges' thing was my third challenge to the Grand Jury system here. I was defending the "Biltmore Six," six young Chicanos who were busted for allegedly trying to burn down the Biltmore Hotel. They were indicted by a Grand Jury and I contended that all Grand Juries are racist since all grand jurors have to be recommended by Superior Court judges and that the whole thing reeks of "subconscious, institutional racism." I was trying to get the indictments squashed on that basis.

To prove my contention I subpoenaed all 109 Superior Court judges in Los Angeles and examined them all under oath about their racism. After almost a year of work on this, the judge on that case, Arthur Alarcón, who is Mexican American, rejected the motion. The way it looks now, I think we're just about finished with that whole legal game.

I'm the only Chicano lawyer here. By that I mean the only one that has taken a militant posture, to my knowledge, in the whole country. When I got here I decided that if I was going to become anything legal I couldn't use the profession as it was. Lawyers are basically peddlers of flesh. They live off of other people's misery. Well, I couldn't do that. I made a decision that I would never charge a client a penny. As a matter of fact, I end up supporting some of my clients. I get money by begging, borrowing, and stealing. Sometimes I get a grant from some foundation like Ford. For a while I was under a Reggie program, although all I was doing was political, criminal work and they knew it. I don't even have an office. I'm in court practically every day.

I relate to the court system first as a Chicano and only seldom as a lawyer in the traditional sense. I have no respect for the courts, and I make it clear to them from the minute I walk in that I have no respect for the system. That I'm against it and would destroy it in one second if I had the physical power to do it. The one thing I've learned to do is use criminal defense work as an organizing tool. That is my specialty. I organize in the courtroom. I take no case unless it is or can become a Chicano Movement case. I turn it into a platform to espouse the Chicano point of view so that that affects the judge, the jury, the spectators. We organize each case, set up defense committees, student groups, and use the traditional methods of organizing.

I don't have much contact with many of the other radical lawyers here. I think a lot of them are still finding themselves. Consequently, they'll often chicken out of something at the last minute. I think it's chickenshit, reactionary, and that they're the enemies of the people. I like them; they're nice guys, but it's too late for these personal things. Too many of them aren't doing the work that has to be done.

Now some of the Chicano law students are thinking of organizing a collective, but I've disagreed because I think it is looking to the future as any other lawyer would do. They are thinking in terms of money to make, cases to take. They're thinking of business. For me, to think of the future is inconsistent with my thinking of the present. It is only the present that is important. I think you develop yourself much more if you don't think of those things, if you think only of the job: defending Chicanos and organizing around the case.

Chapter 48

||||||||||||||||||||||||||||||||||||||||||||||||||||||||||||||||||||||||||||||||||||||||

Legal Violence and the Chicano Movement

Ian F. Haney López

Until the late 1960s, the Mexican community in the United States thought of itself as racially White. That is not how Anglos thought of them, of course. Largely beginning with the nineteenth-century period of intense Anglo-Mexican conflict in the Southwest, Anglo society perceived Mexicans as racially separate and inferior. By the 1920s, the Mexican community responded to this negative racialization by insisting that they were White. Leaders of the community insisted that Mexicans were Caucasian and thus White biologically, deserving the same social status and civic position as the White group. To take one example, although the U.S. Census Bureau enumerated a "Mexican race" in 1930, the Bureau bowed to political pressure from the Mexican community thereafter and in 1950 and 1960 counted that group as "White Persons of Spanish Surname." Despite these gains, in the late 1960s a large segment of the Mexican community reversed its racial self-conception, proclaiming a non-White identity. One of the hallmarks of the Chicano movement of that period was the assertion, still widely subscribed to today, that Mexicans form a separate race from Whites.

How did this transformation occur? Why did an emphasis on non-Whiteness arise in the late 1960s, when the community had fervently claimed a White identity during the relatively more racist 1940s and 1950s, and had even made some progress in garnering official recognition of Mexican Whiteness? Was the claim of non-Whiteness a strategic choice, or did it reflect genuine conviction?

Social Movement Theory

The development of a non-White identity within the Mexican community arose with the Chicano movement, an episode of broad political and cultural mobilization that can be partly explained by social movement theory.

Various social movement theorists have identified the influence of Black mobilization in the 1950s and 1960s on movements for women's liberation, gay and lesbian rights, and disability rights. The southern part of the Black movement stressed the rhetoric of rights over the language of race. In the development of activism in the Mexican community, identity, and in particular racial identity, played a more

From *Protest, Repression, and Race: Legal Violence and the Chicano Movement*, 150 U. Pa. L. Rev. 205 (2001). Originally published in the *University of Pennsylvania Law Review*. Reprinted by permission.

important role than rights. For Chicanos, the most directly influential component of the African-American fight for social rights was not the southern organizing of the 1950s, but the Black Power movement of the mid- to late-1960s. Black Power exercised a direct influence on the Chicano movement because it established racial identity as the principal means of self-conception and group empowerment.

Black Power and the Chicano Movement

Even before the first high school walkouts in East Los Angeles in 1968, local Mexican youth had met with Black Power activists. High school students in East Los Angeles formed a group called Young Citizens for Community Action (YCCA) in 1966. The next year, YCCA opened La Piranya, a coffee house and cultural center where activists introduced their causes to the community. Among the various speakers who met with the young activists of East Los Angeles were Black Power militants H. Rap Brown and Ron Karenga, as well as Stokely Carmichael, one of the architects of "Black Power" as a political rallying cry. In addition to meetings with Black Power advocates, a few Mexicans cut their political teeth in Black organizations. Elizabeth Sutherland Martínez, for instance, worked on civil rights in Alabama and in 1964 became the director of the Student Nonviolent Coordinating Committee office in New York. *East LA Thirteen* lawyer Oscar Acosta also apprenticed in the Black struggle, spending four years working with the Black civil rights movement while attending law school in San Francisco. These direct contacts between the Black Power movement and the leaders of the nascent Chicano struggle reflect the importance of personal networks—interpersonal relations within and between activist groups—in the rise of social movements.

Anti-Black Prejudice

Yet, the experiences, lessons, and strategies of the Black Power movement did not speak exactly to the particularities of Mexican existence. Acosta remarked of his experience in the civil rights movement: "[I]t wasn't really me. I told people that it wasn't just black and white, that there were Chicanos, too . . . ." The frustration Acosta expressed raises a larger point. Mexicans embraced the Black Power movement's model of identity mobilization, but they did so from the distinct social position they occupied in the Southwest. Like the other imitator movements that followed on the heels of, and adapted so much from, the Black fight for equality, the Chicano movement in East Los Angeles reflected many other influences as well.

Perhaps most significantly, the lessons of the Black struggle were filtered through conceptions of Mexican identity already prevalent in that community. Recall that the Mexican-American generation saw themselves as a White group. This self-conception both drew upon and led to prejudice against African Americans, which in turn hindered direct relations between those two groups. In 1964, Mexicans overwhelmingly helped pass California Proposition 14, a voter initiative subsequently overturned on constitutional grounds, which barred local governments from prohibiting discrimination in the housing market. As a contemporary commentator remarked, "Mexican-Americans apparently failed to realize that the measure was directed against them as well as against the Negro." As late as 1965, mainstream Mexican-American civil rights organizations positioned themselves in opposition to Black groups. For instance, shortly after the 1965 Watts riots in Los Angeles, the principal organizations of the Mexican-American generation, including the League of United Latin American Citizens and the GI Forum, sent President Lyndon Johnson a resolution that pointedly contrasted their assimilationist orientation with the militancy of the Black community. "The organizations argued that since Mexican-Americans did not believe in or engage in civil disobedience or violent confrontation, they were good citizens, loyal to the democratic system, and should be included in antipoverty programs."

Thus, to make use of the Black experience, members of the Mexican community had to overcome both a strong assimilationist commitment and a strain of bias against African Americans. Their ability to do so came in part because the social turmoil of the late 1960s highlighted the failure of the Mexican-American generation to achieve social and political equality, despite more than three decades of effort.

Mexican Activism Beyond, and Before, the East Los Angeles Movement

The waning influence of Mexican-American assimilationist ideology both allowed and resulted from the increasing influence of Black activism in the Mexican community. However, other factors also pushed members of the Mexican community in Los Angeles toward an oppositional stance rooted in race. In particular, activism among Mexicans in other parts of the Southwest helped to catalyze the Los Angeles Chicano movement.

For instance, in the fall of 1965, César Chávez organized Mexican laborers in the first major strike against agribusiness in California's Central Valley. The farmworkers' struggle—union activity carried out on a nonracial and nonviolent basis—developed into the largest, and arguably the only, nationally prominent mobilization of Mexicans in this period. Chávez's efforts inspired a wave of activism in Los Angeles and across the Southwest. Chávez traveled and spoke widely to garner support for the farmworkers and to encourage a more widespread political mobilization, appearing several times at rallies in Los Angeles. Two of Chávez's organizers moved to that city to work on *La Raza*, the leading movement newspaper there. Even Acosta felt Chávez's influence: a visit with Chávez during his fast in April 1968 helped Acosta decide to dedicate himself to the full-time defense of Chicano movement activists.

Two other Mexican movements also contributed to Chicano militancy in Los Angeles. In contrast to the nonviolence exemplified by Chávez and the farmworkers, the land grant movement in New Mexico led by Reies López Tijerina provided a model of violent, armed protest. In rural New Mexico in the early 1960s, López Tijerina began to organize his followers around the issue of land titles, arguing that much of the land held by the federal government as national forest had been acquired by fraud from the region's Hispano inhabitants. Under the banner of *La Alianza Federal de Mercedes* (The Federal Alliance of Land Grants), López Tijerina's early strategies involved legal arguments over the meaning of the Treaty of Guadalupe Hidalgo, appeals to the Mexican government for assistance, and political pressure on elected and judicial officials. By 1966, however, these tactics segued into mass demonstrations, including the occupation of national forest land. In one dramatic action in October 1966, López Tijerina and *La Alianza* occupied portions of the Kit Carson National Forest, took two law enforcement officers hostage, tried them for trespassing, and sentenced them to jail, before "mercifully" suspending the sentence and releasing them. Then, on June 5, 1967, while awaiting trial on the 1966 action, López Tijerina and armed members of *La Alianza* stormed the county courthouse in Tierra Amarilla, New Mexico, to make a citizen's arrest of a district attorney they considered abusive. A gun battle ensued, twenty hostages were held for about an hour, and a jailer and a state police officer were wounded. After almost one hundred years of quiescence, the actions of López Tijerina and *La Alianza* represented a resurgence of armed opposition to Anglo domination, and provided Mexicans across the Southwest with a model of authentically Mexican militancy.

The Chicano movement in East Los Angeles also gained impetus from a Denver, Colorado, organization called the Crusade for Justice led by Rodolfo "Corky" Gonzales. Gonzales initially sought to improve the situation of Mexicans by following the route prescribed by the Mexican-American generation. However, by 1965, after stints as a precinct captain for the Democratic Party and as the director of Denver's War on Poverty, Gonzales came to favor increased activism. In 1966 he founded the Crusade for Justice, an organization that spoke not to rural farmworkers or disenfranchised land holders, but to disenchanted Mexican urban youth. Gonzales more than any other brought the question of identity to the forefront of political mobilization. Whereas Chávez stressed labor, and López Tijerina focused on land, Gonzales placed Mexican identity at the center of his organizing. Gonzales was the first prominent activist to attempt to rehabilitate the term "Chicano," theretofore often used pejoratively by Mexicans and Anglos alike. Gonzales' 1967 poem *I Am Joaquín/Yo Soy Joaquín* "became the epic story of the Chicano experience."

The farmworkers, *La Alianza*, and the Crusade all contributed directly and dramatically to the development of Chicano activism in East Los Angeles. When students first marched in protest outside of Garfield High School in early March 1968, their chants included not just salutes to leaders of the Mexican revolution such as Pancho Villa and Emiliano Zapata, but also shouts of *¡Qué Viva!* to the names César Chávez, Reies López Tijerina, and Corky Gonzales.

I contend that twenty years and more of Black activism revealed deep links between community protest, legal repression, and racial identity, and that those in the Chicano movement drew on these conceptual connections as the notion of a Chicano race evolved.

I have argued elsewhere that law constructs race. The Chicano experience suggests that where legal violence against racialized communities is routine, that practice not only draws upon, but spurs, racial constructions. Specific studies must be done to understand the dynamics of racial formation vis-à-vis different communities at various times. Sadly, though, we can be confident that such studies will demonstrate that legal violence contributes to racial construction, both of non-Whites and Whites.

Chapter 49

‖‖‖

Is a Burrito a Sandwich?

Marjorie Florestal

A superior court in Worcester, Massachusetts, recently determined that a burrito is not a sandwich. Surprisingly, the decision sparked a firestorm of media attention. Worcester, Massachusetts, is hardly the pinnacle of the culinary arts—so why the interest in the musings of one lone judge on the nature of burritos and sandwiches? Closer inspection revealed the allure of this otherwise peculiar case: Potentially thousands of dollars turned on the interpretation of a single word in a single clause of a commercial contract.

Judge Locke based his decision in *White City Shopping Center v. PR Restaurants* on "common sense" and a single definition of sandwich—"two thin pieces of bread, usually buttered, with a thin layer (as of meat, cheese, or savory mixture) spread between them." The only barrier to the burrito's entry into the sacred realm of sandwiches is an additional piece of bread? What about the one-slice, open-face sandwich? Or the club sandwich, typically served as a double-decker with three pieces of bread? What about wraps? The court's definition lacked subtlety, complexity, or nuance; it was rigid, not allowing for the possibility of change and evolution. It was a decision couched in the "primitive formalism" Judge Cardozo derided nearly ninety years ago when he said "[t]he law has outgrown its primitive stage of formalism when the precise word was a sovereign talisman, and every slip was fatal. It takes a broader view to-day."

Does it? Despite the title of this piece, my goal is not to determine whether a burrito is a sandwich. Rather, I explore what lies beneath the "primitive formalism" or somewhat smug determination of the court that common sense answers the question for us. I suggest Judge Locke's gut-level understanding that burritos are not sandwiches actually masks an unconscious bias. I explore this bias by examining the determination of this case and the impact of race, class, and culture on contract principles.

The Burrito Brouhaha

The *White City* dispute on its face turns on a traditional commercial transaction. The parties negotiated and executed a lease agreement meant to protect both of their economic interests. In the process, they neglected to define the term "sandwich,"

From *Is a Burrito a Sandwich? Exploring Race, Class, and Culture in Contracts,* 14 MICH. J. RACE & L. 1 (2008). Originally published in the *Michigan Journal of Race & Law.* Reprinted by permission.

an omission which would ultimately prove costly. Without an agreed definition between the parties, the court in *White City* defined the term according to its "ordinary meaning."

In March 2001, Panera—a popular chain of café-style restaurants and bakeries—signed a 10 year lease with White City Shopping Center to occupy retail space in the White City Shopping Center in Shrewsbury, Massachusetts. The lease contained an exclusive use clause preventing the shopping center from leasing space in the same mall to any bakery or restaurant "reasonably expected to have annual sales of sandwiches greater than ten percent (10%) of its total sales. . . ." The original lease allowed for a number of exemptions to the exclusive use provision—for example, a Jewish-style delicatessen was exempt from the provision and thus was free to serve sandwiches. For five years the parties' dealings apparently were amicable, but before the original lease had even expired they decided to renegotiate its terms.

The facts are silent as to why the parties determined to renegotiate the lease early, but what becomes clear is that Panera sought greater protection from competing restaurants, and the shopping center was willing to provide that for a price. During the new round of negotiations, the parties agreed to expand the exclusivity clause to cover more restaurants—the Jewish-style delicatessen lost its exemption, as did near-Eastern restaurants that served gyros (a sandwich utilizing pita bread). But less than one year after signing the amended lease with Panera, the White City Shopping Center entered into a lease agreement with a new client—Qdoba Mexican Grill. Qdoba's menu features salads, tacos, quesadillas, and of course burritos. Upon learning of the new lease, Panera demanded assurance from the shopping center that Qdoba would not become its neighbor. The shopping center's owner refused to provide the requested assurance; rather, it beat Panera to the courthouse seeking a declaratory judgment that it was not in violation of its contractual obligation. Thus began the Burrito Brouhaha.

Despite the volley of claims, counterclaims, affidavits, and charges, the issue before the court was deceptively simple: Does the term "sandwiches" as it appears in the Panera lease include burritos? The court's response on this point consists of a single paragraph:

> Given that the term "sandwiches" is not ambiguous and the Lease does not provide a definition of it, this court applies the ordinary meaning of the word. The New Webster Third International Dictionary describes a "sandwich" as "two thin pieces of bread, usually buttered, with a thin layer (as of meat, cheese, or savory mixture) spread between them." Merriam Webster, 2002. Under this definition and as dictated by common sense, this court finds that the term "sandwich" is not commonly understood to include burritos . . . which are typically made with a single tortilla and stuffed with a choice filling of meat, rice, and beans.

Thus, the court summarily dismisses the conflict between the parties by resort to a dictionary and common sense.

The court's reliance on a dictionary definition at best is a crude attempt at discerning what the parties meant. Words are slippery entities upon which human beings struggle to place concrete meaning. Not surprisingly, the same Webster's Third New International Dictionary upon which the court relies defines "sandwich" as follows:

> *Sandwich*: *1a*. two slices of bread usually buttered, with a thin layer (as of meat, cheese, or savory mixture) spread between them. *1b*. food consisting of a filling placed upon one slice or between two or more slices of a variety of bread . . .

Thus, just a half-step below the definition Judge Locke chose was one that suggests a burrito is a sandwich. How then are we to choose between these competing definitions? The court does so by referencing "common sense" or some shared societal understanding of the word sandwich that transcends the meaning the parties themselves may have attributed to the term. The consequence is to privilege the shopping center's definition merely because it is in line with society's own understanding and not because it is objectively the meaning to which the parties themselves agreed.

Race

It surely surprises no one to say that race has played a central role in the construction of American law. The "Peculiar Institution" of slavery required a series of legal accommodations for its existence, such as the Three-Fifths Compromise, which reduced the personhood of blacks to a fraction of that of whites. During the Reconstruction Era, the Union's legal infrastructure was re-written in an effort to incorporate blacks into the social fabric. The Civil Rights Movement and succeeding generations of the anti-discrimination struggle continue efforts at using law to stamp out discrimination targeting racial and other minorities. Each succeeding wave of race-based social justice litigation has had significant impact on the evolution of contract law.

From Slavery to Freedom: Race and Contracts in Historical Perspective

In contract law, legal doctrines are replete with issues of race. Some prime examples can be found in the racial covenant cases. While northern states generally declined to enact state-sponsored discrimination along the model of the "Jim Crow" laws of the South, private contracts with restrictive covenant clauses served a similar purpose. Racial covenants prevented white homeowners from selling, leasing, or conveying their property in any manner to a member of an "excluded group." The Great Migration of southern blacks from the fields to northern factories in the early twentieth century swelled the number of black families in northern cities. The covenants became a popular tool to preserve "whites only" neighborhoods in the face of this increasing black demand.

But a number of whites breached the covenants and sold their homes to black families who were willing to pay a premium. These families faced lawsuits brought by whites seeking judicial enforcement of their contractual right to be free of black neighbors.

Before *Shelly v. Kraemer*, in which the Supreme Court ultimately banned racial covenants on principles transcending freedom of contract, some courts declined to enforce them based on principles of contract law. For example, in *Hundley v. Gorewitz*, the Court of Appeals for the D.C. Circuit denied enforcement of a restrictive covenant based on the doctrine of changed circumstances, which excuses performance in certain instances when it "can only be done at an excessive and unreasonable cost." The court in *Hundley* concluded blacks had so thoroughly infiltrated the area that plaintiff could not hope to attain his vision of a segregated neighborhood:

> [T]he present appellees are not now enjoying the advantages which the covenant sought to confer. The obvious purpose was to keep the neighborhood white. But the strict enforcement of all five covenants will not alter the fact that the purpose has been essentially defeated by the presence of a Negro family now living in an unrestricted house in the midst of the restricted group, and as well by the ownership by another Negro of a house almost directly across the street. And this is just the beginning.

Does a Burrito Have a Race?

"I know of no chef or culinary historian who would call a burrito a sandwich. Indeed, the notion would be absurd to any credible chef or culinary historian," said Christopher Schlesinger, celebrated New England chef and affiant in the *White City* dispute. Schlesinger's view that the two food items could never be considered part of the same genus comes down to a question of lineage: "A sandwich is of European roots," he asserts, while "a burrito, on the other hand, is specific to Mexico."

Such a categorical statement raises immediate suspicion: Is a New Orleans Po' Boy not a sandwich merely because it is of *American* rather than European origin? And if the American variety is capable of evolving into a bona fide sandwich, then why not the burrito? Embedded in that perspective are certain unconscious notions. Acknowledged or not, burritos are perceived to have a racial status, that of Mexicans; sandwiches are perceived as white.

Admittedly, the most difficult aspect to this discussion is ascribing race to an inanimate object like a burrito. Is this simply taking anthropomorphism too far? Somehow, assigning a certain class or cultural status to an object does not seem to raise the same challenge. The Lamborghini is easily identified as an upper class toy, and a bottle of champagne is synonymous with French culture. But can a burrito be said to have a race? And if so, does Mexican qualify?

Categorizing Mexicans within the U.S. racial framework is a complex task. Assuming Mexican is a race—although it is admittedly difficult to locate in a strictly black/white racial paradigm—the question still remains: Is there really a link between race and *burritos*? Interestingly, the ordinary citizen on the web had little difficulty making the connection. One blogger "pull[ed] out the race card" in questioning the cultural (and culinary) imperialism of the decision:

This is kind of offensive here. OK if burritos are found in northern Mexico. Why didn't they get a Mexican to say "no, that is not a sandwich"? If they did the case would have been settled easily. . . . I am not saying this to be racist (so if you're white, please don't take offense) but why does this government and media use white people to define Mexican culture and food?

In another entry, a blogger cast the shadow of the affirmative action debate over burritos asking, "Doesn't anyone know the difference between 'legislative' and 'judicial'?" then stating, "If it had been legislative, a) it wouldn't be called the White City Shopping Center, and b) diversity foods would be given preference in any case."

And in an even more crude allusion to race, another blog entry asked, "At what moment then, does a burrito become a burrito? When it sneaks across the border in a closed-up box trailer towed by a big rig, then is abandoned, while locked still inside, in the desert without food, water, ventilation or Xbox."

What is illuminating about the blog commentary is that it does identify race as an issue; but only the burrito is assumed to have a race. The sandwich is considered race neutral. I maintain a similar dynamic exists in the *White City* opinion.

How did the race of burritos affect decision making in *White City*? It provided the unspoken gloss that lent legitimacy to the decision. As noted above, because the parties failed to incorporate a meaning of the term sandwich into their agreement, the court properly looked to the ordinary meaning society generally ascribes to the term. Based on the public reaction when the court's decision was announced, the opinion captured the shared understanding of many. The public response to the *White City* decision was an overwhelming "*duh!*" As one blogger put it, the distinction between the two items was so self-evident that "the judge could have deferred to the true experts that were not called . . . [a]ny 12-year old-kid." This chorus of agreement begs further reflection. Is the distinction between burritos and sandwiches really so self-evident that no further analysis is required?

I have already argued the term sandwich is ambiguous, thus the court properly should have examined the context of the agreement—beyond mere dictionaries—to clarify the ambiguity. I digress from contract law for a moment to borrow from international trade law. I find it helpful in order to illustrate my broader point that what the court has deemed self-evident is actually a complex legal question.

Trade dispute panels are often charged with determining whether one product is "like" another. In so doing, they examine not only the tariff heading countries have assigned to a particular product (which would be equivalent to a dictionary definition in this context), but they also look to the function and purpose the two products serve in order to determine whether they are "like" one another. Similarly, the court might well have looked to the function and purpose sandwiches and burritos serve in order to determine whether burritos are sandwiches—or at least their functional equivalent.

Despite their distinct origins—the sandwich was invented by no less venerable a personality than an English Earl, while the burrito was created to feed and strengthen Mexican gold miners—burritos and sandwiches serve the same function and purpose. Of course, they are meant to be eaten, but more specifically, both fall within the same category of "fast casual" food. They are generally cheap, quick, and do not require an elaborate dining set up. In short, burritos and sandwiches serve the same purpose, fall within the same niche market, and cater to the same clientele. Yet they are perceived as completely different products. Interestingly, the wrap sandwich—despite its similarity to burritos—does not face the same perception difficulties; few would argue that a wrap is not a sandwich.

Given the ambiguity in meaning of the term sandwich, as well as the shared function and purpose burritos and sandwiches serve, why did Chef Schlessinger, the court, and popular opinion all converge around the notion that burritos clearly are not sandwiches? Why do so many see the distinction as self-evident? Critical theorists have shown one of the greatest dangers in challenging majority norms is that they seem so . . . well, normal, self-evident, unassailably true. They have effectively demonstrated that the "duh!" response is nothing more than a single frame of reference within which to explore a question; but because that single frame represents the view of the majority, it dominates legal culture such that even calling it into question raises questions of triviality, banality or obviousness.

Little Donkeys and Big Gamblers: A Culinary Tour of Class

Class, like race, played an unconscious but significant role in the *White City* opinion. It is not of course the class of the parties that is relevant, but rather the class of the disputed items—the sandwich and burrito. I set off on the trail of the burrito and sandwich, tracing their origins back to the Motherland. I argue that class-based images of the burrito and sandwich shaped the *White City* decision. In my view, part of the explanation for the chorus of agreement that a burrito cannot be a sandwich —the "*duh!*" response—lies in the difference in class of the two items. Descended from English nobility, sandwiches are generally perceived as "higher class" than burritos. But *White City* also illustrates a broader theme: the convergence of race and class in American society. What is interesting is that the sandwich is able to straddle both the low- and high-class world, while the burrito is consigned exclusively to the low-class realm.

The history of the burrito is decidedly pedestrian. It is said to have originated in northwestern Mexico where it was made popular by gold miners. Originally made using donkey meat, the burrito was a popular meal because it was filling and portable, slipping easily into the miners' saddlebags. In short, the burrito was a cheap and nourishing way to feed people who worked hard for a living and could not afford to spend a great deal of money on food.

The class-bound imagery of the two items stands in marked contrast: The sandwich evokes images of wealthy indolence—a pampered English dandy who fills his days with wine, women, and gambling. Images of the burrito call to mind endless sweat and toil. The word itself—"little donkey"—harkens to a beast of burden laboring under a harsh, burning sun. Indeed, even the bread making process elicits different images for the sandwich than for the burrito.

Class played a role in the *White City* dispute. The court's gut-level reaction that burritos are not sandwiches—and the public's overwhelming support—can be traced back to the burrito's low-class status. But equally compelling is the convergence of class and race in the decision. It is this convergence that helps to explain why the sandwich can straddle high- and low-class status, while the burrito is firmly entrenched in the low-class realm. The burrito meets resistance not just because of its class but also because of its race—and the way the two play off each other.

Chapter 50

||||||||||||||||||||||||||||||||||||||||||||||||||||||||||||||||||||||||||||||||

The Work We Know So Little About

Gerald P. López

I met someone not long ago who too many of us regrettably have come to regard as unremarkable, someone who might well find herself, along any number of fronts, working with a lawyer in a fight for social change. I'll call her María Elena. She lives with her two children in San Francisco's Mission District where she works as a house-keeper. She works as a mother too. And as a tutor of sorts. And as a seamstress. And as a cook. And as a support for those other women—those other Irish-American women, African-American women, Chinese-American women, and most especially those other Latinas—with whom she finds herself in contact. She works in much the same way as many other low-income women of color I've known over the years —women who surrounded me while I was growing up in East L.A., women who helped out in certain fights I participated in while practicing in San Diego, women who largely sustain various formal and informal grassroots efforts that a number of our law students now work with in those communities of working poor that line the east side of Highway 101 on the peninsula, from San Francisco through San Jose.

How María Elena and her children make it from day to day tells us all a great deal about where we live, whom we live with, and even about how people's actual experiences measure up to the "American dream"—a contrast that nowadays tends to get obscured and even denied. Indeed, our own lives are tied inescapably to the María Elenas in our communities. These women are important parts of our economy, indispensable parts of certain of our worklives, and even intimate parts of some of our households. In a very palpable way, María Elena's struggles implicate us. More perhaps than we acknowledge and more perhaps than feels comfortable, she and we help construct one another's identities. We're entangled.

Historically, you'd think that how the María Elenas of our communities make it from day to day should have played an obvious and central role in training those whose vocation is to serve as lawyers in the fight for social change. After all, the lives in which these lawyers intervene often differ considerably from their own—in terms of class, gender, race, ethnicity, and sexual orientation. Without laboring to understand these lives, how else can lawyers begin to appreciate how their profes-sional knowledge and skills may be perceived and deployed by those with whom they strive to ally themselves? How else can they begin to speculate about how their intervention may affect their clients' everyday relationships with employers, landlords, spouses, and the state? And how else can they begin to study whether proposed strategies actually have a chance of penetrating the social and economic situations they'd like to help change?

But, as my niece might say, "Get a clue!" Whatever else law schools may be, they have not characteristically been where future lawyers go to learn about how the poor and working poor live. Or about how the elderly cope. Or how the disabled struggle. Or about how gays and lesbians build their lives in worlds that deny them the basic integrity of identity. Or about how single women of color raise their children in the midst of underfinanced schools, inadequate social support, and limited job opportunities. Indeed, in many ways both current and past lawyers fighting for social change and all with whom they collaborate (both clients and other social activists) have had to face trying to learn how largely to overcome rather than to take advantage of law school experience. What's ultimately extraordinary, I think, is that these relationships work at all and that we can even sometimes fully realize an allied fight for social change.

If you think this overstates all that together confronts the María Elenas of our communities and those lawyers with whom they work, take a brief glimpse through my eyes at María Elena's life and what it seems to say about any future relationship she might have with even the best lawyers. Thirty-one years old, she first set foot in this country a little over eight years ago. She came from Mexico with her husband, their two-year-old son, their three-month-old daughter, and no immigration documents. Not unlike thousands upon thousands of others, the family worked its way from San Diego, through Los Angeles, to Gilroy—picking flowers, mowing lawns, and harvesting fruit—surviving on the many day laborers' jobs that pervade the secondary labor market in this state and living in situations the rest of us would recoil from. Nearly two years later, they finally landed in the Mission District, expecting to reunite with some cousins and gain some stability. Instead, they found only confusing tales from various sources about how their *primos* had been deported after an INS factory raid in the East Bay.

More by force of habit than anything else, María Elena found herself trying to make do—hustling a place to live and her first job as a housekeeper. But the frustrations and indignities of undocumented life already had begun to take their toll on her husband. He couldn't find stable work; he couldn't support his family; he couldn't adjust to the sort of shadowy existence they seemed compelled to endure. Somewhere along the line, María Elena can't quite remember when, he just sort of withdrew from it all. From her, from the children, from trying. He wasn't violent or drunken. He just shrank into himself and didn't do much at all for months. And then one day when María Elena and the kids returned from grocery shopping, he was gone.

That was some four years ago and (it doesn't take much talking to María Elena to realize) many lonely, confused, hurt, angry, scared, and even guilty tears ago. It was also some 1,300-plus housekeeping days ago. For María Elena has come to realize the hard way that housekeeping for her and for so many other women of color no longer serves as the first and worst of jobs in a work career in the United States—as, for example, it once did in the late nineteenth century and still to some degree does for women from Western Europe. It's not that María Elena hasn't tried to find a job that pays better, that offers benefits and job security. She'd be interested, for example, in pursuing a recently publicized opening for some low-level industrial job, except that other Latinas have told her about the employer's so-called fetal protection policy—one that either endangers the health of future children or forces women to get sterilized. And she episodically searches for openings as a custodian and as an electronics assembler—jobs which most of us think of as being on the bottom rung of the job ladder, but which in most regards would be a step up for her and other housekeepers. She's found these jobs very hard to come by, however, except for the occasional openings on night shifts which her obligations to her kids just won't permit her to take.

Though she may be stuck in her job as a housekeeper, there's something unresolved and edgy about María Elena's daily existence. Things are always moving for her and her kids. Getting off to school and work. Coordinating the kids' return with a neighbor's afternoon schedule. Timing her own return with enough space to care for their needs and anxieties, particularly about school. Dealing with their illnesses while still honoring her housekeeping obligations. Often she drags her kids places others would not, and sometimes she leaves them alone when those of us who can afford the luxury of help would never consider it. She never has enough money to buy everything they see around them, but she tries to make sure they get what they need. When times get bad, they cut back. All in all, she seems to be a master of planned improvisation—about food, shelter, and medical care. You can feel her will and drive, and you can easily imagine her children's best efforts to help out. You can also sense, however, the interconnectedness of a range of difficult conditions any one of which might drive most of us to feeling that things had gotten out of control.

So, like so many other people in her position, María Elena does her best to sort her way through the confusion. She's tried to reconcile the cautious advice of certain church and service organizations with the glitzy radio ads promoting private programs that guarantee green cards—all the time remembering to keep her ear to the ground for the ever-evolving rumors that make their way around the Mission. She heard somewhere that certain courses at community colleges and high schools have been or will be certified as meeting the ESL/Civics requirements. But she's found a number of schools increasingly cautious about promising anything, others suspiciously willing to promise too much, and most courses with waiting lists backed up seemingly forever. Meanwhile, to bring matters full circle, she's begun to sense that the employers she now works for would very much like her to get all this taken care of—so that they can know whether they can depend on her or have to hire another housekeeper.

For all her problems, María Elena just can't see herself seeking a lawyer's help, even at places with so positive a reputation as, say, the Immigrant Legal Resource Center, the Employment Law Center, or California Rural Legal Assistance. "Being on the short end and being on the bottom is an everyday event in my life," she says, half-smiling. "What can a lawyer do about that?" That doesn't make it all right, she admits. But she says she's learned to live with it—to deal with it in her own ways. In any event, lawyers and law all seem to conjure up for her big, complicated fights—fights that, as she sees it, would pit her against a social superior, her word against that of a more respected someone else, her lack of written records against the seemingly infinite amount of paper employers seem able to come up with when they must. Because she retains her sense of order by focusing on keeping her family's head above water, lawyers and law most often seem irrelevant to and even inconsistent with her day-to-day struggles.

Were María Elena alone in these sentiments, lawyers might have little cause for concern. But you may be surprised to learn that María Elena is scarcely unique in her views about lawyers and law—though, to be sure, some of her problems may well be peculiarly the product of her immigration status. In fact, we are beginning to discover that many low-income women of color—Asian Americans, Native Americans, Latinas, Blacks—apparently feel much the same way as María Elena, even if they were born here and even when their families have been in this country for generations. Much else may well divide these women—after all, political and social subordination is not a homogeneous or monolithic experience. Still, their actions seem to confirm María Elena's impulses and their words seem to echo María Elena's own.

The little thus far uncovered about whether and how people translate perceived injuries into legal claims seems to confirm what apparently the María Elenas in our communities have been trying to tell us for quite some time, each in her own way. *Low-income women of color seldom go to lawyers, and they institute lawsuits a good deal less frequently than anybody else.* More particularly, they convert their experiences of oppression into claims of discrimination far less often than they (and everybody else) press any other legal claim. Indeed, most learn never even to call oppressive treatment an injury; if they do, many simply "lump it" rather than personally pressing it against the other party, much less pressing a formal claim through a lawyer. For all the popular (and I might add exaggerated) descriptions bemoaning how litigious we've all become, nearly all careful observers concede that low-income women of color seek legal remedies far too infrequently, especially when discriminated against at work. Partly as a result, they still seem to endure regularly the injustice and the indignities that those in high office insist just don't exist much in this enlightened era —at least not in their circles, where everyone seems to be doing just fine.

Most of us presume that this state of affairs bespeaks the unfortunate failure of these women constructively to use lawyers and law—an inability to serve their own needs. You know the litany as well as I do—it almost rolls off the tongue. Lack of information and knowledge about their rights. Limited resources for using legal channels. Limited understanding of the legal culture. And if you're sitting there thinking that this litany still retains real explanatory bite, you're right. The anticipation of rejections by unresponsive agencies, the cost and unavailability of lawyers, the technical obstacles to pursuing causes of action all serve in advance as background assumptions deterring low-income women of color from pressing formal claims. But if you listen carefully to people like María Elena, you begin to realize that they're saying something else is also going on—something that both they themselves and the lawyers with whom they work often find even more difficult to overcome.

Apparently, in order to use law (particularly antidiscrimination law) and lawyers, many low-income women of color must overcome fear, guilt, and a heightened sense of destruction. In their eyes, such a decision often amounts to nothing less intimidating than taking on conventional power with relatively little likelihood of success. It also means assuming an adversarial posture toward the very people and institutions that, in some perverse ways, you've come to regard as connected to you, at least insofar as they employ you when others will not (put aside at what wage, under what conditions, and with what benefits). And it seems inevitably to entail making your life entirely vulnerable to the law—with its powers to unravel the little you've got going for yourself and your family. In effect, turning to law and lawyers seems to signify a formal insurrection of sorts—an insurrection that, at least for these low-income women of color, foreshadows discomfiting experiences and negative consequences.

Instead of using law and lawyers, most low-income women of color often deal with oppressive circumstances through their own stock of informal strategies. Sometimes they tend to minimize or reinterpret obvious discrimination. María Elena, for example, tells me she often chalks up bad treatment to personal likes or dislikes or denies that it could really be about her. At the same time, these women also employ certain more proactive devices in an effort to alter the situations in which they work. For example, the loose network of housekeepers of which María Elena is a part (including both formal work cooperatives and informal support groups), seems to be trying to transform their relationship with employers from master/servant to customer/skilled service provider, all in the somewhat vague but hardly irrational hope that current wages, conditions, and benefits will improve along the way.

Yet for the most part, these low-income women of color have fewer illusions about these strategies than you might first presume. They know that you can't explain away all discriminatory treatment and that you can't alter every oppressive situation through informal devices. And they even seem to sense that while they may perceive their own less formal approach to their problems as self-sustaining, it often turns out to be self-defeating. After all, they know better than the rest of us that too many of them still get paid too little, for too many hours of work, in terrible conditions, with absolutely no health benefits or care for their children, and with little current hope of much job mobility over the course of their lifetimes.

Still, you shouldn't facilely condemn the sense of skepticism many low-income women of color feel about the intervention of lawyers and law, particularly if you appreciate (as no doubt you do) that lawyers and law can hardly ensure them the help they need. These women simply find themselves drawn to those informal strategies more within their control and less threatening than subjecting the little they have to the invasive experience and uncertain outcomes of the legal culture. Their collective past has taught them that seeking a legal remedy for their problems will not likely improve their position, and may well fracture their fragilely constructed lives. If low-income women of color and the very best lawyers at places like the Immigrant Legal Resource Center and the East Palo Alto Community Law Project would seem to offer one another special possibilities, they simultaneously present reciprocally enigmatic challenges. Each potentially threatens the very aspirations that hooking up with the other is meant in part to fulfill.

Somehow in the midst of all this, the María Elenas of our communities and at least the very best lawyers with whom they work still manage more than occasionally to make contact, to get things done, and even to find credible self-affirmation in the collective effort. In some instances, no doubt, they join together out of desperation. If you need or want to help badly enough, you can often figure out ways to hook up and make the relationship work. That is nothing to scoff at. It may well suggest how most things get done in this world, and it certainly says something about the human spirit under pressure.

At its best, this joint effort at fighting political and social subordination can be a story of magnificent mutual adaptation. At those times, both the María Elenas of our communities and those lawyers with whom they work face the enigma of their relationship head on. Both try to be sensitive to, without uncritically acquiescing in, their respective needs and concerns. Both depend on the other to make some sense of how their overlapping knowledge and skills might inform a plausible plan of action. Both try to connect their particular struggle to other particular struggles and to particular visions of the state and the political economy. And both inevitably challenge the other as together they put a part of themselves on the line. In short, when things go well they seem capable of favorably redefining over time the very terms that otherwise circumscribe their capacity to take advantage of one another's will to fight.

Still, you should realize that legal education's historical disregard of practice with the politically and socially subordinated survives in all of us, even as some of us continue to try to break with this past. All of us (practitioners, teachers, students, other lay and professional activists) have learned, to one degree or another, not even really to notice inspired and imaginative work in fights against subordination, much less to study how it happens, how it might be taught, and what it might mean for us all. It's not simply that I think we have screwed-up views about lawyering for social change. More critically, we don't even treat it, because we don't even see it, as remarkably complex and enigmatic work—with multiple and even elusive dimensions, presenting massive conceptual and empirical challenges, and cultural and interpersonal dynamics more daunting and even more self-defining than we are accustomed to handling. Just as we have come to regard María Elena as too unremarkable to pay much attention to, so too have we come to understand working with her as like anything else in law, except (to be truthful) a lot more lightweight, formulaic, and intellectually vapid.

At the heart of the matter, we simply must come to realize that we all make those communities we call our own. That the problems of the María Elenas of this world are our problems, the future of María Elena's children is our future, and that the failure to share what clout we do exercise is ultimately our own failure, and a tragic and even dangerous one at that. We have a rare chance over the next several years to bring to life the systematic study of the work we know so little about, work that in many ways tells us precisely what we need most to know about ourselves—those sorts of things we'd often rather not hear, much less change. If we're big enough as people and honest enough as an institution, then in the near future María Elena and those others with whom she lives and labors might even come to recognize themselves as mattering—as systematically mattering—to the training we provide and the practice of law we help inspire.

‖‖‖

Chapter 51

Should Good People Be Prosecutors?

Paul Butler

When I stopped being a prosecutor I told my friends it was because I didn't go to law school to put poor people in prison. My friends weren't surprised that I quit; they had been shocked that I became a prosecutor in the first place. For a progressive like me—a person who believed in redemption and second chances and robust civil liberties—the work presented obvious pitfalls.

"Locking people up" was practically on the job description. Eric Holder, the first African American U.S. attorney in DC, and now President Obama's attorney general, asked prospective prosecutors during interviews, "How would you feel about sending so many black men to jail?" Anyone who had a big problem with that presumably was not hired.

I began the work, however, as a liberal critic of American criminal justice—the avenging Undercover Brother who would change the system from the inside. What happened instead was that I collaborated with the system's injustice.

Thinking about the business of prosecuting crimes brings questions about the utility and morality of American criminal justice into sharp relief. If too many people languish in prison, how should we feel about the men and women who put them there?

My conclusion is that prosecutors are more part of the problem than the solution. The adversarial nature of the justice system, the culture of the prosecutor's office, and the politics of crime pose insurmountable obstacles for prosecutors who are concerned with economic and racial justice. The day-to-day work of the prosecutor is geared toward punishing people whose lives are already messed up. This does not mean that criminals should be allowed to victimize others; some of the people in prison really belong there, for the protection of society. It suggests, however, that piling on is the main work of prosecutors. It is well intentioned, perhaps even necessary, but piling on nonetheless. Adding up the costs of a lifetime of deprivation and then presenting the bill to the person who suffered it seems an odd job for a humanitarian.

It is true that some prosecutors attempt to mitigate the harshness of the system, either openly or through the covert or subversive measures that I discuss elsewhere. Their principal work, however, is applying the criminal law, not ameliorating its negative effects. Becoming a prosecutor to help resolve unfairness in the criminal justice system is like enlisting in the army because you are opposed to the current war. It's like working as an oil refiner because you want to help the environment. Yes, you get to choose the toxic chemicals. True, the boss might allow you to leave one or two pristine bays untouched. Maybe, if you do really good work as a low-level polluter, they might make you the head polluter. But rather than calling yourself an "environmentalist," you should think of yourself as a polluter with a conscience.

I would not go so far as to call prosecutors "bad people." I know prosecutors who are fair-minded, concerned about economic and racial justice, and even believe that too many people are in prison. Unfortunately, their bodies and souls are working at cross-purposes. Especially for African American prosecutors, the job exacts a terrible toll.

The Cross-Examination

I loved it when the defendant took the stand. The judge would ask, "Does the government have any questions?"

"Yes, Your Honor!" I would leap up from the government's table, stand my full six feet three inches, and stare hard at the bad guy. On the street everybody might be scared of this dude (like they were scared of me, late at night, if I wasn't wearing my suit), but at this moment, I—on behalf of the United States of America—was running the show.

I paced the entire well of the courtroom but avoided going anywhere near the defendant. Later, if my questions got the defendant too riled up and he tried to get smart-ass on me, I would get up in his face—or at least as close as the judge would allow. For now, though, I tried to convey to the jury through my movements as well as my words that the drug dealer on trial was a piece of garbage.

> *Me*: Where were you the night of August 5?
> *Cretin*: Over to my baby mama's house.
> *Me*: What is your wife's name?
> *Cretin*: Her name LaShonda, but she not my wife.
> *Me*: I see. Then you left your baby mama's house and went to stand on the street corner, is that right?
> *Cretin*: I saw my boy and stopped to talk.
> *Me*: What's your boy's name?
> *Cretin*: Lil' Boo. I mean that's what everybody calls him—I ain't know his real name.
> *Me*: And when you and Mr. Boo saw the police, you threw your cocaine on the ground and ran away, didn't you?
> *Cretin*: Naw man.
> *Me*: No further questions, your honor.

Gentle reader, could you hear the slight hint of sarcasm in my voice when I said "wife"? Did you see my eyes roll? Every time the cretin slurred his words and tripped over the conjugation of a verb, my diction became more precise.

Here's what they don't teach you in law school: As you, the black prosecutor, button your jacket and head back to the government table, you look at the jurors and then you glance back over at the defendant. You can't actually say these words, but this is what you mean: Ladies and gentlemen of the jury, I am an African American. You are African Americans. The defendant over there—that's a nigger. Lock him up.

I had the best conviction record in my section.

What happened to that progressive guy who joined the office? My aspirations of changing the system got shot down because I liked winning too much, and I was good at it. I wanted to be well regarded by my peers, to be successful in my career, and to serve my community. And the way to do that, I learned on the job, was to send as many people to jail as I could. I wasn't so much hoodwinked as seduced.

From the Editors *Issues and Comments*

Do you agree with Gerald López that the U.S. Constitution means little to the Chicano community and can only acquire meaning through struggle and fighting?

If the Sleepy Lagoon incident and the zoot suit riots broke out today, how do you think society and the government would respond?

Should radical lawyers, as Michael Olivas puts it, sometimes break the law on principle? Is this any different from similar illegality on the part of the KKK or white supremacist groups?

Oscar "Zeta" Acosta envisioned "a head-on collision with the rest of society" in store for Chicanos as an unavoidable consequence of developing Chicano consciousness and the demands of justice. Was he referring to a purely institutional collision or an actual uprising? Were Martin Luther King, Jr. and Gandhi revolutionaries, even though they both espoused nonviolence? What about Acosta? Do you feel that his "collision" has already taken place? Or is it still waiting to happen?

Do you think that direct action by Latinos—such as high school walkouts and grape boycotts—has been more, or less, successful than similar actions by blacks?

Suppose you are counsel to a group of disgusted radicals insistent on working for racial justice but impatient with the slow pace of progress. Peaceful means of protest, such as boycotts and sit-ins, have brought about little change. The group is now considering introducing a secret virus into every computer in the United States that will disable it for one month. Although the virus is meant to be a nuisance rather a cause of permanent harm, their action will in fact violate federal law. As legal counsel, what do you advise the group? Would you warn them about the possible consequences of their proposed course of conduct? Turn them in? Resign as their lawyer?

Should lawyers for minority communities live in those very communities and send their children to community schools? What if a technically able and deeply committed Anglo lawyer prefers not to? If you were his or her supervising attorney at a storefront law firm serving the community, would you insist that he or she move into the community or resign?

Is a burrito a sandwich? Why or why not? What difference does it make?

How will we know when race is no longer an issue in America and the legal system?

Suggested Readings

Acosta, Oscar "Zeta." "Autobiographical Essay." In *Oscar "Zeta" Acosta: The Uncollected Works,* edited by Ilan Stavans. Houston: Arte Publico Press, 1996.

———. *The Autobiography of a Brown Buffalo.* New ed. New York: Vintage, 1989.

———. *The Revolt of the Cockroach People.* New ed. New York: Vintage, 1989.

Bender, Steven W. *One Night in America: Robert Kennedy, César Chávez, and the Dream of Dignity.* Boulder, Colo.: Paradigm Publishers, 2008.

Cameron, Christopher David Ruiz. "The Labyrinth of Solidarity: Why the Future of the American Labor Movement Depends on Latino Workers." 53 U. *Miami L. Rev.* 1089 (1999).

———. "The Rakes of Wrath: Urban Agricultural Workers and the Struggle against Los Angeles's Ban on Gas-Powered Leaf Blowers." 33 *U.C. Davis L. Rev.* 1087 (2000).

Chávez, César. "The California Farm Workers' Struggle." 7 *Black Scholar* 16–19 (June 1976).

Chávez, Ernesto. *"Mi Raza Primero!"* (*My People First!*): *Nationalism, Identity, and Insurgency in the Chicano Movement in Los Angeles, 1966–1978*. Berkeley: University of California Press, 2002.

Donato, Rubén. *The Other Struggle for Equal Schools: Mexican Americans during the Civil Rights Era*. Albany: State University of New York, 1997.

Escobar, Edward J. "The Dialectics of Repression: The Los Angeles Police Department and the Chicano Movement, 1968–1971." 79 *Journal of American History* 1483 (1993).

———. *Race, Police, and the Making of a Political Identity: Mexican Americans and the Los Angles Police Department, 1900–1945*. Berkeley: University of California Press, 1999.

Fernandez, Ronald. *Prisoners of Colonialism: The Struggle for Justice in Puerto Rico*. Monroe, Maine: Common Courage Press, 1994.

Ferriss, Susan, and Ricardo Sandoval. *The Fight in the Fields: César Chávez and the Farmworkers Movement*, edited by Diana Hembree. New York: Harcourt & Brace, 1997.

Galarza, Ernesto. *Spiders in the House and Workers in the Field*. Notre Dame, Ind.: University of Notre Dame Press, 1970.

Garcia, Ignacio M. *Chicanismo: The Forging of a Militant Ethos among Mexican Americans*. Tucson: University of Arizona Press, 1997.

———. *United We Win: The Rise and Fall of La Raza Unida Party*. Tucson: Mexican American Studies and Research Center, University of Arizona, 1989.

Gardner, Richard. *Grito! Reies Tijerina and the New Mexico Land Grant War of 1967*. Indianapolis: Bobbs-Merrill, 1970.

Gómez-Quiñones, Juan. *Chicano Politics: Reality and Promise, 1940–1990*. Albuquerque: University of New Mexico Press, 1990.

———. *Mexican Students por La Raza: The Chicano Student Movement in Southern California, 1967–1977*. Santa Barbara, Calif.: Editorial La Causa, 1978.

———. *Roots of Chicano Politics, 1600–1940*. Albuquerque: University of New Mexico Press, 1994.

Gonzalez, Gilbert G. *Chicano Education in the Era of Segregation*. Santa Barbara, Calif.: Companion Press, 1990.

Gonzales, Rodolfo "Corky." "Chicano Nationalism: The Key to Unity for La Raza." In *A Documentary History of the Mexican Americans*, edited by Wayne Moquin, 488. New York: Bantam Books, 1972.

———. *Message to Aztlán: Selected Writings*, edited by Antonio Esquibel. Houston: Arte Publico Press, 2001.

Gordon, Jennifer. *Suburban Sweatshops: The Fight for Immigrant Rights*. Cambridge, Mass.: Harvard University Press, 2005.

Greenfield, Alice. *The Sleepy Lagoon Case: A Pageant of Prejudice*. Los Angeles: Citizen's Committee for the Defense of the Mexican-American Youth, 1942.

Griswold de Castillo, Richard, and Richard A. Garcia. *César Chávez: A Triumph of Spirit*. Norman: University of Oklahoma Press, 1995.

Guglielmo, Thomas A. "Fighting for Caucasian Rights: Mexicans, Mexican Americans, and the Transnational Struggle for Civil Rights in World War II Texas." 92 *Journal of American History* 1212 (March 2006).

Gutiérrez, José Ángel. *The Making of a Civil Rights Leader: José Ángel Gutiérrez*. Houston: Arte Publico Press, 2005.

Hammerback, John C., Richard J. Jensen, and José Ángel Gutiérrez. *A War of Words: Chicano Protest in the 1960s and 1970s*. Westport, Conn.: Greenwood Press, 1985.

Huerta, Dolores. "Dolores Huerta Talks: About Republicans, César, Her Children and Her Home Town." 2 *Regeneración* 20–24 (1975).

Jenkins, J. Craig. *The Politics of Insurgency: The Farm Worker Movement in the 1960s*. New York: Columbia University Press, 1985.

Johnson, Kevin R., and George A. Martinez. "Crossover Dreams: The Roots of LatCrit Theory in Chicana/o Studies Activism and Scholarship." 53 *U. Miami L. Rev.* 1143 (1999).

Jourdane, Maurice. *The Struggle for the Health and Legal Protection of Farm Workers: El Cortito*. Houston: Arte Publico Press, 2004.

Kells, Michelle Hall. *Hector P. Garcia: Everyday Rhetoric and Mexican American Civil Rights*. Carbondale: Southern Illinois Press, 2006.

Lazos Vargas, Sylvia R. "The Immigrant Rights Marches (Las Marchas): Did the Gigante (Giant) Wake Up or Does It Still Sleep Tonight?" 7 *Nev. L.J.* 780 (2006–2007).

Levy, Jacques E. *César Chávez: Autobiography of La Causa*. New ed. Minneapolis: University of Minnesota Press, 2007.

López, Ann Aurelia. *The Farmworkers' Journey*. Berkeley: University of California Press, 2007.

López, Gerald P. *Rebellious Lawyering: One Chicano's Vision of Progressive Law Practice*. Boulder, Colo.: Westview Press, 1992.

———. "Reconceiving Civil Rights Practice: Seven Weeks in the Life of a Rebellious Collaboration." 77 *Geo. L.J.* 1603 (1989).

———. "Training Future Lawyers to Work with the Politically and Socially Subordinated: Anti-Generic Legal Education." 91 *W. Va. L. Rev.* 305 (1989).

Marin, Christine. *A Spokesman of the Mexican American Movement: Rodolfo "Corky" Gonzales and the Fight for Chicano Liberation, 1966–1972*. San Francisco: R&E Research Associates, 1977.

Mariscal, George. *Brown-Eyed Children of the Sun: Lessons from the Chicano Movement, 1965–1975*. Albuquerque: University of New Mexico Press, 2005.

Martínez, Elizabeth. "Histories of 'the Sixties': A Certain Absence of Color." 16 *Social Justice* 175–84 (Winter 1989).

Matthiessen, Peter. *Sal Si Puedes: César Chávez and the New American Revolution*. New York: Random House, 1969.

Mazon, Mauricio. *The Zoot-Suit Riots: The Psychology of Symbolic Annihilation*. Austin: University of Texas Press, 1984.

Meléndez, Miguel. *We Took the Streets: Fighting for Latino Rights with the Young Lords*. New York: St. Martin's Press, 2003.

Morales, Armando. *Ando Sangrando (I Am Bleeding): A Study of Mexican American–Police Conflict*. La Puenta, Calif.: Perspectiva Publications, 1972.

Muñoz, Carlos, Jr. *Youth, Identity, Power: The Chicano Movement*. London: Verso, 1989.

Muñoz, Carlos, Jr., and Mario Barrera. "La Raza Unida Party and the Chicano Student Movement in California." 19 *Social Science Journal* 101–20 (April 1982).

Nabakov, Peter. *Tijerina and the Courthouse Raid*. Albuquerque: University of New Mexico Press, 1969.

Navarro, Armando. *The Cristal Experiment: A Chicano Struggle for Community Control*. Madison: University of Wisconsin Press, 1998.

————. *Mexican American Youth Organization: Avant-Garde of the Chicano Movement in Texas*. Austin: University of Texas Press, 1995.

Olivas, Michael A. "Unaccompanied Refugee Children: Detention, Due Process, and Disgrace." 1 *Stan. L. & Pol'y Rev.* 159 (1990).

Oropeza, Lorena. *¡Raza Si! ¡Guerra No! Chicano Protest and Patriotism during the Viet Nam War Era*. Berkeley: University of California Press, 2005.

Orozco, Cynthia E. *No Mexicans, Women, or Dogs Allowed: The Rise of the Mexican American Civil Rights Movement*. Austin: University of Texas Press, 2009.

Pagán, Eduardo Obregón. *Murder at the Sleepy Lagoon: Zoot Suits, Race, and Riot in Wartime L.A*. Chapel Hill: University of North Carolina Press, 2003.

Pardo, Mary. "Mexican American Women Grassroots Community Activists: 'Mothers of East Los Angeles.'" 11 *Frontiers* 1 (1990).

Pawel, Miriam. *The Union of Their Dreams: Power, Hope and Struggle in César Chávez's Farm Worker Movement*. New York: Bloomsbury, 2009.

Peña, Milagros. *Latina Activists across Borders: Women's Grassroots Organizing in Mexico and Texas*. Durham, N.C.: Duke University Press, 2007.

Pizarro, Marcos. *Chicanas and Chicanos in School: Racial Profiling, Identity Battles, and Empowerment*. Austin: University of Texas Press, 2005.

The Puerto Rican Movement: Voices from the Diaspora, edited by Andrés Torres and José E. Velázquez. Philadelphia: Temple University Press, 1998.

Romero, Mary. "El Paso Salt War: Mob Action or Political Struggle." 16 *Aztlán: International Journal of Chicano Studies Research* 119 (1987).

Romo, Ricardo. "George I. Sanchez and the Civil Rights Movement: 1940–1960." 1 *La Raza L.J.* 342 (1986).

————. "Southern California and the Origins of Latino Civil-Rights Activism." 3 *Western Legal History* 379 (1990).

Rosales, Francisco Arturo. *Chicano! The History of the Mexican American Civil Rights Movement*. Houston: Arte Publico Press, 1996.

————. *Dictionary of Latino Civil Rights History*. Houston: Arte Publico Press, 2006.

Rothenberg, Daniel. *With These Hands: The Hidden World of Migrant Farmworkers Today*. Berkeley: University of California Press, 1998.

San Miguel, Jr., Guadalupe. *Brown, Not White: School Integration and the Chicano Movement in Houston*. College Station: Texas A&M University Press, 2001.

Sleepy Lagoon Defense Committee. *The Sleepy Lagoon Case*. Los Angeles: The Committee, 1944.

Stavans, Ilan. *Bandido: Oscar "Zeta" Acosta and the Chicano Experience*. New York: Harper-Collins, 1995.

Symposium: "Latinos and the Law: Twenty Years of Legal Advocacy and Lessons for Advancement." 14 *Chicano-Latino L. Rev.* 1 (1994).

Taylor, Ronald B. *Chávez and the Farm Workers*. Boston: Beacon Press, 1975.

Torres, Rodolfo D., and George Katsiaficas. *Latino Social Movements: Historical and Theoretical Perspectives*. New York: Routledge, 1999.

U.S. Commission on Civil Rights. *Mexican Americans and the Administration of Justice in the Southwest*. Washington, D.C.: Government Printing Office, 1970.

Urrieta, Luis, Jr. *Working from Within: Chicana and Chicano Activist Educators in Whitestream Schools*. Tucson: University of Arizona Press, 2009.

Valdez, Luis. *Zoot Suit and Other Plays*. Houston: Arte Publico Press, 1992.

Vargas, Zaragosa. "Emma Tenayuca and the San Antonio Labor Movement during the Great Depression." 66(4) *Pacific Historical Review* 553–80 (1997).

———. *Labor Rights Are Civil Rights: Mexican American Workers in Twentieth-Century America*. Princeton, N.J.: Princeton University Press, 2004.

Vigil, Ernesto B. *The Crusade for Justice: Chicano Militancy and the Government's War on Dissent*. Madison: University of Wisconsin Press, 1999.

||||||||||||||||||||||||||||||||||||||||||||||||||||||||||||||||||||||||||||||||||||||||

Part VII

Revisionist Law
Does the Legal System Work for Us?

In addition to movements, activism, and resistance, Latino lawyers have challenged racist or unresponsive legal structures through the courts. As well, scholars and historians have analyzed the legal and social structures that have impeded Latinos' civic participation in American society. Part 7 introduces the reader to some of the best of this literature. As we have seen in previous sections, Latinos' racial identity has turned on whether, as a group, they are seen by others or themselves as white. Some of the pieces address the pernicious consequences of the black/white binary view of race, according to which almost everyone thinks of race in the United States in terms of black or white. In nineteenth-century Mexico, however, a different caste system prevailed and influenced the way Mexicans thought about themselves long after they became a part of a white-dominated country. The latter half of these excerpts focuses on the racialization of Latinos in Texas through *Hernandez*, the famous jury participation case, and other cases having to do with school segregation. They show how the paradox of being classified officially as white, yet being socially despised, was used by both whites and Mexican Americans to suit each of their needs. A question running through many of the selections is how much faith an outsider group can place in the legal system.

‖‖‖

Chapter 52

The Black/White Binary Paradigm of Race

Juan F. Perea

Ponder, for a moment, how we are taught to think about race. I believe that most such thinking is structured by a paradigm that is widely held but rarely recognized for what it is and does. It is crucial, therefore, to identify and describe this paradigm and to demonstrate how it binds and organizes racial discourse, limiting both the scope and the range of legitimate viewpoints in that discourse.

The Power of Paradigms

Thomas Kuhn, in *The Structure of Scientific Revolutions*,[1] describes the properties of paradigms and their power in structuring scientific research and knowledge. While Kuhn writes in connection with scientific knowledge, many of his insights are useful in understanding paradigms and their effects more generally. A paradigm is a shared set of understandings or premises which permits the definition, elaboration, and solution of a set of problems defined within the paradigm. It is an accepted model or pattern that, "like an accepted judicial decision in the common law[,] . . . is an object for further articulation and specification under new or more stringent conditions."[2]

Paradigms thus define relevancy. In so doing, they control fact-gathering and investigation. Data-gathering efforts and research are focused on understanding the facts and circumstances that the relevant paradigm has taught us are important.

Describing the Binary Paradigm of Race

Paradigms of race shape our understanding and definition of racial problems. The most pervasive and powerful paradigm of race in the United States is the Black/White binary. I define this paradigm as the conception that race in America consists, either exclusively or primarily, of only two constituent racial groups, the Black and the White. Many scholars of race reproduce this paradigm when they write and act as though only the Black and the White races matter for purposes of discussing race and social policy. The current fashion of mentioning "other people of color," without careful attention to their voices, their histories, and their real presence, is merely a reassertion of the Black/White paradigm. If one conceives of race as primarily of concern only to Blacks and Whites, and understands "other people of color" only through some unclear analogy to the "real" races, this just restates the binary paradigm with a slight concession to demographics.

In addition, the paradigm dictates that all other racial identities and groups in the United States are best understood through the Black/White binary paradigm. Only a few writers even recognize that they use a Black/White paradigm as the frame of reference through which to understand all racial relations. Most writers simply assume the importance and correctness of the paradigm, and leave the reader grasping for whatever significance descriptions of the Black/White relationship have for other people of color. As I shall discuss, because the Black/White binary paradigm is so widely accepted, other racialized groups like Latinos/as, Asian Americans, and Native Americans are often marginalized or ignored altogether. As Kuhn wrote, "those that will not fit the box are often not seen at all."[3]

Andrew Hacker and Two Nations

Andrew Hacker's famous book, *Two Nations: Black and White, Separate, Hostile, Unequal*, provides an excellent example.[4] Its title, proclaiming two nations, Black and White, boldly professes the Black/White binary paradigm. Although Hacker recognizes explicitly that a full perspective on race in America requires inclusion of Latinos/as and Asians, this recognition is, in the context of the entire book, insignificant and underdeveloped. His almost exclusive focus on Blacks and Whites is clearly intentional: "*Two Nations* will adhere to its title by giving central attention to black and white Americans."[5]

Hacker's justification is that "[i]n many respects, other groups find themselves sitting as spectators, while the two prominent players try to work out how or whether they can co-exist with one another."[6] This justifies marginalization with marginalization. What Hacker and so many other writers on race fail, or decline, to understand is that, by focusing only on Blacks and Whites, they both produce and replicate the belief that only "two prominent players," Black and White, count in debates about race. Other non-White groups, rendered invisible by these writers, can thus be characterized as passive, voluntary spectators.

Hacker describes in detail only conditions experienced by White or Black Americans. He first characterizes the White nature of the nation and its culture:

> America is inherently a "white" country: in character, in structure, in culture. Needless to say, black Americans create lives of their own. Yet, as a people, they face boundaries and constrictions set by the white majority. America's version of apartheid, while lacking overt legal sanction, comes closest to the system even now being reformed in the land of its invention.[7]

Of course, Latinos/as, Asian Americans, Native Americans, Gypsies, and all non-White Americans face "boundaries and constrictions set by the white majority," but the vision Hacker advances counts only Blacks as significantly disadvantaged by White racism.

Similarly, Hacker describes Blackness as uniquely functional for Whites:

> As James Baldwin has pointed out, white people need the presence of black people as a reminder of what providence has spared them from becoming. . . . In the eyes of white Americans, being black encapsulates your identity. No other racial or national origin is seen as having so pervasive a personality or character.[8]

According to Hacker, then, Blackness serves a crucial function in enabling Whites to define themselves as privileged and superior, and racial attributes of other minorities do not serve this function.

Hacker's chapter titles largely tell the story of the binary paradigm. Chapter 2, on "Race and Racism," discusses only White and Black perceptions of each other. Chapter 3, "Being Black in America," is followed by a chapter on "White Responses." Hacker's omission of non-Black minority groups in his discussion of specific topics similarly suggests these groups' experiences do not exist. Chapter 9, on segregated schooling, describes only the experience of segregation of Blacks, making no reference to the extensive history of segregation in education suffered by Latinos/as. Chapter 10 asks, "What's Best for Black Children?" with no commensurate concern for other children. Similarly, Chapter 11, on crime, discusses only perceptions of Black criminality and their interpretation. In discussing police brutality, Hacker describes only White police brutality against Blacks. One finds not a single word about the similar brutality suffered by Latino/a people at the hands of White police officers. Nor are there any words in these chapters describing the experiences of Native Americans or Asian Americans.

The greatest danger in Hacker's vision is the implication that non-White groups other than Blacks are not really subject to racism. Hacker seems to adopt the deservedly criticized ethnicity theory, which posits that non-White immigrant ethnics are essentially Whites-in-waiting who will be permitted to assimilate and become White. This is illustrated best in Chapter 8, "On Education: Ethnicity and Achievement," which offers the book's only significant discussion of non-White groups other than Blacks. Asians are described in "model minority" terms, because of high standardized test scores (on a group basis). Latinos/as are portrayed both as below standard, because of low test scores, and as aspiring immigrants. Describing Asian Americans, Latinos/as and other immigrant groups, Hacker writes:

> Members of all these "intermediate groups" have been allowed to put a visible distance between themselves and black Americans. Put most simply, none of the presumptions of inferiority associated with Africa and slavery are imposed on these other ethnicities.[9]

While a full rebuttal of this quotation must wait for another time, its inaccuracy can be quickly demonstrated. Consider how "American visitors to the Mexican

frontier were nearly unanimous in commenting on the dark skin of Mexican mestizos who, it was generally agreed, had inherited the worst qualities of Spaniards and
Indians to produce a 'race' still more despicable than that of either parent."[10] Rufus B.
Sage expressed the common view of Mexicans in 1846: "There are no people on the
continent of America, whether civilized or uncivilized, with one or two exceptions,
more miserable in condition or despicable in morals than the mongrel race inhabiting New Mexico."[11] The common perception of Mexican Americans was that "[t]hey
are an inferior race, that is all."[12]

Incredibly, and without any supporting evidence, Hacker writes that "[m]ost Central and South Americans can claim a strong European heritage, which eases their
absorption into the 'white' middle class."[13] He continues, "[w]hile immigrants from
Colombia and Cyprus may have to work their way up the social ladder, they are still
allowed as valid a claim to being 'white' as persons of Puritan or Pilgrim stock."[14]
Hacker's comments are simply incredible. While some Latinos/as may look White
and may act Anglo (the phenomenon of passing for White is not limited to Blacks),
Hacker's statement is certainly false for millions of Latinos/as. Anti-immigrant initiatives targeted at Latinos/as and Asians, such as California's Proposition 187 and similar federal legislation targeting legal and illegal immigrants, California's Proposition
209, and the unprecedented proposal to deny birthright citizenship to the U.S.-born
children of undocumented persons, debunk any notion that the presence of Latino/a
or Asian people will be accepted or tolerated easily by the White majority.

Cornel West and the Black/White Binary Paradigm

Cornel West is one of the most well known and well regarded philosophers and commentators on race in the nation. While West writes with much more insight than
Hacker, his recent book, *Race Matters,* is also limited by and reproduces the Black/
White binary paradigm of race.[15] A collection of essays West wrote on race and race
relations, its principal subject is the relationship of Blackness to Whiteness and the
exploration of avenues to alter the unsatisfactory state of that relationship. And while
this focus is of course worthy of his attention, he overlooks and ignores relevant subject matter that lies outside the paradigm. West describes the binary nature of our
public discourse about race:

> We confine discussions about race in America to the "problems" black people pose for
> whites rather than consider what this way of viewing black people reveals about us as
> a nation. . . . Both [liberals and conservatives] fail to see that the presence and predica-
> ments of black people are neither additions to nor defections from American life, but
> rather *constitutive elements of that life.*[16]

This statement is accurate, and I would only fault West for not recognizing that exactly the same statement is true of Latinos/as, Asians, and Native Americans as well
as Blacks: we are all constitutive of American life and identity to a degree that has not
been fully recognized, and which is in fact actively resisted.

West's near-exclusive focus on Blacks and Whites, and thus his reproduction of the Black/White binary paradigm, is apparent throughout the book. Chapter 2, entitled "The Pitfalls of Racial Reasoning," presents a powerful critique of racial reasoning within the Black community that immobilized Black leaders, who were generally unable to criticize Clarence Thomas when he was appointed to the Supreme Court. West's binary conception of the nation emerges when he describes the "deep cultural conservatism in white and black America. In white America, cultural conservatism takes the form of a chronic racism, sexism, and homophobia. . . . In black America, cultural conservatism takes the form of an inchoate xenophobia (e.g., against whites, Jews, and Asians), systemic sexism, and homophobia."[17] Like Hacker's conception of "two nations," West sees binary Americas, one White, one Black. In addition, West's reference to Black xenophobia, directed at Whites, Jews, and Asians, sets the stage for his later description of Black distrust of Latinos/as as well.

West also describes the binary paradigm from a Black point of view, referring to the "black bourgeois preoccupation with white peer approval and black nationalist obsession with white racism."[18] Blacks, in their way, are as preoccupied with Whites as Whites are with Blacks.

When West writes about the struggle for Black civil rights in shaping the future of equality in America, he recognizes the need for Blacks to repudiate anti-Semitism and other racisms in order to sustain the moral position garnered through the struggle for civil rights. However, he makes ambivalent comments about the possibilities for coalition with other groups:

> [A] prophetic framework encourages a coalition strategy that solicits genuine solidarity with those deeply committed to antiracist struggle. . . . [B]lack suspicions of whites, Latinos, Jews, and Asians runs deep for historical reasons. Yet there are slight though significant antiracist traditions among whites, Asians, and especially Latinos, Jews and indigenous people that must not be cast aside. Such coalitions are important precisely because they not only enhance the plight of black people but also because they enrich the quality of life in America.[19]

This paragraph warrants probing. Given America's history of racism, Black suspicions of every group may seem well-founded. For example, with respect to Latinos/as, during the nineteenth century as during the present, identification with Anglos by upper-class Mexicans meant becoming more racist and disparaging toward lower-class and darker-skinned Mexicans and Blacks. However, West's characterization of Latino/a, Asian, and Native American resistance to Anglo domination and racism as "slight though significant"[20] seems belittling, ill-informed, and marginalizing of Latino/a, Asian, and indigenous people. This comment can be understood as the kind of "inchoate xenophobia" West himself finds in the Black community.

Another possible reason for this distrust of Latinos/as may stem from a widespread sense that Blacks are being displaced by immigrant Latinos/as. Toni Morrison writes specifically about this distrust. In her essay "On the Backs of Blacks," Morrison describes the hatred of Blacks as the defining, final, necessary step in the Americanization of immigrants. "It is the act of racial contempt [banishing a competing black shoe-shiner] that transforms this charming Greek into an entitled white."[21] Morrison sees Blacks as persistently victimized by Americanizing processes, always forced to "the lowest level of the racial hierarchy."[22] The struggles of immigrants, according to Morrison,

> are persistently framed as struggles between recent arrivals and blacks. In race talk the move into mainstream America always means buying into the notion of American blacks as the real aliens. Whatever the ethnicity or nationality of the immigrant, his nemesis is understood to be African American.[23]

Morrison is right that American "Whiteness" is often achieved through distancing from Blacks. Latinos/as participate in the paradigm, by engaging in racism against Blacks or darker-skinned members of Latino/a communities. Current events, however, belie Morrison's notion of American blacks as "the real aliens." Mexican and other Latino/a and Asian aliens have become targets of state and federal legislation denying them medical and educational resources. The legal attack on entitlement programs and affirmative action programs is an attack on Blacks, Latinos/as, and Asians.

Taken together, these views pose serious problems for Latinos/as. Viewing Latinos/as as aspiring immigrants is, in most cases, a deeply flawed view, for two reasons. First, not all Mexican Americans, Puerto Ricans, and other U.S. Latinos/as, are immigrants. Mexicans occupied the Southwest long before the United States ever found them. Second, this utopian view of immigrant assimilation takes no account of the systemic racism that afflicts Mexican Americans and Puerto Ricans. The utopian view serves White writers like Hacker because they can perpetuate the view that the United States has only a single race problem—the traditional binary problem of the White relationship with Blacks—rather than a more complex set of racisms that, if recognized, would demonstrate that racism is much more systemic and pervasive than is usually admitted.

One can thus discern how the binary paradigm interferes with liberation and equality. If Latinos/as and Asian Americans are presumed to be White by both White and Black writers (a presumption not borne out in the lived experience of most Latinos/as and Asians), then our claims to justice will not be heard or acknowledged. Our claims can be ignored by Whites, since we are not Black and therefore are not subject to real racism. And our claims can be ignored by Blacks, since we are presumed to be, not Black, but becoming White, and therefore not subject to real racism. Latinos/as do not fit the boxes supplied by the paradigm.

[The author goes on to show how the same Black/White paradigmatic thinking operates in law and legal casebooks, then continues as follows—Eds.]

My review of important literature on race establishes the existence of the Black/White binary paradigm and its structuring of writing on race. The "normal science" of race scholarship specifies inquiry into the relationship between Blacks and Whites as the exclusive aspect of race relations that needs to be explored and elaborated. As a result, much relevant legal history and information concerning Latinos/as and other racialized groups end up omitted from books on race and constitutional law.

The omission of this history is extraordinarily damaging to Mexican Americans and other Latinos/as. When this history is omitted, students get no understanding that Mexican Americans have long struggled for equality. The absence of Latinos/as from histories of racism and the struggle against it enables people to maintain existing stereotypes of Mexican Americans. These stereotypes are perpetuated even by America's leading thinkers on race. Paradigmatic descriptions and study of White racism against Blacks, with only cursory mention of "other people of color," marginalizes all people of color by grouping them, without particularity, as somehow analogous to Blacks. "Other people of color" are deemed to exist only as unexplained analogies to Blacks. Uncritical readers are encouraged to continue assuming the paradigmatic importance of the Black/White relationship, while ignoring the experiences of other Americans who also are subject to racism in profound ways.

It is time to ask hard questions of our leading writers on race. It is also time to demand answers to these questions about inclusion, exclusion, and racial presence that go beyond perfunctory references to "other people of color." In the midst of profound demographic changes, it is time to question whether the Black/White binary paradigm of race fits our highly variegated current and future population. Our "normal science" of writing on race, at odds with both history and demographic reality, needs reworking.

NOTES

1. Thomas S. Kuhn, The Structure of Scientific Revolutions (2d ed. 1970).

2. *Id.* at 23.

3. *Id.* at 24; see also Juan F. Perea, *Los Olvidados: On the Making of Invisible People,* 70 N.Y.U. L. Rev. 965 (1995); Anne Sutherland, Gypsies: The Hidden Americans (1986).

4. Andrew Hacker, Two Nations: Black and White, Separate, Hostile, Unequal (1992).

5. *Id.* at xii.

6. *Id.*

7. *Id.* at 4.

8. *Id.* at 30, 32.

9. *Id.* at 16.

10. David J. Weber. Foreigners in Their Native Land: Historical Roots of the Mexican Americans 59 (1973).

11. *Id.* at 72, 74 (quoting 2 Rufus B. Sage: His Letters and Papers, 1836–1847 [LeRoy R. and Ann W. Hafen eds., 1956]).

12. This was the justification offered by Texas school officials for segregating Mexican Americans in 1929. See Jorge C. Rangel & Carlos M. Alcala, *Project Report: De Jure Segregation of Chicanos in Texas Schools,* 7 Harv. C.R.–C.L. L. Rev. 307, 307 (quoting Paul Schuster Taylor, An American Mexican Frontier 219 [1934]).

13. Hacker, at 10.

14. *Id.* at 12.

15. Cornel West, Race Matters (1993).

16. *Id.* at 2–3.

17. *Id.* at 27.

18. *Id.* at 66.

19. *Id.* at 28–29.

20. *Id.* at 28.

21. Toni Morrison, *On the Backs of Blacks*, in ARGUING IMMIGRATION 97 (Nicolaus Mills ed., 1994).

22. *Id.*

23. *Id.* at 98.

Chapter 53

‖‖

The Black/White Binary
How Does It Work?

Richard Delgado

Rodrigo began, "I just got back from a two-day conference hosted by the Latino law students of a major school. It drew an impressive cast, with speakers like Rodolfo Acuña and Carlos Muñoz, as well as the usual complement of law professors. After hours, some of us were talking about the role of Latinos in American politics. We wondered why our relatively large group has had so little impact on national civil rights policy, especially in areas like immigration reform, bilingual education, poverty, and English-only. On all these fronts, we've been relatively ineffectual, compared to blacks. Some thought it had to do with exo-marriage and assimilation, and the way the Latino community lacks cohesion, being made up of so many different national-origin groups. But I think it's something different, namely, the black/white binary."

"What's that?" I asked.

"It's an idea that's just now emerging as a means of understanding American civil rights law and the place of nonblack groups in it," Rodrigo replied. "The idea is that the structure of antidiscrimination law is dichotomous. It assumes you are either black or white. If you're neither, you have trouble making claims or even having them understood in racial terms at all."

"I think I follow you," I replied. "But could you fill it out a little more? Assuming that our system does incorporate such a dichotomy, how does that render nonblack minority groups one-down, as opposed to, say, one-up, compared to blacks?"

"That's the next step," Rodrigo replied. "At the conference, no one had worked that out yet. But it's an important question. America's racial future looks increasingly mixed up. Latinos recently overtook blacks as the most numerous minority. The Asian population, too, is increasing rapidly. Multiracial people are demanding their own voice and census category. A simplistic paradigm of racial relations, based on an either-or, A-or-B model, won't work much longer. I've been trying to figure out how this is so."

"And do you have any inkling?" I asked.

"You remember, Professor, how Critical Legal Studies early on developed the notion of the fundamental contradiction?"

From *Rodrigo's Fifteenth Chronicle: Racial Mixture, Latino-Critical Scholarship, and the Black-White Binary*, 75 Tᴇx. L. Rᴇv. 1181 (1997). Originally published in the *Texas Law Review*. Reprinted by permission.

"Of course," I replied. "At the time a breathtaking breakthrough, it explains many of the strains and tensions running through our system of law and politics. It led to powerful critiques of the public-private distinction, judicial indeterminacy, and rights. Were the Latinos at your conference working on something similar?"

"I think we were," Rodrigo replied. "But without knowing it. And it's that very same black/white binary. People are just starting to talk about it. You may have seen an article or two. If one's paradigm identifies only one group as deserving of protection, everyone else is likely to suffer. Not only that, even members of one's own group are apt to think of themselves as black or white. It's quite a disabling instrument. We may have to blast the dichotomy—embrace the full multifariousness of life—if we're ever going to get anywhere."

"Didn't I read somewhere that early litigators arguing on behalf of Chicanos and other Latino groups embraced something called the 'other white' strategy?" I asked.

"They did," Rodrigo replied. "It's the logical extension of the kind of thinking that the black/white binary predisposes you to. The only way to get relief is to maintain that your client, a Mexican American or Puerto Rican, is white and thus should not be the object of social discrimination."

"Not exactly empowering," I commented wryly. "But I believe you were going to tell me of some other ways the binary does its pernicious work."

"In addition to the way just mentioned—namely that it fetters our own minds," Rodrigo said, "preventing us from articulating, or even imagining, how our victimization is a serious, group-based form of oppression."

"You must do so, and in the most complete fashion possible," I said. "If the binary is to serve as Latinos' fundamental contradiction, you have to spell out exactly how this structure of thought renders Latinos one-down. Otherwise, it's simply an observation, a descriptive statement no more useful than 'many Latinos speak Spanish,' or 'many have ancestors from Latin America or the Caribbean.'"

"I agree," Rodrigo replied. "Without such an explanation, the insight kind of runs out of gas."

"So, what are your ideas on how the black/white paradigm injures Latinos and other nonwhite groups?"

The Black/White Paradigm and the Social Reproduction of Inequality— Doctrine's Role

"As you know, Professor, the mainstay of American civil rights law is the Equal Protection Clause. Rooted in Reconstruction-era activism and aimed at the wholly laudable purpose of redressing slavery, that clause nevertheless produces and reproduces inequality for my people."

"The Equal Protection Clause?" I replied, raising my eyebrows. "That crown jewel in our jurisprudence, centerpiece of justice, and source of civil rights breakthroughs like *Brown v. Board of Education*? It's this that you think subordinates and injures Latinos? That's paradoxical, to put it mildly. I think I need to hear more."

"Let me try," Rodrigo replied calmly. "An analogy occurred to me on the plane.

Consider a different constitutional principle, namely, protection of the right of property. How does that function in a society like ours?"

"I suppose you're going to say that it benefits the haves, while disadvantaging or leaving as they are the have-nots, thus increasing the gap between the propertied and those who have less of that commodity."

"Exactly," Rodrigo replied. "And the same is true of other constitutional principles. The Free Speech Clause increases the influence of those who are articulate and can afford microphones, TV air time, and so on. In the same way, the Equal Protection Clause produces a social good, namely equality, for those falling under its coverage —blacks and whites. These it genuinely helps—at least on occasion. But it leaves everyone else unprotected. The gap between blacks and other groups of color grows, all other things being equal."

"It sounds strange when you first explain it," I said. "The idea of the Equal Protection Clause producing inequality. But you may have a point. As with those other clauses, the black/white paradigm could marginalize Latinos because of the way the clause and the other Civil War amendments were aimed at redressing injustices to blacks, principally slavery."

"I've thought of two other doctrinal sources of inequality," Rodrigo added. "Would you like to hear them?"

"Of course," I said. "I assume they also have to do with the black/white paradigm?"

"They do. The first is the very notion of civil rights. In American law, this means rights bestowed by the civil polity. But Latinos—many of them, at any rate—are not members of that polity. Rather, they want to immigrate here. In this respect they stand on a different footing from blacks. I'm sure you know, Professor, that the plenary power doctrine in immigration law means that someone desiring to immigrate to the U.S. has no power, enforceable in court, to compel equal treatment. U.S. immigration law can be as racist and discriminatory as Congress wants."

"Immigrants have due process rights, rights to a hearing, that sort of thing," I pointed out.

"But only once they're here," Rodrigo replied. "Not to get here in the first place. Since many Hispanics and Latinos, like Asians, come from somewhere else, this limitation affects them drastically. Yet it is inherent in our liberal notion of civil rights and implicit in the black/white binary. Blacks, and even Indians, were here originally or from very early days. Once society decided to count them as citizens, their thoughts and preferences began to figure into the political equation. Even if they were often out-voted and oppressed, their voices at least counted. A Mexican peasant desiring to immigrate in search of a better life, or a Guatemalan village activist fearful that the government wants to kill him, or a Chinese boat person does not count. They can come here only at sufferance, only if Congress decides to let them in."

"For example, through a Bracero program, a student visa, or some other category benefiting the U.S., such as that for investors," I added. "What's your second doctrinal source of inequality?"

"It's related to the one I just mentioned," Rodrigo said. "I'm sure you've heard, Professor, of the self-definition theory of nationhood?"

"In immigration law, you mean?" I asked. Rodrigo nodded. "I have. Going back to an article and a book co-authored by Peter Schuck, the argument holds that nations have the inherent right to decide how to define themselves.[1] Otherwise, according to Schuck, any group could force a nation like ours to undergo radical transformation merely by moving here. This no group has the right to do. Tapping neo-republican principles, the argument has proved influential in the immigration debate by supplying an ostensibly neutral principle for limiting immigration."

"And I suppose you think there's something wrong with it?"

"I do," Rodrigo replied. "The current contours of the U.S. citizenry are shaped by past immigration policies, which were overtly racist. Recently, those policies have been eased somewhat, but only a little. Thus, to ask a body of citizens like ours what sort of person they would like to let in is to invite the answer: as non-threatening and as much like us as possible. And probably in small numbers, too. If we were a more diverse society, that would not be so bad. But the way things stand, the principle of national self-determination that Schuck and others tout merely reproduces more of the same."

"So, Rodrigo, you think you have found the DNA, so to speak, that reproduces inequality for Chicanos and Hispanics. A triple dynamic, inherent in Equal Protection doctrine and contractarianism, that excludes and injures your people."

"Yes, but more than mere doctrine holds us back. If it were just that, we could make gains by working outside the legal arena, by mobilizing and educating, for example. Something happened at the conference that I think you'll find interesting. It illustrates a third way binary thinking injures Latinos. Would you like to hear?"

The Out-of-Mind Phenomenon

I nodded vigorously. "I love conference dynamics. Something zany happens at almost every one. I'd love to hear."

"It's not all that earthshaking," Rodrigo replied. "But I think it captures something. The conference, as I mentioned, featured a star-studded cast. Attendance was fairly good, even though the event was held in the law school, near the edge of campus. The curious thing is that only one law professor from the huge faculty of the host school showed up. The dean, who had been scheduled to introduce the keynote speaker, begged off at the last minute, pleading important business, and sent the associate dean instead. He didn't even stay to hear the address itself."

"Maybe they were just busy," I said a little lamely, trying to excuse my colleagues at that other school, several of whom I knew personally.

"I'm sure that's true," Rodrigo conceded. "But suppose the eminent panel of conferees had been black, consisting of Derrick Bell, Cornel West, John Hope Franklin, Leon Higginbotham, and others of that stature. In fact, the Latino speakers were just as stellar in terms of reputation and standing in their fields."

"Are you saying that attendance would have been better?" I asked.

"I'm not sure it would have been better," Rodrigo replied. "But I suspect the law faculty would have put in at least token appearances. They would have made a point of meeting the speakers, shaken their hands warmly, and told them how glad they were that they were here, how much the students needed them, and so on. They would have shown solidarity and engaged in at least a few minutes of chit-chat before, of course, taking off for their offices and their next manuscripts."

"I hope you're not saying their failure to show up was a deliberate affront?" I asked.

"More likely just a matter of priorities. On any given day, dozens of major events take place at a large university. The professors probably saw the conference as just one of many possible demands on their time, like that reception for the married students or that lecture on Proust being held across campus. No conspiracy or conscious boycott operated, but the result was the same: they didn't show up. If we'd been blacks, they would have. This has happened many times before."

"I know that faculty pretty well," I said. "What you recount is surprising. They're all liberals and deep-dyed supporters of civil rights."

"I wouldn't doubt it," Rodrigo replied. "The faculty know, on some level, that Latinos have terrible troubles and need help. But the classic, the essential racial group is blacks. If you're a liberal law professor, you donate time to the NAACP Legal Defense Fund. When someone mentions 'civil rights,' you immediately think black."

"And so Latinos are simply out of mind because of the black/white binary," I added.

"We're not part of the mindset or discourse. People don't think of us in connection with civil rights struggles. Another mechanism is geographical. Many Latinos, Chicanos for example, don't live in the cities. They're farmworkers or field hands. But when you think of civil rights, you immediately think of city problems like gangs, urban blight, segregated run-down schools, and unemployment—that afflict mainly blacks."

"Puerto Ricans are by-and-large an urban group," I pointed out.

"True, and some urban programs do include them. But many Latinos are not included, especially in the West and Southwest. They fall almost entirely outside traditional civil rights consciousness, even though their struggles with pesticides, insecticides, field sanitation, and education for their kids are just as serious as those of inner-city dwellers."

"I'm beginning to see the force of the black/white paradigm," I interjected. "It looks like it really does disadvantage Latinos."

"And I hope you'll help me figure out more ways that it does. We've touched on three."

"I'm game. Do you have others in mind?"

Practical Consequences of the Black/White Paradigm

"I think the paradigm not only has doctrinal and conceptual consequences, limiting the way we think of race and racism, but it also has highly concrete real-world ones as well."

"Do you have an example?"

"Let's say you're an employer or state bureaucrat. You are distributing assets—things of value, like benefits, contracts, or jobs. You can give a job, say, to one of two equally qualified candidates. One's a black, the other a Hispanic. You probably give it to the black. The black can sue you. He or she has all those civil rights statutes written with him or her in mind. To be sure, courts have held that Hispanics may also sue for discrimination. But the employer may not know that. And the Equal Protection Clause does not protect brown litigants as unconditionally and amply as it does blacks. The binary makes the black the prototypical civil rights plaintiff. When people read of Latinos suing for school or job discrimination, they are always a little surprised."

"Latinos ought to publicize this deficiency," I said.

"That's the problem. We have fewer leaders who could do so. Affirmative action produced a generation of college-trained black leaders and professionals beginning about thirty years ago. Today, these people are mayors of cities and members of Congress. That body boasts a long-standing Black Caucus, but only a much smaller and more recently formed Hispanic one. Also, the entire federal bench includes relatively few Latino judges. It contains many more black ones, even though the two groups' numbers are almost the same in the general population. And the reason is simple: affirmative action started earlier with blacks. Even today, the average employer thinks of affirmative action in black, not Puerto Rican, Laotian, or Chicano terms. A Laotian or Chicano law teaching candidate shows up, and even liberal law faculty have to remind themselves, 'Oh, yes, they qualify for affirmative action, too.'"

"That's a problem of mindset and conception," I said. "The way society thinks of a group—or fails to think about it—influences the way it behaves toward them. If you're out of mind because everyone is thinking in dichotomous terms, how successful will you be in having your needs noticed and addressed? Listeners may even decide you're at fault for your own predicament, a whiner when you call attention to the way no one attended your conference," I warned my young protégé.

Symbol, Myth, and the Role of the Black/White Binary

"I'll be careful," Rodrigo agreed. "But it's interesting to notice why it's necessary. I think the black/white binary conveys to everyone that there's just one group worth worrying about. People conveniently forget that the early settlers exterminated 95 percent of the Indian population, or that many Puerto Rican, Chicano, and Indochinese families are just as poor and desperate as black ones. But only the one group, blacks, has moral standing to demand attention and solicitude. Those others don't. And to make absolutely sure they don't, we deploy appropriate myths and images. Asians are the model minority—smart, quiet, sure to rise in a generation or two; Mexicans are happy-go-lucky cartoon characters or shady characters who sneak across the border, earn some money, and then send it to their families back home. No one today could get away with speaking of blacks in comparably disparaging terms, at least in public. But the national Frito-Lay Corporation used the logo of a sleeping Mexican bandito, hat pulled over his eyes, dozing under a cactus. And the imagery deployed by the political right in the English-only and immigration reform campaigns is nearly as vicious: Latinos come across as criminals, welfare loafers, and drug dealers. If we were part of the civil rights paradigm, no one would dare do this, at least so openly."

"And you think the black/white paradigm is the reason?" I asked.

"Not alone," Rodrigo replied. "But it supplies the conditions that allow it to happen. If one's prevailing cultural image is not that of a noble warrior, like Martin Luther King, but of someone who takes siestas or steals jobs from deserving Americans, why would anyone want to help you?"

"In some ways, those images of Latinos are even more devastating than the ones society has disseminated about blacks, overtly until very recently, and covertly today. They justify society not only in ignoring your misery but in making war against you."

"I'm sure you've heard of the militarized border," Rodrigo interjected.

"I have, and of the imagery that is deployed by the political right to justify it—the 'waves of immigrants,' the 'horde of welfare recipients,' the 'tide' of brown-skinned welfare mothers just waiting to have babies here so they can gain citizenship, the unassimilability of Latino people and their dubious loyalty."

"Even though Latino servicemen and women have given their lives and won medals for heroism far out of proportion to their numbers and exceeding those of every other racial group," Rodrigo interjected. "And consider the issue of language. If an immigrant French couple speaks French to each other or English with a French accent, that's considered a sign of high status and culture. A Mexican worker speaks Spanish and he or she is considered stupid or disloyal."

Later, I kept coming back to this and other conversations Rodrigo and I had had recently about the role of nonblack groups in America's future. Would a country which I had served for more than forty years as a professor and civil rights advocate adjust peaceably to a century in which whites will begin to be outnumbered by blacks and browns? And would those two groups be able to work together toward mutual goals—or would the current factionalism and distrust continue into the future, with the various minority groups competing for crumbs while majoritarian rule continued unabated?

NOTES

1. See Peter H. Schuck and Rogers M. Smith, CITIZENSHIP WITHOUT CONSENT: ILLEGAL ALIENS IN THE AMERICAN POLITY 9–41, 116–40 (1985); Peter H. Schuck, *The Transformation of Immigration Law*, 84 COLUM. L. REV. 1, 1, 4–5, 49–65, 85–90 (1984).

Chapter 54

||||||||||||||||||||||||||||||||||||||||||||||||||||||||||||||||||||||||||||||||

Chicano Indianism

Martha Menchaca

In this chapter I describe forms of racial repression experienced by people of Mexican origin living under the legal system of the United States. Because Mexican-origin people were of mestizo descent (Spanish and Indian ancestry), they were placed in an ambiguous legal position. Their Indian ancestry linked them to people of color, subjecting them to heightened racial discrimination, while their Spanish ancestry linked them to whites, protecting them from the full impact of the racial laws of the period.

U.S. Violation of the Treaty of Guadalupe Hidalgo

When the United States acquired Mexico's northern frontier, the mestizo ancestry of the conquered Mexicans placed them in an ambiguous social and legal position (Tate 1969). In the U.S. government bureaucracy, it became unclear whether Mexicans were to receive the citizenship rights of white citizens or were to be treated as Indian inhabitants. Most government officials argued that Mexicans of predominantly Indian descent should receive the same legal status as the detribalized American Indians (*People v. De La Guerra* 1870; *United States v. Joseph* 1876; *United States v. Lucero* 1869; *United States v. Santistevan* 1874). Mexicans, on the other hand, argued that under the Treaty of Guadalupe Hidalgo and international laws, the U.S. government agreed to extend all Mexican citizens—regardless of their race—the political rights enjoyed by white citizens. These rights fell under the international principle guaranteeing inhabitants of ceded territories the nationality of the successor state unless other provisions are made in the treaty of peace (Kansas 1941).

The Treaty of Guadalupe Hidalgo was exchanged and ratified in Queretaro, Mexico, on May 30, 1848, officially ending the Mexican-American War. It stipulated the political rights of the inhabitants of the ceded territory (including the Indians), set the U.S.–Mexico border, and brought several binational agreements on economic relations to closure. However, Anglo-American legislators violated the treaty and refused to extend Mexicans full political rights. The legislators were able to disenfranchise

From *Chicano Indianism: A Historical Account of Racial Repression in the United States* by Martha Menchaca, pp. 583–87, 599–600. Reprinted by permission of the American Anthropological Association from 20(3) AMERICAN ETHNOLOGIST 583–603 (1993). Not for sale or further reproduction.

many Mexicans by arguing that such people were of Indian descent and therefore could not claim the political privileges of white citizens.

Conflicting Racial Laws in the Conquered Territories

In 1848, with the end of the Mexican-American War, the United States politically disenfranchised all Indians of the Southwest by rescinding Mexico's racial laws in the newly conquered territories. Since 1812, Mexico had given Indians the right to claim citizenship and full political rights (Knight 1990; Morner 1967; *United States v. Lucero* 1869; Weber 1982). Mexico also no longer practiced a legally based racial caste system. Thus, new racial restriction policies instituted in the conquered territories came to threaten the civil rights of the Mexicans because under U.S. laws, Indians and "half-breeds" were not considered citizens (Kansas 1941; Naturalization Act of 1790, ch. 3, sec. 1; see In re *Camille* 1880).

The eradication of Mexico's racial caste system had begun in the late 1700s when the Spanish crown resolved that generations of miscegenation had thoroughly blurred racial distinctions (Knight 1990; Morner 1967). In 1812, the legal basis of the racial ranking order came to an end. The racial caste system, which for two centuries had distinguished individuals on the basis of race, became nonfunctional for political and social purposes. Its gradual breakdown resulted from the growth of the mestizo population and the political power obtained by upper-class mestizos. By the turn of the nineteenth century, the mestizos had become the majority and were heavily represented in the upper classes.

Before the breakdown of the racial caste system, Mexico's population had been divided among Spaniards, *castas*, and Indians (Lafaye 1974; Morner 1967; Vigil 1984). Distinguishing the population on the basis of parental origin had been an adequate legal method of according economic privilege and social prestige to the Spaniards. The Spaniards included both *peninsulares*, individuals who had been born in Spain and were of full European descent, and *criollos*, who were also of full European descent but had been born in the New World. As miscegenation increased among the Spanish elite, the criollo category eventually came to be redefined. The castas were mestizos and other persons of mixed blood. The Indian category included only people of full indigenous descent.

Of the various racial groups, the Spaniards enjoyed the highest social prestige and were accorded the most extensive legal and economic privileges. The legal system did not make distinctions between peninsulares and criollos. Nevertheless, the Spanish crown instituted policies requiring that high-level positions in the government and the Catholic Church be assigned to peninsulares (Haring 1963), on the rationale that they alone were fervently loyal to the Spanish crown. Exceptions were made when a new colony was established in the Americas and when a peninsular was unwilling to accept the appointment. It was required, however, that a criollo taking such an appointment be a son of peninsulares. Peninsulares were appointed to positions such as viceroy, governor, captain-general, archbishop, and bishop, whereas criollos were appointed to less prestigious positions, such as royal exchequer (treasurer, comptroller) and judge, and, after 1618, to mid-level administrative positions in the church (as priests or directors of schools).

The social and economic mobility of the rest of the population was seriously limited by the legal statuses ascribed to their ancestral groups. In theory, Indians were economically more privileged than mestizos because they held title to large parcels of communal land protected by the Spanish crown and the Catholic Church (Haring 1963; Morner 1967). However, regardless of their landed property, the Indians enjoyed little social prestige in Mexican society and were legally confined to subservient social and economic roles regulated by the Spanish elite. Most Indians were placed in *encomiendas* and *repartimientos* (Indian communities where land and labor were controlled by Spanish missionaries or government officials), Indian pueblos, or haciendas and were held in a perpetual state of tutelage. The mestizos enjoyed a higher social prestige than the Indians but were considered inferior to the Spaniards. They were also often ostracized by the Indians and the Spaniards and did not enjoy certain legal privileges accorded to those groups. For example, most mestizos were barred by royal decree from obtaining high- and mid-level positions in the royal and ecclesiastical governments (Haring 1963; Morner 1967). Moreover, the Spanish crown did not reserve land for the mestizos as it did for the Indians. For the most part, the only economic recourse most mestizos had was to enter the labor market or migrate toward Mexico's northern and southern frontiers. Each migrant who was the head of a household received 150 acres and relief from taxation for a period of approximately ten years (León-Portilla 1972; Rubel 1966; Weber 1982). After 1680, mestizos were occasionally allowed to become parish priests in Mexico's frontier settlements or in sparsely populated areas.

By the late 1700s, the rigid racial order had relaxed owing to changes in the interracial sexual and cohabitation practices of the Spanish elite (Bonifaz de Novello 1975; Morner 1967). It had become common for upper-class Spanish males to take mestizo or Indian women as concubines and afterward legitimate their offspring. In such cases the racial status of the child became criollo and not mestizos. These criollos had the racial status of Spaniards but not the corresponding legal privileges. They were barred from positions reserved for the Spaniards of full European descent and suffered certain sanctions for marrying peninsular women. By the early 1800s, large numbers of criollos, mestizos, and Indians were becoming increasingly defiant of bounded social roles and were trespassing their borders with deliberate speed. Criollos attempted to pass for peninsulares in order to obtain more social privileges. Indians often passed for mestizos in order to obtain wage labor in the urban centers, mestizos passed for Indians as a means of acquiring the land titles of the Indians (Bonifaz de Novello 1975; Morner 1967), and mestizos who had amassed great fortunes tried to improve their social standing by passing for criollos. The blurring of the racial distinctions made it difficult for the Spanish crown to enforce the laws and the prescribed social norms, in particular because the majority of the population was indistinguishably mestizo.

The final blow to the racial order came about through the political defection of the masses. By the early 1800s, movements to liberate Mexico from Spanish colonial rule had erupted throughout the country, and as a consequence the Spanish crown

attempted to avert revolutionary action by instituting the 1812 Spanish Constitution of Cadiz. The new constitution legally abolished the casta system and the racial
laws. Theoretically, the constitution conferred on Spaniards, mestizos, and Indians
the same political rights regardless of racial origin. The laws of Cadiz, however, were
unable to avert the national independence movements. In 1821, the masses won the
Mexican War for Independence and instituted a provisional constitution (the Plan de
Iguala) reaffirming the racial philosophy of the Constitution of Cadiz. After the War
of Independence, race could no longer prevent Indians and mestizos from exercis-
ing citizenship rights. For example, it became common for mestizos and full-blooded
Indians to be elected to the presidency. All subsequent Mexican constitutions ratified
the spirit and language of the Constitution of Cadiz.

In northern Mexico, the frontier experienced the same legislative changes as the
interior. Indians were considered Mexican citizens with full political rights. In New
Mexico, southern Arizona, and California the acculturated Indians and the secular-
ized mission Indians actively exercised those rights (Spicer 1962; Weber 1982). In New
Mexico numerous Pueblo Indians were elected to town and county political offices,
and in California acculturated American Indians often held high-ranking posts in the
military. Of course the new laws had limited effects on the majority of the American Indians, because Mexico held title to territories inhabited by unconquered indigenous populations. The majority of the Shoshone, Navajo, Apache, and Comanche
Indians had not been conquered by the Mexican state. And the new legislation did
not eradicate the Mexican elites' attitudes of racial and economic superiority toward
the American Indians and mestizos.

When Mexico ceded its northern territory to the United States, then, it had already abolished all racial restrictions on citizenship. The Indians had theoretically
been incorporated as Mexican citizens. In practice, of course, this legislation had not
abolished racial prejudice and discrimination in Mexico, and the Indians continued
to be stigmatized as uneducated people. However, the mestizo racial category had
taken on a new social meaning. Because most of the population was mestizo, being
mestizo had become a source of pride rather than a stigma. The European race continued to hold high social prestige in Mexico, but the masses no longer considered it
the only prestigious racial group (Knight 1990; Vigil 1984). In the legal domain, race
could no longer serve as a civil rights barrier.

The racial policies of the United States, however, were less liberal than Mexico's.
The United States at that time conferred full citizenship rights on "free whites" only.
Thus, the states' constitutional right to deny Indians U.S. citizenship introduced the
ideological and legal foundation for limiting the Mexican people's political rights.
Moreover, government officials often used the Mexicans' indigenous heritage to undermine the civil rights language of the Treaty of Guadalupe Hidalgo. Article VIII
of the treaty stated that the United States agreed to extend U.S. citizenship to all
Mexican citizens, regardless of ancestry, who remained in the ceded territories. If
individuals did not want U.S. citizenship, they had to so indicate within one year;
otherwise they would become citizens automatically. Under Article IX the United
States further agreed that Mexicans who chose to become U.S. citizens would have
all the attendant rights.

Regardless of the treaty, however, the U.S. government refused to ratify the racial equality laws of Mexico. When the annexed southwestern territories joined the Union, their state constitutions did not extend to American Indians the political rights guaranteed by the Treaty of Guadalupe Hidalgo and the Mexican constitution. And soon after the enactment of the treaty, controversy arose over the citizenship status of the Mexicans. The exclusionary Indian citizenship laws, endorsed by the southwestern legislators, became the legal basis for limiting the political rights of the Mexicans. Government representatives commonly argued that the language of the treaty and the U.S. Constitution was unclear as to whether Mexicans of Indian descent should be treated as American Indians or should be extended the privileges of whites (Surace 1982; *United States v. Joseph* 1876; *United States v. Lucero* 1869; *United States v. Ritchie* 1854; *United States v. Santistevan* 1874).

Ironically, the political privileges that the Spanish and Mexican governments had previously given people in the Southwest were abolished by the U.S. racial laws. The Mexican mestizos and Indians entered a new racial caste-like order in which their civil rights were limited. Given the nature of the U.S. racial system and its laws, the conquered Mexican population learned that it was politically expedient to assert their Spanish ancestry; otherwise they were susceptible to being treated as American Indians (Padilla 1979). At the same time, it became politically expedient for American Indians to pass for Mexican mestizos if they wished to escape the full impact of the discriminatory Indian legislation (Forbes 1973). Let us now examine how the political disenfranchisement of the Indians affected the Mexican population.

The Denial of Citizenship for American and Mexican Indians

After ratification of the Treaty of Guadalupe Hidalgo, government representatives of the annexed region began to pass new racial-restriction citizenship laws. Most American Indians were prohibited from obtaining citizenship, and the anti-Indian legislation adversely affected the Mexicans of partial or full Indian descent. Unless a Mexican was predominantly white, he or she was subject to racial harassment. Those classified as Mexican Indians were not entitled to exercise full political rights or even basic civil rights: they were not allowed to vote, practice law, marry Anglo-American women, or run for political offices such as district judge. They were also subject to severe human rights infringements, such as being placed in debt peonage and being forced to live on reservations.

After the annexation of Mexico's northern frontier, the southwestern territories and states enacted ruthless, discriminatory Indian legislation. The Anglo-American legislators were able to enforce the laws with the help of the U.S. military and the Anglo-American settlers. It became common policy to place American Indians on reservations, drive them out of the southwest, or exterminate them.

Court and legislative records from 1848 to 1947 reveal that the skin color of Mexican-origin people strongly influenced whether they were treated by the legal system as white or as non-white. During the nineteenth century, Mexican-origin individuals who were predominantly of Indian descent were subject to heightened racial discrimination. They were, for example, not allowed to become naturalized citizens if they were immigrants, to vote in the states of California and Arizona, to practice law in the state of Arizona, or to be exempted from segregationist legislation. The segregationist laws continued to affect darker-skinned Mexicans into the mid-twentieth century. Furthermore, nineteenth- and early-twentieth-century legal records indicate that although New Mexican state officials attempted to confer full citizenship privileges on "Mexicanized American Indians," the federal government rescinded their actions. In the legal domain, the federal government failed to acknowledge the existence of people who practiced both Mexican and American Indian traditions; these individuals experienced greater racial discrimination than the rest of the Mexican population. The legal records also indicate that *under the law* Mexican-origin people of predominantly Caucasian ancestry were ostensibly allowed to exercise the full political rights of citizens. In the state of Texas, for example, local governments found alternative legal methods of discriminating against Mexicans who were identified as white. In the *Independent School District v. Salvatierra* court case, it was determined that "white Mexican students" could be legally segregated if they did not speak English.

In sum, the record reveals a history of racial repression and discrimination against the Mexican-origin community in the United States. Government officials used the people's indigenous ancestry to deny them equal citizenship rights and to keep them in a politically subordinate position. Indianism was used to construct an image of Mexican-origin people as inferior and therefore deserving of separate and unequal treatment. I trust that this exploration has demonstrated the value of using legislative and judicial records as evidence that this American minority group has experienced severe racial discrimination in the United States.

REFERENCES

Bonifaz de Novello, Maria Eugenia. 1975. *La Mujer Mexicana: Analysis Historico*. Mexico City: Impresa Mexicana.

Feagin, Joe. 1989. *Racial and Ethnic Relations*. Englewood Cliffs, N.J.: Prentice Hall.

Forbes, Jack D. 1973. *Aztecas del Norte: The Chicanos of Aztlan*. Greenwich, Conn.: Fawcett.

Haring, Clarence H. 1963. *The Spanish Empire in America*. New York: Harbinger.

Hoyt, John P., comp. 1877. *The Compiled Laws of the Territory of Arizona*. Detroit: Richmond, Backus.

Kansas, Sidney. 1941. *U.S. Immigration: Exclusion and Deportation, and Citizenship of the United States of America*. 2d edition. Albany, N.Y.: M. Bender.

Knight, Allen. 1990. "Racism, Revolution, and Indigenismo: Mexico, 1910–1940." In *The Idea of Race in Latin America, 1870–1940*, ed. R. Graham, 71–113. Austin: University of Texas Press.

Lafaye, Jacques. 1974. *Quetzalcoatl and Guadalupe*. Chicago: University of Chicago Press.

León-Portilla, Miguel. 1972. "The Norteño Variety of Mexican Culture: An Ethnohistorical Approach." In *Plural Society in the Southwest*, ed. E. Spicer and R. Thompson, 77–101. New York: Weatherhead Foundation.

Morner, Magnus. 1967. *Race Mixture in the History of Latin America*. Boston: Little, Brown.

Padilla, Fernando. 1979. "Early Chicano Legal Recognition, 1846–1897." *Journal of Popular Culture* 13:564–74.

Rubel, Arthur. 1966. *Across the Tracks: Mexican Americans in a Texas City*. Austin: University of Texas Press.

Spicer, Edward. 1962. *Cycles of Conquest: The Impact of Spain, Mexico and the United States on the Indians of the Southwest, 1533–1960*. Tucson: University of Arizona Press.

Surace, Samuel. 1982. "Achievement, Discrimination, and Mexican Americans." *Comparative Studies in Society and History* 24:315–39.

Tate, Bill. 1969. *The Guadalupe Hidalgo Treaty of Peace 1848 and the Gadsden Treaty with Mexico 1853*. Truchas, N.M.: Tate Gallery and Rio Grande Sun Press.

Vigil, Diego. 1984. *From Indians to Chicanos*. Prospect Heights, Ill: Waveland Press.

Weber, David. 1982. *The Mexican Frontier, 1821–1846: The American Southwest under Mexico*. Albuquerque: University of New Mexico Press.

Chapter 55

|||||||||||||||||||||||||||||||||||||||||||||||||||||||||||||||||||||||||||||||||||

Mexican Americans as a
Legally Cognizable Class

Richard Delgado and Vicky Palacios

Long inured to their status as "the forgotten minority,"[1] few Chicanos find it surprising that, even after decades of intensive civil rights activity on behalf of Blacks, the status of Chicanos as a legally cognizable minority is still in doubt. Indeed, the law's failure strikes a familiar chord; almost every Chicano has experienced at some point in his life having the following reasoning applied against him: (1) Our firm (agency, school district) regards Chicanos as white; (2) we do not discriminate against whites; and (3) therefore, we do not discriminate against Chicanos. This argument rests, of course, on the premise that Chicanos are indistinguishable from members of the majority culture and race and are simply not a minority group for purpose of remedial action.

What is surprising is that in certain areas of civil rights litigation this same argument, albeit in a somewhat more sophisticated form, receives judicial approval. This chapter examines two of these areas: the status of Chicanos under equal protection doctrine and their status under Rule 23 governing class actions [as defined by the Federal Rules of Civil Procedure—Eds.].

Inability of Chicanos to avail themselves of "class" status severely limits the effectiveness of attempts to redress grievances through litigation. Class actions enable a single plaintiff or group of plaintiffs to sue on behalf of an entire class. This procedural device possesses the substantial advantages of economy and res judicata effect as well as considerable political and psychological impact. By the same token, access to equal protection coverage enables a plaintiff to give his complaint constitutional dimensions and thus, in certain circumstances, to secure a stricter standard of judicial review.

Are Chicanos a legally definable class? Among the characteristics common to many Chicanos are: Spanish language as the mother tongue; Mexican ancestry; Spanish surname; a distinct culture and history; a genetic heritage that results in certain recurring physical traits; economic, educational, and political exclusion from the mainstream of American life; perception by Anglos, including many government agencies, as a minority; and perception by Chicanos themselves as a non-Anglo group.

From *Mexican Americans as a Legally Cognizable Class under Rule 23 and the Equal Protection Clause*, 50 Notre Dame L. Rev. 393 (1975). Originally published in the *Notre Dame Law Review*. Reprinted by permission.

The almost mystical significance given the Spanish language as the carrier of Chicano culture has come to the attention of a number of ethnologists. A Chicano university professor has written:

> In the beginning was the Word, and the Word was made Flesh. It was so in the beginning, and it is so today. The language, the Word, carries within it the history, the culture, the traditions, the very life of [our] people. . . . We cannot even conceive of a people without a language, or a language without a people. The two are one and the same. To know one is to know the other.[2]

The refusal of Mexican Americans to surrender their native tongue has at times meant the forfeiture of substantial benefits. In schools, for example, bilingualism has often been suppressed and rarely recognized as an asset. Some states require the ability to speak English as a condition of voting or holding political office. Others require that court proceedings and legal notices be in English. Chicano persistence in retaining the use of Spanish in the face of such pressures testifies to the likelihood that Spanish usage is, and will continue to be, a partial—but highly reliable—index of membership in the Chicano class.

Another characteristic held in common by Chicanos is their ancestry. The precise characterization of this ancestry, however, has been the subject of controversy. In a study on Mexican-American education, the United States Commission on Civil Rights, which used the terms "Mexican American" and "Chicano" interchangeably, declared:

> [T]he term Mexican American refers to persons who were born in Mexico and now reside in the United States or whose parents or more remote ancestors immigrated to the United States from Mexico. It also refers to persons who trace their lineage to Hispanic or Indo-Hispanic forebears who resided within Spanish or Mexican territory that is now part of the Southwestern United States.[3]

This definition suffers from overinclusiveness, since an individual of pure Scandinavian descent who was at one time a Mexican citizen but later immigrated to the United States would qualify as a Chicano. A more accurate definition of Chicanos in terms of ancestry would be "any individual residing in the United States who traces his lineage to Indo-Hispanic or Hispanic ancestors who are living or once lived in Mexico or the Southwestern United States." Such a definition excludes Mexican citizens still living in Mexico but includes those Mexican citizens who are resident aliens. The definition would also include descendants of the colonial Spaniards with little or no Indian blood who, like the Mexican alien, identify with the culture and social goals of the Mexican American. At the same time, the requirement that Hispanic forebears come from the Southwest excludes those of Spanish descent who settled on the East Coast of the United States, since they have generally been assimilated into the dominant society and rarely identify with the culture of the Mexican American.

An additional feature shared by many Chicanos is Spanish surname. The cultural fusion of the native Meso-Americans and the Spanish was such that at one time virtually all residents of the American Southwest carried Spanish surnames. But today not all Chicanos bear Spanish surnames, nor are all persons who do, Chicano. Because of the practice of women taking the husband's surname, those Chicanas who have married Anglos no longer bear Spanish names. Similarly, the Spanish surname of a Chicano husband is carried by his Anglo wife, who may have little attachment to Chicano culture. This blurring obviously increases as generations pass. It is nonetheless true that most Chicanos still bear Spanish surnames. This is due to the tendency of Chicanos, like most ethnic minorities, to limit social interaction to members of their own group. This ethnic closure results in a relatively high incidence of ethnic intramarriage.

The most important of the ties which bind Chicanos is their culture. Culture has been termed the very essence of an individual's social identity. Marcos de Leon, a California educator, has characterized the function of the Chicano culture in the life of the individual member as "all encompassing." It comprises the group's ideas, habits, values, and institutions; it is the force that gives the group cohesion and direction. It supplies the system of beliefs that enables the group to establish social and political structures. Aesthetics also plays a part since culture includes the group's preferences with regard to the graphic and plastic arts, folklore, music, drama, and dance.

Culture, of course, manifests itself differently from community to community and even from individual to individual. Particularly in view of the geographic dispersion of Chicanos, it would be a mistake to assume that the existence of a common culture results in individuals who are carbon copies of each other. Nevertheless, the United States Commission on Civil Rights has found that "Mexican Americans share common traits, common values, and a common heritage which may be identified as components of a general Mexican American cultural pattern."[4] This pattern, the Commission concludes, "sets them apart as a distinct and recognizable group."[5] The unwillingness of the dominant society to recognize the rich culture of the Mexican American creates a tension in the lives of many Chicanos, who see themselves as forced to choose between retaining the traditions of their people and gaining the educational and economic benefits of participation in the dominant society. Most have chosen to keep their culture. However, they have had to do so at the price of being stereotyped as backward, inferior, or, at best, quaint.

An additional feature that binds Chicanos is their physical appearance. Anthropologists Benson E. Ginsberg and William S. Laughlin have written about ethnic populations and the effect of their isolation or mixture on their genetic pools. Regardless of what other implications may follow from the existence of a distinct gene pool, many Chicanos share a phenotype of physical characteristics. This common phenotype bolsters the identifiability of the Chicano class. In writing of the history of the Chicano in this country, one author tells of the halt brought to the migration of Mexican laborers into this country by Depression unemployment. To alleviate the pressures created by unemployment, the Government simply deported Mexican laborers by the carload. Their legal rights ignored, thousands fell victim to a dragnet established and enforced by federal, state, and local agencies. Even Chicanos who were United States citizens were summarily deported. Merely looking "Mexican" sufficed. "Visual identification or stereotype" was the criterion generally employed.

For centuries, Anglos have associated a combination of brown skin and certain other physical traits with people of Mexican ancestry. *Recopilación de Leyes de los Reinos de las Indias*, a 1680 compilation of nearly 200 years of law dealing with the Indians of Meso-America, expressly recognized the existence of a new "race," the mestizo of the Americas.[6] In more modern times, the United States Commission on Civil Rights has also noted the similarities in the appearance of Chicanos: "Many Mexican Americans exhibit physical characteristics of the indigenous Indian population that set them apart from typical Anglos. In fact, some Anglos have always regarded Mexican Americans as a separate racial group."[7]

In the popular mind, Mexicans have long appeared "different" from whites. One study of community attitudes toward Chicanos in Chicago in the 1940s cites a number of examples illustrating these perceptions. One resident of an Italian neighborhood, for example, was quoted as saying, "I don't want my kids to associate with the Mexicans. God made people white and black, and he meant there to be a difference."[8]

Though many of the references to the Chicano's brown color have in the past been negative, Chicanos have turned this derogatory reference into a source of pride and self-awareness, much the same way African Americans have done with the word "black." While this turnabout has done much to improve the Chicano's self-image and sensitize the Anglo to the feeling of pride Chicanos have about themselves, some still equate dark skin with inferiority. So long as this negative attitude persists, physical characteristics will continue to be another source of commonality among Chicano people.

Economic and political disenfranchisement is another aspect of life shared by Chicanos. Chicanos consistently suffer from underparticipation and over-participation in various social institutions. In public education, for example, Chicanos have one of the highest dropout rates of any ethnic group. If present trends continue, barely one-half of the Chicano school population will graduate from high school.

The reasons for this educational gap are not hard to find: poverty, language handicap, migrancy, and cultural insensitivity on the part of teachers and school administrators. Even when an individual Chicano manages to surmount these barriers and obtains a baccalaureate or graduate degree his efforts are typically not rewarded to the same extent as the Anglo's. Because of demands within his group as well as constraints imposed by discriminatory attitudes in the larger society, success-oriented Chicanos have limited opportunities to achieve educational and occupational mobility. Other studies show that minorities who attain a high level of education and enter the professions are likely to find their opinions are not as highly valued by their colleagues as are those of members of the dominant culture.

Mexican Americans have also endured exclusion from the American mainstream in the employment area. Chicanos are markedly underrepresented in the more prestigious and high-paying professions and in many of the trades. That unemployment in the Chicano sector is not merely a lingering residue of bygone discrimination is shown by the disproportionately high unemployment rate among Chicano teenagers.

Regional data indicate that the poverty many Chicanos suffer is severe enough to affect their health and longevity. One Chicano community reported an infant mortality rate five to six times the national rate for white infants. In many southwestern communities, Chicanos fall victim in disproportionate numbers to diseases associated with low socioeconomic conditions.

In certain areas, however, the Chicano can claim the dubious distinction of over-participation in American institutions. One such area is the courts and penal institutions; another, the military service. The Mexican-American casualty rate in the Vietnam war was over 50 percent higher than their proportion to the total population. This figure prompted observers to note that where government agencies have exercised diligence and sincerity in their search for minorities they have been met with success. Unlike jury commissioners and private employers, draft boards have had little difficulty finding qualified people. In Nueces County alone, over 75 percent of the men killed in Vietnam bore Mexican-American names.

In politics, despite a few isolated successes, the Chicano community as a whole remains largely voiceless. Among the reasons are attempts by some to discourage Mexican-American voting. Chicanos in some areas have experienced such discouragement by means ranging from outright intimidation to laws which endeavor to make registration difficult.

A related indicator of class separateness is community attitudes. Chicanos, like other minority groups, can recount a wide variety of personal experiences in which they have been the targets of prejudice. A California school principal told the Civil Rights Commission that he always seated the Chicano students behind the Anglo students at graduation ceremonies because he felt it made for a "better looking stage." A California teacher explained that she asked an Anglo boy to lead a row of Chicano youngsters to an activity because his father was a rancher and the boy needed to get used to giving orders to Mexicans. Another educator reported that she calls on Anglo children to assist their Chicano counterparts who hesitate in recitation because the "American" pupil is more likely to give a correct response and because it is good educational practice to draw out "American" children and give them a feeling of importance by having them help the "Mexicans."

The mass media have also contributed to the formation of negative stereotypes of the Chicano people. Tomás Martinez has analyzed the way in which advertisers promote racism by portraying stereotypes such as the "Frito Bandito." Television and newspaper commercials presenting "typical Mexican villages" or Mexican outlaws reinforce the belief that Mexicans are lazy, unambitious persons in need of underarm deodorant. Such commercials, Martinez suggests, are not harmless jokes or portrayals of cartoon characters. They are caricatures, whose function is to reaffirm symbolically the inferior social status of Mexicans and Mexican Americans in the eyes of the American public. In so doing, the advertisements suggest to the audience that such comical, lazy, and unkempt people want what Anglos have by virtue of their superior culture. The advertisements encourage the viewer to purchase the product because it is the duty of a member of the superior culture.[9]

The final index of the Chicano's separateness is the perception he has of himself and his people. Much of what the Chicano feels about himself can be learned from the terms he chooses to identify his cultural group. One such term which has come into use is *la Raza*. Although literally translated "the race," the phrase more properly connotes the cultural and historical ties which unite Spanish-speaking people. An early forerunner of this designation was "la Raza Cosmica," a phrase coined by the nineteenth-century philosopher Jose Vasconcelos, who believed that Mexicans would form the cosmic, ideal people because of their particular blood mixture. This theory is said to have been the Mexican response to Anglo-Nordic historians who considered the Mexicans inferior half-breeds. Meier and Rivera write of the term la Raza that it connotes "not racial but ethnic solidarity, and a sense of common destiny."[10] Another commentator states: "La Raza has become more than a slogan: it has become a way of life for a people who seek to fully realize their personal and group identity, and obtain equality of rights and treatment as citizens of the United States."[11] It is this sense of a common destiny which illustrates the feeling of community in the use of *la Raza*.

More and more Mexican Americans are choosing to refer to themselves as "Chicano." The word itself is said to be a shortened version of "Mexicano," pronounced perhaps at one time by the Mexican Indians as "Meh-chee-cano." This term has undergone a number of changes in meaning. Originally it was derogatory, and many older Mexican Americans still consider it so and refuse to use it. Later it came into popular use among the more militant Chicanos, and to some it still connotes militancy. More recently, however, "Chicano" has been used by Mexican Americans as a symbol of awareness and pride in their ethnic identity. In *Chicano Manifesto* Armando Rendon writes:

> I am a Chicano. What that means to me may be entirely different from what meaning the word has for you. To be Chicano is to find out something about one's self which has lain dormant, subverted, and nearly destroyed.[12]

Although Chicano problems are not new, Mexican-American self-awareness, so long unvoiced, is perhaps best expressed by activists in the Chicano movement. Rendon characterizes the revolt as "primarily an internal conversion," entailing an expansion of the individual's personality, background, and future as the individual Chicano perceives that all have traveled the same paths, suffered the same indignities, and undergone the same deprivation. He then realizes that while some may have adjusted and survived better than others by adopting the Anglo's ways, all are bound by "a common birthplace; a common history, learned from books or by word of mouth; and a common culture much deeper than the shallow Anglo reservoir."[13] This growing realization increases the Chicano's sense of identity and unity with other Chicanos and strengthens his desire to work for the enhancement of equal opportunity for his people in every phase of American life.

Chicanos have a word to express the kinship they feel—*carnalismo*. The closest literal translation would be "brotherhood," but *carnalismo* expresses much more. Of *pachuco*[14] origin, *carnalismo* carries with it the unique frame of reference the Chicano's history has given him.

Taken together, the class characteristics discussed thus far demonstrate that the Chicano falls outside the mainstream of American life for many purposes. He is not in any sense an average American. His heritage and ancestry, his present welfare and future goals are at variance with those of the dominant society. It is these variances that make the Chicano a separate and identifiable class.

NOTES

1. See, e.g., UNITED STATES COMMISSION ON CIVIL RIGHTS, STRANGER IN ONE'S LAND (1970); Cruz Reynoso, et al., *La Raza, the Law, and the Law Schools,* 1970 U. TOLEDO L. REV. 809, 815–16 (1970).

2. Armando B. Rendon, CHICANO MANIFESTO 29–30 (1971).

3. UNITED STATES COMMISSION ON CIVIL RIGHTS, MEXICAN AMERICAN EDUCATION STUDY, REPORT 1: ETHNIC ISOLATION OF MEXICAN AMERICANS IN THE PUBLIC SCHOOLS OF THE SOUTHWEST 7 n.1 (1971).

4. U.S. COMMISSION ON CIVIL RIGHTS, MEXICAN AMERICAN EDUCATION STUDY, REPORT 3: THE EXCLUDED STUDENT 30 (1972).

5. *Id.*

6. Rendon, at 67.

7. THE EXCLUDED STUDENT, at 11.

8. Rendon, at 24.

9. Tomás M. Martinez, *Advertising and Racism: The Case of the Mexican American,* in VOICES: READINGS FROM *EL GRITO* 48, edited by Octavio Romano-V, 1971.

10. Matt S. Meier and Feliciano Rivera, THE CHICANOS: A HISTORY OF MEXICAN AMERICAN AMERICANS xix (1972).

11. UNITED STATES COMMISSION ON CIVIL RIGHTS, THE MEXICAN AMERICAN 69 (1968).

12. Rendon, at 319.

13. *Id.* at 113.

14. David F. Gomez, SOMOS CHICANOS—STRANGERS IN OUR LAND xii (1973).

‖‖

Chapter 56

Mexican Americans and Whiteness

George A. Martinez

During slavery, the racial divide between black and white became a line of protection from the threat of commodification: whiteness protected one against being an object of property. Even after slavery ended, it continued to be a valuable asset, carrying with it a set of assumptions, privileges, and benefits. Given this, it is hardly surprising that minorities have often sought to "pass" as white—i.e., present themselves as white persons. They did so because they thought that becoming white insured greater economic, political, and social security. Becoming white, they thought, meant gaining access to a panoply of public and private privileges, while insuring that one would avoid being the object of others' domination.

In light of the privileged status of whiteness, it is instructive to examine how legal actors—courts and others—constructed the race of Mexican Americans. In *Inland Steel Co. v. Barcelona*,[1] an Indiana appellate court addressed the question of whether Mexicans were white. The court noted that the *Encyclopedia Britannica* stated that approximately one-fifth of the inhabitants of Mexico are whites, approximately two-fifths Indians and the balance made up of mixed bloods, blacks, Japanese, and Chinese. Given this, the court held that a "Mexican" should not necessarily be found to be a white person.[2] This required a case-by-case determination.

The Texas courts also considered the same question. In *In re Rodriguez*,[3] a Texas federal court addressed whether Mexicans were white for purposes of immigration. At that time, the federal naturalization laws required that an alien be white in order to become a citizen of the United States. The court stated that Mexicans would probably be considered non-white from an anthropological perspective,[4] but went on to note that the United States had entered into treaties with Mexico that expressly allowed Mexicans to become citizens of the United States. Thus, the court held that Congress must have intended that Mexicans were white within the meaning of the naturalization laws. *In re Rodriguez* reveals how racial categories can be constructed through the political process. Through the give and take of treaty making, Mexicans became "white."

Other cases show how politics operated to turn persons of mixed blood into whites or the opposite. In immigration cases, mixed-race applicants often failed to establish their whiteness. For example, in *In re Camille*,[5] the court held that the son of a white Canadian father and an Indian mother was non-white, and therefore not eligible to naturalize. Similarly, in *In re Young*,[6] the son of a German father and a Japanese mother was not a white person within the meaning of the immigration laws.[7] If these cases stand for the proposition that mixed-race persons were not white, Mexicans—a mixture of Spanish and Indian—should not have counted as white. The treaties nevertheless operated to turn them into whites.

The issue of the race of Mexican Americans also arose in connection with school segregation. In *Independent School District v. Salvatierra*,[8] plaintiffs sought to enjoin segregation of Mexican Americans in the city of Del Rio, Texas. There, the court treated Mexican Americans as white, holding that Mexican Americans could not be segregated from children of "other white races, merely or solely because they are Mexicans."[9] Significantly, the court did permit segregation of Mexican Americans on the basis of linguistic difficulties and migrant farming patterns.

Mexican-American jury participation and exclusion also show how the race of Mexican Americans is constructed. For example, in *Hernandez v. State*, a Mexican American had been convicted of murder. He sought to reverse his conviction on the ground that Mexican Americans had been excluded from the grand jury and the petit jury, relying on cases holding that exclusion of blacks from jury service violated due process and equal protection. The court recognized only two classes as falling within the guarantee of the Fourteenth Amendment: the white race and the black. It went on to hold that Mexican Americans are white for purposes of the Fourteenth Amendment. The court reasoned that to hold that the members of the various groups comprising the white race must be represented on grand and petit juries would destroy the jury system.[10] Since the juries that indicted and convicted the defendant were composed of members of his race—white persons—he had not been denied the equal protection of the laws.[11]

On review, the United States Supreme Court also imposed a group definition on Mexican Americans. The court held in *Hernandez v. Texas*[12] that "persons of Mexican descent" are a cognizable group for equal protection purposes in areas where they were subject to local discrimination—but not otherwise.[13] Defining Mexican Americans in terms of the existence of local discrimination hinders Mexican Americans in asserting their rights because not every plaintiff can afford the expense of obtaining expert testimony to prove local prejudice.

Similarly, in *Lopez Tijerina v. Henry*,[14] the court refused to allow Mexican Americans to define themselves as a group. Plaintiffs sought to bring a class action on behalf of a class of "Mexican Americans" in order to secure equal educational opportunity in local schools. The court rejected the claim for class representation, holding that the term "Mexican American" was too vague and failed adequately to define a class within the meaning of Rule 23 of the Federal Rules of Civil Procedure, governing class actions. Since the class was not adequately defined, the court dismissed the class action complaint.

Class actions permit a lawsuit to be brought by large numbers of persons whose interests are sufficiently related so that it is more efficient to adjudicate their rights in a single action. As such, it may represent the only viable procedure for people with small claims to vindicate their rights. The *Lopez Tijerina* case, then, erected a barrier in the way of Mexican Americans wishing to resist oppression.

Subsequently, other courts permitted Mexican Americans to sue as a class under Rule 23 by distinguishing *Tijerina* under the *Hernandez* rationale that local prejudice rendered the class sufficiently identifiable. Thus, the courts defined Mexican Americans in terms of local prejudice, a definition which, for the reasons discussed above, operated to the disadvantage of Mexican Americans in their efforts to assert their rights under Rule 23.

Federal agencies also constructed the race of Mexican Americans. The federal government has long compiled census data on persons of Mexican descent. In 1930, the Census Bureau made the first effort to identify Mexican Americans. The Bureau used the term "Mexican" to classify Mexican Americans, placing it under the rubric of "other races," which also included Indians, Blacks, and Asians. According to this definition, Mexican Americans were not considered "whites." Interestingly, the Mexican government and the United States Department of State both objected to the 1930 census definition of Mexican. Thus, in later years, Mexican Americans were classified as whites.

White identity traditionally has served as a source of privilege and protection. Since the law often recognized Mexican Americans as white, one might have expected that social action would have reflected that status. That, however, was not the case. Legal recognition of the Mexican American as white had only a slight impact on conduct. Far from enjoying a privileged status, Mexican Americans faced discrimination very similar to that experienced by African Americans. Excluded from public facilities and neighborhoods and the targets of racial slurs, Mexican Americans typically lived in one section of town because they were not permitted to rent or own property anywhere except in the "Mexican Colony."[15] Segregated in public schools, Mexican Americans also faced significant discrimination in employment. Mexican Americans were earmarked for exclusive employment in the lowest brackets of employment and paid less than Anglo Americans for the same jobs.[16] Moreover, law enforcement officials have committed widespread discrimination against Mexican Americans, arresting them on pretexts and meting out harassment and penalties disproportionately severe compared to those imposed on Anglos for the same acts.[17] In all these respects, actual social behavior failed to reflect the legal norms that defined Mexican Americans as white. Although white as a matter of law, that law failed to provide Mexican Americans with a privileged status.

At one point, discrimination against Mexican Americans in Texas became so flagrant that the Mexican Ministry of Labor declared that Mexican citizens would not be allowed to go there. In 1943, Mexican Foreign Minister Ezequiel Padilla informed Texas that Mexican citizens would be allowed to go to Texas only after the wave of racial prejudice had subsided. In response, the Texas legislature, on May 6, 1943, passed a resolution that established as a matter of Texas public policy that all Caucasians were entitled to equal accommodations. Subsequently, Mexican Americans attempted to rely on the resolution and sought to claim one of the traditional benefits of whiteness—freedom from exclusion from public places. In *Terrell Wells Swimming Pool v.*

Rodriguez,[18] Jacob Rodriguez sought an injunction requiring a swimming pool operator to offer equal accommodations to Mexican Americans. Plaintiff argued that he could not be excluded from the pool on the basis of his Mexican ancestry because that would violate the public policy expressed in the resolution condemning discriminatory practices against all persons of the white race. The court refused to enforce the policy on the ground that the resolution did not have the effect of a statute. Thus, Mexican Americans could not claim one of the most significant benefits of whiteness —freedom from exclusion from public places.

The legal construction of Mexican Americans as white thus stands as an irony —thoroughly at odds with the colonial discourses that developed in the American Southwest. As happened in other regions of the world the colonizers engaged in epistemic violence—i.e., produced modes of knowing that enabled and rationalized colonial domination from the standpoint of the West.[19]

In sharp contrast to their legal construction as white, writers and other Anglo opinion-makers plainly constructed Mexican Americans as irreducibly Other. The historian David Weber writes:

> Anglo Americans found an additional element to despise in Mexicans: racial mixture. American visitors to the Mexican frontier were nearly unanimous in commenting on the dark skin of the Mexican mestizos, who, it was generally agreed, had inherited the worst qualities of Spaniards and Indians to produce a "race" still more despicable than that of either parent.[20]

Similarly, another commentator described how Anglo Americans drew a racial distinction between themselves and Mexican Americans:

> Racial myths about the Mexicans appeared as soon as Mexicans began to meet Anglo American settlers in the early nineteenth century. The differences in attitudes, temperament and behavior were supposed to be genetic. It is hard now to imagine the normal Mexican mixture of Spanish and Indian as constituting a distinct "race," but the Anglo Americans of the Southwest defined it as such.[21]

Likewise, the dean of Texas historians, Walter Prescott Webb, wrote:

> Without disparagement it may be said that there is a cruel streak in the Mexican nature, or so the history of Texas would lead one to believe. This cruelty may be a heritage from the Spanish of the Inquisition; it may and doubtless should be attributed partly to the Indian blood.[22]

Through this discourse on the Mexican American, Anglo Americans also reformulated their white selves. Anglo judges, as we have seen, did the same, ruling that Mexicans were co-whites when this suited the dominant group—and non-white when necessary to protect Anglo privilege and supremacy.

NOTES

1. 39 N.E.2d 800 (Ind. 1942).

2. *Id.* at 801.

3. 81 F. 337 (W.D. Tex. 1897).

4. *Id.* at 349.

5. 6 F. 256 (1880).

6. 198 F. 715 (1912).

7. *Id.* at 716–17. The court observed:

In the abstractions of higher mathematics, it may be plausibly said that the half of infinity is equal to the whole of infinity; but in the case of a concrete thing as the person of a human being it cannot be said that one who is half white and half brown or yellow is a white person, as commonly understood.

198 at 717.

8. 33 S.W.2d 790 (Tex. Civ. App. 1930). *Salvatierra* was the first case to decide the issue of whether segregation of Mexican Americans in public school was permissible.

9. *Id.* at 795.

10. 251 S.W.2d 531, 532, 535 (Tex. 1952).

11. *Id.* at 536. In *Sanchez v. State*, 243 S.W.2d 700 (1951), a Mexican American had been convicted of murder. He sought to challenge his conviction on the ground that his due process rights had been violated because the county had discriminated against Mexican Americans in the selection of grand jurors. The Texas court held that Mexican Americans are not a separate race, but are white people of Spanish descent. 243 S.W.2d, at 701. Thus the defendant's rights were not violated because whites were not excluded from the grand juries.

12. 347 U.S. 475 (1954).

13. *Id.* at 477–79.

14. 48 F.R.D. 274 (D.N.M. 1969).

15. Pauline R. Kibbe, Latin Americans in Texas 123–24 (1946).

16. Carey McWilliams, North from Mexico 167, 215–16 (1948); Kibbe, at 157.

17. U.S. Commission on Civil Rights, *Mexican Americans and the Administration of Justice in the Southwest* (Summary) 2 (1970).

18. 182 S.W.2d 824 (Tex. Civ. App. 1944).

19. Ruth Frankenberg, White Women, Race Matters: The Social Construction of Whiteness 16–17 (1993). See also Robert Young, White Mythologies: Writing History and the West 127, 158, 173 (1990); Edward W. Said, Orientalism 228 (1978).

20. Foreigners in Their Native Land: Historical Roots of the Mexican Americans 59–60 (David J. Weber ed., 1973).

21. Joan W. Moore, Mexican Americans 1 (1970). See also Rodolfo Acuña, Occupied America: The Chicano's Struggle toward Liberation (1972) at 7.

22. Walter Prescott Webb, The Texas Rangers: A Century of Frontier Defense xv (1965).

Chapter 57

|||||||||||||||||||||||||||||||||||||||||||||||||||||||||||||||||||||||||||||||||||

Mexican Americans and the
Faustian Pact with Whiteness

Neil Foley

In 1980 the U.S. Bureau of the Census created two new ethnic categories of Whites: "Hispanic" and "non-Hispanic." The Hispanic category, an ethnic rather than racial label, comprised Mexicans, Puerto Ricans, Cubans, Panamanians, and other ethnic groups of Latin American descent. Creating a separate ethnic category within the racial category of White seemed to solve the problem of how to count Hispanics without racializing them as non-Whites, as it had done in 1930. To identify oneself today as a "Hispanic" is partially to acknowledge one's ethnic heritage without surrendering one's "whiteness." Hispanic identity thus implies a kind of "separate but equal" whiteness—whiteness with a twist of salsa, enough to make one ethnically flavorful and culturally exotic without, however, compromising one's racial privilege as a White person. The history of Mexican Americans in the Southwest is thus more than the history of their "becoming" Mexican American or Hispanic; for many, especially those of the middle class, it is also the history of their becoming White.

Unlike Black Americans, who experienced de jure segregation throughout the South before 1960, Mexican Americans in the Southwest experienced de facto segregation based on custom rather than statutory authority. Legally, Mexican Americans enjoyed the racial status of White people; socially, politically, and economically, however, they were treated as non-Whites. With the rise of the so-called Mexican American generation of the 1930s, '40s, and '50s, Mexican Americans began insisting on their status as Whites in order to overcome the worst features of Jim Crow segregation, restrictive housing covenants, employment discrimination, and the social stigma of being "Mexican," a label that, in the eyes of Anglos, designated race rather than citizenship status.

Many middle-class Mexican Americans did not object to the segregation of Blacks or challenge the assumptions of White supremacy. On the contrary, they supported strict segregation of Whites and Blacks in the schools and in public facilities. The basis for their claim for social equality was that they were also White, that some unfortunate mistake had been made in regarding persons of Mexican descent as non-Whites.

A group of Mexican Americans, mostly urban and middle class, founded their own organization in 1929 in Corpus Christi, the League of United Latin American Citizens (LULAC), to foster the goals of Americanization in Texas and other states of the Southwest, restricting membership to U.S. citizens and emphasizing English language skills and loyalty to the Constitution of the United States. LULAC members sought to set the racial record straight. In a 1932 article in the *LULAC News* titled "Are Texas-Mexicans 'Americans'?" the author asserted that Mexican Americans were "the first white race to inhabit this vast empire of ours." Another member of LULAC boasted that Mexican Americans were "not only a part and parcel but as well the sum and substance of the white race." As such, LULAC members considered it "an insult" to be associated with Blacks or other "colored" races. In 1936 a LULAC official deplored the practice of hiring "Negro musicians" to play at Mexican *bailes* (dances) because it led to "illicit relations" between Black men and "ill-informed Mexican girls." He urged fellow LULAC members to "tell these Negroes that we are not going to permit our manhood and womanhood to mingle with them on an equal social basis." Not surprisingly, therefore, LULAC, the premier civil rights group for Mexican Americans, turned its back on opportunities to forge ties with the NAACP during its own civil rights battles in the 1940s and 1950s. The African American author and Nobel Prize winner Toni Morrison deserves credit for stating bluntly what many Mexican Americans have been slow to acknowledge: "In race talk the move into mainstream America always means buying into the notion of American blacks as the real aliens."

Unlike the experience of most immigrants, however, discrimination against Mexicans in the United States has been continuous, pervasive, and systemic. After Mexican Americans established LULAC and the G.I. Forum (founded in 1948), they challenged school segregation and other forms of discrimination in state and federal courts. While these organizations and their middle-class Mexican American leaders sought equality based on their constitutional rights as U.S. citizens, increasingly they came to the realization that race—specifically, being White—mattered far more than U.S. citizenship in the course of everyday life.

LULAC members and other urban Mexican Americans constructed new identities as "Spanish American" or "Latin American" in order to arrogate to themselves the privileges of whiteness routinely denied to Mexicans, Blacks, Chinese, and Indians. Becoming Spanish or Latin American also enabled Mexican Americans to distance themselves from recently arrived Mexican immigrants who were often illiterate, poor, non-English-speaking, and dark skinned. Mexican Americans thus began to object strenuously to being labeled as "colored" or forced to share facilities with Black Americans. Increasingly, middle-class Mexican Americans during the thirties and forties began to call themselves "Spanish" and insist on their whiteness.

The discourse on "hispanismo," the movement in the early twentieth century to celebrate Spanish culture in Spain's former colonies, created the cultural context for celebrating "Spanishness" or European whiteness in the Southwest and for denigrating indigenous Indian "Mexicanness," thereby laying the cultural groundwork for Mexicans desiring to pass into "hispanicity." "Old Spanish Days" festivals were invented throughout the Southwest to celebrate Spain's heritage in America while ignoring totally the culture and historical role played by Mexico in the formation of Southwestern culture. The White West discovered Spanish America and created monuments, like Balboa Park in San Diego, for tourists to marvel at, while Spain itself sought to inculcate in its former colonies a love of *la raza hispana.*

Some Mexican Americans were therefore mortified when Anglo Americans made no effort to distinguish between "Spanish" or "White" Mexicans and "Indian" Mexicans, which also became a source of irritation to the Mexican government. Mexican consuls frequently complained that Mexican citizens were not being treated like White people in the United States. In 1933 the Mexican consul in Dallas wrote a county sheriff to protest that a Mexican citizen had been jailed "with the negro prisoners" instead of with the Anglos. "It is my opinion," the Mexican consul general wrote to the sheriff, "that there is no reason for segregating Mexicans from white Americans, inasmuch as they are both of the white race."

Mexican Americans had learned that the courts ended officially sanctioned segregation of Mexicans only when they insisted on their status as Whites. But how was one to become de facto White as well as de jure White? LULAC members had tried just about everything they could to prove how Americanized they were: they spoke English, voted, used the court systems, got elected to office, actively opposed Mexican immigration, and excluded Mexican citizens from membership in LULAC. They organized baseball teams and ate quantities of hot dogs. What more could they do to assimilate whiteness? Assimilation, however, is not only about what one leaves behind; it is also about what one is moving toward, what one acquires in the process of cultural exchange and fusion.

For many immigrant groups, assimilation, in part, meant becoming "American," which is also to say, becoming White. And becoming White, Toni Morrison has written, means that "A hostile posture toward resident blacks must be struck at the Americanizing door before it will open," adding that African Americans have historically served the "less than covert function of defining whites as the 'true' Americans." As with other ethnic groups in the past—Italians, Poles, and Irish, for example—for Mexican Americans the path to whiteness required not so much losing one's culture as becoming wedded to the notion that people of African descent were culturally and biologically inferior to Whites.

Growing numbers of middle-class Mexican Americans thus made Faustian bargains that offered them inclusion within whiteness provided that they subsumed their ethnic identities under their newly acquired White racial identity and its core value of White supremacy. Pedro R. Ochoa, owner of Ochoa Auto Parts and publisher of the weekly six-page paper *Dallas Americano*, was a staunch White supremacist during the 1950s and printed headlines such as "conserva su raza blanca" (preserve your White race) and "segregacion es libertad" (segregation is liberty). In his own column, which he signed "Pedro el Gringo," he urged Latino citizens to identify themselves as "americano" or American because, he wrote, the "Latin, Mexican, and European are foreigners." He regarded Mexican Americans who joined with African Americans in the struggle for civil rights as race traitors and encouraged his readers to join the "Spanish Organization of White People." In a Spanish editorial titled "No use nopal como almohada" ("don't use a cactus as a pillow"), Ochoa wrote: "The American GI Forum, LULAC, the NAACP, chambers of commerce, and other nigger groups ["agrupaciones niggerianas"] have consistently promoted integration to raise the equality, intelligence, and superiority of the black race." Ochoa strongly believed that every improvement in the lives of Black Americans came at the expense of Latino Americans and that only by keeping Blacks down could marginally White Mexicans raise themselves up.

Ochoa sought to lead his people from alien Mexican to native White by rejecting Mexicanness in favor of Americanness and whiteness. Like the protagonist in Américo Paredes's bildungsroman, George Washington Gómez, Ochoa had become the George Washington of White Mexicans. In Paredes's novel of a Mexican American becoming White during the 1930s and '40s, the protagonist, George Washington Gómez, leaves his South Texas home to attend the University of Texas in Austin, where he earns a degree, joins the Army, and is sent back to the border during World War II as an intelligence officer to spy on his own people. When his uncle, Feliciano García, rebukes him for turning his back on his own people, the Mexican Texans or *tejanos*, George Washington Gómez responds angrily: "Mexicans will always be Mexicans. A few of them . . . could make something of themselves if they would just do like I did . . . get rid of their Mexican Greaser attitudes." More recently, Richard Rodriguez, author of the memoir *Hunger of Memory*, viewed the generational gap between himself and his immigrant Mexican parents in ethnoracial as well as cultural terms: they would always be "Mexicans," but he had become "American," a George Washington Rodriguez, whose education and English fluency had given him access to White privilege, which he exalted as the goal of all immigrant groups.

Today many Hispanics enjoy the "wages of whiteness" as a result of a complex matrix of phenotype, class position, culture, and citizenship status, as well as the willingness of many Anglos to make room for yet another group of off-white Hispanics. Still, many persons of Mexican descent, especially recent immigrants, are excluded from the domain of whiteness. A dark-skinned non-English-speaking Mexican immigrant doing lawn and garden work does not share the same class and ethnoracial status as acculturated, educated Hispanics. Hispanicized Mexican Americans themselves often construct a "racial" gulf between themselves and "illegal aliens" and "wetbacks."

The lure of whiteness continues to divide various Mexican constituencies along both race and class lines in their fractured, and often fractious, struggles for civil rights. By examining how law (naturalization, segregation, and miscegenation), comparative civil rights politics (e.g., LULAC and NAACP), labor disputes, culture (e.g., "hispanismo"), religion (e.g., evangelical Protestantism), and literary works have constructed whiteness, often in conflicting and contradictory ways, such a study can illuminate the peculiarly hybrid identities of Mexican Americans and explore the historical roots of the tension between the Hispanic and African American communities, analogous to that which has developed between Jews and Blacks, in the context of these groups' particular orientations toward whiteness.

lll

Race and Erasure
The Salience of Race to Latinos/as

Ian F. Haney López

On September 20, 1951, an all-White grand jury in Jackson County, Texas, indicted twenty-six-year-old Pete Hernández for the murder of another farm worker, Joe Espinosa. Gus García and John Herrera, lawyers with the League of United Latin American Citizens (LULAC), a Mexican-American civil rights organization, took up Hernández's case, hoping to use it to attack the systematic exclusion of Mexican Americans from jury service in Texas.[1] García and Herrera quickly moved to quash Hernández's indictment, arguing that people of Mexican descent were purposefully excluded from the indicting grand jury in violation of the Fourteenth Amendment's guarantee of equal protection of the laws. The lawyers pointed out, and the State of Texas stipulated, that while 15 percent of Jackson County's almost thirteen thousand residents were Mexican Americans, no such person had served on any jury commission, grand jury, or petit jury in Jackson County in the previous quarter century.[2] Despite this stipulation, the trial court denied the motion. After two days of trial and three and a half hours of deliberation, the jury convicted Hernández and sentenced him to life in prison.

On appeal, García and Herrera renewed the Fourteenth Amendment challenge. It again failed. The Texas Court of Criminal Appeals held that "in so far as the question of discrimination in the organization of juries in state courts is concerned, the equal protection clause of the Fourteenth Amendment contemplated and recognized only two classes as coming within that guarantee: the white race, comprising one class, and the Negro race, comprising the other class."[3] The Texas court held that the Fourteenth Amendment did not cover Mexican Americans in cases of jury discrimination.

With the assistance of Carlos Cadena, a law professor at St. Mary's University in San Antonio, the LULAC attorneys took the case to the United States Supreme Court. On May 3, 1954, Chief Justice Earl Warren delivered the unanimous opinion of the Court in *Hernandez v. Texas*, extending the aegis of the Fourteenth Amendment to Pete Hernández and reversing his conviction. The Court did not do so, however, on the ground that Mexican Americans constitute a protected racial group. Rather, the Court held that Hernández merited Fourteenth Amendment protection because he belonged to a class, distinguishable on some basis "other than race or color," that nevertheless suffered discrimination in Jackson County, Texas.[4]

Hernandez is a central case—the first Supreme Court case to extend the protections of the Fourteenth Amendment to Latinos/as, it is among the great early triumphs in the Latino/a struggle for civil rights. *Hernandez* attains increased significance, however, because it is also the principal case in which the Supreme Court addresses the racial identity of a Latino/a group, in this instance Mexican Americans. No Supreme Court case has dealt so squarely with this question, before or since. This point is all the more striking, and *Hernandez* all the more exceptional, because at least on the surface the Court refused to consider Mexican Americans a group defined by race or color. If theorists intend, as I believe we should, to use race as a lens and language through which to assess the Latino/a experience in the United States, we must come to terms with the elision of race in *Hernandez*.

Race and Erasure

In the *United States Reports, Hernandez* immediately precedes another leading Fourteenth Amendment case, *Brown v. Board of Education*, having been decided just two weeks before that watershed decision. Despite extending the reach of the Fourteenth Amendment by unanimous votes, the two cases differ dramatically. In *Brown*, the Court grappled with the harm done through segregation, but considered the applicability of the Equal Protection Clause to African Americans a foregone conclusion. In *Hernandez*, the reverse was true. The Court took for granted that the Equal Protection Clause would prohibit the state conduct in question, but wrestled with whether the Fourteenth Amendment protected Mexican Americans. Nevertheless, as in *Brown*, stark evidence of racism permeates *Hernandez*.

As catalogued by the Court, the evidence in the case revealed the following: First, residents of Jackson County, Texas, routinely distinguished between "white" and "Mexican" persons. Second, business and community groups largely excluded Mexican Americans from participation. Third, until just a few years earlier, children of Mexican descent were required to attend a segregated school for the first four grades, and most children of Mexican descent left school by the fifth or sixth grade. Fourth, at least one restaurant in the county seat prominently displayed a sign announcing "No Mexicans Served." Fifth, on the Jackson County courthouse grounds at the time of the underlying trial, stood two men's toilets, one unmarked, and the other marked "Colored Men" and "Hombres Aqui" ("Men Here"). Finally, with respect to jury selection itself, a stipulation recited that "for the last twenty-five years there is no record of any person with a Mexican or Latin American name having served on a jury commission, grand jury or petit jury in Jackson County," a county 15 percent Mexican American.[5]

In their brief to the Court, Hernández's lawyers placed heavy emphasis on this history of discrimination:

While the Texas court elaborates its "two classes" theory, in Jackson County, and in other areas in Texas, persons of Mexican descent are treated as a third class—a notch above the Negroes, perhaps, but several notches below the rest of the population. They are segregated in schools, they are denied service in public places, they are discouraged from using non-Negro rest rooms. . . . They are told that they are assured of a fair trial at the hands of persons who do not want to go to school with them, who do not want to give them service in public places, who do not want to sit on juries with them, and who would prefer not to share rest room facilities with them, not even at the Jackson County court house.[6]

"The blunt truth," Hernández's lawyers insisted, "is that in Texas, persons of Mexican descent occupy a definite minority status."[7]

The Paradox of Race

Responding to the Texas court's pronouncement that regarding juries the Fourteenth Amendment contemplated only the White and Black races, the Supreme Court could have ruled that the Fourteenth Amendment protected other races as well. But it did not. Instead, while acknowledging that "[t]hroughout our history differences in race and color have defined easily identifiable groups which have at times required the aid of the courts in securing equal treatment under the laws," the Court went on to say that "from time to time *other differences* from the community norm may define other groups which need the same protection."[8] According to the Court, to prevail on his claim Hernández had to show that he was discriminated against as a member of a group marked by inchoate "other differences." Explaining this requirement, the Court suggested that "[w]hether such a group exists within a community is a question of fact,"[9] one that "may be demonstrated by showing the attitude of the community."[10] It is in its effort to assess the community attitudes toward Mexican Americans in Jackson County that the Court recited the litany of racism previously noted. Thus, the Court's finding that Hernández met the other-difference/community-attitude test rested squarely on detailed evidence of what fairly may be characterized as widespread racial discrimination.

In light of the Court's heavy reliance on the abovementioned evidence of racial discrimination, its insistence that Mexican Americans do not constitute a race seems surprising. It seems all the more startling when one recalls that at the time the Court decided *Hernandez*, national hysteria regarding Mexican immigration was running high, and also in light of evidence of possible racist antipathies toward Mexican Americans on the Supreme Court itself.[11] In part, the Court's reticence to acknowledge the cases may have stemmed from the manner in which all parties characterized Mexican Americans as racially White.

In addition, however, the Court's assessment of the evidence in *Hernandez* was no doubt informed by the contemporary conception of race as an immutable natural phenomenon and a matter of biology—Black, White, Yellow, or Red, races were considered natural, physically distinct groupings of persons. Races, the Court no doubt supposed, were stable and objective, their boundaries a matter of physical fact and common knowledge, consistent the world over and across history.

The Court thus could not help but be perplexed by the picture of Mexican-American identity presented in *Hernandez*, an identity that at every turn seemed inconstant and contradictory. Though clearly the object of severe racial prejudice in Texas, all concerned parties agreed Mexican Americans were White; though officially so, the dark skin and features of many Mexican Americans seemingly demonstrated that they were non-White. A biological view of race positing that each person possesses an obvious, immutable, and exclusive racial identity cannot account for, or accept, these contradictions. Under a biological view of race, the force of these contradictions must on some level have served as evidence that Mexican Americans did not constitute a racial group. Thus, the Court insisted in the face of viscerally moving evidence to the contrary that the exclusion of Mexican Americans from juries in Jackson County, Texas, turned neither on race nor color.

Nevertheless, *Hernandez* is virtually unintelligible except in racial terms—in terms, that is, of racial discrimination, of segregation, of Jim Crow facilities, of social and political prejudice, of exclusion, marginalization, devaluation. That despised identity developed in Texas over the course of more than a century of Anglo-Mexican conflict. In the early years of the nineteenth century, White settlers from the United States moving westward into what was then Spain, and after 1821, Mexico, clashed with the local people, eventually giving rise to war between Mexico and the United States in 1846. During this period, Whites in Texas and across the nation elaborated a Mexican identity in terms of innate, insuperable racial inferiority. According to historian Reginald Horsman, "By the time of the Mexican War, America had placed the Mexicans firmly within the rapidly emerging hierarchy of superior and inferior races. While the Anglo-Saxons were depicted as the purest of the pure—the finest Caucasians—the Mexicans who stood in the way of southwestern expansion were depicted as a mongrel race, adulterated by extensive intermarriage with an inferior [Native American] race."[12] These views continued, and were institutionalized, over the remainder of the last century and well into this one. According to historian Arnoldo De León "in different parts of [Texas], and deep into the 1900s, Anglos were more or less still parroting the comments of their forbears. . . . They regarded Mexicans as a colored people, discerned the Indian ancestry in them, identified them socially with blacks. In principle and in fact, Mexicans were regarded not as a nationality related to whites, but as a race apart."[13] Texas institutionalized this racial prejudice against persons of Mexican descent in the various ways catalogued by *Hernandez*. It is in the attitudes toward and the treatment of Mexican Americans, rather than in human biology, that one must locate the origins of Mexican-American racial identity.

In this sense, the solution to the racial paradox posed in *Hernandez* lies within the "community attitudes" test advanced by the Court. The Court propounded this test as a measure of whether Mexican Americans exist as a distinct, though non-racial, group. In fact, no more accurate test could be fashioned to establish whether Mexican Americans, or any group, constitute a race. Race is not biological or fixed by nature; it is instead a question of social belief. Thus, albeit unwittingly, the *Hernandez* opinion offered a sophisticated insight into the nature of race: whether a racial group exists is always a local question to be answered in terms of community attitudes. To be sure, race is constructed through the interactions of a range of overlapping discursive communities, from local to national, ensuring that divergent and conflicting conceptions of racial identity exist within and among communities. Nevertheless, understanding race as "a question of community attitude" emphasizes that race is not biological but social. Therein lies the irony of the Court's position: avoiding a racial understanding of *Hernandez* in part due to a biological conception of race, the Court nevertheless correctly understood that the existence of Mexican Americans as a (racial) group in Jackson County turned, as race does, not on biology but on community attitudes.

Mexican American Racial Identity: White, Then and There

For LULAC, the racial identity of Mexican Americans had long been a troubling question. Founded in 1929 in Texas by members of the small Mexican-American middle class, this organization stressed both cultural pride and assimilation. These twin goals were not without their tensions, however, particularly with respect to the question of racial identity. Emphasizing the former often led LULAC to identify Mexican Americans as a distinct race. For example, LULAC's first code admonished members to "[l]ove the men of your race, take pride in your origins and keep it immaculate; respect your glorious past and help to vindicate your people"; its constitution announced, "[w]e solemnly declare once and for all to maintain a sincere and respectful reverence for our racial origin of which we are proud."[14] On the other hand, focusing on assimilation and the right to be free of widespread discrimination, LULAC often emphasized that Mexican Americans were White. "As descendants of Latins and Spaniards, Lulacers also claimed 'whiteness,'" according to historian Mario García. "Mexican Americans as 'whites' believed no substantive racial factor existed to justify racial discrimination against them."[15] To a certain extent, LULAC resolved the tension between seeking both difference and sameness by pursuing these on distinct planes: difference in terms of culture and heritage, but sameness regarding civil rights and civic participation.

This tension notwithstanding, the decision to defend Pete Hernández constituted part of LULAC's strategy of fighting discrimination against Mexican Americans through the Texas courts. This strategy dictated as well the decision of the lawyers for Hernández to argue that Mexican Americans were White. As Mario García writes: "In [its] antisegregation efforts, LULAC rejected any attempt to segregate Mexican Americans as a nonwhite population. . . . Lulacers consistently argued that Mexicans were legally recognized members of the white race and that no legal or physical basis existed for legal discrimination."[16] For Hernández's attorneys, the decision to cast Mexican Americans as White was a tactical one, in the sense that it reflected the legal and social terrain on which they sought to gain civil rights for their community. On this terrain, being White was strategically key.

While Hernández's lawyers characterized Mexican Americans as White in order to combat discrimination and promote integration, the Texas court did not share those motives in assigning Mexican Americans the same racial identity. The Texas Court of Criminal Appeals' characterization of Mexican Americans as White in *Hernandez* must be viewed in light of that court's prior decisions addressing discrimination against Mexican Americans in the selection of juries. The criminal court had addressed this question on at least seven previous occasions between 1931 and its decision in *Hernandez* in 1952, consistently ruling against the Mexican-American defendant. The court had not, however, been consistent in its racial characterization of Mexican Americans.

One cannot know the exact motivations behind the Texas appellate court's decision in *Hernandez* or the preceding cases to categorize Mexican Americans as White. Certainly, precedent existed for such a racial determination. For example, as early as 1897, a federal district court in Texas recognized persons of Mexican descent as "white persons" in the context of federal naturalization law, under which being White was a prerequisite for citizenship. Moreover, during the period when *Hernandez* was decided both the national government and the government of Texas moved officially to qualify Mexican Americans as White. Thus, in contrast to the 1930 census, which catalogued "Mexicans" as a distinct race, the 1940 census classified "[p]ersons of Mexican birth or ancestry who were not definitely Indian or of some other nonwhite race . . . as white."[17] Contemporaneously, Governor Stevenson of Texas reacted to a decision by the Mexican Ministry of Labor to restrict the migration of *bracero* workers to Texas "because of the number of cases of extreme, intolerable racial discrimination" by initiating a state "Good Neighbor Policy."[18] This policy formally proclaimed Mexican Americans valued state citizens and, more importantly, "members of the Caucasian race" against whom no discrimination was warranted.[19] The Texas Court of Criminal Appeals did not specifically cite these factors in its decisions characterizing Mexican Americans as White. Nevertheless, this larger trend toward according Mexican Americans White status, of which the LULAC campaign was a contributing part, may well have added to the court's growing sense between 1946 and 1952 that Mexican Americans were White persons.

At the time the appellate court in *Hernandez* adopted a White conceptualization of Mexican Americans, the judicial rationale for rejecting claims of racial discrimination against members of that community was fast wearing thin. By 1952, persons challenging the exclusion of Mexican Americans from juries could point, as Hernández's lawyers did, to research indicating that in at least fifty Texas counties with large Mexican-American populations, no Mexican American had ever been called for jury service. They could also demonstrate convincingly that many Mexican Americans qualified for jury service, a point the state stipulated to in *Hernandez*. Finally, a full panoply of Supreme Court cases held that the Fourteenth Amendment prohibited jury discrimination of the sort apparently practiced against Mexican Americans—a roll call of cases on which, as the LULAC lawyers noted in their brief to the Court, "the State of Texas is more than proportionately represented."[20]

Against this backdrop of massive discrimination, purposeful and directed litigation, fast accumulating evidence, and clear constitutional law, the local practices of jury exclusion in Texas counties were increasingly difficult to uphold. Declaring that the Fourteenth Amendment did not protect Mexican Americans in the context of jury selection may have been the most expeditious manner by which the appellate court could immunize such local discriminatory practices. Proclaiming that Mexican Americans were White, and hence, incapable of being the victims of racial discrimination, may have been simply the means to that end. This may not have been the court's sole motivation, but it was likely the principal one.

The Salience of Race

The Supreme Court in *Hernandez* rejected a racial understanding of Mexican Americans in part because it subscribed to a conception of race as something natural and therefore stable, fixed, and immutable. Today we know race is none of these. Instead, race is always contingent on the time, place, and people involved. Racial identity turns not simply or even primarily on genetics or skin color but on the competing social meanings ascribed to ancestry and integument, and assigned as well to other aspects of identity, such as language, dress, religion, and so on. Certainly, all of these different factors contributed to the racialization of Mexican Americans in Texas in the sense of both fueling the belief in Mexican-American difference and in serving as confirmation and signifiers of that difference.

It may seem, however, that given the contingencies of race, the Court nevertheless was ultimately correct in deciding *Hernandez* on a non-racial basis. Even had the Court understood race as a social construction, one might argue, it may still have been the wiser course to decide *Hernandez* without reference to race. After all, the Court struck down the challenged discriminatory practices as it would have under a racial approach, but it managed to do so without inscribing the myth that races are real. Under this reading of the case, *Hernandez* would stand not only for the proposition that race is a social construction, but also for the proposal that, having recognized this, we dispense with the concept of race altogether.

Such a reading of *Hernandez* would not be without proponents. Prominent scholars such as Anthony Appiah have argued that we should abandon the idea of race itself. "The truth is that there are no races," Appiah writes, and "there is nothing in the world that can do all we ask race to do for us."[21] Good reasons argue for the call to discard all notions of race. Race comes to us out of some of the most terrible shadows of our past, only to find us in a present where race continues to justify the centering of some as privileged and empowered, and the expulsion of others as beyond the boundaries of society's care. Retaining race makes the work of racists easier, while it potentially traps anti-racists in injurious myths of difference. Concluding that race is a social construction, it might make sense simply to jettison the entire scheme.

If good reasons argue for repudiating all notions of race, even better ones do so with respect to Latinos/as. Latinos/as historically have not been as consistently racialized as other groups, such as Whites and African Americans. This is especially so regarding Latinos/as or Hispanics as a whole, since these categories are of recent vintage, though it is also true regarding constituent groups such as Mexican Americans or Puerto Ricans. Perhaps the arguments against thinking about groups in racial terms—that it reinforces racism, encourages subscription to false racial essences, and foments balkanization—apply with greater force to a group or groups not already primarily constructed in racial terms. Put differently, if it is true that race can be transcended most easily in the case of a heterogeneous population such as Latinos/as, the arguments for leaving race behind may be all the more difficult to reject with respect to this group. In this way, a praxis of deracination animated by a constructionist understanding of race dovetails with general calls for a non-racial conception of Latinos/as. Should we heed those calls, and eschew race? For a range of reasons, I do not believe so.

The Experience of Race

To begin with, rejecting race as a basis for conceptualizing Latino/a lives risks obscuring central facets of our experiences. Reconsider the evidence of discriminatory treatment at the root of *Hernandez*. In Jackson County, Mexican Americans were barred from local restaurants, excluded from social and business circles, relegated to inferior and segregated schooling, and subjected to the humiliation of Jim Crow facilities, including separate bathrooms in the halls of justice. Each of these aspects of social oppression substantially affected, although of course even in their totality they did not completely define, the experience of being Mexican American in Jackson County at mid-century.

To attempt to fathom the significance of such experiences, imagine being present at the moment that García called his co-counsel at trial, John Herrera, to testify about the segregated courthouse bathrooms. In picturing this episode, keep in mind that Herrera's ties to Texas stretched back at least to the original 1836 Texas Declaration of Independence, which was signed by his great, great-grandfather, Col. Francisco Ruiz, one of two Mexicans to sign that document. As excerpted from the trial court transcript, Herrera's testimony progressed like this:

Q: During the noon recess I will ask you if you had occasion to go back there to a public privy, right in back of the courthouse square?
A: Yes, sir.
Q: The one designated for men?
A: Yes, sir.
Q: Now did you find one toilet there or more?
A: I found two.
Q: Did the one on the right have any lettering on it?
A: No, sir.
Q: Did the one on the left have any lettering on it?
A: Yes, it did.
Q: What did it have?
A: It had the lettering "Colored Men" and right under "Colored Men" it had two Spanish words.
Q: What were those words?
A: The first word was "Hombres."

Q: What does that mean?

A: That means "Men."

Q: And the second one?

A: "Aqui," meaning "Here."

Q: Right under the words "Colored Men" was "Hombres Aqui" in Spanish, which means "Men Here"?

A: Yes, sir.[22]

Under cross-examination by the district attorney, Herrera continued:

Q: There was not a lock on this unmarked door to the privy?

A: No, sir.

Q: It was open to the public?

A: They were both open to the public, yes, sir.

Q: And didn't have on it "For Americans Only," or "For English Only," or "For Whites Only"?

A: No, sir.

Q: Did you undertake to use either one of these toilets while you were down here?

A: I did feel like it, but the feeling went away when I saw the sign.

Q: So you did not?

A: No, sir, I did not.[23]

By themselves, on paper, the words are dry, disembodied, untethered. It is hard to envision the Jackson County courtroom, difficult to sense its feel and smell; we cannot hear García pose his questions; we do not register the emotion perhaps betrayed in Herrera's voice as he testified to his own exclusion; we cannot know if the courtroom was silent, solemn and attentive, or murmurous and indifferent. But perhaps we can imagine the deep mixture of anger, frustration, and sorrow that would fill our guts and our hearts if it were we—if it were we confronted by that accusatory bathroom lettering, we called to the stand to testify about the signs of our supposed inferiority, we serving as witnesses to our undesirability in order to prove we exist.

In this country, the sort of group oppression documented in *Hernandez*, the sort manifest on the bathroom doors of the Jackson County courthouse, has traditionally been meted out to those characterized as racially different, not to those simply different in ethnic terms. It is on the basis of race—on the basis, that is, of presumably immutable difference, rather than because of ethnicity or culture—that groups in the United States have been subject to the deepest prejudices, to exclusion and denigration across the range of social interactions, to state-sanctioned segregation and humiliation. In comparison to ethnic antagonisms, the flames of racial hatred in the United States have been stoked higher and have seared deeper. They have been fueled to such levels by beliefs stressing the innateness, not simply the cultural significance, of superior and inferior identities. To eschew the language of race is to risk losing sight of these central racial experiences.

Racial Conditions

Race should be used as a lens through which to view Latinos/as in order to focus attention on the experiences of racial oppression. However, it should also direct our attention to racial oppression's long-term effects on the day-to-day conditions encountered and endured by Latino/a communities. Consider in this vein the segregated school system noted in *Hernandez*. Jackson County's segregation of Whites and Mexican Americans typified the practices of Texas school boards: although not mandated by state law, from the turn of the century, school boards in Texas customarily separated Mexican-American and White students. In his study of the Mexican-American struggle for educational equality in Texas, Guadalupe San Miguel writes:

> School officials and board members, reflecting the specific desires of the general population, did not want Mexican students to attend school with Anglo children regardless of their social standing, economic status, language capabilities, or place of residence. . . . Wherever there were significant numbers of Mexican children in school, local officials tried to place them in facilities separate from the other white children.[24]

Though it should be obvious, it bears making explicit that racism drove this practice. A school superintendent explained it this way: "Some Mexicans are very bright, but you can't compare their brightest with the average white children. They are an inferior race."[25] According to San Miguel, many Whites "simply felt that public education would not benefit [Mexican Americans] since they were intellectually inferior to Anglos."[26] To be sure, as in Jackson County, school segregation in Texas was most pronounced in the lower grades. However, also as in that county, this fact reflects not a lack of concern with segregation at the higher grades, but rather the practice of forcing Mexican-American children out of the educational system after only a few years of school. The segregated schooling noted in *Hernandez* constitutes but one instance in a rampant practice of educational discrimination against Mexican Americans in Texas and across the southwest.

Using the language of race forces us to look to the pronounced effects on minority communities of long-standing practices of racial discrimination. These effects can be devastating in their physical concreteness, as evidenced by the dilapidated schoolhouse for the Mexican-American children in Jackson County's Edna Independent School District. According to the testimony of one frustrated mother, the "Latin American school" consisted of a decaying one-room wooden building that flooded repeatedly during the rains, with only a wood stove for heat and outside bathroom facilities, and with but one teacher for the four grades taught there. Such effects may also be personal and intangible, though not for those reasons any less real, dire, or permanent. In Jackson County, as in the rest of Texas, the Mexican-American children subject to state-sanctioned segregation no doubt suffered grave harm to their sense of self-worth and belonging—feelings of inferiority embossed on their hearts and minds in ways unlikely ever to be undone, in the language of Chief Justice Warren.[27]

Irrespective of their form, the conditions produced by racism profoundly degrade the quality of life of non-White community members while also limiting their future chances. Consider in this regard the net educational impact of school segregation on Jackson County's Mexican-American community. In their brief to the Court, the LULAC attorneys sought to establish that at least some Mexican Americans residing in Jackson County possessed sufficient education to serve as jurors; the evidence they cited from the 1950 census proved this. Of the 645 persons of Spanish surname in that county over the age of 24, the lawyers informed the Court, "245 have completed from 1 to 4 years of elementary schooling; 85 have completed the fifth and sixth years; 35 have completed 7 years of elementary schooling; 15 have completed 8 years; 60 have completed from one to three years of high school; 5 have completed 4 years of high school; and 5 are college graduates."[28] Although these figures prove that some Mexican-Americans were educationally qualified to serve as jurors, they also demonstrate the impact of that county's systematic educational discrimination against Mexican Americans. The figures tell us, for example, that out of the Mexican American adult population of 645 in Jackson County, only five had completed college. Consider also two additional numbers from the census that the lawyers do not cite: First, out of that population of 645, fully 175 had received no formal education whatsoever; second, the median number of school years completed was a dismal 3.2 years.[29] The net educational impact of segregation on Mexican Americans in Jackson County was nothing short of disastrous.

None but the fewest and most fortunate Mexican Americans raised in the 1950s in Jackson County, Texas, could escape the grinding poverty dictated for them by the racial prejudices of Whites there. Because these conditions circumscribe the lives people can reasonably expect to live in this society, racial language remains a salient vocabulary for discussing socially constituted communities, never more so than when those communities have been severely subordinated in racial terms.

NOTES

1. Gustavo C. García, *An Informal Report to the People*, in A COTTON PICKER FINDS JUSTICE! THE SAGA OF THE HERNANDEZ CASE (Ruben Munguia ed., 1954).

2. Hernandez v. State, 251 S.W.2d 531, 533 (Tex. Crim. App. 1952).

3. *Id.* at 535.

4. Hernandez v. Texas, 347 U.S. 475, 477, 479–80 (1954). The Court suggested, but did not explicitly rule, that this "other basis" corresponded to ancestry or national origin. *Id.* at 479.

5. *Id.* at 481, 480.

6. Brief for Petitioner at 28–29, Hernandez v. Texas 347 U.S. 475 (No. 406).

7. *Id.* at 13.

8. *Hernandez*, 347 U.S. at 478 (emphasis added).

9. *Id.*

10. *Id.* at 479.

11. Mark Tushnet brings to light revealing comments regarding Mexican Americans made by Justice Tom Clark during a 1952 conference discussion of the segregation decisions:
Clark, in a statement which, apart from its racism, is quite difficult to figure out, said that Texas "also has the Mexican problem" which was "more serious" because the Mexicans were "more retarded," and mentioned the problem of a "Mexican boy of 15 . . . in a class with a

negro girl of 12," when "some negro girls [would] get in trouble." Mark V. Tushnet, MAK-
ING CIVIL RIGHTS LAW: THURGOOD MARSHALL AND THE SUPREME COURT, 1936–1961, at 194
(1994). Tushnet adds: "These references capture the personal way the justices understood the
problem they were confronting, and the unfocused quality suggests that they were attempting
to reconcile themselves to the result they were about to reach." *Id.* Clark, formerly the Civil
District Attorney for Texas and a Truman appointee to the Court in 1949, was replaced on the
bench by Thurgood Marshall in 1967. William Lockhart et al., CONSTITUTIONAL RIGHTS AND
LIBERTIES: CASES, COMMENTS, QUESTIONS 1433–35 (8 ed., 1996).

12. Reginald Horsman, RACE AND MANIFEST DESTINY: THE ORIGINS OF AMERICAN RA-
CIAL ANGLO-SAXONISM 210 (1981).

13. Arnoldo De León, THEY CALLED THEM GREASERS: ANGLO ATTITUDES TOWARD
MEXICANS IN TEXAS 1821–1900, at 104 (1983).

14. Mario T. García, MEXICAN AMERICANS: LEADERSHIP, IDEOLOGY, AND IDENTITY,
1930–1960, at 30–31 (1989).

15. *Id.* at 43.

16. *Id.* at 48. The insistence by many in the Mexican-American community that they be
considered White was also fueled by prejudice harbored against Blacks.

17. UNITED STATES DEPARTMENT OF COMMERCE, SIXTEENTH CENSUS OF THE UNITED
STATES: 1940: CHARACTERISTICS OF THE POPULATION 3 (1943).

18. Carey McWilliams, NORTH FROM MEXICO: THE SPANISH-SPEAKING PEOPLE OF THE
UNITED STATES 270 (1949, Greenwood 1972).

19. *Id.* at 270–71.

20. Brief for Petitioner at 29, Hernandez v. Texas, 347 U.S. 475 (No. 406).

21. Kwame Anthony Appiah, IN MY FATHER'S HOUSE: AFRICA IN THE PHILOSOPHY OF
CULTURE 45 (1992).

22. Transcript of Hearing on Motion to Quash Jury Panel and Motion to Quash the Indictment, State v. Hernandez (Dist. Ct. Jackson Co., Oct. 4, 1951) (No. 2091), Record at 74–75.

23. *Id.* at 76.

24. Guadalupe San Miguel, Jr., "LET ALL OF THEM TAKE HEED": MEXICAN AMERICANS
AND THE CAMPAIGN FOR EDUCATIONAL EQUALITY IN TEXAS, 1910–1981, at 54–55 (1987).

25. *Id.* at 32, citing Paul S. Taylor, AN AMERICAN-MEXICAN FRONTIER: NUECES COUNTY,
TEXAS (1934) (specific page attribution not given).

26. *Id.* at 51.

27. Brown v. Board of Education, 347 U.S. 483, 494 (1954).

28. Brief for Petitioner at 19, Hernandez v. Texas, 347 U.S. 475 (No. 406).

29. U.S. Bureau of the Census, U.S. CENSUS OF POPULATION: 1950. VOLUME IV: SPECIAL
REPORTS: PERSONS OF SPANISH SURNAME, 36–67 (1953).

Chapter 59

|||||||||||||||||||||||||||||||||||||||||||||||||||||||||||||||||||||||||||||||||||||

Brown over "Other White"

Mexican Americans' Litigation Strategy in School Desegregation Lawsuits

Steven H. Wilson

The landmark 1954 decision *Brown v. Board of Education* has shaped trial lawyers' approaches to litigating civil rights claims and law professors' approaches to teaching the law's powers and limitations. The court-ordered desegregation of the nation's schools, moreover, inspired subsequent lawsuits by African Americans aimed at ending racial distinctions in housing, employment, and voting rights. Litigation to enforce the *Brown* decision and similar mandates brought slow but steady progress and inspired members of various other minorities to appropriate the rhetoric, organizing methods, and legal strategy of the African American civil rights struggle. Yet Mexican Americans were slow to embrace *Brown*. A prominent minority with a history of successfully litigating, they instead drew upon a different line of judicial opinions to vindicate their own community's civil rights claims.

In the years that followed *Brown*, Mexican American lawyers—in numerous complaints, briefs, and courtroom arguments—continued to rely on this other canon. They disregarded *Brown*'s usefulness to achieving their goals and distanced their clients' particular claims from the constitutional implications of the *Brown* decision. Because the Mexican American lawyers maintained this separate path, the revolution in civil rights litigation that commenced with *Brown* by-passed Mexican Americans until the late 1960s.

The Divide between African and Mexican American Litigation

Attorneys of the NAACP's Legal Defense Fund, Inc. (LDF, or the "Inc. Fund") aimed first to desegregate graduate programs, including law schools, then shifted their efforts to the lower grades. They enjoyed successes and suffered reversals, but steadily laid the groundwork for victory in *Brown*, in which Chief Justice Earl Warren declared for the unanimous U.S. Supreme Court that race-based public school segregation denied the nation's African American students the equal protection of the laws, because "[s]eparate educational facilities [we]re inherently unequal." The Court encouraged high expectations in their follow-up decision, in which the justices charged federal district judges to oversee locally tailored plans for school desegregation. The *Brown* case, in fact, was at once the culmination of one long campaign of organized litigation and the beginning of another struggle that aimed to enforce the ruling and so to fulfill the promise of equal protection embedded in the Fourteenth Amendment.

Like that of African Americans, Mexican Americans' legal activity was shaped by the experience of living in a Jim Crow society. Yet most of the old southern states recognized only two racial categories: "colored" and "white." Under the relevant statutes in Texas, for example, Hispanic Mexican-descended persons were, as judges phrased it, members of one of the "other white races." Mexican Americans faced discrimination by the dominant Anglos despite an equal status under the law, but Mexican Americans clearly experienced discrimination differently than did African Americans. Mexican Americans thus responded to discrimination differently as well. What surprises, looking back from the perspective of the early twenty-first century, is how often lawyers who established the Mexican Americans' legal "canon" employed arguments—which were also based on the Fourteenth Amendment—that called for better policing of the existing boundaries of Jim Crow, rather than for the dismantling of the system. Often, the impetus for a suit was an objection that Mexican Americans had been or were being denied the privileges of their "whiteness" under Jim Crow. This generally meant that Mexican Americans stressed that discriminatory practices that had not been sanctioned by statute were a denial of due process—rather than a denial of equal protection—guaranteed under the Fourteenth Amendment.

Mexican American plaintiffs frequently prevailed in their due process claims. Two drawbacks to this approach emerged over time, however. First, because they led merely to the maintenance of the status quo, such victories could not advance the terms of the argument over Mexican Americans' rights. Second, success bred an overreliance on the winning arguments. Mexican American lawyers continued to employ this strategy even as evidence mounted that a legal argument that had proven sound during the Jim Crow era became counterproductive when Jim Crow was constitutionally doomed. The Mexican American legal community would not abandon the "other white" argument for nearly fifteen years. Only in the late 1960s did they finally seek judicial recognition that Mexican Americans were an "identifiable ethnic minority in the United States" and therefore deserving of equal protection. [*Cisneros v. Corpus Christi ISD*—Eds.]

James DeAnda and the Traditional Approach

James DeAnda, an attorney at the forefront of the late-1960s effort to change the terms of the Mexican American claims from due process to equal protection, himself had often used the "other white" argument in the courtroom. DeAnda was born in 1925 in Houston, Texas, to parents who had been among the thousands of Mexican nationals who migrated north early in the twentieth century to escape the revolutionary chaos in their native country. Yet, although the DeAndas were not native-born Texans, their son had access to the best public education that the state of Texas offered. DeAnda took his B.A. from Texas A&M University in 1948 and earned a law degree at the University of Texas at Austin two years later. His ability to attend these two premier public institutions was unremarkable; middle-class Mexican Americans like DeAnda had been admitted to Texas A&M and U.T. Austin for years. The coincidence that the Supreme Court ordered the desegregation of the U.T. law school, in *Sweatt v. Painter* (1950), the same year that DeAnda graduated, underscored that Mexican Americans fell outside the standard racial equation.

DeAnda recalled decades later that he personally had faced few obstacles in his college career that he clearly could ascribe to an anti-Mexican prejudice. Yet, DeAnda made no overt efforts to enlighten his fellow students if they assumed—as some did, apparently basing the assumption on his Mediterranean-sounding name and olive complexion—that he was of Italian, rather than Mexican, descent. DeAnda's experiences after graduation indicate why he might have chosen to leave mistakes uncorrected. Like many U.T. law graduates, he applied to the elite firms in Houston. He saw promising leads vanish unexpectedly, however, and suspected that the reason was that the prospective employers had learned that his parents had been born in Mexico. DeAnda ultimately did find work in Houston, with another Mexican-descended attorney, John J. Herrera. As he worked with Herrera, DeAnda became aware that less-privileged Mexican-descended persons faced more overt and worse discrimination than he had. This led him to support the economic and social uplift of all Mexican Americans. His support often took the form of lending professional expertise to litigation seeking to vindicate Mexican American civil rights.

DeAnda soon discovered the peculiarities of making Fourteenth Amendment claims in cases featuring Mexican Americans—which meant employing "other white" arguments. A recurring obstacle to these efforts was the difficulty of demonstrating to an individual judge's satisfaction that for Mexican Americans the practical results of "otherness" often trumped the formal status of "whiteness." Lawyers had to accomplish this tricky business without actually undermining their general appeal to the privileges that attached to whiteness. The result was a balancing act, and, ultimately, a self-defeating constitutional argument. Eventually DeAnda came to recognize that "other white" legal arguments were a dead-end and put the Mexican American civil rights effort back on track by appealing to *Brown*.

Becoming an "Official" Minority

Many of the established leaders within the Mexican American community resisted the Chicano movement's innovations. Yet a variety of tools that proved helpful in refashioning ethnic identity became available to the mainstream leaders during the 1960s. The 1964 Civil Rights Act (CRA), for example, which authorized federal officials to withhold funds from states that allowed racial discrimination, also extended similar protections to "national origin" minorities. The statute authorized the U.S. Department of Health, Education, and Welfare (HEW) to issue goals and guidelines for school desegregation. In a 1965 ruling the federal appeals judges for the Fifth Circuit declared that federal district judges should give "great weight" to the HEW standards.

The value of the Fifth Circuit's endorsement was limited for a time by the conservatism of HEW's Office of Civil Rights (OCR). As it investigated allegations of racial discrimination, OCR initially collected and published statistics only within black and white categories. But many school districts had turned the "other white" argument to their own illegitimate purposes. In order to delay the court-ordered desegregation of all-white schools, and also to obscure its slow pace, school district officials in Texas and elsewhere frequently assigned African and Mexican Americans to the same schools, a practice often made easier under a neighborhood school concept by the close proximity of urban ghettos to barrios. School administrators maintained that because Mexican Americans were "white," these schools had been desegregated under *Brown* and its progeny. Federal judges and HEW examiners had accepted this logic.

HEW examiners began to accumulate evidence of discrimination against Mexican Americans only after Hector Garcia, in his new role as a member of the U.S. Civil Rights Commission, rebuked OCR for failing to answer Mexican Americans' complaints. In 1967, HEW began publishing data on black, white, and "other" groups. The last category included "any racial or national origin group for which separate schools have in the past been maintained or which are recognized as significant 'minority groups' in the community." Later, HEW published separate statistics on "Spanish Surnamed Americans" and issued a series of "Mexican-American Studies." Yet, despite the emergence around the same time of a new militant attitude, this shift from official "other white" status to "other minority" confused some Mexican Americans of both the younger and the older generations. One student at Texas A&I University, which later emerged as a hotbed of Chicano activism, wrote a column in the October 1967 issue of the liberal magazine *Texas Observer*. He complained about the Washington bureaucracy's misguided attempt, or perhaps it was a clever ploy, to make "the second largest minority group in the country non-White."

A Legal Defense Fund for Mexican Americans

The year 1967 saw a turning point in litigation strategy, unrelated to James DeAnda's efforts, when San Antonio attorney Pete Tijerina obtained a $2.2 million, multi-year grant from the Ford Foundation. Tijerina used it to found the Mexican American Legal Defense and Educational Fund (MALDEF), which he consciously modeled on the NAACP's LDF. When the U.S. Civil Rights Commission held hearings in San Antonio in December 1968, Commissioner Garcia invited Tijerina to describe why he had organized MALDEF. Tijerina said that his experience in defending Mexican American criminal defendants before all-Anglo juries—and this a decade after the U.S. Supreme Court condemned discriminations in jury selection—had convinced him that a legal defense organization was needed. Tijerina also decried the great expense of private litigation and called on the U.S. government to fight discrimination against Mexican Americans. He assured the commissioners, however, that he sought only to broaden the scope of federal efforts, not to compete with black civil rights efforts.

As contrasted with recently increased federal support of African Americans, Tijerina noted, the government had never intervened in a civil rights lawsuit involving Mexican Americans or filed an *amicus* brief to support them.

Tijerina did not wait for assistance from Washington. Instead, as *amicus curiae,* MALDEF legal expertise and funds ultimately supported a suit filed by DeAnda that finally confronted and overcame the "other white" legacy. The shift required the lawyers to recognize that most of the Mexican American segregation in Texas was not the result of illegitimate testing in schools, but long-term residential patterns. Under the judicially approved "freedom-of-choice" plans for desegregation, Mexican American parents could not transfer their children into Anglo-majority schools—since, according to existing interpretations of laws, all Mexican American students were already enrolled in "white" schools. Before Mexican American civil rights advocates could attack the segregation created by "neighborhood" schools, under the constraints of "freedom of choice," they had to overcome Mexican Americans' equivocal minority status. DeAnda finally led the retreat from the strategic ground that he had helped conquer during the 1950s. In a path-breaking suit against the large urban Corpus Christi Independent School District (CCISD) he formally contended that the *Brown* rationale should apply to—and condemn as a clear denial of equal protection —the widespread segregation of Mexican Americans. [He was successful when a district court held, for the first time in a major school-desegregation case, that Latinos are a minority group under the *Brown* equal protection line of cases, including *Mendez.*—Eds.]

The Legacy of Brown *and the Pragmatism of the Lawyers*

James Patterson reminds readers of his recent reexamination of *Brown v. Board of Education,* whose legitimacy, from the moment that Chief Justice Warren read the unanimous ruling, many contested. But early criticism contributed less to the case's "troubled legacy," as Patterson describes it, than the fact that, fifty years after *Brown,* scholars continued to debate not only the legitimacy, but the social, political, educational, and legal meaning of this controversial milestone. Legal scholar Derrick Bell was more convinced of the decision's basic meaning. In his estimation *Brown* "triggered a revolution in civil rights law," because it increased African American plaintiffs' "leverage" in the nation's courtrooms. The decision ended the constitutional support of state-supported segregation—which existed across the nation but was most notorious in the southern Jim Crow regime—and raised blacks' expectations that federal judges would at long last begin to enforce their rights under the Fourteenth Amendment. Real progress toward formal equality for blacks, of course, required the enactment of civil rights legislation and local litigation to enforce the new laws through judicial decisions. Significant political and social change came slowly and only with boycotts, marches, and martyrdom. Nevertheless, African Americans justifiably celebrate the *Brown* decision as a turning point in their history.

The legacy of *Brown* is more troubled for Mexican Americans. In the years immediately following the decision, it was reasonable for Mexican American lawyers to regard the decision as applicable only to the sort of discrimination suffered by African Americans. Because popular racism as well as some official biracial classifications survived *Brown*, it was also reasonable for them to rely on tried and true approaches. The legal profession is naturally conservative—not in terms of political ideology, but in terms of respecting and recognizing settled and preferably favorable precedent. The changes in African Americans' political and social positions that had developed during the decade after *Brown* did not mean that similarly conservative federal judges would—if asked to do so—agree to overlook a well-established jurisprudence, recognize Mexican Americans as a *de jure* minority, and grant equitable relief under *Brown*.

Why did Mexican Americans lawyers finally seek to appropriate the "revolutionary" *Brown* decision and so stake a claim to the judicially administered equitable remedies available through the equal protection clause? Critics of the legal profession as well as detractors of remedial civil rights programs such as affirmative action would likely argue that the Mexican American lawyers were opportunistic and cynical—that they sought certain legislatively derived benefits and finally hit upon the proper formula for obtaining them. Why else, critics (themselves cynics) might ask, would legal representatives of an ethnic group proud of its historically mainstream identity suddenly seek to obtain judicial recognition that their clients were in fact members of a minority that as a class had been subjected to discrimination by a dominant majority? Part of the answer, I believe, is that lawyers like DeAnda were pragmatic realists, not cynical opportunists. They adopted an "other white" identity because judicial precedents prior to *Brown* dictated that approach as the best for achieving their goals. They did not attack the constitutional foundations of Jim Crow because such an approach would not serve their clients' immediate needs and, in all likelihood, would fail completely. African American lawyers, by contrast, planned and executed a constitutional revolution because they needed one. By the 1960s, frustrated by a general lack of social progress, Mexican American lawyers needed a revolution as well, and so at long last abandoned a dead-end strategy.

Such were the external legal considerations that contributed to a paradigm shift on "other whiteness." But another important impetus for the novel premises of the *Cisneros* suit emerged from social and political pressures that were internal to Mexican American politics (albeit also characteristic of the 1960s). A younger generation of activists began to stake out a new identity as a mystical "bronze race"—the Chicano movement's *La Raza*—that explicitly repudiated the older generations' painstakingly constructed whiteness. The need to combine the internal and external forces came to the fore when Chicano students protested the Anglo hegemony by walking out of classrooms in the late 1960s. Two-thirds of Mexican American students attended Mexican American majority schools. Forty percent were enrolled at schools where the student body was at least 80 percent Mexican American. Twenty percent attended schools that were at least 95 percent Mexican American. Such imbalance was maintained by the reliance by school boards on neighborhood schooling plans for desegregation. No litigation that attacked testing or tracking would have changed this ethnic concentration. The use of the existing biracial (black-white) formulas, moreover—under which administrators transferred African American students into predominantly Mexican American schools and called the schools "desegregated"—promised to isolate both populations even more instead of ending a separation that was, according to *Brown*, inherently unequal. In this way, perhaps, school administrators themselves revealed to Mexican American lawyers the bankruptcy of "other white" arguments and the utility of *Brown*.

The contemporaneous creation of MALDEF had less to do with the shift in thinking than might be expected. The upheavals brought by the black civil rights struggle, the farm workers' movement, and antiwar protests inspired many disaffected Mexican-descended youths to adopt similar goals and direct action tactics—such as walkouts and other disruptive demonstrations—in order to combat the inequities they encountered. As a result, however, activists frequently found themselves sanctioned by school administrators or even law enforcement agencies. Instead of suing schools to change the rules of desegregation, therefore, MALDEF undertook a number of cases that established the new organization as something of an unofficial civil liberties bureau for militant Chicano students. Significantly, in these cases, MALDEF's attorneys did not argue—and in civil liberties cases had no reason to claim—that Mexican Americans were and ought to be considered a group distinct from Anglos. Nevertheless, MALDEF's early victories in this field helped to reestablish litigation as a tool for vindicating Mexican Americans' civil rights.

The recognition that formerly favorable precedents had become counterproductive, combined with the challenges to the conventional wisdom posed by the Chicano movement, led some lawyers to rethink the basis of Mexican Americans' civil rights litigation. The plaintiffs and their lawyers in Corpus Christi opened an important new front in the civil rights struggle by abandoning the dubious benefits of whiteness—thus adopting the heart of the Chicano argument, if not the whole body —and choosing to make fresh claims under *Brown*. The favorable decision in the *Cisneros* litigation established a new precedent that allowed Mexican Americans finally to commence in earnest what Rubén Donato has called the "other struggle for equal schools."

The Mexican Americans' newly reinvigorated legal efforts would continue to evolve in response to changing social, political, and legal conditions. The unfortunate truth, of course, is that Mexican Americans had not missed much actual school desegregation during the fifteen years that they sat on the sidelines—African Americans had in fact made little progress during that first decade and a half after *Brown* was decided. But Mexican Americans nevertheless saw evidence that some slow progress was arriving. In 1979, for example, James DeAnda was appointed to a new judicial seat in the Southern District of Texas and so became the nation's second Mexican American federal district judge. He was sworn in by the first, Reynaldo Garza, who since 1961 had risen by dint of seniority to become the chief judge in the district.

From the Editors *Issues and Comments*

What does history tell us about the way law serves to create and justify the existing social order and the repression of outsider groups? What is gained by recognizing how law is discretionary, contingent, and indeterminate—or the product of a black-white paradigm?

If law is, in fact, indeterminate and highly discretionary, can Latinos and other minorities rely on it as a tool for social advancement?

Does the legal system's insistence on precedent (even when much of it is, in the end, indeterminate) limit that system's ability to remedy longstanding injustices?

Is it only possible to recognize paradigms when they start to break down, and is this beginning to happen with the black/white paradigm?

Do dominant practices and perspectives ever become dysfunctional, even for the dominant group? If so, can outsiders help introduce new ones?

How can one change a paradigm or the way the legal system treats a given issue or group, such as women or Latinos? Do breakthroughs come only when elite self-interest dictates it? Can storytelling or counterstorytelling help blast a paradigm?

Do private choices and law construct whiteness, as Ian Haney López argues? Do they construct Mexican Americans to suit the interests of the majority, now as white, now as nonwhite, as George Martinez argues?

Did Latinos cling as long as possible to whiteness? Do some continue to do so today?

If you were director of litigation for the newly formed Latino Defense Fund (an umbrella organization) and you wanted to challenge the black/white binary, what kind of case would you pick for your challenge?

The date is 150 years in the future. Latinos are the largest group in the United States, slightly larger than whites and considerably larger than Asians and blacks. What legal, political, and social changes do you foresee?

Can Latinos save Anglo society from an otherwise inevitable decline?

Suggested Readings

Acuna, Rodolfo. *Sometimes There Is No Other Side*. Notre Dame, Ind.: University of Notre Dame Press, 1998.

Alvarez, Robert R., Jr. "The Lemon Grove Incident: The Nation's First Successful Desegregation Case." 32(2) *Journal of San Diego History* 116–35 (1986).

Bender, Steven W., Raquel Aldana, Gilbert Paul Carrasco, and Joaquin G. Avila. *Everyday Law for Latino/as*. Boulder, Colo.: Paradigm Publishers, 2008.

Cameron, Christopher David Ruiz. "One Hundred Fifty Years of Solitude: Reflections on the End of the History Academy's Dominance of Scholarship on the Treaty of Guadalupe Hidalgo." 5 *Sw. J.L. & Trade Am.* 83 (1998).

Carter, Thomas P. *Mexican Americans in School: A History of Educational Neglect*. New York: College Entrance Examination Board, 1970.

Cheever, Frederico M. "A New Approach to Spanish and Mexican Land Grants and the Public Trust Doctrine: Defining the Property Interest Protected by the Treaty of Guadalupe Hidalgo." 33 *UCLA L. Rev.* 1364 (1986).

Colloquium: "Representing Latina/o Communities: Critical Race Theory and Practice." 9 *La Raza L.J.* 1 (1996).

"Colored Men" and "Hombres Aquí": Hernandez v. Texas *and the Emergence of Mexican American Lawyering*, edited by Michael A. Olivas. Houston: Arte Publico Press, 2006.

A Cotton Picker Finds Justice! The Saga of the Hernandez Case, compiled by Ruben Munguia. N.p., 1954.

Delgado, Richard. *The Coming Race War? And Other Apocalyptic Tales after Affirmative Action and Welfare*. New York: New York University Press, 1996.

———. "Enormous Anomaly: Left-Right Parallels in Recent Writing about Race." 91 *Colum. L. Rev.* 1547 (1991).

———. "Recasting the American Race Problem." 79 *Cal. L. Rev.* 1389 (1991).

———. *The Rodrigo Chronicles: Conversations about America and Race*. New York: New York University Press, 1995.

———. "Rodrigo's Roundelay: Hernandez v. Texas and the Interest Convergence Dilemma." 41 *Harv. C.R.–C.L. L. Rev.* 23 (2006).

Delgado, Richard, and Jean Stefancic. "California's Racial History and Constitutional Rationales for Race-Conscious Decision Making in Higher Education." 47 *UCLA L. Rev.* 1521 (2000).

———. "Home-Grown Racism: Colorado's Historic Embrace—and Denial—of Equal Opportunity in Higher Education." 70 *U. Colo. L. Rev.* 703 (1999).

Durkee, Ellen. "Special Problems of Custody for Unaccompanied Refugee Children in the United States." 3 *Mich. Yearbk. Int. Leg. Stud.* 203 (1982).

Foley, Neil. *The White Scourge: Mexicans, Blacks, and Poor Whites in Texas Cotton Culture*. Berkeley: University of California Press, 1997.

Garcia, Ignacio M. *White but Not Equal: Mexican Americans, Jury Discrimination, and the Supreme Court*. Tucson: University of Arizona Press, 2008.

Gomez, Laura E. "Off-White in an Age of White Supremacy: Mexican Elites and the Rights of Indians and Blacks in Nineteenth-Century New Mexico." 25 *Chicano-Latino L. Rev.* 9 (2005).

Greenfield, Gary A., and Don B. Kates, Jr. "Mexican Americans, Racial Discrimination, and the Civil Rights Act of 1866." 63 *Cal. L. Rev.* 662 (1975).

Gross, Ariela J. "'The Caucasian Cloak': Mexican Americans and the Politics of Whiteness in the Twentieth-Century Southwest." 95 *Geo. L.J.* 337 (2007).

———. "Texas Mexicans and the Politics of Whiteness." 21 *Law & Hist. Rev.* 195 (2003).

Haney López, Ian F. "Institutional Racism: Judicial Conduct and a New Theory of Racial Discrimination." 109 *Yale L.J.* 1717 (2000).

———. "Race and Colorblindness after Hernandez and Brown." 25 *Chicano-Latino L. Rev.* 61 (2005).

———. *Racism on Trial: The Chicano Fight for Justice*. Cambridge, Mass.: Harvard University Press, 2003.

———. "Retaining Race: LatCrit Theory and Mexican American Identity in Hernandez v. Texas." 1 *Harv. Latino L. Rev.* 297 (1997).

———. *White by Law: The Legal Construction of Race* (10th anniv. ed.). New York: New York University Press, 2006.

———. "White Latinos." 6 *Harv. Latino L. Rev.* 1 (2003).

Haney López, Ian F., and Michael A. Olivas. "Jim Crow, Mexican Americans, and the Anti-Subordination Constitution: The Story of *Hernández v. Texas*." In *Race Law Stories*, edited by Rachel Moran and Devon Carbado, 273. New York: Foundation Press, 2008.

Hernández-Truyol, Berta Esperanza. "Building Bridges: Bringing International Human Rights Home." 9 *La Raza L.J.* 69 (1996).

Johnson, Kevin R. "Driver's Licenses and Undocumented Immigrants: The Future of Civil Rights Law?" 5 *Nev. L.J.* 213 (2004–2005).

———. "The End of 'Civil Rights' as We Know It? Immigration and Civil Rights in the New Millennium." 49 *UCLA L. Rev.* 1481 (2002).

———. "*Hernandez v. Texas*: Legacies of Justice and Injustice." 25 *Chicano-Latino L. Rev.* 153 (2005).

———. "Public Benefits and Immigration: The Intersection of Immigration Status, Ethnicity, Gender, and Class." 42 *UCLA L. Rev.* 1509 (1995).

Latinos and the Law: Cases and Materials, edited by Richard Delgado, Juan F. Perea, and Jean Stefancic. St. Paul, Minn.: West, 2008.

Latinos in the United States: History, Law and Perspective, edited by Antoinette Sedillo Lopez. New York: Garland Publishing, 1995.

López, Gerald P. "The Well-Defended Academic Identity." Working Papers Series. Stanford Center for Chicano Research, 1991.

López, María Pabón, and Gerardo R. López. *Persistent Inequality: Contemporary Realities in the Education of Undocumented Latina/o Students.* New York: Routledge, 2010.

Martinez, George A. "Legal Indeterminacy, Judicial Discretion and the Mexican-American Litigation Experience: 1930–1980." 27 *U.C. Davis L. Rev.* 555 (1994).

Martinez, John. "Trivializing Diversity: The Problem of Overinclusion in Affirmative Action Programs." 12 *Harv. BlackLetter L.J.* 49 (1995).

Menchaca, Martha. *Recovering History, Constructing Race: The Indian, Black, and White Roots of Mexican Americans.* Austin: University of Texas Press, 2001.

Mirandé, Alfredo. "Is There a 'Mexican Exception' to the Fourth Amendment?" 55 *Fla. L. Rev.* 365 (2003).

Mize, Ronald L., Jr. "Reparations for Mexican Braceros? Lessons Learned from Japanese and African American Attempts at Redress." 52 *Clev. St. L. Rev.* 273 (2005).

Moran, Rachel F. "Neither Black nor White." 2 *Harv. Latino L. Rev.* 61 (1997).

———. "Unrepresented." 55 *Representations* 139 (1996).

Olivas, Michael A. "*Hernandez v. Texas*: A Litigation History." In *"Colored Men" and "Hombres Aquí"*: Hernandez v. Texas *and the Emergence of Mexican American Lawyering*, edited by Michael A. Olivas, 209. Houston: Arte Publico Press, 2006.

———. "IIRIRA, the DREAM Act, and Undocumented College Student Residency." 30 *J. College & U. L.* 435 (2004).

———. "Legal Norms in Law School Admissions: An Essay on Parallel Universes." 42 *J. Leg. Ed.* 103 (1992).

———. "Storytelling Out of School: Undocumented College Residency, Race, and Reaction." 22 *Hastings Const. L.Q.* 1019 (1995).

Ontiveros, Maria L. "To Help Those Most in Need: Undocumented Workers' Rights and Remedies under Title VII." 20 *N.Y.U. Rev. L. & Soc. Change* 607 (1993–94).

Padilla, Fernando V. "Early Chicano Legal Recognition, 1846–1897." 13(3) *Journal of Popular Culture* 564–74 (1979).

Perea, Juan F. "Ethnicity and Prejudice: Reevaluating 'National Origin' Discrimination under Title VII." 35 *Wm. & Mary L. Rev.* 805 (1994).

———. "Ethnicity and the Constitution: Beyond the Black White Binary Constitution." 36 *Wm. & Mary L. Rev.* 571 (1995).

Piatt, Bill. "Born as Second-Class Citizens in the U.S.A.: Children of Undocumented Parents." 63 *Notre Dame L. Rev.* 35 (1988).

Rack, Christine. *Latino-Anglo Bargaining: Culture, Structure, and Choice in Court Mediation.* New York: Routledge, 2006.

Ramirez, Deborah A. "The Mixed Jury and the Ancient Custom of Trial by Jury *De Medietate Linguae:* A History and a Proposal for Change." 74 *B.U. L. Rev.* 777 (1994).

Rangel, Jorge C., and Carlos M. Alcala. "Project Report: De Jure Segregation of Chicanos in Texas Schools." 7 *Harv. C.R.–C.L. L. Rev.* 307 (1972).

Ray, Eric L. "Mexican Repatriation and the Possibility for a Federal Cause of Action: A Comparative Analysis on Reparations." 37 *U. Miami Inter-Am. L. Rev.* 171 (2005).

Ressler, Everett, Neil Boothby, and Daniel Steinbock. *Unaccompanied Children: Care and Protection in Wars, Natural Disasters, and Refugee Movements.* New York: Oxford University Press, 1988.

Romero, Victor C. "The Child Citizenship Act and the Family Reunification Act: Valuing the Citizen Child as Well as the Citizen Parent." 55 *Fla. L. Rev.* 489 (2003).

San Miguel, Guadalupe, Jr. *"Let All of Them Take Heed": Mexican Americans and the Campaign for Educational Equality in Texas, 1910–1981.* College Station: Texas A&M University Press, 1987.

Sheridan, Clare. "'Another White Race': Mexican Americans and the Paradoxes of Whiteness in Jury Selection." 21 *Law & Hist. Rev.* 109 (2003).

Soltero, Carlos R. *Latinos and American Law: Landmark Supreme Court Cases.* Austin: University of Texas Press, 2006.

Symposium: "Commemorating the 50th Anniversary of *Hernandez v. Texas.*" 25 *Chicano-Latino L. Rev.* 1 (2005).

Torres, Gerald. "Local Knowledge, Local Color: Critical Legal Studies, and the Law of Race Relations." 25 *San Diego L. Rev.* 1043 (1988).

Valencia, Reynaldo Anaya. *The Legal Construction of a Latino Identity.* Durham, N.C.: Carolina Academic Press, 2007.

Valencia, Reynaldo Anaya, Sonia R. García, Henry Flores, and José Roberto Juárez, Jr. *Mexican Americans and the Law: El Pueblo Unido Jamás Séra Vencido.* Tucson: University of Arizona Press, 2004.

Valencia, Richard R. *Chicano Students and the Courts: The Mexican American Legal Struggle for Educational Equality.* New York: New York University Press, 2008.

Villarreal, Carlos. "Culture in Lawmaking: A Chicano Perspective." 24 *U.C. Davis L. Rev.* 1193 (1991).

———. "Limits on Lawmaking: A Chicano Perspective." 10 *St. Louis U. Pub. L. Rev.* 65 (1991).

Williams, Robert A., Jr. "Taking Rights Aggressively: The Perils and Promise of Critical Legal Theory for Peoples of Color." 5 *Law. & Ineq.* 103 (1987).

Wilson, Steven H. "Some Are Born White, Some Achieve Whiteness, and Some Have Whiteness Thrust upon Them: Mexican Americans and the Politics of Racial Classification in the Federal Judicial Bureaucracy, Twenty-Five Years after *Hernandez v. Texas.*" 25 *Chicano-Latino L. Rev.* 201 (2005).

Wollenberg, Charles. *All Deliberate Speed: Segregation and Exclusion in California Schools, 1855–1975.* Berkeley: University of California Press, 1976.

———. "*Mendez v. Westminster:* Race, Nationality and Segregation in California Schools." 53 *California Historical Quarterly* 317 (1974).

||||||||||||||||||||||||||||||||||||||||||||||||||||||||||||||||||||||||||||||||||||||||||||

Part VIII

Assimilation

Maybe Our Best Strategy Is Just to Duck?

Some scholars and commentators attempt to analogize Latino immigration to that of southern and eastern Europeans during the period 1890–1920, questioning why recent Latino immigrants do not easily assimilate into U.S. society as millions of the Europeans did. Both cohorts suffered nativism—the other side of the assimilationism coin—but Latinos have experienced more of it and for a longer time, as we have seen in part 3. Moreover, the land border between Mexico and the United States is porous, and until recently American agriculture's need for low-wage labor exerted a powerful pull. Unlike other immigrant groups, members of Mexican families have come to the United States and returned to Mexico through many generations, making adaptation more complicated. At the same time, assimilation is a two-way street, dependent on the will, need, and ability of both the immigrant and the receiving country to accept the other. More frequently it is the immigrant who makes the sacrifice of giving up his or her culture, language, and national loyalty in order to conform to a different society. An option, at least for light-skinned Latinos, is to try to fit in, not to make waves, to adopt prevailing manners and inflections, and even to try to pass for white by changing one's name and concealing one's heritage. This strategy imposes costs on those who deploy it and, on occasion, ethical consequences of turning one's back on one's community. Some of the excerpts in part 8 describe questions of identity and the cognitive schizophrenia that arises when children of immigrants begin to enter the American mainstream and try to embrace two cultures. Others analyze the effects of racial discrimination on the path of many of the second generation of immigrants.

Chapter 60

||||||||||||||||||||||||||||||||||||||||||||||||||||||||||||||||||||||||||||

LULAC and the Assimilationist Perspective

David G. Gutiérrez

Even though relatively few Mexicans were formally deported [during the Depression —Eds.], repatriation for most individuals and families was a traumatic, disorienting, and sorrowful event. Many of the repatriates believed that Mexicans had been unfairly blamed for events over which they had no control. Despised and vilified after spending ten, fifteen, or even twenty or more productive years as hard-working, though isolated, members of the American working class, Mexican immigrant workers seemed to bear the brunt of Americans' resentment about the economic catastrophe. A famous *corrido* of the period underscores the sense of injustice and ingratitude many Mexicans clearly felt. "Los Deportados" lamented,

Los güeros son muy malores [*sic*]	The Anglos are very bad fellows
se valen de la ocasión	They take advantage
Y a todos los mexicanos	And to all the Mexicans
nos tratan sin compasión	They treat us without pity
Hoy traen la gran polvareda	Today they bring great disturbance
y sin consideración	And without consideration
Mujeres, niños, y ancianos	Women, children, and old ones
nos llevan a la frontera,	They take us to the border,
nos echan de esta nación	They eject us from this country
Adiós paisanos queridos	Goodbye dear countrymen
Ya nos van a deportar	They are going to deport us
Pero no somos bandidos	But we are not bandits
Venimos a camellar.	We came to toil.[1]

As "Los Deportados" expressed so poignantly, the political climate during the repatriation campaigns placed intense political and social pressures on the ethnic Mexican population of the United States, which continued even after hundreds of thousands of Mexican nationals and their children had returned to Mexico. The scapegoating that occurred at this time rekindled Americans' disdain for working-class Mexicans, and as always, their disdain was directed at Mexican Americans as well as the newer immigrants. For Americans of Mexican descent this situation was like rubbing salt in old wounds. Torn between their cultural ties, their nationality, and their awareness that American citizenship did not necessarily protect them from such excesses, Mexican Americans faced tough decisions as to what their attitudes toward the repatriation campaigns ought to be. As in previous periods of increasing social stress, in the late 1920s and 1930s opinion among Mexican Americans (and the Mexican nationals who remained in the United States) on the complex issues associated with the repatriation crisis remained deeply ambivalent. Between the late 1920s and the mid-1930s, however, opinion and debate on these questions began to harden and polarize.

In the winter of 1921 an article by former Texas Congressman James L. Slayden appeared in an issue of the *Annals of the American Academy of Political and Social Science* that addressed Mexican immigration. A long-time observer of Mexican immigration trends in his state, Slayden proved to be one of the few Americans active in public life perceptive enough to recognize the deep impact mass Mexican immigration was having on the existing Mexican American population. From Slayden's point of view Mexican immigrants represented a threat to the existing Texas Mexican population not so much because immigrants competed with Mexican Americans for jobs and housing as because Anglo Texans generally refused to acknowledge any meaningful distinctions between Mexican Americans and Mexican immigrants. Whether one was a citizen of the United States made no difference: to white Texans a Mexican was a Mexican. As Slayden put it, "In Texas, the word 'Mexican' is used to indicate the race, not a citizen or subject of the country. There are probably 250,000 Mexicans in Texas who were born in the state but they are [defined as] 'Mexicans' just as all blacks are negroes though they may have five generations of American ancestors."[2]

While Slayden was making his observations about the peculiarities of racial classification in Texas, some Mexican Americans in that state were themselves pondering the implications of their ambiguous status. As migration from Mexico continued into the 1920s they began to chafe at the thought that Americans were equating them with immigrants who, in many cases, had just recently entered the United States from the interior of Mexico. Although most of these native-born Texas Mexicans harbored no ill will toward their immigrant neighbors, worsening economic conditions and the intensification of anti-Mexican sentiment caused many of them to wonder whether the new immigrants were undermining their already tenuous position. Having lived in the United States their entire lives, and in many cases having served the United States as members of the armed forces in World War I, increasing numbers of Texas Mexicans began to take exception to Anglo Americans' nonchalant dismissal of them as mere Mexicans. They gradually concluded that the only way to stop this indiscriminate lumping was to take a stand against large-scale immigration from Mexico. This was a painful decision, but from their point of view prudence dictated that Americans of Mexican descent had to be concerned with the immediate well-being and future health of Mexicans already in the United States. Mexico would simply have to take care of its own.

Although similar sentiments had roiled Mexican American communities since the 1850s, these attitudes took on new salience with the establishment of a different type of Mexican American organization in Texas in the years immediately after World War I. Having returned from service in the armed forces, many Mexican Americans were no longer content to accept treatment as second-class citizens. Consequently, in the early 1920s Mexican American community leaders in several Texas cities established a number of civic organizations designed to protect and advance the interests of their people. The three largest of these new groups were El Orden Hijos de América (The Order of the Sons of America), El Orden Caballeros de America (The Order of the Knights of America), and the League of Latin American Citizens. Such groups were formed by lower-middle-class members of the Texas Mexican community, under the leadership of attorneys, restaurateurs, teachers, printers, and small entrepreneurs serving the Spanish-speaking community. By 1927 these groups had established an extensive network of chapters throughout Texas. The Sons of America, for example, had councils in Somerset, San Antonio, Pearsall, and Corpus Christi. The Knights of America were active primarily in the San Antonio area, and the League of Latin American Citizens had established chapters in the south Texas towns of Harlingen, Brownsville, Laredo, Gulf, Penitas, McAllen, La Grulla, and Encino.

As their names indicated, these new organizations espoused a political perspective that departed significantly from that of older Mexican American voluntary associations, such as the *mutualistas* and honorific societies. Unlike earlier groups, which had based their organizations on the principle of mutual cooperation between Mexican immigrants and Americans of Mexican descent, from their inception the new organizations pointedly excluded non-American citizens from membership.

To these organizations, Mexican Americans were American citizens and thus should make every effort to assimilate into the American social and cultural mainstream. Although most were proud of their ethnic heritage, they believed that Mexican Americans had focused too much on maintaining their ethnicity and culture in the United States and, in the process, had hindered their progress as Americans. Thus, while members of these new organizations continued to profess respect for Mexico and for their Mexican cultural heritage, they insisted that the best way to advance in American society was to convince other Americans that they too were loyal, upstanding citizens. In keeping with these beliefs the new organizations carefully cultivated what they considered to be an appropriate image by conducting their proceedings in English, by prominently displaying the American flag in their ceremonies, stationery, and official iconography, by singing such songs as "America" at their gatherings, and by opening their meetings with a recitation of the "George Washington Prayer."

The political agendas of the three groups all reflected these basic premises. For example, the by-laws of the Sons of America recited: "As workers in support of the ideal that citizens of the United States of America of Mexican or Spanish extraction, whether native or naturalized, [we] have a broad field of opportunity to protect and promote their interests as such; [and are committed] to elevate their moral, social and intellectual conditions; [and] to educate them . . . in the proper extension of their political rights."[3] Members hoped to implement these principles by organizing voter registration and poll-tax campaigns, by mounting battles against the segregation of

Mexican Americans in public facilities, and by insisting on greater representation of Mexican Americans on Texas juries.

Such ideas quickly gained currency after some of the Texas-based groups consolidated into a new, larger organization just before the Great Depression. After a preliminary series of meetings in 1927 and 1928 to negotiate the terms of consolidation, the groups united under a new umbrella organization, the League of United Latin American Citizens (LULAC), on February 17, 1929. The original delegates met again at Corpus Christi in May of that year to codify the objectives agreed to in principle at the founding convention. Drafting a constitution and a formal statement of principles they called "The LULAC Code," Texans Manuel C. Gonzales, Alonso S. Perales, Benjamin Garza, J. T. Canales, Luis Wilmot, and others agreed to a series of objectives that came to define the organization's basic philosophy and political program for the next sixty years. Foremost among these was a pledge to promote and develop among LULAC members what they called the "best and purest" form of Americanism. They also resolved to teach their children English, to inculcate in them a sense of their rights and responsibilities as American citizens, and to fight discrimination against Mexican Americans wherever they encountered it.

In many ways the new organization exemplified the integrationist strains of thought that had slowly evolved among some Mexican Americans over the previous years. LULAC's founders believed that Mexican Americans had for too long been denied the full enjoyment of their rights as American citizens and that it was now time to change the situation. Both LULAC's constitution and Code emphasized that the best way to rectify the appalling conditions facing Mexican Americans was to organize as American citizens; thus LULAC's founders rejected outright the notion that they were merely Mexicans who happened to reside in the United States. Although LULAC members insisted that their organization was not a political club, most of the group's goals were clearly political in nature. Thus even though LULAC's by-laws specifically prohibited direct engagement in partisan elections, the group's leaders encouraged members to participate in politics and use their "vote and influence" to support "men who show by their deeds, respect and consideration for our people."[4] They remained extremely sensitive to the anti-Mexican sentiment that was building up in Texas and other parts of the Southwest during the first years of the Depression, however, and so from the outset were careful to disavow the use of political tactics that might be interpreted as radical. Despite such caution, they asserted their strong commitment to "destroy any attempt to create racial prejudices against [Mexican Americans], and any infamous stigma which may be cast upon them [by] demand[ing] for them the respect and prerogatives which the Constitution grants us all."[5]

LULAC leaders consciously chose to emphasize the American side of their social identity as the primary basis for organization. Consequently, in pursuit of much-needed reforms they developed a political program designed to activate a sense of Americanism among their constituents. Considering themselves part of a progressive and enlightened leadership elite, LULAC's leaders set out to implement general goals and a political strategy that were similar in form and content to those advocated early in the century by W. E. B. Du Bois and the National Association for the Advancement of Colored People: for "an educated elite" "to provide the masses with appropriate goals and lift them to civilization."[6] LULAC's political activities varied from chapter to chapter. But in general the organization adopted a three-pronged plan of attack in the 1930s and 1940s that strongly emphasized desegregated public education for Mexican American children; encouraged Mexican American citizens to register, pay their poll taxes, and vote; and supported aggressive local legal campaigns to combat discrimination against Mexican Americans in public facilities and on juries.

Although the Depression constrained LULAC's organizing and proselytizing efforts, the organization proved remarkably successful in expanding its membership base after 1929. Deploying "Flying Squadrons" of organizers who traveled to distant communities in cars or chartered buses, LULAC grew throughout the 1930s in Texas, and by the outbreak of World War II the organization had established viable chapters in New Mexico, Arizona, California, and Kansas. By the early 1940s LULAC claimed at least eighty dues-paying chapters nationwide, making it the largest and best-established Mexican American civil rights organization in the United States.

Despite the generally hostile political environment facing Mexican Americans during this era, LULAC scored a number of significant legal victories in Texas and assisted Mexican Americans in other states in mounting effective challenges against local discriminatory practices. From 1929 through World War II LULAC organized successful voter registration and poll-tax drives, actively supported political candidates sympathetic to Mexican Americans, and aggressively attacked discriminatory measures in communities throughout Texas and the Southwest. More important over the long run, LULAC also achieved a number of notable legal victories in the area of public education. For example, in the organization's first legal challenge in 1930, LULAC lawyers brought suit against the Del Rio, Texas, School District for discriminating against Mexican American students. LULAC ultimately lost most of the major points contested in *Independent School District v. Salvatierra*, but the case was only the opening salvo in what proved to be a long legal struggle in which LULAC and other groups successfully argued that discrimination violated the equal-protection and due-process clauses of the Fourteenth Amendment to the U.S. Constitution. Similar LULAC efforts in the 1940s and 1950s built on this important precedent and helped Mexican Americans and other minority groups attack the separate-but-equal doctrine that was ultimately overturned in the famous *Brown v. Board of Education* case in 1954.[7]

NOTES

1. For this, and for similar examples of *corridos* of the Depression era, see Nellie Foster, *The Corrido: A Mexican Culture Trait Persisting in Southern California* (M.A. thesis, University of Southern California, 1939).

2. James L. Slayden, *Some Observations on the Mexican Immigrant,* ANNALS OF THE AMER-ICAN ACADEMY OF POLITICAL AND SOCIAL SCIENCE 93 (January 1921): 125.

3. Preamble, "Constitución y Leyes de la Orden Hijos de América," 1927, Box 1, Folder 3, O. Douglas Weeks Papers, LULAC Archives, Benson Latin American Library, University of Texas Austin.

4. O. Douglas Weeks, *The League of United Latin American Citizens: A Texas Mexican Civic*

Organization, SOUTHWESTERN POLITICAL AND SOCIAL SCIENCE QUARTERLY 10 (December 1928): 257–78.

5. LULAC Constitution, Box 1, Folder 7, Weeks Papers.

6. August Meier, NEGRO THOUGHT IN AMERICA, 1880–1915: RACIAL IDEOLOGIES IN THE AGE OF BOOKER T. WASHINGTON (Ann Arbor: University of Michigan Press, 1963), 192. Although there is little evidence that Du Bois's ideas directly influenced LULAC's leadership, the similarities between LULAC's evolving political ideas and those of the NAACP during this period are striking.

7. For descriptions of LULAC's general political and legal efforts during this period, see Mario T. García, MEXICAN AMERICANS: LEADERSHIP, IDEOLOGY, AND IDENTITY, 1930–1960 (New Haven, Conn.: Yale University Press, 1989), 40–41, 46–53; and Richard A. García, RISE OF THE MEXICAN AMERICAN MIDDLE CLASS: SAN ANTONIO, 1929–1941 (College Station: Texas A&M University Press, 1991), 282–99.

||||||||||||||||||||||||||||||||||||||||||||||||||||||||||||||||||||||||||||||||||||

Chapter 61

Melting Pot or Ring of Fire?

Kevin R. Johnson

In the spring of 1996, I was sitting in a bar close to the Pacific Coast Highway in Manhattan Beach, California, an upper-middle-class, predominantly white suburb of Los Angeles. Funeral services for my father's uncle, my great-uncle (known as "Brown-eyes" or "Brownie" to distinguish him from his blue-eyed twin), had just finished. I had an hour to burn with my father and stepbrother while I waited for my return flight to Sacramento. Thoughts about my uncle streamed through my mind. He thoroughly enjoyed life. He was always upbeat. But he worried. A life of economic insecurity for him and his family no doubt contributed to the worries. Over the coming days, I wondered how it must have been when he became the first Anglo in his family to marry a Mexican-American woman, Rosie. They had grown up together in a working-class neighborhood near downtown Los Angeles where Mexican Americans and Anglos lived side-by-side. They spent fifty years there before moving to the desert in retirement.

While my mind wandered, a tall Anglo fellow sitting on the barstool next to us rambled to anyone who would listen about a recent visit to Texas. Then came what, in retrospect, was inevitable—a joke, which went something like this: "How do you make sure nobody steals the stereo speakers in your car?" Without waiting for a response, he eagerly offered the punch line: "You put a sign on them saying '*no habla español.*'" Nobody laughed. I wondered why I had to hear this kind of stuff. Why couldn't I grieve with a beer and not have to deal with issues of race that cut to the core of my identity? I wished that, as for many Anglos, my identity could be "transparent," a non-issue in my daily life. The joke made me think of the many Spanish-speakers that I knew and my inability to identify any who stole stereo speakers. This story, in addition to showing that words may hurt and marginalize, demonstrates the limits of assimilation for Latinos.

In recent years, Latinos with high media profiles, such as Linda Chavez and Richard Rodriguez, have unabashedly embraced assimilation for Latinos. In her book *Out of the Barrio,* Chavez explores a "new theory" of assimilation that argues that Latinos, like previous waves of white "ethnic" immigrants, should assimilate, and in fact are doing so. Yet, separate and unequal Latino enclaves in many cities suggest that assimilation is far from complete. Economic disparities show no signs of dissipating. The anti-immigrant backlash, which is in no small part an attack on all persons (immigrants and citizens) of Mexican ancestry in the United States, including persons who trace their ancestry in this country for centuries, is a testament to the limits of assimilation.

On a human level, the experiences of my mother, a most ardent assimilationist, demonstrate the problems confronting Latinas seeking to assimilate. Nor am I, a Harvard-educated law professor, immune to them. Indeed, my experience in the Manhattan Beach bar suggests the contrary.

My experiences exemplify how, because race is a social construction, one has some choice in deciding to be a Latino. For the most part, I was never forced to present myself as Mexican American. Although it may be difficult for some Latinos to "pass" as white due to phenotype, surname, or language skills, I could, if I chose. I might have ignored my background and hoped that nobody would remember, find out, or care. In some circumstances, I could shed my ethnicity and blend in. At other times (for example, with people who knew of my background), this was not possible. To do so, I would have had to deny a family history that was central to my identity during my formative years. Exemplifying the volitional nature of racial identity, my brother, with blond hair and blue eyes, exercised his right to choose in a different way. He never identified as Mexican American.

My wife, Virginia Salazar, is from a traditional Mexican-American family in La Puente, California, east of East Los Angeles, with dark brown hair, brown eyes, and a light complexion. Those in her mother's family generally have fair complexions and light brown hair; those in her father's line generally have dark skin and dark brown hair bordering on black. Although both her parents speak Spanish, she was not taught the language at home. To our surprise, our first two children, Teresa and Tomás, have blond hair and blue eyes and fair complexions. They were embraced by the family proudly, with occasional reference to their being *hueros*, or "white ones." Such references hint at the value of whiteness in U.S. society. Our third child, Maria Elena, looks more like us, with olive-colored skin and brown eyes. Some have referred to her as our "Mexican" baby or *la morena* (the dark one).

The phenotypic diversity among a family of five Mexican Americans under one roof should make it clear that the Mexican-American community is far from one-dimensional. If Mexican Americans are a diverse group, Latinos are even more so. Mixtures of race, national origin, immigration status, class, culture, education, political outlook, and many other characteristics abound.

One aspect of Latino diversity is the large number of those of mixed Latino/Anglo backgrounds. While poignant books by Greg Williams[1] and Judy Scales-Trent[2] have documented the experiences of persons with one black and one white parent, the discussion of mixed-race people has not focused on Latinos of mixed parentage. This is true despite the high rates of intermarriage between Latinos and Anglos and the many mixed Latino/Anglo people in the United States. As the Latino population in the United States increases, one can expect the number of intermarriages and children of mixed race to increase as well.

Some of my experiences exemplify the difficulties of forcing people into hard-and-fast categories, which law and society inevitably attempt to do. Mixed-race people regularly face this difficulty. For example, in the United States census, what demographic box should a person check who does not fit neatly into any of the enumerated racial or ethnic categories? Or consider admission to educational programs and employment. None of the recognized categories fully nor accurately describes a mixed-race/ethnicity person. One hates to be in the unsavory position of denying one's background. At the same time, one fears being accused of claiming to be a minority simply to obtain a "special" preference.

The Myth of Spain and Assimilation through Denial

Despite their Mexican roots, my mother and grandmother were ardently assimilationist in outlook. Marrying Anglo men was part of the assimilationist strategy. Another aspect of the plan was for my mother and grandmother to claim that they were not of *Mexican*, but *Spanish*, ancestry.

Always the storyteller, one of my grandmother's favorite stories concerned her mixed Spanish-French background, with particular emphasis on the Spanish. This theme, in fact, found its way into many of her stories. My mother also emphasized her "Spanish" ancestry. My grandmother, with her indigenous phenotype, and my mother, with her olive-colored skin, seemed no different from the other Mexican Americans in the San Gabriel Valley. My great grandmother, who never mentioned her Spanish ancestry in my presence, was a Mexican citizen who lived in Mexico during my younger years. All of our relatives in the Imperial Valley, only a few miles from the U.S./Mexico border, were Mexican American. My mother's magical Spanish ancestry was thus very much an exaggeration.

This claim of Spanish heritage is not at all uncommon. Many Latinos understand that being classified as Mexican is disfavored in the United States, especially so in the Southwest before development of the civil rights consciousness of the 1960s. The phenomenon of Latinos attempting to "pass" as Spanish, and therefore as white, is a variation of the "passing" of other minorities as white. To many Anglos, being "Spanish" is more European, and therefore more acceptable, than being of Latin American ancestry. My mother and grandmother knew the southern Californian world in which they lived and the racial hierarchy that reigned there, even if they recognized it in simplified terms (i.e., that many people did not like Mexicans and that they had better convince them they were not Mexicans).

This Spanish mythology was part of my mother's assimilationist leanings. To this day, rather than pronounce her maiden name (Gallardo) in proper Spanish, which requires a special "ll" sound similar to "y," she says it as it would be said in English, as in the word "fallen." Consequently, the word "lard" and all of the images that it connotes stick out right in the middle.

In no small part because of her assimilationist approach, my mother consciously avoided teaching her children Spanish. She spoke Spanish, though she lost some of it over the years. Like many in her generation, she considered Spanish an educational impediment. The theory was that we needed to master English (which would not be possible if we learned Spanish) so that we could succeed in school, a view held to this day by some Latinos. In my mother's generation, it was not uncommon to suffer punishment for speaking any language other than English in the public schools. When I was growing up, my mother and grandmother spoke Spanish only when they wanted to have a private conversation in our presence. My mother would become irritable, rare for her, when my brother and I teased her for speaking "Mexican." "It is *Spanish*," she would emphasize. "There is no *Mexican* language."

While my mother and grandmother lived in a state of denial, the Anglo men in the family often emphasized their Mexican-ness, though in dramatically different ways. When my grandmother talked about her Spanish background, my stepgrandfather would sarcastically respond: "Get off it. You're a Mexican like the rest of them." Weakly saying that he did not know anything and laughing uncomfortably, my grandmother would appear wounded. In a much more constructive way, my father would emphasize the positiveness of my mother's Mexican background to me. He told me in my younger years that the mixture of his "Swedish" (an exaggeration) and my mother's Mexican bloodlines was good.

My mother's and grandmother's assimilationism also meant adoption of the dominant society's racial attitudes. From an early age, my grandmother reminded me never to bring home an African-American girlfriend. She jokingly would say things to me like "don't bring home anyone who wants pork chops." Though she said this with a laugh, I understood her seriousness. Although my mother would never say such things, I sensed her agreement. My mother and grandmother also considered immigrants from Mexico as lessers, referring to them (jokingly, of course) as "wetbacks" or "Julios." These distinctions between themselves and Mexican immigrants were part of their denial of their Mexican ancestry and efforts to "pass" as Spanish.

NOTES

1. Gregory Howard Williams, LIFE ON THE COLOR LINE (1995).

2. Judy Scales-Trent, NOTES OF A WHITE BLACK WOMAN: RACE, COLOR, COMMUNITY (1995).

Chapter 62

||||||||||||||||||||||||||||||||||||||||||||||||||||||||||||||||||||||||||||||

Assimilation and Demographic Replenishment

Mary Waters

In the past forty years the largest immigration flow in the nation's history has profoundly transformed U.S. society. For some, this influx of predominantly nonwhite
immigrants is nothing short of a social, economic, and cultural disaster, displacing
native workers, swelling the largely minority underclass, and exacerbating racial and
ethnic conflict. For others, the new immigrants strengthen and reinforce the best in
American traditions, revitalizing decaying neighborhoods and stagnant industries
and adding new talents and energies to the U.S. civic culture.

Because few people are willing to argue that past immigration was bad for America, the debate about immigration restrictions in our own time hinges on the question of how immigration today differs from that of earlier periods. Are today's immigrants fundamentally different from those who arrived during the nineteenth and
early twentieth centuries? Are historical conditions fundamentally different now than
they were before?

Wayne Cornelius [see part 2—Eds.] directs our attention to the specific antipathies
and fears with which Anglo Americans regard Latinos as a group. Some Americans,
he argues, believe that Latinos find it particularly difficult to integrate into U.S. society because of their strong linguistic and cultural distinctness. Cornelius suggests that
many Americans believe that even though earlier waves of European immigrants successfully assimilated, the concentration and numbers of current Latino immigrants,
along with the proximity of the border, make it possible that the United States will
fail to integrate Latino immigrants.

Two themes are key in the political debates over immigration: (1) the ethnic cultural distinctness of current immigrants and the difficulties they are thus presumed
to have with assimilation and (2) the increasing role of transnationalism in current
immigrant experiences. These themes are relevant to all current immigrant groups.
Yet Latinos, by their sheer numbers and by their origins in America's closest neighbors—Mexico, the Caribbean, and Central and South America—bring these differences into stark relief. Social science theories and models of immigration developed
in the twentieth century largely to illuminate the experiences of the great wave of
immigrants from Europe, and most did not deal with Latinos, even though Latinos

were also immigrating to the United States at that time. These theories of immigrant assimilation focused on changes between generations. But those generational changes reflected the drastic slowing of European immigration from the late 1920s onward.

The immigration restrictions of the 1920s meant that after three generations, the flow of immigrants from Europe essentially stopped. The cutting off of immigration from Europe eliminated the supply of raw material for ethnicity, so what it means to be Jewish or Italian or Polish in the United States reflects what happened in the United States over those 50 to 60 years. Without new immigrants arriving in any appreciable numbers, successive generations dominated the population. Thus, by the 1980s and 1990s the overwhelming majority of Italian Americans and Polish Americans were second-, third-, and fourth-generation U.S. residents. As they became less occupationally and residentially segregated, as they intermarried more, and as their ethnic identities became more symbolic and more a matter of choice, few if any "more ethnic" new immigrants arrived to take their place.

New immigrants from Latin America and Asia face different incorporation experiences. Because of a constant supply of new immigrants, these ethnic populations are heterogeneous on measures of assimilation. Individuals may undergo marked assimilation, but new arrivals keep the ethnic group "fresh." Ethnic neighborhoods such as East Los Angeles and Spanish Harlem will not shrink like Little Italy did, becoming quaint shrines to an earlier way of life. Rather they will remain vibrant neighborhoods. But that does not mean that the same people will stay in them. A third-generation Mexican American might intermarry, move to the suburbs, achieve substantial social mobility, and develop a "symbolic" identity as Latino American. Yet he or she will be replaced with a first-generation Mexican American who will live in a Mexican neighborhood, speak little English, and live a richly and very visibly ethnic Mexican lifestyle.

This demographic replenishment and the resulting heterogeneity of what it means to be Latino clearly affect American public opinion on immigration policy, as Cornelius shows. Because ongoing immigration means a constant fresh, new first generation of immigrants, it will appear to the average American that the new immigrants are not assimilating in the same way that European immigrants did in earlier times. This is because the most visible aspects of ethnicity—speaking a language other than English, occupational specialization, and residential concentration—will not be diluted even when a great deal of assimilation is taking place among the second and third generations.

Hence the demographic patterns of current Caribbean, Latin American, and Asian immigrants will be more complex than those of earlier immigrants. Some intermarriage and identity changes are already occurring among the descendants of these immigrants. Yet the ongoing nature of immigration means that there may be two stories to tell—one story of new arrivals and the replenishment of an ethnic culture and another story of the quiet assimilation of individuals into a much more integrated and blended culture. The danger is that the ongoing assimilation of the new immigrants and their children and grandchildren will be obscured by the replenishment of the immigrant generation. In that case, public support for restricting immigration may increase because people are not aware of the sometimes hidden assimilation that is occurring.

Mexican Americans exhibit the greatest degree of generational diversity: some come from families that have been present in the United States for many generations, but a large number are foreign-born. Accordingly, they might serve as a lightning rod for the type of cultural anxieties Cornelius describes. Cuban Americans, by contrast, because of the paucity of current immigration from Cuba, are aging generationally in a way reminiscent of the European immigrants. (Of course, this could change dramatically when Cuba experiences a change in its current government, possibly allowing more immigration.)

Yet regardless of the variation among groups, Latino Americans as a whole will be integrating into American society within a setting of constant immigration and replenishment. This means that the assimilation that does occur among individuals —especially later-generation individuals—will be obscured, and the kinds of cultural anxieties Cornelius outlines will probably persist. Their economic, cultural, and political incorporation into American society proceeds apace, but the constant supply of new immigrants may make much of that assimilation invisible to the broader public.

Chapter 63

||||||||||||||||||||||||||||||||||||||||||||||||||||||||||||||||||||||||||||

A Scholarship Boy

Richard Rodriguez

I stand in the ghetto classroom—"the guest speaker"—attempting to lecture on the mystery of the sounds of our words to rows of diffident students. "Don't you hear it? Listen! The music of our words. '*Sumer is i-cumen in. . . .*' And songs on the car radio. We need Aretha Franklin's voice to fill plain words with music—her life." In the face of their empty stares, I try to create an enthusiasm. But the girls in the back row turn to watch some boy passing outside. There are flutters of smiles, waves. And someone's mouth elongates heavy, silent words through the barrier of glass. Silent words—the lips straining to shape each voiceless syllable: "*Meet meee late errr.*" By the door, the instructor smiles at me, apparently hoping that I will be able to spark some enthusiasm in the class. But only one student seems to be listening. A girl, maybe fourteen. In this gray room her eyes shine with ambition. She keeps nodding and nodding at all that I say; she even takes notes. And each time I ask a question, she jerks up and down in her desk like a marionette, while her hand waves over the bowed heads of her classmates. It is myself (as a boy) I see as she faces me now (a man in my thirties).

The boy who first entered a classroom barely able to speak English, twenty years later concluded his studies in the stately quiet of the reading room in the British Museum. Thus with one sentence I can summarize my academic career. It will be harder to summarize what sort of life connects the boy to the man.

With every award, each graduation from one level of education to the next, people I'd meet would congratulate me. Their refrain always the same: "Your parents must be very proud." Sometimes then they'd ask me how I managed it—my "success."

(How?) After a while, I had several quick answers to give in reply. I'd admit, for one thing, that I went to an excellent grammar school. (My earliest teachers, the nuns, made my success their ambition.) And my brother and both my sisters were very good students. (They often brought home the shiny school trophies I came to want.) And my mother and father always encouraged me. (At every graduation they were behind the stunning flash of the camera when I turned to look at the crowd.)

As important as these factors were, however, they account inadequately for my academic advance. Nor do they suggest what an odd success I managed. For although I was a very good student, I was also a very bad student. I was a "scholarship boy," a certain kind of scholarship boy. Always successful, I was always unconfident. Exhilarated by my progress. Sad. I became the prized student—anxious and eager to learn. Too eager, too anxious—an imitative and unoriginal pupil. My brother and two sisters enjoyed the advantages I did, and they grew to be as successful as I, but none of them ever seemed so anxious about their schooling. A second-grade student, I was the one who came home and corrected the "simple" grammatical mistakes of our parents. ("Two negatives make a positive.") Proudly I announced—to my family's startled silence—that a teacher had said I was losing all trace of a Spanish accent. I was oddly annoyed when I was unable to get parental help with a homework assignment. The night my father tried to help me with an arithmetic exercise, he kept reading the instructions, each time more deliberately, until I pried the textbook out of his hands, saying, "I'll try to figure it out some more by myself."

When I reached the third grade, I outgrew such behavior. I became more tactful, careful to keep separate the two very different worlds of my day. But then, with ever-increasing intensity, I devoted myself to my studies. I became bookish, puzzling to all my family. Ambition set me apart. When my brother saw me struggling home with stacks of library books, he would laugh, shouting: "Hey, Four Eyes!" My father opened a closet one day and was startled to find me inside, reading a novel. My mother would find me reading when I was supposed to be asleep or helping around the house or playing outside. In a voice angry or worried or just curious, she'd ask: "What do you see in your books?" It became the family's joke. When I was called and wouldn't reply, someone would say I must be hiding under my bed with a book.

(How did I manage my success?)

What I am about to say to you has taken me more than twenty years to admit: *A primary reason for my success in the classroom was that I couldn't forget that schooling was changing me and separating me from the life I enjoyed before becoming a student.* That simple realization! For years I never spoke to anyone about it. Never mentioned a thing to my family or my teachers or classmates. From a very early age, I understood enough, just enough about my classroom experiences to keep what I knew repressed, hidden beneath layers of embarrassment. Not until my last months as a graduate student, nearly thirty years old, was it possible for me to think much about the reasons for my academic success. Only then. At the end of my schooling, I needed to determine how far I had moved from my past. The adult finally confronted, and now must publicly say, what the child shuddered from knowing and could never admit to himself or to those many faces that smiled at his every success. ("Your parents must be very proud. . . .")

Chapter 64

‖‖‖

Masks and Acculturation

Margaret E. Montoya

[The author invites the reader to consider how culture and stories interweave in the lives of outsiders, now combining to create masks, now to "create new options for expression, personal identity, cultural authenticity and pedagogical innovation." She then continues as follows:]

> I put on my masks, my
> costumes and posed for each
> occasion. I conducted myself
> well, I think, but
> an emptiness
> grew
> that no thing
> could fill. I think
> I hungered for myself.[1]

One of the earliest memories from my school years is of my mother braiding my hair, making my *trenzas*. In 1955, I was seven years old and in second grade at the Immaculate Conception School in Las Vegas, New Mexico. Our family home with its outdoor toilet was on an unpaved street, one house from the railroad track. I remember falling asleep to the subterranean rumble of the trains.

Nineteen fifty-five was an extremely important year in my development, in my understanding of myself in relation to Anglo society. I remember it as the year I began to think about myself in relation to my classmates and their families. I began to feel different and to adjust my behavior accordingly.

My sister, brother, and I dressed in front of the space heater in the bedroom we shared. Catholic school girls wore uniforms. We wore blue jumpers and white blouses. I remember my mother braiding my hair and my sister's. I can still feel the part she would draw with the point of the comb. She would begin at the top of my head, pressing down as she drew the comb down to the nape of my neck. "Don't move," she'd say as she held the two hanks of hair, checking to make sure that the

From *Mascaras, Trenzas, y Greñas: Un/Masking the Self while Un/Braiding Latina Stories and Legal Discourse*, 17 Harv. Women's L.J. 185 (1994); 15 Chicano-Latino L. Rev. 1 (1994). Originally published in the *Harvard Women's Law Journal* and the *Chicano-Latino Law Review*. Reprinted by permission.

part was straight. Only then would she begin, braiding as tightly as our squirming would allow, so the braids could withstand our running, jumping, and hanging from the monkey bars at recess. "I don't want you to look *grenudas*," my mother would say. ["I don't want you to look uncombed."]

Hearing my mother use both English and Spanish gave emphasis to what she was saying. She used Spanish to talk about what was really important: her feelings, her doubts, her worries. She also talked to us in Spanish about gringos, Mexicanos, and the relations between them. Her stories were sometimes about being treated outrageously by gringos, her anger controlled and her bitterness implicit. She also told stories about Anglos she admired—those who were egalitarian, smart, well-spoken, and well-mannered.

Sometimes Spanish was spoken so as not to be understood by Them. Usually, though, Spanish and English were woven together. *Grenuda* was one of many words encoded with familial and cultural meaning. My mother used the word to admonish us, but she wasn't warning us about name-calling: *grenuda* was not an epithet that our schoolmates were likely to use. Instead, I heard my mother saying something that went beyond well-groomed hair and being judged by our appearance—she could offer strategies for passing that scrutiny. She used the Spanish word, partly because there is no precise English equivalent, but also because she was interpreting the world for us.

The real message of *grenudas* arrived through the use of the Spanish word—it was unspoken and subtextual. She was teaching us that our world was divided, that They-Who-Don't-Speak-Spanish would see us as different, would judge us, would find us lacking. Her lessons about combing, washing, and doing homework frequently relayed a deeper message: be prepared, because you will be judged by your skin color, your names, your accents. They will see you as ugly, lazy, dumb, and dirty.

As I put on my uniform and my mother braided my hair, I changed; I became my public self. My *trenzas* announced that I was clean and well-cared-for at home. My *trenzas* and school uniform blurred the differences between my family's economic and cultural circumstances and those of the more economically comfortable Anglo students. I welcomed the braids and uniform as a disguise which concealed my minimal wardrobe and the relative poverty in which my family lived.

As we walked to school, away from home, away from the unpaved streets, away from the "Spanish" to the "Anglo" part of town, I felt both drawn to and repelled by my strange surroundings. I wondered what Anglos were like in their big houses. What did they eat? How did they furnish their homes? How did they pass the time? Did my English sound like theirs? Surely their closets were filled with dresses, sweaters, and shoes, *apenas estrenados*.[2]

I remember being called on one afternoon in second grade to describe what we had eaten for lunch. Rather than admit to eating *caldito* (soup) *y tortillas,* partly because I had no English words for those foods, I regaled the class with a story about what I assumed an "American" family would eat at lunch: pork chops, mashed potatoes, green salad, sliced bread, and apple pie. The nun reported to my mother that I had lied. Afraid of being mocked, I unsuccessfully masked the truth, and consequently revealed more about myself than I concealed.

In those days before certain ecumenical reforms, Catholicism still professed great concern about sinning. Although elementary school children were too young to commit most sins, lying was a real spiritual danger. Paradoxically, we were surrounded by Truth disguised in myriad ways. Religious language was oblique and filled with multiple meanings: Virgin Mother, Risen Son, bread that was the Body and wine that was the Blood. Our teachers, the nuns, were completely hidden—women without surnames, families, friends, or homes of their own. They embodied the collapsing of the private into the public. Their black and white habits hid their breasts, waists, legs, hair color, and hair texture.

Our school was well integrated with "Spanish" students because it stood in a town with a predominantly Latino population. The culture of the school, however, was overwhelmingly Anglo and middle class. The use of Spanish was frowned upon and occasionally punished. Any trace of an accent when speaking English would be pointed out and sarcastically mocked. This mocking persisted even though, and maybe because, some of the nuns were also "Spanish."

I remember being assigned to tutor another second-grader in reading. He wore denim overalls, had his hair shaved for some medical procedure and spoke mostly Spanish. I think of him now, and perhaps thought of him then, as being exposed— exposed by not being able to read, exposed by not having a uniform, exposed by not having hair, exposed by not knowing English. From my perspective as a child, it all seemed connected somehow—Spanish-ness, sickness, poverty, and ignorance.

By the age of seven, I was keenly aware that I lived in a society that had little room for those who were poor, brown, or female. I was all three. I moved between dualized worlds: private/public, Catholic/secular, poverty/privilege, Latina/Anglo. My *trenzas* and school uniform were a cultural disguise. They were also a precursor for the more elaborate mask I would later develop.

Presenting an acceptable face, speaking without a Spanish accent, hiding what we really felt—masking our inner selves—were defenses against racism passed on to us by our parents to help us get along in school and in society. We learned that it was safer to be inscrutable. We absorbed the necessity of constructing and maintaining a disguise in public. We struggled to be seen as Mexican but also wanted acceptance as Americans at a time when the mental image conjured up by that word included only Anglos.

Mine is the first generation of Latinas to be represented in virtually every college and university and in anything approaching significant numbers. But, for the most part, we find ourselves isolated. Rarely has another Latina gone before us. Rarely do we find another Latina whom we can watch to try and figure out all the little questions about subtextual meaning, about how dress or speech or makeup are interpreted in this particular environment.

My participation in the Chicano student movement in college fundamentally changed me. My adoption of the ethnic label as a primary identifier gave me an ideological mask that serves to this day. This transformation of my public persona was psychically liberating. This nascent liberation was, however, reactive and inchoate. Even as I struggled to redefine myself, I was locked in a reluctant embrace with those whose definitions of me I was trying to shrug off.

When I arrived as a student at Harvard Law School, I dressed so as to proclaim my politics. During my first day of orientation, I wore a Mexican peasant blouse and cutoff jeans on which I had embroidered the Chicano symbol of the *aguila* (a stylized eagle) on one seat pocket and the woman symbol on the other. The *aguila* reminded me of the red and black flags of the United Farm Worker rallies; it reminded me that I had links to a particular community. I was never to finish the fill-in stitches in the woman symbol. My symbols, like my struggles, were ambiguous.

As time went on, my clothes lost their political distinctiveness. They signified my ambivalence: perhaps if I dressed like a lawyer, eventually I would acquire more conventional ideas and ideals and fit in with my peers. Or perhaps if I dressed like a lawyer, I could harbor for some future use the disruptive and, at times, unwelcome thoughts that entered my head. My clothing would become protective coloration. Chameleon-like, I would dress to fade into the ideological, political, and cultural background rather than proclaim my differences.

Academic success traditionally has required that one exhibit the linguistic and cognitive characteristics of the dominant culture. Until challenged by recent empirical research by Chicano social scientists, retention of traditional Mexican-American culture was believed to impede successful adjustment within mainstream American society. This "damaging-culture" model provided a rationale for advocating the complete assimilation of Latinos into the mainstream culture.

The widespread acceptance of assimilationist thought fueled social and familial pressure on Latinos to abandon traditional values and lifestyles in order to achieve educational and economic upward mobility. Acculturation into the dominant culture is a concomitant of education. Virtually all Latino students with a college-level education appear to be highly assimilated into Anglo culture.

To support their academic progress, Latinos have encouraged their children to speak English well and have tolerated other aspects of acculturation, such as changes in friends, clothes, and recreational preferences. Students learn to adopt masks of the dominant culture which avoid the negative values ascribed to traditional Latina/o culture. Latina/o history is replete with stories about those who changed their names, lost the Spanish language and with it any trace of a Spanish accent, or deliberately married out of the culture. In short, some did whatever was necessary to be seen as not different by the majority.

Feeling masked because of ethnic and racial differences is directly linked to the process of cultural assimilation, and to the pervasive Latina/o resistance against assimilation; against being seen as *agringada*, of becoming a *gringa*, of being taken for something one never wanted to become. Assimilation has become yet another mask for the Latina/o to hide behind. I have a clay mask made by Mexican artisans that captures this idea but from a different perspective. The outermost mask is a white skeleton face wearing a grimace. The second layer shows a face with an aquiline nose and a goatee suggesting the face of the Spaniard, the colonizer of indigenous Mexico. This second mask parts to show the face of a pensive Aztec. This clay sculpture suggests the indigenous Indian preserved behind the false masks, the death mask, the conquistador mask. In other words, the sculpture represents all of us who have been colonized and acculturated—who have succeeded in withholding a precious part of our past behind our constructed public personas.

Belonging to a higher economic class than that of one's family or community and affecting the mannerisms, clothing styles, or speech patterns that typify the privileged classes can strain familial and ethnic bonds. Families, even those who have supported the education and advancement of their children, can end up feeling estranged from them and resentful of the cultural costs of their academic and economic success. Accusations of *vendida*, "selling-out," forgetting the ethnic community, and abandoning the family can accompany academic success.

Even when family or friends do not recriminate, internal doubts plague the student about what one has given up in order to achieve academic success. Concerns about ethnic identity and personal authenticity are imbedded within the question "Who am I really?" We have been told, "You don't seem Latina," or have been asked, "How Latina are you?" Such comments, when made by Anglos, imply that we have risen above our group. We are special, better, acceptable. When made by Latinos, however, the question carries an innuendo of cultural betrayal and the threat of cultural excommunication.

There are times when the strands of our lives resist being woven into a neat braid. Recently I happened upon an autobiography, *Always Running: La Vida Loca, Gang Days in L.A.*, written by Luis J. Rodriguez. I found the book while on a trip to Cambridge as an elected director of the Harvard Alumni Association. I had attended a long day of meetings in the rarefied seclusion of the Harvard Faculty Club, where I always feel like a spectator rather than a participant. The building evokes the "clubiness" of its name: dark wood paneling, well worn rugs, rooms called libraries. I can never seem to dress well enough or choose words, accents, or voices carefully enough to feel that I belong there. Occasionally, I can give voice to my experience—to one Latina's experience.

After one such day, I wandered into a bookstore in Harvard Square. I leafed through the Rodriguez book. Suddenly, I focused on my cousin's name, Rodolfo "Sonny" Gomez, listed among those to whom the book was dedicated. Rodriguez didn't state it explicitly, but it was, presumably, a list of his homeboys and homegirls who didn't survive *la vida loca*. I knew that but for the grace of God . . . Sonny could have had my fate and I, his.

Standing in the bookstore, my eyes filled with tears. We both stood with a foot in two worlds. I remembered Sonny; he drove a yellow MG convertible, introduced me to the music of Bob Dylan, talked about Karl Marx and Chicanismo.

My multiple identities do not usually clash as violently as they did at that particular moment. Those moments set me apart from the privileged majority, the experience of being yanked back unpredictably into powerlessness. Throughout the last decade, Latinos and others have challenged the efficacy of the assimilationist model, pointing out the heterogeneity of orientations and experiences among Latinos. They have demonstrated that "integration with one's ancestral culture is conducive to success and adjustment in American society."[3] Sociocultural adjustment is now understood as a multifaceted process that depends upon complex variables rather than a unilevel process whereby the customs of one culture are merely substituted for those of another.

Latinos have long exhibited bicultural behavior and values, but until recently no body of literature established the validity of such cultural integration. Contemporary Latina/o poetry and fiction exhibit this bilingual and bicultural character. Latina/o public discourse increasingly mirrors private speech.

As Latinas/os begin to construct our varied identities, we can still feel caught between the traditional understanding of what "real Latinas/os" are like and the strategies we invoke to respond to novel situations. Resolution of these issues need not be an isolating, individualistic, or secretive process, alienating us from our families or our communities. Despite important historical, ethnic, and linguistic differences, stories of assimilation told from the various perspectives of subordinated groups have strains of similarities. In addition to the personal and collective pain that we experience because of societal pressures to assimilate, Latinas/os face the disquietude of being masked for some of the same reasons as other Outsiders.

Being masked may be a universal condition in that all of us control how we present ourselves to others. But a fundamental difference marks feeling masked because one is a member of one or more oppressed groups within the society. When members of the dominant culture mask themselves to control the impressions they make, such behavior is not inherently self-loathing. But when we attempt to mask immutable characteristics of skin color, eye shape, or hair texture because they historically have been loathsome to the dominant culture, then the masks of acculturation can take on shades of self-hate. Moreover, unmasking for members of the dominant culture does not spark the fear or depth of humiliation that it does for the subordinated, for whom the unmasking is often involuntary and unexpected.

For Outsiders, unmasking is a holistic experience: I do not have separate masks for my female-ness and Latina-ness. The construction of my public persona includes all that I am. My public face is an adjustment to the present and a response to the past. Any unmasking resonates through the pathways of my memory. For Outsiders, the necessity of unmasking has been historical. Strategies are passed on from one generation to another to accommodate, to resist, to subvert oppressive forces. Involuntary unmasking is painful, it evokes echoes of past hurts, hurts one has suffered, and hurts one has heard stories about.

Outsiders also live with the gnawing suspicion that the public identities available to them are limited to those reflecting the values, norms, and behavior of the dominant ideology. Through my cultural disguise, I sought to mirror the behavior of those who mattered more than I. As a child, I altered or denied my language, my clothes, my foods. My *trenzas* helped me to fit in, to get by, to move up. As an adult, I still alter or deny myself/selves, both consciously and unconsciously.

A significant aspect of subordination is the persistence with which we mimic the styles, preferences, and mannerisms of those who dominate us, even when we have become aware of the mimicry. Lost to the Outsider are those identities that would have developed but for our real and perceived needs to camouflage ourselves in the masks of the Master. Lost to all are the variety of choices, the multiplicity of identities that would be available if we were not trapped by the dynamics of subordination, of privilege.

NOTES

1. Alma Villanueva, *Mother, May I?* in CONTEMPORARY CHICANA POETRY 303, 324 (Marta Ester Sanchez ed., 1985).

2. *Apenas estrenados* is a Spanish concept that has no English equivalent. *Estrenar* connotes wearing something for the first time and conveys the special privilege that attaches to the first wearing. We had few opportunities to *estrenar* new clothes.

3. Raymond Buriel, *Integration with Traditional Mexican-American Culture and Sociocultural Adjustment,* in CHICANO PSYCHOLOGY 95, at 97 (Joe L. Martinez, Jr., & Richard H. Mendoza eds., 2d ed. 1984).

|||||||||||||||||||||||||||||||||||||||||||||||||||||||||||||||||||||||

Chapter 65

The Mexican Case

The Story of the Immigrant
Second Generation

Alejandro Portes and
Rubén G. Rumbaut

The first girl born in California in 2000 was born to Mexican parents. She was named Anayeli de Jesús. Her parents, Elena and Javier, came from Mexico in the 1990s looking for a better life and hope the same for their daughter: "To be a good student and to go to the university."

—Kate Folmar and Scott Martelli, "The New Faces of
Orange County's Future," p. 1.

"If one takes out the Mexicans, there will be no evidence for segmented assimilation." This is a statement often heard among immigration specialists. It is buttressed by the size of the Mexican-origin population, by far the largest among contemporary immigrant groups, and by its low human capital. Some observers believe that signs of dissonant acculturation, low ambition, and the emergence of oppositional attitudes concentrate mainly among second-generation Mexicans. This is erroneous since other groups that have experienced negative modes of incorporation are also at risk. In different contexts, we have examined evidence to that effect among other sizable immigrant minorities, including Nicaraguans, Haitians, and post-Mariel Cubans.

Nevertheless, the Mexican immigrant population is defined by several attributes that make it unique and deserving of special attention. It is worth reviewing what these are and how they affect the second generation, particularly in relation to the ideological battles now raging. In California, in particular, nativist and assimilationist policies have been directed primarily at Mexicans and their offspring with consequences that, as just seen, have been the opposite of those intended. The Mexican population of the United States is marked by three characteristics that make it unique:

It is the product of an uninterrupted flow lasting more than a century. Mexicans are the *only* foreign group that has been part of both the classic period of immigration at the beginning of the twentieth century and the present movement. Accordingly, Mexicans are also the only group among today's major immigrant nationalities to have spawned an earlier second and even third generation.

Mexicans come from the only less-developed country sharing a land border with the United States. This geographical contiguity has facilitated both labor recruitment and subsequent mass labor displacements, mediated by social networks. The facility of such movements across a land border accounts for the lower average human capital of Mexican immigrants relative to other groups, who come from even poorer but more distant countries.

Because of their numbers, poverty, and visibility, Mexican immigrants were targets of repeated waves of nativist hostility throughout the twentieth century. These attacks included organized government campaigns aimed at their repatriation or at forcefully preventing their settlement. Mexican immigrants have thus experienced a negative mode of incorporation not only at present but for over 100 years. Demand for Mexican migrant labor has been equally persistent, but the conditions under which it has been employed have been marked by the social inferiority and political vulnerability created by this negative setting.

Results of our study offer abundant evidence of the consequences of these features. Mexican immigrants represent *the* textbook example of theoretically anticipated effects of low immigrant human capital combined with a negative reception. It is worth summarizing these results for what they tell us about the specific experiences of the group and, by extension, of those to be anticipated for other disadvantaged foreign minorities:

Adult Mexican immigrants not only receive low earnings, but their economic disadvantage also endures even after controlling for their human capital. Net of human capital factors, Mexican parents in our sample earn $1,910 less per year than other adult immigrants.

This economic disadvantage compounds because whatever human capital Mexican immigrants possess has a lower return than that among more successful groups. Thus, years of U.S. residence do not increase incomes for Mexican parents in our sample, and knowledge of English yields a lower payoff than for immigrants from other countries.

Mexican parents are significantly more likely to report low bonds of solidarity and low levels of support from their co-ethnics, reflecting the weak communities that have emerged under their precarious conditions of arrival and settlement. Aspirations for their children are also significantly lower than for other groups.

Mexican-American children are the only Latino group in the sample to lack a positive nationality effect on fluent bilingualism, and they have the lowest average self-esteem. Controlling for other factors, Mexican origin makes no positive contribution to either adaptation outcome.

Mexican-American children are the most likely to have shifted self-identities away from any American label and toward an unhyphenated national (i.e., Mexican) identity. They are also the group most prone to racialize their national origin. Both trends reflect a strong process of reactive formation to perceived external hostility.

Reflecting their parents' low aspirations, Mexican-American children have significantly lower educational expectations than average and the lowest among Latin-origin groups. This disadvantage persists after controlling for other factors. Net of them, second-generation Mexican students are still 10 percent less likely to believe that an advanced college degree is within their reach than other students.

Corresponding to these low aspirations and cumulative disadvantages, Mexican-origin students are less likely to perform well in school. Their lower-than-average grades and test scores cannot be explained by individual, family, or school predictors. In junior high school, Mexican students fell behind a net 12 points in standardized math scores and 15 points in reading scores, after controlling for these predictors; they also had a significant net disadvantage in grades. This inferior performance continues in late high school, where Mexican-American students suffer a significant handicap after controlling for a wide array of individual and family factors.

These cumulative results clearly point to a difficult process of adaptation and to the likelihood of downward assimilation in many cases. The high optimism of parents and the superior school performance and lower dropout rates of second-generation Mexicans relative to their native-parentage peers do not modify this conclusion. This optimism and relatively better academic record reflect a residual immigrant drive that weakens with the passage of time under the continuous influence of an adverse social environment. It is worth emphasizing that the second-generation Mexican advantage is only observable in comparison with their native counterparts, that is, third-generation and higher Hispanics who perform even worse than the more recent arrivals. This comparison offers no grounds for expecting that academic performance will improve and dropout rates decline over time.

The danger of downward assimilation for Mexican-American youths is only compounded by the policies that have captured the imagination of mainstream voters. For reasons already examined, nativism and forceful assimilationism yield programs that undermine successful adaptation by increasing dissonant acculturation or provoking an adversarial reaction. In light of the present evidence, there is no second-generation group for which selective acculturation is more necessary than for Mexican Americans. This would entail educational programs that combine learning of English and acculturation with preservation of Spanish and understanding and respect for the parents' culture. In particular, there should be ample external support for the immigrant family and for its incipient attempts at building strong community bonds. In many Mexican families, the *only* thing going for the children is the support and ambition of their parents. These aspirations should be strengthened rather than undermined.

From a long-term perspective, current policies toward Mexican immigration verge on the suicidal. Demand for Mexican migrant labor continues unabated, and its arrival is guaranteed by various legal loopholes and the strong social networks created over a century. Once here, however, migrant workers and their children are heavily discriminated against, blamed for their poverty, and subjected either to nativist ire or pressures toward immediate assimilation. The results are not hard to discern in the spectacle of the impoverished barrios of Los Angeles, San Diego, Houston, and other large southwestern cities and in consistent results from our study.

Chapter 66

||||||||||||||||||||||||||||||||||||||||||||||||||||||||||||||||||||||||||||||||

Harvard Homeboy

Ruben Navarrette, Jr.

I'm a homeboy now. At Harvard, I didn't fit.
　　　　　　　　　　　　—J.R. (Harvard Class of 1989)

A writer friend warned me that this case brings no easy answers. No "obvious conclusions" can be drawn by the story of J.R., the former Harvard student who was convicted of armed robbery in Orange County two months ago. "The whole thing seems problematic," my friend cautioned. "My hunch is that the kid's shoulders can't stand much metaphor. Forget it." Still, I fear that much remains unsaid. So I say it.

The day after the Harvard Class of 1989 received the golden passports that would open any door of their choosing, J.R., who would have been among them, was instead in a courtroom in Santa Ana facing a possible fifteen years in prison.

So came to an end the drama, two years after it first played out in the national media, of the Latino honors student from La Habra who, a jury decided, held up at least six stores and fast-food restaurants during school breaks over the course of eighteen months.

If one seeks tragedy—dishonor, if you will—the drama will not disappoint. The wasted future of a bright young man imprisoned in a correctional system that leaves those it punishes scarred and beaten, seldom corrected. The pain of a family that sacrificed much of their own lives to enhance his. The white alumni offended by his abuse of Ivy League benevolence—"See what happens when. . . ."

People following the story can only guess at the "why" of J.R.'s turning from the educational fast track to armed robbery. Psychologists offer simplistic theories about self-destructive "sun children"—bright minority students who excel beyond expectation and then turn away from the guiding light of success to burn out like a shooting star. In New York, a writer draws what seems an insightful comparison between the J.R. case and that of E.P., a black honors student from Exeter, bound for Stanford on a scholarship, who was killed as he was mugging an undercover policeman near

Harlem. J.R. himself says he felt "alienated" in Cambridge. Harvard, in characteristic fashion, disclaims responsibility. "An isolated case," Harvard says. Ah. . . .

Four years ago, J.R. and I entered Harvard as two of thirty-five or so Mexican Americans in the Class of '89. Some of those students were from wealthy families and private schools in the Southwest; others were from poor, Spanish-speaking families. Some wanted to take their Harvard degree "back to the community"; others intended to take it only as far as Wall Street. In Harvard's eyes, we were similar; in fact, we had our differences.

Unfortunately, at Harvard as in the world in general, what makes people different is not always respected. Insecurity as to whether you really "belong" in a foreign environment can breed intolerance toward others. At its extreme, it becomes a kind of contest to "fit in"—a contest that seems to have only one kind of winner.

At Harvard, J.R. and I were friends. Yes, I think that's fair to say. Sometimes we argued politics or talked football over a few beers; we felt comfortable with one another, I think. It was our school that my friend never felt comfortable with. He seemed to pass through a stage that many scared and alienated young people in elite schools go through—wearing his ethnicity like a badge. Or was it more like a shield? I remember him in the costume of an East L.A. "homeboy"—the khaki pants, the Pendleton shirt, the bandanna around his head. I remember his tattoos and his homesickness for La Habra. I remember seeing him with a black eye and learning that he had been in a fistfight with a couple of local "townies" because of a racist remark they made. Young working-class whites sometimes resent the presence of Chicanos on an elite hometown campus that remains largely closed to them. It's ironic that J.R. felt shut out from the campus, too.

Harvard Chicano. Twenty years in existence and the term still seems an enigma, a paradox that doesn't lend itself to a neat definition. Two concepts, once as distinct as oil and water, now are joined in the name of educational progress. Who are the people who bear the weight of that label? A policy-maker's "model minority," one whose excellence will make affirmative action easier. A "teacher's pet" always waving her arm with the right answer. A high school counselor's "overachiever" needing little guidance. Most of all, a tearful parent's pride and joy, proof that with hard work anything is possible.

Since the central character in this tragic play is a personification of this paradox, one is tempted to romanticize his experience. A respected Chicano studies professor who knows neither J.R. nor Harvard speculates that "Ivy League racism made J.R. miserable at Harvard; he committed those crimes to get out." I've heard others say that J.R.'s story is really one of a scared young man who wanted off the fast-moving treadmill that a well-meaning society had placed him on. Maybe. But gaps appear in the drama that aren't filled by even the most sweeping of "obvious conclusions." At Harvard, J.R.'s rebellious appearance was not unusual. Many freshmen adopt a costume, a mannerism, a way of presenting themselves to others. In the Commune on the Charles, the extraordinary is ordinary. But not every student who sports torn Levi's, or a serape, around Harvard Yard commits armed robbery during summer vacation. There must be more.

At his trial, mention was made of J.R.'s dabbling in drugs. Seeking shelter from his somewhat charmed life, he entered the hallucinogenic world of PCP. For him, this world promised acceptance. It is, after all, a world already inhabited by hundreds of thousands of young Latinos like him, or unlike him—those that he had always been told he didn't have to be like.

With the emergence of drugs into the drama, many people lost interest. He was no longer a "good victim."

It is tempting to take the complex human experience that began to unfold during J.R.'s trial and reduce it to a more manageable drug story, but the critical onlooker presses for more.

Some of us know, and few will admit, that J.R. experienced a kind of double alienation while at Harvard. Confused and alone, he instinctively sought refuge in the one corner of that foreign world that appeared familiar.

The Mexican-American students' association at Harvard is called Raza; its professed goal for twenty years has been to provide a support system for students who, on their application, checked the box marked "Mexican American/Chicano." Raza works with the admissions office to ensure active recruitment of Latino high school students, and the organization's rhetoric promises that it will make every effort to provide emotional support when they arrive in Cambridge. In short, Raza is supposed to help create a nurturing environment in which Latinos can adjust to life at Harvard without necessarily surrendering their cultural identity at the front gate.

Yet those who know these types of student organizations also know that sometimes they become as intolerant of individual differences as they accuse the campus community at large of being. Ethnic organizations do sometimes develop an image deemed "proper" for their group and exclude those who appear to contradict that image.

To those members of Raza eagerly awaiting their admittance to the world of BMWs and designer suits, J.R. and his East L.A. look represented that sort of contradiction. He was an embarrassment to some, a reminder of how close they still were to the world they'd left behind. He dressed like the kid whose fate, we had been told, we could escape if we studied hard. So we did. And when, through all our effort, we arrived safely in the ivy-covered world of cashmere and Kennedys, there he was —staring us in the face and forcing us to deal with the painful realization that we had not progressed nearly as far as we thought we had. He made us feel uncomfortable, then guilty for feeling uncomfortable.

I remember my last conversation with him before finals in our sophomore year— the boyish expression on his face as he described his eagerness to go home. He asked if I had time for lunch; I frowned and said no, some errand in the Square. He understood. None of us ever had time for him.

A few weeks later I was in California, clerking for the state attorney-general's office. My father called and asked if I'd read the morning paper. "A guy from Harvard was arrested," he said. "Did you know him?" Yes, I did.

As I punch out the painful impressions of that time, my father looks over my shoulder and seems intrigued by the element of betrayal. "This happened at Harvard?" he asks. "Are you saying that the higher we climb, the less united we become?" Maybe that is what I am saying. Or maybe this is personal. Maybe this is just guilt, another confession by another Latino at Harvard. Maybe.

Maybe I just want people to think about what happens when a young man walks a tightrope between two very different worlds. Each has a claim on him. Harvard homeboy. Between the worlds that those two words represent is, perhaps, a barrier that should not be crossed.

Chapter 67

||||||||||||||||||||||||||||||||||||||||||||||||||||||||||||||||||||||||||||||

Dropping the Hyphen?

Tanya Golash-Boza

At a rally in Siler City, North Carolina, one chilly afternoon in February 2000, David Duke told an attentive, although sparse, crowd that foreign elements wanted to take over America. In Duke's diatribe about the failure of Latin American immigrants to blend into the melting pot, he did not mention that Irish and Italian immigrants had also been deemed incapable of assimilating in the early 20th century. Duke did make himself clear that when he refers to America and American values, he is referring only to the direct descendants of European-Americans. By doing this, he elucidated what normally goes unspoken—that the unmarked label "American" in most cases means European-American. For this reason, when we refer to African-Americans or Asian-Americans, we specify with hyphenated labels. On the other hand, when we are referring to European-Americans, "American" usually suffices. For example, Feagin (2000:100) reports that, in a six-month study of 65 U.S. newspapers, the term "American" was found many times, but the expression "white American" was exclusively used in juxtaposition to another racial category, usually "African-American."

If the unhyphenated label is reserved for white Americans as Feagin argues, then to what extent can Latin American immigrants and their descendants become Americans? Feagin contends that the unhyphenated American label refers to those people in the United States who have the luxury of pretending they do not have a racial or ethnic status. Pamela Perry's (2002) ethnographic study of racial identities among high school students reveals that many whites see themselves as not having a racial status or identity. For Perry's informants, those who were attuned to the prevalence of discrimination in U.S. society were more likely to recognize their white privilege, and thus their racial status as white. Among Bonilla-Silva's (2003) informants, one of the primary distinctions between the racial attitudes of blacks and whites was the recognition of the existence and prevalence of discrimination. His analyses demonstrate that only a small percentage of whites are aware of the omnipresence of discrimination in U.S. society. All these writers demonstrate that the recognition of discrimination plays a key role in the awareness of one's racial status.

I will argue that the recognition of discrimination plays a fundamental role in determining not only one's racial attitudes, but also one's racial or ethnic identification.

From *Dropping the Hyphen? Becoming Latino(a)-American through Racialized Assimilation,* 85 Social Forces 27–29, 31, 33–34 (Sept. 2006). Copyright © 2006 by the University of North Carolina Press. Used by permission of the publisher. www.uncpress.unc.edu.

Part of being white is being able to ignore the prevalence of racial discrimination in U.S. society. In the United States, the ethnic identity "American" is an unmarked ethnic identity just as is white. As such, part of being American is being able to ignore the prevalence of discrimination based on national origin in the United States. While whites self-identify as Americans, non-white Americans recognize that they are not Americans, but African-Americans, Native-Americans, Asian-Americans or Latino/a-Americans. In this sense, how one becomes American or how one assimilates into American society depends in large part on one's racial status. Nevertheless, scholars of immigration have not given sufficient consideration to racial status when studying patterns of immigrant adaptation.

Hispanics and Discrimination in the United States

It should come as no surprise that Hispanics face discrimination in the United States. Many people in the United States view Hispanics as poor, uneducated, unclean, illegal aliens and prone to teenage pregnancy. Popular media have contributed to these perceptions. In a study of the portrayal of Hispanics in the media, Lichter and Amundson (1997) found that, "compared to both Anglos and African Americans, television's Hispanics were low in number, low in social status, and lowdown in personal character, frequently portraying violent criminals" (71).

Survey analysis has demonstrated the prevalence of stereotypes about Hispanics. Members of this group are often perceived as less intelligent or culturally advanced than Anglos, less affluent than whites or Asians, less intelligent, more prone to be on welfare, and more likely to be engaged in drugs or other criminal activity than whites or Asians. In addition, blacks and Asians have a more negative view of Latinos/as than they do of whites. These widespread stereotypes are bound to influence interactions between non-Hispanics and people perceived to be Hispanics. They are also likely to affect the ethnic identifications of Hispanic Americans.

Given the prevalence of prejudicial beliefs in the United States about Hispanics, one can surmise that people who are labeled as such are likely to experience discrimination at some time in their lives. However, within the segment of the U.S. population that the Office of Management and Budget defines as Hispanic, only some of the individuals actually have the physical and cultural features that result in their being considered Hispanic in daily interactions. Because not all Hispanics are easily categorized as such, Hispanics experience varying levels of discrimination. Those who do experience discrimination are less likely to self-identify as American because this discrimination increases their awareness of their non-white status in the United States. I will also argue that Hispanics who do experience discrimination are more likely to self-identify as Hispanic or Latino/a, because experiences of discrimination teach Hispanics that they are labeled as such by others in the United States.

The analyses presented in this paper are based on ethnic self-identifications in national surveys. I acknowledge that survey analysis is not adequate to gain an in-depth understanding of the respondent's identity. Nevertheless, it is reasonable to propose that individuals who self-identify on a survey as Hispanic or as American have some attachment to these labels. This attachment, or lack thereof, provides a window into which we can glimpse a key part of their ethnic identity. If a person chooses not to identify as American when asked if that can be used to describe them, then we can safely assume that American-ness is not an integral part of his or her identity. This is important since the core assumption of traditional assimilation theory is that immigrants will eventually become un-hyphenated Americans.

Becoming American?

Proponents of assimilation theory insist that ethnic distinctiveness will eventually disappear for the children of immigrants in the United States. However, a number of other scholars have found that many immigrants associate being American with being white. For example, Rumbaut (1994) recounts that a sixteen-year-old Cambodian girl, when asked about her American identity responded: "How could I be American? I have black skin, black eyes, black hair. . . . My English is not good enough and my skin color black" (750). In addition, a Hispanic-looking appearance entails treatment as a foreigner even for native-born Americans. For example, Prudence Carter's (2005) Dominican informant, despite having been born in the United States, said that she was Hispanic and not American because American society does not accept her. Patricia Zavella (1996) recounts the story of a Chicano, who despite three generations of his ancestors having been born in the United States, was deported to Mexico, because he could not produce his birth certificate. One can clearly see here how this man's non-whiteness prevented him from being perceived as an American. This would never happen to the great-grandson of an Irish immigrant, for his Americanness would not come into question.

The association of Hispanicity with foreignness can also be seen in questions Latinos often get about their origins. Many U.S.-born Latinos and Latinas report that when they are asked where they are from, the answer California or Texas only begets the well-known follow-up: "But, where are you *really* from?"

In contemporary U.S. society, we learn our racial place through interactions with others. If others classify us as white, we learn to expect preferential treatment. If others classify us as something other than white, we learn to expect marginalization. This marginalization plays out in different ways, depending on a wide variety of factors, including skin color, manner of speaking, body language, hair texture and facial features. There is no "monolithic minority" experience; people of color experience marginalization in distinct ways. Little research has examined how racism works in different ways for blacks and Latinos in the United States. Nevertheless, it is clear that Latinos experience different forms of oppression, according to whether or not they are perceived to be white, black or Hispanic. Turnovksy, for example, recounts that black Panamanians had to perform Latinidad in order to be deemed eligible for day labor position (and not to be confused with African-Americans), while Ecuadorians mistaken for Mexicans were presumed to be hard-working and willing to work for low pay. Aranda and Rebollo-Gil (2004) tell readers that their phenotypically white Puerto Rican informants often evoked surprise when they informed people that they were Puerto Rican. Some of these white Puerto Ricans have the option of passing for white, while others did not because of their accent or forms of expressiveness. These and other studies show that only phenotypically white people born in the United States who speak Standard Received English and don't move their hands too much can call themselves unhyphenated Americans without this label being questioned by others.

It is important to point out that, even though external categorizations affect identity, each individual has the ability to accept, embrace or reject these categorizations. For example, Aranda and Rebollo-Gil's informants rejected others' assumptions that they were white, and insisted that they were Puerto Rican. Likewise, Turnovksy's (2004) Panamanian informants rejected others' labeling of them as black by emphasizing their non-African-American ethnic attributes. These and other studies also show that people's categorizations are situational. Some people may be alternatively categorized as black, Latino or Dominican in distinct settings. In addition, some individuals know how to manage these categorizations to exert some control over them. In any case, whether people choose to accept, embrace or manipulate their categorizations, they influence how individuals think of themselves and how they understand their social location. Latinos who are categorized as non-white are more likely to experience discrimination. Many of these Latinos will interpret this discrimination as an indication that they are not welcome in white American spaces and are thus more likely to reject the label "American" as a self-identifier.

REFERENCES

Aranda, Elizabeth, and Guillermo Rebollo-Gil. 2004. "Ethnoracism and the 'Sandwiched' Minorities." *American Behavioral Scientist* 47 (7): 910–27.

Bonilla-Silva, Eduardo. 2003. *Racism without Racists: Color-Blind Racism and the Persistence of Racial Inequality in the United States.* New York: Rowman & Littlefield.

Carter, Prudence L. 2005. *Keepin' It Real: School Success beyond Black and White.* New York: Oxford University Press.

Feagin, Joe. 2000. *Racist America: Roots, Current Realities and Future Reparations.* New York: Routledge.

Lichter, S. Robert, and Daniel R. Amundson. 1997. "Distorted Reality: Hispanic Characters in TV Entertainment." In *Latin Looks,* ed. Clara Rodriguez, 57–72. Boulder, Colo.: Westview.

Perry, Pamela. 2002. *Shades of White: White Kids and Racial Identities in High School.* Durham, N.C.: Duke University Press.

Rumbaut, Rubén. 1994. "The Crucible Within: Ethnic Identity, Self-esteem, and Segmented Assimilation among Children of Immigrants." *International Migration Review* 28 (4): 748–95.

Turnovsky, Carolyn Pinedo. 2004. "Making the Queue: Latino Day Laborers in New York's Street Corner Labor Markets." Center for Comparative Immigration Studies. Working Papers. Accessed April 1 at http://repositories.cdlib.org/ccis/papers/wrkg98.

Zavella, Patricia. 1996. "Reflections on Diversity among Chicanas." In *Race,* ed. Steven Gregory and Roger Sanjek. New Brunswick, N.J.: Rutgers University Press.

Chapter 68

||||||||||||||||||||||||||||||||||||||||||||||||||||||||||||||||||||||||||||||||||

Going to School
"Two Struggles"

Julio Cammarota

School holds a different meaning for Latinos than for Latinas; it is a place in which they are policed, contained, and treated as if they are a social and criminal threat. This experience of containment makes them feel uneasy in social/public spaces and willing to avoid or resist the uncomfortable feeling of being perceived as a menace. Their responses are often drawn from certain notions of urban masculinity that find meaning in rebelling against mainstream life and institutions such as schools.

My central argument in this chapter is that gender influences school experiences for Latina/o youth and offers different cultural resources for males and females to use against the structural constraints of inferior and racist schooling. Although male and female youth in this study attend the same horrid schools and face the same teacher apathy and uncaring attitudes, their individual experiences reveal important gender distinctions. Specifically, for young men, the negative racial treatment they go through at school is made worse by their being labeled as dangerous.

The Strategy of Avoidance

When they speak about school, Latinos fail to offer much in the way of details that pertain to classrooms or relationships with teachers. In comparison to the number of Latinas who explain their school experiences, the Latinos' discussions of school are quite sparse and flat. However, cutting class is one aspect of school that many Latinos in the study thoroughly explain. The substantial evidence of skipping school among Latinos is a critical factor in understanding the qualitative disparity between the Latinos' and Latinas' descriptions of schooling.

High school is peripheral for most Latinos participating in the research. They spend a considerable amount of school-time outside the campus with other male peers and far from the action of daily school life. As their grade school career comes to a close, they increasingly withdraw from attending class. Their attendance rate

From Sueños Americanos: Barrio Youth Negotiating Social and Cultural Identities by Julio Cammarota, pp. 138–43, 145, 147–49, 151–52. Copyright © 2008 by the Arizona Board of Regents. Reprinted by permission of the University of Arizona Press.

diminishes so much in the latter part of grade school that when they reach fifteen or sixteen years of age, many spend substantially more time cutting classes than attending them. Ishmael Ramirez feels somewhat guilty about totally withdrawing from school; he wants to attend class, but somehow he cannot get himself to go.

> I started messin' up. I'm on probation and not sure if I'm gonna pass this year? I don't know? 'Cause I've been trying to go to class, but I missed the whole year. Yeah, I missed a lot of classes this year. If I do good, which I'm trying to, and if I do good and my teachers see I'm doing good, I could probably pass. And if I pass I'm going to pass straight to the twelfth. That's why. If I pass straight to the twelfth and then I have just another year on the twelfth grade, and then—see if I graduate, and that'll be it. But I be messin' up.

Cutting rarely occurs in isolation, meaning that it is more of a social activity usually involving other males. As Rolando Garcia explained, friends meet each other at school and then decide together to cut class.

> I used to go to classes and, you know, between lunch breaks, I'd go out somewhere and then I bumped into this guy and they go, Oh, I don't want to go class, can you hang with me? We had like, next to the school there was like a little canyon with trees, you know, we had like this . . . this bark from the trees in the wood and the tree was kind of bent and you could sit there, a trunk, a old trunk there? Yeah. And they—people over the years took a mattress there, man, like a mattress, used to be like lay down and relax there and we used to kick back.

Cutting class is a common and shared practice among Latinos. However, one rarely finds clear indication that cutting is completely enjoyable for them. Rather, their statements suggest that cutting is a troublesome activity in which Latinos engage in order to enact and sustain friendships, a time to be together for social interaction but with serious costs. This was evident in a statement made by Julian Guerro:

> I was doing good in school until I got to high school with the people I was hanging out with. I guess it was a bad crew or whatever you want to call it. That's when the trouble started. I did my work, but I just got suspended and in trouble with teachers more times for cutting school or just little stuff like that. Most of them were my neighbors or my cousins, and they were already living here, so I knew them and I just started hanging around with them because they were like family. My teachers and everybody around me always thought I was bad because I hanged around with them, and I just cut a lot. I was just hanging with them and cutting, but I was used to being into school even though I did bad things.

Cutting school is obviously not something Julian thoroughly enjoys doing. He knows that missing class is wrong and a possible reason for his trouble with school. However, he joins other Latinos in cutting class because they represent family.

Although many Latinos spoke to me of cutting class, Latinas in this study rarely mentioned it. Out of the entire sample of twenty females participating in this research

—both fast-food and community center workers—only one stated that she cut class regularly. This Latina, Kiri Souza, was a community center worker, who commented on how school became meaningless for her so she stopped attending: "I used to cut, go where all my friends were, and I'd hang around with my friends, because I didn't want to go to class. There was no class anymore I really wanted to stay in; I wasn't learning anything so why should I go?"

Kiri's reason for cutting and the reasons presented by the males in the study differ in one important respect. For Kiri, it was a matter of wasting time or "not learning anything" that drove her to skip classes and hang out with friends. However, males suggest that cutting is a desired or necessary social activity for enacting, symbolizing, and sustaining friendships or familiar relationships.

Although Latinos use cutting class for social gatherings, they are ambivalent about its consequences. They understand that skipping class means that they are missing their education. Therefore, cutting has both the positive side of being with friends and the negative side of forfeiting one's education. It is evident among Latinos that an education would be important for future employment and opportunities. But the school's treatment of Latinos as a criminal threat reinforces the drive to avoid school.

Policing the "Threat" of Latinos

After several months of researching, I understood the particular social experience of Latino youth. To become "close" with my research participants, I shaved my head and wore extremely baggy clothes.

Although they are only a few miles apart, the university and my neighborhood near El Pueblo represent two distinct spaces that hold almost opposite meanings for me. The university seems hostile, a place in which I need to be circumspect and ready for someone to falsely accuse me of some malfeasance and try to banish or castigate me. My neighborhood, in contrast, is a place in which I am safe from accusation, the fears of others, and criminal treatment.

However, the feeling of safety in my neighborhood endures only until the police enter it. Police pull over, question, and harass young men who are simply walking down my street, minding their own business. During the summer months, when youth are out socializing on the streets, the policing occurs daily. I cannot count the times that I see the police from my front window doing something with male youth—questioning, arresting, or harassing them.

During my research, I would sometimes borrow a friend's car to visit research participants that lived more than twenty or so blocks from my apartment. The car was a new Japanese model that tended to get stolen. While I drove through El Pueblo, police regularly pulled right behind me, tailgating inches away from the car and checking my license plate to see whether I had stolen it. Seeing police constantly outside my front window or speeding up behind me in the rearview mirror made me feel as if someone was always watching and ready to take me away.

I realized that the policing of Latinos is extremely widespread. Many people, including store workers, employees at recreation centers, police, and even Fish and

Game wardens, perceive the young Latino in California as a potential threat. Ishmael Rivera described how others in society perceive Latinos: "Like troublemakers. Like regular young people, up to no good, dumb people who aren't interested in school, just interested in drugs and money. Like they don't really think of us like the future. They don't really look at us like the future. And they're afraid of us." The image of the Latino youth conjures fear in many; it is a fear based on assumptions of criminality. Whatever public space a young Latino enters, he often becomes immediately stereotyped as dangerous. Social life for a young Latino includes the normal everyday occurrence of being watched, searched, and treated as a plague in need of containment.

Frequently, Latinos in this study mentioned contentious encounters with the police. Arturo Chavez stated that the police regularly pull him over in his car without reason. When I interviewed Nestor Cruz and Salvador Portolla, I asked them if the police had ever harassed them.

> *NC*: Yeah, just this morning! I was dropping my sister off at work in front of Happy Burger; we parked the car and waited for them to open up. All of a sudden this police comes right up to my window and taps on it real loud. I said, "What's up." He said something like what the hell was I doing here. I told him I was dropping my sister off for work.

> *SP*: I was walking with the homies [in a white neighborhood] you would see white bars, with all these white people outside, just drinking and happy, and then I hear, we come walking, and we have this little small radio, and the cops would come by. And they would ask us to sit on the sidewalk, kneeled down and ask us all these information. And here you have this group of white people; just drinking, makin' lots of noise, but the cops don't do a thing with them.

Others police Latinos, as well. Workers in retail stores, private security in companies, and everyday citizens contribute to monitoring and containing the potential threat that Latinos supposedly pose to society. Salvador commented on his feeling that he is under surveillance in public almost every day, everywhere, and by everyone.

> Every day, man, just every day when I dress the way I dress and go into a department store, it's like eyes and cameras—you know what I'm saying? It's now like people hate me so much where I'm used to it, and so, I don't really trip as much. I just start seeing this shit, like how people just looking at me, and just watching me. I used to wonder, why always looking at me, and why saying stuff about me over here? It's just happened to me so much, that I just take it for granted.

Salvador has become inured to the surveillance in order to diminish the stressful feelings that accompany being constantly under suspicion. Accepting that policing is an everyday part of life is a way for Latinos to downplay its significance and thus attempt to ignore it.

The policing of Latinos is such a pervasive and well-accepted social practice that the experience of being monitored and contained happens at school as much as it does anywhere else. National data reveal that teachers often assume young Latinos are in gangs, whether they know this to be a fact or not. El Pueblo High School hires security personnel for surveillance purposes, and city police appear on campus or patrol in front of the school almost daily. Being policed is a significant part of the school experience for many Latinos.

With their schools participating in the social practice of policing, Latinos understandably use cutting class as a way to escape this enforcement. As mentioned, cutting allows Latinos to gather socially and interact. In the face of such intense policing at school, it becomes a practice of separation from the hostility imposed by the police, teachers, and school personnel. Many Latinos in this study believe that schools represent institutions not much different from police stations or prisons. Because policing is the most troublesome aspect of their social experiences, schools become places to avoid.

The greater participation of females in community-run programs explains the higher college enrollment rate among females in this study. It is clear that one reason that Latinas attend class more frequently than males is that they are less likely to be targets of policing, enforcement, and intense discipline. Latinas do not have to contend with the specific anguish of criminal treatment, so they are less fearful of schools and attend class more frequently.

However, Latinas in the study do experience unfair treatment that bears the potential to discourage them from attending school. Since they are present more often in the classroom, Latinas experience more intensely uncaring relationships with teachers and school personnel stemming from assumptions of inferiority and incompetence. Because racism often influences these relationships, Latinas have enough reason to drop out without being treated as criminals. However, many females in this study persevered, negotiated their way through the harsh treatment, and graduated from high school.

Generational and Cultural Change among Latinas

According to my research, the foundation of Latinas' perseverance is a feminist drive for cultural, generational, and social change. Latinas have a particular feminist perspective concerning the family economy. Families in this study are financially strapped because of severe economic conditions, so a mother often adopts the role of provider as well as that of primary caretaker. Because the Latina/o culture and general society are uncritical of men or fathers who are oppressive as well as negligent with their family responsibilities, Latina mothers are often burdened by male oppression while raising and supporting their families. Many Latinas in this study know that their mothers' dual burden results from male domination and sexist oppression, and are determined to relieve their mothers from this unfairness by earning money and contributing to the family economy.

Mothers recognize their daughter's contributions to the family economy but clearly prefer that their daughters avoid being consumed by this role of family provider. They want them to take some initiative for themselves, for the future, for their education. Latina mothers can play an important role in motivating their daughters. They also hope that their daughters will struggle against and overcome male oppression. Latinas understand the importance of their mothers' messages because they are conscious of the female suffering of previous generations.

> *Aura Gabriela*: Because the mothers—my mom is a strong woman, and I think I'm a strong woman, and my mom she teaches me. The strength comes from my family and my mom. It's weird because in my family, three generations ago, it was like my grandmother, she used to get abused by my mom's dad. And there was one day where my mom's dad hit her mom, right? Not my grandma, but my great-grandmother. So, my grandma was like, "This is it!" After that, it was like the women in my family— you won't see families where the men hit the women, the men abuse the women—it's different.

> *Rogelia Silva*: I don't want to be stuck at home, being a housewife like my mom. So, that's why I graduated high school and go to college.

Latina youth know that they may suffer the same fate as their mothers, and changes in power and status are therefore critical. This is evident in a statement made by Kiri Souza:

> I feel like Latinas, we have two struggles. Being Latina, and being a Latino woman, so if we get discriminated because we are Latinas—if a man can get discriminated against because they're Latinos, a woman gets discriminated two times more because they're a woman and they're Latinos. So, women, we have two struggles because we are women. Because they see us as low and even in our culture, like our parents—they teach us that men are more than women. Like, why do men go out, and I don't go out? Because he's a man. Why do my brothers do these, and I don't? Because he's a man. And they teach that, so we have two struggles, because we're a woman, and because we're Latinas. And we don't hear this only from other people, whatever, but in our families, in our own culture, because our culture, they see a woman as low.

Kiri's thoughts on her own culture embody a feminist criticism of gender oppression.

Indeed, it is obvious to many Latina youth that their mothers and previous generations of women in the family have spent their lives subservient to men as well as to the capitalist system. Yet through education, they enter a new generation of Latinas that achieve for themselves and attain a status through which they can challenge male domination and economic subservience. Graduating from high school is a crucial step in the feminist project of generational, cultural, and societal change. Often, a high school degree for a Latina youth means that she has achieved more than any other woman in the family. This achievement offers a Latina more control over her life.

Conclusion

This chapter presented "two struggles" for Latina and Latino youth. On one side, the Latinas I interviewed brought from their homes and community a feminist drive to achieve that helped them challenge and overcome their school's silencing and negligence. This determination to remain in school, despite a poor quality of education, kept them attending and on track to graduate. Most importantly, their presence in school allowed them contact with cultural organizers and the few caring school personnel who entered and worked to bring change. These compassionate agents picked up the slack left by an uncaring system and provided Latinas with the guidance, encouragement, information, and support to help them onto the college track. It is safe to say that without the help of these cultural organizers and compassionate agents, many Latinas in this study would not have made it to college.

On the other side, the Latinos I interviewed drew from peer groups and popular notions of urban masculinity to resist and avoid schooling altogether. Since these Latinos were escaping the policing experienced at school and were frequently cutting class, they, unlike the Latinas, had very limited exposure to cultural organizers from the community. Therefore, they missed important assistance that could have helped them negotiate their way through the institutional constraints intent upon containing their urban maleness. Instead of getting help, they faced limited options that tended to lead them to escape by avoiding school and eventually dropping out. Reinforcing this reaction was an urban male culture commanding them to be tough and to rebel against mainstream life.

From the Editors *Issues and Comments*

Is it common to want to appear normal—to fit in—in whatever group we find ourselves? If so, what is wrong with the assimilationist impulse? Can it not be an advantage to be light-skinned enough, and speak English well enough, to "pass"? Have you ever attempted to pass?

Do you think LULAC would have made as much progress in their fight for rights if they had included noncitizens? Do you agree with their tactics?

Suppose you are of indeterminate ethnicity. By wearing your hair a certain way and adopting a certain manner of dress and posture, you can appear Latino; another way, Anglo. Which would you choose, and why?

Who decides what the perfect balance of assimilation and nonassimilation is? How much do you think is too much or too little?

Is assimilation in the sense of a conscious effort to appear Anglo or "Spanish" contemptible, a refusal to stand with the underdog, and a form of near-treason?

Can *anti*-assimilationist pressures—such as pressures within Latino organizations to be radical—be just as suffocating as those emanating from mainstream society to embrace the dominant culture?

What's wrong with being a "scholarship boy/girl"? Are you one?

Do we all use masks to hide something we feel others will not approve of?

Why do you think being able to speak a second language, through study or foreign travel or residence, holds great value in the professional world, and yet one who speaks that language from birth finds this ability devalued?

Do you think people who discriminate against a Latino would stop if the Latino could present a birth certificate conclusively proving that he or she is Spanish? A U.S.-born citizen?

If you are a member of a minority group, how do you feel when a close friend says, "I don't think of you as a . . ."?

Why is assimilation a more painful process for Latinos than for white immigrants?

Can Harvard (or any other elite organization) drive a Latino crazy?

"Harvard Homeboy" made a public spectacle of JR and provided ammunition for critics of affirmative action. Was it irresponsible journalism—or did it raise legitimate issues? Note that many white youths have run-ins with the police—why is this case any different?

Does experiencing racism radicalize a person and cement his or her identification with an outgroup? Or does it do the opposite—make him or her wish more fervently that he or she were white?

Why are the children of many Latino immigrants "assimilating downwards"—doing worse than their working-class parents on most measures of social well-being?

Describe the perfect society where no implied or explicit pressures coerced one to assimilate. What language would people use when speaking with different communities? Would people of different cultures live together or separately? Would assimilation happen eventually?

Suggested Readings

Allsup, Carl. *The American G.I. Forum: Origins and Evolution*. University of Texas Center for Mexican American Studies Monograph no. 6. Austin: University of Texas Press, 1982.

American G.I. Forum of Texas and Texas State Federation of Labor. *What Price Wetbacks?* Austin: G.I. Forum of Texas, 1954. Reprinted in *Mexican Migration to the United States*, edited by Carlos Cortes, New York: Arno Press, 1976.

Aparicio, Ana. *Dominican Americans and the Politics of Empowerment*. Gainesville: University Press of Florida, 2006.

Barrera, Mario. *Beyond Aztlán: Ethnic Autonomy in Comparative Perspective*. Notre Dame, Ind.: University of Notre Dame Press, 1990.

Cammarota, Julio. *Sueños Americanos: Barrio Youth Negotiating Social and Cultural Identities*. Tucson: University of Arizona Press, 2008.

Cammarota, Julio, and Augustine Romero. "A Critically Compassionate Pedagogy for Latino Youth." 4 *Latino Studies* 305–12 (2006).

Chavez, Linda. *Out of the Barrio: Toward a New Politics of Hispanic Assimilation*. New York: Basic Books, 1991.

Chicano School Failure and Success: Past, Present, and Future, edited by Richard R. Valencia. London; New York: Routledge/Falmer, 2002.

Crosnoe, Robert. *Mexican Roots, American Schools: Helping Mexican Immigrant Children Succeed*. Palo Alto, Calif.: Stanford University Press, 2006.

Davis, Mike. *Magical Urbanism: Latinos Reinvent the U.S. City*. London and New York: Verso, 2000.

de la Garza, Rodolfo O. *Chicano Elite Perceptions of the Undocumented Worker: An Empirical Analysis*. Working Papers in U.S.–Mexican Studies, no. 31. La Jolla: Center for U.S.–Mexican Studies, University of California, San Diego, 1981.

De León, Arnoldo. *Ethnicity in the Sunbelt: A History of Mexican Americans in Houston*. Houston: University of Houston Press, 1989.

Diaz, David R. *Barrio Urbanism: Chicanos, Planning, and American Cities*. New York: Routledge, 2005.

Ethnicities: Children of Immigrants in America, edited by Rubén Rumbaut and Alejandro Portes. Berkeley: University of California Press, 2001.

Ethnicity: Theory and Experience, edited by Nathan Glazer and Daniel Moynihan. Cambridge, Mass.: Harvard University Press, 1975.

"Exceptional Outcomes: Achievement in Education and Employment among Children of Immigrants." 620(1) *Annals, American Academy of Political and Social Science* 7–310 (November 2008).

Fernandez, Carlos A. "La Raza and the Melting Pot: A Comparative Look at Multiethnicity." In *Racially Mixed People in America*, edited by Maria P. P. Root, 126. Newbury Park, Calif.: Sage Publications, 1992.

Fox, Geoffrey. *Hispanic Nation: Culture, Politics, and the Constructing of Identity*. Tucson: University of Arizona Press, 1997.

Garcia, Juan Ramon. *Mexicans in the Midwest, 1900–1932*. Tucson: University of Arizona Press, 1996.

Garcia, Mario T. "The Californios of San Diego and the Politics of Accommodation." 6 *Aztlán: International Journal of Chicano Studies Research* 69–85 (Spring 1975).

———. *Mexican Americans: Leadership, Ideology, and Identity, 1930–1960*. New Haven, Conn.: Yale University Press, 1989.

Garcia, Richard A. *Rise of the Mexican American Middle Class: San Antonio, 1929–1941*. College Station: Texas A&M University Press, 1991.

Garza, Edward D. *LULAC: The League of United Latin American Citizens*. San Francisco: R&E Research Associates, 1972.

Gonzales, Manuel G. *The Hispanic Elite of the Southwest*. El Paso: Texas Western Press, 1989.

Grebler, Leo, Joan Moore, and Ralph Guzman. *The Mexican American People: The Nation's Second Largest Minority*. New York: Free Press, 1970.

Grogger, Jeffrey, and Stephen J. Trejo. *Falling Behind or Moving Up? The Intergenerational Progress of Mexican Americans*. San Francisco: Public Policy Institute of California, 2002.

Gutiérrez, David G. *Walls and Mirrors: Mexican Americans, Mexican Immigrants*. Berkeley: University of California Press, 1995.

Hanson, Victor Davis. *Mexifornia: A State of Becoming*. 2d ed. New York: Encounter Books, 2007.

Hayes-Bautista, David E. *La Nueva California: Latinos in the Golden State*. Berkeley: University of California Press, 2004.

Hollinger, David A. *Postethnic America: Beyond Multiculturalism*. New York: Basic Books, 1995.

Kaplowitz, Craig W. *LULAC, Mexican Americans, and National Policy*. College Station: Texas A&M University Press, 2005.

Karst, Kenneth L. *Belonging to America: Equal Citizenship and the Constitution*. New Haven, Conn.: Yale University Press, 1989.

Latino Americans and Political Participation: A Reference Handbook, edited by Sharon Ann Navarro and Armando Xavier Mejia. Santa Barbara, Calif.: ABC-CLIO, 2004.

Latino Cultural Citizenship: Claiming Identity, Space and Rights, edited by William V. Flores and Rina Benmayor. Boston: Beacon Press, 1997.

Latino Immigrants and the Transformation of the U.S. South, edited by Mary E. Odem and Elaine Lacy. Athens: University of Georgia Press, 2009.

Latinos and Citizenship: The Dilemma of Belonging, edited by Suzanne Oboler. New York: Palgrave Macmillan, 2006.

Latinos and the Political System, edited by F. Chris Garcia. Notre Dame, Ind.: University of Notre Dame Press, 1988.

Latinos in New England, edited by Andrés Torres. Philadelphia: Temple University Press, 2006.

Latinos in New York, edited by S. Baver and G. Haslip Viera. Notre Dame, Ind.: University of Notre Dame Press, 1996.

Latinos in the New South, edited by Heather A. Smith and Owen J. Furuseth. Aldershot, U.K., and Burlington, Vt.: Ashgate, 2006.

Latinos: Remaking America, edited by Marcelo M. Suárez-Orozco and Mariela M. Páez. Berkeley: University of California Press, 2002.

Macias, Thomas. *Mestizo in America: Generations of Mexican Ethnicity in the Suburban Southwest*. Tucson: University of Arizona Press, 2006.

Mantero, José María. *Latinos and the U.S. South*. New York: Praeger, 2008.

Marquez, Benjamin. *Constructing Identities in Mexican-American Political Organizations: Choosing Issues, Taking Sides*. Austin: University of Texas Press, 2003.

————. *LULAC: The Evolution of a Mexican American Political Organization*. Austin: University of Texas Press, 1993.

Martinez, George A. "Immigration and the Meaning of United States Citizenship: Whiteness and Assimilation." 46 *Washburn L.J.* 335 (2007).

————. "Latinos, Assimilation and the Law: A Philosophical Perspective." 20 *Chicano-Latino L. Rev.* 1 (1999).

Mexican Immigration to the United States, edited by George J. Borjas. Chicago: University of Chicago Press, 2007.

Multiple Origins, Uncertain Destinies: Hispanics and the American Future, edited by Marta Tienda and Faith Mitchell. Washington, D.C.: National Academies Press, 2006.

Navarrette, Ruben, Jr. *A Darker Shade of Crimson: Odyssey of a Harvard Chicano*. New York: Bantam Books, 1993.

Olivas, Michael A. "Torching Zozobra: The Problem with Linda Chavez." 2(2) *Reconstruction* 48–51 (1993).

Polinard, Jerry L., Robert D. Wrinkle, and Rodolfo O. de la Garza. "Attitudes of Mexican Americans toward Irregular Mexican Immigration." 18 *International Migration Review* 782–99 (Fall 1984).

Portes, Alejandro, and Rubén G. Rumbaut. *Immigrant America: A Portrait*. 3d ed. Berkeley: University of California Press, 2006.

————. *Legacies: The Story of the Immigrant Second Generation*. Berkeley: University of California Press, 2001.

Ramos, Henry A. J. *The American G.I. Forum: In Pursuit of the Dream, 1948–1983*. Houston: Arte Publico Press, 1998.

Rieff, David. *The Exile: Cuba in the Heart of Miami*. New York: Simon & Schuster, 1993.

Rivera, Rick. *A Fabricated Mexican*. Houston: Arte Publico Press, 1995.

Rodriguez, Gregory. *Mongrels, Bastards, Orphans, and Vagabonds: Mexican Immigration and the Future of Race in America*. New York: Knopf, 2007.

Rodriguez, Richard. "An American Writer." In *The Invention of Ethnicity*, edited by Werner Sollors, 3. New York: Oxford University Press, 1989.

————. *Days of Obligation: An Argument with My Mexican Father*. New York: Viking, 1992.

————. *Hunger of Memory: The Education of Richard Rodriguez*. Boston: D. R. Godine, 1981.

Sanchez, George J. *Becoming Mexican-American: Ethnicity, Culture and Identity in Chicano Los Angeles, 1900–1945*. New York: Oxford University Press, 1993.

"The Second Generation in Early Adulthood" (Special Issue). Edited by Alejandro Portes and Rubén G. Rumbaut. 28(6) *Ethnic & Racial Studies* 983–1214 (November 2005).

Suárez-Orozco, Carola, and Marcelo M. Suárez-Orozco. *Children of Immigration*. Cambridge, Mass.: Harvard University Press, 2001.

Suárez-Orozco, Carola, Marcelo M. Suárez-Orozco, and Irina Todorova. *Learning a New Land: Immigrant Students in American Society*. Cambridge, Mass.: Harvard University Press, 2008.

Suro, Roberto. *Strangers among Us: Latino Lives in a Changing America*. New York: Vintage, 1999.

Telles, Edward E., and Vilma Ortiz. *Generations of Exclusion: Mexican Americans, Assimilation, and Race*. New York: Russell Sage Foundation, 2008.

Trueba, Enrique T. *Latinos Unidos: From Cultural Diversity to the Politics of Solidarity*. New York: Rowman & Littlefield, 1999.

Valdes, Dennis N. *Al Norte: Agricultural Workers in the Great Lakes Region, 1917–1970*. Austin: University of Texas Press, 1991.

Vasquez, Richard. *Chicano*. Garden City, N.Y.: Doubleday, 1970.

Villarreal, Jose Antonio. *Pocho*. New York: Doubleday, 1959.

Villasenor, Victor. *Rain of Gold*. Houston: Arte Publico Press, 1991.

Weyr, Thomas. *Hispanic U.S.A.: Breaking the Melting Pot*. New York: Harper & Row, 1988.

Zlolinski, Christian. *Janitors, Street Vendors and Activists: The Lives of Mexican Immigrants in Silicon Valley*. Berkeley: University of California Press, 2006.

II

Splits and Tensions within the Civil Rights Community

What is the relationship between Latinos and African Americans? Are they friends and allies in the civil rights struggle, marching hand in hand in pursuit of common objectives such as better schools, voting rights, and stronger civil rights enforcement? Or are they sometimes at each other's throats, battling for the few crumbs such as jobs, political appointments, and social programs that society is prepared to scatter in their direction? Sometimes African Americans have opposed immigration, believing that Latinos take jobs away from working-class blacks. Others have not welcomed coalition with Latinos, seeing them as Johnnies-come-lately who let blacks do all the work and then sought to join the civil rights movement after gains had already arrived. A few African-American writers hold that Latinos are, basically, whites or white wannabes. Some Anglo writers take this position, as well. For their part, Latinos sometimes accuse African Americans of narrow nationalism and a refusal to consider the needs of any group other than their own. Still others, recognizing that many Latinos have black ancestry, challenge all Latinos to forgo identifying as white. Part 9 addresses these and related issues, including whether it might not be best to get beyond race altogether.

|||||||||||||||||||||||||||||||||||||||||||||||||||||||||||||||||||||||||||||||||||||

Chapter 69

Over the Rainbow

Neil Foley

In the aftermath of the 2004 presidential election, many wondered why President Bush received over forty percent of the Latino vote compared to only twelve percent of the African American vote. The notion persists that minorities, like African Americans and Latinos, often share similar political views that reflect a similar history of racial discrimination and civil rights struggles against Jim Crow practices. The picture is much more complicated than that, of course, and always has been.

Some of the differences that divide many blacks and Latinos today, such as the dominance of African Americans on school boards and city councils in districts and cities where Latinos greatly outnumber blacks, stand in contrast to the efforts of both groups to find common ground in their earliest civil rights struggles, especially school desegregation cases in California and Texas. In the 1946 Mexican school desegregation case in Orange County, California, *Mendez v. Westminster*, Thurgood Marshall and the NAACP submitted an amicus curiae brief that many legal scholars acknowledge was a dry run for *Brown v. Board of Education*. And in Corpus Christi, in the late 1960s, parents of African American and Mexican American school children brought suit against the school district for busing ethnic Mexicans to predominantly black schools and African Americans to predominantly Mexican schools, while leaving Anglo schools alone [*Cisneros v. Corpus Christi Independent School District*]. These black-brown legal collaborations represent high water marks in the relations between African Americans and Mexican Americans.

However, Mexican American commitment to a Caucasian racial identity from the 1930s through the 1950s complicated, and in some ways compromised, what at first appeared to be a promising start to interracial cooperation. African Americans can hardly be faulted for failing to find common ground with a civil rights strategy based on the premise that Mexican Americans were Caucasians, and whose goal it was to end de facto segregation of Mexicans—not de jure segregation of blacks. Of significant importance in the evolution of this Caucasian identity was the finding of the 1930 U.S. census that for the first time, persons of Mexican descent, born in the United States, outnumbered Mexican immigrants. Second-generation Mexican Americans, the so-called Mexican American generation, thought of themselves as "Americans"

From *Over the Rainbow:* Hernandez v. Texas, Brown v. Board of Education, *and* Black v. Brown, 25 CHI-CANO-LATINO L. REV. 139 (2005). Originally published in the *UCLA Chicano-Latino Law Review.* Reprinted by permission.

and stressed their American citizenship as the basis for being treated equally under the law. The Mexican American generation was quick to learn a fundamental lesson of American life: being white was not just a racial identity; it was a property right that conferred concrete privileges and rights denied to those, like African and Asian Americans, who could not lay claim to a white identity.

The first Mexican American civil rights organizations, both founded in Texas, the League of United Latin American Citizens (LULAC) and the American GI Forum, argued to anyone within earshot that Mexican Americans were white and citizens of the United States.

The Mexican American generation had two decades of success in litigating against school segregation in the courts before 1954, and in all these cases the courts acknowledged, whether implicitly or explicitly, the membership of Mexicans in the Caucasian race. In response to pressure from LULAC to end discrimination against Mexican Americans in Texas and the Mexican government's deep concern over the mistreatment of *braceros*, the Texas state legislature passed the Caucasian Race Resolution in 1943, declaring that "all persons of the Caucasian Race" are entitled to "equal accommodations" and that "whoever denies to any [Caucasian] person" these equal accommodations "shall be considered as violating the good neighbor policy of this state." While the resolution did not have the force of law, it did reflect the urgency of reaching an accommodation with the Mexican government to import *braceros* at a critical moment for the United States' World War II war effort. LULAC took advantage of this emergency farm worker program to press its case for official recognition of their status as Caucasians, much as the courts and the census, with the exception of 1930, had been doing for decades.

With this brief history in mind, African Americans can be forgiven for not always recognizing Mexican Americans as people of color. That is not to imply, however, that blacks were unmindful of discrimination against Mexican Americans, particularly in states like Texas and California. Rather, African Americans had to contend with a Supreme Court decision, *Plessy v. Ferguson*, that allowed states to enforce segregated accommodations on public transportation, which became the basis for the separate but equal doctrine in education.

Let us briefly look at three Mexican American school desegregation cases. We begin in 1930 when Mexican American parents in Del Rio, Texas, brought the first desegregation suit in Texas, *Independent School District v. Salvatierra*. They charged school officials with enacting policies designed to accomplish "the complete segregation of the school children of Mexican and Spanish descent . . . from the school children of all other white races in the same grade. . . ." The parents did not question the quality of the instruction or the condition of the separate school house; their suit was aimed exclusively at the school district's policy of separating Mexican American children from their Anglo counterparts. The district superintendent argued that the district had a "peculiar situation as regards people of Spanish or Mexican extraction here," because of their English language deficiency and their missing a lot of school because most followed the cotton crop during the fall. He assured the court that separate schooling "was not actuated by any motive of segregation by reason of race or color. . . ." In fact, he continued, Mexican children had teachers specialized in "the matter of teaching them English and American citizenship," revealing that citizenship was something even U.S.-born Mexicans needed to learn. He also told the segregated Parent Teachers Association of the Latin American Association that "Spanish speaking children are unusually gifted in music" and possessed "special facilities" for art and handicrafts, talents he hoped to develop with the hiring of new teachers. Never did the superintendent mention the word race or refer to Mexican children as anything other than "Latin Americans" or "children of Spanish or Mexican descent."

The Texas Court of Appeals reversed the lower court's ruling, but warned that "school authorities have no power to arbitrarily segregate Mexican children, assign them to separate schools, and exclude them from schools maintained for children of other white races, merely or solely because they are Mexicans." The arbitrary exclusion of Mexican American children from "other whites," the court ruled, constituted "unlawful racial discrimination." Segregation, in other words, was unlawful when Anglo whites treated Mexican whites as a separate racial group. The Texas Court of Appeals recognized that Mexicans constituted a distinct white "race" distinguished "from all other white races." Almost twenty-five years later, the Supreme Court ruled in *Hernandez* that Mexicans constituted a "distinct class" that had been discriminated against in jury selection. While the *Hernandez* case avoided references to Mexicans as a race, the wording of the *Salvatierra* ruling could have easily been adapted to *Hernandez*: That is, jury commissioners "have no power to exclude" Mexicans from juries, "merely or solely because they are Mexicans."

The understanding that Mexicans could not be arbitrarily segregated as a separate race from whites, like blacks in the South or Chinese and Native Americans in California, was affirmed in 1947 when the United States Ninth Circuit Court of Appeals ruled in *Westminster School District v. Mendez* that segregation of Mexican-descent children, in the absence of state law mandating segregation of Mexicans, deprived them of "liberty and property without due process" and "denied them the equal protection of the laws." Judge Stephens noted that California law authorized segregation of children "belonging to one or another of the great races of mankind," which Stephens identified as Caucasoid, Mongoloid, and Negro. Stephens further noted that California law permitted segregation of Indians and "Asiatics" (as well as blacks), but that no state law authorized the segregation of children "*within* one of the great races." Although European Americans rarely regarded Mexican Americans as "within" the white race, in the eyes of the law, Mexican Americans were "Caucasoid" who could not be arbitrarily segregated from "other whites." In other words, the Court of Appeals for the Ninth Circuit ruled in favor of Mexican American children not on the ground that the separate-but-equal provision of *Plessy* was invalid, but that no California statute mandated the segregation of Mexican Americans.

While the Ninth Circuit narrowly tailored its ruling to the illegality of segregation of Mexicans in the absence of state law, the lower district court ruling attacked segregation on much broader grounds. In ruling that segregated education violated the Fourteenth Amendment, Judge McCormick cited the 1943 Supreme Court decision *Hirabayashi v. United States*, which held that singling out citizens of Japanese descent for restriction of movement during curfew hours was constitutional in time of warfare. Nevertheless, the Court did so reluctantly and acknowledged the offensiveness of making distinctions based on race: "Distinctions between citizens solely because of their ancestry are by their very nature odious to a free people whose institutions are founded upon the doctrine of equality." After citing the internment cases, Judge Mc-Cormick went on to state that

> "equal protection of the laws" pertaining to . . . California [public schools] is not provided by furnishing in separate schools the same technical facilities, text books and courses of instruction to children of Mexican ancestry. . . . A paramount requisite in the American system of public education is social equality. It must be open to all children by unified school association regardless of lineage.[1]

In other words, a California district court had just ruled that separate but equal was unconstitutional.

Here, the trajectories of Mexican American civil rights intersected with those of African Americans. During the 1940s, after a decade of litigation, the NAACP shifted its strategy of forcing school districts to provide equal facilities for black children to attacking the separate-but-equal doctrine of *Plessy* head-on. In the *Mendez* decision they had found a court willing to rule that segregation based on race was unconstitutional. Thurgood Marshall seized on the language of the *Mendez* lower court ruling to argue in his brief that "separation itself [is] violative of the equal protection of the laws . . . on the grounds that equality cannot be effected under a dual system of education." In that brief, Marshall skillfully combined the goals of African Americans and Latinos, namely, "equality at home" as well as the "equality which we profess to accord Mexico and Latin American nationals in our international relations." For added measure, Marshall reminded the Ninth Circuit Court that the United States had ratified and adopted the Charter of the United Nations in 1945, which states that our government is obligated to promote "[u]niversal respect for . . . human rights and fundamental freedoms for all without distinction as to race. . . ." Seven years later, in *Brown v. Board of Education*, Marshall would hammer home the idea, using social science literature, that segregation was inherently unequal because of the damaging effects of discrimination on black children.

The *Mendez* case, for all of its historical and juridical importance, was not cited in *Brown v. Board of Education* principally because *Brown* occurred within the familiar black-white binary. The *Brown* decision was premised on racial segregation, which was not the central issue in the *Mendez* case. The Mexican American claim that they could not be segregated because they were Caucasians and that no state law specifically mandated their segregation was virtually irrelevant to the legal argument being made by Marshall and the NAACP.

The influence of the *Mendez* case, however, went beyond California. Thurgood Marshall and other NAACP lawyers were preparing a desegregation case in Hearne, a small town in east Texas, in 1948, while LULAC, Mexican American attorney Gus García, and University of Texas Professor George I. Sánchez were preparing the first desegregation case in Texas since the 1930 *Salvatierrra* case. With financial support from LULAC and the legal assistance of Gus García, Minerva Delgado and twenty parents of Mexican American children from five segregated school districts filed a complaint alleging that the school districts had "prohibited, barred and excluded" children "from attending the certain regular schools and classes . . . [with] other white school children . . ." and that segregation was "unjust, capricious, and arbitrary and in violation of the Constitution . . . and denies them the equal protection of laws . . . as guaranteed by the Fourteenth Amendmen. . . ."[2] Judge Rice ruled on June 15, 1948, that the five school districts named in the suit and the state superintendent of public instruction were "permanently restrained and enjoined from . . . segregating pupils of Mexican or other Latin American descent in separate schools or classes." Two weeks later, Professor Sánchez received a letter from Thurgood Marshall asking for access to the case file in preparation for the desegregation case in Hearne, Texas, that was going to trial later that month. Sánchez wrote back that he would be happy to cooperate, but that the affidavits in the case would not be useful "in an issue such as being raised in Hearne." Affidavits in the *Delgado* case, Sánchez wrote, are "pointed specifically towards a denial of the pedagogical soundness of segregation that is based on the 'language handicap' excuse." In other words, the strategy in the *Delgado* case was not to challenge segregation on the grounds that distinctions based on race were odious to a free people, but rather on the grounds that segregation on the basis of a "language handicap" was pedagogically unsound. Sánchez abhorred discrimination of all kinds, but his pedagogical approach to ending segregation did not resonate with Marshall's direct challenge to *Plessy* that separate schooling was inherently unequal.

A few years after the *Mendez* and *Delgado* cases, attorneys Gus García and Carlos Cadena chose to challenge the court conviction of Pete Hernández on the grounds that Mexican Americans had been systematically excluded from jury service in Jackson County, Texas. The details of the case are well known. [See part 7—Eds.] What is important is that García and Cadena relied heavily on numerous jury discrimination cases brought by African Americans who had won their cases by demonstrating that blacks had been systematically excluded from jury service. So why were Texas courts ignoring these cases (particularly *Norris v. Alabama*) in ruling against García and Cadena? Texas courts consistently ruled that the Fourteenth Amendment applied only to the interplay between blacks and whites in discrimination cases. Since Mexican Americans had for two decades argued that they were white, they could not claim discrimination. In their brief García and Cadena strenuously objected to the appeal court judge's ruling in these words: "If, then, this Court holds that, while such statutes forbid exclusion of Negroes [from jury service], they allow exclusion of persons of Mexican descent because the latter are members of the white race, the Court is in effect saying that the statutes protect only colored men, and allow discrimination against white men."[3] The attorneys concluded their brief in these words: "All of the talk about 'two classes'; all of the verbal pointing with alarm at a 'special class' which seeks 'special privileges' cannot obscure one very simple fact which stands out in bold relief: the Texas law points in one direction for persons of Mexican descent . . . and in another for Negroes."[4] Mexican Americans wanted to be accorded the same treatment as African Americans, at least where the law and the Fourteenth Amendment were concerned.

Two weeks after the *Hernandez* ruling, African Americans won their case in *Brown v. Board of Education*. Mexican Americans wondered if the law applied to them, or if the courts might rule, as the lower courts in Texas had ruled in the *Hernandez* case, that desegregation applied only to black and white schools. Mexican Americans sought the answer twelve years later. In 1968 African Americans and Mexican Americans in Corpus Christi joined together in a suit against the practice of busing Mexican children to predominantly black schools to achieve integration, while leaving predominantly white schools alone. School officials had used the "other white" argument to justify grouping black and Latino children to achieve integration. But the judge in the case ruled otherwise: As "an identifiable, ethnic-minority group . . . *Brown* can apply to Mexican-American students in public schools."[5] The Corpus Christi desegregation case coincided with the Chicano/a Movement's evocation of "la raza," signifying their rejection of a white racial identity and embracing their mestizo heritage.

Perhaps the single greatest obstacle to black-brown cooperation had stemmed from the Mexican American insistence on a white racial identity. In a letter to Roger Baldwin, the Director of the ACLU, urging continued support for Mexican American civil rights activities, George Sánchez wrote in 1958:

> Let us keep in mind that the Mexican-American can easily become *the front-line defense* of the civil liberties of ethnic minorities. The racial, cultural, and historical involvements in his case embrace those of *all . . . other minority groups*. Yet, God bless the law, he is "white"! So, the Mexican-American can be the wedge for broadening of civil liberties for others (who are not so fortunate as to be "white" and "Christian"!).[6]

He concluded, "I am sorry that Thurgood Marshall and the NAACP have not seen fit to consult with us in these matters." Perhaps Marshall had good reason not to. Marshall, after all, did not bless the law that granted white privilege to Mexican Americans but denied it to blacks, nor could he bless a strategy that opposed segregation on the narrow ground that Mexicans could not be segregated from other whites.

In more recent times the possibilities for collaboration and cooperation between blacks and Latinos in the political sphere seem remote, though not implausible. African Americans and Mexican Americans often support different political candidates for local and national elections. It is no secret that many African Americans resent the "minority" status of Mexican Americans who, they believe, have not suffered the degree of discrimination and exclusion they have. They also point out that forty-eight percent of all Latinos in the United States chose "white" as their race in the 2000 census. Many Latinos, on the other hand, were troubled when almost half of all African Americans in California voted for Proposition 187 in 1994 to deny undocumented Mexican immigrants basic public services, including education and health care. In many cities, African Americans and Latinos continue to regard each other with mutual suspicion over competition for municipal employment and private sector jobs, representation on school boards and in city councils, and supporting candidates for political office, especially when one of their own is running.

Tensions between blacks and Latinos surfaced in the mayoral election in Los Angeles in 2001 when African Americans joined ranks with Anglos to elect James

Hahn over Antonio Villaraigosa, the former speaker of the California state assembly, thus denying Latinos the opportunity to have a Mexican American mayor for the first time since the nineteenth century. It was an especially bitter loss because Latinos constituted forty-five percent of the population compared to eleven percent for African Americans. Four years later, however, Villaraigosa defeated Hahn decisively, in large part because of Hahn's extreme unpopularity and the ongoing investigation of corruption during his term, but also because Villaraigosa ran in 2005 as a non-ideological pan-ethnic who played down his ethnic roots and won the support of the African American community. It is too early to predict if this election represents a meaningful political re-alignment of Latinos, Anglos, and African Americans in the nation's second largest city.

Voting for one's own, regardless of party affiliation or political beliefs, may merely be an expression of ethnic or racial pride, but the suspicion nevertheless remains that Latinos do not trust African American politicians to look after their interests any more than African Americans trust Latinos who are in office. Ask any African American or Haitian resident of Miami. Looking back on early black and brown civil rights struggles in Texas, we have to wonder if African Americans and Mexican Americans can find common ground again.

NOTES

1. Mendez v. Westminister Sch. Dist., 64 F. Supp. 544, 549 (D. Cal. 1946), aff'd, 161 F.2d 774 (9th Cir. 1947).

2. Complaint to Enjoin Violation of Federal Civil Rights and for Damages, Delgado v. Bastrop Indep. Sch. Dist., Civil Action No. 388 (W.D. Tex. June 15, 1948) (unpublished order).

3. Brief for Appellant at 16, Hernandez v. State, 251 S.W.2d 531 (Tex. Crim. App. 1952) (No. 25816).

4. Brief for Petitioner at 30, Hernandez v. State, 347 U.S. 475 (1954) (No. 406).

5. Cisneros v. Corpus Christi Indep. Sch. Dist., 324 F. Supp. 599 (S.D. Tex. 1970), aff'd in part, modified in part, 467 F.2d 142 (5th Cir. 1972), cert denied, 413 U.S. 922 (1973).

6. Letter from George I. Sánchez, to Roger N. Baldwin (Aug. 27, 1958) in George I. Sánchez Papers, Box 31, Folder 8 (Benson Latin American Collection, General Libraries, University of Texas at Austin) (italics in original).

Chapter 70

||||||||||||||||||||||||||||||||||||||||||||||||||||||||||||||||||||||||||||||||||

Who Counts?
Title VII and the Hispanic Classification

Alex M. Saragoza, Concepción R. Juarez, Abel Valenzuela, Jr., and Oscar Gonzalez

At nearly eight in the evening of July 1, 1991, few people remained in the chambers of the San Francisco Civil Service Commission when that body began its final deliberations on the definition of the term *Hispanic* for the purposes of Title VII of the Civil Rights Act. After months of intermittent discussion, several articles and editorials in the local media, and even national coverage in various magazines and newspapers, the issue was finally to come to a head. Were persons of Spanish descent covered by the Hispanic classification? The meeting was prompted by a complaint by Pete Roybal, a native of New Mexico and a veteran of the San Francisco Fire Department, who argued against the inclusion of Spaniards in the Hispanic category for the purposes of affirmative action. That night, nearly thirty years after the original passage of the legislation regarding affirmative action, in a city laced with reminders of its Spanish and Mexican past, the debate over the Hispanic classification turned bitter and deeply emotional.

Firefighters argued vehemently against inclusion of Spaniards, contending that historically Spaniards have not been among the oppressed; rather they were responsible for the destruction of the indigenous culture in Latin America. Others countered that exclusion of those of Spanish origin would be unjust and arbitrary. The controversy in San Francisco serves as a metaphor for a larger problem regarding the use of generic racial and ethnic terms in civil rights legislation. None perhaps is more difficult than the term *Hispanic*, given its peculiar history and the complex patterns of racism and prejudice against that group in the United States. The use of the Hispanic classification, however, is not confined to problems related to employment. Latino advocacy groups, such as the Mexican American Legal Defense and Educational Fund (MALDEF) and the National Council of La Raza, for instance, have relied on aggregated statistics to push for district elections as a means of increasing the political representation of Latinos. Thus, the uses of the Hispanic classification hold repercussions beyond affirmative action.

The politics of group identity in the 1960s framed the assumptions, including the

From *History and Public Policy: Title VII and the Use of the Hispanic Classification*, 5 LA RAZA L.J. 1 (1992). Originally published in the *La Raza Law Journal*. Reprinted by permission.

notion of the homogeneity of Hispanics, surrounding legislation such as Title VII and the subsequent uses of the Hispanic classification. Those assumptions were in many respects mistaken or misinformed, and the flaws inherent in that legislation have surfaced in the controversy over affirmative action. In fact, the debate over the term itself fails to address a more fundamental question: how do we apply civil rights law to diverse groups of people that are aggregated under generic terms, such as *Hispanic*, *Asian American*, and arguably, *Native American*, and even perhaps *African American*?

The diversity of the groups commonly covered by the term *Hispanic* is complicated by a number of factors, including the particular aspects of the history of relations between the U.S. and Mexico, Puerto Rico, Cuba, and the seven distinct countries that make up Central America. Immigration from these areas has been directly affected by domestic and foreign policies of the U.S. This is not to mention the individual histories and cultures of the rest of Latin America, including the Portuguese-speaking nation of Brazil, as well as the French and British influenced islands of the Caribbean. Furthermore, the wide range of patterns of race, ethnicity, and cultural expression in Latin America, extending from the Rio Bravo (Rio Grande) to the Patagonia, defy easy generalization. More specifically, in the American Southwest a host of terms have emerged over time to describe a variety of groups currently covered by the Hispanic classification.

In short, no indelible physical characteristics, language, or cultural forms are shared by all of the people south of the U.S.–Mexico border that would invariably unify them under one ethnic or racial term. Yet, the term *Hispanic* suggests that such commonalities exist, and that these commonalities have been the subject of similar racist or discriminatory practices in the U.S. Title VII was written without regard to the problems of applying such legislation to aggregated, diverse groupings such as Hispanics. The overwhelming reference point for the civil rights act was African Americans, not Latin Americans. As a result, the courts were forced to clarify the applications of Title VII for a diverse group of people, a diversity not anticipated by the legislative language of that time.

The operable terms in the Civil Rights Act of 1964 were "race" and "color." Congress, however, failed to define these terms precisely. For the groups currently included in the term *Hispanic*, both race and color were problematic categories of definition and identification. Congressional discussion over the legislation focused on Blacks, as certain assumptions framed the use of race and color. Even for Blacks, these categories presumed manifest physical similarities that held less often than generally thought. Nevertheless, for most legislators in 1964 civil rights legislation referred primarily to Blacks, despite the amorphous use of the terms "race" and "color."[1] This ambiguity led to disputes "over whether a person is a member of a particular race . . . or indeed whether a certain classification, e.g. Hispanic, is a racial or other classification."[2]

Unity and Nationalism

The civil rights movement of the 1960s, more so perhaps than in the past, emphasized the importance of unity and common struggle in overcoming institutional racism. As many studies have shown, sharp disagreements took place within the Black civil rights movement over tactics, strategy, and ultimate goals. In this respect, the differences between Martin Luther King, Jr. and Malcolm X have become the usual example, but lack of consensus punctuated the civil rights movement throughout the 1960s and into the subsequent decade. Thus, the tendency to use the singular "movement" was a misrepresentation of actual events and processes at that time. Nonetheless, such differences consistently met with efforts, both public and private, to lessen if not eliminate the conflicting possibilities of political differences within or among civil rights organizations. Repeatedly, it was argued that division among African Americans and other minority groups only held benefits for "white racists"; division was both a tool and an advantage of institutional racism and its supporters. The exaltation of this principle—though more often observed in the breach than in practice—led to the lumping of subgroups into monolithic communities as a politically expedient tactic.

Rhetoric portraying the African American community as singular marked the political strategy of Black civil rights advocates during the 1960s. Other ethnic and racial groups paralleled African Americans in this strategy, though with much less public notoriety. This political essentialism among African Americans quickly became widespread, due especially to the news media. For most of the American public the issue of race in this country generally implied Blacks. The "other" minority groups failed to achieve in this period the visibility or political clout, particularly in Congress, afforded Blacks. This frustrated Mexican American legislators, as indicated in the remarks of Senator Montoya of New Mexico in 1972:

> We are the "invisible minority." While the black man has made the crying needs of his Ghetto children part of the nation's known history and collective conscious, we remain unseen. . . . Our efforts are fragmented. . . . And so in fragmented disorder we remain impotent; given hand-me-down programs; counted but not taken into account; seen with hindsight but not insight; asked but not listened to; a single brown face in a sea of black and white.[3]

As suggested in Montoya's comments, the strategy of Blacks to stress their group experience had been effective, pushing the senator from New Mexico to acknowledge a lack of such cohesion among "Hispanics." In sum, Mexican American legislators desired their own form of political essentialism—Hispanic versus white—with the same level of political privileges granted to Blacks.

A crucial impetus to political essentialism in the civil rights arena came from the resurgence of nationalism among Blacks, Chicanos, and other groups. Among Mexican-origin and Puerto Rican–based civil rights groups this new nationalism often came couched in cultural terms, leading to forms of cultural essentialism. These forms varied in expression and content, with everything from the vernacular (the celebration of "pachuco" talk) to traditional Mexican music and dance (the ubiquitous appearance of mariachi bands and folkloric dancers) at Chicano student-sponsored "cinco de mayo" events at innumerable college campuses by the late 1960s and into the present. Hence, the "Chicano" *movimiento* (and its corollaries among "Boricuas" [Puerto Ricans—Eds.] for example) sought to emphasize the commonalities among

"Latino" groups as an extension of cultural essentialism and as a political ploy. As Felix Padilla has shown for Chicago, this quickly led to a new style of political activism, what he has termed "situational" Latino politics.[4] Where expedient or necessary, Mexican-American and Puerto Rican groups in Chicago forged alliances in order to increase their collective access to governmental programs, political decision-making, and publicly funded services.

On the other hand, the essentialist, nationalist discourse unleashed by the *movimientos* created certain tensions in this new group politics that encompassed more than one ethnic subgroup under a generic term. Padilla noted the reasons for this generic group identity:

> [T]he politicization of a situational Latino ethnic identity and consciousness entails almost a related irony and paradox. It stresses, ideologizes, and sometimes virtually recreates the distinctive and unique national-cultural identities of the groups that it mobilizes, precisely at the historical moments when these groups are being asked to take on a Latino ethnic consciousness.[5]

Thus, the nationalism of the *movimiento* implied an expansive notion of group identity, La Raza, that both reified particular identities ("Chicanismo" for instance), as well as a more inclusive concept embracing other Latin American origin groups (such as Puerto Ricans). Not insignificantly, the critique of the role of the United States in Latin America added to this notion of group identity. In this view, Latin Americans were oppressed by the consequences of U.S. policy in that region, not unlike the oppression of Latinos living in this country.

Despite the anomalies and ambiguities of this new style of group politics, the benefits led to the increased use of the group identity, especially during the community action program era of the late 1960s and early 1970s. The political benefits of "lumping" the group allowed for aggregate figures to justify resources for community action groups, welfare rights organizations, and manpower training programs, among other initiatives. Distinctions due to immigration, class, national origin, length of residence in the United States or legal status were subsumed under the political expediency of generic terms. Hence, Chicano activists spoke of the Chicano community with scant attention to the importance of differentiation among people of Mexican origin in the United States. Moreover, when politically useful, Chicano advocates of civil rights legislation aggregated all Latino subgroups as one. Differences were glossed over by the rhetoric of "Brown power" and similar notions. If only implicitly, the assumptions of this strategy suggested that all the groups suffered equally and similarly from past racist practices directed at people of Latino background.

NOTES

1. F. James Davis, WHO IS BLACK: ONE NATION'S DEFINITION (1991); Allen J. Matusow, THE UNRAVELING OF AMERICA: A HISTORY OF LIBERALISM IN THE 1960S (1984).

2. Stephen N. Shulman & Charles F. Abernathy, THE LAW OF EQUAL EMPLOYMENT OPPORTUNITY § 4.02[1], at 4–3 (1990).

3. 118 Cong. Rec. S26664 (1972).

4. Felix M. Padilla, LATINO ETHNIC CONSCIOUSNESS: THE CASE OF MEXICAN AMERICANS AND PUERTO RICANS IN CHICAGO 4–8 (1985).

5. Felix M. Padilla, *On the Nature of Latino Ethnicity,* 65 SOC. SCI. Q. 651, 662 (1984).

ıı

Latinegras

Desired Women—Undesirable Mothers, Daughters, Sisters, and Wives

Marta I. Cruz-Janzen

Latinegras are Latinas of obvious black ancestry and undeniable ties to Africa, whose ancestral mothers were abducted from the rich lands that cradled them to become and bear slaves, endure the lust of their masters, and nurture other women's children. They are the mothers of generations stripped of their identity and rich heritage that should have been their legacy. Latinegras are women who cannot escape the many layers of racism, sexism, and inhumanity that have marked their existence. Painters, poets, singers, and writers have exalted their beauty, loyalty, and strength, but centuries of open assaults and rapes have also turned them into concubines, prostitutes, and undesirable mothers, daughters, sisters, and wives.

Latinegras are marked by a cruel, racialized history because of the shades of their skin, the colors and shapes of their eyes, and the textures and hues of their hair. They are the darkest *negras*, *morenas*, and *prietas*, the brown and golden *cholas* and *mulatas*, and the wheat-colored *trigueñas*. They are the light-skinned *jabás* with black features and the *grifas* with white looks but whose hair defiantly announces their ancestry. They are the Spanish-looking *criollas*, and the *pardas* and *zambas* who carry indigenous blood.

Latinegras represent the mirrors that most Latinos would like to shatter because they reflect the blackness Latinos don't want to see in themselves. I am a Latinegra, born to a world that denies my humanity as a black person, a woman, and a Latina; born to a world where other Latinos reject me and deny my existence even though I share their heritage. Racism and sexism have been with me all my life.

Growing up biracial in Puerto Rico, I became aware of Latino racism at a very young age. As the child of a white Puerto Rican mother, whose family counted their drops of pure Spanish blood and resented our dark presence, and a very *prieto* (dark black) Puerto Rican father, I became aware of the social and economic gulf that prevails within this supposedly harmonious, integrated society. My paternal grandparents were educated, considered middle-class, and lived in a white neighborhood of paved streets and nice homes. Theirs was a neat wooden house with electricity, indoor plumbing, and a telephone. A large concrete balcony and front fence were decorated with ornamental wrought iron. Grandma kept a beautiful front flower garden. They were the only blacks in the neighborhood, always conscious of their neighbors' watchful and critical eyes. We were careful never to set foot outside the house unless we were impeccably groomed. In contrast, the rest of my father's family lived in a predominantly black slum on the outskirts of town. In that neighborhood, everyone was *puro prieto* (pure black). The dirt streets, the dilapidated houses, the numerous domestic and farm animals running loose, and the lack of electricity and sanitary facilities unequivocally punctuated the differences.

My siblings and I grew up in predominantly white neighborhoods and moved back and forth between two realities that seemed worlds apart. I do not recall a time when both sides of the family got together. Teachers and other adults in the community openly commented to me and my siblings that my mother had disgraced her family by marrying a black man while my father had elevated himself and his family by marrying a white woman. It was then that I learned how identity labels reveal the rancor of white Latinos toward Latinos of obviously nonwhite heritage. White Latinos are light-skinned Latinos who are usually the product of racial mixing, who profess white racial purity, and who are usually accepted as white ("social white"). While my father's family called me *trigueña*, signifying a "step up" from being black, my mother's called me *negra* (black) and *mulata*, signifying a step down from being white. On one side of the family we were *negros finos* (refined blacks), while on the other side we were *una pena* (a disgrace, sorrow, and shame). Both sides of the family continually judged our looks; whoever had the most clearly defined white features was considered good-looking. I was constantly reminded to pinch my nose each day so it would lose its roundness and be sharper like those of my brothers and sisters. My younger sister received praise for her long flowing hair while I endured pity for my *greñas* (long mane of tangly hair). I felt fortunate, though, that at least it was long and not considered *ceretas* (short and knotty, like raisins).

When I was four my father took me to my first day of school. Later, when my mother came to pick me up and I jumped up happy to see her, my teacher exclaimed, "That can't be your mother. That woman is white." I realized for the first time that I was not like my mother or a lot of other people around me, including classmates and teachers. I recall holding hands with my parents, thereafter comparing skin colors, seeing that I was not like either one of them. I realized that our different skin colors would always be an issue. I recall the cruel taunts of classmates, adults, and even teachers who called me *negativo*, meaning photo negative, because, while I resembled my mother, they joked that we were opposites. They often called me *Perlina* (pearly white), referring to a bleaching detergent with the picture of black children dressed in white on the label. Peers teased that I was *una mosca en un vaso de leche* (a fly in a glass of milk) because I stood out among them. They also teased that my father was *retinto* (double-dyed black) and *moyeto*, meaning black and ugly.

In retrospect, I realize that having a white mother was an asset. Our mother was easily accepted in the community, whereas our father was not. As public ambassador of the family, Mami dealt with neighbors and negotiated opportunities for us, especially at school. She always managed to place us with the advanced students. I learned that a black mother would not have been able to do this because Latinegras have been socialized, through generations, to accept their inferiority to all men and whites. As occupants of the lowest rungs on the social ladder, they are looked down upon, expected to be docile, subservient, uneducated, and ignorant. I always sensed others' resentment toward Papi (Father), especially by white men. Latino men challenge each other's machismo constantly, even in unspoken ways, and the authority of a black man is not accepted on equal terms. They commented to me that Papi thought himself *parao* (uppity), *presumio* (presumptuous), and *alzao* (elevated) because he married a white woman. I dreaded my father's presence in public because he didn't elicit the warmest of responses and was only superficially treated with respect. Behind his back, peers, teachers, neighbors, and other adults called him *negro come coco* (coconut-eating black man) an expression alluding to a popular cartoon that depicted a very dark monkey eating coconuts on a palm tree. It was clear to me that they were mocking my father for marrying a white woman.

When we moved to the United States mainland in the 1960s, Latino friends advised me to emphasize my Latinness and to downplay my African traits to avoid being confused with African Americans. Some teachers advised that I might as well be black because I would be treated like one by white Latinos and mainstream white Americans. They felt that I should prepare myself for what inevitably awaited me. I deliberately spoke with a Spanish accent even though schools kept placing me in speech courses; I learned to use a fan gracefully, and wore my hair long and straight. Many Latinos distanced themselves from me by calling me *morena* (Moorish black), a derisive term reserved for dark-skinned blacks, especially African Americans.

Time has passed, but some things remain constant. Two years ago a Latino educator in Colorado told me that I was not one of them: "Hispanics are from Spain. You are not Hispanic. Everyone knows you're black." At a Latino meeting where I raised concerns about the educational needs of African American children, I was addressed with contempt: "You ought to know; you're black like them." A Latina friend explained, "Some Hispanics here don't want to see you as one of them because you represent everything they do not want to be. They see you as a black person, and they don't want to be black. They want you to stop saying you're like them."

In the United States blacks are usually identified as African American and often considered the racialized group most discriminated against. For Latinos, to be black in the United States is a perceived liability. Regardless of skin color and physical appearance, in the United States one drop of nonwhite blood makes the person loo percent nonwhite, while in Latin America one drop of white blood makes the person whiter, or at least no longer black or Indian. In Latin America "racial impurity" can be "cleansed" and "expunged" in ascending stages; in the United States racial "impurity" designates the person and his or her future generations as unfit and undesirable. In a society where "color supersedes ethnicity and culture," black Latinos in the United States find themselves identified as African Americans by both whites and Latinos. The more Latinos become immersed in the racial ideology of the United States, the sharper and more unyielding the black /white dichotomy becomes, and the more powerful is their need and desire to free themselves of any and all vestiges of African ancestry. Many Latinegros try to deny their blackness and identify themselves as Hispanic. ·

Two years ago at a conference in California I got on an elevator with two Latinas who, upon seeing me, switched their conversation from English to Spanish. When I asked them a question in flawless Spanish, they seemed surprised and remarked, "You don't look Latina!" They attempted to conceal their embarrassment and explained their surprise by telling me, "*Nosotros tenemos personas como usted en nuestro pais*" (We [Latino whites] have persons like you [Latino blacks] in our own country). Since few black Latinos from Latin American countries besides Puerto Rico are financially or legally able to migrate to the United States, these Latinas assumed that I was African American. I found their explanation neither comforting nor flattering. It reaffirmed my belief that Latinos in the United States prefer to deny my legitimate group membership. Within their native countries and within Latino groups in the United States, Latinegros live as "foreigners of both locations." "You don't look Latina/o [or Hispanic]" is something Latinegros hear often not only from white Americans but from other Latinos as well.

Upon entering Cornell University in 1968, I tried joining several Latino student organizations. When that failed, I tried to establish a club for Puerto Ricans. It became apparent that Puerto Ricans from the island and those from the United States mainland did not view themselves in the same way. Puerto Ricans from the island did not want to be perceived as black and rejected me, quite shamelessly. In contrast, Puerto Ricans from the United States mainland saw their strength through unity with African American students. Many flaunted even the minutest African heritage with Afro hairstyles and African clothing. I severed ties with most Latinos from Latin America, including Puerto Rico, and sought out the African and African American communities. I styled my hair in an Afro and began wearing African clothes. I found myself in a constant struggle to find my identity. I felt obliged to prove my blackness to other African Americans, even when they looked just like me. I was the victim of jokes because my hair would not stay up, and called "flat-top" and "lame-fro." I tried all sorts of styling chemicals; I even wore hairpieces and wigs. Finally, I cut my hair as short as possible. Repeatedly, African Americans told me that I must be ashamed of my African heritage because I tried to conceal it by claiming to be Latina and speaking Spanish.

The culmination of my search for a legitimizing identity came when I visited Africa, "the homeland." Ironically, the search that took me halfway across the world brought me right back home. What began as a journey to establish my identity proved instead to be a dead end—I was not, nor could I ever be, an African: I was a Latinegra living among Africans in Africa.

Mestizaje represents an interracial heritage manifest in white and indigenous unions. Many Spanish-speaking Latin American countries, especially Mexico, call themselves nations of mestizos but forget their African bloodlines. Even Latin American scholars endorse the doctrine of two "worlds," the Spanish and the indigenous, meeting on American soil. The concept of mestizaje sheds light on the historical rejection of Latinegros within most Latino cultures. Many Latinos, aware of their interracial heritage, may admit to their indigenous legacy, the mestizo, but few will admit to a black ancestor.

Chapter 72

Mestizaje and the Mexican *Mestizo* Self
No Hay Sangre Negra, So There Is No Blackness

Taunya Lovell Banks

Many who write about Mexican *mestizaje* omit references to Afromexicans, Mexico's African roots, and anti-black sentiments in the Mexican and Mexican American communities. At the end of the twentieth century a number of writers advanced *mestizaje* as a unifying principle that moves beyond the conventional binary (black-white) discussions of race. This uncritical and ahistorical invocation of *mestizaje* has serious implications for race relations in the United States given the growing presence and political power of Mexican Americans, because substituting *mestizaje* for racial binarism when discussing race in the United States reinforces, rather than diminishes, notions of white racial superiority and dominance.

I argue that scholars should replace their uncritical celebration of *mestizaje* with a focus on colonialism and capitalism, the twin ideologies that influenced racial formation from the late fifteenth through the twentieth century in the Americas. I argue that Spanish colonialists, disturbed by a growing population composed of offspring from relations between Spaniards, Africans and Indigenous people in colonial Mexico, developed a complex set of rules creating a race-like caste system with a distinct anti-black bias reinforced through art. Even after the end of colonial rule and the abolition of slavery and caste-based laws, this anti-African bias remained. Post-colonial officials and theorists in shaping Mexico's national image were influenced not only by the Spanish colonial legacy, but also by the negative image of Mexico and Mexicans articulated in the United States during the early nineteenth century. Thus, being Mexican becomes being *mestiza/o,* defined as European and Indian, with an emphasis on the European roots.

After examining how Mexicans came to be constructed in both Mexico and the United States from the mid-nineteenth through the twentieth century, I conclude that in the United States, Mexican nationals and Mexican Americans often were classified as white for political purposes. Nevertheless, many prominent members of the dominant American society considered persons of Mexican ancestry non-white, and in the nineteenth century some politicians saw some Mexicans as possessing African ancestry and thus theoretically akin to black Americans.

From Mestizaje *and the Mexican* Mestizo Self: No Hay Sangre Negra, *So There Is No Blackness,* 15 S. Calif. Interdisc. L.J. 199 (2006). Originally published in the *Southern California Interdisciplinary Law Journal.* Reprinted by permission.

I then posit that some Latino scholars are reluctant to admit or address evidence of anti-black bias in contemporary Mexico and within the Mexican American and larger Latina/o communities in the United States. The uncritical use of *mestizaje* or mestiza/o as a substitute for the traditional black-white binary racial analytical framework reinforces the denial of anti-black bias. This unexamined use of *mestizaje* ignores or trivializes the colonial baggage that accompanies the term. *Mestizaje*, unexamined and unreconstructed, also essentializes the African component of the racializing process in Latin America and the Caribbean, reinforcing conscious and unconscious notions of white superiority. Thus I call on scholars to engage in conversations about whether *mestizaje*, defined or undefined, can ever be an all-purpose substitute for the black-white binary racial analytical framework in the United States, the Caribbean, or Latin America.

The Evolution of Mestizaje *in Colonial Mexico*

Black Africans and their descendants were brought to New Spain, the formal name for the Spanish colony that later became Mexico, in the early sixteenth century. Initially, the Spanish Crown encouraged intermarriage between Spanish "explorers" and indigenous people "as a tool to promote peaceful cultural interaction in the Caribbean."[1] In contrast, early in the colonial period the Crown discouraged, but did not forbid, intermarriage between Spaniards and Africans. According to Mexican anthropologist Gonzalo Aguirre Beltrán, initially African women slaves were more numerous than male slaves, serving as concubines for the Spaniards. He writes that during "the first year of the conquest . . . [,] 99% of the individuals of white stock were males, as were 6% of those of Negro stock."[2]

According to some historians, by the mid-eighteenth century, mulattoes, the last of the African-descent slaves in Mexico, *disappear* or become assimilated into Mexican society. This assimilation came about so quickly, they argue, because the Afromexican population was so small, never exceeding two percent of the total population during the colonial period. But the size of the Afromexican population vis-à-vis Spanish colonialists is still a subject of dispute. Thus, the alleged disappearance or assimilation of Afromexicans warrants closer examination.

During the colonial period the Spanish colonists seemed highly concerned with drawing distinctions between the products of miscegenation. They divided offspring of mixed couples into three general groups: *mestizo* (Spanish-Indian), *mulatto* (Spanish-Black), and *zambo* or *zambaigo* (Black-Indian). But even the Spaniards realized that these categories might overlap. For example, there were black mestizos and subdivisions within this category. Hue often was used to distinguish between the types of mulattos and mestizos. These offspring of miscegenation unions, often illegitimate as well, were called *las castas*.

A legal classification system based on hue or phenotype was bound to cause confusion and misidentification between groups, especially for persons with African and Indian ancestry. According to Beltrán, darker-hued Afro-mestizos consistently tried to conceal their African ancestry because under colonial rule, Indians had a higher socio-economic status than *castas*. To prevent Afro-mestizo slaves passing as Indians, masters often used hot irons to brand "the insignia of servitude" on slaves' faces, or other places readily apparent to the observer.

Even free Afro-mestizos had an interest in hiding their African ancestry since by law mulattoes, but not mestizos, were subject to paying tribute in the form of head-taxes. In the words of art historian Ilona Katzew, the extensive racial classification system represented by the *sociedad de castas* suggests that "Spanish or white blood is redeemable . . . [and] inextricably linked to the idea of 'civilization.' Black blood, bear[s] the stigma of slavery, [and] connote[s] atavism and degeneracy."[3] Some colonial public and private art reinforced this idea.

I join with those scholars who argue against the unexamined use of the *mestizaje* paradigm to replace U.S. binary racial analysis because the uncritical use of mestizos or *mestizaje* papers over the role of the Atlantic slave trade in shaping and perpetuating racialized color-caste neo-colonial hierarchies in the United States and the post-colonial hierarchies in other parts of the Americas. Discussions of the racing process, whether in the United States, Caribbean, or other Americas, benefit from a colonial analysis that is grounded in the Atlantic slave trade. As I point out, recent scholars' wholesale condemnation of the black-white racial binary analysis, prominent in U.S. race jurisprudence, tends to overlook how that binary analysis affects other racialized groups, especially mixed-raced ethnic groups from Latin America and the Caribbean. Thus, an anti-African bias found in many Latin American and Caribbean nations goes unexamined.

The failure to acknowledge and examine this bias means that race issues among Latino/as receive scant treatment in the celebration of Latino/a *mestizaje*. In discussing the concept of *mestizaje* in Latin American and U.S. society, it is essential to determine not only what *mestizaje* moves toward, but more importantly from what *mestizaje* moves away. In 1993, Peter Skerry argued that the movement among Mexican Americans to identify themselves as an ethnic group and minority would impede their political assimilation, identify them more closely with the black minority, and distance them from earlier European-American ethnic populations. Sociologist Orlando Patterson might argue that many Latina/os have chosen the assimilation route.

Writing in the *New York Times*, Patterson disagrees with those commentators who assert that with the increasing Latina/o population the United States is becoming a non-white country. He argues that these commentators "fail to take account of the fact that nearly half of the Hispanic population is white in every social sense of the term; 48 percent . . . classified themselves as solely white . . . to the census taker."[4] Patterson also argues that second-generation "Hispanic whites" are intermarrying and assimilating American language and culture faster than earlier second-generation European migrants. But Miriam Jiménez Román and Gina Pérez write in response, "That Latinos are not considered 'true whites' is evident by their classification as Hispanic whites, a conditional whiteness bestowed on (or claimed by) only some (and not all, as Mr. Patterson suggests)."[5]

Patterson's comments evidence the real fear among blacks that Latina/os, a growing political power within the United States, prefer to occupy a middle racial position, a buffer between whites and blacks, who will side most often with whites against the interests of blacks. Román and Pérez's response reminds *New York Times* readers that Latina/os, whether classified as conditional whites or not and not withstanding any economic and political power, will continue to retain their non-white status. So even though they seem at cross purposes, as my prior discussion suggests, Patterson, Román and Pérez are correct in their analysis of Latina/os' situation in the United States as not fully assimilated.

Thus, by not adopting a more global analytical perspective when discussing race, ethnicity, gender, and perhaps sexuality, U.S. legal scholars have started at least a century too late. When discussing race, ethnic, and gender subordination in the Americas, scholars must acknowledge the lingering effects of war, colonialism, capitalism, and slavery, as well as the way in which different imperial powers, like Spain, England, and more recently, the United States, have dominated the Americas during different eras over the past five centuries.

NOTES

1. Susan Kellogg, *Depicting Mestizaje: Gendered Images of Ethnorace in Colonial Mexican Texts*, 12 J. WOMEN'S HIST. 69, 73 (2000).

2. Gonzalo Aguirre Beltrán, *Races in 17th-Century Mexico*, 6 PHYLON 212 (1945).

3. Ilona Katzew, NEW WORLD ORDER: CASTA PAINTING AND COLONIAL LATIN AMERICA 10 (1996).

4. See Orlando Patterson, *Race by the Numbers*, N.Y. TIMES, May 8, 2001, at A27.

5. Miriam Jiménez Román & Gina Pérez, Letter to the Editor, *A Category, Not a Race*, N.Y. TIMES, May 15, 2001, at A26.

Chapter 73

||||||||||||||||||||||||||||||||||||||||||||||||||||||||||||||||||||||||||||||||

Inventing Race

John D. Skrentny

Our seemingly endless debate about the justice of affirmative action has kept a related and increasingly important issue off the national agenda: If we are to have affirmative action, which groups should be included? Americans almost always debate
affirmative action as if African Americans were the only beneficiary. The logic behind
this assumption has been that this group has experienced uniquely severe oppression
and disadvantage, and was the original intended beneficiary of affirmative action and
of the civil rights laws introduced in the 1960s.

But almost from the beginning of the affirmative-action era, the federal government included other ethnic and racial groups in its regulations. In the late 1960s,
these regulations established what would become, with some adjustment, America's
"official minorities": blacks, Latinos, Asian Americans, and American Indians. These
are the groups included in federal employment affirmative action and set asides
for businesses, as well as affirmative action in university admissions, though Asian
Americans have been dropped from the affirmative-action admissions programs of
most colleges and medical schools on account of their high representation.

The scope of affirmative action is a matter of some importance. The question of
how many and which groups are classified as victims, or as different enough from
mainstream whites to contribute to "diversity," is what political scientist Steven Teles
calls a "regime-level issue"—an issue that touches on "basic issues of citizenship and
social system maintenance" and American national identity. Second, immigration
is drastically changing the shape of affirmative action. National policy now allows
nearly one million immigrants into the United States every year, more than three-
quarters of them Latinos and Asians who would be eligible for affirmative action.
The 2000 census confirmed that Latinos alone already outnumber blacks in the
United States.

This convergence of immigration policy and affirmative action has led to conflicts.
These have mostly occurred among the "official minorities" themselves, as when Latinos use affirmative action to make inroads into areas like government employment
where blacks predominate. The sociologist Orlando Patterson has called for the exclusion from affirmative action of all Asian Americans except Chinese Americans descended from pre-1923 immigrants, the exclusion of all Hispanics except for Puerto

From *Inventing Race*, 146 THE PUBLIC INTEREST 97 (Winter 2002). Reprinted excerpts from pp. 97–99, 110–
13 by permission of the author and the publishers of *National Affairs*, successor to *The Public Interest*.

Ricans and second generation or later Mexican Americans, and the exclusion of immigrants from Africa and the Caribbean.

Patterson's effort to narrow the scope of affirmative action raises difficult questions: If affirmative action is not only for the descendants of American slaves, then what degree of past (or present) suffering should serve as the dividing line? And once that line is drawn, is it right to offer the included groups equal help? Should religious differences be completely ignored, as they are now? Do white ethnic groups, such as Italians, Jews, and Poles, as well as Iranians and other Middle Easterners, encounter discrimination, or have they already achieved equal representation? Do these groups contribute to diversity?

Though these subjects have drawn little public debate, the courts have begun to show concern about the criteria for inclusion in affirmative-action policies. Some programs have been struck down for being overly broad. It appears that both defenders of affirmative action and its critics will have to pay more attention to who is included in affirmative action and why.

But the historical record of affirmative-action policymaking offers astonishingly little guidance for what to do today. Scarcely any study went into deciding which groups would be considered "minorities" eligible for affirmative action. Instead, this is a story of some quiet lobbying, and of policymaking based on the largely unquestioned assumption that certain groups were in some unspecified way analogous to blacks. The nonblack groups were at the time small, the problems of black America very large, and few paid attention as American society was classified in an entirely novel way. Over the years, and with an equal absence of thought, these classifications became entrenched in government and university policies. Now this strange lack of attention to fundamental questions may lead to affirmative action's undoing.

University elites embraced the desirability of reaching out to minority groups, and with zeal and creativity they developed reasons why it was a good idea. Yet their views on both counts were limited by the government's approach to affirmative action. All minorities were seen as equally disadvantaged, the mixture of ethnicities within a minority category did not matter or mattered far less than race, there were no mixed-race persons, and all "whites" were the same—"socially and ethnically homogeneous," as one Supreme Court brief put it. Persons of British, Italian, Arab, Armenian, Greek, and Polish ancestry were understood to be essentially similar in their histories, viewpoints, and experience with past discrimination, and none of these groups was thought to contribute anything meaningful to the educational experience of diversity. Distinctions between Protestants, Catholics, and Jews were ignored as well.

Who Was Left Out?

Representatives from certain white ethnic groups protested the direction of affirmative-action policy. In 1967, Vincent Trapani, the head of a New York Italian-American organization, complained to the EEOC that its EEO-1 form violated the Civil Rights

Act by specifying only four minority groups and demanded that it be revised or eliminated. In 1968, the Jewish Labor Committee argued that Jews should be included on
the form, and the Anti-Defamation League conducted studies of Jewish employment
in New York. Jews received some attention at the EEOC's hearings on white-collar
employment in New York City, but never gained the status of "official minorities."

Polish-American leaders were the most active, especially the Polish American
Congress (PAC) lawyer Leonard Walentynowicz. Upset by the popularity of "Polish
jokes," and resentful that Poles were frozen out of top positions in society while simultaneously being blamed for keeping blacks down, the PAC lobbied the EEOC, the
OFCC [Office of Federal Contract Compliance], and the U.S. Commission on Civil
Rights for attention. Poles and Italians also joined forces in Chicago to produce studies that showed underrepresentation of these groups in executive and government
positions.

These groups had some allies in Congress, including Democratic congressmen Roman Pucinski of Chicago and Mario Biaggi of New York. New York senator James
Buckeley complained that the OFCC's primary affirmative-action regulation used the
word "minority" more than 65 times without ever defining it.

But except for an OFCC proposal that firms with government contracts remedy
underutilization of Catholics, Jews, and eastern and southern Europeans—a plan that
was rejected by the Nixon White House—civil rights agencies mostly brushed off
these efforts. They and administration aides stated that adding more groups would be
too burdensome to businesses, that preferences for Catholics and Jews would violate
the Constitution by giving preference to certain religions, and that it was harder to
determine who was Italian and Jewish and Polish than it was to determine who was
black. But their principal argument, stated but never elaborated, was that these groups
had not suffered as much as blacks had. These rebuffs invariably avoided the more
difficult comparisons among and between white ethnics (and, later, Middle Eastern
groups), Latinos (50 percent of whom say they are white), Asian Americans (wealth-
ier and more educated on average than almost any white ethnicity), and American
Indians (who show very high rates of intermarriage).

Affirmative Action on the Ropes

Affirmative-action policy separates government-designated minorities from other
Americans through an undefined standard of victimhood. The logic of the policy is
based on an unexamined assumption equating black Americans with Latinos, Asian
Americans (sometimes), and American Indians.

This probably makes sense to most Americans. Some of these groups can lay claim
to unique experiences with state-sanctioned oppression, discrimination, and segregation that white ethnics, Jews, and Arab or Middle-Eastern Americans cannot. Why,
then, should we care that these latter minorities are not included in affirmative-
action programs, while so-called "people of color" are? I offered two answers at the
outset of this essay: first, that these policies make permanent victims of the included

populations; and second, that high immigration levels among Hispanics and Asians have dramatically transformed affirmative action, bringing it far from its original goals. In closing, I offer another: If affirmative action is dismantled on a national basis, the policy's over- or underinclusiveness will likely be the reason.

The lack of any specification, analysis, or clear rationale for official minority status has troubled the courts in ways that it has not troubled legislators. In the famous reverse-discrimination case *Regents of the University of California v. Bakke* (1978), the plaintiff challenged the Medical School of the University of California at Davis's affirmative-action plan, which gave preferences to the EEO-1's four minority groups even though Asians did well enough not to need the preferences. Leonard Walentynowicz, writing for various Polish-American groups, filed a blistering amicus brief that complained of the lack of clear basis for minority-group selection and charged a violation of due process. The brief also argued that if protections were to be given, they should go to all groups experiencing discrimination, and such a decision should not be made simply because a group is more vocal, or better organized, or because of the emotions of the day. It should be made by an open political process in which public confidence can be secured and divisiveness avoided.

Few justices or legal analysts took note of the problem of affirmative action's scope (Justice Thurgood Marshall, for instance, discussed only blacks in his opinion). Justice Lewis Powell, however, took Walentynowicz's argument seriously. In his opinion in the *Bakke* case, Powell chose to embrace the "diversity" rationale for affirmative action precisely because it avoided the question of which groups had suffered sufficient discrimination to warrant preferential treatment—any underrepresented group could add to the diversity of a student body. Powell wrote:

> There is no principled basis for deciding which groups would merit "heightened judicial solicitude" and which would not. Courts would be asked to evaluate the extent of the prejudice and consequent harm suffered by various minority groups. Those whose societal injury is thought to exceed some arbitrary level of tolerability then would be entitled to preferential classifications at the expense of other groups.

Powell suggested that a constitutional "diversity" preference might, in some circumstances, offer preference to an Italian American.

It has taken two decades for Powell's warning to come to pass. When Americans criticize affirmative-action programs, they generally make their case against preferences for blacks, the group which, arguably, needs them most. But the adoption of strict scrutiny as a standard of judicial review for public affirmative-action programs has led to increased examination of affirmative action's inclusiveness. Many judges have begun to demand a clearer rationale for racially based preferences. Some of them are less sympathetic to affirmative action than was Powell; applying the strict scrutiny standard, they demand that affirmative action be narrowly tailored to achieve a compelling government purpose. In 1989, in the case of *City of Richmond v. J. A. Croson*, the Supreme Court struck down Richmond, Virginia's set-aside program for its lack of a clear rationale. Richmond included nonblack minorities without providing any evidence of past discrimination against these groups, and even included Eskimos in its American-Indian category despite the absence of Eskimos in the city's population. More than a decade has passed since this decision, and there is still no widely accepted and coherent theory to justify why some groups should be included in affirmative action while others should not. The continuing confusion over the scope of affirmative action weakens a policy that may still be very important for black Americans.

Chapter 74

||||||||||||||||||||||||||||||||||||||||||||||||||||||||||||||||||||||||||||||||||||||

Locating Latinos in the Field of Civil Rights
The Neoliberal Case for Radical Exclusion

Richard Delgado

Poor Latinos! Nobody loves them. Think-tank conservatives like Peter Brimelow, joined by a few liberals and a host of white supremacist websites, have been warning against the Latino threat: Because our dark-skinned friends from south of the border insist on preserving their peculiar language and ways, they endanger the integrity of our Anglocentric culture. In order to guard against Balkanization and associated disorders, we should limit immigration from Latin America and police the southern border even more vigilantly than we do now.

Recently this group of scholars has been joined by a second group. Composed for the most part of moderate liberals, these writers argue that Latinos pose a different kind of threat. Classified as minorities by many university and public administrators, members of this group nevertheless consume social services and affirmative action slots intended for the country's historic minorities—blacks and Native Americans. Precisely because Latinos assimilate, according to these commentators, they have little claim on our civil rights sympathies. Latinos, then, come under fire from the right for not assimilating and from the left for doing the exact opposite. The right uses unassimilability as a rationale for keeping Latinos out; the left, their success in fitting in as a reason for denying public benefits and places in colleges and universities to ones who are already here. Individualistic, no-nonsense Americans have a limited stock of empathy, this group writes. Why risk compassion fatigue by extending our civil rights sympathies to groups who do not really need them?

The former group includes Brimelow, Patrick Buchanan, Samuel Huntington, liberal Arthur Schlesinger, the anti-immigrant organization FAIR, and a legion of white supremacist websites that inveigh against the evils of "mud people." The second, somewhat softer-edged school includes scholars such as Paul Brest, John Skrentny, Orlando Patterson, Mari Matsuda, and columnist Charles Krauthammer, who warn of the danger of dilution when well-meaning activists and administrators extend civil rights programs to groups beyond their original beneficiaries.

A recent book by George Yancey typifies this new movement. *Who Is White?: Latinos, Asians, and the New Black/Nonblack Divide*[1] offers an extended argument,

From *Locating Latinos in the Field of Civil Rights: Assessing the Neoliberal Case for Radical Exclusion*, 83 Tex. L. Rev. 489 (2004). Originally published in the *Texas Law Review*. Reprinted by permission.

complete with footnotes, charts, graphs, and survey material, for limiting civil rights remedies to blacks alone. Other chapters in this volume review the recurring admonitions of nativist writers that Latinos are incompatible with America. This chapter, by contrast, considers the recent school of liberal critics who reason that Latinos assimilate—intermarry, move into white neighborhoods, learn English—so successfully that they can safely be ignored. The first group's arguments are weak normatively—their vision of America as a sanitized, Anglicized nation with little diversity of thought, culture, or ethnicity is simply out of keeping with contemporary ideals.

The second group's are not. Normatively strong, they rise or fall on the strength of their factual predicate and what follows from it. Are Latinos, in fact, assimilating, and if so, in what ways? Are they following the same path as that of earlier European groups, such as Irish, Italians, and Jews, who were first considered nonwhite, culturally inferior, and incapable of higher intellectual functioning, but soon secured social acceptance and admission to the white race? And, if Latinos are coming to terms with America in some respects, what does that mean for social justice? Should we quietly but firmly write them out of the civil rights equation in favor of those more needy? After considering these questions, I close by offering a few observations for the benefit of the second-largest minority group about the fate that may befall them if they make common cause with moderate liberals who urge just that, as well as some directions critical scholarship should take in light of America's multiracial future.

As we have seen, Anglo society has not readily accepted, much less welcomed, brown-skinned newcomers from Mexico or most other parts of Latin America. Except for the agricultural sector, which periodically needed their labor, U.S. society deemed Latinos dull, unclean, and slow to acquire American ways. Despite their poor reception, however, Latinos have continued to migrate to the United States and, once here, to have children so that their numbers have grown rapidly. That growth has sparked a new attitude toward Latinos on the part of a certain sector of the population. Concerned that this large and growing group is poised to exert real influence on American society, this sector, which includes a number of academics, liberals, and concerned African Americans, wishes simply to write them out of the civil rights equation. In this view, Latinos would enjoy the right to remain here, work, attend school, and intermarry with whites, but they would have little claim on our civil rights sympathies.

Too Successful for Their Own Good? Neoliberal Racism and the Emerging Argument against Latino Recognition

Preservation of Affirmative Action

The new argument for excluding Latinos from civil rights consideration holds that they are little different from former immigrant groups. This "immigrant analogy" suggests that, just as earlier groups of European immigrants from Greece, Italy, Ireland, and Poland found their places in American society, so too, in time, will Latinos.

Society need make few special provisions for them. In particular, it should exclude them from affirmative action programs designed for real minorities—blacks.

For example, in a syndicated column, Charles Krauthammer argues in favor of cutting affirmative action back to its core—blacks—in order to preserve it from attack and to conserve scarce social resources and sympathy. Without addressing how Latinos will fare if left alone, Krauthammer urges that this is justified because they lack the moral standing of blacks, and including them in affirmative action would dilute that program and raise its costs beyond what America is prepared to pay.

Political scientist John Skrentny echoes many of these sentiments in a 2002 article. Observing that affirmative action was originally designed to benefit only blacks, he questions the wisdom of its recent expansion to new groups, particularly the children of immigrants from Latin America and Asia. This approach makes "permanent victims" of these groups, while threatening affirmative action for others. If the public ultimately rejects affirmative action, he warns, its "over- or underinclusiveness will likely be the reason."[2]

Distraction from More Pressing Matters

Critical race theorist Mari Matsuda and former Stanford Law School dean and sometime critical legal studies fellow traveler Paul Brest argue along similar lines. Matsuda warns that the black/white binary paradigm of American racial thought retains much of its original descriptive force despite the country's rapidly diversifying population. While the issues facing nonblack groups such as Latinos and Asians deserve consideration, policymakers should focus first on the larger problems of African Americans, the alleviation of which can give other racial minority groups resolve to combat their own social injustices.[3] Brest and his coauthor argue that Latinos lack the unique history of oppression that blacks endured; the lesser version they suffer may be addressed in other ways.[4] In a similar vein, Orlando Patterson argues that "race by the numbers," in which college administrators aim for a student body composed of all the country's minority groups in proportion to their representation in the population at large, will lead to administrative chaos and the program's ultimate downfall.[5]

Not Deserving

A final group of writers, including University of Michigan Professor J. B. White,[6] Peter Skerry,[7] and, at least by implication Brest and Oshige, make arguments casting doubt on Latinos' entitlement to civil rights solicitude, including affirmative action, because they are not deserving. As nonblack minorities with light skin, middle-class aspirations, and no history of slavery or intense discrimination, they are more likely to pursue the same upward course that earlier waves of European immigrants did. Brest and Oshige concede that Latinos might warrant consideration in regions of the country where their numbers are high, but only by showing economic disadvantage. Blacks would qualify for affirmative action without that showing.

George Yancey and the Coming Black/Nonblack Divide

Recently, George Yancey, one of the editors of *The Cornel West Reader*, has offered an extensive argument against including Latinos and Asian Americans in the civil rights equation, except, perhaps, as cheerleaders and supporters of black causes. In *Who Is White?: Latinos, Asians, and the New Black/Nonblack Divide*, Yancey builds on the scholarship of all the above authors, but goes on to pose the issue of non-black minorities in an especially provocative way. Because Yancey's book constitutes the most detailed exposition of the emerging argument against Latinos, Asians, and other nonblack groups, it deserves special scrutiny.

Yancey begins by reminding his readers of the familiar prediction that by the year 2050, minorities of color will for the first time outnumber whites. In an astonishing twist, Yancey takes issue with this piece of conventional wisdom. Whites will not re-main passive in the face of the impending shift. Instead, they will enlist Asians and Latinos as members of the white race, leaving blacks at the bottom of the social lad-der. Members of these two other groups will not join whites merely in a strategic sense, making common cause with them on particular issues. Rather, they will liter-ally become white, just as the Irish, Greeks, Italians, and Jews did in the decades fol-lowing the advent of heavy immigration in the early years of the twentieth century. At first marginalized, despised, and excluded from the best neighborhoods, schools, and jobs, these groups were treated much like blacks and actually seen that way; only by a process that included acquiring wealth (sometimes through organized crime), swearing loyalty to the Democratic Party, and agreeing to join in the suppression of blacks were they permitted to join the white race. Just as their social construction changed when white self-interest dictated it, that of Asians and Latinos will as well.

By 2050, Yancey writes, the number of what today are regarded as whites will in-deed slip below that of what we now consider people of color. But by then, Latinos and Asians will have achieved admission to the white race, so that the number of whites will continue to exceed that of the nation's historic and truest minority. The demographers' predictions then, while literally correct, ignore that race is malleable, that a group's contours are subject to change, and that immigrant groups have always moved into and out of the white race when it suited whites' purposes.

But will Asians and Latinos succumb to the siren song of whiteness, rather than, for example, pursue civil rights in coalition with blacks and Native Americans? Yes; in fact, they have already begun doing so, according to Yancey, just as whites have be-gun seeing them as racial allies. The same will not happen with blacks, Yancey writes, for they suffer a degree of alienation unlike that of other minorities. Even as Latinos and Asians move smoothly up the ladder of whiteness, blacks will continue to occupy the bottom rung. Uniquely stigmatized, alienated, and marginalized, they will remain specially in need of assistance from white sympathizers and the government.

Examining the Neoliberal Argument against Latino Recognition

Each of the authors mentioned above—White, Krauthammer, Yancey, Skrentny, Matsuda, Skerry, and Patterson—argues for some version of two propositions: (1) blacks are different from Asians and Latinos—more victimized by discrimination and cruel stereotypes, they are exceptional; and (2) because of this exceptionality, blacks are more deserving of civil rights solicitude and affirmative action. Some of these writers also subscribe, either implicitly or explicitly, to the immigrant analogy according to which Asians and Latinos will follow the path of earlier groups like the Irish and Italians, who made their peace with America, learned American ways, and today are virtually indistinguishable from the descendants of Anglo-Saxon immigrants who came to this country in its early years. Each of these propositions is open to question.

The Immigrant Analogy

Some of the core weaknesses of the latter-day argument against Latinos stem from the immigrant analogy, which holds that, like earlier waves of European immigrants, Latinos will blend into American society in a generation or two, whether or not this country makes special efforts on their behalf. Beyond ordinary decency, society owes them very little—certainly not the full protection of our civil rights laws or affirmative action programs designed for other purposes. "If my ancestors made it," some of these writers seem to reason, "they (Latinos and Asians) can, too."

And of course they can, after a fashion. But many Latinos are not immigrants. With U.S. roots extending back for several generations, indeed in some cases since before the Anglo settlers arrived, their poverty and stigmatization cannot be explained as the product of a temporary unfamiliarity with mainstream culture. And with those who are immigrants, the path for many is not linear. In particular, immigrants from Mexico, and perhaps other Latin American countries as well, are assimilating downwards—the second and third generations worse off than the first. To hope that Latin poverty and misery will abate, by itself, in a short time, flies in the face of current knowledge.

Latino social mobility is different from the European kind, for a number of reasons. As mentioned earlier, the group's history is inextricably linked with conquest and American imperialism. From the first encounters, Anglo society demonized the Mexicans they found living in the Southwest, coining stereotypes that they would soon use to rationalize military aggression and the plunder of Mexican lands. Latinos were treated as inferior and deserving of subservient roles from the beginning. Italians, Greeks, and Irish, although scarcely welcomed with open arms, met no precisely comparable fate. Their "story of origin" includes hardship and struggle, but they were not conquered people nor despised as such.

Further, the Mexican border (and that with Guatemala) is near, making passage from one side to the other easy. Many Mexican Americans and others take advantage of the border's proximity and porosity to make frequent repeat visits to their villages. Many send some of their precious savings home, employing one of dozens of telegraph and money delivery services that have sprung up in large U.S. cities. Others arrange to have favorite foods cooked by mothers-in-law in their native villages 2,200 miles away sent to them in New York or Hartford. Most immigrants retain a place in their heart for their homeland, intending to return there someday to retire, build a home, or buy a small farm. This makes forming unconditional attachment to the United States difficult, something that was not true of the early wave of immigrants.

Even in death, many Mexicans seek reunion with their home country. A recent *New York Times* article described a booming business among mortuaries in certain large cities that prepare and send the bodies of Mexicans who die in the United States back to their village graveyards in Mexico. And when Mexico recently decided to permit its émigrés to hold dual citizenship, Mexicans living in the United States flocked to their consulates to fill out an application, even ones who had lost their Mexican citizenship and gained the U.S. variety.

Other grounds differentiate Latinos from the earlier wave of immigrants from eastern and southern Europe. Many Latinos are very dark or indigenous looking, with broad cheekbones, slightly slanted eyes, black hair, and short, stout bodies—as far from the idealized image of Eurocentric beauty as one could be and as much so as many blacks. Many of the early European immigrants, although uprooted and poor, looked white. They also arrived without the devastating social stigma many Latinos, particularly Mexicans, bore, dating back to the time of conquest when the early settlers disparaged them as a lazy, stupid, and mongrelized race. Latinos were stigmatized in the prevailing Anglo "story of origin." European immigrants were not.

Still other features differentiate the experiences of the early European immigrants from those of today's Latinos. The early Europeans received help from settlement houses, social workers, and a small cottage industry of "Americanization" agents, self-appointed and otherwise, who taught them American standards of cleanliness, recipes, dress, and social behavior. *Today's* Latinos benefit from nothing comparable. Indeed, a militarized border with searchlights, motorized vehicles, barbed wire, police dogs, helicopters, and sensors places unauthorized entrants in mortal danger. In some areas of the Southwest, murderous, Mexican-hating vigilantes, some of whom move to the region expressly because they enjoy the prospect of engaging in human target practice, step in where they believe the border patrol is not doing its job. Early U.S. immigration law favored Europeans; today, it is stacked against Latinos seeking entry. Once inside the country, the Europeans found U.S. law either neutral or on their side. Domestic laws today formally disadvantage Latinos, ranging from California's Proposition 187, which would have cut off schooling and other state benefits to immigrants, to English-only laws in many states and workplaces, and school policies that prohibit bilingual education beyond a very brief period.

Unlike the early twentieth-century European immigrants or blacks today, Latinos lack role models or a large middle class. The Europeans left countries that might have been suffering famine, war, or revolution, but that were otherwise culturally intact. Many boasted proud histories of artistic and cultural achievement. Many of today's Latino immigrants come from sending nations that are in economic turmoil due to histories of U.S. meddling and imperialism. Blacks count role models in the form of entertainment and sports stars and the occasional media celebrity, as well as a large and growing middle class. Latinos have little of either. Blacks benefited from the Civil

Rights Movement and still enjoy support from white sympathizers, including a legion of teachers and school counselors on the lookout for black talent. Latinos have far fewer allies of this sort. Popular culture disparages Latinos through explicitly and consciously demeaning roles in movies, jokes, putdowns, and mocking of the Spanish language through expressions such as "hasta la vista, baby," "no problemo," "numero uno," and "no way, Jose"—features that others do not have to endure, at least as frequently and unapologetically.

Social Attitudes and Whiteness—What Does It Mean to Think White?

Some years ago, I published a law review article entitled *Minority Law Professors' Lives: The Bell-Delgado Survey*,[8] which examined how law professors of color were faring. With questions dealing with career satisfaction, burn-out, relations with colleagues and students, and material support at their law schools, the questionnaire provided a snapshot of the fortunes and well-being of blacks, Latinos, and Asians teaching at the nation's law schools.

Some years later, a young African American woman obtained my permission to replicate the survey. It turned out that she did not use the same questions I had asked, so the results of her survey would shed little light on changes in the legal academy during the interim. When I received my own questionnaire, I was struck by how little relevance some of the questions bore to Latinos. One question, in particular, asked whether, when growing up, my parents had suffered because of the legacy of Jim Crow laws. I wrote the author, explaining that, while they had not suffered under that particular regime, the country's formal legal structure had disadvantaged them—and me—in countless ways, including many of the ones discussed above. I pointed out that most Latinos would probably have the same reaction and suggested a few questions to add if she were interested in eliciting information for that group. Whether she took me up on my suggestion, I do not know; her article still awaits publication.

This incident suggests that scholars need to take care when assessing the civil rights experiences of Latinos. Yancey, for example, supports his argument against including Latinos in the civil rights agenda by citing survey data professing to show that Latinos are beginning to think like whites. But consider how he came to that conclusion. One of his questions asked respondents whether they thought there was too much talk about race. According to Yancey, very few blacks think this is true, although most whites do. When many of his Latino and Asian respondents agreed with the proposition, Yancey concluded that Latinos and Asians are beginning to think like whites.

But might it not be that Latinos and Asians, realizing that the country implicitly subscribes to a black/white binary paradigm of race, interpret the question, not unreasonably, as asking whether they believe the United States has too much conversation about blacks? Answering yes to that question would not, then, be an indication of political conservatism, much less of identification with the white race. It might mean, instead, that the respondent believes discussion of racial minority groups ought to be broader than it is now and include groups other than African Americans. Similarly, Yancey asked his respondents how they felt about increasing welfare spending and integration of the nation's churches. Evidently, many blacks believe in both, while large numbers of whites do not. Because Yancey's Latino and Asian respondents gave answers more like those given by whites than by blacks, he concludes that they are beginning to adopt white attitudes. But bear in mind that Latinos, as a group, prize families and cultural solidarity. Asked whether they favor integrating churches or spending on social welfare programs, they may reply tepidly, not because they identify with whites but rather because they identify with their own culture and believe that families and churches should be the first resort of those who suffer misfortune.

One could imagine a different test of cultural attitudes that asked African Americans how they feel about immigration, bilingual education, accent discrimination, or workers speaking languages other than English on the job. On learning that many respond to these measures in much the same way whites do, one could conclude that blacks were taking on white attitudes, were on their way to assimilation, and that society's first order of business ought to be to take care of those nonblack minority groups that represent the real bottom of the social ladder. Of course, this would be preposterous, but the point is that one's choice of questions, as well as how one interprets the answers, must be approached with care. If one's object is to see whether Asians and Latinos are "beginning to approach racial issues from a majority group perspective," one must avoid using racial issues as synonymous with black ones, for then one would come perilously close to using the black/white binary of race to justify itself.

Yancey committed exactly this error in his selection of questions. He first examined questions to see if they generated a large black/white gap in the responses he received. When he found such a question, he proceeded to ask it of a population of Asians and Latinos to see if their responses were more like those of whites than blacks. The fallacy of such an approach should be obvious: It ends up measuring a group's attitudinal similarity to whites by imagining that they were blacks answering the same questions. But a group like Latinos may be attitudinally vastly different from whites in a host of respects that the researcher did not ask about—precisely because the researcher designed questions merely to show that Latinos differ from blacks. That, of course, does not exhaust all the possibilities. Because Latinos do not respond as blacks do to certain questions, it does not follow that they are like whites. To make such an assertion simply recapitulates the black/white binary paradigm of race.

Yancey, like other liberals who oppose including Latinos in the civil rights agenda, finds it highly significant that blacks are still the most segregated group when it comes to housing. But Latinos hold that dubious distinction with respect to schooling—more Latino children attend dominantly minority schools than do any other group. They also suffer the highest high school dropout rate by far. Who is to say which group is most marginalized and separated from the mainstream? Or, again, consider the marginally lower opposition to intermarriage rates that Yancey cites for Asians and Latinos vis-à-vis blacks as indications of their assimilation. Yet, might those rates not reflect, in some cases, white males pursuing a "Suzy Wong" stereotype of the obedient, non-feminist Asian woman, or Anglo women acting on unconscious stereotypes, for example, of the Latin lover?

NOTES

1. George Yancey, WHO IS WHITE? LATINOS, ASIANS, AND THE NEW BLACK/NONBLACK DIVIDE (2003).

2. John D. Skrentny, *Inventing Race*, 146 PUB. INT. 97, 97–99, 109–12 (Winter 2002) (reprinted, in part, this volume).

3. Mari Matsuda, *Beyond and Not Beyond Black and White: Deconstruction Has a Politics*, in CROSSROADS, DIRECTIONS, AND A NEW CRITICAL RACE THEORY 393, 393–94, 396–97 (Francisco Valdes et al. eds., 2002).

4. Paul Brest and Miranda Oshige, *Affirmative Action for Whom?* 47 STANFORD L. REV. 855, 873–74, 875, 883–90, 900 (1995).

5. Orlando Patterson, *Race by the Numbers*, N.Y. TIMES, May 8, 2001, at A27.

6. James Boyd White, *What's Wrong with Our Talk about Race?: On History, Particularity, and Affirmative Action*, 100 MICH. L. REV. 1927, 1935n.16, 1936 (2002).

7. Peter Skerry, MEXICAN AMERICANS: THE AMBIVALENT MINORITY 297–99 (1993).

8. Richard Delgado, *Minority Professors' Lives: The Bell-Delgado Survey*, 24 HARV. C.R.–C.L. L. REV. 349 (1989).

African-Americans, Latinos, and the Construction of Race
Toward an Epistemic Coalition

George A. Martinez

Latinos recently became the largest minority group in the United States. African-Americans may therefore be about to give up political clout to Latinos. This prospect has generated tension between African-Americans and Latinos. Given this shift, it is important to consider the African-American/Latino relationship. Specifically, the legal construction of Mexican-Americans as white has generated tensions that form a barrier to coalition building between African-Americans and Latinos. I contend that Mexican-Americans should embrace a non-white identity to facilitate coalition building with African Americans. Indeed, I contend that the racialization of African-Americans cannot be fully understood without considering the racialization of Latinos. As a result, I call for an epistemic coalition comprised of all minority groups so that each group achieves knowledge about themselves and their place in the world.

How Is the Relationship between African-Americans and Latinos Affected by the Construction of Race?

I want to focus on the example of Mexican-Americans. Mexican-Americans have been legally classified as white. That legal classification endangers the relationship between African-Americans and Mexican-Americans. It creates a barrier to coalitions with African-Americans and other non-white minorities.

An example from Dallas, Texas is instructive. In that city, African-Americans and Mexican-Americans are at odds over the direction of the Dallas School District. African-Americans have recently expressed resentment toward Mexican-Americans as free riders who ride their coat tails and share in the benefits.

This resentment stems from the legal construction of Mexican-Americans as white. Recently, some African-American leaders in Dallas have argued that Mexican-Americans should not share in the benefits or gains achieved by African-Americans

From *African-Americans, Latinos, and the Construction of Race: Toward an Epistemic Coalition,* 19 UCLA CHICANO-LATINO L. REV. 213 (1998). Originally published in the *UCLA Chicano-Latino Law Review.* Reprinted by permission.

because Mexican-Americans have been legally classified as white. Thus, the relationship between African-Americans and Mexican-Americans suffers because of a particular construction of race. The legal designation of Mexican-Americans as white raises a barrier to coalition building between African-Americans and Mexican-Americans.

In order to help build a coalition between African-Americans and Mexican-Americans, it makes sense for Mexican-Americans to reject their legal designation as white. Although white identity has been a traditional source of privilege and protection, Mexican-Americans did not receive the usual benefits of whiteness. Mexican-Americans have experienced segregation in schools and neighborhoods and discrimination in employment.

Given this, it does not make sense for Mexican-Americans to retain the legal designation of white. If Mexican-Americans embraced a non-white legal identity, then Mexican-Americans and African-Americans would be able to build a better relationship.

It is pointless for Latinos and African-Americans to divide themselves over the issue of Latino "whiteness." Indeed, to preserve the current racial hierarchy, mainstream white society often attempts to create divisions among minority groups. Latinos and African-Americans must work together as a coalition in order to dismantle racial subordination. By rejecting the legal designation of white, Latinos would be taking a step toward building such a coalition.

It is inevitable that society consider the racialization of Latinos. Currently, a worldwide movement—the Politics of Recognition and Multiculturalism—generates a "demand for recognition." One leading philosopher, Charles Taylor, ties this demand to a person's notion of their identity. The idea is that one's identity is partially determined "by recognition or . . . misrecognition of others."[1] Thus, people can suffer harm if the community reflects back to them a disparaging image of themselves. "Nonrecognition or misrecognition," then, can be a form of oppression. Proper recognition, then, is an essential requirement for human beings. Given this demand for recognition, race theorists must recognize Latinos and consider how Latinos have been racialized.

This does not require that the interests of African-Americans be marginalized. Indeed, I believe that the racialization of African-Americans cannot be fully understood without considering the racialization of Latinos and other groups. According to philosopher W. V. O. Quine's holism, "the truth of any one statement or proposition is a function not of its relationship to the world but of the degree to which it 'hangs together' with everything else we take to be true." Thus, for Quine, it is incorrect to talk about the meaning of a single statement. One cannot talk about the truth of a statement separate and apart from other propositions in the web of belief. In particular, we cannot talk about the truth of statements about African-Americans in isolation from propositions about Latinos within the web of belief. We cannot ascertain the truth about African-Americans without considering propositions regarding the racialization of Latinos. As Ludwig Wittgenstein explained, the world "wax[es] and wanes as a whole."[2]

Quine's holism provides powerful support for the importance of establishing a coalition to combat the epistemic violence that has been practiced against minority groups. Scholars of western colonialism have emphasized the importance of the generation of knowledge—*i.e.*, the writings and discourses of the white colonizers on the non-white Others—that justified the subordination of such Others. The production of such knowledge has been termed "epistemic violence." The Quinean insight —that the truth about the various minority groups (Latinos, Asian-Americans, Native Americans and African-Americans) cannot be ascertained without considering propositions about the various groups—means that minority groups must develop an epistemic coalition to learn the truth about themselves in order to fight against epistemic violence. Each group must contribute to that effort. They must develop knowledge about themselves. Only by considering the knowledge developed about each group will it be possible to learn the truth about any one racialized group.

Thus, minority groups must establish more than coalitions to achieve political results. Latinos, African-Americans, Asian-Americans and Native Americans must establish an epistemic coalition to achieve knowledge about themselves and their place in the world.

I have argued that the relationship between African-Americans and Latinos turns on the construction of race. In particular, the legal construction of Mexican-Americans as white has generated tensions that form a barrier to coalition building. As a result, Mexican-Americans should embrace a non-white identity to better enable coalition building with African-Americans. Race scholars can benefit by considering the racialization of Latinos. Indeed, the racialization of African-Americans cannot be fully understood without considering the racialization of Latinos. Minorities need to establish an epistemic coalition to achieve knowledge about themselves and their place in the world.

NOTES

1. See Charles Taylor, *The Politics of Recognition*, in MULTICULTURALISM: EXAMINING THE POLITICS OF RECOGNITION 25 (Amy Gutmann ed., 1994).

2. Ludwig Wittgenstein, TRACTATUS LOGICO-PHILOSOPHICUS 72 (D. F. Pears & B. F. McGuinness trans., 1974).

|||||||||||||||||||||||||||||||||||||||||||||||||||||||||||||||||||||||||||||||

Chapter 76

Do Immigrants Take Away Black Jobs?

Kevin R. Johnson and Bill Ong Hing

Understanding the Continued Discrimination against African Americans

Much of the call for African Americans to support immigrant rights is based on an appeal to African Americans to understand and sympathize with the plight of immigrants. Of course, it helps to understand the similarities that African Americans have with immigrants. But in reaching out to African Americans, immigrant rights advocates would do well to understand the perspectives of members of that group.

In the aggregate, the entire economic system may benefit from the presence of immigrants; but do low-income African Americans suffer in the process? It is difficult to confront stories of African American job displacement, especially when faced with the individual story of an African American whose old job is now filled by an immigrant who is working for lower pay. Arguing that we should be interested in aggregate outcomes for the entire black community is plainly inadequate. By so doing, one ignores that certain individuals at the bottom or at the margin are the ones most vulnerable to hard times and the most likely victims. Keeping the true causes of African American job loss in perspective is critical, but this may prove unsatisfying —especially to those who appear to be victims of displacement by immigrants.

Although it is simplistic for anti-immigrant groups to make sweeping claims that immigrants take jobs away from native workers, the claims of pro-immigrant groups that immigrants take only jobs that native workers do not want are equally simplistic. The pro-immigrant claim may be true generally, but willingness to take a job also depends on the wage, a person's age, stage in life, attitude, opinion of the job, and work conditions. Moreover, native workers' willingness to take certain jobs could change drastically if job conditions changed even minimally, such as by raising the pay or improving work conditions. Differences of opinion exist within the African American community over whether or not blacks should or would take low-paying jobs, and commentators and policymakers should not overgeneralize about who might or might not take such jobs.

Native workers who have been displaced because of the recession or structural adjustments in major industries are generally not in competition with immigrants.

From *The Immigrant Rights Marches of 2006 and the Prospects for a New Civil Rights Movement*, 42 Harv. C.R.–C.L. L. Rev. 99 (2007). Originally published in the *Harvard Civil Rights–Civil Liberties Law Review*. Reprinted by permission.

Thus the low-wage, unstable, menial jobs held by most immigrants are not long-term solutions for the natives who have lost jobs. Certainly, some displaced workers might be willing to take such jobs temporarily, but few would accept the humiliation of the small income and permanent drop in social status. Ultimately, they need retraining and relocation assistance.

Twenty years ago, Michael Piore argued that social status is critically important to understanding African American youth:

> Employers perceived a change in black attitudes toward the work which made them difficult to manage, and recruited migrants to replace them. Black attitudes changed because an older generation, raised in the rural south with a background and motivations similar to the immigrants of today, was replaced by a new generation who grew up in northern urban areas. These younger workers associated the jobs with the inferior social status to which their race had been condemned in the United States and feared that they would be confined in them permanently through prejudice and discrimination.[1]

Piore's argument holds special force today. The popular view that immigration restrictions serve to help disadvantaged native workers by freeing up low-wage, low-skilled (dead-end) jobs for African Americans is offensive. Anti-immigrant forces that toe this line appear to be unconcerned with broader social goals, such as achieving equal opportunity for socioeconomic advancement for African Americans. Certainly some blacks might, and do, take these jobs, but many understandably would not. Because immigrants are concentrated in the secondary labor market, reducing immigration might increase the numbers of native workers in the secondary sector. Although access to secondary sector jobs may provide a basis for social mobility among the disadvantaged, social pressures that isolate that sector from primary sector jobs persist.

When we view immigrants' impact on African American unemployment in the aggregate, little evidence surfaces of any significant impact on black employment resulting from immigration. Blacks still face severe unemployment and poverty in parts of the country, including areas relatively untouched by immigration. In places with large numbers of immigrants such as New York and Los Angeles, African Americans have not lost jobs in the aggregate but instead have moved into the public sector.

Economic studies confirm that African American job prospects are not a function of immigration levels. In 1980, about 125,000 migrants from Cuba arrived in the United States as part of the "Mariel Boatlift." About half of these migrants settled in Miami, creating an overnight increase of 7% in the city's labor force. The influx, however, had no detectable effect on the wages or unemployment rates of low-skilled native workers or earlier Cuban immigrants. The unemployment rate in Miami increased from 5% in April 1980 to 7.1% in July, the same as the increase in state and national unemployment rates over these months. Although unemployment rates fluctuated between 1982 and 1984, the rates returned to pre-1980 lows by 1985; the Cuban unemployment rate followed the same pattern. Real wages for whites between 1979 and 1985 remained constant in Miami and comparable cities. Wages for African Americans in Miami were constant from 1979–81, dropped in 1982–83, but then increased to previous levels by 1984; in comparable cities, African American wages steadily declined during this period. Thus, in the long run, the influx of low-wage workers may have helped blacks in Miami by stimulating the local economy.

In Los Angeles, young African Americans and those with limited education have experienced a small increase in unemployment due to the influx of Latina/o immigrants with limited education. However, that increase may have resulted from racial discrimination by employers. When low-skilled Latina/o workers became available employers hired them and rejected African American job applicants.

In a study of poverty and employment rates in Chicago, economist Robert Aponte sought explanations for why persons of Mexican ancestry had lower poverty rates than Puerto Ricans and African Americans and higher employment rates than those groups as well as whites. He found that this success defied conventional predictors of poverty and unemployment: Mexican Americans were the group with the least education, English proficiency, skills, work experience, and access to automobiles for commuting. About half of the African Americans surveyed held low-wage, low-skill jobs with poor working conditions. About the same proportion of Mexicans had similar jobs. However, unlike African Americans, Mexican Americans were not "mired in prototypically 'secondary' jobs": Median wages for Mexicans were about the same as for Puerto Ricans but higher than for African Americans, contradicting the theory that Mexican Americans are favored by employers because of a willingness to work for lower wages. The discriminatory predispositions of Chicago employers were examined, and the study found that they consistently preferred immigrant workers— whether of Mexican, Asian, or Eastern European descent. Employers conspicuously discriminated against African American workers.

These studies confirm that, in certain instances, employers discriminate against African Americans in favor of immigrant workers. Thus, in areas of the country such as Los Angeles and Chicago, with a ready supply of low-wage immigrant workers, employers with discriminatory instincts against African Americans can be expected to choose immigrants over low-skilled, less-educated blacks. One might argue that employers would hire more African Americans if immigrants were absent from the employment market. But do we honestly believe that this would be the case? At the very least, we should think carefully about whether excluding immigrants, if it were possible, is the best option for improving the status of African Americans. Policy efforts and resources might be better devoted to ending racial discrimination in the workplace.

Claims of job loss must, however, be considered in light of other findings that support the hypothesis that immigrants are *not* taking jobs from African Americans. An analysis of hotel and restaurant sectors suggests that African Americans have opted out of the service sectors. For example, some employers perceive that African American employees "just expected more." One employer noted, "They either have an attitude you owe them a job because they're black male, or they kick back and say if you fire them they'll sue for discrimination and you can't do anything about it." But does all this only mean that employers think immigrants are more "flexible" and have better attitudes, while African Americans have become too "uppity"? Undoubtedly, employers who view African Americans in this discriminatory fashion have exacerbated black unemployment.

In Chicago and Los Angeles, employers have relied on word-of-mouth for hiring, which reproduces the characteristics of the existing work force and systematically narrows opportunities for many African Americans. Employers operate with a hierarchy of ethnic preferences, with native whites at the top, followed by immigrant whites, immigrant Latina/os, and native African Americans at the bottom.

Unequal numbers of African Americans and immigrants in particular industries reduce the likelihood of direct competition between the groups. For example, poor blacks generally work in fast-food outlets and chains, while immigrants work in ethnic restaurants. Likewise, African Americans are concentrated in public sector jobs in many cities while immigrants are found in low-wage private sector employment.

Of course, the occupational division is far from complete, so there is likely some competition. For example, with fewer immigrants and ethnic restaurants, other restaurants would presumably pick up most of this business. Similarly, were it not for nonunion immigrant construction, unionized businesses that employ large numbers of African Americans would presumably have more opportunities. In addition, relatively heavy immigrant employment in hotel cleaning and landscaping could represent jobs that would be filled at higher wages were immigrants not available. Thus, African Americans may feel the effects, even though immigrant workers in certain instances are not directly competing with them.

On the other hand, if they were unable to use immigrant labor, many businesses would simply dissolve, move abroad, or substitute technology for labor. In these cases, immigrants do not directly displace native workers. That phenomenon has been demonstrated in Los Angeles automotive parts firms, the garment industry, other light manufacturing, and assembly jobs. As a result, immigrants who are employed as transitional workers or who comprise certain industries' disposable labor forces are probably not hurting African Americans.

What is the extent of this capital flight threat? If it is less than one hundred percent, one could at least argue that substitution is taking place, and that wages are being pushed downward. Second, where do these businesses obtain their capital? If banks and other investors would otherwise place part of their capital in investments that paid higher wages and employed native African Americans, then there may be a tangible effect on the economic life of blacks. If we look primarily at the effect that immigration has on African Americans, instead of the total economic activity due to immigration, the argument that "nearly all" or "most" or even "much" immigrant employment displaces native workers might hold less persuasive power.

We need to know about other employment options available to African American workers. We also need to know the other ramifications of the higher wages that would result if they were part of the workforce. In downtown Los Angeles buildings, higher maintenance fees would result in higher rents. If so, might some business tenants at the margin move their operations or go out of business as a result? A similar set of possibilities can be envisioned in other industries. We cannot assume that a manager's decision to hire low-wage immigrant workers is unhealthy for the overall economy or that firm survival is at stake.

If one's goal is full and fair employment of African American workers, one must demand the hiring of more blacks at all levels of the labor market, particularly in the primary sector. Better public schools and job training for all workers must be a top priority. To guard against managerial decisions to exploit low-wage workers, insisting on better wages and work conditions in the secondary sector and organizing immigrant workers (as exemplified by the Justice for Janitors campaign) must be high on the agenda as well.

NOTES

1. Michael J. Piore, *Can International Migration Be Controlled?*, in ESSAYS ON LEGAL AND ILLEGAL IMMIGRATION 21, 39 (Susan Pozo ed., 1986).

Chapter 77

Our Next Race Question

The Uneasiness between Blacks and Latinos

Jorge Klor De Alva, Earl Shorris, and Cornel West

The angry and confused discourse about American race relations often blindly assumes that the only major axis of racial division in America is black-white. Strangely ignored in the media backwash is the incipient tension between blacks and Latinos.

Each group constitutes an ever greater percentage of the total population; each is large enough to swing a presidential election. But do they vote with or against each other, and do they hold the same views of a white America that they have different reasons to distrust?

Knowing that questions of power and ethnicity are no longer black-and-white, *Harper's Magazine* invited three observers—a black, a Latino, and a white moderator —to open the debate.

Anglos May Be of Any Race

Shorris: We've just demonstrated one of the tenets of this conversation. That is, we have discussed almost exclusively the question of blacks in this society. But we started out saying we would have a black-brown dialogue. Why does that happen? And not only in the media. Why did it happen here, among us?

Klor De Alva: Part of the answer, as Cornel was pointing out, is that blacks are the central metaphor for otherness and oppression in the United States. Secondly, in part I take your question, when focused on Latinos, to mean, Don't Latinos have their own situation that also needs to be described if not in the same terms, then at least in terms that are supplementary?

I'm not sure. The answer goes to the very core of the difference between Latinos and blacks and between Cornel and myself: I am trying to argue against the utility of the concept of race. Why? Because I don't think that's the dominant construct we need to address in order to resolve the many problems at hand. Cornel wants to construct it in the language of the United States, and I say we need a different kind of language. Do you know why, Earl? Because we're in the United States and blacks are Americans. They're Anglos.

West: Excuse me?

Klor De Alva: They're Anglos of a different color, but they're Anglos. Why? Because the critical distinction here for Latinos is not race, it's culture.

West: Speaking English and being part of American culture?

Klor De Alva: Blacks are more Anglo than most Anglos because, unlike most Anglos, they can't directly identify themselves with a nation-state outside of the United States. They are trapped in America. However unjust and painful, their experiences are wholly made in America.

West: But that doesn't make me an Anglo. If I'm trapped on the underside of America, that doesn't mean that somehow I'm an Anglo.

Klor De Alva: Poor whites similarly trapped on the underside of America are also Anglos. Latinos are in a totally different situation, unable to be captured by the government in the "five food groups" of racial classification of Americans. The Commerce Department didn't know what to do with Latinos; the census takers didn't know what to do with Latinos; the government didn't know what to do with Latinos, and so they said, "Latinos can be of any race." That puts Latinos in a totally different situation. They are, in fact, homologous with the totality of the United States. That is, like Americans, Latinos can be of any race. What distinguishes them from all other Americans is culture, not race. That's where I'm going when I say that Cornel is an Anglo. You can be a Latino and look like Cornel. You can be a Latino and look like you, Earl, or like me. And so, among Latinos, there's no surprise in my saying that Cornel is an Anglo.

West: But it seems to me that "Anglo" is the wrong word.

Klor De Alva: Hey, I didn't make it up, Cornel.

West: "Anglo" implies a set of privileges. It implies a certain cultural formation.

Klor De Alva: I'm trying to identify here how Chicanos see "Anglos."

West: But I want to try and convince those Latino brothers and sisters not to think of black folk as Anglos. That's just wrong. Now, they can say that we're English-speaking moderns in the United States who have yet to be fully treated as Americans. That's fine.

Klor De Alva: My friend, Cornel, I was speaking of one of the more benign Latino names for blacks.

West: Let's hear some of the less benign then, brother.

What Color Is Brown?

Klor De Alva: Do you think of Latinos as white?

West: I think of them as brothers and sisters, as human beings, but in terms of culture, I think of them as a particular group of voluntary immigrants who entered America and had to encounter this thoroughly absurd system of classification of positively charged whiteness, negatively charged blackness. And they don't fit either one: they're not white, they're not black.

Shorris: What are they?

West: I see them primarily as people of color, as brown people who have to deal with their blackness-whiteness.

Shorris: So you see them in racial terms.

West: Well, no, it's more cultural.

Shorris: But you said "brown."

West: No, it's more cultural. Brown, for me, is more associated with culture than race.

Shorris: But you choose a word that describes color.

West: Right. To say "Spanish-speaking" would be a bit too vague, because you've got a lot of brothers and sisters from Guatemala who don't speak Spanish. They speak an indigenous language.

Klor De Alva: You have a lot of Latinos who aren't brown.

West: But they're not treated as whites, and "brown" is simply a signifier of that differential treatment. Even if a Latino brother or sister has supposedly white skin, he or she is still Latino in the eyes of the white privileged, you see. But they're not treated as black. They're not niggers. They're not the bottom of the heap, you see. So they're not niggers, they're not white, what are they? I say brown, but signifying culture more than color. Mexicans, Cubans, Puerto Ricans, Dominicans, El Salvadorans all have very, very distinctive histories. When you talk about black, that becomes a kind of benchmark, because you've got these continuous generations, and you've got very common experiences.

Now, of course, blackness comprises a concealed heterogeneity. You've got West Indians, you've got Ethiopians. My wife is Ethiopian. Her experience is closer to browns'. She came here because she wanted to. She was trying to get out from under a tyrannical, Communist regime in Ethiopia. She's glad to be in a place where she can breathe freely, not have to hide. I say, "I'm glad you're here, but don't allow that one side of America to blind you to my side."

So I've got to take her, you know, almost like Virgil in Dante's *Divine Comedy*, through all of this other side of America so that she can see the nightmare as well as the dream. But as an Ethiopian, she came for the dream and did a good job of achieving it.

Klor De Alva: So you are participating in the same process as the other Americans, other Anglos—to use that complicated term—that same song and dance of transforming her into a highly racialized American black.

West: It wasn't me. It was the first American who called her "nigger." That's when she started the process of Americanization and racialization. She turned around and said, "What is a nigger?"

Klor De Alva: And you're the one who explained it.

LBJ's Other Dilemma

Shorris: How do you see yourself, Jorge?

Klor De Alva: I'm an American citizen. What are you, Cornel?

West: I am a black man trying to be an American citizen.

Klor De Alva: I'm an American citizen trying to get rid of as many categories as possible that classify people in ways that make it easy for them to be oppressed, isolated, marginalized. Of course, I'm a Chicano, I'm a Mexican-American. But for me to identify myself that way is not much help. More helpful is my actually working to resolve the problems of poor folks in the United States.

If I were black, I would heighten the importance of citizenship. Why? Because every time we've seen huge numbers of immigrants enter the United States, the people most devastated by their arrival, in terms of being relegated to an even lower rung on the employment ladder, have been blacks.

Shorris: Are you defining "black" and "Latino" as "poor"?

Klor De Alva: No, no. I'm not defining them that way at all.

West: What's fascinating about this issue of race is the degree to which, in the American mind, black people are associated with instability, chaos, disorder—the very things that America always runs from. In addition, we are associated with hypersexuality, transgressive criminal activity—all of the various stereotypes and images.

Klor De Alva: No matter what kind of policy you set in place, there has to be something in it for everybody or the policy is not going to last very long. And I'm not even going to get into the issue that affirmative action has been essentially an African-American thing, not a Latino thing.

West: But who have the major beneficiaries been? White women. And rightly so. More of them have been up against the patriarchy than black and brown people have been up against racism.

Klor De Alva: Affirmative action has had the capacity to create a black middle class. Many of these folks also have been the dominant group in the civil rights arena and in other human rights areas. The net effect has been to create a layer, essentially of African-Americans, within the public sphere that has been very difficult for Latinos to penetrate and make their complaints known.

West: That's true, and I think it's wrong. But at the same time, blacks are more likely to register protests than Latinos are. Black people are more likely to raise hell than brown people.

Klor De Alva: But having been blocked from the public sector, I am concerned that Latinos turning to the private one will buy deeply into U.S. concepts of race and will be even less willing than Anglos to employ blacks. So for me, any new social or public policy must begin with dismantling the language of race.

One Night of Love

Shorris: We've been talking about conflicts. Let's stipulate, unless you disagree, that the advantage to the people in power of keeping those at the bottom at each other's throats is enormous. That's the case in all societies. So we have blacks and browns, for the most part, at the bottom. And they are frequently at each other's throats. They're fighting over immigration, fighting over jobs, and so on. A group of young people comes to you and says, "Tell us how to make alliances, give us a set of rules for creating alliances between blacks and browns." What would you answer?

West: I'd appeal to various examples. Look at Ernesto Cortés and the Industrial Areas Foundation in Texas or the Harlem Initiatives Together in New York City, which have been able to pull off black-brown alliances of great strength, the "breaking bread" events of the Democratic Socialists of America. Or I'd talk about Mark Ridley-Thomas in South-Central Los Angeles and look at the ways in which he speaks with power about brown suffering as a black city councilman, the way in which he's able to build within his own organization a kind of black-brown dialogue. Because what you really see then is not just a set of principles or rules but some momentum at work.

Shorris: But how do you do that? What's the first step?

West: Well, it depends on what particular action you want to highlight. You could, say, look at the movement around environmental racism, where you have a whole host of black-brown alliances. With Proposition 187 you had a black-brown alliance among progressives fighting against the conservatives who happened to be white, black, and brown. In the trade-union movement, look at the health-care workers union here in New York City. That's a very significant coordinated leadership of probably the most important trade union in the largest city in the nation. So it depends on the particular issue. I think it's issue by issue in light of a broad vision.

Shorris: What is the broad vision?

West: Democracy, substantive radical democracy in which you actually are highlighting the empowering of everyday people in the workplace and the voting booth so that they can live lives of decency and dignity. That's a deeply democratic sensibility. And I think that sensibility can be found in both the black and brown communities.

Klor De Alva: Unless there's a dramatic shift in ideology, linkages between people who are identified as belonging to opposing camps will last only for the moment, like the graffiti I saw during the L.A. riots: "Crips. Bloods. Mexicans. Together. Forever. Tonite [*sic*]," and then next to that, "LAPD" crossed out and "187" underneath. That is, the alliances will work only as long as there's a common enemy, in this case the L.A.P.D., whose death the graffiti advocated by the term "187," which refers here to the California Criminal Code for homicide.

As long as we don't have a fundamental transformation in ideology, those are the kinds of alliances we will have, and they will be short-lived and not lead, ultimately, to terribly much. Clearly, the progressive forces within the United States must be able to forge ideological changes that would permit lasting linkages. At the core of that effort lies the capacity to address common suffering, regardless of color or culture. And that cannot be done unless common suffering, as the reason for linkages across all lines, is highlighted in place of the very tenuous alliances between groups that identify themselves by race or culture.

Shorris: Let's see if anything happened in this conversation. Cornel, are you a black man?

West: Hell yes.

Shorris: Jorge, is he a black man?

Klor De Alva: Of course not.

From the Editors *Issues and Comments*

Why are tensions between Latinos and blacks increasing?

When Latinos and blacks feud, does this just play into the hands of white power, or are there sometimes genuine issues between them?

Do blacks and Latinos experience racism at the hands of white society in the same way?

Are the conflicts between Latinos and blacks caused by the same forces that cause conflicts between whites and minority groups? Why or why not? What are these forces?

If one (say, a Latino) has been the victim of discrimination, does that make one more, or less, likely to inflict that evil on another (say, a black)? In other words, does racism "trickle down?" Does victimization predispose, or inoculate against, victimizing others in the same way?

How do divisions within the Latino group compare in intensity to those within the African-American or Asian-American communities? Do Mexicans, Puerto Ricans, and Cubans have different activist agendas? If so, do they ever come in conflict?

Is it more helpful or harmful to aggregate smaller minority groups into larger ones? At which level and for what purposes would it be most efficient to stop aggregating?

Is the increasing number of people who identify themselves as multiracial a good or a bad thing?

Why do you hear so little about Latinos who are black or have black ancestors?

In order to preserve affirmative action from its critics, should we cut it back to just one or two of the most deserving, long-suffering groups?

Do Latinos take away black jobs?

Is the system set up so that Latinos, blacks, and Asians are constantly fighting for crumbs rather than confronting the systems of hierarchy and privilege that oppress them all? If so, is a pan-ethnic coalition the answer?

What are the advantages and disadvantages of building a coalition among all minority groups? What motivations do Latinos and African Americans have to work together against oppression? Are these motivations powerful enough to overcome their conflicts?

In the colloquy between Jorge Klor de Alva and Cornel West, Klor de Alva says that African Americans are Anglos—their culture more American than American. Is this so? Which group—Latinos, some of whom are light-skinned and can pass for white; or blacks, who have been here a long time and whose music, styles, and literature have influenced mainstream shopping habits and musical tastes—is more Anglo than the other?

Is it more helpful or harmful to rank different minority groups according to the degree of oppression in our society? Why or why not?

Do you know of any successful long-term coalitions between minority groups?

Suggested Readings

Black/Brown/White Relations: Race Relations in the 1970s, edited by Charles V. Willie. New Brunswick, N.J.: Transaction Books, 1977.

Blacks, Latinos, and Asians in Urban America: Status and Prospects for Politics and Activism, edited by James Jennings. Westport, Conn.: Praeger, 1994.

Comas-Díaz, Lillian. "LatiNegra: Mental Health Issues of African Latinas." In *The Multiracial Experience: Racial Borders as the New Frontier*, edited by Maria P. Root. Thousand Oaks, Calif.: Sage Publications, 1996.

Davis, Mike. *City of Quartz: Excavating the Future in Los Angeles*. London: Verso, 1992.

De Genova, Nicolas, and Ana Y. Ramos-Zayas. *Latino Crossings: Mexicans, Puerto Ricans, and the Politics of Race and Citizenship*. New York: Routledge, 2003.

Delgado, Richard. "Derrick Bell's Toolkit: Fit to Dismantle That Famous House?" 75 *N.Y.U. L. Rev.* 283 (2000).

Espinoza, Leslie, and Angela Harris. "Embracing the Tar-Baby: LatCrit Theory and the Sticky Mess of Race." 85 *Cal. L. Rev.* 1585 (1997).

Esteva-Fabregat, Claudio. *Mestizaje in Ibero-America*. Tucson: University of Arizona Press, 1995.

Ethnic Los Angeles, edited by Roger Waldinger and Mehdi Bozorgmehr. New York: Russell Sage Foundation, 1996.

Guinier, Lani, and Gerald Torres. *The Miner's Canary: Enlisting Race, Resisting Power, Transforming Democracy*. Cambridge, Mass.: Harvard University Press, 2003.

Hernández, Tanya Kateri. "'Too Black to Be Latino/a': Blackness and Blacks as Foreigners." 1 *Latino Studies* 152 (2003).

Hing, Bill Ong. "Beyond the Rhetoric of Assimilation and Cultural Pluralism: Addressing the Tension of Separatism and Conflict in an Immigration-Driven Multiracial Society." 81 *Cal. L. Rev.* 863 (1993).

Hutchinson, Earl Ofari. *The Latino Challenge to Black America: Towards a Conversation between African Americans and Hispanics*. Los Angeles: Middle Passage Books, 2007.

Johnson, James H., Jr., and Walter C. Farrell, Jr. "The Fire This Time: The Genesis of the Los Angeles Rebellion of 1992." 71 *N.C. L. Rev.* 1403 (1993).

Johnson, Kevin R. "The Case for African American and Latina/o Cooperation in Challenging Racial Profiling in Law Enforcement." 55 *Fla. L. Rev.* 341 (2003).

———. "Immigration and Latino Identity." 19 *Chicano-Latino L. Rev.* 197 (1998).

———. "Law and Politics in Post-Modern California: Coalition or Conflict between African Americans, Asian Americans, and Latina/os?" 4(3) *Ethnicities* 381 (2004).

———. "Puerto Rico, Puerto Ricans and LatCrit Theory: Commonalities and Differences between Latina/o Experiences." 6 *Mich. J. Race & L.* 107 (2000).

———. "Racial Hierarchy, Asian Americans and Latinos as 'Foreigners,' and Social Change: Is Law the Way to Go?" 76 *Or. L. Rev.* 347 (1997).

———. "Some Thoughts on the Future of Latino Legal Scholarship." 2 *Harv. Latino L. Rev.* 101 (1997).

———. "The Struggle for Civil Rights: The Need for, and Impediments to, Political Coalitions among and within Minority Groups." 63 *La. L. Rev.* 759 (2003).

Lemann, Nicholas. "The Other Underclass." *Atlantic Monthly*, December 1991, p. 96.

Loewen, James. "Levels of Political Mobilization and Racial Bloc Voting among Latinos, Anglos, and African-Americans in New York City." 13 *Chicano-Latino L. Rev.* 38 (1993).

Maharidge, Dale. *The Coming White Minority: California's Eruptions and the Nation's Future.* New York: Times Books, 1996.

Martinez, Elizabeth. "Beyond Black/White: The Racisms of Our Time." 20 *Social Justice* 22 (1993).

———. *De Colores Means All of Us: Latina Views for a Multi-Colored Century.* Cambridge, Mass.: South End Press, 1998.

McClain, Paula D., et al. "Racial Distancing in a Southern City: Latino Immigrants' Views of Black Americans." 68(3) *Journal of Politics* 571–84 (2006).

McDaniel, Antonio. "The Dynamic Racial Composition of the United States: An American Dilemma Revisited." 124(1) *Daedalus* 179–98 (1995).

Miles, Jack. "Blacks vs. Browns: African Americans and Latinos." *Atlantic Monthly,* October 1992, p. 41.

Mindiola, Tatcho, Jr., Yolanda Flores Niemann, and Nestor Rodriguez. *Black-Brown Relations and Stereotypes.* Austin: University of Texas Press, 2003.

Moran, Rachel F. "Getting a Foot in the Door: The Hispanic Push for Equal Educational Opportunity in Denver." 2 *Kan. J. L. & Pub. Pol'y* 35 (1992).

Neither Enemies nor Friends: Latinos, Blacks, Afro-Latinos, edited by Anani Dzidzienyo and Suzanne Oboler. New York: Palgrave Macmillan, 2005.

Nelson, William E., Jr., and Jessica L. Lavariega Monforti. *Black and Latino/a Politics: Issues in Political Development in the United States.* Miami: Barnhardt & Ashe, 2005.

No Longer Invisible: Afro-Latin Americans Today, edited by Minority Rights Group. London: Minority Rights Publications, 1995.

O'Brien, Eileen. *The Racial Middle: Latinos and Asian Americans Living beyond the Racial Divide.* New York: New York University Press, 2008.

Oh, Angela E. "Race Relations in Los Angeles: 'Divide and Conquer' Is Alive and Flourishing." 66 *Cal. L. Rev.* 1647 (1993).

Pastor, Manuel, Jr., Lisa Magana, Amalia Cabezas, and Morgan Appel. *Latinos and the Los Angeles Uprising: The Economic Context.* Claremont, Calif.: Tomás Rivera Center, 1993.

Patterson, Orlando. "The Race Trap." *N.Y. Times,* July 11, 1997, p. A27.

Piatt, Bill. *Black and Brown in America: The Case for Cooperation.* New York: New York University Press, 1997.

Portes, Alejandro, and Alex Stepick. *City on the Edge: The Transformation of Miami.* Berkeley: University of California Press, 1993.

Pulido, Laura. *Black, Brown, Yellow, and Left: Radical Activism in Los Angeles.* Berkeley: University of California Press, 2006.

Ramirez, Deborah A. "Multicultural Empowerment: It's Not Just Black and White Anymore." 47 *Stan. L. Rev.* 957 (1995).

Rieff, David. *Los Angeles: Capital of the Third World.* New York: Simon & Schuster, 1991.

Robinson, Toni, and Greg Robinson. "*Mendez v. Westminster*: Asian-Latino Coalition Triumphant?" 10 *Asian L.J.* 161 (2003).

Romero, Tom I., II. "¿La Raza Latina? Multiracial Ambivalence, Color Denial, and the Emergence of a Tri-Ethnic Jurisprudence at the End of the Twentieth Century." 37 *N.M. L. Rev.* 245 (2007).

Samora, Julian. Mestizaje: *The Formation of Chicanos.* Palo Alto, Calif.: Stanford Center for Chicano Research, 1996.

Skrentny, John D. *Ironies of Affirmative Action: Politics, Culture, and Justice in America.* Chicago: University of Chicago Press, 1996.

Stepick, Alex, Guillermo Grenier, Max Castro, and Marvin Dunn. *This Land Is Our Land: Immigrants and Power in Miami.* Berkeley: University of California Press, 2003.

Torres, Rodolfo D., and ChorSwang Ngin. "Racialized Boundaries, Class Relations, and Cultural Politics: The Asian-American and Latino Experience." In *Culture and Difference: Critical Perspectives on the Bicultural Experience in the United States*, edited by Antonia Darder, 55–69. New York: Bergin & Garvey, 1995.

Vaca, Nicolas C. *The Presumed Alliance: The Unspoken Conflict between Latinos and Blacks and What It Means for America*. New York: Rayo, 2004.

Wiessner, Siegfried. "¡Esa India!: LatCrit Theory and the Place of Indigenous Peoples within Latina/o Communities." 53 *U. Miami L. Rev.* 831 (1999).

Yancey, George A. *Who Is White?: Latinos, Asians, and the New Black/Nonblack Divide*. Boulder, Colo.: Lynne Rienner, 2003.

|||||||||||||||||||||||||||||||||||||||||||||||||||||||||||||||||||||||||||||||||||||||||||||

Part X

Sex, Gender, and Class
Sure I'm a Latino, but I'm Still Different from You—
How about It?

The Latino group contains not only men but also women, gays and lesbians, and children. Not all of these stand on the same footing with respect to issues like immigration, social welfare, and civil rights. Many issues that are foremost on the agenda of one subgroup, say Cuban men in Miami, may not be particularly important to Chicana single mothers in California or lesbian Puerto Rican office workers in Queens, New York. The Latino community struggles to come to terms with "machismo," a kind of exaggerated masculine bravado, and Marianismo, a syndrome in which women accept undue burdens and suffer in silence. Women are saddled with spiritual responsibilities and made to feel guilty if they are not Catholic enough. Men do too little housework. Latino school boys drop out to be with their buddies and listen to misogynist rap music. As with many relatively poor communities, spousal abuse and neglect are all too common. Fears that a Latino population explosion will engulf the United States add to nativistic hostility toward Latinas, most of whom are low-level, unskilled workers, and have little legal protection. Cultural differences such as the Latin American practice of naming stir confusion and irritation as well. The chapters in part 10 address some of these issues.

Chapter 78

||||||||||||||||||||||||||||||||||||||||||||||||||||||||||||||||||||||||||||

Mexican Gender Ideology

Adelaida R. Del Castillo

Traditionally, gender in culture is part of a dichotomy in which sex is a biological given and gender is a cultural construction. As such, gender in culture is expressed through individuals who are bearers of prescribed male/female social roles. In the past, anthropologists have identified, described, and explained gender roles through the observation of the patterned, recurrent, and typical, contributing to the reification of predictable and fixed gender roles. This approach offers a binary frame of reference, which posits the oppositional (he's strong, she's weak) as universal in male/female gender-based norms and relegates all other gendered possibilities to the realm of the exceptional, the unexplainable, or the deviant. For although tradition may express expected practices, beliefs, and cultural ideals, it cannot account for cultural flexibility, contradiction, and indeterminacy.

According to gender-based norms, the family in Mexico is hierarchical in structure, asymmetrical in social and gender relations, genealogical in patterns of residence, and loyal to itself in its moral economy.[1] According to the traditional ideal, men wield authority over women, the husband enjoys authority over his wife as does the brother over his sister; and while the older have authority over the younger, the father remains the ultimate authority over the household and family matters.

It is significant that Mexico's most distinguished authors and pundits (mostly males) have also had something to say about the character, status, and gender-based norms of the Mexican male and female, thus contributing to the social construction of sex/gender ideology in Mexican society.[2] Their conceptualizations cannot go unnoticed because they are probably more widely read internationally than any other literature of social scientific significance.

The most notable of these authors is Nobel Prize laureate Octavio Paz. Through the use of various forms of literary license, Paz offers insights into the character and motives of the *macho* by positing a dialectical relationship between men and women whose relational duality is as "closed" is to "open." "The ideal of manliness is never to 'crack,' never to back down. Those who 'open themselves up' are cowards. . . . Women are inferior beings because, in submitting, they open themselves up. This inferiority is constitutional and resides in their sex, their submissiveness, which is a wound that never heals."[3]

For Paz, the sexual encounter itself speaks to a socio-moral asymmetry between the sexes, reified in physiology: "The *macho*, the male . . . rips open . . . the female, who is pure passivity, defenseless against the exterior world."[4] Thus, a woman who transcends passivity is a cultural anomaly representative of gender chaos. Here, also, Paz offers a portrayal of the bad woman, *la mala mujer*, which serves logocentric propositions of unchaste female behavior in a Mexican context. The *mala mujer*, he tells us, is a woman who does not conform to the traditional female ideal and assumes male attributes such as the independence of the macho. Mexican gender ideology, its observations and portrayals, expresses cultural ideals of gender-appropriate behavior which may or may not have correlations in actual behavior.

NOTES

1. Beverly Chiñas, THE ISTHMUS ZAPOTECS: WOMEN'S ROLES IN CULTURAL CONTEXT (New York: Holt, Rinehart & Winston, 1973); May N. Díaz, TONALÁ: CONSERVATISM, RESPONSIBILITY, AND AUTHORITY IN A MEXICAN TOWN (Berkeley: University of California Press, 1966); Larisa A. Lomnitz, NETWORKS AND MARGINALITY: LIFE IN A MEXICAN SHANTYTOWN (New York: Academic Press, 1977).

2. Many of these concepts have been based on Mexican psychological and family studies, including the work of María E. Bermúdez, LA VIDA FAMILIAR DEL MEXICANO (México, D.F.: Antigua Libería Robredo, 1955); Rogelio Díaz-Guerrero, ESTUDIOS DE LA PSICOLOGÍA DEL MEXICANO (México, D.F.: Editorial F. Trillas, 1967); and Samuel Ramos, PROFILE OF MAN AND CULTURE IN MEXICO (Austin: University of Texas Press, 1934).

3. Octavio Paz, THE LABYRINTH OF SOLITUDE: LIFE AND THOUGHT IN MEXICO (New York: Grove Press, 1961), 29–30.

4. *Ibid.*, 77.

Chapter 79

||||||||||||||||||||||||||||||||||||||||||||||||||||||||||||||||||||||||||||||||

Latinas and Religion
Subordination or State of Grace?

Laura M. Padilla

Catholicism has oppressed many women through its conservative insistence on male domination, yet devout Catholics have challenged that domination through liberation theology. Can religion, in fact, liberate Latinas without oppressing them?

Latinas' cultural background includes reverence for family. Although such reverence has been exposed as a source of oppression, not all Latinas accept this charge. "Maintaining our families is an intrinsic part of our struggle. Therefore, we are not willing to accept fully the Anglo feminist understanding of the family as the center of women's oppression."[1] Rather than blindly accepting others' pronouncements about what family should mean for them and the appropriate relationship between family and religion, Latinas must decide for themselves the significance of family.

Latinas' view of family also colors their religiosity. As mothers, Latinas are primarily responsible for inculcating religious values into their children. "It has been characteristic of the role of women, whether as mother or catechist, to instruct children in the faith, to see to it that they receive the sacraments. And to instill in them the values and virtues consonant with a good Christian life."[2] Regardless of family status, religion is a central part of many Latinas' lives. Researchers consistently find that Latinas/os consider themselves highly religious, with Latinas even more likely than their male counterparts to do so. The centrality of religion for Catholic Latinas/os appears in both orthodox doctrine and popular religiosity. The former takes the form of many Latinas/os' belief in heaven, hell, the virginal birth of Jesus, and Jesus's resurrection, as well as Latinas/os' participation rates in sacraments such as baptism and church weddings. The latter is illustrated in many ways, including through devotion to the Virgin Mary, a strong belief in the intercession of saints, and the habit, particularly among women, of lighting candles or establishing home altars.

Thus, "Latinas' relationship with the divine is a very intimate one. This intimate relationship is a matter not only of believing that God is with us in our daily struggle, but that we can and do relate to God the same way we related to all our loved ones."[3] In other words, Latinas' God is a personal, living figure with whom they converse daily—upon awakening, while driving to work, booting up a computer, reprimanding

From *Latinas and Religion: Subordination or State of Grace?* 33 U.C.-Davis L. Rev. 973 (2000). Originally published in the *University of California at Davis Law Review*. Reprinted by permission.

children, and wondering how they will get through another day. They can harm this divine relationship through apathy and excessive autonomy, thus distancing themselves from a source that could provide meaning in their lives. These sins of indifference and selfishness cause individual and collective harm by preventing Latinas from both living up to their potential and co-creating healthier communities. To avoid these sins,

> Latinas need to actualize our sense of *comunidades de fe* [faith communities] by setting-up communities which are praxis-oriented, which bring together personal support and community action, and which have as a central organizing principle, our religious understandings and practices as well as our needs.[4]

Latinas/os and Religion in the Americas

Early settlement of the Americas took the form of colonization, including the religious variety. The missionaries had many goals, including conquering indigenous populations in the name of God. While the goal was sometimes well meaning, the colonizers always acted in a dominating and intolerant manner that assumed both superior knowledge of what was right for the indigenous and a conviction that local practices and religious beliefs had no redeeming qualities. The priests, even those who were genuinely concerned about the welfare of the indigenous, systematically destroyed the natives' religious traditions, thus depriving them of meaning and significance in their lives and leaving them spiritually untethered. In the process of converting natives, their

> [g]ods, their religion, and the ways of their ancestors were . . . discredited, insulted, maligned, and totally destroyed. . . . Like other conquerors, the Christians burned the conquered people's temples and imposed their gods. But they refused any sharing, demanded the annihilation of local cults, and kept for themselves an absolute monopoly of the priesthood and the sacred. This radical opposition to everything that had been sacred to Indian people was the deepest source of their collective trauma.[5]

In addition to assimilating through religion, assimilation came about through education, intermarriage, and interbreeding, though often with the understanding that "they" could not truly be assimilated, and that "their" worth would always be a function of the amount of European blood that ran in their veins—the larger the amount, the more valuable.

Although the resulting class system dictated some forms of oppression, other forms of it were gender-based. All women, regardless of class, shared many forms of oppression and subordination, and no woman could exercise leadership within the Church.

> [A] poor, rural *india* shared with the *española* of the upper classes the prevailing norm of exclusion from participation in the new system. The universal function of women

during this period was to serve in the home as procreators, housekeepers, wives and mothers. Other common grounds of exclusion shared by *indias* and *españolas* were the universal denial of participation in religion, government, and education.[6]

Accordingly, all women were considered inferior to men, especially native women. Yet in spite of the disdain with which Europeans viewed the indigenous and mestizos, particularly women, efforts at assimilation, including religious assimilation, continued. Religion's development in the New World became increasingly complicated, partly because of an event that occurred shortly after the Spanish invasion.

In the predawn hours of an early December day, the Virgen de Guadalupe (Virgin of Guadalupe) revealed herself to Juan Diego, a poor, dark *campesino* (farmer or countryman). She asked him to convey to the bishop her presence and her request that the bishop build a hermitage at the site. After the bishop rejected Juan Diego's request, she twice more revealed herself to Diego. He continued to make the same request of the bishop, who continued to resist until Juan Diego's third interview with him. At that interview, as a sign from the Virgen, Juan Diego presented to the bishop brilliant flowers from the desolate hilltop where she had revealed herself to Juan Diego. And as Juan Diego unfolded his white mantle to present the flowers, "she painted herself: the precious image of the Ever-Virgin Holy Mary, Mother of the God Teotl. . . ." The bishop then believed and ordered the hermitage built. Hundreds of millions of pilgrims have already journeyed to this site, and thousands continue to make the journey.

By choosing to reveal herself to Juan Diego, a poor and oppressed Nahuatl Indian, the Virgen illustrated the importance of reaching and serving the oppressed, the downtrodden—those at the bottom. When the Virgen chose him, she chose someone who

> stands for every person whose self-dignity has been crushed, whose credibility has been destroyed, whose sense of worth has been trampled. As he will tell us himself, he is nothing; he is a bunch of dry leaves. He has been made to think of himself as excrement. . . . He no longer knows himself as he truly is, seeing himself only through others' eyes as totally worthless and useless.[7]

The Virgen story replicates biblical teachings in which God favors the poor and outsiders. In the Old Testament, the Lord declares that He "will assemble the lame, and gather the outcasts, even those whom I have afflicted. I will make the lame a remnant and the outcasts a strong nation."

The Virgen story additionally illustrates the potential for synthesis as a mode of liberation for Latinas because it respects elements of indigenous religion and culture while teaching Christianity. The Virgen told Juan Diego, "[k]now and be certain in your heart, my most abandoned son, that I am the Ever-Virgin Holy Mary, Mother of the God of Great Truth, Teotl, of the One through Whom We Live, the Creator of Persons, the Owner of What is Near and Together, of the Lord of Heaven and Earth." By using the names of Nahuatl Gods, the very ones that the Spanish missionaries first disrespected and then dismissed, the Virgen acknowledges those Gods and thus grants them the respect that had formerly been stripped away from them. In the process, she neither discredits the natives' Gods nor denies the Christian one. Thus, she moves out of the "either/or, us or them" paradigm into one of acceptance. This contrasted with early conquerors' and missionaries' zeal for destroying all vestiges of the old religion and marked a new tolerance for alternate ways of seeing and believing.

Although Latinas/os have remained at the margins of Catholic leadership, the Church has gradually turned its attention to Latinas/os' specific needs. For example, the Church has been active in social justice issues affecting Latinas/os.

> It has at times provided extensive welfare services for the Mexican-American commu-
> nity, has sponsored citizenship classes and youth organizations, . . . and has recently
> seen some of its clerical representatives demonstrate in picket lines on behalf of strik-
> ing Mexican-American farm workers, directing antipoverty programs, and testifying on
> minimum-wage legislation before Congressional committees.[8]

Although the Church has not uniformly embraced these causes, a critical mass within the Church has done so. This is consistent with the "Latino Religious Resurgence" which followed the Second Vatican Council, and allowed Latinas/os to proclaim a new role for their religion.

Liberation theology in Latin America preceded and coincided with the development of the Latino Religious Resurgence in the United States. No discussion of Catholicism in the Americas would be complete without a brief introduction to liberation theology. One legal academic laid out the fundamentals of liberation theology as follows:

1) People's response to God is impeded by oppressive economic and social conditions.
2) Where the institutions we have in place create such oppressive conditions, we have a duty as Christians to do what we can to reform them.
3) Inherent in oppressive institutions is a class struggle between the beneficiaries and the victims of those institutions. The institutions cast the beneficiaries, like it or not, in the role of oppressors of the victims.
4) Reform of the institutions in question liberates the beneficiaries from their role as oppressors just as it liberates the victims from their role as persons oppressed.
5) Efforts to bring about such liberation have eschatological (religious and eternal) value even if their historical fruition is problematic.

"One goal of liberation theology is to reconcile human beings so that injustice and oppression caused by people and institutions are replaced with a more just society in which the dignity and the right to a flourishing human existence for all are respected."[9] For Latinas/os, liberation theology and movements which are similarly based on a desire to liberate subordinated persons from oppression provide an opportunity for religion to serve as part of an antisubordination crusade.

Women/Latinas within the Church

Judeo-Christian religions generally are traditional patriarchal institutions which have subordinated and oppressed women. This subordination is rooted in the bible, and has been extended through biblical interpretation and subsequently developed Church doctrine and policy. In response to Eve's transgression in the first book of the bible, the Lord God said to woman, "I will greatly multiply your pain in childbirth, in pain you shall bring forth children; yet your desire shall be for your husband, and *he shall rule over you.*" Thus appears the first directive from God that man shall rule over woman. It is not the only such directive. The book of Ephesians orders that:

> Wives, be subject to your own husbands, as to the Lord. For the husband is the head of the wife, as Christ also is the head of the Church, He Himself being the Savior of the body. But as the church is subject to Christ, so also the wives ought to be to their husbands in everything.

In the *Book of Timothy*, Paul exhorted women to maintain certain roles.

> [L]et a woman quietly receive instruction with entire submissiveness . . . do not allow a woman to teach or exercise authority over a man, but to remain quiet. For it was Adam who was first created, and then Eve. And it was not Adam who was deceived, but the woman being quite deceived, fell into transgression. But women shall be preserved through the bearing of children if they continue in faith and love and sanctity with self-restraint.

Women also experience oppression at the hands of the Church through limits it places on their leadership, such as prohibiting their ordination as priests. Thus, at a fundamental legal level, doors within the Church are closed to women. This not only officially limits women's roles in the Church, it sends a message about women's position and their (in)abilities.

The Catholic Church also prohibits birth control and abortion. That leaves Latinas few procreative options if they want to comply with Church doctrine.

Considering biblical teaching about women, limited Church-defined roles for women, and women's relative lack of power in the Church, it would be easy to conclude that within the religious realm, women are destined to a life of subordination. Yet, "contrary to some current stereotypes, women have always had a religious role for autonomous decision-making, especially in clergy-controlled Catholicism." While Latinas are generally not recognized as Church leaders, their role remains significant.

Women frequently hold leadership positions in grass-roots movements. Thus, to view Latinas as powerless in the Church oversimplifies a more complex dynamic.

> [S]uch a view leaves little room for differentiating between the institutionalized form of religion, on the one hand, and popular religiosity with its roots in the beliefs and traditions of the people, on the other. Upon a closer examination of how power unfolds, it

becomes clear that women exercise a productive function in religion; one that subverts and transforms social values.[10]

Even prior to recent feminists' assertions that Latinas play a significant unofficial role in religious life, others had acknowledged the importance of Latinas in the Church.

> When through lack of interest or numbers, the priests, sisters and other religious personnel [v]anish from Latino communities, or fail to provide adequate ministry it is business as usual for the local *"espiritista"* [spiritual healer], *"curandera"* [healer] and *rezadora* [prayer leader], as they continue . . . to give counsel so much needed in times of crisis. . . . Despite the patriarchy of the clergy, particularly within Catholicism, women's input continues to shape the transmission of social values among Latinas today. As in the past, the sustaining sources of popular religiosity are not the priests, nor even lay male leaders, but women.[11]

Latinas accordingly are central in the transfer of religious and moral values, even when not formally recognized as religious leaders.

NOTES

1. Ada María Isai-Díaz, *Latina Women's Ethnicity in Mujerista Theology, in* OLD MASKS, NEW FACES: RELIGION AND LATINO IDENTITIES 93, 97 (Anthony M. Stevens-Arroyo & Gilbert R. Cadena eds., 1995).

2. Ana María Díaz-Stevens, *The Saving Grace: The Matriarchical Core of Latino Catholicism,* LATINO STUD. J., Sept. 1993, at 60, 64.

3. Isai-Díaz, at 105.

4. *Id.*

5. Virgil Elizondo, GUADALUPE: MOTHER OF THE NEW CREATION 29 (1997).

6. Alfredo Mirandé & Evangelina Enríquez, LA CHICANA: THE MEXICAN-AMERICAN WOMAN 37–39 (1979).

7. Elizondo, at 52.

8. Leo Grebler, et. al., THE MEXICAN-AMERICAN PEOPLE: THE NATION'S SECOND LARGEST MINORITY 454 (1970).

9. Robert R. Araujo, S.J., *Political Theory and Liberation Theology: The Intersection of Unger and Gutierrez,* 11 J.L. & RELIG. 63, 68 (1994–95).

10. *Id.*

11. *Id.* at 75

Chapter 80

"In the Beginning He Wouldn't Lift Even a Spoon"

Beatríz M. Pesquera

[Consider] the relationships between the ideology and the practice of professional, clerical, and blue-collar Chicana workers, in particular, "gender strategies"—that is, peculiarities in types of strategies used by wives and husbands in the struggle over "who will do what." These tactics—such as "stalling" (used by men) and "coaching" (used by women)—illustrate the ideological underpinnings in the political struggle over household labor. By *ideology*, we mean the belief system that incorporates what women "think" husbands ought to do and what they concretely "expect" them to do. The *practice* of household labor refers to behavior, including devices used in the struggle over household chores. The term *political struggle* is borrowed from Heidi Hartmann, who proposes using housework to illustrate the conceptualization of family as a "locus of political struggle" over the fruits of labor.

The overwhelming majority of women in this study think that their husbands should participate equally in household labor. Expectations of actual performance, however, differ considerably. Thus, at the level of thought, the responses are uniform. At the level of expectations, however, this ideological convergence dissipates. In particular, clerical workers did not expect their husbands actually to perform household labor on an equal basis.

Differences in the level of expectation reflect what takes place in practice within these families. Professional and blue-collar Chicana workers harbor greater expectations and observe greater male participation in household tasks. The different levels of male participation reflect not only different expectations but also the women's willingness to engage in conflict and struggle with their husbands in order to increase their share of household work. That is, professional and blue-collar Chicana workers not only expect more but are willing to demand more from their husbands. Therefore, their husbands do considerably more than the husbands of clerical workers. The high level of expectation did not, however, translate into an equal division within these households. Although these women were firm in expressing their expectations, half of them admitted that these expectations were dashed. As one woman stated, "It doesn't mean it's going to happen."

To understand the complex dynamic between ideology and behavior, we must examine the gender strategies of these households by occupation. As pointed out, at the level of ideology, we see a divergence by occupation; differences also appear at the behavioral level.

Professional Workers

Households of Chicana professionals are the least sex-role segregated of this sample. Nonetheless, these women perform more of the household labor than their husbands do. Although professional women's expectations are not translating into equitable household division of labor, half of these women reported a high degree of satisfaction with existing arrangements. The reported level of satisfaction came into question, however, as Chicana professionals articulated their frustrations, conflicts, and struggles during the interview. Furthermore, the reported level of male participation in the division of household labor on the scaled questionnaire often did not coincide with the women's descriptions of daily activities in the home.

The struggle over the division of household labor among professional couples tends to generate various levels of conflict. For some, it was minimal; for others, it was open warfare. Perhaps Linda was most adamant in expressing this conflict:

> Well, he says that I need to do more around the house. I'm sure that whatever he says, it is because he is feeling that I'm not putting in my part. But frankly, I don't give a shit. I mean, I do, but I'm thinking I'm doing a lot, too. I tell him I'm not superwoman. And if I start taking what he says really seriously, then I would probably have a nervous breakdown. I wouldn't be able to function.

Yolanda felt that she was doing more of the household work than she should. Her husband's lack of participation and his cultural expectations were constant sources of conflict. She complained that her husband consistently compared her to other women in order to discredit her expectations. She also has come to believe that other women are willing to accept a minimal amount of male participation.

> What happens, what blows my mind, is I consider the fact that my husband does what to me is a minimal amount of work around the house, and my friends will come over and it will blow their minds at how much he does. Oh, Tony cooks, and washes dishes. Yeah, and it blows their mind, because their husbands do even less.

Stalling or not completing the task properly are strategies men employ to avoid doing housework. Women sighed with resignation and said that often it was just easier to do the work themselves. Teresa Godinez explained:

> The balance between how much is done or expected to be done creates tension. I think at any point when something isn't done there is a "who will do it." In his mind the easiest answer is that no one does it and that's okay with him. In my mind if it doesn't get

done, then I'm unhappy about it, so I end up doing it. It's not so much an argument of "who will do it," but just it has to be done. It probably goes back to the superwoman image. I want a good house. I don't want somebody to walk in and see this mess. It is not going to be Mike that they think didn't clean up the mess. It's going to be me.

Celia, who has difficulties with her husband's stalling, rationalized his behavior as "casual, laid-back." She stated that her husband was extremely committed to his career and spent several hours every evening on his work. His zeal and commitment to his work call into question his laid-back attitude toward household labor. Rather, his casual attitude toward housework appears to be a strategy to avoid the work.

Overall, men married to professional Chicanas do more household work than other men in this sample. In a few families, their participation is not a product of constant tension. For the most part, however, the only way women have altered the distribution of labor has been through conflict and confrontation.

Clerical Workers

In marked contrast, men married to clerical Chicanas do much less housework than all other husbands in the sample. Although women were solely or primarily responsible for the household tasks, only three expressed dissatisfaction. The division of household labor in these households did not generate the same level of conflict as was found in households of Chicana professionals. Instead of open conflict, clerical workers thankfully accepted whatever their husbands were willing to give or attempted to "school" their husbands through gentle tactics. Their behavior reflects a clear ideological division between what they think and expect regarding household labor. Some women said that they did not expect equal sharing because of their cultural upbringing. Gloria, for example, said:

I think if I was raised differently and he had been raised differently I would, but I don't expect it. I'm not going to be the type that nags and says you do your share. I don't because it makes the house a little more comfortable, rather than have the constant nagging.

Laura, a swing-shift worker at the telephone company, whose husband is a full-time student, does not expect him to take equal responsibility and attempts to avoid conflict. Before she leaves for work in the afternoon, she usually prepares dinner for her husband and nine-year-old son. Although she arrives home after midnight, she gets up in the morning to take care of her son's needs and drives him to school.

There are times when I wish I could come home and the sink was clean and there were no dishes from dinner. But I overlook it. They are going to get done, I'm going to do them, and I see no sense in making an upheaval about it. I never hold him accountable. So if it gets done, fine; if it doesn't, well it will get done somehow. It's not something I harp on.

Norma, a secretary, talked about how men had to be "retrained." She also attempts to avoid conflict, nagging, or demanding tactics. Instead, she has taken the advice of older Mexican women, who have told her that "*tienes que hacerlo por la buena*" (you have to do it on good terms).

> I usually try to do it *a la buena*. I kind of play little tricks, get him into a good mood or whatever. I just make sure that everything feels kind of neutral, like at night when no one is feeling grouchy or angry. And I will say, "Oh, help me with this, or bring me that, and can you do this for me. Oh, thank you, honey" or whatever and I kind of pat him on the back.

Norma's efforts have met with some success, in that her husband is beginning to become more active in household labor. Juan is now working a four-day, ten-hour shift and is home Fridays. "On Fridays, when he is home, he fixes his own breakfast, and he will clean up a little bit, like he washes the dishes, vacuums, and fixes things up." Norma also recently began to school him on how to do the laundry. While she feels responsible for laundering his work and personal clothing, she decided that he could take care of his athletic clothing. Juan belongs to a soccer team that plays every weekend and practices several times a week, so extra work is required for the upkeep of his gym clothes. Recently, after gentle prodding from her, he began to take responsibility for doing his own gym clothes.

The division of labor has also changed somewhat over the course of the marriage in Flor's household, but she is still responsible for the majority of the work, with help from her teenage daughter.

> It's changed. In the beginning he wouldn't lift even a spoon. As they say in Spanish: "*No levanta ni una cuchara*." That's true. He wouldn't babysit his own children; he wouldn't pick up his things; he wouldn't take his dish to the sink. Everything had to be done for him. It remained like that while I was at home. After I started working, things weren't getting done by me. After a long time he finally decided he could carry his dish to the sink by himself, and he could watch his own kids. Little by little he has just kind of gotten into doing things for himself. If there wasn't a pair of pants ironed, well, he just had to iron them himself. He has also learned to prepare his own breakfast and lunch for himself. So now he does for himself, and he doesn't really get into any household things for anybody else. If he does, then we hear about it.

Flor's husband, like Norma's, takes part in sports tournaments and practices several times a week. Like Norma, Flor also recently decided that she should not have to be responsible for his gym clothes.

Clerical workers also complained that their husbands stall. Even though women recognize these tactics, they nevertheless fall prey to their husbands' strategies. As Yvette explained:

> There were times when the garbage is there and I'll ask him, "Victor, will you please take out the garbage?" and he will say, "OK babe, I'll do it later." It's two hours later and I look and the garbage is still there and I will think, "I'll fix that." I'll get another bag and

I'll start making another little garbage bag. And it's already in the evening and I'll ask him, "Aren't you going to take out the garbage?" "Oh yeah, babe, I'll do it later." Then I'll think, "I'll fix this guy, I'll do it myself." I feel like I'm torturing him because I didn't give him the opportunity to take out the garbage, but all along I'm torturing myself, right?

While clerical workers do expect their husbands to "fill in their shoes" when necessary, they cling to traditional gender-role ideology. Although Yvette's situation has changed over the course of the marriage, with her husband taking on more responsibilities, a clear division of "his" and "her" realms persists, and both view his participation as a help to her.

Things have changed. Now if he takes off his clothes and leaves them around, I just put them into a little pile. So a few days later, he will say, "Where are my slacks?" You see that pile over there? Well, what are they doing there? Look, I don't wear them, those are your clothes. If you know they are clean, you hang them up, and if they are dirty, then I will get to them.

Clerical workers in particular bring up gender-role socialization to explain contemporary gender behavior and realms of responsibility. As Yvette explained:

In my house my father did nothing, my mother did everything. The house was the responsibility of my mother and the children. So in my mind, the father was to go to work and bring home the bread and butter, and it was the mother's responsibility to have the bread and butter on the table. That is why I say, my dishes, my laundry, because those are my responsibilities up front.

Chicana clerical workers differ from women in both professional and blue-collar jobs in their acceptance of traditional gender-role divisions. They uniformly did not expect their husbands to share equally in the division of household labor, relied on gender-role ideology to explain their situation, and deployed nonconfrontational strategies to attempt to change this division of labor.

Blue-Collar Workers

Chicana blue-collar and professional workers articulated similar expectations and willingness to engage in household struggle. Although husbands of blue-collar workers do less housework than husbands of Chicana professionals, the level of satisfaction with the division of household labor was similar for both groups. Half of the blue-collar women expressed a high level of satisfaction.

One blue-collar worker declared that she expected her husband to do his equal share "right from the beginning," but most of the blue-collar workers adopted a militant stance on household labor later in their marriages. The overwhelming majority of blue-collar marriages started out highly sex-role segregated. During the course of the marriage, however, women began demanding—and receiving—more help from their husbands to accommodate their working schedules.

Christina, a delivery truck driver, who has the most egalitarian relationship in this sample, was clear about what she expected from her husband from the beginning of her marriage.

> Well, in the beginning we would have arguments, but I told him, I can't do everything. Right from the beginning we said what was expected. I wanted to work but I didn't want to come home to clean up the house. Like some of my girlfriends, their husbands work and they come home and that is it. They don't do anything. And on Friday nights they go out and have fun with their friends and the women have to stay home with the kids. I can't accept that. That is not right.

Christina reported joint division of labor on almost all items on the questionnaire. However, when she talked about what occurred on a daily basis, it was clear that although her husband does a considerable amount of work, she does more. At the end of the interview, she became aware of this contradiction, looked up at me, and said: "I think I do more. But he doesn't just sit around the house. He puts his share in, but I do more."

Perhaps the most dramatic change has occurred in Maria's family as a result of her demands. Maria has a full-time job in a furniture factory, working the swing shift. She also works on-call at a motel during the week and works two eight-hour shifts on the weekends. Of the women interviewed in this sample, she had the most oppressive relationship. Prior to her newfound militancy, she did all the household labor, but then things changed. As she says,

> This just started recently, about two years ago. Before, I used to do everything. Now I put my cards on the table and he is doing his chores. In other words, we have made an agreement that he does so much and I do so much. I have worked hard for this, that is why it has changed.
>
> When I asked her what brought on the change, she replied:
>
> I just got tired of it. *I'm nobody's slave.* Like I told him, I never used to take care of myself. Now I'm taking care of me. Before, I was too busy taking care of everything. I didn't have time, now I have time. Before, he demanded that I get up at 4:00 A.M. to prepare his breakfast and lunch, and now he does it himself. So now I get a full rest. I don't have to worry about washing clothes because he washes every week. If I prepare dinner, he will wash dishes. And when I don't feel like preparing dinner, he makes dinner and washes dishes too.

Like Chicana professionals, blue-collar women have had to fight an uphill battle that has gained them some tangible results. But even though men are doing more than they used to, most of the women are still responsible for the majority of household labor. Victoria discusses resistance and change in gender relations in her marriage:

> It hasn't been easy. Richard was brought up *muy macho.* When I started working, I told him, "I'm tired. Why don't you help me do this?" At first he would say, "You can do it." It was getting to be too much. To this day Richard does not bathe the girls, Richard does

not cook, he doesn't wash the toilet. I do that. But he washes clothes, mops the floor, and vacuums.

Richard's subversive techniques are similar to those employed by other husbands in this sample. Victoria, like other women, falls prey to these strategies, ultimately doing the job herself.

> For Richard to give the girls dinner, he will go to Wendy's and feed them. For him to be able to pay the PG&E bill, he will wait for two months to pay it. For Richard to make sure that the floor is clean, he will let it go. He will eventually do it but not when it needs to be done. I know he can do it, *pero se hace tonto* [but he plays dumb]. So I'll say, "Get out of here and let me do it."

Victoria has attempted a variety of techniques in her struggle. Outright confrontation and nagging have netted some results. Recently she has become increasingly impatient with her husband and has gone on strike.

> So I found another way of doing it, which is I don't wash for him, I don't cook for him. I'm getting to the point at which I only make certain foods for the girls and I. Then he will come to, he gets the message.

Not only are blue-collar Chicanas willing to make demands on their husbands, but also at the ideological level they label their husbands' attitude as sexist. Victoria very adamantly told me: "One day I called Richard a male chauvinist pig. Boy, was he shocked."

Like other husbands, blue-collar men compare their wives to other women as a mechanism of social control. Lisa related an incident that happened at her mother-in-law's house.

> He tries to pull these little numbers. Like "That is not the way my mother does it." Well, once we were at his mother's house and she had some beans on the stove, and he told his mother the way he wanted the beans cooked. And I thought to myself, if he had told me that, he would have been wearing the beans. I just thought, no way. I'm not going to put up with that, no way.

The data reveal that both men and women employ a variety of gender strategies to manipulate the situation to their advantage. Men use stalling tactics and perform tasks in a slipshod manner to avoid domestic work. They attempt to compare their wives to other women as a means of social control and in order to discredit their wives' requests. Women also employ a variety of strategies in their daily struggle: they retrain, coach, and praise husbands for a job well done. At times, they resort to slowdowns or work stoppages, so that eventually men are forced to contribute more to household labor.

Clerical workers are unique in their underground approach, which, for the most part, avoids verbal confrontations and open power struggles. Professional and blue-collar workers also mount underground resistance in combination with confrontation techniques. This tactic has been successful for blue-collar and professional women; they have been able to alter the distribution of household labor on their behalf to a much greater degree than clerical workers. A strong relationship emerged between women's willingness to engage in political struggle and the level of male participation in household labor.

The analysis of the household division of labor in this sample illustrates the complexity of the relationship between ideology (the belief system that incorporates what women think and what they expect) and practice (as expressed in their behavior). At the ideological level, all the respondents believe that their husbands should have equal responsibility for household chores. However, clerical workers unanimously stated that they did not expect equal sharing, whereas blue-collar and professional workers expected equal sharing but did not believe it would actually happen. "Expectations" operate at two levels: what women want, and what they think will happen realistically. At the level of practice, clerical workers behaved according to their nonexpectations. They did not demand or struggle for male involvement. They also articulated more sex-linked attitudes regarding male and female roles in the family. At the abstract level, they embrace an egalitarian stance on household labor. At the same time, they also expressed strong ideological and emotional ties to sex-typed roles. Perhaps this commitment to traditional roles accounts for their lack of expectations and their nondemanding attitudes. They could not expect their husbands to participate equally, since they themselves were not convinced that equal participation should be the rule. Professionals and, to a lesser degree, blue-collar workers were more successful in translating their beliefs and expectations into practice. Their willingness to struggle with their husbands also attested to the strength of their convictions and expectations.

Women's earnings and work demands are thus contributing factors, at the ideological and behavioral levels, in the political struggle over the distribution of household labor. They are not the only factors, but they represent two plausible links between employment and the division of household labor that emerged from this sample.

Chapter 81

||||||||||||||||||||||||||||||||||||||||||||||||||||||||||||||||||||||||||||

Domestic Violence against Latinas

Jenny Rivera

After about two months he started . . . hitting me again. This time I was going to do something, so I told Yolanda, my best friend. She said, and I'll never forget it, "So what, you think my boyfriend doesn't hit me? That's how men are." It was like I was wrong or weak because I wanted to do something about it. Last time he got mad he threatened me with a knife. That really scared me.[1]

Although domestic violence has received tremendous attention, the form of it inflicted upon Latinas by their spouses and male partners has not. This specific issue deserves consideration because differences of gender, race, and national origin shape Latinas' experiences with this form of violence.

Latinas' Experiences and Expressions of Male Violence

Racial and cultural differences are critical in analyzing and responding to the crisis of domestic violence. These differences are not merely cosmetic or superficial, much less mere grounds to support demands for assistance. Differences based on race and culture are both internal[2] and external,[3] and represent primary factors affecting the experiences of violence by women of color. Latinas are best situated to describe the nature of the violence against them by their male partners. As one put it:

I have never called the police here because [he] told me that they will deport us if I do. I've thought about learning some English, but between work and the kids there is hardly any time. So I've never really asked anybody for help. Anyway sometimes he goes months without hurting me and I try to forget about it and just work.

From *Domestic Violence against Latinas by Latino Males: An Analysis of Race, National Origin, and Gender Differentials*, 14 B. C. THIRD WORLD L.J. 231 (1994). Originally published in the *Boston College Third World Law Journal*. Reprinted by permission.

Latinas are differently situated from white and black women. They experience vulnerability and helplessness because of a dearth of bilingual and bicultural services from social service providers and shelters. In addition, Latinas may experience cultural isolation. These differences have led one researcher to conclude that Latinas need support services—targeted to their specific needs—to a greater extent than other battered women. Understanding the interplay of race and ethnicity in Latinas' lives first requires an analysis that focuses on Latina experiences and needs.

Stereotypes: "El Macho" and the Sexy Latina

Historically, stereotypes have depicted Latinos, especially males, as irrational, reactive, hot-blooded, passionate, and prone to emotional outbursts. "Macho" is the accepted—and expected—single-word description synonymous with Latino men and male culture. For their part, Latinas are presented as both innocent virgins and sexy vixens. Accustomed to a male-centered community, the Latina is constructed as docile and domestic. In order to satisfy her hot-blooded, passionate partner, however, the Latina must also be sensual and sexually responsive. One commentator succinctly summarized these caricatures as they developed through film: "[They] established and repeated other stereotypes, including the violent-tempered but ultimately ineffective Puerto Rican man; the mental inferior; the innocent, but sensual Puerto Rican beauty; and the 'loose,' 'hot-blooded mama.'"[4]

Within the Latino community, Latinas' identities center on their roles as mothers and wives. By encouraging definitions of Latinas as interconnected with and dependent upon status within a family unit structure, the Latino patriarchy denies Latinas individuality on the basis of gender. For Latinas, cultural norms and myths of national origin compound patriarchal notions of a woman's role and identity. A Latina must serve as a daughter, a wife, and a parent, who places the needs of family members above her own. She is the foundation of the family unit, treasured as a self-sacrificing woman who will always look to the needs of others before her own. The influence of Catholicism throughout Latin America solidifies this image within the community, where Latinas are expected to follow dogma and to be religious, conservative, and traditional. The proliferation of stereotypes, which are integral to institutionalized racism, obstructs the progress and mobility of Latinas. Assumptions about Latinas' intellectual abilities and competence are formed on the basis of stereotypes, and justified by pointing to poor educational attainment statistics. Unless these myths and misconceptions are dispelled, the reality of Latinas as targets of Latino violence will remain unexplored, and Latinas' critical problems will remain unsolved.

Legal Strategies

Many of the strategies and responses to domestic violence evidence a lack of understanding of the needs of Latinas and other women of color. When Latinas receive poor treatment at the hands of law enforcement officials or are turned away by domestic violence shelters because of language and cultural differences, or when Latinas do not even take the first step of seeking assistance because there is no place to turn, the domestic violence movement fails.

Legislation

Consider the obstacles that Latinas must surmount in order to exercise their rights to security and protection. First, state law enforcement officers and judicial personnel continue to reflect the Anglo male society. Latinos and bilingual personnel are rarely found within the legal system, and women continue to represent only a small percentage of the police force. Second, even when state laws are adequate, domestic violence legislation remains susceptible to poor enforcement by police and judicial personnel.

Law Enforcement

Law enforcement officials' failure to respond appropriately to violence against women has come in for harsh criticism. Discussions of appropriate techniques and mechanisms for ensuring women's protection have failed to address Latinas. Instead, the debate has focused on women as a monolithic class with similar patterns of conduct and common concerns. When women of color enter the discussion, they have been treated without reference to race-specific differences and experiences. Their treatment has focused primarily on their economic status and lacked a detailed analysis of the role of race—including the entrenched racism of law enforcement institutions nationally. As a result, the different experiences and realities of women of color are not taken into account when designing effective guidelines on enforcement in domestic violence situations. This absence creates the risk that strategies aimed at all women will fail to address adequately the needs of Latinas.

Latinos in the United States have had a long, acrimonious history of interaction with local police and federal law enforcement agencies. Latinas are understandably suspicious of police who have acted in a violent and repressive manner toward the community at large. In addition, a Latina must decide whether to invoke assistance from an outsider who may not look like her, sound like her, speak her language, or share cultural values.

A second factor is the failure of activists to consider the role of race in police response. Officers often fail to make an arrest, minimize the seriousness of the situation, or treat the woman as if she were responsible for the violence. Battered women's activists have criticized male police officers for their sympathetic attitudes toward batterers. But they rarely consider the race of the batterer, which is a relevant factor in the police response to a domestic violence situation. The history of aggression toward Latino males by police officers cannot be ignored, nor can the police's belief that violent behavior is commonplace and acceptable within the Latino community. No definitive research examines the impact of these stereotypes on arrest patterns, yet they are important factors in patterns of arrest for domestic violence.

Against this backdrop, the first issue regarding the impact of Latinas' political status becomes clear: if a Latina decides to go beyond her community and seek assistance from persons already considered representatives of institutional oppression, the community may view her act as a betrayal. A Latina, therefore, may tolerate abuse rather than call for outside help. This hesitation to seek assistance provides the community with an excuse for ignoring or denying violence against Latinas, as well as for trivializing and resisting Latina activists' efforts to create a community strategy to end the violence.

Second, law enforcement officials may not give adequate consideration to calls received from poor neighborhoods and neighborhoods with significant populations of people of color, believing such work either highly dangerous or unrewarding. Although a misperception, this attitude engenders a sense within the community that seeking police assistance is futile.

The Criminal Justice System

Local prosecutors and judges react differently to domestic violence cases than to other criminal cases. They often treat these cases as inconsequential or private matters, ill suited to state intervention. Gender bias in the courts therefore results in the disparate treatment of domestic violence crimes compared to other crimes of violence.

Numerous obstacles based on language and culture lie in the way of a Latina seeking to use the criminal justice system effectively and ensure a criminal prosecution against her batterer. First, the shortage of bilingual and bicultural personnel—prosecutors, judges, clerks, and psychologists, all of whom are crucial and can influence the ultimate outcome of a Latina's case—creates a system unprepared to address claims by Latinas. Second, Latinas have limited resources to fill the gaps in available support services to assist them. Third, Latinas face racial and ethnic barriers. Neither white women victims nor white male batterers receive discriminatory treatment on account of their race. Latinas do. Devalued and dehumanized, they lack connections to those who have been assigned to prosecute and adjudicate their complaints. Fourth, the "cultural defense" raised by men in response to prosecution for killing their wives represents another barrier to Latinas.[5] The defendant's theory in each of these cases is that violence against women is normal and sanctioned by the culture.

Such an approach, by requiring legal institutions to consider all relevant factors and to judge the defendant from his or her actual perspective, may initially appear inherently fair and just. With violence against women, however, a cultural defense serves only to promote violence within the community. Even if violent actions against women are common in a particular culture, legitimizing them only reinforces patriarchy, and exposes women to more of the same. It also runs counter to a legal system allegedly founded on equality.

Social Services

Social services, including counseling, assistance in securing entitlements and health coverage, and temporary or permanent housing for women who leave their homes, are especially critical for Latinas, whose access to judicial and law enforcement remedies are also limited. Because of linguistic, cultural, and institutional barriers, Latinas have limited access to such services.

A recent study found that Latina shelter residents were the least likely to contact a friend, minister, or social service provider for assistance prior to entering the shelter. It also found that Latinas' actions comported with marital norms, which differed from those of other shelter residents. Specifically, Latinas appear bound by a norm of "loyal motherhood." They tend to get married younger, have larger families, and stay in relationships longer. They are correspondingly poorer, have completed fewer years of formal education, and suffer more extensive periods of abuse than their non-Latino counterparts. Moreover, when Latinas try to enter shelters, many are turned away because they speak little or no English. Indeed, the lack of bilingual and bicultural personnel represents a major barrier to Latinas' access to programs and shelters. Shelters without such personnel insist that they would do a disservice to Latinas by accepting them, because the language barrier would prevent personnel from providing Latinas with adequate services. Shelters thus turn away Latinas on the basis of national origin.

When accepted into a shelter, Latinas find themselves in foreign and unfamiliar surroundings, because a shelter rarely reflects a Latina's culture and language. For purposes of safety, women are often placed in shelters outside their community, which contributes to Latinas' sense of loneliness and isolation. Without bilingual and bicultural personnel and a familiar community environment, these shelters can provide only the barest, most temporary, services. Insensitivity based on racism or on a lack of knowledge about or exposure to other cultures, by both shelter personnel and other residents, further isolates Latinas and heightens their sense of unwelcomeness.

Nor do shelters facilitate the Latina's return to her own community. Because most lack Spanish-speaking personnel, the Latina cannot develop the skills and strengths necessary to escape the violence permanently and establish a new, independent life. These shelters currently provide only temporary, short-term services. They can scarcely hope to ameliorate the dependency and disempowerment that brought about the Latina's predicament in the first place. Women of color should be at the center of feminist reform movements. The current lack of services available to Latinas reflects the consequences of failing to do so.

Responses

The Latino community has not yet begun to develop a comprehensive strategy to end violence within itself. This failure reflects more than mere oversight. Historically, activists and leaders within the community have confronted racism and national origin discrimination with clear, focused strategies. Moreover, Latinos have vehemently opposed the characterization of those in their community as violent and uneducated. This commitment to equality and civil rights stops short, however, of addressing issues such as "women's rights" that are of specific importance to Latinas. Struggles within the Latino community to recognize the pervasiveness of domestic violence and its impact upon the lives of women and their families must continue. Unfortunately, demands for a community response to the violence have been met with insistence that such issues are private matters that cause division within the community and impair the larger struggle for equality. This approach skirts the real issue: Latinas are physically, emotionally, and psychologically abused on a daily basis by the men who are closest to them. These are not private matters—just as the lack of adequate health care, education, and living wages are not.

The development of strategies to address domestic violence must proceed aware of the reality and experiences of all women, recognizing the tensions and conflicts associated with developing reforms. A reform movement that recognizes these realities and experiences will acknowledge the need to work in unison, but only from a strong base. Latino community-based organizations must be strengthened and provided with the financial and political flexibility to develop and establish domestic violence shelters and services. The Latino community must place a high priority on domestic violence initiatives. The lives of women and the well-being of an entire community depend on it.

NOTES

1. Myrna M. Zambrano, MEJOR SOLA QUE MAL ACOMPANADA 140 (1985).

2. Common characteristics of ethnic and racial groups—such as English as a second language—provide an example of internal differences.

3. External differences are demonstrated when the treatment accorded to particular individuals or groups is based on their membership in a racial or ethnic category.

4. Richie Perez, *From Assimilation to Annihilation: Puerto Rican Images in U.S. Films*, 2 CENTRO BULL. 8, 13 (1990).

5. Sarah Eaton & Ariella Hyman, *The Domestic Component of the New York Task Force Report on Women in the Courts: An Evaluation and Assessment of New York City Courts*, 19 FORDHAM URB. L.J. 391, 487 (1992).

Chapter 82

||||||||||||||||||||||||||||||||||||||||||||||||||||||||||||||||||||||||||||

Chicano Rap
Machos y Malas Mujeres

Pancho McFarland

The Gendered Image

I had the good fortune to speak with young people about rap music. Our discussions were illuminating. We began by playing rap songs and discussing the lyrics. Together we examined violent and sexist lyrics. Since many of these youths identified as gang members, they preferred the style and lyrics of Chicano gangsta rappers such as Brownside and Proper Dos. They found nothing wrong with the violence discussed in the lyrics. In fact, the opposite was true. The more graphically violent the lyrics, the more most tended to like the music.

The same could be said about the sexist messages in the songs. They saw no problem with the way women were depicted in the music. "That's life," they said. The words and sentiments were nothing new to these thirteen- to seventeen-year-olds. When I asked them about the names that were often used to label women—names like "ho," "hoodrat," "hoochie," and "bitch"—I received several interesting responses. One particularly articulate young man began by apologizing to my research assistant, Leonor, saying that he hoped he would not offend her with what he was about to say. He explained that the word "bitch" was just another word for woman. He and his friends meant no harm by the term. According to him, the word did not mean anything derogatory, nor did it cause him to see women as inferior. Most of the other young men in the group nodded or verbalized their agreement. They saw this as an unimportant issue and wanted to move on to talk about other issues including police brutality, the education system, and gangbanging.

Sexist representations of women abound in U.S. popular culture and everyday discourse. These young men made it clear that the images of women in the Chicano rap that we listened to were nothing new and nothing to be concerned about. "Bitch," referring to women, was a normal part of their everyday speech. They had heard it all before. The question is, Where had they heard this language and picked up these images? How did words like "ho" and "hoochie" and images of women as sex objects become naturalized, normalized, and internalized in the minds of these adolescents?

Gender Socialization

Scholars have focused on understanding gender socialization as a key component of the development of youth identity and worldview. Many powerful agents—mass media, families, schools, and churches among them—teach adolescents to abide by patriarchal notions of what it means to be a man or woman and how women and men should relate to each other. I examine Chicano rap music to develop a picture of the ways Chicanos understand masculinity, femininity, and gender relations.

Previous research suggests that if gender socialization for Chicanos results from misogyny and hypermasculinity in the surrounding culture, then we should expect to find in the musical production of young Chicanos representations of women that reflect these attitudes. Specifically, we should find representations of women as sexual objects, as "good women" (*mujeres buenas*), as "bad women" (*mujeres malas*), and in relation to men and not as autonomous subjects. Men will be represented as dominant, violent, and otherwise hypermasculine.

Contextualizing Gender in Chicano Rap

A study of misogyny in Chicano rap music must take into account the representation of woman and gender in broader U.S. society.

Hypermasculinity is a defining trait of manhood in today's society. Acts of violence and daring are part of male gender performance that prove to young men that the risk-taking adolescent boy is not weak, feminine, or gay and is instead tough, hard, and violent. The result for boys is often deadly. Drunken driving, suicide, male violence, schoolyard bullying, road rage, binge drinking, and similar behaviors have dramatically increased since the 1970s. These efforts to prove and perform one's manhood also harm women, as incidents of rape, murder, and other acts of violence against women remain commonplace. The National Crime Victimization Survey (NCVS) found that between 1992 and 2000, attempted rapes, completed rapes, and sexual assaults against women averaged 366,460 per year in the United States. Hypermasculinity as the marker of manhood has led to stricter notions of gender and created a much more dangerous environment for teenage boys and girls and adult women and men.

Hypermasculinity has become the norm by which other male behaviors are evaluated. For young men of color the pressures to be hypermasculine are even more intense. Old racist notions of the Black Buck, the Black rapist, the criminal, and the gangster have been recycled in contemporary popular culture through the gang exploitation genre of film and corporate rap music. Moreover, many young Black men see themselves depicted in these ways and imitate them, recognizing that in our society power is intimately linked to violence and domination. They are thus influenced to model hypermasculine behaviors in order to establish themselves as men and to approximate the power and influence of big-screen heroes and real corporate and government power brokers.

Much the same holds true for the way popular media influence young Chicanos' gender socialization. In our popular imaginary, males of Mexican descent are extremely violent and deviant. Hollywood movies have depicted Mexican men as savages, dumb children, or criminals. On television, Mexican American men appear most commonly as perpetrators or victims of violence. Scholars of Mexican American culture have found that our history of Catholicism, rugged individualism, and patriarchal notions of Mexicanness has presented Chicano boys with few models of manhood. But in sports and popular culture, such a man is strong and protective and uses violence when necessary to solve problems. The ubiquity of boxing clubs in our barrios is a case in point. Boxing, for many, is deeply intertwined with nationalism and manhood.

The same cultural forces have defined womanhood in similarly narrow ways. Maria Herrera-Sobek has used feminist archetypal criticism to examine and codify the ways in which the Mexican American *corrido* genre of music has represented women. In examining Chicano film culture, Rosa Linda Fregoso shows that depictions of gender have a long history of male-centeredness. This male-centered lineage forms an ideological foundation in Mexican/Chicano culture that informs contemporary notions of masculinity, femininity, and gender relations. The patriarchal values and behaviors of Mexican American men (and some women) are reinforced and transmitted through the generations, in part via our popular culture, where idealized representations often serve as morality tales for proper gendered behavior.

Importantly, contemporary ideas about gender roles and relations in Chicano youth culture have another influence that we must consider when examining Chicano rap music. The degree of cultural exchange and influence between inner-city Chicanos and Blacks has led to lowriding, Chicano rock music, fashion, rap music style, attitude, and language, and other aspects of their expressive cultures. Through Black gangsta rap, badman and pimp folk characters have influenced young Chicanos' ideas about masculinity and gender relations. These hypermasculine figures have served as models of Black social banditry that appeal to young men of color who are denied success through conventional channels in the United States. Many young men of color see hypermasculinity in the form of the pimp or gangster as their only possible road to success.

The corporate music industry has championed music that presents this model of Black masculinity. The old racist stereotypes of the dangerous Black man find new fertile ground in gangsta rap. Alternative models of Black masculinity are rarely marketed by record companies eager to cash in on this new twist on an old stereotype. The record-buying public, including Chicanas/os, is much more willing to consume these images of Black hypermasculinity than more representative and diverse models of manhood. The combination of a hypermasculine and misogynist street mentality and commodified Black manhood influences young inner-city Chicanos who consume the violent and sexist images of corporate rap music. In turn, we find narratives of the pimp and player and the irreverence of the Black badman in Chicano rap.

Images of Masculinity and Misogyny

In my sample of 470 songs, 56 percent contain some discussion of women; of these, 37 percent represent women as objects of the male gaze and talk about women's bodies, beauty, sexiness, and clothing. In these songs women are represented simply as objects of male desire and pleasure. Of the songs that mention women, 37 percent discuss sexual intercourse. In none of these are women represented as having sexual agency or having the right to define their own sexuality. Instead, Chicano rappers place women in submissive positions and demonstrate pride in deceiving women into having sex with them. Women who have sex with Chicano rappers and the fictional characters in their rap stories are most often depicted as "sluts," "whores," and "freaks." In fact, 36 percent of all 470 songs I examined refer to women by such epithets. Other "bad" women are fortune-seekers ("gold-diggers"), unfaithful, or the cause of men's downfall. Lyrics that represent "good" women usually appear in the context of discussing familial relations—wives, mothers, grandmothers, daughters, or other family members.

Masculinity as Domination: Violence

Men's studies scholars argue that violence and domination are the central characteristics of contemporary notions of masculinity. Michael Kimmel, borrowing from Judith Butler's ideas about gender as performance, writes that masculinity is a highly unstable trait. One must continually prove his masculinity by distancing himself from femininity and homosexuality and by engaging in acts of daring and aggression; boys and men must continually "perform" masculinity. While I found that 71 percent of the songs in my sample discuss violence, certainly 71 percent of the activities in Chicano barrios are not related to violence. Why, then, do Chicano rappers spend so much of their time rapping about violence? What is it that they are saying about violence?

In many songs, violence did not serve as a vehicle to tell a cautionary tale but rather becomes the protagonist of the narrative. Violence is sold Hollywood-style. The Funky Aztecs' "Is This Real?" (on *Day of the Dead*, 1995) exemplifies the influence of the action film. The narrator of this story wakes up to gunshots and runs from violent situation to violent situation throughout his day. The protagonist uses several high-powered weapons, including two machine guns at once à la Sylvester Stallone's Rambo character. He eventually gets shot in the leg but escapes by jumping five stories into a hotel swimming pool. In true Hollywood style, the hero of the song surrounds himself with women. At one point he has two women in bed. One of his "bad" women looks out the window and is shot in the head. The imagery and pace of the song, its urgency and graphic detail call to mind any number of action movies over the past two decades. To further draw our attention to the fantasy nature of the song, between verses the rapper asks, "Is this shit real / or am I just trippin'?" Clearly the story is fictional, as such superhuman feats rarely occur and instead are reserved for big-screen fantasies. This type of violence abounds in Chicano rap. Rappers such as Brownside, Knightowl, and Darkroom Familia and Low Profile artists scarcely let a song go by without graphic depictions of how, where, and when they commit violent acts. For example, the Brownside CD *Payback* (1999) has a total of eleven songs; ten detail violent actions, and the other is a lament about a dead friend.

While it is hard to quantify the amount of gratuitous violence in Chicano rap, it is safe to say that many discussions of violence take their lead from Hollywood movies. Consider, for example, the use of names of notoriously violent characters from movies, references to rappers' similarity to action superstars Schwarzenegger, Stallone, and others, and samples of dialogue from war movies and gangster movies like *Scarface, Serpico, American Me,* and *The Godfather* trilogy. Moreover, a great deal of the rappers' iconography represents violent exploits. Album covers, posters, symbols, and webpages of many Chicano rap artists and recording labels display images of guns, blood, homeboys in menacing poses, and the like.

Violent metaphors are also common in Chicano rap. Because they are intended as metaphor and not as actual violence, this type of song has the potential to reveal the ubiquity of violence in our culture. Chicano rappers use metaphors to communicate their superiority to other young men. As the focus is verbal ability and cleverness, any type of metaphor would serve the purpose of demonstrating one's microphone skills. Curiously, though, rappers choose to talk about "blastin"—leaving opponents bloody on the ground—and knocking people out rather than using metaphors devoid of violence and domination. This demonstrates an understanding of masculine power as "domination over" rather than alternative notions of power as uplifting, enlightening, and enabling.

Masculinity as Domination over Women

Chicano rappers distinguish themselves from the sexual Other, woman, who is the passive sexual partner. Men are the active agents who have sex with many women without getting emotionally involved. This attitude mirrors Michael Kimmel's argument that two key traits of contemporary masculinity are repudiation of femininity and controlling one's emotions. Men lure and trick women into having sex with them, thus demonstrating their superior knowledge and ability. For many young Chicanos, gender relations involve trying to bed females without any suggestion of longer-term relationships. They demonstrate their masculinity by not becoming emotionally engaged with women and conquering more women than their friends do.

The epitome of such notions of gender relations is the "pimp-ho" relationship. The pimp figure is the ideal hypermasculine man. He obtains money his own way without recourse to the legitimate market economy and without fear of the law. Thus, some see him as a social bandit figure. Devoid of emotion, he has sex with many women but loves none. He does not shy away from violence and sees anything associated with femininity as weakness. He is aggressively heterosexual. He is stylish and intelligent. The women with whom he associates are inferior spiritually, emotionally, intellectually, and physically. They obey his every command and give their bodies and money to him.

Women serve as gauges of male power in a different way. Feminist authors study-ing rape and sexual violence against women point out that in patriarchal societies, men see women as their property. Men in their wars of domination with each other commonly struggle for control of women, using them as instruments to defeat the enemy. Controlling women signals to other men that one is powerful and in charge and that other men are impotent and weak.

Control of women is a central means by which men maintain and understand their masculinity. Chicano rappers compete with other men by attempting to take away each other's women. This type of competition appears in the songs like Dark-room Family's 2001 "DRF por Vida" by asserting, for example, that an inferior man's woman ("bitch") is having sex with the superior man ("ridin' my dick"), or the com-petition can be inferred by the rapper boasting about the number of women with whom he has had sex. While the second type is nearly unquantifiable because of the sheer number of times rappers talk about women they have bedded, I found thirty-seven examples of Chicano rappers using women as competition between them and other men. In other words, in 14 percent of the songs that discuss women, Chicano rappers overtly use women as objects of competition between men.

Other rappers take dominance and repudiating femininity a step further by de-picting misogynist violence. I found twenty songs in which violence against women appears. Only one, South Park Mexican's "SPM vs. Los," laments or critiques it. All seem to celebrate this type of violence as an example of male domination and their own superiority. For example, Street Platoon opens its misogynist "Pink (Pastrami Strips)" (2002) with a monologue by a young woman who begs to be raped, called dirty names, spanked, tied up, and choked during sexual intercourse. The entire song is laden with vitriol aimed at women who are described as "dirty bitches," "filthy sluts," "sexual cannibals," "snakes," and "dirty hoodrats." They describe women engag-ing in oral sex and other sexual acts with multiple partners and conclude that women were made for intercourse.

The need for young men to define themselves against women and to use women to demonstrate their dominance leads Street Platoon to argue that women love being abused. Misogynist songs, the pimp figure, and songs that use women as weapons in male competition provide evidence that dominant corporate popular cultural no-tions of masculinity as hypermasculinity influence Chicano rappers' understanding of gender. In their respective films with director Sut Jhally, bell hooks and Jackson Katz show that since the 1980s, misogynist violence has become commonplace in Hollywood movies and link its rise to the backlash against women. The ubiquity of hypermasculinity and misogyny in Chicano rap mirrors that found in movies, tele-vision, and other aspects of our communication and entertainment media. Chicano rap combines and rearticulates ideas of hypermasculinity and misogyny found in the dominant popular culture and patriarchal Black and Mexican male culture and tradition.

I found that of the sixty-seven rappers included in the sample, thirty-five had songs that discuss women's bodies as objects of male desire. This contrasts sharply with the relatively small number of rappers who speak of other aspects of women; for example, only eleven rappers in this sample had songs that discuss "good" women.

The data clearly illustrate that Chicano rappers understand their masculinity in relation to womanhood in simple and degrading ways. For young Chicano rappers, as for many men in U.S. society, womanhood is valued for controlled sexuality and reproduction.

The "Good" Woman: Mothers, Wives, and Other Familia

In Chicano male culture and patriarchal culture generally women are not only valued for their ability to satisfy men sexually. Mothers, daughters, wives, and grandmothers are also highly valued. Thirty-one songs in my sample refer to women in seemingly appreciative ways as nurturers, loved ones, and loyal wives. While initially this seems like a positive trend, further examination of the lyrics and the uses of the "good woman" archetype reveal that these images of women are often just the flip side of attempts to keep women in subordinate roles.

The cult of the Virgin of Guadalupe, or *marianismo*, has disseminated throughout Mexican society a gender ideology that allows for only two possible female roles. Ideal women are the "strong, long-suffering women who endured social injustice, [and] maintained the family as a safe 'haven in a heartless world.'" Women's proper role in family and in the community is one of subordination to husband and devotion to family. Against this *mujer buena* or Ideal Woman, patriarchal Mexican culture created *la mujer mala*, the aggressive, independent, and "sexually loose" woman outside of male control.

The Mexican woman is valued for her status as the wife and mother who assists the Mexican man and "nourishes and sustains [his] machismo." Thus, her positive status results from her relationship to men. She has little value outside of these relationships. For ethnic Mexicans, the "good" mother is the most important person in the world, while the "bad" woman, *la escandalosa*, is among the most despised. The good-mother figure presents an ideal of womanhood that is almost impossible to fulfill. Young women, then, are socialized into a gender role that they inevitably fail to realize. Nonetheless, the pressures to comply are overwhelming, as they are found throughout all aspects of ethnic Mexican culture—in our religion, oral and literary traditions, and music.

Maria Herrera-Sobek has identified a central female archetype in the Western and Mexican literary traditions in the suffering mother, *mater dolorosa*. She finds that in the *corrido*, "the basic imagery is that of the weeping mother at the death of her son." Even in death, the male hero of the *corrido* is supported by his mother. The weeping mother is the most common good-woman figure in Chicano rap. For example, South Park Mexican discusses this figure in five songs ("Ghetto Tales," "Filthy Rich," "Revenge," "Comin' Up, Comin' Down," and "Hustle Town"), and Latin Bomb Squad's first compact disc (1998) has three songs in which the figure appears. In "Temptations," "Deal with Tha Madness," and "Whatcha Missin'" the weeping mother image symbolizes a culture and a community that suffers from gun violence. In their laments about gang culture and macho Mexican and Chicano culture, Latin Bomb Squad (LBS) equates goodness with mothers and evil with irresponsible and violent men. They equate the young Chicano narrator of "Whatcha Missin'" with the irresponsible father figure when the rapper states that he is like his father ("Pops") because in his death he, too, abandons his mom. Throughout the CD the only moral figure and hope for the future is the mother. Every other character participates in violence, drug use, gang activity, or impersonal sex. LBS reiterates long-held Mexican beliefs that the mother is the repository of all that is good and that she is responsible for the future direction of the race—a burden that furthers male privilege and domination by allowing men to eschew responsibility for changing violent and misogynist behaviors.

Chapter 83

||||||||||||||||||||||||||||||||||||||||||||||||||||||||||||||||||||||||||||||||||||

Latina Sexuality, Reproduction, and Fertility as Threats to the Nation

Leo R. Chavez

On October 17, 2006, a woman gave birth to a baby that would take the United States population to 300 million.

If one thing appeared certain in the news coverage it was that the 300 millionth person would probably be Latino and would probably be born or living in Los Angeles, or at least somewhere in the U.S. Southwest. This pronouncement had been made a full ten months earlier in a *New York Times* article by William Frey, a demographer with the University of Michigan's Population Studies Center: "The 300 millionth [baby] will be a Mexican Latino in Los Angeles County, with parents who speak Spanish at home and with siblings who are bilingual." A senior demographer with the Population Reference Bureau explained why: "While most Americans are still Anglo-Saxon Protestants, Hispanic mothers have higher birth rates, and no state has more births than California, where most newborns are of Hispanic origin. There, Jose ranked fourth in 2004 among the most popular baby names for boys after Daniel, Anthony and Andrew."

Many of the news stories chronicling the event included information on historical immigration trends, contrasts to the 200-millionth-person milestone, current immigration patterns, changing demographics and the proportional increase in Latinos, the probability that the 300 millionth person would be Latino, and a photograph of Latinos, usually either Mexican immigrants participating in the immigrant marches earlier that year or a Latino family with a baby. Such reporting underscored Latino fertility and immigration as key components of population growth and other demographic changes. As the *Washington Post* put it, "Hispanics from Latin America, by far the largest share of recent immigrants, are driving the natural increase [in population] here. On average, Hispanic women have one more child than non-Hispanic white women." *WorldNetDaily* put it more bluntly: "Invasion USA: Illegals Push U.S. to 300 Million Mark."

Fears of immigrants' sexuality and their reproductive capacities are not new. Race, immigration, and fertility have formed a fearsome trinity for much of U.S. history.

During each wave of immigration, "natives" (typically the children or grandchildren of immigrants) have feared that the new immigrants would have deleterious impacts on American culture and society. During the great migration from southern and eastern Europe, for example, a wary American public perceived immigrant fertility levels as dangerously high and thus a threat to the education, welfare, and medical care systems, as well as a harbinger of demographic shifts leading to the diminishing of the power of the dominant Protestant, northern European–American racial/ethnic group. In addition, immigration authorities inspected immigrant women closely, suspecting them of loose morals, engaging in prostitution, becoming public charges, and other examples of moral turpitude.

During the most recent, post-1965 wave of immigration, Latina reproduction and fertility, especially of Mexican immigrant women, have been ground zero in a war of not just words but public policies and laws. Indeed, anti-immigrant sentiment during the last decades of the twentieth century and the first decade of the twenty-first focused specifically on the biological and social reproductive capacities of Mexican immigrant and Mexican-origin (U.S.-born) women. The post-1965 period witnessed a steady fertility decline among U.S. women, which has contributed to a demographic shift such that the proportion of white, non-Hispanic Americans in the overall population has decreased. Latina reproduction and fertility have been center stage in the often vitriolic public debate over the causes and meanings of demographic change.

The biological reproduction of Latinas combines with their social reproduction in the popular imagination to produce fears about Latino population growth as a threat to the nation—that is, "the American people," as conceived in demographic and racial/ethnic terms. This threat materializes not merely because of Latino population growth, but also because Latino babies transgress the border between immigrants and citizens. It is here that the metaphor of leaky national borders converges with that of porous bodies (producing babies) and the permeable category of citizenship. These transgressions make immigration a hot political issue, especially when the mother is an undocumented immigrant.

In California, for example, the perceived threat of Latina fertility, especially among immigrants, was central to the "Save Our State" movement that led to Proposition 187, which sought to curb undocumented immigration by denying undocumented immigrants social services, particularly prenatal care and education for their children. As Bette Hammond, one of the organizers of Proposition 187, put it: "They come here, they have their babies, and after that they become citizens and all those children use social services." Pete Wilson, governor of California from 1991 to 1999, made the denial of prenatal care for undocumented immigrant women a top priority of his administration. The 1996 welfare reform law also targeted medical services for immigrant women. As we shall observe, the popular discourse of Latina reproduction is decidedly alarmist in that it becomes part of a discourse of threat and danger to U.S. society and even national security, which is underscored in a post-9/11 world. Thus discourses not only filter reality but help construct what is taken for "real."

Sexuality, Reproduction and Latinas

Residents of Albuquerque, New Mexico, awoke to a Cinco de Mayo surprise in 2004. Around the city stood a number of large billboards advertising Tecate beer, which were placed by Labatt USA, the company that imports the beer. The ads featured an ice-cold beer bottle, with cold water beaded up on it, tilting sideways as if falling down, perhaps into a reclining position. What raised local ire was the words attached to the image: FINALLY, A COLD LATINA.

The sexual innuendos in the Tecate ad were anything but subtle. The "cold Latina" was being offered as a pun, but it worked only because what was unsaid but understood was that Latinas are "hot." This reference to supposedly "hot" Latinas built upon commonly held and taken-for-granted stereotypes of Latina sexuality and reproductive behavior. What "hot Latina" means has always been constructed in relation to other taken-for-granted assumptions about normative behavior of non-Latina whites. Thus the unspoken "hot" of the advertisement conjured up a plethora of images and referents to Latinas as exotic, sexually aggressive, flirtatious women who engage in sexual activities at an early age and thus have babies younger than white women, and who have more sexual partners (are more promiscuous) than their white counterparts. To finally find a "cold Latina," the ad suggested, would be a remarkable event, underscoring the assumed innateness of the "hot" attributes associated with Latinas. These personality and behavioral characteristics were, so to speak, part of the Latina's nature.

The assumption of an innate, or genetic, basis for the Latina's "hot" characteristics is part of common discourse, especially the "it's in their blood" observation. Consider the following exchange between Arnold Schwarzenegger, governor of California, and Susan Kennedy, Schwarzenegger's chief of staff. The topic is California assemblywoman Bonnie Garcia. The only Latina Republican in the California legislature, Garcia was born in New York, where her parents had moved from Puerto Rico. The candid conversation was tape-recorded and obtained by the *Los Angeles Times*:

Kennedy: Bonnie Garcia is great. She's a ball-buster. She's great. Is she Puerto Rican?
Schwarzenegger: She seems to me like Cuban.
Kennedy: She's not Mexican.
Schwarzenegger: No.
Kennedy: But she said something and I thought, I thought she was Puerto Rican.
Schwarzenegger: She maybe is Puerto Rican or the same thing as Cuban. I mean, they are all very hot. They have the, you know, part of the black blood in them and part of the Latino blood in them that together makes it.

Governor Schwarzenegger had offered up a theory of genetics (blood) as the basis for cultural behavior that goes well beyond the eye of the beholder's personal views. Both Schwarzenegger and the Tecate beer advertisement were articulating assumptions and taken-for-granted "truths" about Latina sexuality. Characterizing Latinas as "hot" objectifies and sexualizes them in a way that sets them up as society's Others, in distinct opposition to the normative sexuality and morality of white women. Latinas are reduced to their biological essences, which are narrowly defined along the lines of sexual attraction.

Latina Reproduction in the Post-1965 Era

Paul Ehrlich, a biologist at Stanford University, struck a societal nerve when his book *The Population Bomb* appeared in 1968. Ehrlich meant his book as a wake-up call about the dangers of population growth and the need to control fertility levels. His cataclysmic tone is best expressed in his own prose:

> Our position requires that we take immediate action at home and promote effective action worldwide. We must have population control at home, hopefully through a system of incentives and penalties, but by compulsion if voluntary methods fail. We must use our political power to push other countries into programs which combine agricultural development and population control. And while this is being done we must take action to reverse the deterioration of our environment before population pressure permanently ruins our planet. The birth rate must be brought into balance with the death rate or mankind will breed itself into oblivion. We can no longer afford merely to treat the symptoms of the cancer of population growth; the cancer itself must be cut out. Population control is the only answer. (p. 12)

Ehrlich leaves no doubt about the catastrophic outcomes should society fail to curb population growth. What he means by the ominous-sounding control "by compulsion" is not clear, but examples might include the draconian population control programs such as the one-child rule implemented in China and forced sterilizations among Latinas in the United States. Such actions may seem justified within a discourse that treats population growth as a "cancer" that will kill humankind through environmental degradation, famines, pestilence, and wars between rich and poor. Ehrlich further warned that, "If the pessimists are correct, massive famines will occur soon, possibly in the early 1970s, certainly by the early 1980s. So far most of the evidence seems to be on the side of the pessimists, and we should plan on the assumption that they are correct."

Ehrlich argued that re-channeling the meanings attached to sexual activity was a key goal of controlling fertility. Sexual activity, according to Ehrlich, is one of man's least animal functions. Sexual activity is a "peculiarly human activity" (that is, cultural) insofar as it has functions beyond reproduction, such as reinforcing interpersonal relationships, inducing pleasurable feelings, and functioning as a means of recreation. A rational approach, according to Ehrlich, would be to emphasize these nonreproductive aspects of sexual activity and to de-emphasize the reproductive role of sex, especially the satisfaction that comes with childbearing and "excessive" fatherhood. In other words, when it comes to sex, recreate—don't procreate.

Ehrlich's views not only helped ignite a social movement—zero population growth —but they also helped establish the movement's enemy: women who had supposedly high fertility levels and who continued to value childbearing. In this way, Ehrlich's *Population Bomb* contributes to an understanding of developments that would stigmatize Latinas as hot (hypersexual) and as possessing abhorrently high fertility rates (not to mention the stigmatizing of "welfare mothers").

In 1979 Paul Ehrlich followed *The Population Bomb* with *The Golden Door*, which focused on Mexico and Mexican migration to the United States. According to Ehrlich and his coauthors, Mexico's population growth was a major problem for Mexico, and thus for the United States, because it combined with social inequalities and inadequate job creation to produce intense pressures on emigration. Mexico's high fertility rate was the result of an "unusually pronatalist cultural tradition," which meant that Mexicans placed an abnormally high value on having children. Because of machismo and Marianismo, the argument went, men were dominant and women were submissive, and having more children increased the social status of both. "Motherhood is viewed as the essential purpose for a woman's existence," Ehrlich and his colleagues wrote, adding that these pronatalist cultural values receive reinforcement from the Catholic Church.

However, Ehrlich was also cautiously optimistic about Mexico's future fertility patterns. Based on his travels in that country, he observed that the Mexican government was taking population control seriously and implementing programs to change cultural values toward smaller families. He noted that such programs were already having some effect and that these efforts "will be felt in the long run." Moreover, Ehrlich's overview of Mexican history and the U.S.–Mexico relationship led him to warn against alarmist anti-Mexican rhetoric. In fact, he appeared to be speaking against a *U.S. News & World Report's* cover, which carried the headline "Time Bomb in Mexico: Why There'll be No End to the Invasion of 'Illegals.'" As Ehrlich noted:

> Mexico is in one of the worst demographic situations of any nation—something that should worry any humane person regardless of Mexico's geographic position. . . . But because of the myths about Mexicans, in many people concern has taken the form of outright fear of an invasion. This fear is rooted in ignorance of our southern neighbors, their past, and our past involvement with them. Some knowledge of them as a *people*, rather than caricatures, should help to calm that fear and allow legitimate concerns to be handled sensibly.

Despite Ehrlich's call for calm, his work reaffirmed already taken-for-granted assumptions about the family values and fertility rates of Mexican women. Soon after *The Golden Door* appeared, *Time* magazine's August 6, 1984 issue devoted a cover to Mexico and its population problem. The cover's image begins with the headline: "Mexico City, The Population Curse." Below the headline is a sun behind two Aztec twin pyramids. The sun the Aztecs worshipped, however, is being engulfed in smoke pouring out of chimneys from either factories or oil fields, since a number of oil derricks surround the smoking towers in the middle of the image. To the left is an urban landscape of tall buildings that continues to the edge of the image in the fashion of an infinity line (a line of people, animals, or things that seems to go on without end), thus giving the appearance of endless growth. To the right spreads an endless line of suburban-style housing. Below the buildings and smoking towers is a four-lane highway filled with cars snaking off into the distance, once again with the visual metaphor of the infinity line emphasizing that the line of cars is unending. Below the highway of cars is a mass of people flowing without end across the page. The message the *Time* cover imparts to its readers is that Mexico's population curse is also the readers' curse because of pressure it creates for Mexican emigration.

Increasingly in the 1980s, the growth of the U.S. Latino population came in for mention in conjunction with the declining proportion of whites in the U.S. population and declines in European immigration. For example, *Newsweek's* January 17, 1983 issue reported that between 1970 and 1980, the Latino population in the United States grew by 61 percent, largely because of immigration and higher fertility rates and because since the mid-1960s 46.4 percent fewer immigrants arrived from Europe. In addition, fertility took center stage in the invasion and reconquest narratives. Both *U.S. News & World Report* (March 7, 1983) and *Newsweek* (June 25, 1984) published covers with photographs of Mexican women being carried across water into the United States. *U.S. News & World Report's* cover announced, "Invasion from Mexico: It Just Keeps Growing," and *Newsweek's* title read, "Closing the Door? The Angry Debate over Illegal Immigration; Crossing the Rio Grande." The message was that the invasion carried the seeds of future generations. Women would have babies, create families, and soon communities of Latinos who would remain linguistically and socially separate and clamoring for a reconquest of the United States.

By the late 1980s and early 1990s, the "browning of America" was achieving increasing currency. For instance, in 1990 *Time* magazine noted, "The 'browning of America' will alter everything in society, from politics and education to industry, values and culture. . . . The deeper significance of America becoming a majority nonwhite society is what it means to the national psyche, to individuals' sense of themselves and the nation—their idea of what it is to be American." What is even more telling of the role of fertility in the "browning of America" narrative was the advertisement for this issue that *Time* created.

The image in *Time's* advertisement consisted of thirty-eight newborn babies arranged ten to a row, except for the bottom row, which had eight babies and a small copy of *Time's* cover for April 9, 1990. The babies were a mix of various shades of brown. Although framing the question this way, in conjunction with the flag image, is racially divisive, it pales in comparison with the words of the advertisement:

> Hey, whitey, your turn at the back of the bus. Sometime soon white Americans will become a distinct minority in a largely brown cultural and racial mix. A hard story for many of our readers. But then again TIME has never tried to be easy. It's what our readers expect. Call it relevance. Call it perspective. If it's important to you, you'll find it on this cover and inside these pages.

Most of the authors writing about the Mexican invasion and reconquest focused on fertility and reproduction. For example, Peter Brimelow found that Hispanics were particularly troublesome because of biological and social reproduction issues. Using Latinos as a whipping boy, he launched into a diatribe about bilingualism, multiculturalism, multilingual ballots, citizenship for children of illegal immigrants, the abandonment of English as a prerequisite for citizenship, the erosion of citizenship as the sole qualification for voting, welfare and education for illegal immigrants and their children, and congressional and state legislative apportionment based on populations that include illegal immigrants.

Victor Hanson blamed a blind adherence to culture for what he considered the curse of large families:

> The greatest hazard to the illegal immigrant is a large family—the truth that is never mentioned, much less discussed. Everything that he was born into—parents, priest, reigning mores—tells him to have five boys, better six or seven, to carry on the family name, ensure help in the fields, give more souls to God, provide visible proof of virility, and create a captive audience at the dinner table. In contrast, everything America values —money, free time, individual growth, secular pleasure—advises the opposite.

For Hanson, Mexican identity and values were the polar opposite of American identity and values, and both were locked into unchanging, essentialized types.

An appropriate end to this section is *Foreign Policy* magazine's 2001 article on "The Population Implosion." It is appropriate in two senses. First of all, the article resonates with my own observations below that low fertility is no panacea for society's problems and that it generates pressure for more immigration. Fertility levels worldwide experienced a dramatic drop of over 40 percent between the early 1950s and the end of the twentieth century. But the decline in fertility rates has been especially acute in the industrialized nations, where they are at "subreplacement" levels. When low fertility combines with rapidly aging populations, new problems emerge. The way that *Foreign Policy* chose to represent this problem on its cover also summarizes a key point of the discussion so far. The magazine cover's headline stated: "Wanted: More Babies. Why the end of the population explosion is a mixed blessing." The sort of babies that were needed was not-too-subtly suggested by the white, blue-eyed cherubic infant that almost fills the cover. White babies were needed to counter the browning of America, a perceived threat underlying much of the anti-immigration discourse on invasions and reconquests.

Anchor Babies

One final issue related to Latina reproduction is citizenship for children born in the United States. Based on the principle of jus soli, any baby born in the United States is automatically a U.S. citizen. As Section 1 of the Fourteenth Amendment to the U.S. Constitution states:

> All persons born or naturalized in the United States, and subject to the jurisdiction thereof, are citizens of the United States and of the State wherein they reside. No State shall make or enforce any law which shall abridge the privileges or immunities of citizens of the United States; nor shall any State deprive any person of life, liberty, or

property, without due process of law; nor deny to any person within its jurisdiction the equal protection of the laws.

Although this may sound straightforward, public debate has focused on conferring birthright citizenship for the children of undocumented immigrants. Changing this principle would entail changing the U.S. Constitution, but that has not deterred public debate on TV and radio talk shows or websites. The term that has emerged in these debates is *anchor babies,* a metaphor that is meant to capture the alleged strategy among undocumented immigrants of having a baby in order to have a U.S. citizen who will someday be able to apply for their family's legal residence through the preferences for family reunification. Those who promote this interpretation have not been distracted by the fact that such a child could not assist its parents in obtaining legal residence for at least twenty-one years, and the process could take years from that point. In addition, many undocumented immigrants who migrate with the short-term goal of work and then return to their country of origin may fear apprehension if they deliver their babies in hospitals, or they may not even be aware of advantages of having a U.S.-born child.

In response to the clamor over birthright citizenship, politicians have at various times introduced legislation to disallow automatic citizenship to the children of undocumented immigrants. An early proponent of this policy was Representative Elton Gallegly (Republican from Simi Valley, California), who in June 1995 recommended an amendment to the U.S. Constitution to end automatic citizenship for U.S.-born children whose parents are undocumented immigrants. Although unsuccessful, Gallegly continued his efforts in later congressional sessions. More recently, bills were introduced in Congress—the U.S. Citizen Reform Act of 2005 and Birthright Citizenship Act of 2007—both of which would deny U.S. citizenship to children born to undocumented immigrants.

Although the idea of anchor babies raises alarm for some, even more troubling would be the legal construction of a group of U.S.-born, nationality-less outcasts. Scholars such as Judith Butler and Sarah Willen have pointed to the effects of living as abject subjects. The definition of *abject* comes to us from the Latin "to cast away" or "to throw away" and is used to describe those with the lowest, most contemptible, and most wretched social status. Denying birthright citizenship to those who would undoubtedly continue to live among us would cast them as the most liminal and miserable subjects in the nation. Even 1.5 generation undocumented immigrants, those who have been raised in the United States since they were young children and who often feel despair at the obstacles they face, would be displaced by this new class of nationless, and thus even more abject, residents.

Cracks in the Discourse

I became suspicious of the veracity of this discourse on Latina sexuality and reproduction for a number of reasons. I began to ask, is the story more complicated than we are led to believe? First of all, it may be true that overall Latinas have more children than white women, but one cannot help but think about the relationship between the "graying of America" discourse and fertility statistics. Is it really that surprising that Latinas have more children per 1,000 women under age 45 in a place like Orange County, California, when the 2000 census indicates the average adult white woman is between 40 and 44 years of age and Latinas are in their 20s? Latinas are in the peak reproductive ages, whereas white women, on average, are toward the end of their reproductive lives. Even using "under 45 years of age" as a category, one would find, on average, more white, non-Latinas closer to age 45 and more Latinas, on average, much younger.

Also raising suspicion was that I often ask students in class and audiences in the many talks I give around the country how many children they would like to have. Few want ten, nine, or eight children and so on. I always start at ten children, but almost all want one or two, a preference that runs across the racial/ethnic mosaic.

Finally, I have become increasingly interested in the fertility and immigration relationship. In capitalist economic systems, such as that of the United States and most of the industrialized nations of Europe and also Japan, the basic premise is that economic growth is not only good but essential. There is tremendous pressure to maintain even a modicum of economic growth, which translates into creating more jobs today than yesterday. Creating more jobs avoids the social, political, and economic problems that come with economic recessions and depressions. For example, young people want jobs when they enter the labor market, and older people want their social entitlements, such as Social Security and medical care. Economic growth helps to accomplish these desires. However, cultural values, based on economic considerations, are such that declining fertility rates are the rule in the industrialized nations and in the world more generally.

This gap between fertility and economic growth creates a demand for immigrant labor. This gap will increase as U.S. baby boomers begin to retire in large numbers. Why? There are only two ways to get workers for a labor market. You can either birth them or import them. This is true locally, regionally, and globally. Local labor markets can draw workers from other regions of the country, but they also draw foreign workers if the demand for labor persists. What is clear is that countries with below replacement fertility rates (less than two children per woman) often experience pressure for immigration. Only the United States is listed as being at replacement level, but this rate is actually lower if only women under 45 years of age, the reproductive years, are considered. For some nations, such as Spain and Italy, fertility decline, combined with economic growth, has resulted in a rapid shift from being an emigrant-sending nation to an immigrant-receiving nation. Although 4 to 5 percent foreign-born in a population may not seem excessively high, the sudden visibility of immigrants can raise concerns. In Spain, for example, where the proportion of immigrants from northern Africa is relatively small, Spaniards view them as a threat to Spanish language, identity, and culture. Japan, a nation that guards its borders carefully, has what it considers an "immigration problem," even though the foreign born account for only 1.6 percent of its population.

If a nation does not produce workers but has a desire for economic growth and job creation, then there is pressure to provide workers through immigration. The anti-immigration discourse blames immigrants for responding to this labor demand with little consideration to homegrown pressures for immigrant flows. What influences the demand for immigrant labor is values, not just the value of having fewer children, but the desire for more education, a meaningful job, and more time for personal goals, as well as a desire for services such as fast food, child care, lawn care, elder care, manicures, and hair care. Along with these desires are equally strong desires not to do certain jobs. I often ask students, "How many of you are going to spend your summer helping farmers harvest their crops?" None raise their hands. This was once a common practice. We generally do not educate youth to desire low-income, semiskilled jobs in agriculture and food production, construction, manufacturing, and services. These are the default jobs for those we fail to educate properly. The bottom line is that fertility is related to immigration in a way that receives scant treatment in anti-immigrant discourse.

Chapter 84

‖‖

Maid in the U.S.A.

Mary Romero

Mexican Immigrant and Chicana Domestic Workers in the Modern Period

Attitudes and practices developed in the Americanization programs of the 1920s and 1930s continued as part of the racial etiquette between Mexican domestic workers and their Anglo employers. The 1959 publication entitled *Your Maid from Mexico* offers valuable insight into race relations between employees and employers in domestic service. Written as a practical handbook for Anglo housewives on how to supervise servants, it is also replete with suggestions and advice for the employees. Perhaps some employers gave a copy to the maid to read. More probably, employee suggestions were a strategy for developing the role expectations of the housewife employer. Thus, when a maid is advised to let her employer search her purse, we should probably read this as affirming and enhancing Anglo employers' "rights" as supervisors and the kind of deference that they should expect from their Mexican maids. In a similar vein, the following statement, although addressed to maids, actually suggests a strategy for employers: "Always try to remember that the man or lady of the house is probably trying to help you—not criticize you."

Your Maid from Mexico is a rich source of data on the folkways, mores, norms, values, and racial etiquette governing domestic service in the Southwest. Dos and don'ts provide insight into racial and gender hierarchies in the employer's home. Under the heading "Obligations of the Employer," for instance, the authors caution against common practices that may cause employee-employer problems: keeping workers beyond the agreed upon time, rearranging work schedules, changing days off, promising to raise salaries, training maids in the presence of the family or guests, and accusing maids of stealing. The authors' solutions to these issues are similarly informative. Rather than suggest that employers keep promises to raise salaries, the authors advise them to "explain why you do not or cannot do so." Although the book acknowledges that public reprimands and training of the maid are humiliating, the reason for avoiding these tactics is that children are likely to replicate such behavior, reducing the maid's effectiveness as a babysitter. Employees are warned against taking even the smallest item, such as a bobby pin, in order to maintain trust and avoid "misunderstandings." Furthermore, employees are urged to forgo privacy by showing employers the contents of their bags when they leave for their day off.

Gender construction appears in a section entitled "The Man of the House." Maids are expected to maintain and support patriarchy. The maid is informed that "the man of the house" pays the bills and her salary. He is the "king" of the house and, presumably following the housewife's lead, the maid should do everything to make him feel that way. She is expected to serve dinner when the man wants to eat, regardless of any imposition on her or the rest of the family. She is even warned to expect his occasional escapades at cooking and instructed to "smile, and clean up after him willingly."

As with mistresses at the turn of century, employers hiring Mexican domestics in the 1950s and 1960s expected to purchase broadly defined labor power rather than labor services: "Remember that your employer pays you for your time, and though you may consider a task unnecessary, it may be important to her." The job was therefore defined to include any task or personal service the employer or her family required: shampoo and set employer's hair, give permanents, sew dresses for children, give manicures, shine all the family shoes, wash the family car, etc. General housecleaning also encompassed ritual cleaning: "In many households, one day each week is set aside for the cleaning of silver, brass, copper, chandeliers, etc."

Elements of the cult of domesticity resurface throughout *Your Maid from Mexico*. All aspects of the occupation emerged as opportunities for the maid's self-enhancement and fulfillment. Domestic service emerged as the most rewarding occupation for Mexican women and the ideal training ground for learning middle-class ideas of motherhood and womanhood:

> You girls who work in homes can soon become more valuable to your employers than girls who work in offices, stores, or factories, because our homes and families are the closest to our hearts.
>
> Remember, as you learn new skills day by day, you are not only learning how to become a better wife and mother yourself, but you are learning to support yourself and your family in a worthwhile career in case you must be the breadwinner.

The authors adopted language that reinforced racial and ethnic hierarchies. Employers are women or ladies, employees "girls." The section on "how to act on the job" illustrates how racial domination in the employer's home operates on a daily basis. Mexican household workers are instructed to act out the "non-person" role that Erving Goffman described: "The classic type of non-person in our society . . . is defined by both performers and audience as someone who isn't there." Thus, Mexican maids are to be invisible: "Give them privacy with one another and with their friends, but be available when they call you." "Be considerate by not playing the radio or television loud when people are talking or reading. Run the noisy appliances when no one is around to be disturbed." The most condescending and racist section in the book is one called "how to look on the job," subtitled "cleanliness":

> if you stay clean, you will not only look better, but feel better. Your employer will show you where she wants you to bathe. She will want you to take a bath or shower regularly,

and wash your hands with soap. You will be furnished a washcloth and towel for your own use.

The manual specifies the occasions when the maid should wash her hands: "after you use the toilet," "after you use your handkerchief," "before you handle dishes, food, or other utensils in the kitchen," "after handling pets," "before you pick up the baby," and "before you handle the baby's clothes or things." The maid should provide her own toilet articles, particularly deodorant, however, sanitary napkins will be provided by the "lady of the house." No explanation is given for this curious division of toiletries. Perhaps the employer can use Kotex to keep track of her employee's menstrual cycle and dismiss her if she becomes pregnant.

Your Maid from Mexico is a distillation of a century of management techniques Anglo housewives used to manipulate Mexican domestic workers. Employers learn how to maneuver employees into doing more work through gifts, tips, and symbolic generosity: "Deeds of loyalty and sympathy are so much more important than words. You will always be rewarded, and you will find that they will help you as well when *you* need help." The employee is assured that the employer "will probably give you many things *she wants you to have* [emphasis added]." Domestics are told to expect extra work and "to do small favors for house-guests, such as light laundry or pressing or even serving coffee in the bedroom in the morning." In payment for the extra work, they may receive a gift or money.

The maid's rights as a worker never appear. The discussion on extra work, which includes caring for special guests and the sick, does not advocate additional pay. Instead, the worker is told to ingratiate herself in hopes of tips or emotional rewards. Of course, the section on "the man of the house" makes no reference to sexual harassment, a common problem particularly among live-in domestics. This is a major omission in a manual about an occupation plagued with sexual stereotypes of the worker "as sexual initiator for the young males in the family," and "as object of the fantasies of the more mature males." The section covering "accident prevention at home" discusses safety in the home but makes no mention of health insurance for the worker.

Your Maid from Mexico is not a historical artifact. Two recent publications aimed at Anglo homemakers hiring Spanish-speaking maids have been widely circulated throughout the Southwest. Apron Pocket Press sold 100,000 copies of *Home Maid Spanish*, which instructed monolingual English speaking employers how to train their Mexican maids. The manual consists of introductory phrases for informing the worker where the local Catholic Church is, a list of her days off, and detailed instructions on how to do the work. Instructions to the maid include thirteen different sets for the bedroom and guidelines for child care that entail picking up after the children. Tasks include polishing the silver and doing the marketing. In the 1980s, Linda Wolf published a similar book, entitled *Tell-A-Maid*, aimed at Los Angeles area employers and an estimated 100,000 Spanish-speaking household workers. A hit with homemakers, *Tell-A-Maid* consists of twenty-eight pages of Spanish and English clip-out phrases that can be left throughout the employer's home as a method of communication.

Given the level of servitude expressed in *Your Maid from Mexico*, it is not surprising to discover that Chicanas leave the occupation as soon as other job opportunities became available. Chicanas seek industry and office jobs because domestic service lacks any opportunity for advancement and because the work is monotonous with long and irregular hours. More importantly, even though Chicanas and Mexican immigrants are usually hired for low-level and unskilled factory jobs, employers outside domestic service do not demand the same level of deference and servility. As David Katzman explained: "Others held it in low regard because of those who performed the work—immigrants in cities, blacks in the South, women everywhere. Many women considered it degrading because it was women's work, done by unskilled poorly educated women who couldn't find other work."

In Southwestern communities, as native-born Chicanas found other employment, Mexican immigrant women filled positions in domestic service. But working conditions of Chicana and Mexican immigrant domestics tend to be quite different. Since the 1940s, the trend in domestic service has been toward day work; however, live-in conditions are still common among immigrant women. Moreover, Mexican immigrants have not entirely replaced Chicanas in domestic service because limited job opportunities have locked many Chicanas into the occupation.

Mexican immigrant women tend to predominate in larger cities, particularly along the border. Researchers estimate that anywhere from 18,000 to 26,000 domestics are employed in private residences in El Paso. In El Paso and other areas near the border, labor is so cheap that most middle-class families have at least one servant, and some also employ a laundress, nursemaid and yardman. Although average wages for undocumented workers in all positions are well below the minimum wage, domestic workers are paid the least. Sasha Lewis reported that in the 1970's the highest-paid underground jobs were found in the construction industry, where undocumented men workers made an average of $2.98 per hour. Undocumented women domestic workers earned an average of $1.63 per hour.

Household workers in El Paso's suburbs include both commuter maids with green cards and undocumented Mexicanas who dodge *la Migra* (the Border Patrol and the INS agents) as they cross the border. The extent of economic interdependency appeared in March of 1979, when Mexican nationals blockaded the bridge between Mexico and the United States to protest *la Migra's* deportation of some 140 maids. Lewis described the incident as the "strongest border protest against the U.S. in recent memory" and noted that "some of the Mexican border towns seem to have only one reason for being where they are: to supply the U.S. with cheap temporary workers. They supply the maids for Juarez, who earn enough money in El Paso to support their families."

In 1983, the *El Paso Herald-Post* published a report called "The Border," which included an article on domestics entitled "Mexican Maids: El Paso's Worst-Kept Secret." Journalists Michael Quintanilla and Peter Copeland interviewed maids, housewives, government officials, academic experts, and social workers on both sides of the border in an attempt to uncover the plight of domestics in El Paso: "While no figures are available on how many maids work in El Paso, there may well be more maids per home in the city than anywhere else in the nation. The reason is the low wages and shortage of jobs in Juarez. At $40 plus room and board a week, many El Pasoans can afford them, not just the rich."

Maids in El Paso receive little, if any, vacation and no workmen's compensation, health benefits or retirement pension. Live-in domestics usually receive no more than forty dollars a week. Day workers rarely receive minimum wage. Employers commonly threaten to deport undocumented domestics if they refuse to do more work, reject sexual advances, or attempt to return home. Isabel Garcia-Medina recalled an employer who threatened to call the immigration when she refused "to clean her house and iron two big plastic bags full of clothes—do everything for $5." She responded by pulling out her resident alien card and telling the employer to call whomever she wanted. However, the fear of deportation serves to silence many undocumented workers.

Across the board, the income of domestic workers is below the federal poverty level. Thus, in 1978, the wages for a sample of 583,000 African American household workers averaged $2,729, slightly below the poverty level of $2,884. Moreover, these wages did not include social security, health insurance, or other benefits. Altogether, 54 percent of women reported incomes below the poverty level; a majority were heads of household. Sherrie Rossoudji and Susan Rainey reported that Mexican immigrants employed as household workers earned less than ten dollars a day. In her study of Mexican immigrant women in California, Pierrette Hondagneu-Sotelo found that domestics were paid between minimum wage and fifteen dollars an hour. Leslie Salzinger found the hourly wage to fluctuate between five and ten dollars an hour for day work and one and three thousand dollars a month for live-in domestic work among Central American immigrant women employed through cooperatives in the Bay area.

|||||||||||||||||||||||||||||||||||||||||||||||||||||||||||||||||||||||||||||

Chapter 85

Three Perspectives on Workplace Harassment of Women of Color

Maria L. Ontiveros

For women of color, sexual harassment is rarely, if ever, about sex or sexism alone; it is also about race. For us, racial epithets are spoken in sexist terms, and sexual or sexist comments target our race and our culture. Marcia Gillespie, speaking for African-American women, but with words applicable for many other women of color, wrote,

> We say, I am a Black Woman, I cannot separate my race from my sex, cannot separate racism from sexism. They are rarely separate, never indivisible. So don't ask me to choose, I cannot; I am myself, I am not you. Nor will I let you choose for me. And I will not let you pretend that racism and sexism are not inseparable issues in all of our lives.[1]

This indivisibility was noted by early victims of workplace harassment who, when they were asked if they were filing racial or sexual harassment claims, responded that they could not tell. While everyone agrees that sexual harassment is about sexism and power, for us it is also about race and culture. From the viewpoint of the harasser, women of color appear less powerful, less likely to complain, and the embodiment of particular notions of sexuality. From the perspective of the women, attitudes in their community and lessons learned in their culture may make it more difficult for them to respond forcefully to discrimination. Finally, the judicial system's perspective on both women of color and relationships between men and women of color often influences the outcome of such cases.

The Harasser

Since workplace harassment is an exercise of power, women of color serve as likely targets because they are the least powerful participants in the workplace. Unlike

From *Three Perspectives on Workplace Harassment of Women of Color,* 23 GOLDEN GATE U. L. REV. 817 (1993). Originally published in the *Golden Gate University Law Review.* Reprinted by permission.

white women, they are not privileged by their race. Unlike men of color, they are not privileged by their gender. Although a white man might harass any woman, a man of color is not likely to feel that he has the prerogative to harass a white woman because of his lack of racial status or because he knows he could be subject to the harsh, vengeful treatment society has visited in such cases. If the harasser is a man of color, the victim is likely to be a woman of color. Harassers may also prefer those women of color, such as Latinas and Asian-American women, whom they view as passive and unlikely to complain.

Additionally, racism and sexism can blend together in the mind of the harasser and form an inseparable whole. The types of statements used and actions taken incorporate the unique characteristics of women of color, subjecting each race and ethnicity to its own cruel stereotype of sexuality. Harassment of African-American women incorporates images of slavery, degradation, sexual availability, and natural lasciviousness. In *Brooms v. Regal Tube Co.*, the defendant showed the victim several photocopies of racist pornography including bestiality, gave her pornographic pictures depicting an interracial act of sodomy and told her that she was hired for the purposes indicated in the photograph because it showed the "talent" of a black woman.[2] In *Continental Can Co. v. Minnesota*, the harasser told his African-American victim that "he wished slavery days would return so that he could sexually train her and she would be his bitch."[3]

A parallel stereotype portrays Asian-American women as exotic, submissive, and naturally erotic. This attitude most likely grows out of the 1870s racist portrayal of all Asian women as prostitutes, seeking to enter the United States to engage in "criminal and demoralizing purposes."[4] Unfortunately, several examples illustrate that these historical stereotypes survive and affect women today. Hearings on sexual harassment sponsored by the California Women's Caucus included the testimony of an "Asian construction worker whose co-workers shoved a hammer between her legs, who was taunted with racial slurs, who was repeatedly grabbed on her breasts while installing overhead fixtures, and who was asked whether it was true that Asian women's vaginas were sideways."[5]

In another case, a young Japanese-American receptionist's harasser told her he had a foot fetish, stroked and kissed her feet, and kissed the nape of her neck. He told her, "I thought Oriental women get aroused by kissing the back of the neck."[6] Finally, a Taiwanese-American banking executive won a settlement from a Los Angeles bank because, among other things, a co-worker said that she was best suited to a job as a "high-class call girl" and the bank's president once introduced her as "vice president in the real estate and sex department."[7]

Like African-American and Asian-American women, society considers Latinas naturally sexual, in this instance evoking the image of the "hot-blooded" Latin. In addition, Latinas are often perceived as readily available and accessible for sexual use, with few recriminations for abusing them. Sonoma County District Attorney Gene Tunney has seen this perception become reality. In commenting on one case which typifies this situation, he stated, "[W]e've become aware of people who have imported Mexican women, usually from rural villages in the middle of nowhere, and brought them here for sexual reasons. My suspicion is there is a lot of it going on."[8]

Women of Color as Members of the
Minority Community

The community in which a woman lives and the culture in which she grows up influence her reaction to workplace harassment. For example, some women of color have been raised to become passive, defer to men, and not bring attention to themselves. This may be particularly true in the traditional Asian value system that includes obedience, familial interest, fatalism, and self-control, and which tends to foster submissiveness, passivity, pessimism, timidness, inhibition, and adaptiveness. Similar barriers may face Latinas growing up in a "macho" culture. For these women to resist an act aggressively or to pursue a legal remedy requires confronting those cultural issues. Additionally, many women wrestle with feelings that they will be blamed for the harassment. For Asian-American women, philosophies like "Shikata ga nai"[9] and "If something happens to you, it is your fault for putting yourself in that position" exacerbate the victim's guilt and self-doubt. One Mexican immigrant victim of harassment, when asked why she did not report it earlier, told a rape counselor that "a woman who is raped in Mexico is the one at fault, maybe because her parents didn't watch her."[10] Upon learning of the harassment, her husband denounced her as a permanent shame to her family.

Immigrant or illegal status and a lack of understanding of their legal rights further handicap women of color. Marie DeSantis, a community advocate for Sonoma County Women Against Rape, notes that immigrant women are often victims of what she terms "rape by duress."[11] They do not report such crimes because they are too intimidated by their fear of deportation, ignorance of their legal rights, and presumed power of their employers. One Mexican housekeeper explained that because she was here illegally and was paid by her employer, she had no place else to go. She worried that "He could have cut me up in a million pieces, and no one would have known."[12]

The failure to understand their legal rights is further compounded by the differing ideas of sexuality which permeate different cultures. Sex is discussed less frequently and openly by Asian-American women; sexual harassment is therefore not something to be discussed either. In fact, no words for "sexual harassment" exist in Japanese, Mandarin, or Cantonese. In cultures that do not even have words to encompass the concept of sexual harassment, it is predictable that many women in those cultures are less likely to recognize harassing behavior when it occurs. Finally, victims recognize that accusations of workplace harassment will reflect badly on their cultures and likely bring adverse community response. For example, one Latina community worker was urged by two female co-workers (who had also been harassed and remained silent) not to report an incident of harassment "for fear that exposing the perpetrators would undermine their movement and embarrass the Latino community."[13] This adverse community response may be especially painful for women of color, to whom community is particularly important.

The Legal System

Once an incident of workplace harassment becomes a lawsuit, the legal system provides the final construct of the event in at least three ways: judges and juries may tend to disbelieve what the women of color say; the dominant culture's construct of their sexuality influences the cases' outcomes; and the entire justice system misperceives relationships between men and women of color, thereby excusing discriminatory acts by men of color.

For example, a Mexican immigrant woman told the Sonoma District Attorney that she believed her employer was "a doctor . . . and that is a title of some esteem and high position in Mexico. . . . If you're a peasant girl, and it's your word against his, you don't have a chance."[14] African-American women also have a hard time convincing the legal system that they are telling the truth. Judges have been known to tell jurors to take a black woman's testimony "with a grain of salt."[15] A recent study of jury members in rape trials indicated the lack of credibility given black women's testimony. One juror said of black rape victims, "you can't believe everything they say; they're known to exaggerate the truth."[16]

Penalties are often light because women of color are believed to have been "asking for it," to not be greatly affected by the abuse, or simply to not be worthy of the same legal protection afforded the rest of society. One study concluded that defendants who assault African-American women are less likely to receive jail time than those who assault white women. Another found that assailants of African-American women receive an average sentence of two years, compared to one of ten years for defendants who assault white women. One juror, sitting in the case of a rape of a black pre-teen, stated "being from that neighborhood she probably wasn't a virgin anyway."[17]

A final problem occurs when the legal system misinterprets relationships between men and women of color. The so-called "cultural defense" has been used by people of color to explain why their action is understandable and even excusable in their culture, even when it offends American values. In *People v. Chen*,[18] a Chinese man, after learning of his wife's adultery, killed her by hitting her on the head eight times with a hammer. The defense argued that, in traditional Chinese culture, a man is often driven to violence upon hearing of his wife's infidelity, but, unlike this defendant, is stopped by someone in the community before he can actually hurt her. The court took this defense into account and sentenced him to five years' probation. In another case, two Korean youths were acquitted on the charge of rape after arguing that the victim, a Korean woman, tacitly consented to the rape because her visit to bars with the men would communicate consent in Korea.[19] Although many protested that these rulings misinterpreted Chinese and Korean social norms and views of justice, the legal system accepted them, thereby devaluing women of color in the process.

Following the Hill-Thomas hearings, the issue of sexual harassment has risen to the forefront of social consciousness, yet sexual harassment only describes part of what happened to Anita Hill and continues to happen to many other women. Race or national origin affects the way a woman is perceived by the harasser, her ability to respond to the incident, and the judicial system's eventual resolution of the matter. We need to reconstruct our perception of sexual harassment to include that of women of color. This transformation must take place because the elements of a sexual harassment case are different from and more onerous than those in a racial harassment case. Treating these cases as sexual harassment, then, not only misstates the dynamic but further disadvantages these women. Such a solution could arrive either by modifying the rules governing sexual harassment or by creating a new cause of action prohibiting discrimination against women of color as such.

This reform would address some of the problems discussed here, but true solutions are not so simple because the problems and interrelationships are so complex. Deeply held notions of race, gender, identity, sexuality, and power must come in for reexamination. Furthermore, this must take place both within and across cultural and class boundaries. Only in this way will we be able to answer the challenges raised by the Hill-Thomas hearings and, as Marcia Gillespie said, no longer pretend that racism and sexism are neatly compartmentalized issues in all of our lives.

NOTES

1. Marcia A. Gillespie, *We Speak in Tongues,* Ms., Jan.–Feb. 1992, at 41–42.

2. 881 F.2d 412, 417 (7th Cir.1989).

3. 297 N.W.2d 241, 246 (1980).

4. Sucheta Mazumdar, *General Introduction: A Woman-Centered Perspective on Asian American History,* in MAKING WAVES: AN ANTHOLOGY OF WRITINGS BY AND ABOUT ASIAN AMERICAN WOMEN 1, 2–3 (1989).

5. Kimberlè Crenshaw, *Race, Gender and Sexual Harassment,* 65 S. CAL. L. REV. 1467, 1474 (1992).

6. California Dept. of Fair Employment and Housing v. Guill, et al., (1989) FEHC Oct. No. 89–15 (CEB 11). Modified on remand, (1991) FEHC Feb. No. 91-16 (CEB 10).

7. Kim Murphy, *Bank Will Pay $400,000 in Sexual Harassment Suit,* L.A. TIMES, Oct. 7, 1986, Part 2, at 1.

8. Carla Marinucci, *Despair Drove Her to Come Forward,* S.F. EXAMINER, Jan. 10, 1993, at A11.

9. Japanese for "it can't be helped."

10. Marinucci.

11. *Id.*

12. *Id.*

13. Crenshaw, at 1474.

14. Marinucci.

15. Crenshaw, at 1470.

16. *Id.*

17. *Id.*

18. No. 87-7774 (N.Y. Sup. Ct. Mar. 21, 1989).

19. Melissa Spatz, *A "Lesser" Crime: A Comparative Study of Legal Defenses for Men Who Kill Their Wives,* 24 COLUM. J.L. & SOC. PROBS., 597, 625 n.200 (1991).

Chapter 86

‖‖‖

What's in a Name?

Retention and Loss of the Maternal Surname

Yvonne M. Cherena Pacheco

Where is our history?
What are the names washed down the sewer
In the septic flood?
I pray to the rain
Give me back my rituals
Give back truth
Return the remnants of my identity
Bathe me in self-discovered knowledge
Identify my ancestors who have existed suppressed
Invoke their spirits with power . . .

—Sandra Maria Esteves[1]

Consider the difficulties that confront millions of Latino citizens and residents of the United States in their attempts to gain recognition of their complete names, and the impact of those difficulties for Latinas. Human beings generally receive names within their first days of life. Traditions regarding naming vary considerably from one culture to another, reflecting ancestral, religious, or linguistic customs. In any given state, the traditional naming patterns of the dominant culture or cultures will appear in the laws and the official behavior of that state.

The names originally given to a child usually reflect her parentage or lineage, clan membership, place of origin, as well as individual identity. Whatever the tradition within which the child is named, her name serves as the cornerstone of her identity as she grows toward maturity. Naming issues arise when the desire of the individual to be known by a particular name comes into conflict with social practice. Naming issues have a long history in North America, dating to at least colonial times. Enslaved

From *Latino Surnames: Formal and Informal Forces in the United States Affecting the Retention and Use of the Maternal Surname,* 18 T. Marshall L. Rev. 1 (1992). Originally published in the *Thurgood Marshall Law Review.* Reprinted by permission.

Africans routinely were renamed by those who bought them, while Native American names quickly came to be shortened, mispronounced or translated into English or French. With the dominance of Anglo-Saxon culture well established from the beginning of the republic, European immigrants from other traditions had similar experiences of renaming, particularly if they hailed from Southern or Eastern Europe. What all of the targets of these practices had in common was their relative powerlessness, and the desire of those representing the dominant culture to force them to conform.

Very little has changed over the years regarding the value that an individual places on his name. Poet Sandra Maria Esteves seeks the true names of her ancestors in order to be able to name herself as an individual. In recent decades, women inspired by the feminist movement have asserted their right to retain their birth names after marriage or to resume their use upon divorce or widowhood. At the same time, many couples have opted to combine their surnames after marriage to form a new, hyphenated version which is then borne by their offspring.

In the case of Latinos, the principal naming conflict centers on the use or non-use of a two-part surname representing the lineages of both parents. More precisely, the question is whether, as a practical matter, an individual living in the United States who has been named in the traditional Latin American style can retain both parental surnames or must submit to use of the father's surname only. This issue holds special poignance for the Latina, because the application of the Anglo-cultural tradition to a traditional Latin surname eradicates the maternal or female identity of the individual.

Latin American Naming Tradition: The Form and the Substance

The Latina's name is made up of one or more given names together with a two-part surname (consisting of a patronymic and a matronymic), which is more than the traditional Anglo-American first name, middle name, and single surname combination. For the Latina, both parts of the two-part surname are essential in making her entire family name. The involuntary dropping of either part constitutes an unwanted name change. Many American individuals of all traditions prefer to use their complete name—the one given at birth, or during christening or formal naming. Among these are perhaps millions of Latinas in the United States, including both those who came to the United States from Latin America (i.e., Mexico, Central America, South America, and the Caribbean) and those born on the mainland.

The Latina positions both the paternal name and maternal name, respectively, in the place generally reserved in the North American custom for the single last name. For example, if an individual's name is Maria Iris Rivera Sancho then the name is ordered as follows:

(1) Maria, the given name or *nombre;*
(2) Iris, the *segundo nombre* or "second given name," not considered a middle name;
(3) Rivera, her paternal surname, known as the *primer apellido,* which translates as the "first last name"; and

(4) Sancho, the maternal surname, known as the *segundo apellido,* the "second last name."

The positioning indicates that Maria Iris is the daughter of a father named Rivera and a mother named Sancho. Sometimes the letter 'y' (as the word 'and') separates the *primer apellido* and the *segundo apellido,* e.g. Maria Iris Rivera y Sancho. However, each surname is considered part of the family name; one is not subordinate to the other. The position of the *primer* or *segundo apellido* indicates the paternal and the maternal order respectively. The Latina's birth name is made up of two names; her complete surname is used as a unit. In fact, until about 150 years ago, Spanish women did not take their husband's name after marriage. Today some of them retain both the mother's and the father's *apellidos.* For example, Sra. Leticia Maria Rios-vega de Borrero's name indicates: her *primer nombre* is Leticia, *segundo nombre* Maria; her father's surname is Rios; her mother's surname is Vega; and she is married to one named Borrero.

It is not a novelty for an individual to use both paternal and maternal surnames nor is it an attribute solely belonging to one class, ethnic or racial group. In fact, by far the dominant custom throughout all of Latin America and Spain is to use both paternal and maternal surnames. For the Latina it is important culturally that both surnames appear; they represent both families to which the individual belongs. As the family unit is central to the identity of the individual so, too, is the name that each family unit bears. By custom, the use of both surnames is essential to self-identification. The two names appear in all official documents such as birth certificates, baptismal certificates, marriage licenses, drivers' licenses, death certificates, professional licenses, etc. Not all Latinos may be interested in using both paternal and maternal surnames but my purpose is to give that choice to all Latinos.

Involuntary Name Changes: How and Why They Occur

The Latino who emigrates to the United States finds himself caught between these two naming traditions—desiring to keep his Latino tradition but facing a different dominant practice.

Although tradition or custom is not necessarily law, the custom of using the first, middle, and surname in the United States inhibits other name practices or at best ignores them. The customary becomes the familiar, the expected, the appropriate, and the legitimate, even if it does not take on the full force of law. No law in the United States restricts the use of surnames or precludes the Latina's right to cling to her full, original surname. Likewise, no official policy or other formal directive consciously sheds the *segundo apellido* or requires a Latina to depart from full adherence to familial traditions.

Yet, cultural supremacy, bureaucratic laziness, racism and simple ignorance combine to make it exceptionally difficult for the Latino, as a practical matter, to obtain recognition for both last names. The United States' tradition of one surname is so well-entrenched that any deviation from it is immediately deemed awkward and odd, and subtle—but pervasive and quite powerful—forces will operate to change it. Actions by governmental units, by large and small private business organizations, by individual people—and ultimately by the Latina herself—will tend to drop the matronymic half of the surname, squeezing the Latina into the Anglo-Saxon mold.

How does American society accomplish this? Federal and state governments prefer using a single surname, despite lack of any statutory proscription against more. Administrative personnel may view those with multi-part surnames as un-American. Government forms may have insufficient space to register a complete Latino name, and the instructions and format of the form may suggest that only a single word should be entered into the place for "last name." Teachers may regularly refer to students by only a single last name. Military officers may likewise assume that a single word can suffice for a Latino soldier or sailor, as for an Anglo-Saxon, and the second last name is omitted. On alphabetical lists, on court papers, on government notices, the Latino can regularly anticipate inclusion of only the first half of his surname. No official rules require the shortening, but every Latino person in the United States has experienced it, and many have now grudgingly accepted the official system.

Even more than governmental action, the practices of private business and individuals reinforce the social norm of using a single last name. Telephone companies, banks, and credit agencies all act as if they expect every customer to adhere to the Anglo-Saxon style. If anyone objects, he could probably succeed, but many will not "rock the boat" when confronting a large, powerful organization. In applying for a job or for an apartment, a special incentive presses to conform. To the Latino, it may seem more prudent to go along with the popular culture, to acquiesce in the name change, even at the cost of cultural identity.

The Impact of Involuntary Name Changes

Three types of problems accompany the unwanted deletion of the second last name. Sometimes, these can be comical. But more often, they are serious and traumatic with long-range effects in economic, cultural, and personal terms.

Costs of Being Different

Costs are associated with simply being different, being reminded—every time someone says or writes your name—that your heritage derives from a culture unlike that of the numerically and economically dominant groups in the country.

First is the economic, social, and political disadvantage in perpetuating an identity at odds with the North American norm. Because peoples of British background were the principal early colonizers of the United States, a prejudice developed in favoring Americans with English-rooted names. Job opportunities benefited those with names that were identifiable as English, and early immigrants, such as the Irish, the Italians, and the Eastern Europeans, felt the effects of discrimination in the struggle for employment. Eventually this discrimination lessened within the second and third generations as they have grown more homogeneous, especially socioeconomically. Although many immigrants kept their family names, significant numbers succumbed to the pressures of a name change.

Second, costs are associated with going in the opposite direction: attempting to conform to an Anglo-American society, assimilate into its practices, and adopt its naming patterns. When an individual simplifies or streamlines the family name, she may do so after assessment of the effects it will have on the individual and her culture. This assessment may include focusing on the origins of the family name, how the individual may see herself connected to that name, what impact changing the name or not being able to continue to use the name may have on the individual, and how the individual sees herself and therefore how she chooses to name herself.

Third, use of one's own name—and the misuse, modification, or appropriation by others—speaks volumes about "control" and "empowerment." An individual needs to rely on his sense of self and enjoy the privacy that brings self-control and self-empowerment. For the individual to decide for himself what he should be named is a matter of privacy. The right as an individual to one's privacy is encompassed in the term "personhood." Brandeis points out in *Olmstead v. United States*[2] that the makers of the Constitution held dear the "pursuit of happiness." They recognized the significance of man's spiritual nature, of his feelings and of his intellect. They knew that only a part of the pain, pleasure, and satisfaction of life are to be found in material things. They sought to protect Americans in their beliefs, their thoughts, their emotions, and their sensations. They conferred, as against the Government, the right to be let alone—the most comprehensive of rights and the one most valued by civilized men. To protect that right, every unjustifiable intrusion by the Government upon the privacy of the individual, whatever the means employed, must be deemed a violation of the Fourth Amendment.

Costs of Not Being Accepted

The Latino and the Latino naming tradition are not merely treated as being "different" by the dominant society; they are treated as "inferior," subject to capricious, unwanted alteration to fit the expectations of mainstream society. Both racism and sexism play a role in this operation. Most members of the dominant society may respond that they are not racists, because they have never intended to treat those from the non-white races discriminatorily. However, Americans who share a common historical and cultural heritage harbor many ideas, attitudes, and beliefs that attach significance to an individual's race and induce negative feelings and opinions about non-whites.[3] Any unconscious racism or negative feelings towards Latinos may affect how members of the dominant society view the Latino name and whether or not they may "unconsciously" modify the name. By the same token, a society that has valued the male name more than the female is asked to value the way in which both the Latino and Latina prefer to use their name. In addition to the Latina, the Latino becomes a victim of sexism, when he is denied the usage of his maternal surname.

Costs of Being Compelled to Conform—Invisibility

Unfortunately, not much has been written about the plight of the women and men who have not been able to completely use the names which identify them. They have been made invisible. In Ralph Ellison's *Invisible Man,* the protagonist reflects:

> It is sometimes advantageous to be unseen, although it is most often rather wearing on the nerves. Then too, you're constantly being bumped against by those of poor vision. Or again, you often doubt if you really exist. You wonder whether you aren't simply a phantom in other people's minds. . . . It's when you feel like this that, out of resentment, you begin to bump people back.[4]

Not having her complete name recognized is part of a greater reality of not being seen, for the Latina struggles with a denial of her identity that goes far beyond the loss of a name. The Latina remains invisible each time her life experience and her input are considered inferior, when her diversity and culture are not welcomed, and when she is discriminated against because she does not belong and her opinion does not matter.

It is never easy to reform a social practice that is as widespread, as subtle, and as basic as the dominant United States practice of insisting upon single-word surnames. This form of repression is so elusive and insidious that few people are even aware of it. This story boasts no overt villain, no blatantly racist government actions, no xeno-phobic community leaders attempting to resist Latino surnames, not even very many scrupulous clerks and form-filers who object to anything out of the ordinary. Instead, the Latina naming issue presents an unusually subtle phenomenon, which will have to be dealt with through concerted action by three different sets of actors.

First, the government will have to play a role. No name-purist statutes remain on the books, but official actions are still too unfriendly to the Latino tradition. Per-haps a persuasive argument for freedom in naming is that the government has other means of identifying an individual—i.e., use of social security number and the date and place of birth, together with the use of the family name. Additionally, if the use of a complete family name causes fear of an administrative nightmare, then the solu-tion lies in upgrading data through the use of computer rather than manual collec-tion of journal entries in books.

Second, society as a whole will have to be more accommodating. An imperfect "melting pot," society can do more to accommodate this form of diversity. Telephone books could regularly carry two last names. Newspapers could alter their conven-tions, and start referring to Latinos by two last names. All of us can be more aware of the Latino's preference and more respectful of it. Finally, and most importantly, the Latina herself must take the lead in promoting use of both surnames. She must clearly indicate her name preference to the world at large, consistently adopting the full Latin tradition and requesting that others do so, too. This will require effort, pa-tience, and persistence—and quite often she will have to educate others about the reasons for her choice.

NOTES

1. Sandra Maria Esteves, *It Is Raining Today,* in Tropical Rains: A Bilingual Downpour 5 (1984).

2. 277 U.S. 438 (1928), overruled, Katz v. United States, 389 U.S. 347, 352–53 (1967).

3. Charles R. Lawrence, III, *The Id, the Ego, and Equal Protection: Reckoning with Unconscious Racism,* 39 Stan. L. Rev. 317, 322 (1987).

4. Ralph Ellison, Invisible Man 3 (1989).

From the Editors *Issues and Comments*

Is a Latina woman essentially a woman, or a member of her racial group? That is, which affiliation is more vital to her identity, or is the answer neither?

You are a Latina. An expedition of Space Traders offers you one of two pills that, introduced into the water system, will solve either racism or sexism permanently and completely. Which practice causes you more misery, and which pill would you choose? If you were a Latino, which pill would you choose?

Is Latino culture homophobic and even harder on gays and lesbians than white culture is? If so, why?

Can religion liberate Latinas without oppressing them?

Why don't Latina clerical workers expect equal sharing of work in their households, as do their professional and blue collar counterparts?

Do women, especially women of color, suffer forms of violence that we simply do not call by that name?

Considering the shortage of funding for domestic violence programs, what changes can advocates make to ensure that they are meeting the needs of Latinas?

Why do some Latino men affect a super-macho persona or stance? Why do some stereotypes of minority men—for example, hapless Mexican clown or buffoon—depict them as desexed neuters? Are the reasons possibly related?

Should Latino rappers be encouraged to change their lyrics to be more respectful of women? How? What happens if they don't?

Is the high fertility rate of Latinos a threat to society?

Do Latina maids need a union? A few good lawyers? In addition to the examples in *Maid in the U.S.A.*, recall the story of Maria Elena in part 6.

Do black and Latina women suffer a "double whammy," or is their status sometimes an advantage in that employers reap a two-for-one benefit in hiring them and also view them as less threatening than men of color?

Are illegal immigrants at increased risk of sexual oppression because of their fear that reporting the crime could lead to deportation? If so, is the solution that the police overlook their illegal status when immigrants report crimes against them?

If a practice is sexual harassment in one culture but not another, should the law punish it anyway?

Is it racism if a government official, agency, or the phone book discourages Latino double surnames? Is it sexism in that the name invariably cut is that of the mother?

Suggested Readings

Arriola, Elvia R. "Gendered Inequality: Lesbians, Gays, and Feminist Legal Theory." 9 *Berkeley Women's L.J.* 103 (1994).

———. "Voices from the Barbed Wires of Despair: Women in the Maquiladoras: Latina Critical Legal Theory, and Gender at the U.S.–Mexico Border." 49 *DePaul L. Rev.* 729 (2000).

Between Borders: Essays on Mexicana/Chicana History, edited by Adelaida R. Del Castillo. Encino, Calif.: Floricanto Press, 1990.

Beyond Stereotypes: The Critical Analysis of Chicana Literature, edited by María Herrera-Sobek. Binghamton, N.Y.: Bilingual Press, 1985.

Blackwelder, Julia Kirk. *Women of the Depression: Caste and Culture in San Antonio, 1929–1939.* College Station: Texas A&M University Press, 1984.

Bonilla-Santiago, Gloria. *Breaking Ground and Barriers: Hispanic Women Developing Effective Leadership.* San Diego, Calif.: Marin Publications, 1992.

Building with Our Hands: New Directions in Chicana Studies, edited by Adela de la Torre and Beatriz M. Pesquera. Berkeley: University of California Press, 1993.

Castillo, Ana. *The Mixquiahuala Letters.* Binghamton, N.Y.: Bilingual Review Press, 1986.

Cervantes, Lorna Dee. *Emplumada.* Pittsburgh: University of Pittsburgh Press, 1981.

Chicana Creativity and Criticism: New Frontiers in American Literature, edited by María Herrera-Sobek and Helena María Viramontes. Rev. ed. Albuquerque: University of New Mexico Press, 1996.

Chicana Critical Issues, edited by Norma Alarcon et al. Berkeley, Calif.: Third Woman Press, 1993.

Chicana Feminisms: A Critical Reader, edited by Gabriela F. Arredondo, Aída Hurtado, Norma Klahn, Olga Nájera Ramírez, and Patricia Zavella. Durham, N.C.: Duke University Press, 2003.

Chicana Feminist Thought: The Basic Historical Writings, edited by Alma Garcia. New York: Routledge, 1997.

Chicana Lesbians: The Girls Our Mothers Warned Us About, edited by Carla Trujillo. Berkeley, Calif.: Third Woman Press, 1991.

Chicana Voices: Intersections of Class, Race, and Gender, edited by Teresa Cordova et al. Austin: Center for Mexican American Studies, University of Texas, 1990.

Chicanas in the 80's: Unsettled Issues, edited by Mujeres en Marcha. Berkeley: Chicano Studies Library Publications Unit, University of California, 1983.

Compañeras: Latina Lesbians, An Anthology, edited by Juanita Ramos. New York: Routledge, 1994.

Coto, Virginia P. "LUCHA, The Struggle for Life: Legal Services for Battered Immigrant Women." 53 *U. Miami L. Rev.* 749 (1999).

Delgado, Richard. "Rodrigo's Sixth Chronicle: Intersections, Essences and the Dilemma of Social Reform." 68 *N.Y.U. L. Rev.* 639 (1993).

Deutsch, Sarah. *No Separate Refuge: Culture, Class, and Gender on an Anglo-Hispanic Frontier in the American Southwest, 1880–1940.* New York: Oxford University Press, 1987.

Diaz-Cotto, Juanita. *Gender, Ethnicity, and the State: Latina and Latino Prison Politics.* Albany: State University of New York Press, 1996.

Díaz-Stevens, Ana María, and Anthony M. Stevens-Arroyo. *Recognizing the Latino Resurgence in U.S. Religion.* Boulder, Colo.: Westview Press, 1997.

Espinosa, Gaston. *Rethinking Latino(a) Religion and Identity.* Cleveland, Ohio: Pilgrim Press, 2006.

Gándara, Patricia. *Over the Ivy Walls: Educational Mobility among Low Income Chicanos.* Albany: State University of New York Press, 1995.

García, Alma M. "The Development of Chicana Feminist Discourse, 1970–1980." 3 *Gender and Society* 217–38 (1989).

Gender on the Borderlands: The Frontiers Reader, edited by Antonia Casteñada, with Susan H. Armitage, Patricia Hart, and Karen Weathermon. Lincoln: University of Nebraska Press, 2007.

Gil, Rosa Maria, and Carmen Inoa Vazquez. *The Maria Paradox: How Latinas Can Merge Old World Traditions with New World Self-Esteem*. New York: G. P. Putnam's Sons, 1996.

Girman, Chris. *Mucho Macho: Seduction, Desire, and the Homoerotic Lives of Latin Men*. New York: Routledge, 2005.

Gonzalez, Deena J. "Chicana Identity Matters." In *Culture and Difference: Critical Perspectives on the Bicultural Experience in the United States,* edited by Antonia Darder, 41–53. New York: Bergin & Garvey, 1995.

Gonzalez, Rosalinda M. "Chicanas and Mexican Immigrant Families 1920–1940: Women's Subordination and Family Exploitation." In *Decades of Discontent: The Women's Movement, 1920–1940,* edited by Lois Scharf and Joan M. Jensen, 59. Westport, Conn.: Greenwood Press, 1983.

Grillo, Trina. "Anti-Essentialism and Intersectionality: Tools to Dismantle the Master's House." 10 *Berkeley Women's L.J.* 16 (1995).

Gutiérrez, Elena R. *Fertile Matters: The Politics of Mexican-Origin Women's Reproduction*. Austin: University of Texas Press, 2008.

Gutiérrez, Ramón A. *When Jesus Came, the Corn Mothers Went Away: Marriage, Sexuality, and Power in New Mexico, 1500–1846*. Stanford, Calif.: Stanford University Press, 1991.

Gutman, Matthew. *The Meanings of Macho: Being a Man in Mexico City*. 2d ed. Berkeley: University of California Press, 2006.

Hawkins, Gladys, Jean Soper, and Jane Henry. *Your Maid from Mexico*. San Antonio, Tex.: Naylor, 1959.

Hernández-Truyol, Berta Esperanza. "The Gender Bend: Culture, Sex, and Sexuality: A LatCritical Human Rights Map of Latina/o Border Crossings." 83 *Ind. L.J.* 1292 (2008).

———. "Sex, Culture, and Rights: A Re/Conceptionalization of Violence for the Twenty-First Century." 60 *Alb. L. Rev.* 607 (1997).

Herrera-Sobek, María. *The Mexican Corrido: A Feminist Analysis*. Bloomington: Indiana University Press, 1990.

Hondagneu-Sotelo, Pierrette. *Domestica: Immigrant Workers Cleaning and Caring in the Shadows of Affluence*. Berkeley: University of California Press, 2001.

———. *Gendered Transitions: Mexican Experiences of Immigration*. Berkeley: University of California Press, 1994.

Hurtado, Aída. *Voicing Chicana Feminisms: Young Women Speak Out on Sexuality and Identity*. New York: New York University Press, 2003.

Iglesias, Elizabeth M. "Rape, Race, and Representation: The Power of Discourse, Discourses of Power, and the Reconstruction of Heterosexuality." 49 *Vand. L. Rev.* 869 (1996).

———. "Structures of Subordination: Women of Color at the Intersection of Title VII and the NLRA. Not!" 28 *Harv. C.R.–C.L L. Rev.* 395 (1993).

Isasi-Díaz, Ada María, and Yolanda Tarango. *Hispanic Women: Prophetic Voice in the Church*. Scranton, Penn.: Scranton University Press, 1988.

Johnson, Kevin R. "Racial Restrictions on Naturalization: The Recurring Intersection of Race and Gender in Immigration and Citizenship Law." 11 *Berkeley Women's L.J.* 142 (1996).

Katz, Susan Roberta. "Presumed Guilty: How Schools Criminalize Latino Youth." 24(4) *Social Justice* 77–96 (1997).

Latina Issues: Fragments of Historia(ella) (herstory), edited by Antoinette Sedillo López. New York: Routledge, 1999.

Latinas in the United States: A Historical Encyclopedia, edited by Vicki Ruíz and Virginia Sánchez Korrol. Bloomington: Indiana University Press, 2006.

Lebell, Sharon. *Naming Ourselves, Naming Our Children: Resolving the Last Name Dilemma.* Freedom, Calif.: Crossing Press, 1988.

Luna, Guadalupe T. "'This Land Belongs to Me': Chicanas, Land Grant Adjudication, and the Treaty of Guadalupe Hidalgo." 3 *Harv. Latino L. Rev.* 115 (1999).

Making Face, Making Soul/Haciendo Caras: Creative and Critical Perspectives by Women of Color, edited by Gloria Anzaldúa. San Francisco: Aunt Lute Foundation Books, 1990.

McFarland, Pancho. *Chicano Rap: Gender and Violence in the Postindustrial Barrio.* Austin: University of Texas Press, 2008.

Mirande, Alfredo. *Hombres y Machos: Masculinity and Latino Culture.* Boulder, Colo.: Westview Press, 1997.

Mirande, Alfredo, and Evangelina Enriquez. *La Chicana: The Mexican American Woman.* Chicago: University of Chicago Press, 1979.

Moore, Joan W. *Gangs, Drugs, and Prison in the Barrios of Los Angeles.* Philadelphia: Temple University Press, 1978.

———. *Going Down to the Barrio: Homeboys and Homegirls in Change.* Philadelphia: Temple University Press, 1991.

Muy Macho: Latino Men Confront Their Manhood, edited by Ray González. New York: Anchor Books, 1996.

Nabhan-Warren, Kristy. *The Virgin of El Barrio: Marian Apparitions, Catholic Evangelizing, and Mexican American Activism.* New York: New York University Press, 2005.

Now the Volcano: An Anthology of Latin American Gay Literature, edited by Winston Leyland. San Francisco: Gay Sunshine Press, 1979.

Old Masks, New Faces: Religion and Latino Identities, edited by Anthony M. Stevens-Arroyo and Gilbert R. Cadeña. New York: Bildner Center for Western Hemisphere Studies, 1995.

Ontiveros, Maria L. "Fictionalizing Harassment—Disclosing the Truth." 93 *Mich. L. Rev.* 1373 (1995).

———. "Rosa Lopez, David Letterman, Christopher Darden, and Me: Issues of Gender, Ethnicity, and Class in Evaluating Witness Credibility." 6 *Hastings Women's L J.* 135 (1995).

Paz, Octavio. *The Labyrinth of Solitude.* New York: Grove Press, 1961.

Pesquera, Beatriz M., and Denise Segura. "There Is No Going Back: Chicanas and Feminism." In *Chicana Critical Issues: Mujeres Activas En Letras Y Cambio Social,* edited by Norma Alarcon, 294. Berkeley, Calif.: Third Woman Press, 1993.

———. "With Quill and Torch: A Chicana Perspective on the American Women's Movement and Feminist Theories." In *Chicanas/Chicanos at the Crossroads: Social, Economic and Political Change*, edited by David R. Maciel and Isidro D. Ortiz, 231. Tucson: University of Arizona Press, 1996.

The Puerto Rican Woman: Perspectives on Culture, History and Society, edited by Edna Acosta-Bélen and Barbara R. Sjostrom. New York: Praeger, 1986.

Rivera, Jenny. "The Politics of Invisibility." 3 *Geo. J. Fighting Poverty* 61 (1995).

———. "The Violence against Women Act and the Construction of Multiple Consciousness in the Civil Rights and Feminist Movements." 4 *J. L. & Pol'y* 463 (1996).

Rodríguez, Juana María. *Queer Latinidad: Identity, Practices, Discursive Spaces.* New York: New York University Press, 2003.

Rodriguez, Luis J. *Always Running: La Vida Loca—Gang Days in L.A.* Willimantic, Conn.: Cubstone Press, 1993.

Rodriguez, Richard. *Next of Kin: The Family in Chicano/a Cultural Politics*. Durham, N.C.: Duke University Press, 2009.

Romany, Celina. "Ain't I a Feminist." 4 *Yale J. L. & Fem.* 23 (1991).

———. "Women as Aliens: A Feminist Critique of the Public/Private Distinction in International Human Rights Law." 6 *Harv. Hum. Rgts. J.* 87 (1993).

Romero, Mary. "Immigration, the Servant Problem, and the Legacy of the Domestic Labor Debate: 'Where Can You Find Good Help These Days!'" 53 *U. Miami L. Rev.* 1045 (1999).

———. *Maid in the U.S.A.* 10th anniv. ed. New York: Routledge, 2002.

Ruiz, Vicki L. "By the Day or Week: Mexicana Domestic Workers in El Paso." In *"To Toil the Livelong Day": America's Women at Work, 1780–1980,* edited by Carol Groneman and Mary Beth Norton, 269. Ithaca, N.Y.: Cornell University Press, 1987.

———. *Cannery Women, Cannery Lives: Mexican Women, Unionization, and the California Food Processing Industry, 1930–1950*. Albuquerque: University of New Mexico Press, 1987.

———. *From Out of the Shadows: Mexican Women in Twentieth-Century America*, 10th anniversary ed. New York: Oxford University Press, 2008.

Saldivar-Hull, Sonia. *Feminism on the Border: Chicana Gender Politics and Literature*. Berkeley: University of California Press, 2000.

Sanchez, George F. "'Go after the Women': Americanization and the Mexican Immigrant Woman, 1915–1929." In *Unequal Sisters: A Multicultural Reader in U.S. Women's History*, edited by Ellen C. DuBois and Vicki L. Ruiz, 250. New York: Routledge, 1990.

Saucedo, Leticia M. "The Employer Preference for the Subservient Worker and the Making of the Brown Collar Workplace." 67 *Ohio St. L.J.* 961 (2006).

The Sexuality of Latinas, edited by Norma Alarcon, Ana Castillo, and Cherríe Moraga. Berkeley, Calif.: Third Woman Press, 1993.

Situated Lives: Gender and Culture in Everyday Life, edited by Louise Lamphere, Helena Ragoné, and Patricia Zavella. New York: Routledge, 1997.

Symposium on the Feminization of Poverty: The Hispanic Perspective. Cosponsored by the New York State Division for Women and the National Conference of Puerto Rican Women, Inc., June 1986.

Tamayo, William R. "Role of the EEOC in Protecting the Civil Rights of Farm Workers." 33 *U.C. Davis L. Rev.* 1075 (2000).

Terrorizing Women: Feminicide in the Americas, edited by Rosa-Linda Fregosa and Cynthia Bejarano. Durham, N.C.: Duke University Press, 2010.

This Bridge Called My Back: Writings by Radical Women of Color, edited by Cherríe Moraga and Gloria Anzaldúa. 2d ed. New York: Kitchen Table, Women of Color Press, 1983.

Valdes, Francisco. "Queers, Sissies, Dykes, and Tomboys: Deconstructing the Conflation of 'Sex,' 'Gender,' and 'Sexual Orientation' in Euro-American Law and Society." 83 *Cal. L. Rev.* 1 (1995).

Women and Migration in the U.S.–Mexican Borderlands, edited by Denise A. Segura and Patricia Zavella. Durham, N.C.: Duke University Press, 2007.

||||||||||||||||||||||||||||||||||||||||||||||||||||||||||||||||||||||||||||||

Part XI

English-Only, Bilingualism, Interpreters
You Mean I Can't Speak Spanish?

Latinos are perhaps more attached to their language than is any other non-English-speaking group. Why is this so? And how legitimate is the desire to maintain the mother language in a country whose dominant language is English? Part 11 addresses the United States' history as a multilingual nation and problems that arise because of varying degrees of commitment to adopting English as the official language at the national level. Our society in many eras has tolerated and given official sanction to the speaking of foreign languages such as French and German, but it has also displayed nativist antagonism toward non-English speakers such as Indians, southern and eastern Europeans, and Latinos. Essays also examine English-only laws that would forbid speaking Spanish or other foreign languages in connection with certain official functions, seating jurors who speak or do not speak English or Spanish, and the role of court interpreters. Other essays discuss the right to speak Spanish in the workplace and in school. When a Spanish-language TV program features a handsome actor or a suave, glib-tongued broadcaster, will the production company insist on a "Latin look" or "Walter Cronkite Spanish"? If so, is this an expression of the same sort of language orthodoxy we find in the English-only movement?

Chapter 87

||||||||||||||||||||||||||||||||||||||||||||||||||||||||||||||||||||||||||||||||||||||

Hold Your Tongue

James Crawford

Nothing is new about ethnic intolerance. But beginning in the 1980s, it assumed a guise we had not seen before: the politics of English Only.

Traditionally taken for granted, our national tongue emerged as a cause célèbre, a civic passion touching nearly every state house, the U.S. Congress, and numerous municipalities. The fervor was not so much *for* English as *against* the growing prominence of other languages. "Bilingualism" had arrived, to the dismay of many monolingual Americans. Some claimed it was now easier to function in English when traveling abroad than in the immigrant ghettos of U.S. cities. Apparently today's newcomers, unlike their predecessors, felt no obligation to learn our language. Did they expect us to learn Spanish? shocked Anglo-Americans wanted to know. Whose country was this, after all? Most amazing, government was pursuing policies that seemed to discourage English acquisition: bilingual schooling, bilingual driver's tests, bilingual welfare forms, even bilingual assistance in the voting booth. Could we afford to accommodate millions of new Americans—literally scores of different language groups—each in their own tongue? Would Congress soon be translating its proceedings, United Nations–style, with every member listening through a headset? Where would it end?

Such anxieties and resentments have given rise to a movement to declare English the nation's official language. While the objective may seem innocuous, the means are not. A constitutional English Language Amendment seeks to prohibit most uses of other tongues by government (federal, state, and local) and, in some circumstances, by individuals. Whether it would achieve these aims no one can say with certainty. But, if adopted, the measure would jeopardize a wide range of rights and services now available to non-English speakers, from bilingual clerks at city hall to the freedom of speech itself. At a symbolic level, Official English would be a way of telling newcomers, "Conform or get out."

Americans are not accustomed to quarreling over language. Earlier generations of nativists were usually too preoccupied with immigrants' race or religion to worry whether their English skills were up to snuff. Contrary to melting-pot mythology, newcomers often maintained their native tongues for generations on U.S. soil. Many fought for and, depending on their political clout, won concessions like bilingual public education, which was commonplace in nineteenth-century "German America." Moreover, this country has a kind of libertarian tradition where language is concerned—a democracy is not supposed to tell its citizens how to talk—which may explain the Founders' "oversight" when it came to mandating an official tongue.

This is not to say the tradition has been consistent. At various points in our history, linguistic minorities have faced policies of exclusion or coercive assimilation or both. Yet, unlike today's campaigns, these were normally aimed at particular groups for particular purposes—for example, in the 1880s, when federal authorities decided that "the first step . . . toward teaching the Indians the mischief and folly of continuing in their barbarous practices" was to force their children to attend English-only boarding schools; or in 1897, when Pennsylvania enacted an English-proficiency requirement for miners, seeking to bar Italians and Slavs from the coal fields; or in 1921, when Republicans in New York pushed through an English literacy test for voting, hoping to disfranchise one million Yiddish speakers who had an annoying habit of electing Democrats.

What distinguishes today's English Only phenomenon is the apocalyptic nature of its fears: that the American language is "threatened" and, with it, the basis of American nationhood. We are warned that unless action is taken to halt our "mindless drift toward a bilingual society," the United States will soon be balkanized, divided, at war with itself.[1] Ostensibly to defend "the primacy of English," a new cadre of zealots is working to restrict speech in other tongues. And such proposals could become law; in several states, they already have.

Worries about the slipping status of English come, ironically, at a time when English continues to spread as a world language, the undisputed medium of international business, science, and statecraft. To be sure, this country is more diverse, linguistically and otherwise, than it was a generation ago. Immigration is the major reason. Exotic cultural enclaves have appeared not only in coastal cities, but throughout the heartland. In 1960, how many citizens of Fort Smith, Arkansas, or Garden City, Kansas, would have foreseen a Vietnamese community in their midst? (How many had even heard of Vietnam?) Just as in the past, the newcomers find it natural to preserve remnants of their homelands—food, customs, religion, and language—that some Americans find jarring. The number of U.S. residents who speak a minority tongue at home has increased rapidly. Yet, at the same time, all available evidence shows that today's immigrants are learning English faster than ever before. By objective measures, bilingualism is no more prevalent now than in several earlier periods of U.S. history.

So what accounts for the new English Only mentality? Some say bigotry. It is no coincidence that the targets of antibilingual campaigns are frequently racial as well as linguistic minorities. Leaders of U.S. English, the major lobby promoting an English Language Amendment, have expressed an animus toward Hispanics in particular. This organization is an outgrowth of the immigration restriction movement. One of its founders has warned that Spanish speakers may use their "greater reproductive powers" to seize political control in the United States. ("Perhaps this is the first instance in which those with their pants up are going to get caught by those with their pants down!")[2] A similar group, English First, complains: "Tragically, many immigrants these days refuse to learn English! They never become productive members of American society. They remain stuck in a linguistic and economic ghetto, many living off welfare and costing working Americans millions of tax dollars each year." It goes on to claim that "radical activists have been caught sneaking illegal aliens to the polls on election day and using bilingual ballots to cast fraudulent votes." The fact that U.S. English and English First have raised millions of dollars with such appeals suggests a sizable nativist constituency.

Nevertheless, it is a mistake to assume that enthusiasm for Official English is driven solely, or even primarily, by such prejudices. According to opinion polls and election results, about three Americans in four are inclined to endorse the idea. Many ask: Shouldn't newcomers learn English, for their own good and the country's? What's racist about that? Nothing whatsoever. Bilingual accommodations are the issue. Should government be able to provide them, as needed, to ease immigrants' transition into this society? Should there be an affirmative *right* to certain services in minority tongues? Or should public-sector bilingualism be banned by law? When Congress passed the Bilingual Education Act of 1968 and the bilingual voting rights amendments of 1975, it galloped headlong into this arena with little foresight and almost no public discussion. Such an abrupt turn in policy was bound to provoke debate sooner or later. At last, language issues are beginning to receive some needed attention. It is only unfortunate that vital programs, for example, the schooling of limited-English-proficient children, are now held hostage to symbolic politics.

English Only flows from feelings of insecurity. Now that demographic changes of all kinds—greater mobility, nontraditional families, mass culture—are disrupting Americans' sense of community, one sees a renewed search for unifying institutions. With ethnic warfare spreading in eastern Europe, many are wondering when it will reach our shores. Already one hears talk of "tribalism" and "the disuniting of America" from those who fear that common ties are giving way to group claims of all descriptions. Many fair-minded people, who otherwise cherish individual rights and cultural pluralism, are beginning to wonder whether the national tongue may be an exceptional case. Perhaps "unilingualism" is our best hope of managing diversity, the one bond that might keep us together. If so, it becomes too precious to risk and legislating conformity becomes justifiable.

It is my aim to show how mistaken, how shortsighted, and how disastrous that view can be.

NOTES

1. Gerda Bikales, Presentation to Georgetown University Round Table on Languages and Linguistics, March 12, 1987.

2. John Tanton, "Memorandum to WITAN IV Attendees," Oct. 10, 1986.

Chapter 88

||||||||||||||||||||||||||||||||||||||||||||||||||||||||||||||||||||||||||||||||||||||

The English Language Movement

Steven W. Bender

U.S. residents have long been hostile to languages other than English. In the early 1900s, protectors of the English language targeted immigrants from southern and eastern Europe with laws declaring English the official language and others requiring the use of that language in schools. Nebraska's 1920 constitutional amendment declaring English the official state language arose from a World War I anti-German sentiment so intense that restaurants called sauerkraut "liberty cabbage" and frankfurters "hot dogs." By 1923, thirty-four states had enacted laws declaring English the language of school instruction and prosecuted teachers who committed the crime of educating their students in non-English languages.

Enthusiasm for these laws dampened the same year when the U.S. Supreme Court struck down Nebraska's school instruction law as an unconstitutional violation of a teacher's due process rights, declaring that the law failed to promote a proper legislative purpose.

The U.S. assimilation agenda even swept up Native American children. The federal commissioner of Indian affairs in 1887 explained the imperative to teach Native American children in English: "The first step to be taken toward civilization, toward teaching the Indians the mischief and folly of continuing in their barbarous practices, is to teach them the English language." These forced assimilation efforts encompassed Mexican American children, as well as adults who were processed in the early 1900s through so-called Americanization programs with the dual purpose of teaching them the English language and "American" ideals.

Hostility still rages today. In 2005 a Kansas City public school suspended a teenager for speaking Spanish in the hallway—the youth merely replied "no problema" when asked to lend a friend a dollar. In 2008 a remote Nevada school district prohibited high school students from speaking Spanish on their daily three-hour bus ride, until the ACLU intervened.

Continuing language hostility has taken several forms. First, the current English language movement has become more formalized through national organizations such as U.S. English that oversee restrictionist agendas. The movement has also become aligned with the anti-immigrant movement and shifted its sights almost squarely to Mexican and other Latino immigrants after the chairman of U.S. English, John Tanton, published his notorious "pants down" memo.

Linda Chavez and iconic newsman Walter Cronkite resigned from its Advisory Board. U.S. English then appointed Chilean-born immigrant Mauro Mujica, light-skinned, grey haired, and an architect by trade, its CEO in 1993. Under Mujica, the organization took on a "tough love" flavor that cast language accommodation as hampering the earning potential of immigrants by keeping them linguistically isolated.

The modern English language movement started with the idea of prompting a federal constitutional amendment proclaiming English as the national language. Although about 28 states have embraced some form of comprehensive English-language regulation, thus far Congress has resisted it. In response, the English language movement looked beyond so-called Official English laws (those deeming English the official language) and English-Only laws (those prohibiting the government from acting in languages other than English) to other language frontiers in the states, particularly language in the classroom. Borrowing from lessons unlearned in the early 1900s school language laws, voters in California (1998) and Arizona (2000) adopted citizen initiatives that effectively abolished bilingual education by mandating English-Only classrooms.

The language movement has also reached the workplace and privately owned establishments and spilled onto the streets and even entered private homes. In the workplace, several employers have instituted English language policies for their employees. Typically, these rules require employees to speak English on the job in order to ensure worker safety, ease workplace tensions, or cater to customer prejudice by sparing them from overhearing workers conversing in Spanish. Several businesses have gone further and implemented English-Only rules for their customers. A Washington state tavern attracted national attention in the 1990s when its sign "In the U.S.A. It's English or Adios [*sic*] Amigo" prompted an unsuccessful civil rights lawsuit from Latino Spanish-speaking customers kicked out of the tavern for refusing to converse in English. As one Anglo customer put it: "They start speaking their own language, and we don't know what they're saying. They could be insulting us, making fun of our wives, or figuring out a way to rob the place."

Language vigilantism on the streets occurs throughout the U.S., including one incident retold by an editorial writer in Florida in which an elderly passerby insisted that the writer and his wife "[t]alk English" because "[y]ou are in the United States." English language tensions broke out on a Massachusetts baseball field in 2005 when little league baseball officials prohibited coaches from instructing players in Spanish, prompting a national little league spokesperson to confirm no rule prohibited players from speaking Spanish on the baseball field. English vigilantism can also reach into the home. For example, a Florida cooperative apartment building voted to deny residency to non-English speakers because they didn't want "undesirables" living there. An increasing number of judges are requiring criminal defendants to learn English and requiring parents to speak only English to their children. Such was the case with a Texas judge in a child custody case who deemed a mother speaking Spanish to her five-year-old daughter guilty of child abuse.

U.S. English officials profess to disdain any private restriction of non-English languages. For example, U.S. English chairman John Tanton assured in 1988 that "[n]o one wants to regulate the languages used in homes, businesses, or churches, or to prevent newspapers or books from being published in any language." Yet, the adoption of English language laws has sparked private language vigilantism throughout the United States. After the 1986 passage of California's English language initiative declaring English the official state language and prohibiting the legislature from making any law diminishing the role of English, civil rights organizations received complaints that employers adopted English-Only rules to gag their employees in such private businesses as hospitals, hotels, manufacturing firms, insurance companies, banks, and charitable organizations. Following enactment of Colorado's 1998 English-language initiative declaring English the official state language, a Colorado school bus driver told students that speaking Spanish on the bus was illegal. Colorado schoolchildren told their Latino playmates they were now "unconstitutional" and had to leave the country.

Notables have sounded the alarm against supposed ethnic separation in recent years, leveling much of the blame on the Spanish language. In the 1990s, Newt Gingrich argued that bilingualism posed a challenge to the "very fabric of American society," while Harvard professor Samuel Huntington proclaimed:

> Spanish is joining the language of Washington, Jefferson, Lincoln, Roosevelts, and Kennedys as the language of America. If this trend continues, the cultural division between Hispanics and Anglos will replace the racial division between blacks and whites as the most serious cleavage in American society. A bifurcated America with two languages and two cultures will be fundamentally different from the America with one language and one core Anglo-Protestant culture that has existed for over three centuries.

But Americans need not fear the Spanish language because we've already embraced it more than we'll acknowledge. We've welcomed it into our television shows and music and into our cinema favorites. We've welcomed it into our taverns and fast-food restaurants. Our libraries, celebrations, the names of states and cities, city streets, parks, zoos, map books, and even our homes exhibit the language.

The Spanish influence in the English language contributes to the uniqueness of American English as distinct from British English—England doesn't have the benefits of the linguistic contributions of a significant Latino immigration nor of sharing a border with a Spanish-speaking country. Thus, we should abandon futile efforts to suppress the Spanish language by laws and social policy, and instead accept the Spanish influence in our culture and revel in the ongoing and future creation of a uniquely "American" blend of English with Spanish flavoring.

Chapter 89

|||||||||||||||||||||||||||||||||||||||||||||||||||||||||||||||||||||||||||||||||

American Languages, Cultural Pluralism, and Official English

Juan F. Perea

The demand for bilingual education dates back to the inception of our nation. In 1787, the German college at Lancaster was established to provide bilingual education in German and in English. In 1837, the Pennsylvania legislature authorized the founding of German-language schools on an equal basis with English-language schools, both at public expense. Louisiana, prior to 1864 and after 1879, provided for public education in English and French. Many schools of this time, and earlier, were monolingual in languages other than English. Whatever the merits of the current debate about bilingual education, it has existed as a legitimate, state-supported form of education since our nation's beginning. The statement that this is a demand "never voiced by immigrants before" is simply false for two reasons: false, because bilingual education, at least in German and French, has been a feature of our educational landscape for centuries; and false, because Hispanic populations have lived within the current borders of the United States since before this nation existed. The Hispanic population is both a colonial population with ancient ties to this country, in the same sense as the English colonists, and an immigrant population, with reference to current immigrants. To refer to the entire Hispanic population, and particularly the Mexican-American population of the Southwest and California, as "immigrants" denies the longevity of the Hispanic populations of this country.

American nativism and racism have, of course, targeted many groups throughout our history. Native Americans, African Americans, Mexican Americans, and Asian Americans, among other groups, have been subjected to unequal treatment and oppression because of their differences from the majority culture. This chapter discusses the restrictive use of literacy and language requirements in our immigration laws, describes the official English movement and its use of language to exclude certain Americans from political participation, and concludes with an evaluation of official English.

Despite the absence of federal laws declaring English the official language, a number of federal laws do, in effect, produce this result. Our current federal immigration and naturalization laws require English literacy for naturalized citizenship and a

From *Demography and Distrust: An Essay on American Languages, Cultural Pluralism, and Official English,* 77 MINN. L. REV. 269 (1992). Originally published in the *Minnesota Law Review*. Reprinted by permission.

literacy requirement for admission to the United States. In addition, the Immigration Reform and Control Act of 1986 required aliens newly legalized under its amnesty provision to demonstrate "minimal understanding of ordinary English" in order to become permanent resident aliens.[1]

The English-literacy requirement for citizenship is of great symbolic importance. It is through our naturalization laws that, in clearest form, the nation spells out the criteria that must be met by those who would join the American nation. English literacy has not, however, always been a requirement for citizenship. Nor has literacy always been a requirement for initial admission to the nation. The evolution of the English-language literacy requirement further demonstrates that nativism finds expression through language restrictions.

A strong popular movement favoring coerced assimilation sprang up for the first time near the beginning of the twentieth century. Until around 1880, immigration to the United States had been open and unrestricted. Most assumed that American society would simply assimilate new immigrants. Indeed, because most of the immigrants until this time were from northwestern Europe, and especially from Great Britain, Germany, and Scandinavia, their racial and cultural characteristics matched those of the existing population, allowing them to assimilate with relatively little friction.

By 1890, immigrants from these countries began to be outnumbered by ones from southern and eastern Europe: Italy, Poland, and the Austro-Hungarian empire. These new immigrants brought with them their distinctive cultural traits. In response, a strong popular movement developed in favor of restrictions on immigration to the United States. The first goal of proponents of restricted immigration was a literacy test that, in theory, would exclude a large proportion of those seeking admission to the United States. The test, "though ostensibly selective in theory, would prove restrictive in operation."[2] The purpose was clear: to exclude people whose ethnicity differed from that of the majority. Advocates hoped the test would reduce immigration by 25 percent.[3]

Opponents of the new European immigration tried three times, without success, to enact legislation that included a literacy requirement in some language for admission to the United States. Such legislation passed the Congress on three occasions. It was consistently vetoed by successive presidents because it was such a departure from prior policy. Congress, however, enacted a provision requiring a literacy test over President Wilson's veto in 1917, on the eve of America's entry into World War I. The test excluded "[a]ll aliens over sixteen years of age, physically capable of reading, who cannot read the English language, or some other language or dialect, including Hebrew or Yiddish."[4] Increasing literacy rates in southern Europe and the postwar migration of educated Europeans, however, made a simple literacy test ineffective as an exclusionary device.

When this failure became apparent, new legislation established numerical quotas for immigrants. The justification was that national unity depended on racial "homogeneity," which appeared to mean preservation of the existing racial character of the country. This illustrates the theme, repeated throughout our history, that our national identity, unity, and loyalty to our government depend on uniformity—sometimes racial, sometimes linguistic. "Foreign influences," persons whose ethnicity differs from that of the majority, are perceived as a threat to the nation. An identical theme underlies the official English movement's claim that national unity depends on linguistic uniformity or purity.

The controversy over a literacy test for admission to the United States illustrates two of the principal themes of this chapter. First, the repeated exchanges between several presidents and several Congresses illustrate the tension between a pluralist view of America and one based on a need to restrict difference and encourage conformity. These exchanges illustrate the dialectic between plurality and conformism. The repeated presidential vetoes of legislation including the literacy test drew from the tradition of liberty that includes freedom for ethnically different peoples within our shores. By reaffirming the view of America as a land of opportunity for different peoples, these presidents reaffirmed the view of America as a pluralistic society. Congress, in contrast, responded to a strong popular movement supporting coerced assimilation, or increased conformity to some image of the desirable American. During this period, pressures for conformity within American society ran high.

Second, the controversy over the literacy tests illustrates the use of language as a proxy for the exclusion of immigrants on the basis of national origin. The literacy test, in effect, operated as an indirect, disguised device for exclusion. The first statutory requirement of English ability for naturalized citizenship appeared in 1906. The rationale for the statute was that a requirement of ability to speak English would improve the "quality" of naturalized citizens. The Commission on Naturalization of 1905 expressed the prevailing view: "[T]he proposition is incontrovertible that no man is a desirable citizen of the United States who does not know the English language."[5]

The initial requirement was that an applicant be able to speak English. Some courts, however, added a gloss requiring literacy to the statutory provision. For example, in *Petition of Katz*, the federal district court found that a successful Polish immigrant, unable to read English, could not fulfill the statutory requirement of attachment "to the principles of the Constitution of the United States."[6] The Nationality Act of 1940 also contained the requirement that an applicant for citizenship speak English. Section 304 of the Act stated: "No person . . . shall hereafter be naturalized as a citizen of the United States upon his own petition who cannot speak the English language."[7]

In 1950, at the height of hysteria over communism, Congress stiffened the language requirements for naturalization. The Subversive Activities Control Act of 1950 amended section 304 to demand full literacy in English. The provisions of the naturalization statute remain essentially the same today.

The symbolic importance of an English literacy requirement for naturalization should not be underestimated. It is in the naturalization laws that the criteria for belonging to America, for participating in its government, are most clearly set out. As one leading commentator put it, "[a]n English literacy requirement . . . establishes the fact that the United States is an English culture and that its citizens will have to learn English in order to participate fully in it. The very existence of a literacy test establishes the 'official' character of the language."[8] To date, this represents the maximum degree to which English receives official and legal recognition as the language of the United States.

From the panorama of the legal treatment of ethnicity and language several distinctive features of nativist movements stand out. Nativism tends to grow and flourish at times of national stress, often in response to unwelcome immigration or wartime. Nativism triggers restrictive laws aimed at persons whose ethnicity differs from that of the core culture, ostensibly to serve the goals of national unity or national security. Nativist movements seek to reinforce their narrow view of American cultural identity by restricting cultural traits deemed "foreign." They also strive to disenfranchise certain Americans, or to impede the naturalization of others, because of their difference from the core culture.

The official English movement of the 1980s is part of this tradition. Former Senator S. I. Hayakawa, acting through U.S. English, an organization he founded with Dr. John Tanton, sought an amendment to the Constitution making English the official language of the United States. Subcommittees of the Senate Judiciary Committee, in 1984, and the House Judiciary Committee, in 1988, conducted hearings on proposed official English amendments. Despite persistent efforts and publicity, proponents of official English have not yet succeeded in achieving a federal constitutional amendment.

The official English movement now appears to have a two-fold strategy: first, to enact official English laws or constitutional amendments in the states, and, second, to pass a federal statute making English the official language of the federal government. Since the movement's ultimate goal is still a federal constitutional amendment, it appears that official English proponents will attempt to strengthen their position by arguing that the presence of many state laws and a possible federal statute increases or proves the necessity for a federal constitutional amendment.

The official English movement has been quite successful at the state level. One-half of all states now have laws declaring English the official language within their borders. These laws have usually been enacted by direct popular votes on referenda by overwhelming margins. Moreover, a federal statute to codify English as the official language of the federal government was introduced in 1990 and 1991. These legislative efforts of U.S. English continue unabated.

The official English movement belongs squarely within the matrix of American nativism, in modern form. The cause of the official English movement is the immigration of people unpopular in the eyes of the majority. Its manifestations are those of earlier nativist movements: a desire to restrict immigration; an appeal to national unity or, conversely, the familiar spectre of national disunity and the disintegration of American culture caused by new immigration; and, most important, the desire to disenfranchise certain Americans.

Many commentators agree that the cause of the official English movement is the large, and largely unwelcome, immigration of many Hispanics and Southeast Asians during recent decades. Since the repeal of national origin quotas in 1965, increasing numbers of immigrants have come from non-European countries, thus changing the racial and cultural balance carefully preserved by the prior quota system. In addition to legal immigration, a large influx of undocumented aliens from Latin America arrived, many of whom subsequently were legalized during the amnesty offered in 1987 and 1988. Like all other such groups, these immigrants have brought with them their native languages. The influx of Spanish-speaking Hispanic immigrants has antagonized many Americans. Immigrants from Southeast Asia have also encountered hostility, violence, and language restriction. The racial and cultural differences of recent immigrants from the core culture have not gone unnoticed.

Part of U.S. English's original program was to "control immigration so that it does not reinforce trends toward language segregation."[9] The organization intended to lobby for legislation to restrict immigration that would reinforce the maintenance of certain languages, particularly Spanish, which, after English, is the second most-used language in this country. This means limiting the immigration of Hispanics, whom they consider advocates of "language segregation." The group's original emphasis on restricting immigration is not surprising. This has been a long-time goal of Dr. John Tanton, founder and former chairman of U.S. English.

The official English movement renews the claim that national unity depends on ethnic purity—really conformity with the Anglo core culture—this time in the form of language. This perceived threat to the English language, however, is not supported by fact. English is ubiquitous. Between 94 and 96 percent of the American population is English-speaking. Fully 85 percent of the population claims English as its mother tongue. Furthermore, English enjoys virtual hegemony as an international language of business, commerce, and interaction between nations. The unparalleled international status of English as "the world's most prestigious, most effective, and most sought-after vehicle of communication" only reinforces its importance. Given the national and international status of English, concerns about its submergence, echoed throughout our history, are greatly overstated. Since fact does not support claims of deterioration of the English language, nor of national disunity, something else must be going on.

Voting

Since its inception, one of the official English movement's principal goals has been to eliminate bilingual, or more correctly, multilingual voting ballots. This can happen only through the Congress's repeal, or refusal to extend, provisions in the 1975 amendments to the Voting Rights Act. Proponents of official English argue that English-only ballots create incentives for citizens to learn English and to realize that they cannot enjoy full participation in American life without doing so. Furthermore, multilingual ballots supposedly impair the political process because they make some voters dependent on "interpreters or go-betweens," because they preserve "minority voting blocs," and because voters whose primary language is not English will not be "as fully informed as possible" when they go to the polls.[10] Proponents of official English thus charge that multilingual ballots reduce political participation, an assertion glaringly at odds with the obvious access to political participation that multilingual ballots provide to non-English speakers.

These arguments deserve brief response. First, English-only ballots create no meaningful incentive to learn English, particularly given the overwhelming social and economic incentives to learn English. English-only ballots disenfranchise citizens who, for various reasons, have retained a language other than English. Second, voters who rely on American newspapers printed in languages other than English, such as Miami's main newspaper, the *Miami Herald*, which is published daily in both Spanish and English editions, can be fully informed about the issues in an election. The movement's concern about "minority voting blocs" defined by language both expresses fear of the political power of Hispanics and the offensive assumption that minority group members think and vote alike. If proponents of official English are truly concerned about ethnic voting blocs, they should also be equally concerned about English-speaking ethnic voting blocs. Their concern, however, is only about ethnicity, Hispanic or Asian, different from that of the core culture.

Language as Symbol

The historical record demonstrates both the significant legal recognition and protection given to different languages and the nativist restrictions imposed through the law on language. While many aspects of this history are virtually unknown within the legal academy, scholars of language and politics and sociolinguistics have long been aware of the political significance of language. The work of scholars in these disciplines provides a framework within which to assess the current meaning and symbolism of the official English movement.

Language is both our principal means of communication and a social symbol, malleable and capable of manipulation for the achievement of social or political goals. In America we have (and always have had) many languages coexisting, with English dominant. Spanish, for example, is the second most-used American language. Sociolinguists sometimes refer to this situation as diglossia, defined as "[a] situation where two languages coexist in the same speech community but differ in domains of use, attitudes toward each, and patterns of acquisition and proficiency."[11] As we can infer from this definition, coexistence does not imply equal dominance, prestige, or spheres of influence.

Discussions of different languages and other aspects of ethnicity are discussions of human differences. And "it is almost an axiom of human society that . . . [h]ierarchy is found everywhere superimposed upon difference."[12] So it is with languages. Different languages have very different prestige values in our society. These differences manifest themselves through bias, conscious or unconscious, for or against certain languages. The perceived intelligibility, for example, of languages is influenced by these prestige rankings. For instance, if the people who speak a particular language have prestige and power, people perceive their language as easy to understand. Conversely, the languages of groups perceived as lacking in prestige and power, or groups who are the objects of prejudice, are often perceived as difficult to understand.

Discourse itself, the expression of ideas, and the ordering of discourse, who gets to express ideas, who gets to express them first, and which ideas get expressed, also reflect hierarchy and relationships of power in society. According to Michel Foucault, "as history constantly teaches us, discourse is not simply that which translates struggles or systems of domination, but is the thing for which and by which there is struggle. . . . [D]iscourse is the power which is to be seized."[13] For example, access to public forums or the press is an ample power indeed. The presence or absence of certain languages, their encouragement within or elimination from certain public forums, like the ballot in public elections, reflect the results of this struggle and the presence or absence of domination. Furthermore, discourse and the order of discourse are governed by ritual, and are thus endowed with social significance. Accordingly, we pay more attention to those discourses made significant through rituals with social sanction than to others.

Given the symbolic and psychological values attached to language, important consequences attend governmental intervention and establishment of language policies. In a democracy, the attitudes and feelings of "government" are those of the majority or its representatives. Thus the majority can manipulate language and language laws to express its approval or disapproval of favored or disfavored groups within the society. Often in our society favored and disfavored groups are defined by their ethnicity: race, national origin, religion, ancestry, and language. Language often has been the basis for discrimination against groups whose language is not English. Language is a fundamental symbol of ethnicity. This is just as true of English as of Spanish or any other language. English is a crucial symbol of the ethnicity of America's dominant core culture. Language can be a symbol of group status, dominance, and participation in or exclusion from the political process. Campaigns to make a language standard or official thus emerge as attempts to create or reinforce the dominance of the culture of which the language forms an integral part.

As we have seen, legal history demonstrates that many American languages have co-existed within these borders. Yet, different languages have never threatened the unity of the nation. Indeed, even if one accepts the assumption that other languages somehow threaten the dominance of English, then the threat to English is currently at its minimum point, given the unprecedented domestic and international prestige and influence the English language holds.

The official English movement appears to be, then, another round in the "dialectic of plurality and conformism," the paradox generated by the confrontation of American cultural pluralism with the demand for conformity to core culture. Official English is the demand for national identity through linguistic homogeneity, a homogeneity that has never existed in America's people. It is a demand clearly at odds with pluralism and core principles of American liberty.

Our country, and its government, must include all who belong. Cultural pluralism need not lead to distrust. To disenfranchise Americans, or to exclude Americans "symbolically" because of the language they speak, is an old wrong of exclusion. Rather than repeat this wrong, we must expand the concept of "American" to include the full measure, linguistic, racial, and cultural, of Americans.

NOTES

1. See Immigration Reform and Control Act of 1986, Pub. L. No. 99-603, 100 Stat. 3359, 3394 (codified at 8 U.S.C. § 1255a(b)(1)(D)(i) (1987 & Supp. 1992)).

2. Robert Divine, AMERICAN IMMIGRATION POLICY, 1924–1952 at 4 (1957).

3. *Id.* at 5; Denis Baron, THE ENGLISH-ONLY QUESTION 57 (1990).

4. IMMIGRATION ACT OF 1917, ch. 29, § 3, 39 Stat. 874, 877 (repealed 1952).

5. Commission on Naturalization, *Report to the President* (Nov. 8, 1905), reprinted in H.R. DOC. NO. 46, 59TH CONG., 1ST. SESS. 11 (1905).

6. 21 F.2d 867, 868 (E.D. Mich. 1927).

7. NATIONALITY ACT OF 1940, ch. 876, § 304, 54 Stat. 1140 (repealed 1952).

8. Arnold H. Leibowitz, *English Literacy: Legal Sanction for Discrimination,* 45 NOTRE DAME LAW. 7, 14 (1969).

9. Guy Wright, *U.S. English,* S.F. CHRON., Mar. 20, 1983, at B3.

10. The English Language Amendment: Hearing on S.J. Res. 167 Before the Subcomm. on the Constitution of the Senate Comm. on the Judiciary, 98th Cong., 2d Sess., at 20 (testimony of Sen. Huddleston).

11. Joan Rubin, *Language and Politics from a Sociolinguistic Point of View,* in LANGUAGE AND POLITICS, 389 (William O'Barr and Jean O'Barr eds., 1976).

12. William O'Barr, *Boundaries, Strategies, and Power Relations,* in LANGUAGE AND POLITICS, at 405, 415.

13. Michel Foucault, *The Order of Discourse,* in LANGUAGE AND POLITICS 108, 110 (Michael J. Shapiro ed., 1984).

Chapter 90

||||||||||||||||||||||||||||||||||||||||||||||||||||||||||||||||||||||||||

How the García Cousins Lost Their Accents

Christopher David Ruiz Cameron

This is the story of how the federal law of equal opportunity failed to protect three bilingual, distant cousins, each of whom bears the family name García, when they spoke Spanish in the workplace.

The first cousin is Hector García, "a native-born American of Mexican descent."[1] Employed as a salesman by Gloor Lumber and Supply, Inc., at its retail store in Brownsville, Texas, Mr. García was among the seven of eight Gloor salesmen who were "Hispanic"—a business decision perhaps influenced by the fact that three-quarters of the company's customer base is also Latino "and many of Gloor's customers wish to be waited on by a salesman who speaks Spanish."[2]

Mr. García, who speaks English perfectly but prefers Spanish because that is the language spoken *en casa*, was hired "precisely because he was bilingual."[3] Eventually, he was fired for the same reason. This happened after Gloor adopted a work rule forbidding any on-duty employee from speaking a language other than English unless he was waiting on a non-English-speaking customer. Soon thereafter Mr. García was asked a question by another Mexican-American employee about an item sought by a customer. Mr. García replied "in Spanish that the article was not available."[4] Alton Gloor, a company officer and stockholder, overheard the conversation; Mr. García was promptly discharged.

The second cousin is Priscilla García, "a fully bilingual" employee of the Spun Steak Company of South San Francisco, California.[5] Of Spun Steak's thirty-three employees, Ms. García is among the twenty-four who speak Spanish, "virtually all of whom are 'Hispanic.'"[6] As a production line worker, she stands in front of a conveyor belt and places poultry and other meats into packages for resale. The company's production line workers have little contact with the general public, and "Spun Steak has never required job applicants to speak or to understand English as a condition of employment."[7]

Ms. García's production line *compañera*, Maricela Buitrago, is also "fully bilingual," but the two prefer communicating with one another in Spanish. Two co-workers, one African American and the other Chinese American, who apparently did not understand Spanish, nevertheless complained that García and Buitrago had made "derogatory, racist comments in Spanish."[8] The company's president, Kenneth Bertelsen, formulated a new workplace rule, mandating that employees communicate only in English "in connection with work."[9] The rule permits conversation in languages other than English when speaking in situations outside the work setting, such as at lunch and on breaks. After catching Ms. García and Ms. Buitrago speaking in Spanish while working, the company issued warning letters and prohibited the pair from working next to each other for two months. The workers' union unsuccessfully filed suit, charging that Spun Steak's English-only policy violates Title VII of the Civil Rights Act of 1964.

The third cousin is Yolanda García de la Torre, a fictional American poet who as a young girl emigrated from the Dominican Republic to New York with her parents and sisters Carla, Sandra, and Sofía. The lifelong adventures of the Misses García de la Torre are brought to life by novelist and literature professor Julia Alvarez in her novel *How the García Girls Lost Their Accents*.[10] Although Professor Alvarez weaves the García family tapestry in all its intricate and variegated splendor, the singular thread in the life of each girl—and especially the poet Yolanda, or "Yo"—is her transformation from a comfortable Spanish-speaking immigrant child into an unsure bilingual American adult, who in struggling with her dual identity cannot help but keep one foot firmly planted in the Old Country and the other in the New.

Soon after their move to the United States, several incidents with a neighbor introduce the Misses García to America's resistance toward biculturalism—and, by extension, bilingualism. *La Bruja,* the old woman "with a helmet of beauty parlor blue hair" who lives in the apartment below them, has been complaining to the building superintendent since the day the family moved in that the Garcías should be evicted. Their food smells. They speak loudly and not in English. The kids sound like a herd of wild burros. One day *La Bruja* stops Mrs. García and the four girls in the lobby and spits out that ugly word the kids in school sometimes used: "Spics! Go back to where you came from!"[11]

The stories of the three cousins García are unremarkable merely because they are, or could be, true. Even in what we sometimes suppose to be these enlightened times, tales of overt discrimination against American citizens and legal residents who look, speak, or act in a manner that the Anglo cultural majority considers "foreign" could be told by all too many folks, whether native-born or immigrant, professional or *campesino,* Latino or non-Latino. Rather, the Garcías' stories are remarkable because, according to the leading federal appellate decisions, none of them states a claim for illegal national-origin discrimination.

In the real-life cases of Hector and Priscilla, the United States Court of Appeals for the Fifth and Ninth Circuits, respectively, each held that a private employer's English-only rule could not be considered discriminatory. The Garcías, these courts reasoned, are bilingual and therefore can "easily comply" with the directive.[12] Under the law, neither García has the right to speak Spanish while on duty—to supervisors, co-workers, or even customers—unless communicating with somebody else who speaks Spanish only. So Mr. García stays fired, and Ms. García remains segregated from her Spanish-speaking *compañera* for as long as her boss sees fit.

Even in the fictional case of Yolanda García, were the super to placate *La Bruja* by putting the García family out on the street, a legal challenge might well fail. In the eyes of the law, the family's ancestry, and especially its bilingualism, is more of a liability than an asset. Nearly twenty-five years ago, the United States Supreme Court held that Title VII's ban on "national origin" discrimination does not mean what it appears to say, thereby permitting an employer to deny a job to a lawful resident alien from Mexico based solely upon her alienage.[13] Unfortunately for the García family, Title VIII of the Civil Rights Act of 1968, which purports to outlaw "national origin" discrimination in public housing, contains language similar to that found in Title VII and is practically indistinguishable.

Under Title VII, a work rule whose adverse effects fall exclusively upon the most widely accepted class of protected workers—African-American men—ordinarily would raise a prima facie violation of the statute. In most of our courts, an attempt to defend such a rule by claiming it could easily be complied with would be rejected, if not mocked, as the equivalent of telling an African American that she may lawfully be "required to sit at the back of a bus" because she could easily do so. How, then, can a work rule which effectively requires a bilingual employee "to sit at the back of the bus" escape the grasp of the employment discrimination laws?

That English-only rules have a discriminatory impact on Latinos ought to be obvious. The Spanish language is central to Latino identity. People whose primary language is Spanish constitute a cognizable group—a "discrete and insular minority"—who historically have been, and continue to be, subject to discrimination. Therefore, English-only policies that appear to be neutral workplace regulations are actually language discrimination against bilingual employees, including Spanish-speakers. This is illegal national-origin discrimination, as many commentators have argued.

The question, then, is not *whether* English-only rules are national-origin discrimination, but why courts have consistently refused to find them so. I believe the explanation lies in the tendency of judges toward "racial dualism"—the tendency to view civil rights discourse in terms of Blacks and Whites only. Racial dualism is a world view that infects judicial decision making, as reflected in the reported opinions of cases dealing with challenges to English-only rules brought under Title VII. This view embraces, among other things, reliance on false dichotomies, such as the traditional jurisprudential distinction between "mutable" and "immutable" personal characteristics. Decisions approving English-only rules in the workplace are based largely on judges' limited understandings of the forms that national-origin discrimination can take: after all, for a bilingual employee, isn't the ability to speak Spanish a mutable characteristic, changeable without causing serious inconvenience?

Racial dualism is problematic not only because it limits judges' understanding of national-origin claims but also because it makes Latinos and their problems in the workplace invisible. If racial dualism were a coin, then its flip side would be blank. When culture allows only two ways of seeing things—Black or White—other colors, such as Brown, are bound to remain hidden from view.

By their use of language—phraseology, choice of metaphor, or silence—parties and judges offer insights into why the bilingual population receives a second-class (if any) form of protected status. These insights yield a rich harvest of information about their, and our, belief systems respecting the treatment of minority cultures in the workplace. By confronting these values and prejudices, combatants and courts alike may begin to change them and accord victims of national-origin discrimination the respect they truly deserve.

NOTES

1. García v. Gloor, 618 F.2d 264, 266 (5th Cir. 1980) (*García I*).

2. *Id.* at 267.

3. *Id.* at 269.

4. *Id.* at 266. Precisely what the offending Spanish words or phrases were does not appear in the decision—a remarkable omission in itself since uttering them got Mr. García fired.

5. García v. Spun Steak Co., 998 F.2d 1480 (9th Cir. 1993) (*García II*). The opinion does not specify Ms. García's ancestry, other than to suggest she is "Hispanic."

6. *Id.* at 1483.

7. *Id.*

8. *Id.*

9. *Id.*

10. Julia Alvarez, How the García Girls Lost Their Accents (1991).

11. *Id.* at 171.

12. *See García I,* 618 F.2d at 270; *García II,* 998 F.2d at 1487–88.

13. Espinoza v. Farah Mfg. Co., 414 U.S. 86, 95 (1973).

Chapter 91

||||||||||||||||||||||||||||||||||||||||||||||||||||||||||||||||||||||||||||||||||

The Law of the Noose

A History of Latino Lynching and Its Relation to Official English

Richard Delgado

Introduction

Recent research by reputable historians shows that Latinos, particularly Mexican Americans in the Southwest, were lynched in large numbers during roughly the same period when lynching of blacks ran rampant. Few people know this. Every school child knows that blacks suffered that fate. Why do so few know about the lynching of Latinos?

The numbers the authorities report are remarkably similar—597 lynchings or slightly more[1]—most of them dating to the same period when black lynching ran rampant, Reconstruction and the years immediately following it. Moreover, the reasons that motivated the lynchings were similar for the two groups—acting "uppity," taking away jobs, making advances toward a white woman, cheating at cards, practicing "witchcraft," and refusing to leave land that Anglos coveted—with one exception. Mexicans were lynched for acting "too Mexican"—speaking Spanish too loudly or reminding Anglos too defiantly of their Mexicanness. Even Mexican women, often belonging to lower economic classes, were lynched, often for sexual offenses such as resisting an Anglo's advances too forcefully.

Lest one think that physical brutality and harassment of Latinos ended with Reconstruction and the years immediately following it, a similar but less deadly form of violence took place during World War II, when U.S. servicemen in Los Angeles attacked young Mexican American men who loitered on street corners wearing distinctive "Zoot suits," gold watch chains, and slicked-back hair. Although the violence amounted to beatings, forcible undressings, and other forms of nonlethal humiliation, the attacks went on for several days without official intervention. As with the earlier wave of lynching, the World War II–era attacks targeted Mexican youths who displayed their identity too proudly and openly.

The numbers of African Americans lynched during the period in question were, of course, higher—around 3,400 to 5,000. But the Latino group in the United States

From *The Law of the Noose: A History of Latino Lynching,* 44 HARV. C.R.–C.L. L. REV. 297 (2009). Originally published in *Harvard Civil Rights–Civil Liberties Law Review.* Reprinted by permission.

was much smaller then (and the Mexican American group smaller still), so that the rate of lynching for the two groups was similar. As with blacks, Latino lynching went on with the knowledge and, in some cases, active participation of Anglo law enforcement authorities.[2]

Moreover, the lynching of Mexicans, like that of blacks, was often marked by hilarity and an atmosphere of righteous celebration or "public spectacle." Those conducting the events believed they were acting in full accord with community wishes and meting out a type of informal justice. One historian even describes Anglo vigilantism toward Mexicans as a means of solidifying society and reinforcing civic virtue. As with black lynchings, the ringleaders would often mutilate the bodies of the victims and leave them on display in a practice of "ritual torture and sadism." Accounts describe how lynch mobs would often burn or shoot the bodies of the Mexicans even after they were dead. Others dismembered the remains and cut off body parts for souvenirs. Even the Anglo press often enthusiastically supported the events.

Most lynchings of Latinos took place in the Southwest, especially in the states or territories of Texas, California, Arizona, and New Mexico, all of which had substantial Mexican or Mexican American populations. Smaller numbers took place in Colorado and Nevada, with a few scattered cases in Nebraska, Oklahoma, Oregon, Kentucky, Louisiana, Montana, and Wyoming. Similarly, most lynchings of blacks were concentrated in one region, namely the South.

William Carrigan writes that many lynchings began with a mob snatching a Mexican from the hands of the authorities, removing him from a prison cell or courthouse, and then executing him. In June 1874, a Latino man named Jesus Romo was arrested for robbery and other crimes in La Puente, California. Later, a group of masked men seized him from the arresting officers, took him outside, tied a rope around his neck, and hanged him to death. Local opinion held that Romo was a "hardened and bloodstained desperado" who richly deserved his fate.[3] Of course, the mob acted on unsubstantiated assertions, not a judicial trial.

Many lynchings, like Romo's, took place near jails and courtrooms when vigilante mobs could not wait for formal justice to proceed. Others occurred in isolated mining camps or sparsely settled ranch areas, often with the assistance (formal or informal) of the authorities, such as the Texas Rangers. Carrigan estimates that the number of Mexicans murdered by members of that organization may have run into the thousands. Very few, if any, Anglos seem to have been made to stand trial for playing a part in the lynching of a Mexican.

Lynching was so rampant and uncontrolled that the Mexican government and even the U.S. consul in Matamoros, Mexico, lodged official complaints. Some local Mexicans fought back. Latino civil rights organizations lodged protests. Some, such as mythic outlaw Joaquin Murietta, took matters into their own hands, avenging the lynching of compatriots by murdering the Anglos responsible. Juan Cortina and Gregorio Cortes, the heroes of several *corridos*, did the same, if not always quite so violently. Still other Mexicans organized secret, conspiratorial societies, such as the Plan de San Diego, which called on Mexicans to overthrow Anglo society.[4] Anglos generally met these acts of resistance with ruthless, organized force and murder.

The few U.S. historians who write about lynching of Latinos ascribe it to simple racial prejudice, protection of turf, and Yankee nationalism left over from the Mexican War. Rodolfo Acuña compares the operative Anglo sentiment to anti-black racism and the form of special hatred that accompanies unjust wars. Another authority, after reviewing the evidence, concludes that Latino lynchings are a relatively unknown chapter in United States history and part of a worldwide pattern of shaping discourse so as to avoid embarrassment of the dominant group.

Official Obscurity: Why These Events Are So Little Known

Why are these events not better known, and why have they come to light only recently? One key reason is that the primary accounts of the *linchamientos* appeared in community newspapers, which were printed in Spanish.[5] Since relatively few mainstream historians read Spanish or consulted these sources, Latino lynching remained beyond the ken of most mainstream readers. Mexicans and Mexican Americans, of course, knew full well about them. Oral culture, including *corridos*, *actos*, and *cantares*, told of the deaths of brave Mexicans who defied Anglo authority and paid the price. Sung at parties, funerals, and other ritual occasions, these laments kept alive the memory of the events generation after generation. They also celebrated heroes like Juan Cortina who stood up for their rights or exacted revenge for the murder of a friend.

Many in the Mexican and Mexican-American community knew of the lynchings, either by word of mouth or by reading about them in a community newspaper. But the events were largely missing from mainstream histories. A few early scholars, such as Carey McWilliams and Arnoldo De León, mentioned them. But in contrast to black lynchings, that of Mexicans is largely absent from America's collective record and memory.

Why would this be? The oversight, as mentioned, may be in part a product of many Americans' simply not speaking Spanish. Another explanation may be that some authorities in the academic mainstream may have come across evidence of the practice but minimized it, instead focusing overwhelmingly on black lynching and slavery. Still others might have failed to examine it out of sheer inertia. Scholars of all disciplines adhere, consciously or not, to a paradigm or common understanding of events. Since Latino lynching falls outside the dominant paradigm of American history, the few historians and writers who came across reference to it may have afforded it scant treatment.

For some scholars, the invisibility of Latino lynching is neither accidental nor surprising. An emerging school of scholarship known as postcolonial theory describes how colonial societies almost always circulate accounts of their invasions that flatter and depict them as bearers of justice, science, light, and humanism. The native or colonial subjects, by contrast, emerge as primitive, hapless, or even bestial in their depictions. These natives are in need of the civilizing force of the invading power, which arrives in the form of superior administration, better use of the land and its resources, and, of course, a higher form of justice.

One such scholar, Edward Said, writes that the West paints the Orient as exotic, unknowable, and foreign in order to legitimize its hegemony over that region and its people, and to persuade itself that its history of imperialism is entirely justifiable. Scholars from other previously colonized regions, including India, Pakistan, Africa, and Latin America, and a few from the West, sound many of the same themes. The colonial subject emerges as unruly, dark, untrustworthy, and in need of tutelage, discipline, and punishment. In such accounts, if the conqueror oversteps, beating a native to death, for example, or punishing an innocent victim, the act is often excused as a mere matter of excess—the right idea gone awry.

Naturally, the official histories of colonization are written from the perspective of the conqueror and, understandably, show him in the best possible light. Might this account, in part, for the invisibility of Latino lynching in standard American history books? Rodolfo Acuña writes that Latinos living in the United States are, for all practical purposes, an internal colony of the United States. If so, postcolonial theory may explain key elements of the relationship between the conquering Anglos and the subjugated Latinos, particularly in the Southwest, including the prevalence of lynching and vigilante justice. To what extent does this legacy live on today?

English-Only Movements and Their Connection to Latino Lynching

Movements to declare English the official language of the United States have gathered momentum beginning with the early advocacy of U.S. Senator and former university president S. I. Hayakawa and political operative John Tanton. Currently, over half the states declare English their official language, and the current wave of anti-immigrant sentiment has spurred a movement in Congress to pass national legislation to that effect. Meanwhile, many cities and towns gripped by anti-immigrant fervor have enacted ordinances forbidding behavior thought to be associated with Latino immigrants, including the speaking of Spanish. A number of workplaces have begun insisting that their employees speak English exclusively, either when interacting with the public or each other. Even a few taverns and other places of public accommodation have begun requiring patrons to speak English while on their premises.

Those who support this movement argue that declaring English the official language will promote Americanism and civic values. They also believe it will encourage immigrants to assimilate and acquire a proficiency in English, thereby avoiding the formation of permanent ghettos and a balkanized national culture.

At the same time that the English-Only movement has been gaining force, a related movement urges the abolition of bilingual education in public schools. According to them, allowing immigrant schoolchildren to learn in both languages will slow their acquisition of English and send the message that adoption of American ways is a choice rather than a practical and patriotic necessity. Both the English-Only and anti-bilingual movements sprang up around the time that Latino immigration increased and gained national attention. Many of the same organizations and leaders who back one movement also back the other.

Given that the policy underpinnings of these measures seem insecure and alarmist, what is really going on? It would seem that, in addition to sending signals and parceling out validation—who belongs to America—one of these laws' functions might be to regulate history and knowledge of the past. For example, they send a message that the U.S. is an inherently English-speaking country, when, in fact, it is a product of many different streams of immigration, ethnicities, and tongues. Although the literature on Official English devotes little attention to this feature, when one thinks about that movement in connection with historic events, its regulatory function emerges clearly.

Consider how a Latina child brought up in a Spanish-speaking household is apt to acquire knowledge about the group's treatment in the United States through discussion with parents and grandparents. That treatment is full of matters such as: a war of aggression; seizure of lands in the Southwest; broken treaty obligations; Jim Crow laws directed against Mexicans; brutal Texas Rangers; crooked lawyers and land surveyors who conspired to deprive Latinos of their ancestral lands; and one hundred ten years of colonial status for Puerto Rico. And then there is lynching, the most lethal form of mistreatment of all.

But imagine a Latina child who does not speak Spanish, or only speaks it poorly because the surrounding culture punishes her for speaking it, and the school authorities do not provide the education that would enable her to preserve fluency in the two languages as she matures. Such a child would be unable to converse with her grandparents about life in the Southwest or Puerto Rico. She would be unable to absorb the cultural record through newspapers like *La Opinion* that carried accounts of all the events described above. Such a child could easily grow up believing that lynching was largely a problem for blacks, that civil rights and the struggle for equal dignity were largely black affairs, and that racism and stereotypes maligning Spanish-speaking people were simply cases of bad luck or tasteless humor unconnected with a history of colonialism and oppression.

Postcolonial scholars from several continents have identified language as a principal field on which the subaltern citizen struggles for recognition and equal treatment. Writers such as Trinh Minh-ha, Chinua Achebe, Haunani-Kay Trask, Ngugi wa Thiong'o, and Frantz Fanon point out how the colonial subject who is forced to speak the colonizer's tongue loses contact with her own people. Indeed, until recently, American and Australian administrators required young Indian or aboriginal children to attend boarding schools, where they learned to reject their own culture, acquire English, and forget their native language.[6]

In recent years, United States civil rights scholars have made similar arguments for a distinctive "black voice" and for storytelling and narrative analysis in legal scholarship. Recent studies of the second generation of Latino immigrants in the United States show that their children who are born here exhibit much higher rates of depression, drug-taking, and crime than their parents, who immigrated to the United States as adults. Might the severed connection with their culture and history, accelerated by failure to learn Spanish, be contributing to this increase in pathology and social distress? My suspicion is that it is, and that this constitutes an implicit form of lynching.

Conclusion

English-Only laws and practices, then, emerge as much more than misguided efforts to achieve national uniformity or a pleasing linguistic sameness. Rather, reminiscent of lynching and other harsh practices, they inhibit adults in the ordinary business of work and conversation, and convey the message that outsiders are not welcome unless they behave according to standards set by others. They sever the cultural cord from one generation to the next and hide histories of aggression, unprovoked war, lynching, segregated schools, and stereotypical treatment at the hands of media and the entertainment industry going back at least 150 years. They inhibit righteous indignation and efforts to achieve redress, while leaving the young defenseless against mistreatment that they are ill-equipped to understand or counter.

English-Only orthodoxy is, thus, a form of lynching in at least two senses. Although not in itself physically lethal, it can inflict great psychic and cultural damage. Further, it conceals from view events—including actual lynchings—that call out for exposure and reparative justice. English-Only laws and workplace rules are aspects of the law of the noose. They are like a silken cord that tightens the more one struggles. If one stands still and does not resist, the cord will not choke. But the price is to go through life with a rope around one's neck.

We should emphatically reject any such laws and practices. Moreover, scholars should unearth other laws and customs that operate on distinct minorities the way language regulation operates on Latinos. Otherwise, marginalized groups will find themselves in a condition similar to that which the postcolonial scholars describe —alienated from themselves, co-opted, and unable to mount serious, concerted resistance to illegitimate authority, if not dead.

NOTES

1. See, e.g., William D. Carrigan & Clive Webb, *The Lynching of Persons of Mexican Origin or Descent in the United States, 1848 to 1928*, 37 J. Soc. Hist. 411, 413 (2003); Rodolfo Acufia, *Crocodile Tears: Lynching of Mexicans*, HispanicVista.com (July 20, 2005); William D. Carrigan & Clive Webb, *"A Dangerous Experiment": The Lynching of Rafael Benavides*, 80 N.M. Hist. Rev. 265, 268 (2005); Ken Gonzales-Day, Lynching in the West: 1850–1935, at 206 (2006).

2. Carrigan & Webb, *Mexican Origin*, at 416, 420–22; Armando Navarro, Mexicano Political Experience in Occupied Aztlan 108–12, 120–21, 173 (2005); Richard Delgado, *Rodrigo's Corrido: Race, Postcolonial Theory, and U.S. Civil Rights*, 60 Vand. L. Rev. 1691, 1738 (2007) (discussing oral literature complaining of brutal treatment at the hands of this group).

3. Carrigan & Webb, *Mexican Origin*, at 416 (quoting *L.A. Star*, June 13, 1874, at 1); Carrigan & Webb, *"Dangerous Experiment,"* at 275 (describing local coverage of lynching as a form of "noble and patriotic service" (quoting *Farmington Times Hustler* (N.M.), Nov. 30, 1928, at 16).

4. See Benjamin Heber Johnson, Revolution in Texas: How a Forgotten Rebellion and Its Bloody Suppression Turned Mexicans into Americans (2005); Navarro, at 100, 113–15 (describing the secret organization known as Las Gorras Blancas (The White Caps)), 317; Carrigan & Webb, *Mexican Origin*, at 425; Carrigan & Webb, *"Dangerous Experiment,"* at 278.

5. Acuña, *Crocodile Tears*. When Anglo newspapers covered lynchings of Latinos, the coverage was often matter of fact or favorable; Carrigan & Webb, *"Dangerous Experiment,"* at 271, 274–75. The literature on Latino lynching is, thus, sparse.

6. See, e.g., Allison M. Dussias, *Let No Native American Child Be Left Behind: Re-envisioning Native American Education for the Twenty-First Century*, 43 ARIZ. L. REV. 819 (2001).

Chapter 92

‖‖‖

Hernandez

The Wrong Message at the Wrong Time

Miguel A. Méndez

In *Hernandez v. New York*,[1] the United States Supreme Court dealt a serious blow to the cause of bilingualism and equal access to jury service. The Court confronted the question of whether prosecutors could eliminate from jury service bilingual persons whom they "feel" might not abide by the official interpretation of the testimony of non-English-speaking witnesses. A plurality held that unless the accused persuades the trial judge that the prosecutor removed these prospective jurors, known as venire-persons, on account of their race or ethnicity, their removal would not violate the Equal Protection Clause.

The Court's holding prescribes the wrong remedy for correcting inaccuracies by court interpreters. Disqualifying from jury service individuals who can call attention to such inaccuracies defeats the truth-seeking function of a jury trial. It also reinforces a deeply embedded fear that retaining a language in addition to English might undo the fragile bonds of our society. The United States is one of the few developed nations which views the mastery of a foreign language with suspicion. This is especially true if the speakers acquired their foreign language skills from their families rather than through formal study. To these speakers, the Court's decision is but another painful reminder of how proficiency in another language is a liability, not an asset. As even the plurality concedes, "It is a harsh paradox that one may become proficient enough in English to participate in a trial . . . only to encounter disqualification because he knows a second language as well."[2]

The Court's standard guarantees that most defendants will be unsuccessful in challenging the State's use of peremptories to exclude bilingual venirepersons who happen to know the language spoken by non-English-speaking witnesses. Since many, if not most, of these venirepersons will be members of minority groups, the Court's holding will ensure the disproportionate exclusion of members of these groups from serving as jurors.

Presumably, the justification for *Hernandez* is that jurors should employ a common fund of information to arrive at their verdict. Under our adversary system, the parties bring all helpful information to the trier of fact, while the judge deletes

From Hernandez: *The Wrong Message at the Wrong Time*, 4 STAN. L. & POL'Y REV. 193 (1993). Originally published in the *Stanford Law and Policy Review*. Reprinted by permission.

inadmissible data from the information presented. Such a process helps ensure that all jurors reach a verdict based on the same facts. The court routinely instructs jurors to draw from this common nucleus of information. They are routinely told to avoid news accounts of the trial and to refrain from discussing the case with anyone until they begin deliberations. In addition, if they have heard about the case prior to trial, they are instructed to set aside any pre-formed impressions about it. Underlying the common fund view is the assumption that in an adversary system it is the parties who challenge and test the information upon which the jury will rely. Jurors who use information "outside the record" become untested evidentiary sources.

Jurors who rely on their own interpretation of what a non-English-speaking witness says pose a serious challenge to the concept of shared information. Seemingly, bilingual persons who insist on relying on their own interpretation should not serve on the jury since they have announced their intention not to abide by the evidence presented in the case. That, however, was not the situation presented in *Hernandez*. In response to the prosecutor's questions, the venirepersons said that they "would try" to abide by the official interpretation.[3] When questioned by the judge, they said that they "could."[4] The prosecutor nonetheless struck them peremptorily because he "just felt from the hesitancy in their answers and their lack of eye contact that they would not be able to do it."[5] Yet, as defense counsel pointed out, any honest venireperson would have answered the prosecutor's questions in the same way. Without knowing anything about the interpreter's ability to interpret accurately, they could only promise to try to abide by the official interpretation.

But, if a bilingual juror believes that an official interpretation is incorrect, why should he or she ignore the error? If in fact the interpreter is wrong, *Hernandez* would require the bilingual juror to ignore the error and refrain from bringing it to the attention of the other jurors. Accurate fact-finding would dictate a different rule: one that would not disfavor the selection of bilingual jurors who can bring serious errors in interpretation to the judge's attention. Indeed, Justice Stevens advocated such a rule in his *Hernandez* dissent.[6]

In *Hernandez*, the accused argued that because Spanish-language ability bears a close relationship to ethnicity, the peremptory removal of bilingual venirepersons was tantamount to removal on account of ethnicity. The Court declined to address this argument. It did concede, however, that removal of bilingual venirepersons whom the prosecutor felt would not abide by the official English translation "might well result" in the disproportionate removal of Latino venirepersons. But it concluded that this would not violate the Equal Protection Clause of the Constitution unless the accused proved that the prosecutor's true motive was to prevent bilingual Latinos from serving on the jury. Thus, even if foreign language proficiency correlated perfectly with ethnicity, this would be of scant use to the accused. The problem, then, is not the degree of correlation, but the Court's use of standards far removed from the realities of the courtroom.

Precise data on the number of adult bilinguals who may be subject to exclusion under *Hernandez* are unavailable. [As of the time of writing] Census data indicate that approximately 17.3 million persons over the age of five speak Spanish in the home. Of these, approximately two-thirds are bilingual. If the same proportion of Latinos eighteen and over are also bilingual, then roughly 66 percent of Latinos who qualify for jury duty may be excludable under *Hernandez*. Countless others who speak English and some other language are also subject to exclusion. Many, if not most, bilinguals claim an ethnic background that qualifies for protection under the Equal Protection Clause. The actual number subject to removal, while lower, cannot be known. Available data do not show the probability that an ethnic bilingual will be called for jury service; the percentage of ethnic bilinguals who would meet jurisdictional requirements for jury service; the probability that in a given trial a non-English speaker will be called as a witness; or whether an ethnic bilingual called for jury service will understand the language spoken by a non-English-speaking witness. The point, though, is not the difficulty in arriving at precise figures. Members of ethnic groups who happen to know or understand the language of a non-English-speaking witness are, by reason of that knowledge, excludable from jury service.

Hernandez reinforces a provincial American view that the retention of languages other than English is bad. We admire the multilingual abilities of Europeans but view American children who start school knowing only a foreign language as a problem. Rather than help them retain this asset, we immerse them in programs designed to convert them into monolingual English speakers in the shortest time possible. In the process, we strip them not only of an asset but of a sense of self that would benefit them and society as well. We are a multicultural, multilingual society that draws much of its strength from its diversity. Exploiting this strength fully will require a respect and tolerance for our differences which we have yet to achieve.

NOTES

1. 111 S.Ct. 1859 (1991).
2. *Id.* at 1872.
3. *Id.* at 1865.
4. *Id.*
5. *Id.*
6. *Id.* at 1877 (Stevens, J., dissenting).

Chapter 93

llllllllllllllllllllllllllllllllllllllllllllllllllllllllllllllllllllllllllllllllll

Attorney as Interpreter

Bill Piatt

Should an attorney serve as an interpreter for a non-English-speaking client in a criminal prosecution? Out of an apparent sense of duty to the court or client, some bilingual attorneys have been willing to assume that role. Moreover, trial courts which have imposed such an obligation upon counsel have generally been upheld on appeal. Ponder the potential harm to the client, counsel, and the administration of justice when an attorney acts as an interpreter for a client in litigation.

As with other language rights issues, problems with interpreters develop because courts and counsel seem not to understand the significance of the interests at stake. The lack of a coherent recognition of language rights in this country and the absence of any United States Supreme Court decision defining the right to court interpreters add to the uncertainty. Yet, the use of interpreters is becoming increasingly important to the administration of justice. In a recent year, interpreted proceedings constituted 6 percent of all federal court hearings.[1] Examining the issues that arise when an attorney is called upon to interpret for a client first requires some understanding of the nature of the right to an interpreter. An understanding of the extent to which an attorney-interpreter fulfills the obligation of zealous advocacy is also required.

Through the middle of the twentieth century, courts generally held that appointment of an interpreter in a criminal proceeding rested solely in the trial court's discretion. However, in 1970, the Second Circuit Court of Appeals in *United States* ex rel. *Negron v. New York*, determined that the sixth amendment's confrontation clause, made applicable to the states through the fourteenth amendment's due process clause, requires that non-English-speaking defendants be informed of their right to simultaneous interpretation of proceedings at the government's expense.[2] Otherwise, the trial would be a "babble of voices,"[3] the defendant would not understand the testimony against him, and counsel would be hampered in effective cross-examination.

The right to an interpreter in the federal courts expanded with the Court Interpreters Act in 1978.[4] The Act requires judges to employ competent interpreters in criminal or civil actions initiated by the government in a United States district court. An interpreter must be appointed when a party or witness speaks only or primarily in a language other than English or suffers from a hearing impairment, so as to inhibit the person's comprehension of the proceedings. The Director of the Administrative

From *Attorney as Interpreter: A Return to Babble,* 20 N.M. L. REV. 1 (1990). Originally published in the *New Mexico Law Review.* Reprinted by permission.

Office of the United States Courts is required to prescribe, determine, and certify the qualifications of persons who may serve as interpreters. The Director maintains a list of interpreters and prescribes a fee schedule for their use.

Courts have repeatedly determined that no constitutional right guarantees an interpreter in civil or administrative proceedings. However, various state constitutional and legislative provisions do so, in most cases leaving the determination to the trial court's discretion. Under traditional views of zealous advocacy, counsel for a party with a language barrier should be ethically required to urge the Court to exercise its discretion in a manner favorable to that client regarding these interpretation issues. Before turning to a discussion of counsel as interpreter, it is important to consider how counsel who is not also required to serve as an interpreter should ordinarily proceed regarding interpretation issues in litigation.

The first issue is whether a client is entitled to an interpreter. Courts will ordinarily not appoint one in the absence of a request, and failure of an attorney to request an interpreter for a qualifying client has been held to constitute ineffective assistance of counsel. A client need not be totally ignorant of the English language in order to be entitled to an interpreter. The federal test is basically whether the client speaks only or primarily a language other than English. Thus, even though a client may be able to function in English in a social conversation, he or she may still be entitled to an interpreter in litigation. Zealous advocacy would seem to require counsel to seek an interpreter when a language barrier may inhibit his or her client's comprehension of the proceedings or interfere with presentation of evidence on the client's behalf.

Counsel must also ensure that the interpreter is qualified. As mentioned, the federal Director of the Administrative Office examines and maintains lists of certified interpreters; some states do as well. In the absence of such certification, an attorney should require the interpreter to demonstrate that he or she can make a competent translation. Although interpreters with obvious conflicts of interest, such as a family relationship to a witness, may be allowed to serve, opposing counsel should identify such conflicts and object, in order to preserve a record for appeal.

Assuming the court appoints a competent, unbiased interpreter, counsel's work is still not done. Counsel should ordinarily insist on a simultaneous translation. Because the court reporter only transcribes the English dialogue, counsel should insist on a "first-person" translation to avoid a garbled record. Further, counsel should adamantly insist on having two interpreters in the courtroom. One would translate witness testimony and proceedings for the record. The other would facilitate communication between counsel and client and advise counsel of any translation errors made by the first, or "court" interpreter. Finally, counsel should insist that testimony be tape-recorded for correcting errors at trial or for transmission with the record on appeal if necessary.

In some pre-*Negron* cases, courts encountered no difficulty in finding that the right to confront witnesses in a criminal proceeding was satisfied where defense counsel was bilingual, or understood the testimony even though the defendant did not. Thus, the presence of counsel who could communicate with their respective clients in French, Italian, or Polish, as well as Spanish, was held to obviate the need for the appointment of an interpreter. The "bald assertion" that an attorney who was forced to act as the client's interpreter could not thereby function effectively as counsel was found to be without merit in a case with a Spanish-speaking defendant and bilingual counsel.[5] And the presence of a bilingual judge was held to satisfy the constitutional right of a Spanish-speaking defendant to confront witnesses in a criminal proceeding.[6]

Even though the Supreme Court has never recognized a constitutional right to an interpreter, it has found a due process right to state-furnished "basic tools," including psychiatric experts on behalf of indigents. Similarly, a showing of particularized need for an interpreter coupled with a showing as to why a bilingual attorney cannot fulfill the need should lead to a conclusion that the failure to appoint a separate interpreter violates due process. In addition, *Negron* teaches that confrontation clause and due process violations occur when a language minority client does not have an interpreter to confront adverse witnesses. *Negron* also refers to a standard of "simple humaneness."[7] Counsel should invoke these concerns as well in resisting the dual appointment as attorney and interpreter.

Equal protection considerations also support this conclusion. The only apparent reason why courts require counsel to also serve as interpreters is to save the money which the court would otherwise pay to independent interpreters. Assuming that such a scheme effectively deprives the client of either the attorney or the interpreter to which the client would otherwise be entitled, the situation appears analogous to equal protection problems identified by the Supreme Court where state court schemes denied indigent defendants appellate transcripts.[8]

Moreover, even though trial courts have enjoyed wide discretion to appoint as interpreters persons with obvious bias, inherent conflict issues stemming from the attorney-client relationship loom large. For example, the attorney who interprets for a client at trial may well end up testifying against the client on appeal if an issue arises as to the adequacy of the translation. Even though the issue of effective assistance of trial counsel is occasionally raised in criminal appeals, no good reason argues for counsel to agree to inject an additional potential area of conflict between themselves and clients.

Given the many serious problems that surface when counsel serve as interpreters for their own clients, one cannot help but wonder why the situation has continued. Monolingual judges may have been unaware of the inherent difficulties in the understanding of courtroom testimony and the presentation of an effective case in the presence of a language barrier. The lack of any United States Supreme Court decision defining and applying the right to an interpreter undoubtedly adds to uncertainties as to the exact nature and parameters of the right. Viewing the situation somewhat less charitably, judges may have been aware of the difficulties, but chosen not to rectify them because of the same fear, apprehension, and hostility monolingual people exhibit toward a language and speakers they do not understand.

Whatever the motivations of court and counsel, it should appear obvious that it is unfair to the client when his or her attorney must serve as interpreter in court. The client, obviously, cannot enter his or her own objection because of a lack of understanding of the language and the process. Thus it becomes incumbent upon counsel and the courts to protect the due process and confrontation rights of clients who are not fluent in English.

NOTES

1. H.R. REP. NO. 100-889, 100th Cong., 2d Sess., reprinted in 1988 U.S. CODE CONG. & ADMIN. NEWS 6018, 6019. Spanish is by far the most widely used language in these proceedings. Interpreted proceedings employing languages other than Spanish accounted for only one-third of 1 percent of all federal court hearings in 1986.

2. United States *ex rel.* Negron v. New York, 434 F.2d 386, 390–91 (2d Cir.1970).

3. *Id.* at 388.

4. 28 U.S.C. § 1827 (1988).

5. United States v. Paroutian, 299 F.2d 486, 490 (2d. Cir. 1962).

6. United States v. Sosa, 379 F.2d 525, 527 (7th Cir.), cert. denied, 389 U.S. 895 (1967).

7. 434 F.2d, at 390.

8. Griffin v. Illinois, 351 U.S. 12 (1956).

Chapter 94

||||||||||||||||||||||||||||||||||||||||||||||||||||||||||||||||||||||||||||||

Buscando América

Why Integration and Equal Protection Fail to Protect Latinos

Juan F. Perea

During the 1940s, Gonzalo and Felícitas Méndez moved to Westminster, California. When they tried to enroll their children in the all-White Westminster elementary school, officials refused to admit them because they were dark-skinned. Instead, the children were offered admission to the Hoover school. Taking a stand against segregation, the Méndezes refused to enroll their children in the Hoover school and complained to the school board. The board offered the Méndezes "special admission" to the Westminster school, which they refused. Instead, "tired of being pushed around," the Méndezes organized a boycott of the schools by local parents who wanted to send their children to the schools of their choice. Ultimately, Gonzalo Méndez hired an attorney and filed suit against the school board, demanding that Westminster County's schools be desegregated.

The ensuing case, *Mendez v. Westminster School District*,[1] proved an important chapter in the struggle to overturn *Plessy v. Ferguson*. In *Mendez*, several Mexican-American families sued the school district to end the segregation of their children into schools with facilities inferior to those in neighboring White schools. The federal district court's opinion in the case was remarkable in that it rejected for the first time the basic premises of the *Plessy* opinion and anticipated closely the reasoning in *Brown v. Board of Education*. Judge McCormick wrote that "[a] paramount requisite in the American system of public education is social equality. It must be open to all children by unified school association regardless of lineage." He also wrote:

> [C]ommingling of the entire student body instills and develops a common cultural attitude among the school children which is imperative for the perpetuation of American institutions and ideals. . . . [M]ethods of segregation prevalent in the defendant school districts foster antagonisms in the children and suggest inferiority among them where none exists.[2]

Judge McCormick's opinion anticipated ideas that would later be important in the reasoning of *Brown*: the notion of an indivisible equality, the ideals of assimilation

From *Buscando America: Why Integration and Equal Protection Fail to Protect Latinos,* 117 HARV. L. REV. 1420 (2004). Originally published in the *Harvard Law Review*. Reprinted by permission.

and integration, and the accurate assessment of the meaning of segregation, which is to attempt to suggest inferiority where none exists.

The national importance of the *Mendez* case was not lost on the legal community. A Note on the case in the *Yale Law Journal* commented that the *Mendez* opinion "questioned the basic assumption of the *Plessy* case and may portend a complete reversal of the doctrine." Another Note, in the *Columbia Law Review*, noted that the *Mendez* court broke sharply with the approach in *Plessy* in "find[ing] that the 14th Amendment requires 'social equality' rather than equal facilities." The NAACP also recognized the importance of the case in its struggle against segregation. When the case was appealed, Thurgood Marshall, Robert L. Carter, and Loren Miller, on behalf of the NAACP, filed an amicus brief supporting the plaintiffs and urging the desegregation of the schools. Robert Carter used this brief to try out the argument that segregation was unconstitutional per se. Judge Constance Baker Motley, then an attorney for the NAACP, recalled that "[t]his new approach to attacking segregation, per se, in education had been inspired by *Mendez v. Westminster School District.*" The district court's opinion in *Mendez* was affirmed on appeal.

Ultimately, the *Mendez* opinions resulted in the repeal of California's segregation statutes. The repealing legislation was signed by then-Governor Earl Warren. Through its reasoning and its connection to Earl Warren, the *Mendez* case is an important part of the intellectual history of the *Brown* decision.

Despite its connection to the *Brown* case, it is likely that most readers have never heard of the *Mendez* case, nor of the history of educational segregation of Mexican Americans and other Latinos. At least since the 1930s, Latinos have struggled hard against school segregation and educational inequality. *Brown*'s legacy of integration has been even less successful for Latinos than it has been for Blacks. Because of the relative lack of knowledge about Latinos, it may surprise readers to learn that, among the largest racial groups in the United States, Latinos are clearly the worst off as measured by educational attainment. The statistics paint an undeniable picture of inferior education received by both Black and Latino children. Today, Latinos are more segregated by race, poverty, and language than any other ethnic group. Latinos, by far, have the highest high school dropout rates of any group. In 2000, the status dropout rate for Latino students was 27.8%, more than twice the rate for Blacks and four times the rate for Whites. Put another way, only 56% of Hispanics graduated from high school in 2000, while 88% of Whites earned high school diplomas. Latinos rank last among major U.S. racial groups in their average level of educational attainment. In 1997, Whites demonstrated by far the highest rate of college graduation (33%), followed by Blacks (14%), and then Latinos (11%). The college graduation rates of Blacks and Latinos fell even further behind those of Whites during the rest of the 1990s.

Many dismal statistics reflect the current effects of past and present discriminatory practices in Southwestern schools. For example, Latino students tend to be held back in school much more often than their peers and are overrepresented in low-ability groups and classes. In 1986, Latino students were 13% more likely to be placed in classes for the educable mentally retarded than Whites.

The interesting questions are why integration has failed for Latino students, and why we as a society have chosen, and continue to choose, not to educate Latino students effectively. I have been puzzled by these questions: we have known for many years how to educate Latino students effectively, yet as a society we have rarely done it. One reason is that effective education demands recognition of and attention to the cultural particularity of Latinos. As one would guess intuitively, students learn best in the language they understand best, which for many but certainly not all Latino students is Spanish. Yet bilingual education in our schools—particularly the more effective type that seeks the maintenance of Spanish and the acquisition of English —runs directly counter to strong traditions of Anglocentric assimilation and homogenization, as well as majoritarian hostility toward Spanish speakers.

The Spanish language lies at the heart of the Latino experience in the United States. As a heritage language, Spanish remains significant even for Latinos who do not speak it. Recent census figures show that 46.9 million, or 17.9%, of U.S. residents speak languages other than English at home, and of these, 28.1 million, or 10.7% of U.S. residents, speak Spanish. Latinos account for 70.9% of school-age children who speak a language other than English at home. After English, Spanish is by far the most prominent language spoken in the United States.

The linguistic subordination of Spanish speakers has a long history in the United States. Language is much more than just words. Properly understood within historical context, it is a symbol of political struggle, status, and domination and subordination. Latinos continue to be subordinated in school, in the workplace, and in the law itself, because of their language. Language is thus inseparable from race for Latinos. Indeed, for Latinos and other language minority groups, language discrimination is race discrimination, and courts should treat it as such.

Language and Race

Spanish speakers, historically and in the present, have been treated as inferior and discriminated against by English-speaking America. I argue, therefore, that language should be treated as an aspect of race and that language discrimination should be treated as race discrimination.

It is a gross oversimplification to consider language as merely a utilitarian means of communication. Language is the carrier and vessel of culture, which in turn shapes language and perception. Language constitutes a primary symbol of cultural identification. For Mexican Americans and other Latinos, the Spanish language is an emblem of their culture. The same is true, of course, for English speakers. Otherwise, European Americans would not be so tied to English as the exclusive language of proper American identity.

Language use, dominance, and status must be recognized as dynamic sites of political struggle and subordination. Because of the United States's history of conquest and enslavement, the languages of the conquered and the enslaved—indigenous languages, African languages, Black English, and Spanish—carry the low status assigned to their historically subordinated speakers. As the language of the conquerors, English is obviously the dominant and most prestigious language in the United States. The relationship between the high status of English and the low estate of Spanish illustrates the form of oppression Iris Marion Young labels "cultural imperialism." "[T]he universalization of a dominant group's experience and culture, and its establishment as the norm. . . . The dominant group reinforces its position by bringing the other groups under the measure of its dominant norms."

Thus, it is the history of the relationships between peoples speaking different languages that enables us to understand more fully the status of a language and the layered meanings in language conflicts. The United States' aggressive war of conquest against Mexico from 1846 to 1848 and the ensuing colonization of formerly Mexican lands provide important context for understanding the current status of the Spanish language and the meaning of debates over its use in the United States. After the conquest, Mexican Americans struggled, and continue to struggle, with Anglos for the survival of their culture and language.

The presence of large numbers of Spanish-speaking citizens and residents of the United States means that language conflicts between Spanish and English speakers will arise regularly. These conflicts, and their resolution, are not just about abstract, decontextualized language choice. Rather, language conflicts, in historical perspective, constitute the linguistic part of the unresolved legacies of the conquests of Mexico and Puerto Rico and American immigration policy. Struggles over bilingual education, English-only rules in the workplace, and campaigns to make English the official language of the United States (known as the "Official English" movement) can be understood as continuing linguistic and cultural aspects of the U.S. conquest of Mexico.

New Mexico took sixty-two years to achieve statehood, longer than any other state. From approximately 1900 to 1912, the principal objections to New Mexico's statehood were the presence of Mexicans and the ubiquity of Spanish. Mexicans in the territory were deemed unfit for state citizenship and consequent participation in national politics. Senator Albert Beveridge, Chairman of the Senate Committee on Territories, strongly opposed New Mexico's admission for reasons of race and language. In the Senate report discussing statehood for the territory, Senator Beveridge wrote: "Since we are about to admit [New Mexico] as a state of the Union, the disposition of its citizens to retain their racial solidity, and in doing so to continue the teaching of their tongue, must be broken up."

Puerto Rico came under the ambit of the United States through military occupation by U.S. forces during the Spanish-American War. Under the Treaty of Paris of 1898, Spain ceded control of the island to the United States. Like other colonial rulers, the United States was interested in educating the people of Puerto Rico primarily for the purpose of preparing them for the social and cultural transformation that would accompany colonial control. The goal of Americanization was "the substitution of one set of cultural traits for another."

The goal of the American administrators of Puerto Rico was to accomplish Americanization through the schools. Prior to U.S. intervention, Puerto Ricans were a Spanish-speaking people. American authorities thus declared from 1900 to 1905 a strict English-only policy in schools that taught only Spanish-speaking students. Puerto Ricans who migrated to the U.S. mainland also faced language discrimination and lack of support for their academic achievement.

Although territorial expansion and colonialism have receded as overt policy goals of the U.S. government, the legal, linguistic, and cultural ramifications of conquest, colonialism, and assimilationism continue. Cultural imperialism is evident in the continuing linguistic subordination of Spanish speakers in schools, workplaces, and the law. The persistence of linguistic subordination and the Supreme Court's inadequate recognition of language discrimination as race discrimination demand reconsideration of the Court's conceptual tools for understanding language difference and language discrimination.

Segregation, Education, and Latinos

Language-based subordination has plagued Latinos in the educational system. In the realm of schooling, a variety of techniques burden or exclude Spanish speakers. Some of these can be characterized as assimilative in nature—pressuring Spanish speakers to abandon their language and culture or to integrate into Anglo society as an underclass. Some of the techniques are not assimilative, but rather discriminatory—residential or educational segregation, or teacher prejudice against Spanish-speaking students. All of these techniques, intentionally or not, reflect and enforce a racist, subordinating attitude toward Latino students.

Segregation was practiced throughout the Southwest to isolate Mexican-American children and to retard their educational progress. The purpose of the educational system was to reproduce the caste society of the Southwest, with Anglos at the top and Mexicans, Indians, and Blacks at the bottom. Equal education was inconsistent with the need for uneducated Mexican laborers. In the words of one Texas school superintendent: "Most of our Mexicans are of the lower class. They transplant onions, harvest them, etc. The less they know about everything else the better contented they are. . . . If a man has very much sense or education either, he is not going to stick to this kind of work." Anglo farmers, many of whom sat on school boards, used the schools to keep Mexicans uneducated, thereby guaranteeing a plentiful labor supply for their cotton fields.

Assimilation, conceived as one-way adaptation by persons of color to the norms of Whiteness and English monolingualism, was an important initial goal of American education for conquered peoples. Just as lessons supporting slavery and Black inferiority were the most important ones taught in schools to Black children, lessons supporting conquest and subordination were the most important ones taught to Mexican school children. Because Mexican culture and the Spanish language were major impediments to progress and learning, public schools were at pains to exclude and eliminate the culture and language of Mexican students. According to Thomas Carter, "the full force of the educational system in the Southwest has been directed toward the eradication of both the Spanish language and the Spanish-American or Mexican-American cultures."

Wherever Mexicans lived in large numbers, segregation was the rule. Carey McWilliams described the segregated conditions in the California citrus belt:

Throughout the citrus belt, the workers are Spanish-speaking, Catholic, and dark-skinned, the owners are white, Protestant, and English-speaking. The owners occupy the heights, the Mexicans the lowlands. . . . While the towns deny that they practice segregation, nevertheless, segregation is the rule. Since the Mexicans all live in jim-town, it has always been easy to effect residential segregation. The omnipresent Mexican school is, of course, an outgrowth of segregated residence. The swimming pools in the towns are usually reserved for "whites," with an insulting exception being noted in the designation of one day in the week as "Mexican Day." . . . Mexicans attend separate schools and churches, occupy the balcony seats in the motion-picture theaters, and frequent separate places of amusement. . . . The whole system of employment, in fact, is perfectly designed to insulate workers from employers in every walk of life, from the cradle to the grave, from the church to the saloon.[3]

Segregated schools for Mexican-American children were the rule in the Southwest. Often Mexican Americans and Blacks were grouped together, separate from Whites. Ironically, despite the fact that California's Education Code did not even mention them, Mexican-American children were the largest and most frequently segregated ethnic group in California's schools.

Mexican-American children were regularly retained in first grade for two or three years, which automatically placed them behind their Anglo peers. While this retention policy was often justified for linguistic reasons, in many instances the linguistic competence of the children was tested in a hasty and inconclusive fashion, if at all. Today, Latinos continue to be held back in school much more often than their peers. Mexican-American students continue to be physically, culturally, and intellectually segregated even within supposedly integrated classrooms.

Teachers who intentionally or unintentionally reinforce stereotypes of Mexican-American children perpetuate subordination. The common assumptions that Chicano children are inherently culturally disadvantaged or that they come from a "simple folk culture" are racist judgments imposed on cultural differences. Another common stereotype is that Latino parents do not care about the education of their children.

Studies demonstrate that Anglo teachers viewed their Mexican-American students as lazy and favored Anglo students in class participation and leadership roles. Such leadership opportunities, according to the teachers, were necessary to teach Anglos how to control and lead Mexicans. Many Anglo teachers and parents saw Mexican-American children as dirty and diseased. One teacher advocated mandatory baths for "dirty Mexican kids because it will teach them how nice it feels to be clean." Another teacher refused to let her Mexican-American students hug her without first inspecting their hair for lice. These attitudes on the part of Anglo teachers only reinforced stereotypes of inferiority that subordinated Mexican-American children.

One Texas school imposed an extensive disciplinary system for speaking Spanish. A student caught speaking that language was first detained for an hour or more. If the child spoke it again, the principal spanked him. Repeat offenders who persisted in speaking Spanish might ultimately be suspended or expelled from school. Other punishments for speaking Spanish included physical abuse and public humiliation. These kinds of punishments were, and continue to be, meted out in schools with large Mexican-American populations. In jurisdictions that have repealed bilingual education by referendum, including Massachusetts, Arizona, and California, some educators are enforcing the new laws in the old ways by prohibiting the use of Spanish among students on school campuses.

Another facet of the educational campaign to extinguish native Spanish has been the persistent devaluation of bilingualism in general and of the native ability to speak Spanish in particular. Many teachers, perhaps most, see childhood bilingualism as a deficit and an impediment to learning. Many also believe that Spanish-speaking or bilingual Mexican-American children speak no language at all. Regardless of their linguistic abilities, Mexican-American children are often considered deficient from the start. The value judgments teachers make of the languages spoken by their Latino students are consistently negative, likely reflecting the teachers' stereotypical judgments about the social status of their students. These "no Spanish" rules and disparaging attitudes toward native Spanish speakers are part of a system of behavioral controls intended to banish manifestations of "Mexicanness" from the public schools.

Recent news reports about local legal disputes provide ample evidence of the continuing devaluation of bilingualism and Spanish-speaking ability in schools, workplaces, and courtrooms. For example, a Texas judge hearing a custody dispute threatened a Mexican-American mother with the loss of her daughter because she spoke Spanish at home:

> [Y]ou're abusing that child and you're relegating her to the position of a housemaid. Now get this straight. You start speaking English to this child because if she doesn't do good in school, then I can remove her because it's not in her best interest to be ignorant. The child will hear only English.

In this judge's eyes, a five-year-old Mexican-American girl who spoke Spanish was ignorant, incapable of good school performance, and destined to be a housemaid. His opinion lays bare the pervasive assumptions that knowledge of the Spanish language is no knowledge at all and that Mexicans are unintelligent and fit only for menial labor. More recently, a Nebraska judge warned that he would limit severely a Mexican-American father's rights to visit his daughter if he continued speaking to her in Spanish. The judge insisted that "[t]he principal form of communication . . . is going to be English and not the Hispanic language."

In another recent case, a New York judge rejected a constitutional challenge to the poor quality of education provided to Latino youngsters who had dropped out of school by the eighth grade. The judge explained that completion of the eighth grade constituted a "sound basic education," because "[s]ociety needs workers in all levels of jobs, the majority of which may very well be low level." The judge's satisfaction with blatantly unequal education for Latino and Black students, and his blithe contentment with their futures in menial labor, echo the exploitive purposes for which Mexican-American education was originally designed.

The education of Mexican-American children in the Southwest provides a powerful illustration of Derrick Bell's interest-convergence hypothesis. For most of the twentieth century, Latinos and Blacks lacked high-quality education because their education was not in the interests of Whites, who needed them only as manual labor-ers. Whites were interested in educating Mexican Americans only for the purpose of teaching them to believe in their own inferiority and to be satisfied with roles as manual laborers; indeed, Anglos saw Latino education as a threat to their labor force and to their sense of White supremacy. The troubling question we must ask today is: to what extent has this state of affairs changed? The maintenance of White privilege, and Brown and Black subordination, though no longer overt goals, are clearly ob-servable in our unequal educational system and in our failure to enact meaningful reforms.

NOTES

1. 64 F. Supp. 544 (S.D. Cal. 1946), aff'd, 161 F.2d 774 (9th Cir. 1947).

2. *Id.*

3. Carey McWilliams, SOUTHERN CALIFORNIA COUNTRY: AN ISLAND ON THE LAND 219 (1946).

Chapter 95

|||||||||||||||||||||||||||||||||||||||||||||||||||||||||||||||||||||||||||||

The Latin Look and "Walter Cronkite Spanish"

Arlene Dávila

That there is a generic or pan-Hispanic "look" as well as universal Spanish is taken for granted by almost everyone I talked to in this industry, from producers to creatives and casting directors. This construct dates back to the 1970s and the first nationwide TV campaigns, although it did not achieve its present dominant status until after an interlude in the 1980s, when the customization and regionalization of campaigns reached their zenith as marketing strategies. Thus today, even when few may know how to define it, everyone I spoke with took for granted and made constant reference to some sort of generic "Latin look" that any Hispanic can recognize and identify upon seeing. But who and what constitutes the generic Hispanic? A casting director explained, "You know what they want when they ask you for models; it's unspoken. What they want is the long straight hair, olive skin, just enough oliveness to the skin to make them not ambiguous. To make them Hispanic."

What makes anyone Hispanic in advertising, however, is more than olive skin. The so-called generic look is a product of the beauty-obsessed world of advertising, as well as of the demand that this industry be (or appear to be) representative of its target consumer. Specifically, in contrast to advertising images for Latin American or other North American audiences, images for the U.S. Hispanic market have to be both aspirational (in the sense of showing beautiful, educated, or accomplished individuals) and also representative. Blondes and Nordic types, which are common in Latin American ads, supposedly would not work for U.S. Hispanics who, as minorities, I was told, were looking at ads for representation and confirmation. This does not mean that ad models are indeed representative of U.S. Hispanics—a quick look at Hispanic media images would surely attest to this—but that advertisers make a concerted effort to cast aspirational models who are still somewhat representative of the "Hispanic consumer," or at least to sell and stress to clients the need for models who are representative, not just beautiful.

As an anonymous casting director tired of always being asked for "light-skinned Latinas" noted,

> What they want is a very conservative, anglicized look, a Hispanic in an anglicized garb. It's very much what in the general market we used to call the "P and G look" [Procter

& Gamble look], the very clean-cut, all-American, blond and blue eyes, that was not representative of the United States. That was changed a long time ago, but it's not been thrown out in the Hispanic market. It's been replicated. They are trying to make the squeaky clean, perfect, boxed Latina look, not too dark and not too light.

And when in doubt, she continued, her clients would surely select the lighter over the darker Latina. Standards of beauty within Latin America which favor whiteness and straight, or "good," hair are very much at play here, as are those in the United States, especially beauty trends marked by Hollywood which become dominant in the modeling industry at large. As she insisted, "You also have to consider existing trends in beauty and looks. My roster is full of Jennifer Lopez types, because she's hot, and before that I had a lot of Julia Roberts or Jennifer Anniston types. A client will also ask you for an Antonio Banderas type or a cool Nicolas Cage, and this makes it easy because no one can go through the entire roster of models."

Making reference to Hollywood stars may facilitate communication between casting director, agency, and client, but it also translates into the casting of whiter models and actors. There are, after all, few black and Latina Hollywood stars who can be independently recalled as "types." Indeed, seldom does an indigenous or black face appear in Hispanic ads, unless in group shots. Even ads targeting the Central American and Mexican constituencies in the West feature whiter, mestizo types. For nationwide campaigns, however, it is the generic/Mediterranean look that rules. When more recognizably "ethnic" types are shown, they tend to be presented as signifiers of cultural authenticity, never of beauty or generic appeal. Thus an ad for Banco Popular shows a woman with Indian traits making tortillas only as part of a collage of people to denote its status as the bank for the people; channel 41's thirty-year anniversary ads present Andean performers and Puerto Rican folk musicians in authentic garb to mark their authenticity as performers in order to appeal to specific subgroups in New York—but they do not speak.

The so-called generic Latin look meets its linguistic match in "Walter Cronkite Spanish"—unaccented, generic, or universal Spanish, supposedly devoid of regionalism or of traceable accent, which is generally believed to be the most effective medium for campaigns reaching the entire market. This is also the Spanish that most creatives and ad executives I spoke with were convinced they themselves had cultivated, in order to corroborate their own pan-ethnicity and thus their authority to address this pan-ethnic market. In this way, Hispanic marketers acted as a "linguistic community," united by their allegiance to the existence and promotion of a "standardized" language, which they treated as a "realizable asset" that they themselves had cultivated and mastered. This "standard" Spanish was conceived as Standard English and is, in the United States, perceived as correct speech and valorized as an instrument of clarity and rational thought. Most of all, it was regarded as the optimum means to avoid the potential double meanings and malapropisms that could ensue from the various speech patterns and codes of different Latin American nationalities. Their adherence to this construct was apparent in marketers' avoidance of regionally marked terminology, in their boasting about their lack of accent, and in the pride with which they reacted to my inability to discover their national background from their speech.

Yet, like any putative standard form of language, "Walter Cronkite Spanish" is not an empirical fact but a "discursive project," reproducing particular language ideology and social distinctions; as such, it meets ready acceptance by all in the industry. Walter Cronkite Spanish is slightly influenced by English at the level of structure, vocabulary, and grammar, and English's lingering threat to Spanish is one factor that guides the hiring of Latin American–born staff. Moreover, although many advertising personnel have reduced their native Latin American accents as a result of their immigration experience and their engagement in the "linguistic community" of advertising, the origin of their accents is still perceptible under scrutiny. In addition, their nationalities are never shed when they reduce their national accents; in fact, Hispanic marketers are quite adept at "reading" each other's camouflaged accents to expose knowledge of each other's background, a knowledge that remains important for social interactions within the industry at large.

In fact, some advertising staff I spoke with admitted that the so-called Walter Cronkite Spanish was a cloak for the "Mexicanization" of the language, a perception that is not at all unfounded. Given that Mexican Americans constitute 65 percent of all Hispanics and that many ads are filmed in Mexico with Mexican actors, ads for the national market often end up with a Mexican flavor which, combined with the central role of Mexican soap operas and programming on the U.S. Hispanic airwaves, further strengthens Mexican language, accent, and mannerisms as the embodiment of generic Latinidad. What we therefore have is the dissemination of a media register of a sociolect of mostly upper-class Mexican Spanish, where Mexican (mostly *chilango*, or from the capital) mannerisms and accents emerge as "representative" of the market, whereas Caribbean Spanish is hardly heard in generic advertisements and is highly edited in the Hispanic networks' programming. For example, both the Cuban Cristina Saralegui and the Puerto Rican Ray Arrieta, popular Univision entertainers, have publicly revealed the pressure they faced to tone down their accents. Cristina, who has achieved considerable influence in this industry, struggled and was able to keep her Cuban accent and have it accepted as a trademark of her TV personality, but Raymond had to shed his Puerto Rican "*Ay bendito*" after the first filming of his new Univision program *Lente Loco*.

For others, generic Spanish is but a myth that never fully appeals to all Hispanics. This view is most prevalent among radio professionals, who work in a more regional medium and are thus inherently less likely to embrace the generic Spanish idea. According to Eduardo Caballero, a primary figure in the development of national Hispanic radio, "The problem is that the generic Spanish is a myth. It's like Walter Cronkite, who, wanting to reach all, would not reach anyone. That's the problem. It's generic, but it is not absolutely relevant or direct." Connecting to consumers, he argued, entails speaking to their "souls" through their particular type of Spanish, enhancing rather than diminishing accents.

From the Editors *Issues and Comments*

Is the English language the tie (or a tie) that holds the United States together? Or, on the contrary, are English-only laws insulting and racist? Suppose that in 150 years, Latinos are a majority of the U.S. population; could they then impose a Spanish-only regime in order to unify the nation?

If a significant number of U.S. residents spoke French, would the English-only movement be as strong as it is now?

Can you imagine the United States as an officially multilingual society? What would that be like? What would be the official language(s)? Would different ethnic and racial groups be more or less segregated? Would the U.S. function as India does with its multiple languages? Or would it be more like Europe?

Do some consumers affirmatively prefer not to patronize businesses where some of the employees are audibly speaking a foreign language, even if the counter clerk speaks perfect English?

What is wrong with a bilingual juror's hearing testimony in a foreign language and giving it as much weight as the official translation by a court interpreter, full of mistakes?

Should government make special efforts to employ emergency personnel—police, firefighters, paramedics—who speak foreign languages? Is this a form of affirmative action?

Does bilingual instruction slow the ability of immigrant schoolchildren to acquire the English they will need to flourish in the United States? Who should decide the answer to this question?

Can a non-Anglo culture survive in an English-only environment, or is culture inextricably tied with language, so that loss of the language eventually causes the culture to wither?

If Puerto Rico joins the United States as the fifty-first state, will its official language (now Spanish) have to change, or will the United States have to tolerate a Spanish-speaking state?

Suggested Readings

Alvarez, Julia. *How the García Girls Lost Their Accents*. Chapel Hill, N.C.: Algonquin Books, 1991.

Baron, Denis. *The English-Only Question: An Official Language for Americans?* New Haven, Conn.: Yale University Press, 1990.

Barry, Ellen. "Learn English, Judge Tells Moms." *L.A. Times*, Feb. 14, 2005, p. A14.

Bender, Steven W. Comprende?: *The Significance of Spanish in English-Only Times*. Mountain View, Calif.: Floricanto Press, 2008.

———. "Consumer Protection for Latinos: Overcoming Language Fraud and English-Only in the Marketplace." 45 *Amer. U. L. Rev.* 1027 (1996).

———. "Direct Democracy and Distrust: The Relationship between Language, Law, Rhetoric, and the Language Vigilantism Experience." 2 *Harv. Latino L. Rev.* 145 (1997).

Berk-Seligson, Susan. *The Bilingual Courtroom: Court Interpreters in the Judicial Process.* Chicago: University of Chicago Press, 1990.

———. "The Importance of Linguistics in Court Interpreting." 2 *La Raza L.J.* 14 (1988).

Bragg, Melvyn. *The Adventure of English: The Biography of a Language.* New York: Arcade Publishing, 2003.

Bratton, William. "Law and Economics of English Only." 53 *U. Miami L. Rev.* 973 (1999).

Califa, Antonio J. "Declaring English the Official Language: Prejudice Spoken Here." 24 *Harv. C R.–C.L. L. Rev.* 293 (1989).

Colon, Mark. "Line Drawing, Code Switching, and Spanish as Second-Hand Smoke: English-Only Workplace Rules and Bilingual Employees." 20 *Yale L. & Pol'y Rev.* 227 (2002).

Crawford, James. *At War with Diversity: U.S. Language Policy in an Age of Anxiety.* Clevedon, U.K.: Multilingual Matters, 2000.

———. *Bilingual Education: History, Politics, Theory and Practice.* 2d ed. Los Angeles: Bilingual Educational Services, 1991.

———. *Hold Your Tongue: Bilingualism and the Politics of English Only.* Reading, Mass.: Addison-Wesley Longman, 1992.

Del Valle, Sandra. *Language Rights and the Law in the United States: Finding Our Voices.* Clevedon, U.K.: Multilingual Matters, 2003.

The Elusive Quest for Equality: 150 Years of Chicano/Chicana Education. Cambridge, Mass.: Harvard Educational Review, 1999.

Frought, Carmen. *Chicano English in Context.* London: Palgrave Macmillan, 2003.

Galindo, René, and Jami Vigil. "Language Restrictionism Revisited: The Case against Colorado's 2000 Anti-Bilingual Education Initiative." 7 *Harv. Latino L. Rev.* 27 (2004).

Gonzalez, Norma. *I Am My Language: Discourses of Women and Children in the Borderlands.* Tucson: University of Arizona Press, 2006.

Hayakawa, S. I. *One Nation . . . Indivisible? The English Language Amendment.* Washington, D.C.: Washington Institute for Values in Public Policy, 1985.

Jacobson, Rodolfo. "The Social Implications of Intra-Sentenial Code-Switching." In *New Directions in Chicano Scholarship*, edited by Richard Romo and Raymond Paredes, 227. La Jolla: Chicano Studies Program, University of California, San Diego, 1978.

Johnson, Kevin R., and George A. Martinez. "Discrimination by Proxy: The Case of Proposition 227 and the Ban on Bilingual Education." 33 *U.C. Davis L. Rev.* 1227 (2000).

Kleven, Thomas. "Democratic Right to Full Bilingual Education." 7 *Nev. L.J.* 933 (2006–2007).

Kloss, Heinz. *The American Bilingual Tradition.* Rowley, Mass.: Newbury House, 1977.

Language Ideologies: Critical Perspectives on the Official English Movement, edited by Roseann Dueñas González with Ildikó Melis, vols. 1–2. Urbana, Ill.: National Council of Teachers of English, 2001.

Language Loyalties: A Source Book on the Official English Controversy, edited by James Crawford. Chicago: University of Chicago Press, 1992.

Latinos and Education: A Critical Reader, edited by Antonia Darder, Rodolfo D. Torres, and Henry Gutierrez. New York: Routledge, 1997.

Lopez, Maria Pabon. "The Phoenix Rises from El Cenizo: A Community Creates and Affirms a Latino/a Border Cultural Citizenship through Its Language and Safe Haven Ordinances." 78 *Denv. U. L. Rev.* 1017 (2000–2001).

Macedo, Donaldo. "The Colonialism of the English Only Movement." 29(3) *Educational Researcher* 15–24 (2000).

Macedo, Donaldo, Bessie Dendrinos, and Panayota Gounari. *The Hegemony of English*. Boulder, Colo.: Paradigm Publishers, 2003.

Martinez, Glenn A. *Mexican Americans and Language: Del Dicho al Hecho*. Tucson: University of Arizona Press, 2006.

Matsuda, Mari J. "Voices of America: Accent, Antidiscrimination Law, and a Jurisprudence for the Last Reconstruction." 100 *Yale L.J.* 1329 (1991).

McCrum, Robert, William Cran, and Robert MacNeil. *The Story of English*. 3d ed. New York: Penguin Books, 2002.

McWhorter, John. *Word on the Street: Debunking the Myth of a "Pure" Standard English*. New York: Basic Books, 2001.

Méndez, Miguel A. "Lawyers, Linguists, Story-Tellers, and Limited English-Speaking Witnesses." 27 *N.M. L. Rev.* 1 (1997).

Meyer, Doris. *Speaking for Themselves: Neomexicano Cultural Identity and the Spanish-Language Press, 1880–1920*. Albuquerque: University of New Mexico Press, 1996.

Mirande, Alfredo. "'*En la Tierra del Ciego, el Tuerto Es Rey*' ('In the Land of the Blind, the One-Eyed Person Is King'): Bilingualism as a Disability." 26 *N.M. L. Rev.* 75 (1996).

———. "'*Now That I Speak English, No Me Dejan Hablar*' ('I'm Not Allowed to Speak'): The Implications of *Hernandez v. New York*." 18 *Chicano-Latino L. Rev.* 115 (1996).

Moran, Rachel F. "Bilingual Education as a Status Conflict." 75 *Cal. L. Rev.* 321 (1987).

———. "Of Democracy, Devaluation, and Bilingual Education." 26 *Creighton L. Rev.* 255 (1993).

———. "The Politics of Discretion: Federal Intervention in Bilingual Education." 76 *Cal. L. Rev.* 1249 (1988).

Navarrette, Ruben, Jr. "A Bilingual-Education Initiative as a Prop. 187 in Disguise?" *L.A. Times*, July 6, 1997, p. M6.

Perea, Juan F. "English-Only Rules and the Right to Speak One's Primary Language in the Workplace." 23 *U. Mich. J. L. Reform* 265 (1990).

———. "*Hernandez v. New York*: Courts, Prosecutors, and the Fear of Spanish." 21 *Hofstra L. Rev.* 1 (1992).

———. "Killing Me Softly, with His Song: Anglocentrism and Celebrating Nouveaux Latinas/os." 55 *Fla. L. Rev.* 441 (2003).

———. "*Los Olvidados*: On the Making of Invisible People." 70 *N.Y.U. L. Rev.* 965 (1995).

Pew Hispanic Center. "Fact Sheet: Hispanic Attitudes toward Learning English." Washington, D.C.: Pew Hispanic Center, http://pewhispanic.org/files/factsheets/20.pdf.

Piatt, Bill. *Language on the Job: Balancing Business Needs and Employee Rights*. Albuquerque: University of New Mexico Press, 1993.

———. *¿Only English? Law and Language Policy in the United States*. Albuquerque: University of New Mexico Press, 1990.

———. "Toward Domestic Recognition of a Human Right to Language." 23 *Hous. L. Rev.* 885 (1986).

Porter, Rosalie Pedalino. *Forked Tongue: The Politics of Bilingual Education*. New York: Basic Books, 1990.

Portes, Alejandro, and Lingxin Hao. "E Pluribus Unum: Bilingualism and Loss of Language in the Second Generation." 71 *Sociology of Education* 269–94 (October 1998).

Ramirez, Deborah A. "Excluded Voices: The Disenfranchisemnt of Ethnic Groups from Jury Service." 1993 *Wis. L. Rev.* 761.

Rodriguez, Cristina M. "Accommodating Linguistic Difference: Toward a Comprehensive Theory of Language Rights in the United States." 36 *Harv. C.R.–C.L. L. Rev.* 133 (2001).

———. "Language and Participation." 94 *Cal. L. Rev.* 687 (2006).

———. "Language Diversity in the Workplace." 100 *Nw. U. L. Rev.* 1689 (2006).

Salinas, Lupe S. "Immigration and Language Rights: The Evolution of Private Racist Attitudes into American Public Law and Policy." 7 *Nev. L.J.* 895 (2006–2007).

———. "Linguaphobia, Language Rights, and the Right of Privacy." 3 *Stan. J. C.R.–C.L.* 53 (2007).

Schmid, Carol L. *The Politics of Language: Conflict, Identity, and Cultural Pluralism in Comparative Perspective.* New York: Oxford University Press, 2001.

Schmidt, Ronald., Sr. *Language Policy and Identity Politics in the United States.* Philadelphia: Temple University Press, 2000.

Spanish Loanwords in the English Language: A Tendency towards Hegemony Reversal, edited by Félix Rodriguez González. Berlin: Mouton de Gruyter, 1996.

Speaking Chicana: Voice, Power, and Identity, edited by D. Letticia Galindo and María Dolores Gonzales. Tucson: University of Arizona Press, 1999.

Stavans, Ilan. *Spanglish: The Making of a New American Language.* New York: HarperCollins, 2003.

Suarez, Debra. "The Paradox of Linguistic Hegemony and the Maintenance of Spanish as a Heritage Language in the United States." 23(6) *Journal of Multilingual & Multicultural Development* 512–30 (2002).

Trujillo, Armando L. *Chicano Empowerment and Bilingual Education: Movimiento Politics in Crystal City, Texas.* New York: Garland Publishing, 1998.

Valdes, Guadalupe. "The Language Situation of Mexican Americans." In *Language Diversity, Problem or Resource? A Social and Educational Perspective on Language Minorities in the United States*, edited by Sandra L. McKay and Sau-Ling C. Wong, 111. Cambridge, Mass.: Newbury House, 1988.

———. *Learning and Not Learning English: Latino Students in American Schools.* New York: Teachers College Press, 2001.

Walsh, Catherine E. *Pedagogy and the Struggle for Voice: Issues of Language, Power, and Schooling for Puerto Ricans.* South Hadley, Mass.: Bergin & Garvey, 1991.

Weeden, L. Darnell. "Less Than Fair Employment Practice of an English-Only Rule in the Workplace." 7 *Nev. L.J.* 947 (2006–2007).

Zentella, Ana Celia. *Growing Up Bilingual: Puerto Rican Children in New York.* New York: Blackwell, 1997.

Contributors

Oscar "Zeta" Acosta, a legal aid attorney in Oakland, became a political activist in the Chicano community in Los Angeles, defending the LA Thirteen. After an unsuccessful campaign for sheriff of Los Angeles County, he traveled through the West with the writer Hunter Thompson and wrote *The Autobiography of a Brown Buffalo* and *The Revolt of the Cockroach People*. He disappeared during a journey to Mazatlán, Mexico, in 1973.

Rodolfo Acuña, one of America's leading scholar-activists, is professor emeritus of Chicano studies at California State University at Northridge. His book, *Occupied America*, now in its seventh edition, is one of twenty books and hundreds of articles, book reviews, and essays he has written on issues of racial justice.

Tomás Almaguer, sociologist, is professor of ethnic studies at San Francisco State University and former dean of its College of Ethnic Studies. A leading scholar of racial formation in the United States, he focuses his work on the Latino community and identity, gender, and sexuality.

Gloria Anzaldúa was a poet, essayist, fiction writer, editor, and feminist critic. Her autobiography, *Borderlands/La Frontera: The New Mestiza*, became a classic in Chicano border studies, feminist theory, gay and lesbian studies, and cultural studies. She edited *Making Soul/Haciendo Cara*, an anthology of critical writings by women of color, and, with Cherríe Moraga, *This Bridge Called My Back: Writings by Radical Women of Color*.

Taunya Lovell Banks is the Jacob A. France Professor of Equality Jurisprudence and the Francis & Harriet Iglehart Research Professor of Law at the University of Maryland, where she teaches and writes in the areas of constitutional law, torts, law in popular culture, and critical race theory. Prior to entering legal education, she worked as a civil rights lawyer in Mississippi.

Steven W. Bender is the James and Ilene Hershner Professor of Law and Director of Portland Programs at the University of Oregon. An author of books on Latino stereotypes, Spanish and the English-only movement, and the relationship between Cesar Chavez and Robert Kennedy, he has also published a casebook on real estate transactions and a treatise on real estate financing.

Charles Ramirez Berg, Distinguished Teaching Professor and Joe M. Dealey, Sr. Professor in Media Studies at the University of Texas at Austin, is an authority on Latinos in film as well as film history in general. Author of *Latino Images in Film* and

Cinema of Solitude: A Critical Study of Mexican Film, 1967–1983, he has also served on the Executive Council of the Society for Cinema.

Homer Brooks, Communist Party organizer and 1938 Texas gubernatorial candidate, was married to Emma Tenayuca from 1937 to 1941.

Paul Butler teaches in the areas of criminal law, civil rights, and jurisprudence at George Washington University law school. His scholarship has been published in the *Yale Law Journal, Harvard Law Review, Stanford Law Review, UCLA Law Review*, and by *The New Press*.

Christopher David Ruiz Cameron, the Irwin R. Buchalter Professor of Law at Southwestern University, is an authority on employment law, bankruptcy, immigration, and entertainment and sports, and speaks frequently on challenges facing Latino workers. He has published articles on the law of the workplace in top law journals, and is coauthor of two books.

Julio Cammarota is assistant professor in the Bureau of Applied Research in Anthropology and the Mexican American Studies and Research Center at the University of Arizona, where his research focuses on Latina/o youth, institutional factors in academic achievement, and liberatory pedagogy. He also codirects the Social Justice Education Project in Tucson, Arizona.

Gilbert Paul Carrasco teaches civil rights law, immigration law, and constitutional law at Willamette University law school. The author of casebooks and law review articles, he served in the U.S. Department of Justice and as a trial attorney in the Civil Rights Division, and later as a directing attorney of the National Center for Immigrants' Rights.

Leo R. Chavez, professor of anthropology at the University of California–Irvine, explores issues related to transnational migration, including immigrant families and households, labor market participation, motivations for migration, the use of medical services, and media constructions of "immigrant" and "nation." His publications include *Shadowed Lives: Undocumented Immigrants in American Society* and *Covering Immigration: Popular Images and the Politics of the Nation*.

Yvonne M. Cherena Pacheco, assistant dean for enrollment management and director of admissions at CUNY law school, was formerly associate dean of admissions at St. Mary's University law school. She has taught clinical courses, jurisprudence, and legal method.

Wayne A. Cornelius is director emeritus of the Center for Comparative Immigration Studies at the University of California–San Diego, as well as Theodore Gildred Distinguished Professor of Political Science and U.S.–Mexican Relations. An expert on Mexican immigration, he is the author of groundbreaking work on immigrant sending and receiving communities in Mexico and the United States.

James Crawford has specialized in the politics of language as an independent writer, lecturer, and consultant over the past twenty years. The author of *Educating English Learners* and the editor of *Language Loyalties: A Source Book on the Official*

English Controversy, he has also served as Washington editor of *Education Week*. In 2006 he cofounded the Institute for Language and Education Policy, which is devoted to research-based advocacy for English and heritage-language learners.

Marta I. Cruz-Janzen, professor of multicultural education at Florida Atlantic University, is coauthor of *Meeting the Needs of Multiethnic and Multiracial Children in Schools* and *Educating Young Children in a Diverse Society*. Her research focuses on identity, ethnicity, and racial formations, including that of Latinegros.

Roger Daniels is the Charles Phelps Taft Professor Emeritus of History at the University of Cincinnati and past president of the Society for Historians of the Gilded Age and Progressive Era as well as of the Immigration History Society. He served as consultant to the Presidential Commission on the Wartime Relocation and Internment of Civilians and is a planning committee member for the immigration museum on Ellis Island.

Antonia Darder, professor of educational policy studies and Latino/a studies at the University of Illinois at Urbana–Champaign, examines cultural issues in education with an emphasis on identity, language, and popular culture. Her current work focuses on comparative studies of racism, class, and society.

Arlene Dávila is professor of anthropology and of social and cultural analysis at New York University, where she teaches and writes in the areas of urban and ethnic studies, the political economy of culture and media, and consumption studies. Her work focuses on Puerto Ricans in the eastern United States, and Latinos nationwide.

Arnold De León, the C. J. "Red" Davidson Professor of History at Angelo State University in San Angelo, Texas, is the author and editor of critically acclaimed books and monographs. One of the top ten books on Texas history, *They Called Them Greasers: Anglo Attitudes toward Mexicans in Texas, 1821–1900*, shaped contemporary understandings of that state, particularly as it relates to Mexican Americans.

Adelaida R. Del Castillo, associate professor and department chair of Chicana and Chicano Studies at San Diego State University, is the editor of *Between Borders: Essays on Mexicana/Chicana History*. Her research focuses on gender relations.

Richard Delgado is University Professor at Seattle University law school. Author of articles and books on Latinos and civil rights, including *The Rodrigo Chronicles*, he is also one of the founders of critical race theory. Winner of several book awards and prizes, he is considered a pioneer of narrative theory and legal storytelling.

Leslie G. Espinoza, formerly a clinical professor of law at Boston College, taught health-care law and women and the law. Author of articles on race, ethnicity, and higher education, she has served as an officer or member of committees devoted to community and minority affairs.

Joe R. Feagin, the author of nearly fifty books and 150 articles, many examining the development and structure of racial and gender prejudice and institutional and systemic discrimination, is currently the Ella C. McFadden Professor of Liberal

Arts at Texas A&M University. He recently served as president of the American Sociological Association.

Marjorie Florestal, associate professor at McGeorge law school at University of the Pacific, teaches contracts and lectures widely on the WTO and the impact of globalization on developing countries, focusing particularly on economic development in Africa.

Neil Foley, associate professor of history and American studies at the University of Texas, writes and teaches about Mexican-American history, the American Southwest, social and cultural history of the U.S.–Mexico border, and Mexican immigration and civil rights politics in the twentieth-century United States.

René Galindo serves as associate dean at the School of Education & Human Development at the University of Colorado–Denver. His research interests include language policy, the future of bilingual education, nativism as a forgotten ideology, and the politics of immigration and immigration rights.

Tanya Golash-Boza, assistant professor in the departments of sociology and of American studies at the University of Kansas, focuses on the racial identities of Latinos and Latinas in the United States and in Latin America.

Guillermo J. Grenier, associate professor of sociology at Florida International University, directs the Florida Center for Labor Research and Studies. Author of books and articles on labor and ethnic issues in the United States, he also conducts yearly surveys on the attitudes of the Cuban-American community towards Cuba.

David G. Gutiérrez, professor of history at the University of California–San Diego, teaches Chicano history, comparative immigration and ethnic history, and politics in the twentieth-century United States. He has served as editor of *The Columbia History of Latinos in the United States since 1960*.

Ian F. Haney López, the John H. Boalt Professor of Law at the University of California–Berkeley, is the author of ground-breaking books on the social and legal construction of race, including *White by Law: The Legal Construction of Race* and *Racism on Trial*. His current research examines the emergence and operation of colorblindness as a new racial ideology.

George Hartley, associate professor in the English Department of Ohio University, teaches contemporary poetry, critical theory, and Chicano poetry.

Berta Esperanza Hernández-Truyol, Levin Mabie & Levin Professor of Law at the University of Florida, writes and teaches in the areas of international law, race, gender, and employment discrimination. Her books, *Moral Imperialism*, an edited reader, and *Just Trade*, with Stephen Powell, apply a human rights framework to domestic civil shortcomings and U.S. trade agreements.

Bill Ong Hing, professor of law at the University of San Francisco, is the author of books and articles on immigration policy and race relations, including *Deporting*

Our Souls: Values, Morality and Immigration Policy. A founder of the Immigrant Legal Resource Center in San Francisco, he also serves on the National Advisory Council of the Asian American Justice Center.

Reginald Horsman recently retired from the University of Wisconsin–Milwaukee. He has written extensively on American history, with an emphasis on the early national period, westward expansion, and racial attitudes. His book *Race and Manifest Destiny* is considered a milestone in the development of critical studies of whiteness.

Kevin R. Johnson is dean, professor of law and Chicana/o Studies, and the Mabie-Apallas Public Interest Law Chair at the University of California–Davis. In addition to his work on immigration law and policy and civil rights, he has written *How Did You Get to Be Mexican? A White/Brown Man's Search for Identity*.

Jorge Klor De Alva became Senior Vice President for Academic Excellence and Director of the University of Phoenix National Research Center in August 2007. Before joining the university's parent organization, he taught at the University of California–Berkeley, Princeton University, State University of New York–Albany, the University of Californina–Santa Cruz, and San Jose State University.

Robert Koulish, an interdisciplinary political scientist in the School of Liberal Arts at Philadelphia University, chairs the Law and Society program. His research and writing focus on immigration and the border, human rights abuses and political asylum applicants, and sovereignty and the privatization of immigration control.

Gerald P. López is professor of law at UCLA. His book *Rebellious Lawyering: One Chicano's Vision of Progressive Law Practice* describes perspectives on lawyering that he developed as cofounder of the Program in Public Interest Law and Policy at UCLA and the Lawyering for Social Change Program at Stanford law school.

George A. Martinez, professor of law at Southern Methodist University, teaches and writes about legal history, philosophy and law, and Latino legal theory, and serves as associate editor of *NAFTA: Law and Business Review of the Americas*.

Pancho McFarland teaches sociology of race, gender, and culture at Chicago State University. His book *Chicano Rap* combines formal and field research in the previously understudied genre of Chicano hip hop culture.

Carey McWilliams served as editor of *The Nation* from 1955 to 1975. His books on Mexican Americans include *Factories in the Field, Ill Fares the Land, Southern California Country*, and *The Education of Carey McWilliams*. A leading figure in the history of disempowered people in the United States, he also practiced law.

Martha Menchaca is an anthropologist at the University of Texas. Her recent book *Recovering History, Constructing Race: The Indian, Black, and White Roots of Mexican Americans* describes how Spanish, Mexican, and U.S. authorities constructed racial status hierarchies that marginalized Mexicans of color and restricted their rights of land ownership.

Miguel A. Méndez is professor of law at the University of California–Davis. Author of articles and materials for practicing lawyers, he has held positions at MALDEF (Mexican American Legal Defense and Educational Fund) and in state and local government.

Gustavo Chacon Mendoza was a member of the University of La Verne law review and is now a member of the California bar.

Margaret E. Montoya, professor of law at the University of New Mexico, focuses on affirmative action and critical race pedagogy. She has worked in corporate law, legal services, and academic administration, and served as interim director of the Southwest Hispanic Research Institute.

José Luis Morín is professor in the Department of Latin American and Latina/o Studies and a member of the faculty in the Ph.D. Program in Criminal Justice at John Jay College of Criminal Justice, CUNY, where he teaches domestic and international criminal justice, civil and international human rights, race and ethnicity in the United States, Latina/o studies, and U.S.–Latin American relations.

Ruben Navarrette, Jr., is a columnist and editorial board member of the *San Diego Union-Tribune* and writes for various national publications. A graduate of Harvard and its Kennedy School of Government, he is a widely sought speaker on Latino affairs and serves as a regular contributor to NPR's *Morning Edition.*

Suzanne Oboler teaches Latino/Latina studies and Latin American literature and culture at John Jay College of Criminal Justice, CUNY. She is the founding editor of *Latino Studies* and coeditor-in-chief of the *Oxford Encyclopedia on Latinos and Latinas in the United States.*

Michael A. Olivas holds the William B. Bates Distinguished Chair of Law at the University of Houston, where he directs the Institute of Higher Education Law and Governance. The author of books and articles on immigration law, higher education law, and civil rights, he serves as a director of MALDEF (Mexican American Legal Defense and Educational Fund) and on boards of service organizations and scholarly journals.

Maria L. Ontiveros, professor of law at the University of San Francisco, teaches and writes on immigrant workers' rights, workplace harassment of women of color, organized labor, and access to education for children of undocumented workers.

Ángel R. Oquendo, Olimpiad S. Ioffe Professor of International and Comparative Law at the University of Connecticut, teaches and writes about comparative law and jurisprudence. In addition to his J.D. from Yale, he earned a Ph.D. in philosophy at Harvard. He has taught in Germany and Brazil and published in German, French, and Latin American journals as well as American law reviews.

Laura M. Padilla, associate dean and professor of law at California Western, writes and teaches in the areas of property, race, gender, spirituality, and Latino issues. She has served on the Stanford Associates Board of Governors and received the Stanford University Governors' Award.

Vicky Palacios, associate professor of law at Southern Methodist University, served as Hastie Fellow at the University of Wisconsin law school. Her areas of scholarship include sentencing, the death penalty, and civil rights.

Juan F. Perea, Cone, Wagner, Nugent, Johnson, Hazouri & Roth Professor of Law at the University of Florida, writes on American language policy, nativism, and ethnic identity, and is the editor of *Immigrants Out! The New Nativism and the Anti-Immigrant Impulse in the United States* and coeditor of two casebooks on race and law.

Beatriz M. Pesquera is retired from the University of California–Davis, where she was associate professor and director of the Chicana/Chicano Studies Program. She has published articles on Chicana feminism, focusing on employment and familial experiences, and coedited *Building with Our Hands: New Directions in Chicana Studies.*

Bill Piatt, professor of law at St. Mary's University, is author of *¿Only English? Law and Language Policy in the United States* and *Language on the Job: Balancing Business Needs and Employee Rights.* His areas of expertise include immigration law, law and language policy, corporations, and family law.

Alejandro Portes is professor and past chair of sociology at Princeton University and a faculty member of the Office of Population Research. He cofounded and directs the Center for Migration and Development. His research and writing include books and articles on immigrant assimilation, Latin American politics, and United States/Cuba relations.

Jenny Rivera, professor of law and founder and director of the Center on Latino and Latina Rights and Equality at CUNY, teaches and writes about civil and women's rights. A former Sonia Sotomayor judicial clerk, she served as lead author of the Hispanic National Bar Association's review of the judge's record for her Supreme Court nomination.

Clara E. Rodriguez, professor of sociology at Fordham, is the author of articles and books in the areas of race, media studies, Latino studies, labor markets, migration, and regional studies. Her book, *Changing Race*, is considered a classic study of Latinos, the Census, and the history of ethnicity in the United States.

Richard Rodriguez is a contributing editor at New America Media in San Francisco. In addition to an autobiographical trilogy on class, ethnicity, and race—*Hunger of Memory*, *Days of Obligation*, and *Brown*—he writes for several newspapers and magazines, both in the United States and in England. He is also a frequent commentator on the PBS *NewsHour.*

Mary Romero is Professor of Justice Studies and Social Inquiry at Arizona State University and affiliate faculty of Women and Gender Studies. Her research focuses on the unequal distribution of reproductive labor as a paid commodity and its role in reproducing inequality among families within countries and between nations.

Rubén G. Rumbaut, professor of sociology at the University of California–Irvine, is an internationally known scholar and author of books and articles on immigration and refugee movements and on the adaptation of immigrants and refugees in the United States. He currently codirects the landmark Children of Immigrants Longitudinal Study and a new large-scale study of *Immigration and Intergenerational Mobility in Metropolitan Los Angeles.*

Otto Santa Ana is associate professor of Chicana and Chicano Studies at UCLA with a concentration in linguistics. His current research encompasses the history of the languages and dialects of Chicanas and Chicanos, focusing on the social and educational implications of language variation among Latino communities.

Alex M. Saragoza, associate professor of history in the Department of Ethnic Studies at the University of California–Berkeley, investigates the privatization of the Mexican economy in general, and the tourism industry in particular. Through UC Extension he has led study tours that focus on early Mesoamerican history and Cuba.

Earl Shorris is founder and chairman of the advisory board of the Clemente Course in the Humanities, a college-level course for poor people. During his career as a journalist, social critic, lecturer, and novelist, his articles have appeared in *Harper's Magazine,* where he has been a contributing editor since 1972, as well as in many other publications.

John D. Skrentny, professor of sociology at the University of California–San Diego, codirects the Center for Comparative Immigration Studies. His work focuses on public policy, law, and inequality, especially as they relate to immigration and civil rights. His current research includes a study of the impact of immigration on discrimination law in the United States.

Ilan Stavans is Lewis-Sebring Professor of Latin American and Latino Culture at Amherst College. Born in Mexico City, he has produced many publications, including *Imagining Columbus: The Literary Voyage* and *The Hispanic Condition.* He edited *Becoming Americans: Four Centuries of Immigrant Writing* and *The Norton Anthology of Latino Literature,* and coedited *Growing Up Latino.*

Jean Stefancic, research professor of law at Seattle University, is the author of articles and books on civil rights, law reform, and social change, including *No Mercy: How Conservative Think Tanks and Foundations Changed America's Social Agenda.*

Ronald Takaki, grandson of Japanese immigrant plantation laborers in Hawaii, served as professor of ethnic studies at the University of California–Berkeley for three decades. Author of the critically acclaimed *Iron Cages* and the prize-winning *Strangers from a Different Shore,* he was a nationally recognized scholar of multicultural studies.

Emma Tenayuca, shaken by the ill treatment of Mexican migrant workers during the Depression, became a labor organizer in Texas at the age of seventeen. During a cigar factory strike, she cofounded the Workers Alliance, spearheading the three-month pecan shellers' strike in San Antonio in 1938. Harassed and threatened with death because of her activism and short-lived but controversial Communist Party membership, she left for San Francisco. After returning to San Antonio in 1962, she continued her lifelong work of educating migrant children, and died there in 1999.

Rodolfo D. Torres is Professor of Urban & Regional Planning, Political Science and Urban Studies in the School of Social Ecology at the University of California–Irvine, where he employs a Marxist critique to analyze the future of cities, the decline of the public domain, racism and class relations in the United States and Western Europe, the changing nature of work and Mexican American labor, and the systemic logic of American capitalism and global disorder.

Abel Valenzuela, Jr., holds joint appointments in the Department of Urban Planning and the César E. Chávez Department for Chicana/o Studies at UCLA and directs the Center for the Study of Urban Poverty. He writes and teaches in the areas of immigration and labor markets, poverty and inequality, and immigrant settlement patterns.

Jami Vigil is executive director and managing attorney of Socorro, which provides legal services for immigrant women and children in Denver. She served as program director for the Rural Immigrant Outreach Project, a nonprofit agency providing free legal clinics to Spanish-speaking immigrant communities in rural Colorado.

Mary Waters, the M. E. Zukerman Professor of Sociology at Harvard University, studies intergroup relations, the formation of racial and ethnic identity among children of immigrants, and how to measure race and ethnicity. Two of her current research projects are the New York Second Generation Project, which focuses on New Yorkers with Latin American, Chinese, and Caribbean roots, and *Coming of Age in America*, a study of the transition to adulthood.

Cornel West, the Class of 1943 Professor at Princeton University, teaches in the Center for African American Studies and in the Department of Religion. His writing, speaking, and teaching combine traditions of the black Baptist Church, progressive politics, and jazz. His book, *Race Matters,* has become a contemporary classic, selling more than half a million copies to date.

Steven H. Wilson, associate dean of Liberal Arts at Tulsa Community College, has also been a consultant in Houston specializing in litigation research and analysis.

Index